P9-EJH-742

The Literature of the Sages
Part One

Compendia Rerum Iudaicarum ad Novum Testamentum

SECTION TWO

THE LITERATURE OF THE JEWISH PEOPLE
IN THE PERIOD OF THE SECOND TEMPLE AND THE TALMUD

I. MIQRA
Reading, Translation and Interpretation of the Hebrew Bible in Ancient Judaism and Early Christianity
Editor: M. J. Mulder

2. JEWISH WRITING OF THE SECOND TEMPLE PERIOD
Apocrypha, Pseudepigrapha, Qumran Sectarian Writings, Philo, Josephus
Editor: M. E. Stone

3. THE LITERATURE OF THE SAGES
FIRST PART: Oral Tora, Halakha, Mishna, Tosefta, Talmud,
External Tractates

SECOND PART: Midrash, Aggada, Midrash Collections, Targum, Prayer
Editor: S. Safrai

Advisory Editors:
Y. Aschkenasy, D. Flusser, J. Goldin, H. Kremers, Th. C. de Kruyf,
R. Le Déaut, G. W. MacRae (deceased), K. Stendahl, E. Tov

Executive Editors:
W. J. Burgers, H. Sysling, P. J. Tomson

Published under the Auspices of the
Foundation Compendia Rerum Iudaicarum ad Novum Testamentum,
Amsterdam

The Literature of the Sages

First Part:
Oral Tora, Halakha, Mishna, Tosefta,
Talmud, External Tractates

Editor: Shmuel Safrai
Executive Editor: Peter J. Tomson

1987
Van Gorcum, Assen/Maastricht
Fortress Press, Philadelphia

© 1987 by Stichting Compendia Rerum Iudaicarum ad Novum Testamentum

No parts of this book may be reproduced in any form, by print, photoprint, microfilm or any other means without written permission from the publisher.

Library of Congress Cataloging-in-Publication Data

The Literature of the Sages.

(Compendia Rerum Iudaicarum ad Novum Testamentum; 11/3a–   )
Bibliography: v. 1, p.
Contents: v. 1. Oral tora, Halakha, Mishna, Tosefta, Talmud, External Tractates.
1. Rabbinical literature—History and criticism.
I. Safrai, Shmuel, 1919–   . II. Series: Compendia Rerum Iudaicarum ad Novum Testamentum; section 2, etc.
BM496.5.L57   1987   296.1   86–45910

ISBN 0–8006–0605–1 (Fortress Press: v. 1)
ISBN 90–232–2282–2 (Van Gorcum: v. 1)

Printed in The Netherlands by Van Gorcum, Assen

Foreword

In the foreword to Volume Two, the first to have appeared in Section Two, the Board of the *Compendia* Foundation apologized for the long delay that had occurred since the completion of Section One. A number of reasons which today have only a historical interest caused this delay. The Board is happy to be able to present another volume after a much shorter interval.

The present work is actually the First Part of Section Two, Volume Three, which deals with The Literature of the Sages. While work on this volume was in progress, it became clear that the subject matter was too voluminous to be managed in one book. The Board then decided to split Volume Three into two Parts, the first of which has now been realized. In order to enhance the usefulness of the separate Parts, both are provided with an accumulative bibliography and indices.

The Board of the Foundation wishes to thank most heartily Professor S. Safrai of the Hebrew University of Jerusalem who, having cooperated actively in the *Compendia* project as a whole from the beginning, is the Editor of the present work. The Board is aware of the heavy burden of this task and it is equally aware of the unique character of the volume which, through his learning and insight, can now be presented to the learned and interested public. Much gratitude is also due to the authors of the various parts of this work. They are all specialists in their own fields, and we are convinced that their contributions in many cases break new ground.

No work of scholarly quality can be published without the assistance of its Executive Editors. The Board wishes to express its indebtedness to Dr. W. J. Burgers without whose keen insight and great experience the production of this Section, including the present work, would have been hardly possible, and Mr. P. J. Tomson who carried out the actual editing with great expertise and exactitude.

This publication was made possible through grants from various institutions, of which we wish to mention specially the Prins Bernhard Fund, Amsterdam and the Anne Frank Fonds, Basle.

The Board expects the publication of Section Two, Volume One, to take place in the first half of 1988, and of Volume Three, Part Two, in another year. The Board accepts full responsibility for this order of publication.

R. A. Levisson, President
Y. Aschkenasy, H. de Bie, L. Dequeker, J. van Goudoever (Secretary), A. van der Heide, H. Kremers, Th. C. de Kruijf, H. E. Oving (Treasurer). H. van Praag.

V

A Note on Transliteration

Transliteration of Hebrew and Aramaic follows a most simple system with a dual aim: to produce the modern Hebrew pronunciation for anglophones, and not to bother the reader with illegible pedantry. The specialist will know for himself. Where necessary, Hebrew types are used.

This same system is also used for titles of rabbinic documents and names of Sages. German transliterations common even in English scholarly literature have been eliminated: thus *Tsitsit* and not *Tzitzit*; *Yonatan* instead of *Jonathan*. Names not typical for the world of the Sages, however, such as biblical names, are given in their usual form: hence Joshua, Judah and Ezekiel.

For Hebrew book titles see bibliography.

Acknowledgements

The contributions by S. Safrai were translated from the Hebrew by J. Schwartz and P.J. Tomson; Ms. V. de Rijk-Chan assisted in language editing. The sections written by M. Krupp were translated from the German by K. Smyth. Ms. T.L. Bak re-typed several chapters. Indices were prepared by H.L.M. Ottenheim.

Translations of Hebrew sources were often adapted to give a more effective rendition. Otherwise, the Revised Standard Version of the Bible and H. Danby's translation of the Mishna are followed. Translations of Philo and Josephus follow the Loeb edition.

The Editors gratefully acknowledge permission to publish reproductions of manuscript pages from the following libraries: Leiden, Universiteitsbibliotheek; Cambridge, University Library; Budapest, Magyar Tudományos Akadémia Könyavtáre. The Israel Department of Antiquities graciously provided a photograph of a mosaic floor with the permission to publish it.

Finally, the Editor wishes to express his gratitude to the Netherlands Institute for Advanced Study in the Humanities. The facilities it offered him during the academic year 1980-81 greatly helped in laying the foundations for this book and creating part of its contents.

Contents

List of Illustrations

Introduction

This section of the *Compendia* is devoted to Jewish literature from the periods of the Second Temple and the Talmud. We perceive two basic forms: 1) the varied group of apocryphal and pseudepigraphic writings and Hellenistic Jewish literature; 2) the literature of the Sages.[1]

The first category, which was treated in Volume Two of this Section, has usually survived in the Greek, either having been written in that language or translated from the original Hebrew or Aramaic. In many cases only the translations into Greek, or other languages, have survived. This literature has for the most part reached us through Christian literary tradition and not via Jewish sources. In fact, this type of literature was basically lost to Jewish tradition.

In this category we included the literature of the Qumran sect which has survived in its original Hebrew. This literature was not transmitted by Jewish or Christian tradition but was discovered in the course of archeological investigations and, additionally, by chance discoveries from ancient *genizot* or storehouses for discarded books in synagogues.

The second category, the literature of the Sages, was originally created wholly in Palestine, and from the third century c.e. also in Babylonia. It was composed in Hebrew and Aramaic, and has reached us via Jewish tradition. It is to this body of literature that the two parts of this volume are devoted.

There are several features unique to the literature of the Sages. The various documents – Mishna, Tosefta, the Talmudim, the midrash collections and other items – were on the whole not composed by individual authors. Rather, each of these is the final result of a collective creative process which took place over the course of many generations. The material evolving in this process was finally collated or edited by some Sage, in one or another House of Study (*Beit Midrash*), and usually included material descending from many other Sages as

---

[1] We prefer the term 'Sages' and 'literature of the Sages'. Not only does this follow Hebrew usage more closely. It also avoids both the methodical difficulties of the relationship between Pharisees and rabbis, and the anachronistic confusion with medieval rabbinism. For lack of an adjective derived from 'Sages', we also use the term 'rabbinic literature' or, less frequently, 'talmudic literature'.

well as from many Houses of Study. Occasionally, tradition has recorded the period in which a particular work was composed, and the Sage or House of Study responsible for it. But for the most part there are no reliable traditions regarding this most vital information.

The final editing of this literature does not predate the end of the second century C.E. or the beginning of the third. However, as a result of the extended creative process most of these works contain material which derives from the Second Temple period. In this period, unlike the preceding one, the Pentateuch acquired a place of prime importance among the people. This engendered a ramified social and intellectual process aimed both at the application of the Pentateuch in practical life and its studying and commenting. Both activities, moreover, went hand in hand with the creation of novel teachings and literary forms inspired by the Pentateuch yet independent from it. Thus practical implementation and literary creation developed side by side. This process can be perceived in various Second Temple writings, as is demonstrated in our chapters on Halakha and Oral Tora.

Thus a halakhic or aggadic tradition found in a late collection, or even one with an explicit late attribution, does not necessarily have a late origin. It may date to a much earlier period or reflect a situation from that period. Sometimes this can be proven through a comparison with early sources outside of talmudic literature. Such a tradition, preserved in a first or second century source, may then turn out to be the consummation of a religious idea or custom which had been developing for a long time and originated somewhere in the early Second Temple period. In the present work, as well as in the previous volumes, many examples of this literary phenomenon are to be found.

The order of chapters in the two parts of this volume is based, among other things, upon the known or approximate date at which the various collections received final editing. But, as we have just indicated, this does not necessarily inform the reader about the date of origin of individual traditions contained in any collection.

The literature of the Sages, as we shall see, includes many categories: halakha (law), aggada (legend), midrash (exposition of Scripture), targum (translation of Scripture), prayer, and others. However, the division into separate literary categories was a rather late phenomenon in the development of this literature and, certainly in the initial stages, all categories developed together. In a later stage, when the division between the various categories was felt and consciously maintained, a marked reciprocity continued to exist even across the borderlines separating them. Thus we find midrash and aggada in such a strictly edited halakhic collection as the Mishna, and halakha in outstanding aggadic midrash collections. Therefore a correct understanding of this literature necessitates not only a treatment on the basis of the division into separate categories and individual collections, but also from the perspective of a basic coherence.

This insight is borne out in the design of this volume. Apart from the chapters which treat the various documents and bodies of literature, we have devised chapters on general aspects of the literature of the Sages. Considerations of expediency made us decide to divide this volume into two parts appearing separately. This resulted in the removal to the second part of general chapters originally designed for the beginning of the volume. Thus the present part has the chapters on Oral Tora and Halakha, while those on Midrash and Aggada will appear in the forthcoming part.

The present part opens, after a description of the historical background (Chapter One), with the treatment of one fundamental feature which left its imprint on this literature in various ways. This feature is expressed in the name used by the Sages to refer specifically to their own literary tradition: Oral Tora. Chapter Two is devoted to this phenomenon and the major historical and literary problems connected with it. Next is a chapter on what the Sages considered a central subject area of their tradition: halakha (Chapter Three). The Halakha is treated not as a mere literary category but as a religious legal tradition which developed within the historical realities of Jewish society, and sprang from the desire of the Sages to fulfill the Tora and its precepts

After these two general chapters, there follow the chapters dealing with the various halakhic collections: the Mishna (Chapter Four), Tosefta (Chapter Six), the Palestinian (Chapter Seven) and the Babylonian Talmud (Chapter Eight). The tractate Avot, which wholly consists of aggada yet was incorporated in the prime halakhic collection, the Mishna, is treated in a separate chapter (Chapter Five). We conclude this part with a discussion of the so-called external or minor tractates, and of Palestinian post-talmudic halakhic compositions (Chapter Nine). Much of the latter was edited at a rather late period, but it represents a marked continuation of the halakhic and aggadic literary traditions of the Tannaim and Amoraim in the Land of Israel.

The chapters dealing with the specific collections all have sections on textual criticism. This field of research, which has been greatly expanding during recent decades, is of vital importance for the scholarly study of the literature of the Sages. Due to the extended process of creating and editing, as well as the oral nature of this literature which allows flexibility and change, textual versions and variants abounded early on. Furthermore, the text of many talmudic traditions was adapted or corrupted in the subsequent transmission process. One striking phenomenon is the increasing adaptation of the text of the Palestinian Talmud to readings from the much more influential Babylonian during the Middle Ages. As a matter of fact, any research work, commentary or translation which is not based on painstaking analysis of the extant textual witnesses can have only very limited value. Research on the text of rabbinic literature is based first of all on the many *Geniza* fragments which are being identified and published and, in addition, on renewed textual and philological analysis of codices which have been known for a longer time.

Chapter One, as we said, discusses the historical background of the literature of the Sages. It covers a rather long period, beginning with the Second Temple era and extending until the end of the Byzantine period. It is not a full historical survey of this long period, but an attempt to relate to the literary activity of these times within a historical perspective, elucidating the social frameworks in which Oral Tora as a whole functioned and took shape.

The forthcoming part is to be seen as integral to this volume. It will contain the chapters dealing with midrash, aggada and other categories. This part will be similar in format, first treating the categories of midrash and aggada *per se*, and then going on with the chapters on the individual documents: the halakhic midrash collections of the Tannaim and the aggadic ones of the Amoraim.

As we shall explain in Chapter Two of the present part, additional genres which developed during the Second Temple period and the centuries following should be seen as a part of Oral Tora: targum, prayer, and to some extent even *piyut*. These genres were created by the same authors, or authors closely associated with the world of the Sages. Their development is also quite similar to that of halakha and aggada. They evolved in the world of the Sages, as a part of the broader phenomenon of Oral Tora – either in the course of study in the Beit Midrash, or of the reading of the Tora, the sermon (*derasha*) and prayer in the synagogue. They were also transmitted in the form of oral teachings. Furthermore, the ideas and opinions expressed in them reflect the world of the Sages as found in the various forms of talmudic literature, both in halakha and aggada. It is true that there are also minor differences between the Targumim and the Halakha or Aggada of talmudic literature. But for the most part these differences reflect a historical development which took place between the periods in which the various works were edited. The points in common far outweigh the differences.

At the end of Part Two, those types of literature that were not edited in specific collections shall be discussed: mystical traditions, legal deeds, inscriptions and mosaics, and traditions in the field of medicine, agriculture, geography, astronomy and astrology, and magic. Again, a part of the material discussed in this volume, such as *Megillat ha-Tsumot* and the developed forms of *piyut,* received its extant form only after the talmudic period. But the large amount of earlier material contained in them has warranted their inclusion in these volumes.

Part Two will also contain a chapter, relevant to both parts, on the languages of Oral Tora.

The wide scope of rabbinic literature, its complex form, and the long creative process, as well as its great practical significance for the life of the nation, drew the critical attention of the learned as early as the Gaonic period. Important elements of the study of rabbinic literature developed in the period following the completion of the main documents. The reader will thus find throughout this book reference being made to scholars beginning from the Gaonic period.

In addition to the natural interest in the history of the halakhic process and the development of the intellectual world of the Sages, attention was paid – although to a lesser extent – to the literary history of these works and the periods in which they flourished. Thus the different stages of literary creation were studied, the relationships between the various works, the use made of early sources in late works, and the nature of the earliest collections.

In Jewish circles, study of the Talmud was more widespread than that of the Bible. In the first place, this was certainly because, in most periods and places, the Talmud was more widely read. In the second place, main parts of the Bible have the form of a work of history or are ascribed, in the Bible itself, to a specific author or historical period. Thus the Bible itself (when read naively) seemingly answers many of the questions relating to authorship and date. The study of rabbinic literature, however, by its very nature raises many problems and questions of this kind which cannot be solved by a simple perusal of the texts.

In de Middle Ages, many scholars engaged in the research of talmudic literature. A number of lexica of talmudic language, introductions to talmudic literature, lists of Sages of the Talmud period, and biographies of some of them, date from this period. Many authors added introductions to the Talmud to their commentaries on the Mishna, on *Massekhet Avot* or on the Talmud.

In the modern period, beginning in the 19th century with the advent of the scientific study of Jewish history and philology, talmudic research played a rather large role in Jewish scholarship, much more so than biblical research. Strides and advances in the study of general history and philology, in the sciences, the classics and philosophy, helped the scientific study of Talmud. The first modern scholars of rabbinic literature endeavoured to implement these advances in general scholarship in the study of the literature of the Sages. Most of these founding fathers of the *Wissenschaft des Judentums*, particularly those from Eastern Europe, had received the intensive talmudic education of the traditional *yeshivot*, and having become acquainted with the methods of modern scholarship, they applied these to talmudic literature.

The academic study of Judaism at this time, in particular talmudic study, was motivated to a great extent by the cultural and political conditions of the Jewish people. The critical re-evaluation of Jewish tradition was pursued by some in light of the development of Reform Judaism at that time. Others were interested in presenting a new positive face to Judaism for the outside world in light of recent cultural and political developments. The various branches of orthodox Judaism also evinced an interest in the academic and scientific study of the Talmud. This was often part of the polemic against other Jewish movements, or out of the desire to study their own roots with the methods of modern scholarship.

All of this interest and study resulted in the development of a variety of approaches and evaluations of the literature of the Sages, whether in general outlook, in the perception of the history of Oral Tora and of halakha and aggada, or in particulars such as the meaning of terms and concepts. In the course of time, scientific Talmud study emancipated from the explicit or implicit religious and cultural interests of the scholars, and many of the scholarly achievements became part of the common canon of the scientific study of rabbinic literature.

In recent decades, there have been great advances in the scientific study of rabbinic literature. Not only were new literary and philological methods created, but the scope of research was also widened, particularly regarding the social or historical background of the period and the study of the *realia* of the time. Thus, talmudic research began to apply and enhance the study of political, social, economic and linguistic circumstances in which rabbinic literature was created. Archeology, historical geography, and the study of ancient agriculture, labour, crafts and sciences became of concern to the talmudic scholar.

The recent period has also seen the publication of new texts from the Cairo Geniza or other *genizot*. Many of these are simply earlier or different versions of texts which were already known, but others had previously not been known. A large part have been published recently in scientific editions.

Unlike most of scholarship involved in biblical literature and the apocryphal and Hellenistic Jewish writings, talmudic research is largely written in Hebrew. While a number of early works were written in German, such as those of ZUNZ and GEIGER, or in French and English, most of the important works appeared in Hebrew. Even scholars who published many works in German or in English, such as BÜCHLER or GINZBERG, wrote their works on talmudic research for the most part in Hebrew. This is especially the case regarding modern commentaries on talmudic literature, including GINZBERG's *Commentary*. LIEBERMAN, who published important books and studies in English on a variety of topics of ancient Judais, wrote his long and classic commentary, *Tosefta ki-Fshutah*, in Hebrew. Moreover, the scientific editions of almost all forms of rabbinic literature, whether published in pre-war Germany, in America or in Israel, are for the most part published in Hebrew, and so are most publications of newly discovered texts. The same goes, naturally, for the classic works of modern talmudic scholarship published in Israel, such as the works of EPSTEIN which laid the foundations of modern-day critical scholarship, and those of ALON which provided a new historical framework for the study of Tannaic literature. It is unfortunate that these outstanding works of research and commentary do not always find full expression in the translations of rabbinic literature and the research works which have been appearing in modern European languages.

There are many points of agreement among the various scholars of rabbinic literature, particularly as regards literary and philological methods. But there are also great differences in approach which result in different conclusions regarding the date and provenance of various categories, especially targum, piyut and early mystical literature. This also regards the place of these genres within the general framework of rabbinic literature. Marked differences exist in the evaluation of the stages of development of rabbinic literature, the role of midrash and legislation in the development of halakha, or the editing process of the Mishna and other collections.

Limitations of space made it impossible to give full expression to every bibliographical detail or fully to evaluate the contributions made by all scholars. The considerations of each author, by himself or in discussion with the editor, have led to a presentation which takes into account every serious innovation in scholarship – even if, in the footnotes and the bibliographies concluding each chapter, this may result in tacit rejection.

The authors and the editor do not belong to the same school, assuming that such could exist, and do not always share the same opinions on major historical and literary problems. This may occasionally make for contradictions between some of the chapters. We have tried to be sensitive to such matters, without striving for uniformity.

In presenting this volume, we hope to fulfil our responsibility both to scholarship and the general reader of the *Compendia*.

Shmuel Safrai
January 1987

Chapter One

The Historical Background

Isaiah M. Gafni

Defining the Rabbinic Period

Establishing chronological boundaries for the historical background of rabbinic
literature is well nigh an impossible task, due in no small measure to the
amorphous nature of what we choose to include under the rubric of 'rabbinic
tradition'. If, for instance, we embrace a maximalist approach equating rabbinic
tradition with 'Oral Tora'[1] and defining the latter as any comment or statement
touching or elaborating on a portion – however small – of the written Bible, our
terminus a quo for the history of rabbinic tradition may find us not far removed
from Mt. Sinai itself. Indeed, it was just this premise that served as the basis for
the 'chain of tradition' drawn up by the Sages and linking them to Moses at
Sinai.[2] Rabbinic tradition in the eyes of its propounders was no less than the sum
of all those explanations, qualifications and clarifications of the frequently
obscure or all-too-brief text of God's Tora, and it was only natural for them to
assume that such traditions made their initial appearance almost contemporaneous with the divine revelation itself.[3]

By necessity, then, we find ourselves forced to embrace, at least for the
purposes of this chapter, a more limited task, i.e. providing a brief historical
outline of the salient stages that lead to, and ultimately produced, organized
tracts of rabbinic material. Here too, however, we encounter a developmental
process that must not be ignored, and a clear distinction is required – albeit not
easily applied along purely chronological lines – between the earlier formative
stages of rabbinic tradition, and the later stages that actually spawned literary
corpora of rabbinic material. The latter stage, roughly embracing the first five

---

[1] For a brief history of the term Oral Tora and its early uses cf. Urbach, *Sages*, 290ff.; Blidstein,
'Note'.
[2] *Avot* 1:1; the 'Tora' received by Moses and handed down to Joshua etc., clearly refers to the 'Oral
Tora' or to the amalgam of written and oral Tora, cf. Herr, 'Continuum', 44f., for the implications of
the chain of tradition drawn up by the Sages.
[3] E.g. *B.T. Meg.* 19b: 'The Holy One Blessed He showed Moses the minutiae of the Tora and the
minutiae of the scribes, and the innovations which would be introduced by the scribes'; cf. *Sifra,
Behukotai* 2 (112c).

1

or six centuries of the common era, is frequently designated as the 'Mishna and Talmud Period'[4] of Jewish history, and indeed it was during those years that the monumental works of the Sages – the Mishna, Tosefta, two Talmudim and the Midrashim – were crafted and shaped into the *literary* forms we recognize today. But to accurately assess the nature of this literature as we now possess it, we must remain cognizant of the processes that both preceded and followed the Mishna and Talmud period. On the one hand, while rabbinic literature may have taken on a literary format in the first five centuries of the common era, the *contents* of this material may at times reflect ideas, practices and even statements handed down from earlier phases of Jewish development, most particularly the days of the second Jewish commonwealth, which commenced with the return to Zion (538 B.C.E.) and building of the Second Temple (c. 516 B.C.E.), and concluded with the destruction of Jerusalem by Titus (70 C.E.). While this statement does nothing to diminish the enormous contribution of the Tannaim and Amoraim, it nevertheless takes into account the fact that by the first century C.E. there already existed within the Jewish community a significant body of oral tradition, both in the form of biblical commentary as well as 'regulations handed down by former generations and not recorded in the Laws of Moses'.[5] Rabbinic literature thus frequently serves as a conduit for the transmission of ideas and statements whose genesis preceded the rabbinic era by decades or even hundreds of years. For the student of rabbinic history the fact that a statement issuing – in literature – from the mouth of R. Akiva may have its roots in the teachings of an anonymous Sage hundreds of years earlier is indeed inhibiting,[6] but it is only after we accept this basic premise that rabbinic literary development can be placed in its proper perspective.

No less crucial for our understanding of rabbinic literary development are the processes that accompanied and followed the stages of rabbinic activity. The unique systems involved in the transmission of 'oral' traditions, whereby whole corpora of statements were organized, preserved and publicly disseminated in a non-written form,[7] gave rise to a situation whereby many of the rabbinic works we refer to were in fact finally redacted and transcribed in the post-talmudic period. Thus, for example, we frequently refer to 'aggadic midrashim' such as the various *Rabbot* (*Genesis Rabba*; *Leviticus Rabba* etc.) as Amoraic midrashim, and this is correct to the extent that we take note of the persons whose

---

[4] Neusner's observation (*History of Religions* 8 [1968] 164 and elsewhere) that historians were thus employing literary categories to define historical periods is correct, but his contention that 'Talmud does not define an age' may be qualified. Designation of the 'Talmudic Era' is no less natural than the rendering of portions of the 2nd and 1st millenia B.C.E. as 'The Biblical Period'; cf. also Neusner, *Method and Meaning*, 6. For support of a 'Talmudic Period' cf. Goodblatt, 'Rehabilitation', 32.

[5] Josephus, *Ant.* 13:297.

[6] Cf. Urbach, *Sages*, 3; no less sobering is the converse possibility, i.e. that a statement attributed to R. Akiva may have been placed in his mouth generations *after* the fact; cf. Green, 'What's in a Name'.

[7] Cf. Lieberman's classic study on 'The Publication of the Mishnah' in his *Hellenism*, 83-99.

statements are recorded in these works. But if indeed midrashim such as *Genesis Rabba* or *Leviticus Rabba* were compiled in the Land of Israel towards the end of the talmudic era (c. 5th to 7th cent.), other *Rabbot* and 'Amoraic midrashim' were redacted hundreds of years later. While a midrash such as *Numbers Rabba* is commonly included among Amoraic midrashim, its final redaction does not precede the 12th century. Similarly, many other Amoraic midrashim were compiled in the Geonic era (7th-11th cent.), and it goes without saying that such works frequently allude to events or ideas of that later era. It is not surprising, therefore, that we find references to the Islamic conquest in works commonly categorized as 'Amoraic',[8] but again, the converse is also a fact: midrashim redacted at a later date frequently preserve much earlier material, the antiquity of which may be established through a comparison with early non-rabbinic Jewish or Christian literature.[9]

Second Temple Institutions and the Sages

As noted, the period of the second Jewish commonwealth clearly served as a major context for the development and propagation of what ultimately found its way into the literary tradition of the Sages. In political terms, the period is at times overly projected as the last vestige of total Jewish independence in the Land of Israel. In fact, for most of the period, Jews in the Land of Israel found themselves ruled by various conquering regimes: Persia (536-332 B.C.E.), Alexander the Great and the Hellenistic monarchies (332-141 B.C.E.) and Rome (63 B.C.E.- 70 C.E.).[10] Only during eighty years of Hasmonean rule (141-63 B.C.E.) did Jews experience total self-rule, but it would be a mistake to focus only on this period as conducive to the development of extra-biblical traditions.[11] On the contrary, lack of real political freedom may even have enhanced a devotion on the part of certain authorities to religious concerns, and as far back as the days of Ezra and Nehemiah religious adherence was linked to instruction in the Tora in public. Chapters 8 to 10 in the Book of Nehemiah describe the elaborate gathering of the nation, wherein Ezra's public reading of the Tora 'from early morning until midday' (Neh 8:3) engendered a national re-commitment to the covenant (Neh 10:29). The assembly, however, was not confined to a verbatim reading of the Tora, but placed stress on a clear understanding of the text (Neh 9:7-8), and later Sages would see this – in light of their own oral tradition – as an

---

[8] Thus we find the Amora R. Yitshak describing the military confrontations between the 'King of Persia', 'King of Arabia' and 'Edom', *Pes. R.* 36 (162a); cf. Bamberger, 'Messianic Document'.

[9] A primary example is the midrash *Pirkei de-R. Eliezer*; while clearly edited no earlier than the 8th or 9th century, the book has been shown to draw heavily on the Apocryphal and Pseudepigraphical tradition of the Second Temple Period, cf. G. Friedlander's introduction to his English translation, London 1916, xxi-liii.

[10] Cf. Gafni in *Compendia* II/2, 2-3.

[11] Although later rabbinic tradition would come to look upon portions of the Hasmonean era ('the days of Shimon ben Shatah and Shlomtsion the Queen') as a 'golden age' in terms of Jewish behaviour and consequent divine rewards; cf. *Lev. R.* 35,10 (p. 829); *B.T. Taan.* 23a.

explicit allusion to the various components of Oral Tora.[12] It is hardly surprising, therefore, that the Sages would ultimately consider Ezra a major link between themselves and the first teacher of the Tora, Moses.[13] While Ezra was a priest, he was also a 'scribe' (Neh 8:9, 12:26), and his activity in elaborating and teaching Tora would ultimately be linked to his second title,[14] so that in time the term 'words of the scribes' דברי סופרים would be juxtaposed with the 'written Tora'.[15] This process, in retrospect, was a crucial phase in the formative stages of rabbinic tradition, for it allowed – possibly for the first time – the creation of a non-priestly cadre of Tora teachers, whose activity could transcend the physical confines of a temple or holy-city, and whose mobility would serve to spread their teachings even among Jews who did not maintain links with the priestly oligarchy. Moreover, it was precisely when portions of the priesthood would be stigmatized as being either too cosmopolitan (e.g. the Hellenistic, pre-Hasmonean period)[16] or too politicized (the later Hasmoneans and priests of the Roman-Herodian period)[17] that such teachers might enjoy enhanced reverence on the part of the masses, and thus a perceived distance from political contamination may have served to promote the spread of oral tradition among certain elements of Jewish society.[18]

While a designated 'period of scribes' is still doubtful as a distinct phase in the history of post-biblical Judaism,[19] the activities attributed to Ezra, i.e. teaching Tora as well as establishing ordinances (*takkanot*) would remain linked as two of the primary functions of the emerging Pharisaic-rabbinic movement. The Second Temple period provided a number of institutional frameworks for teaching as well as legislation by the Sages. On a national level, the two major institutions wherein their activity might be conducted were the Temple and the Sanhedrin. Just as Ezra publicly taught Tora on the Temple Mount at the beginning of the Second Commonwealth, tradition also describes Rabban Yohanan ben Zakkai, the renowned Sage of the late Temple period, teaching 'in the shadow of the sanctuary'.[20] Similarly, the Gospels project Jesus as well as members of the early Christian community teaching at the Temple,[21] and clearly the various pilgrimages and other religious ceremonies linked to the Temple provided these teachers and preachers with a considerable audience.

---

[12] *B.T. Meg.* 3a.
[13] *T. Sanh.* 4:7 – 'Ezra was worthy for the Tora to have been given by him, had not Moses come before him'; cf. *B.T. Sukka* 20a.
[14] Cf. Schürer, *History* 2, 323-5.
[15] E.g. *M. Orla* 3:9; cf. *B.T. Meg.* 19b.
[16] Cf. 1 Macc 1:11.
[17] *T. Men.* 13:21; *B.T. Pes.* 57a.
[18] Cf. Urbach, 'Class Status', 46.
[19] See Safrai, below 148-53. For a summary of the various functions attributed to the *sofrim* see: Mantel, 'Development', 52-57.
[20] *B.T. Pes.* 26a.
[21] Luke chaps. 20-21; cf. Safrai in *Compendia* I/2, 905.

As distinct from the function of public preaching, the legislative (and academic) activities of Second Temple Jerusalem are obviously to be linked to the court system established in that city. Here, however, the sources leave much open to speculation. At least one literary source of the early Hellenistic period, Hecataeus of Abdera, seems to suggest that at that time 'guardianship of the laws and customs' was still entrusted to the priests who served as 'judges in all major disputes'.[22] In the later Hellenistic and Hasmonean period a *gerousia* emerges in Jerusalem,[23] and while its responsibility for the nation's internal affairs would slowly be superseded by that of the Hasmonean dynasty,[24] it continued to function until the late Hasmonean period. With the Roman conquest of Judaea we encounter for the first time in a Jewish context the phrase Sanhedrin,[25] but as repeatedly noted by scholars, the different sources project divergent pictures of the functions, components and leadership of this body.[26] No conclusive evidence exists to support the well-known theory of a plurality of legislative and rabbinic-academic bodies in Jerusalem,[27] and a more likely explanation of the discrepancies between the sources (Josephus, the New Testament and rabbinic literature) must take into account both the varied aims and perspectives of those sources, as well as the ever-shifting political balance that existed in late Second Temple Jerusalem, and that undoubtedly manifested itself in the composition and orientation of the Sanhedrin.[28] And yet, for the purpose of our discussion, even the various changes undergone by the Sanhedrin to not diminish the fact that within the context of the high courts of Jerusalem (and possibly of local courts as well)[29] a framework was provided for legislative and academic activity – both serving to enhance the scope of the extra-biblical tradition that ultimately would be incorporated in rabbinic literature. One can also assume that various ordinances attributed to particular Second Temple Sages such as Shimon ben Shatah, Hillel, and Rabban Gamliel

---

[22] Cf. Stern, *Greek and Latin Authors* 1, 26.

[23] *Ant.* 12:138; 1 Macc 12:6; the *gerousia* may represent the continuation of a 'coucil of elders' from Persian times, cf. Stern, *Ha-Teudot*, 34; for the various theories linking the *gerousia* with the 'Great Assembly' cf. Mantel, 'Development', 44-49; *id. Anshei Knesset Hagedola*, 63-79.

[24] The Hasmonean era effected a formal change in the hierarchical relationship between the high-priesthood and the *gerousia*; cf. Schürer, *History* 2, 203-4; Stern (*ib.*).

[25] Under Gabinius (57-55 B.C.E.) the Jewish territory of Palestine was divided into five συνέδρια (*Ant.* 14:91; cf. *War* 1:170) which seems to suggest administrative units. As a court of Jerusalem the phrase appears initially in connection with the trial of Herod (*Ant.* 14:165-179).

[26] Cf. Safrai in *Compendia* I/1, 379-82; Schürer, *History* 2, 204-26.

[27] First suggested by Büchler, *Synedrion*; for a summary of the various other theories cf. Mantel, *Studies*, 54ff.

[28] Cf. Alon, *The Jews* 1, 185-205.

[29] The local court system is referred to in later – and schematic – rabbinic traditions on the judicial hierarchy that functioned before the destruction, cf. *T. Sanh.* 7:1 (compare *Ant.* 4:214f.). Josephus (*War* 2:569f.) also describes the establishment of local courts as well as a Galilean court of 70 prior to the Great War; the nature of Josephus' history, however, and his propensity for dwelling on national issues, leaves us with only fragmentary information on the local frameworks of Second Temple Jewish life; cf. Safrai in *Compendia* I/1, 394.

the Elder, were in fact carried out, or at least supported, by some official court body, although what the relationship was to a 'High Court' or 'Sanhedrin' in each case remains unclear.[30] Nevertheless, the tradition of the Sages, both in the form of legislation as well as biblical interpretation, thrived in Second Temple Jerusalem, for learning and teaching were by now inseparably linked to the worship of God, and the authority vested in the site of the Temple rendered the teachings emanating from that site equally authoritative.[31]

On a local level, the emergence of the synagogue clearly presents one of the most significant contributions to the growth of the influence of the Sages. The roots of the synagogue phenomenon are unclear,[32] and a distinction may be made between activities ultimately associated with synagogue functions – such as regular gatherings for the purpose of reading the Tora or preaching – and the actual establishment of fixed settings for such activity. The Book of Kings (2 Kgs 4:23) already alludes to regular assemblies around the prophets on Sabbath and the New Moon, and Ezra's public reading of the Tora may also have served as a precedent for the institution of periodic readings from Scripture.[33] These, however, did not necessarily require a fixed institution or building, and indeed the earliest archaeological and literary evidence of synagogues does not precede the Hellenistic period.[34] Later talmudic sources would assume that the first synagogues were established in post-First-Temple Babylonia,[35] but this was based on the assumption that the earliest synagogues were established as a replacement for the destroyed Temple. Scholars have noted, however, that this perception may be anachronistic,[36] deriving from a post-Second-Temple reality when indeed prayers as the replacement for sacrificial worship emerged as the central component of synagogue activity. This, however, was not the situation during the Second Temple period itself, and almost all extant sources project the institution as being complementary to the Temple, rather than serving to take its place. For first century Jerusalem the Theodotus inscription is particularly illuminating, with its forthright statement that the synagogue was built 'for the reading of the Law and for the teaching of the commandments'.[37] This two-fold educational enterprise – reading and teaching – is similarly described in the New Testament,[38] and Josephus also maintains that the Tora requires 'that

---

[30] Alon, *The Jews* 1, 201; Safrai, *ib.* 388; Albeck, 'Semikha', 92-3, suggests that these *takkanot* were established by the 'private courts' of the presiding Sage, rather than by a national Sanhedrin; see also Urbach, 'Class Status', 49-50.

[31] For the link between the judiciary and Temple worhip cf. *B.T. Sanh.* 52b; *Mekh. de-R. Sh.b.Y.* p. 171; see most recently Urbach, *Ha-Halakha*, 10.

[32] Cf. Guttmann, *The Synagogue*, 3-76.

[33] Safrai in *Compendia* I/2, 912-3.

[34] The earliest inscriptions attesting to synagogues are from the rule of Ptolemy III (247-221 B.C.E.); *CPJ* 3, no. 1440 (p. 141), no. 1532A (p. 164); cf. Schürer, *History* 2, 425 n. 5.

[35] *B.T. Meg.* 29a.

[36] Cf. Safrai, 'The Synagogue', 67-70; Gutmann, 'Origin', 36-40.

[37] *CII* 2 no. 1404 (p. 332-5); Reinach, 'L'inscription'.

[38] Luke 4:16-22; Acts 13:15.

every week men should desert their other occupations and assemble to *listen to the Law* and to obtain a *thorough and accurate knowledge* of it'.[39] The situation in the diaspora is succinctly described by Philo: The Jews 'assemble in the same place on these seventh days... (and) some *priest* or one of the *elders* reads the holy laws to them and *expounds* them point by point'.[40] Philo's description is noteworthy not only for its reference to the exposition that follows the reading, but in that *en passant* we encounter here the emerging prominence of elders (i.e. sages) alongside priests. Common to all the sources, in any event, is the realization that what ultimately may be classified as rabbinic material – whether in the form of direct biblical interpretation (reading from Scriptures and translating or explaining the text) or in the more elaborate form of the sermon[41] was now provided with a major setting for its propagation among the population. It is hardly surprising, therefore, that later rabbinic sources would assume that each of the '480' synagogues of Second Temple Jerusalem maintained a 'Beit Sefer' and 'Beit Talmud',[42] i.e. a framework for biblical as well as rabbinic studies.

The Pharisaic Movement

The central institutions cited above served only as a partial framework for the intellectual activity that was to produce rabbinic material. Clearly, not all teachers operated within an official context, nor need we assume that all Jews adhered to the decisions that issued from bodies such as the Sanhedrin. The degree to which the Pharisaic-rabbinic movement in fact influenced Second Temple Jewry has been heatedly debated by scholars, with opinions running the gamut from a maximalist approach that equated rabbinic teaching with normative Jewish behaviour,[43] to a minimalist camp that would portray the Sages of the Second Temple period as merely one of a host of splinter groups (alongside Essenes, Sadducees, etc.) exerting a negligible influence on the masses.[44] Inasmuch as our purpose here is not to present a 'history of Judaism' but rather a sketch of the stages leading up to rabbinic literary activity, it is not incumbent upon us to align our survey with any particular camp. Nevertheless, one issue is central in this context, and that is to seek the Second Temple forerunners of the later rabbinic movement.[45] Notwithstanding all the doubts and hesitation on the

---

[39] *Ag. Ap.* 2:175.

[40] Philo, *Hypothetica, apud*: Eusebius, *Praep. evang.* 8:7, 11-13; cf. Philo, *Spec. leg.* 2:62.

[41] Not all synagogues, however, necessarily included a sermon as part of the weekly service; cf. Safrai in *Compendia* I/2, 932-3.

[42] *P.T. Meg.* 3, 73d. The number 480 is a midrashic exaggeration based on *gematria*.

[43] Alon, *Jews, Judaism*, 22 ('the Pharisees constituted the vast majority of the nation').

[44] Smith, 'Palestinian Judaism'.

[45] This issue is far from simple, given the later rabbinic tendency to 'rabbinize' earlier Jewish history, and particularly Jewish heroes from as far back as biblical times. For a recent brief treatment cf. Cohen, 'Parallel Tradition'.

issue,[46] there appears to be a progression from the Pharisaic movement of the second commonwealth to the rabbinic circles of the Mishna and Talmud periods.[47] To be sure, the Sages usually refrain from referring to themselves as 'Pharisees', using this name preferably in connection with their Sadducean adversaries. They clearly preferred the title 'Sages';[48] moreover, in drawing the chain of rabbinic tradition they preferred to designate persons rather than groups or parties.

The history of the Pharisees as a group remains clouded. As in so many other areas, the Persian period offers precious little information on who was involved in either developing or teaching extra-biblical traditions, save for what has already been noted in relation to the days of Ezra and Nehemiah. Following the enigmatic reference to 'Men of the Great Synagogue', the first named Sage in the famous list at the beginning of Mishna *Avot* is Shimon the Just. Here again we are uncertain as to the provenance of this Sage-priest, alternately dated to either the early Hellenistic period[49] or to approximately 200 B.C.E., and thus possibly the high-priest Shimon ben Yohanan described by Ben Sira (50:1ff.).[50] Chapter 39 of Ben Sira's work is of particular interest, as it projects – possibly for the first time – the activities and behaviour that would come to be identified with that of the rabbinic Sage: '... Not so he that applieth himself to the fear of God, And to set his mind upon the Law of the Most High'. The author goes on to praise the attributes of the Sage who 'pours forth wise sayings ... directs counsel and knowledge and sets his mind on their secrets ... declares wise instruction and glorifies in the Law of the Lord. His understanding many do praise ...'.

Following Shimon the Just, the Mishna (*Avot* 1:3) lists Antigonos of Sokho, for whom we have no historical context,[51] but only a statement pertaining to the manner in which one ought to serve God. Antigonos is succeeded by Yose ben Yoezer and Yose ben Yohanan, the first in a series of five 'pairs' among the Sages, leading up to Hillel and Shammai, contemporaries of Herod. Yose ben Yoezer's statement in *Avot* ('Let thy house be a meeting-place for the Sages, and sit amid the dust of their feet and drink in their words with thirst') would again seem to suggest the appearance of a class of Sages, and it is with Yose ben Yoezer that legal statements are first listed in connection with particular mas-

---

[46] E.g. Neusner, 'Formation'.

[47] This statement takes into account the shift in rabbinic self-consciousness following the destruction, and the widely different roles of the Second Temple Pharisees and post-Temple rabbis; cf. Cohen, 'Significance'.

[48] Cf. Herr, 'Boethusians', 13-14 and n. 97.

[49] Shimon is the high-priest who greets the great conqueror on his journey through Palestine, cf. *B.T. Yoma* 69a and parallels; compare *Ant.* 12:43, 157, where Shimon the Just is a contemporary of Ptolemy I.

[50] For literature on Shimon the Just cf. R. Marcus, Josephus, Loeb ed. vol. 7, 732-6.

[51] A later source would link his disciples with the formation of the Sadducees and Boethusians, see *A.R.N.* a 5 and b 10 (13b).

ters.[52] Yose ben Yoezer's death is recorded in the midrash in connection with
יקים איש צרורות *Yakim ish tserorot*.[53] The latter has commonly been identified as the high-priest Alkimos, appointed by the Seleucid monarchy during the
last years of Judah the Maccabee (c. 162 B.C.E.) and ultimately responsible for
the slaughter of sixty members of the group of Hasidim.[54] Thus there may have
been some social framework for the activities of Sages as far back as the pre-
Hasmonean period, and prior to the formation of a Pharisaic party. However,
while the line from 'scribes' to 'hasidim' to 'Pharisees' has frequently been
suggested, the rigidity of such a progression probably requires some
qualification.

Nevertheless, by the late 2nd century B.C.E., if not earlier,[55] we are confronted with a definite social mosaic comprised of those parties that would remain
active until late Temple times. The background for the appearance of the
Pharisces (as well as that of the Sadducees and Essenes) was thus the formation
of the Hasmonean state and the ensuing political, cultural and social changes
that transpired in Judaea. By 142 B.C.E. under Simon, the last surviving son of
Mattathias, the Jews of Judaca had in effect removed themselves from the rule
of the Seleucid Empire.[56] A new dynasty emerged, transplanting the earlier
priestly families and linking military and social leadership with the priesthood (1
Macc 14). There is no evidence for a Pharisaic movement diametrically opposed
to all the ensuing components of a political entity,[57] and under the Hasmonean
Queen Salome the Pharisees seem to have enjoyed a position of enhanced
power.[58] More importantly, even when the Pharisees were out of favour in
Hasmonean eyes, such as during portions of the reign of Alexander Yannai,[59]
we do not find them taking the route of ultimate sectarians who chose – as did
the Essenes – to irrevocably sever ties with Jerusalem and the ruling establishment. Indeed, the striking characteristic of many of the early Sages is that they
maintain an independent and implied moral stand regarding issues of the day,

---

[52] *M. Ed.* 8:4; *Sifra, Shemini* 8 (55a); *B.T. Shabb.* 14b.

[53] *Gen. R.* 65,22 (p. 724f.).

[54] 1 Macc 7:16. Inasmuch as the activities of the third 'pair', Shimon ben Shatah and Yehuda ben
Tabbai, are contemporaneous with Alexander Yannai (103-76 B.C.E.) and Alexandra Salome (76-67
B.C.E.), the first 'pair' would have been active two generations earlier, i.e. the middle of the 2nd
century B.C.E., and thus fit easily into the early days of the Hasmonean movement.

[55] Josephus first refers to Pharisees, Sadducees and Essenes within the context of Jonathan's rule
(160-142 B.C.E.; *Ant.* 13:171-3); the first historic event, however, that projects the Pharisees as an
identifiable group, was their clash with John Hyrcanus I (134-104 B.C.E.; *Ant.* 13:288-96). While the
source quoted by Josephus in relation to Jonathan's leadership does not elaborate on the involvement of the groups in the social history of the time, it is possible that in its original form it related the
opposition of Essenes and Sadducees to the perceived usurpation of the high-priesthood by Jonathan. Cf. Schwarz, 'Josephus and Nicolaus', 161-2.

[56] Gafni in *Compendia* II/2, 12.

[57] Alon, *Jews, Judaism*, 23-26 and n. 43.

[58] *Ant.* 13:408-409; the hostile tone of the description may be attributed to Nicolaus.

[59] For relations between Yannai and the Pharisees cf. Schürer, *History* 1, 223-5 and n. 22 for possible
references in the Dead Sea Scrolls.

while frequently operating within traditional frameworks. Shimon ben Shatah seems to have been particularly active in establishing ordinances touching on major social issues, while at the same time seeking to avoid the wrath of the Hasmonean king.[60] At the trial of the young Herod before the Sanhedrin (47 B.C.E.), the Galilean governor as well as the other judges are reproached by Samaias,[61] and later we hear that the two Pharisaic leaders, Pollion and Samaias, refuse to swear allegiance to Herod.[62]

The Hasmonean state fell to the Roman legions of Pompey in 63 B.C.E., and for 23 years the Jews of Judaea were granted a small vassal state under the 'ethnarchy' of John Hyrcanus II. Following the Parthian invasion of the Near East (40 B.C.E.) Roman influence was temporarily removed from Jerusalem, and Mattathias Antigonos ruled briefly as the last Hasmonean monarch. With reconquest of Judaea by Herod (37 B.C.E.) the Land of Israel enters a second stage of Roman influence, and while politically Herod would stifle any independent activity, the Pharisaic-rabbinic movement – although also attacked by the King – nevertheless continued to grow.

Hillel and 'The House of Hillel'

It was precisely during Herodian rule that a central Sage, Hillel the Babylonian, was able to flourish, although one suspects that his Babylonian roots may have been to his advantage. STERN has graphically described the social revolution that took place in Herod's time in the Jerusalem hierarchy and religious establishment.[63] While that monarch systematically attempted to eradicate Hasmonean influence, a new aristocracy, based in part on Jews from the Hellenistic and Parthian diaspora, was created in Jerusalem to fill the void.[64] Hillel's emergence on the scene coincides with this phenomenon,[65] and with him our corpus of Pharisaic-rabbinic tradition grows considerably.[66] Later generations would claim that Hillel already assumed an official position of *Nasi* (Patriarch). That such an office even existed in Second Temple times is questionable, and even more so given the limited powers delegated by Herod to anyone – let alone a rabbinic Sage spiritually close to those who refused to take an oath of allegiance. Nevertheless, we are witness to an impressive list of disputes between

---

[60] *Gen. R.* 91,3 (p. 1115); *P.T. Ber.* 7,11b (= *P.T. Naz.* 5,54b); *B.T. Ber.* 48a. For the *takkanot* cf. *P.T. Ket.* 8, 32c.

[61] *Ant.* 14:172-3; in *Ant.* 15:3 it is Pollion the Pharisee who spoke at Herod's trial; *Ant.* 15:3, 370 describes Samaias as a disciple of Pollion the Pharisee.

[62] *Ant.* 15:370; much has been written on the possible connection of Samaias and Pollion with the rabbinic figures of the 4th pair, Shemaya and Avtalion, or the 5th pair, Hillel and Shammai; cf. Feldman, 'Identity'; Schalit, *Herodes*, 768-71.

[63] Stern, 'Realignments'.

[64] Stern, *ib.* 49f.

[65] Stern, *ib.* 58.

[66] For a list and discussion of Hillel and Shammai traditions cf. Neusner, *Rabbinic Traditions* 1, 185-302.

Hillel and Shammai,[67] and an even more impressive corpus (over 300 cases) of disputes attributed to the two schools bearing the names of these two luminaries. Granted, many of the disputes probably emerged years, decades or even generations after Hillel's death (c. 10 C.E.), and the debates would not be conclusively resolved until after the destruction.[68]

In any case, major developments within the movement of the Sages, socially as well as in the literary and legal sphere, seem to have been advanced with the appearance of Hillel. Hillel's name is connected with a series of ordinances,[69] as well as with new exegetical systems applied for the first time as a means not only of producing new biblical interpretation, but also – or even primarily – for the purpose of providing solutions to new halakhic problems.[70] But beyond these developments in the realm of midrash and halakha, which will be closely examined in this work, Hillel's appearance serves as a major crossroad in the social history of the rabbinic movement. The 'House of Hillel' will ultimately serve not only as a designation of a school of disciples, but also as an emerging dynasty.

If until now we encountered individual Sages or small groups whose power hinged on either personal charisma or relations with the ruling regime, Hillel's advent may signify something of an ideological revolution. Not only must Tora be taught publicly, but attached to Hillel's name is the notion of a popular movement, where one encourages disciples regardless of family background or social status. This clearly contrasts with a priestly oligarchic leadership based on hereditary authority It also appears to be diametrically opposed to the elitist attitude expressed by Shammai and his followers.[71] (An additional difference with Beit Shammai is the apparent proximity of the latter with the Zealot movements in the last years of the Second Temple.[72]) What is interesting, however, is that this same popular rabbinic movement would produce from within its ranks a dynasty – Beit Hillel – ultimately to assume political as well as spiritual predominance in the post-Temple Jewish community. Paradoxically,

---

[67] For these disputes, as well as traditions comparing the two Sages' ideals and behaviour, Neusner, *ib.* 303-40.

[68] Nor was there a one-time decree resolving the issues; rather, the process seems to have been an ongoing one, spread over much of the Mishna period; cf Safrai, 'Decision'.

[69] *B.T. Shabb.* 14b; *P.T. Pes.* 1, 27d; *M. Shev.* 10:3-4; *M. Ar.* 9:4.

[70] The famous example – resolving the halakhic issues incurred when the Passover sacrifice falls on Sabbath – is discussed in parallel rabbinic traditions: *P.T. Pes.* 6, 33a; *B.T. Pes.* 66a; *T. Pes.* 4:13; a copious bibliography on this source has accrued over the years, inasmuch as it was seen to relate to a major phase in the development of rabbinic systems of legal debate, cf. the literature cited by Safrai, 'Tales', 220 n. 38; cf. also Fraenkel, 'Hermeneutic Problems'.

[71] *A.R.N.* a 3 (7b).

[72] This is based primarily on the rabbinic tradition on the Shammaites who forced Beit Hillel to accept the '18 decrees', *T. Shabb.* 1:16-22; *P.T. Shabb.* 1, 3c; *B.T. Shabb.* 13b. These decrees, formulated at 'the upper chamber of Hananya ben Hizkia ben Garon' (*M. Shabb.* 1:4) were intended to place a further distance between Jews and gentiles; cf. Graetz, *Geschichte* III/2, 797-9. See also Epstein, *Tannaitic Literature*, 746 for a possible rabbinic connection between Beit Shammai and the Idumean Zealots.

then, the same movement that stressed behaviour and knowledge over bequeathed, geneological authority,[73] would slowly find itself functioning along the same social lines as its priestly predecessors. At least two generations – and the destruction of the Jerusalem – would pass, however, before the crystallization of a dynastic house would reach the stage of assuming an official, recognized position. While the descendants of Hillel[74] – Gamliel I and Shimon ben Gamliel – appear to have enjoyed a revered status among the Sages of late Second Temple Jerusalem, in neither case do we note an *official*, bureaucratically recognized role of leadership on their part. Gamliel I (the Elder) appears in Acts 5:34 merely as a Pharisaic member of the Sanhedrin, albeit 'held in honour by all the people'. Similarly, Josephus describes his own contemporary, Shimon ben Gamliel, as 'a native of Jerusalem, of a very illustrious family and of the sect of the Pharisees ... a man highly gifted with intelligence and judgement',[75] but again, without any reference to an official position. The meaningful change in the status of the Sages would evolve only in the wake of the destruction.

Hasidim and Zealots

The world of the Sages in the Second Temple period was not only lacking of any overall organizational structure, it was also far from homogeneous. The present work focuses primarily on those elements whose orientation was towards the study and teaching of Tora, ultimately resulting in the creation of rabbinic literature. However, we also encounter individuals who, while seemingly of kindred spirit with the Sages, nevertheless placed a greater stress on behaviour or political activism. In certain instances such individuals are projected as being invested with supernatural powers, and appear capable of either effecting miracles or enjoying heavenly protection from danger. Of particular interest in this context are a number of individuals – from different stages of the Second Temple period as well as the post-Temple era – referred to as *hasidim* (pious).[76] One of the earliest examples of such behaviour are the stories linked with the name of 'Honi the Circlemaker' or 'the hasid' who induced rain by means of prayer and invocation of the Holy Name.[77] Other hasidim maintained rulings that either deviated from generally accepted halakha or demanded increased

---

[73] E.g. *B.T. Yoma* 71b; cf. Urbach, 'Class Status', 46-9.

[74] Cf. *B.T. Shabb.* 15a. It has recently been posited that the patriarchal dynasty goes back only to Gamliel I, and that the 'House of Hillel' is in reality comprised of Gamliel's descendants; see Goodblatt, 'Origins'. The present author is not entirely convinced by Goodblatt's arguments on these points, but accepts the contention that a 'Patriarchate' in the later sense did not exist before the destruction.

[75] Jos., *Life* 191.

[76] חסידים ראשונים 'First Hasidim' or חסידים ואנשי מעשה 'Hasidim and Men of Deeds'. The sources are listed and analyzed by Safrai, 'Teaching of Pietists'. It is far from certain if any connection may be made between these individuals and the 'Congregation of hasidim' mentioned in 1 Macc 2:42, 7:13; 2 Macc 14:6; cf. Schürer, *History* 1, 150 n. 46.

[77] *M. Taan.* 3:8; *T Taan.* 2:13. Honi (Onias) is also mentioned by Josephus, *Ant.* 14:22.

strictness (regarding Sabbath in particular). Some were outstanding for their personal piety or devotion, frequently accompanied by an exaltation of poverty as a virtue, while others were involved in healing the sick or devoting themselves to various charitable deeds. What is outstanding in most cases was that the study of Tora was considered by these pietists as subservient to personal behaviour and individual charisma. This gave rise to the question of their original links to the Pharisaic-rabbinic world, some scholars refusing to accept any distinction between the hasidim and the early Sages,[78] while others would claim that this particular type of piety and miracle-working was in fact antithetical to early rabbinic ideology.[79] If, however, we accept the variegated and fluid nature of the rabbinic world before the destruction, embracing different groups who – while adhering to the general 'philosophy' of the Pharisees – carved out their own particular niche within the Jewish community,[80] we can understand that the proximity between the Sages and the hasidim would not have precluded tension between the two branches, and even a rabbinic reaction to what was perceived as a too strenuous relegation of learning and intellectual activity.[81]

It has recently been shown that the hasidim were primarily a Galilean phenomenon.[82] This throws light on the position of Jesus and his disciples. While clearly given to a Pharisaic-rabbinic orientation, they were nevertheless closer to the 'hasidic fringe' of that movement.[83]

Yet another example of a Galilean group loosely connected to the Sages and yet pursuing a particular political-religious agenda, is the group of Zealots referred to by Josephus as the 'Fourth Philosophy': 'This school agrees in all other respects with the opinions of the Pharisees, except that they have a passion for liberty that is almost unconquerable'.[84] Josephus claims that this group was founded by Judas the Galilean,[85] and it appears that the forerunners of this particular group had been active in Galilee for some time, as opponents of the Roman regime.[86]

In any case, regional factors seemed to have played a certain role in creating a variety of groups or individuals, all supportive of the major tenets of Pharisaic-rabbinic Judaism, while at the same time pursuing more particular lifestyles or political goals.

[78] Büchler, *Piety*.

[79] Cf. most recently Green, 'Palestinian Holy Men'.

[80] Another example of distinct groups within the broader Pharisaic fold are those who banded together with the common goal of maintaining ritual purity or refraining from the use of untithed food; cf. *M. Dem.* 2:2-3; Oppenheimer, *Am-Ha'aretz*.

[81] In which case the rabbinic saying in *M. Avot* 2:5 – 'An ignorant man cannot be saintly' – represents the Sages' response to the phenomenon of unlearned piety; cf. the most recent re-examination of the issue by Safrai, 'Hasidim'.

[82] Safrai, *ib.* 134-8.

[83] Safrai, *ib.* 137.

[84] *Ant.* 18:23.

[85] In *Ant.* 18:2 – Judas the Gaulanite and Zadok the Pharisee.

[86] Cf. Stern, 'Sicarii and Zealots', 262f.

The Destruction and the Yavne Period

The fall of Jerusalem and destruction of the Second Temple, following decades of turmoil and four bitter years of revolt throughout the Land of Israel (66-70 c.e.),[87] demanded the immediate establishment of new social and religious frameworks, if the Jewish people were to survive and retain their national identity. That the destruction of the Temple serves as a major turning point in Jewish history cannot be denied. Defining, however, the precise nature of the trauma that was felt at the time, as well as of the nature of the changes that were introduced into the world of the Sages, has engendered lively debate among scholars.[88] Echoes of the devastation that was felt seem to imply that for some Jews, the lack of a Temple and cessation of sacrificial worship were interpreted as the severing of all real and ongoing ties between the nation and its God: 'Woe unto us' declared one of the great Sages of the day, 'that this – the place where the iniquities of Israel are atoned for – is laid waste'.[89] Yet other Jews, writing at the time, express a feeling of total despair and loss of life's meaning without a Temple,[90] and this in turn induced some groups to undertake a position of perpetual mourning and asceticism.[91] To be sure, the war itself did not effect a mass exodus of Jews from the land, and the fact that the province continued – at first – to be called Judaea points to the lack of any major demographic shift at this stage. While certain administrative steps would ultimately be taken by the Roman government as a result of lessons learnt in the wake of the Great War,[92] our interests in this volume lay primarily with the spiritual leadership that emerges in the aftermath of the destruction.

The first stages of restoration in Judaea are commonly linked to the imposing figure of Rabban Yohanan ben Zakkai.[93] While the facts surrounding his arrival at Yavne are shrouded in legend,[94] his policy in rebuilding the religious foundations of the community are clear and well defined. The underlying premise of Rabban Yohanan's undertaking was that Jewish existence need not cease – even without a social and religious focal point in the form of a Temple. An analysis of the numerous *takkanot* attributed to this Sage reflects the common

---

[87] Cf. Gafni in *Compendia* II/2, 27.

[88] See for example Cohen, 'Significance', for conclusions vastly different from what is commonly accepted in modern scholarship.

[89] The speaker is R. Yoshua ben Hananya, a disciple of Rabban Yohanan ben Zakkai; see *A.R.N.* a 4 (11a) and cf. Alon, *The Jews* 1, 50-1. Cf. also *B.T. Ber.* 32b; 'R. Elazar also said: Since the day the Temple was destroyed, a wall of iron has intervened between Israel and their Father in heaven'; on this statement, however, cf. Bokser, 'The Wall'.

[90] Cf. 2 Bar 10:6-19 (Charlesworth, *Pseudepigrapha* 1, 624-5).

[91] *T. Sota* 15:11-15; *B.T. Bava B.* 60b.

[92] For the political status and administration of Roman Judaea cf. Stern, 'Roman Administration'.

[93] Cf. Alon, *The Jews* 1, 86-118; *id.*, *Jews, Judaism*, 269-343; Safrai, 'New Research'; Neusner, 'Life'; Urbach, 'Class Status', 54-6. For further literature see also Schürer, *History* 2, 369 n. 55.

[94] Cf. Safrai in *Compendia* I/1, 404-5.

denominator for most of his enactments. The void created by the destruction was to be filled both with regards to the outright worship of God,[95] as well as through the establishment of a new apparatus to oversee Jewish communal life.[96] In this context one of the issues that demanded an immediate solution was the ongoing responsibility for regulating and periodically intercalating the calendar,[97] and Rabban Yohanan ben Zakkai's takkanot deal both with the decision-making process, as well as the steps to be taken in informing the community of the center's decisions. Rabban Yohanan ben Zakkai's activities serve, in a sense, as a harbinger of the major halakhic and theological re-evaluation that would characterize the rabbinic world after the destruction.

As noted elsewhere[98] the project begun at Yavne by Rabban Yohanan ben Zakkai and carried on by Rabban Gamliel II[99] was a unique exercise in which the leaders of the community would stress continuity with Jerusalem and the past, while simultaneously setting up an authority structure and religious framework that clearly evolved out of a radically new situation. Thus, customs once performed only at the Temple and Jerusalem[100] would now be decentralized and performed in synagogues throughout the land, but would be justified as a means of 'perpetuating the memory of the Temple' זכר למקדש;[101] a new Sanhedrin would be established at Yavne which – while not enjoying proximity to Temple worship as a source of authority[102] – would nevertheless be deemed authoritative and in fact a direct continuation of the Jerusalem Sanhedrin.[103] As already pointed out, even the Patriarchate would assume a 'history' going back at least three or four generations, although it was only at Yavne that the office began to

---

[95] Cf. his reply to R. Yoshua's above-quoted statement: 'My son, do not be grieved, we have another atonement as effective as this (= sacrificial worship), and what is it? Acts of loving kindness', A.R.N. a 4 (11a); cf. also Urbach, Sages, 667.

[96] For Rabban Yohanan ben Zakkai's takkanot see: M. Rosh H. 4:1-4; B.T. Rosh H. 21b, 31b; for an analysis see Safrai, 'New Research'.

[97] The urgency of the issue is succinctly expressed in the dialogue between the 'Sons of Bathyra' and Rabban Yohanan ben Zakkai, B.T. Rosh H. 29b; for the importance of the calendar and its regulation in Jewish life at the time, cf. Herr in Compendia I/2, 843-57.

[98] Gafni in Compendia II/2, 28-31.

[99] The precise dates of Rabban Yohanan ben Zakkai's activity at Yavne and Rabban Gamliel's succession are uncertain. Alon, The Jews 1, 119, limits R. Yohanan's tenure to only 10-15 years (c. 70-85 C.E.), while Safrai, 'New Research', 30-1 maintains that it is untenable that a scion of such an illustrious family as Gamliel's would have been allowed by the Flavian dynasty to assume such a powerful position; hence he suggests that Gamliel's appearance came only after Domitian's death, 96 C.E. See also Safrai in Compendia I/1, 406.

[100] E.g. sounding the shofar on the New Year – even on Sabbath; taking up the lulav for the full seven days of the Feast of Tabernacles.

[101] M. Rosh H. 4:3.

[102] Cf. above n. 31.

[103] Cf. B.T. Rosh H. 31a-b; Gen. R. 97 (p. 1220-1) for the removal of the Sanhedrin 'from Jerusalem to Yavne' and subsequently on to the Galilee. For the powers of the Sanhedrin at Yavne cf. Safrai in Compendia I/1, 407; on the question of whether, indeed, the new body was deemed a 'Sanhedrin', see some recent doubts raised by Levine, Rabbinic Class, 47-52.

enjoy its unique powers, deriving from a combination of political recognition and spiritual authority.[104]

The world of the Sages could not help but react at Yavne to the social upheaval and changes brought about by the Great War and destruction. Not only did particular social and religious groups – such as the Essenes or Sadducees – disappear from the scene, but the entire structure of the ruling classes of the Jewish community was shattered. To the extent that the descendants of the house of Herod, such as Agrippa II, had any influence among Jews until the war, that impact was now negligible or non-existent.[105] A similar fate was met by the aristocratic families of late Second Temple Jerusalem, who likewise fade from the scene. While priests as a social class would still maintain a position to be reckoned with,[106] the high-priesthood was no longer a factor in the social hierarchy. The Sages, it appears, were among the few social classes whose communal position could transcend the destruction of the Temple, precisely because – as we have noted – their powers did not emanate from any formal ties with the Temple. The mobility of the Sage, together with the displacement of the Temple and its worship with prayer in the synagogue, and even the mobility of the central body of Sages, are all signs of a new, and potentially decentralized Jewish community.[107] These developments led the Sages to search for a redefinition both of their own particular world, as well as a redefinition of the social and religious boundaries of the Jewish nation at large. The process, it appears, had a definite impact on the development of rabbinic literature as well.

In terms of their immediate circles, the Sages at Yavne begin to take on a more formal, almost bureaucratic image – which of course fits their newly augmented status within the community. While some sort of ordination ceremony may have existed in late Second Temple times,[108] it is only at Yavne that we encounter outright evidence of a Sage (Rabban Yohanan ben Zakkai) ordaining his disciples (R. Eliezer and R. Yoshua).[109] Ultimately, this will become the prerogative of the Patriarchate[110] (beginning probably with Yehuda the Patriarch), and the latter could effectively curtail the career of a budding Sage by pronouncing his refusal to confer ordination.[111] Similarly, and as a

---

[104] See above, n. 74.

[105] On Agrippa II after the destruction cf. Schürer, *History* 1, 479-83.

[106] Cf. Kimelman, 'Conflict'.

[107] Thus lending – at least at first glance – support for the argument that Jewish *galut* (exile) commences with the year 70 C.E.; cf. Urbach, 'The Jews in their Land'; for a rebuttal of the notion cf. Alon, *The Jews* 1, 3-17. Urbach's opinion was presented in a review of the original Hebrew version of Alon's book.

[108] Note the custom of 'laying on of hands' in appointing apostles, Acts 6:6, and cf. Daube, '*Exousia*'. See also Lohse, *Ordination*, 29ff. (sources on earlier Jewish ordination); Mantel, 'Ordination and Appointment'.

[109] *P.T. Sanh.* 1, 19a.

[110] Cf. Alon, *Jews, Judaism*, 401ff.

[111] Cf. *P.T. Taan.* 4, 68a; *P.T. Moed K.* 3, 81c; cf. also *Eccl. R.* 1,30 and compare with *B.T. Sanh.* 38a.

direct result, it is at Yavne that we encounter for the first time the bestowing of a title – Rabbi – on the ordained Sage.[112] The practical result of receiving ordination, beyond the title and the honour, was one's appointment as member of the Sanhedrin[113] as well as other communal functions.[114] What emerges, in any case, is a self-awareness of the Sages as a definite social class within the community, as opposed to the charismatic individual of the Second Temple period.

Self-definition, however, transcended the immediate circle of the Sages and ultimately was applied to the community at large. As noted by scholars, the Yavne period ushers in a negation of the very legitimacy of sectarian Judaism.[115] The impression one gets at Yavne is of concerted efforts to minimize fragmentation within the community, and while calling this 'the creation of a normative type of Judaism'[116] would suggest an exaggerated degree of uniformity, the tendency to remove perceived deviants from the community and at the same time to resolve disputes within the rabbinic fold manifests itself in numerous ways.

On the broader, national level, certain statements issuing from the Sages, as well as concrete steps taken, seem to point to an active stance against heretics (minim).[117] Stories about R. Eliezer's punishment for having discourse with a disciple of Jesus,[118] as well as other statements requiring the maintenance of a distance between minim and Jews,[119] seem to reflect a wish to isolate and render illegitimate, certain Jewish elements. While the birkat ha-minim, the benediction inserted into the liturgy by Rabban Gamliel, may have been intended as a general curse against all heretics,[120] one nevertheless is impressed by certain statements – beginning as early as the second century – that Christians conside-

---

[112] As noted already in *Iggeret Rav Sherira Gaon*, 125; Alon, *The Jews* 1, 226 n. 51 notes that in the Gospels Jesus is called *rabbi* by his disciples; this, however, is not intended as a formal title, but as a form of address: 'My master ...'.

[113] Hence the term in the Land of Israel for ordination, *minui*, i.e. appointment. The Babylonians seems to have preserved the archaic from *semikha* (laying on of hands), although by talmudic times there was no longer a 'laying of the hands' on the appointee (cf. *B.T. Sanh.* 13b). This may be explained by the fact that there was no formal ordination in Babylonia or the diaspora (*B.T. Sanh.* 14a; *P.T. Bikk.* 3, 65d), hence the Babylonians were not conscious of the import of contemporary ordination, and retained instead the biblical description linked to the laying of hands (Num 27:33); cf. Alon, *Jews, Judaism* 399; Albeck, 'Semikha', 86 and n. 5.

[114] Alon, *Jews, Judaism*, 413.

[115] Cf. Baron, *History* 2, 129ff.

[116] Cf. Moore, *Judaism* 1, 3.

[117] For a comprehensive examination of the term *min* cf. Kimelman, '*Birkat Ha-Minim*'.

[118] *T. Hull.* 2:24; *B.T. Av. Zar.* 16b-17a; for an analysis of the tradition cf. Lieberman, 'Roman Legal Institutions'.

[119] *T. Hull.* 2:22-23; *B.T. Av. Zar.* 27b; *T. Shabb.* 13:5; *B.T. Shabb.* 116a; *P.T. Shabb.* 16, 15c.

[120] On the *birkat ha-minim* cf. *T. Ber.* 3:25; *B.T. Ber.* 28b; *P.T. Ber.* 4, 8a; for the various possible targets see Kimelman, '*Birkat Ha-Minim*'.

red themselves a major target of synagogue pronouncements.[121] The distancing of the community from Christian influences would seem to lay at the heart of another act taken by the Sages at the time (possibly after the death of Rabban Gamliel), namely the decision to commission a new translation of the Bible into Greek.[122] Inasmuch as the Septuagint had evolved into the widely accepted version of the growing Christian community,[123] it had now fallen into disfavour with the Sages, and thus the new translation by Aquila was intended to supplant the Septuagint, while meeting the needs of Greek speaking Jews, primarily in the Greco-Roman diaspora.[124]

Closer to home, a seeming re-evaluation on the part of the Sages led to a new conception of how the world of Tora functions. A far greater stress would now be placed on the collective will or opinion of the Sages, leading to the suppression at times of minority opinions. Two famous tales depict the ostracizing of individual Sages who refused to accede to majority rule,[125] and to these we may add the series of clashes between Rabban Gamliel and the Sages[126] which reflect a different type of authoritarian attitude: the predominance of the 'Patriarch' over the Sages of the academy. Both examples, however, seem to express a need for arriving at a more fixed halakhic norm than had previously existed, and this may be yet another phase in the process of redefinition that followed the destruction. As already noted, the gradual process of deciding halakha in favour of Beit Hillel was linked to the activity of the Sages at Yavne,[127] but this may have been only one factor in a broader development: the collation of the vast amount of oral traditions that had accrued over the years. In this context one particular statement in the Tosefta has frequently been cited:[128]

> When the Sages entered the Vineyard at Yavne they said: A time will come when a man will seek a Tora teaching and not find it, a ruling of the

---

[121] Cf. Justin Martyr, *Dial.* 16:4 (Eng. transl. and notes by A.L. Williams, London 1930 p. 33 n. 3): 'And now you reject ... those that set their hope on him ... cursing in your synagogues them that believe in Christ'; later Christian sources (Epiphanius, *Adv. Haer.* 29:9; Jerome, *Commentary to Isaiah* 52:5) are even more explicit in referring to the denouncement of Christianity in Jewish prayer. Cf. also the Geniza fragments of the prayer (J. Mann, *HUCA* 2 [1925] 306) which include the word נוצרים; and see Alon, *The Jews* 1, 288ff.

[122] *P.T. Meg.* 1, 71c.

[123] Cf. *Tanh. Tissa* 34 (127a): 'The Holy One Blessed He foresaw that the nations of the world would translate the Tora and read it in Greek, and they say: We are Israel ...'

[124] Cf. Jellicoe, *Septuagint*, 76-83. There are other examples of the Sages re-evaluating and changing traditional customs that were embraced by *minim*; see for example the removal of the Ten Commandments from the liturgy 'on account of the contention of the *minim*, lest they say: These alone were given to Moses at Sinai' (*P.T. Ber.* 1, 3c). These *minim* may have also been connected to Christian groups, cf. Urbach, *Sages*, 361-2; cf. Vermes, 'Decalogue'.

[125] Akavya ben Mahalalel, *M. Ed.* 5:6 (possibly during the tenure of Rabban Yohanan ben Zakkai at Yavne, cf. Urbach, *Sages*, 598-9); R. Eliezer ben Hyrcanus, *B.T. Bava M.* 59a-b (seemingly during Rabban Gamliel's rule).

[126] *M. Rosh H.* 2:8-9; *B.T. Bekh.* 36a; *B.T. Ber.* 27b-28a.

[127] *P.T. Ber.* 1, 3c and parallels; cf. Safrai, 'Decision', 22 n. 7.

[128] *T. Ed.* 1:1. For a recent – and divergent – study of this text cf. Halivni, *Midrash*, 44-7.

Scribes and not find it ... so that one precept of the Tora would not be like another. (Hence) they declared: Let us begin with Hillel andShammai. Modern scholars are divided on the literary and historical implications of this text. One opinion considers this to be a clear reference to the first impulses leading to the redaction of the Mishna, thereby assuming that until now rabbinic teaching was transmitted in a myriad of forms and systems, lacking any uniform organization. Were this not the case, they claim, there would be no cause for the fears expressed in the Tosefta.[129] Others, however, would limit the literary innovation intended here, citing for example the fact that collected halakhot are already apparent from the late Second Temple period, and were incorporated later in our Mishna. Rather, they maintain, we are now confronted for the first time with a systematic collation of rabbinic traditions, beginning with the disputes of Hillel and Shammai, not merely for the purpose of organization, but with the goal of *rendering decisions*.[130] No one would deny, however, that a major impetus towards the final redaction of Oral Tora in the form of our Mishna may be linked to the re-organization of the world of the Sages beginning at Yavne. The process would be hindered, however, both by the lack of a strict centralization within the world of Tora, as well as by political events that would plunge the Land of Israel and the Jewish people at large into further turmoil.

The center at Yavne, it must be remembered, was not universally embraced, at least initially, by all Sages or even by all of Rabban Yohanan ben Zakkai's disciples. One Sage, R. Elazar ben Arakh, preferred Emmaus, 'a pleasant place with pleasant waters', to Yavne and, according to tradition, subsequently forgot 'his Tora'.[131] Other students may have expressed a personal dissent towards Rabban Yohanan ben Zakkai, but emerge at Yavne under Rabban Gamliel.[132] Yet others – and among them the most prominent of the generation – established schools in their own places of residence: Lydda (R. Eliezer ben Hyrcanus), Pekiin (R. Yoshua ben Hananya), Bnei Brak (R. Akiva), and in Galilee: Sepphoris (R. Halafta), Sikhnin (R. Hanina ben Teradyon) etc.[133]

In general, the academy at Yavne, for all its importance at the time, seems to have functioned as a major center for no more than one and a half generations. With the demise of Rabban Gamliel (c. 114 c.e.) we perceive a certain decentralizing force, with yet more Sages, as well as the younger Yavnean corps, re-establishing local schools. This generation, spanning the death of Rabban Gamliel and the Bar Kokhba uprising (114-135 c.e.), is represented by one of

---

[129] Cf. Albeck, *Untersuchungen*, 89ff.; *id., Introduction*, 82.

[130] Cf. Epstein, *Tannaitic Literature*, 428f.; cf. also Urbach, *Sages*, 598: 'The purpose of the convention was not therefore literary – it was not to systemize the halakhot – but to arrive at decisions regarding disputed halakhot.' For remnants of pre-70 collections of Mishna cf. Epstein, *ib.* 25-58.

[131] *A.R.N.* a 14 (25a).

[132] Cf. Alon, *The Jews* 1, 103-4.

[133] Cf. Safrai, 'Restoration', 36; cf. Also Avi-Yonah - Safrai, *Atlas*, 77 for a map of the rabbinic dispersion during the Yavne period.

the giants of the rabbinic world: R. Akiva,[134] who together with his disciples served as a major conduit of rabbinic tradition, from the early post-Temple days to the generation of Yehuda the Patriarch (c. 180-220 c.e.) and the final redaction of the Mishna. Scholars have described R. Akiva as 'the Father of the Mishna',[135] and he is credited not merely with transmission and elaboration of oral tradition, but with the introduction of a systematic categorization of all halakhic material.[136] His disciples Meir, Yehuda, Yose, Shimon *et al.*, would serve as the link between the pre- and post-Bar Kokhba eras,[137] and as the teachers of Yehuda the Patriarch, thereby emerging as the most frequently quoted authorities in the Mishna.

Bar Kokhba and the Later Tannaic Period

The generation of R. Akiva, both in Judaea and the diaspora, was destined to suffer through two of the most cruel wars fought by Jews in all of antiquity, and the devastation resulting from these clashes would have no less an impact on subsequent Jewish history than the Great War of 66-70 c.e. During the last years of the Roman emperor Trajan (115-117 c.e.) – while that ruler was involved in an extensive campaign deep into Parthian territory – the Jews of Cyrene and Egypt, later joined by their brethren in Cyprus, embarked on a major military confrontation aimed primarily against their Greek fellow-countrymen, but ultimately spilling over into a war against the ruling Roman legions of those territories.[138] The clashes, probably the culmination of a long history of Jewish-Greek hostility in much of the Greco-Roman world, are documented not only in literary accounts, but also with impressive epigraphical and papyrological evidence.[139] Furthermore, it appears that at the same time the Jews of Mesopotamia played a central role in a Parthian uprising against the invading Roman forces, which subsided only with Trajan's retreat in 117 c.e.[140] The final outcome of these hostilities, however, was no less than a major catastrophe for diaspora Jewry,[141] and the prosperous Jewish communities of much of the Hellenistic world – most particularly Alexandria – ceased from this moment to play a major role in the social and literary development of the Jewish people. The relevant point for the present volume is clear. Whereas the documents in our possession testify to an impressive literary production by Hellenistic Jews

---

[134] Cf. Finkelstein, *Akiba*; Safrai, *Akiva*.
[135] Cf. Epstein, *Tannaitic Literature,* 71ff.
[136] *A.R.N.* a 18 (34a).
[137] E.g. *B.T. Sanh.* 13b.
[138] Cf. Schürer, *History* 1, 529-34; Smallwood, *The Jews*, 389-427.
[139] Fuks, 'Aspects'; *CPJ* 2, 225-260.
[140] On the Parthian war cf. Lepper, *Trajan's Parthian War*; for the Jewish role in the uprising cf. *ib.* 88ff; Schürer, *History* 1, 532 n. 83.
[141] A more limited role for Judean Jewry, referred to in rabbinic literature as the '*Polemos* of Quietus', has been posited; cf. Alon, *The Jews* 2, 413-29.

during the Second Temple period, literary activity in the following period would be practically confined to two communities: the Land of Israel and Babylonia.

The second Jewish war (132-135 C.E.)[142] had a more immediate impact on the world of the Sages, and its results touch on almost every aspect of subsequent Jewish life. The Bar Kokhba uprising was the last major armed conflict undertaken by the Jewish nation in antiquity, but a heated controversy surrounds almost every facet of this conflagration: its immediate causes, its military and geographical scope, the nature of the Jewish supporters of Bar Kosiba (his actual name, as found in the documents of the Judean desert) and the degree of messianic fervour surrounding the Jewish general. Most relevant to this survey, however, is the rabbinic activity in response to the needs of the devastated community. One of the awe-inspiring developments of the war was the refusal on the part of numerous Sages to succumb to the systematic religious persecution introduced by Hadrian towards the end of the war. The ideology of martyrdom, going back in Jewish history at least to the days of the Hasmoneans, would now be formulated according to fixed criteria, and the acts of martyrdom of the Bar Kokhba war thus remained etched in Jewish consciousness.[143]

The demographic results of the war effected a major shift in the ethnic balance of the Judean population. Even if the numbers of casualties supplied by Cassius Dio are exaggerated,[144] it is certain that the Jewish population of the Land of Israel – and particularly Judaea – was decimated. This situation was exacerbated not only by thousands of Jews being sold into slavery, but also by a growing number of Jews who apparently opted for emigration, whether to the major Jewish diaspora community of Babylonia, or to other portions of the Roman Empire.[145] The issue would be tackled head-on by the Sages, who only now addressed themselves in a sweeping manner to the question of centrality of the Land of Israel in Jewish life, and the requirement incumbent on every Jew to reside in the Land.[146] Their success in this enterprise is impressive, and within one generation we are witness to a reversal of the trend, with frequent immigrants arriving in Erets Israel, frequently to take up major positions in the restored rabbinic institutions. While a sizable Jewish population remained in portions of southern Israel (= Judaea),[147] the central rabbinic institution, i.e. the Sanhedrin, was now transferred to Galilee, where it would remain throug-

[142] For general overviews of the Bar Kokhba war cf. Schürer, *History* 1, 534-57; Smallwood, *The Jews*, 428-466; Alon, *The Jews* 2, 592ff. A copious and ever growing bibliography exists on the Bar Kokhba uprising. For the most recent and comprehensive list cf. Mor - Rappoport, 'Bibliography'.

[143] Cf. Herr, 'Persecutions'; Lieberman, 'On Persecution'; Safrai, 'Kiddush Ha-Shem'.

[144] '580,000 were slain in raids and battles; while ... the number of those that perished by famine, disease and fire was past finding out'; Cassius Dio, *Hist. Rom.* 69:14,1; cf. Stern, *Greek and Latin Authors* 2, 391ff.

[145] Cf. Avi-Yonah, *The Jews*, 15ff.

[146] Cf. Gafni, 'The Status of Eretz Israel'.

[147] Cf. most recently Schwartz, *Jewish Settlement*.

hout the Talmudic period and beyond.[148] Rabbinic tradition describes the movement of the Sanhedrin north to Usha, and from there to Shefaram, Beit Shearim, Sepphoris and Tiberias.[149] The list is noteworthy, inasmuch as the first three choices were small, rather insignificant towns. While scholars have suggested that this was a deliberate move, intended to keep out of public – i.e. Roman – view, it may also signify stages in the re-settling of rabbinic leadership in the north. The Sages, it would seem, chose at first to re-establish themselves as a viable academic and legislative body, without confronting the entrenched Galilean leadership of the major centers.[150] Only when the Patriarchate reached its peak in terms of political as well as spiritual authority, in the days of Yehuda the Patriarch (180-220), did that leader feel sufficiently confident to set up the major rabbinic apparatus in the Galilean metropolis of Sepphoris.[151]

The first stages of restoration after Bar Kokhba are far from clear. The early gatherings of Sages – disciples of R. Akiva – took place without a 'patriarch', with the intercalation of the calendar again serving as the immediate focus of attention.[152] Another gathering – this time at Usha but also without a patriarch – addressed itself to the broader issue of re-establishing a rabbinic academy.[153] Rabban Shimon ben Gamliel would finally assume his position at Usha, but later sources would infer that he never attained the equivalent predominance of his father at Yavne, and certainly not of his son Yehuda.[154] Nevertheless, it was under R. Shimon ben Gamliel that the Land of Israel met and overcame the first potential challenge to its hegemony over the Jewish world, made by one of the Babylonian Sages.[155]

As noted, the contemporaries of Rabban Shimon ben Gamliel served as a critical generation in the transmission of Oral Tora, and it was their disciple and Shimon's son, Yehuda the Patriarch, that would be credited with the definitive

---

[148] The movement from Judaea north was not without a certain traumatic element, for while all of the Land of Israel was deemed sacred, a certain geographical 'hierarchy' had developed over the years, with Judaea attaining a preferred status due to the proximity of the Temple. This explains why, for decades after the rabbinic center had moved to Galilee, intercalation of the calendar would be carried out and announced from Judaean sites; cf. Safrai, 'Localities'.

[149] Cf. Schürer, *History* 2, 323-5.

[150] Büchler, *Political and Social Leaders*.

[151] Cf. Safrai, 'Beth She'arim', 209.

[152] *P.T. Hag.* 3, 78d; the absence of the Patriarch, Rabban Shimon ben Gamliel, has given rise to numerous theories, either of his hiding from Roman eyes, or of his relations with the students of R. Akiva; cf. Baumgarten, 'Opposition'. One wonders, however, to what extent the existence of a 'patriarchate' had already become entrenched in the rabbinic world, given the fact that only one such precedent, that of Rabban Gamliel at Yavne, had existed – and he too had deceased for years *before* the Bar-Kokhba war.

[153] *Cant. R.* 20,16; compare to *B.T. Ber.* 63b-64a.

[154] For the Babylonian tradition about an attempt to depose the Patriarch cf. Goodblatt, 'Story'; on the relatively weak position of Rabban Shimon ben Gamliel vis-a-vis his court cf. Alon, *The Jews* 2, 668ff.

[155] See the attempt by Hananya, the nephew of R. Yoshua, to regulate the calendar in Babylonia; *P.T. Sanh.* 1, 19a; *B.T. Ber.* 63a-b.

redaction of a vital part of Oral Tora into the Mishna. Inasmuch as the halakhic and literary aspects of Yehuda's enterprise will be dealt with extensively elsewhere in this work, we will briefly take up only the salient political and social conditions that contributed to Yehuda's powerful position within the Jewish community, unequalled by any other Judean figure of the post-Temple period.[156]

Rabbinic tradition keenly notes the unique concentration of religious and political powers maintained by Yehuda the Patriarch (commonly referred to in the sources as 'Rabbi').[157] Most of his tenure coincided with the reign of the dynasty of the Severans in Rome (193-235 C.E.), a family which for political reasons as well as cultural proclivities deriving from its eastern roots, cultivated a positive relationship with the Judean community and its leaders. This support was acknowledged both in rabbinic sources that describe a 'personal' relationship between Yehuda and a Roman emperor called 'Antoninus',[158] as well as in Latin sources that allude to the religious syncretism and pro Jewish tendencies of the Severans.[159] This would explain the apparently favourable mention of the Emperor Septimius Severus and his sons in an inscription from 197 C.E. found in Galilee,[160] as well as mention of a 'Severan synagogue' in the midrash.[161] One result of this relationship was the enhanced economic position of the Patriarchate,[162] as well as the general perception that the central governing bodies of the Jews enjoy the implicit support of the Roman authorities.[163] Clearly, a certain *rapprochement* between the heretofore hated Rome and the Jewish people began to emerge, and the relaxed relations probably served to enhance the status of the Patriarch even more. On the social front, Yehuda was cognizant of the need to broaden the popular base of support for the offices of Jewish leadership, and not only moved the seat of government (Patriarchate and Sanhedrin) to Sepphoris but openly courted support of the wealthier classes.[164] Among his *takkanot*, on the other hand, there is a clear attempt to alleviate the plight of those farmers who apparently were hardpressed to pay taxes, especially during the Sabbatical Year, and a series of steps were introduced to lighten that particular burden – possibly even to the extent of abrogating the

[156] For brief surveys of Yehuda's role cf. Alon, *The Jews* 2, 705-37; Avi-Yonah, *The Jews*, 39-88. On the chronology of Yehuda the Patriarch cf. Guttmann, 'The Patriarch'; Safrai, 'The *Nesiut*'.

[157] B.T. Sanh. 36a: 'From the days of Moses to the days of Rabbi, we do not find Tora and greatness in one place.'

[158] A large number of traditions describe the discourse between the Jewish and Roman leaders, touching even on the possibility of the emperor's conversion; they were the topic of numerous scholarly articles bent on discovering the 'historical' Antoninus, a tenuous enterprise at best; cf. Krauss, *Antoninus*; Avi-Yonah, *The Jews*, 39-42.

[159] Cf. Scriptores Historiae Augustae, *Alexander* 29:2; *ib.* 28:7 (where he is referred to as the 'Syrian Archisynagogus').

[160] Frey, *CII* 2, 157-8; cf. Alon, *The Jews* 2, 685f.

[161] *Bereshit Rabbati* p. 209; for similar, corroborating evidence see Alon, *The Jews* 2, 685.

[162] Avi-Yonah, *The Jews*, 59; Levine, 'Period', 100-102.

[163] Alon, *The Jews* 2, 693.

[164] B.T. Er. 86a: 'Rabbi respects the wealthy'.

prohibition of certain agricultural activities in the Seventh Year (although here rabbinic opponents drew the line).[165]

Yehuda the Patriarch's position was, in fact, so overwhelming, that while rabbinic opposition filters through the sources every now and then, the converse is also true, and certain statements began to attach to the Patriarch's person messianic potential.[166] His death and funeral are described in far greater detail than those of any other Sage,[167] signifying a later perspective that considered his passing the end of an era.[168]

By Yehuda's death (c. 225 C.E.), the Patriarchate had emerged as the universally recognized office of Jewish leadership, and it would retain that position for another 200 years. Patriarchs would be influential in appointments throughout the Land of Israel.[169] By the fourth century – and probably earlier – the Patriarchs were actively involved in diaspora affairs; *apostoli* were sent to Jewish communities, where they not only collected funds for the center, but also appointed or removed local officials.[170] It is not surprising that the office would serve as a major target of attacks by Christian leadership, beginning in the fourth century and culminating with the abolition of the office, in the first quarter of the fifth.[171]

The Amoraic Period in the Land of Israel

The Amoraic era in the Land of Israel extends over a period of roughly two centuries, from the death of Yehuda the Patriarch (c. 225 C.E.) to the abolition of the Patriarchate (c. 425 C.E.). A precise delineation of the period is impossible, given the uncertain state of our knowledge regarding the last phase of Amoraic activity in the Land of Israel, leading up to the redaction – if indeed that is the correct word – of the Palestinian Talmud.

---

[165] *T. Shev.* 4:17-19; *P.T. Shev.* 6, 37a and parallels; *P.T. Taan.* 3, 66c (= *P.T. Dem.* 1, 22a); cf. Safrai, 'Sabbatical Year' (2).

[166] E.g. *P.T. Shabb.* 16, 15c; *B.T. Sanh.* 98b; *B.T. Rosh H.* 25a. It is only under Yehuda the Patriarch that outright mention is made of the Patriarch's family indeed being descended from the House of David; cf. *P.T. Taan.* 4, 68a = *Gen. R.* 98,8 (p. 1259). The same *sugya*, a few lines earlier, describes the ceremony of *salutatio,* well known in Roman circles, being carried out daily at the court of the Patriarch. For the issue of the Patriarchate's Davidic lineage cf. Liver, *Toledot,* 37-41.

[167] *B.T. Ket.* 103a-104a; *P.T. Kil.* 9, 32a-b; *P.T. Ket.* 12, 34d; *Gen R.* 96,5 (p. 1198); *Gen. R.* 100,2 (p.1284); for a recent discussion of R. Yehuda's last testament cf. Cohen, 'Patriarchs'.

[168] *B.T. Sota* 49b.

[169] Cf. *Gen. R.* 81,2 (p.969); *P.T. Yev.* 8, 9b.

[170] Patriarchs and Sages had travelled to the diaspora as far back as the days of Rabban Gamliel II, cf. Safrai, 'Visits'. On messengers dispatched by patriarchs cf. *P.T. Hag.* 1, 76d. The powers of the messenger are described by Joseph the Comes, cf. Epiphanius, *Adv. Haer.* 30:3,4, and by the late 4th century these functions are also attacked by the Roman legislator, cf. *Cod. Theod.* 16:8,14; 16:8,15; 16:8,29. The position of the Patriarch in diaspora communities is also reflected in the letters of Libanius, cf. Stern, *Greek and Latin Authors* 2, 580ff., and esp. 598-9. For a summary of the offices of the Patriarch cf. Mantel, *Studies,* 175-253.

[171] Avi-Yonah, *The Jews,* 225-9; Dan, 'Leadership'.

The Amoraic period in the Land of Israel may be divided into two distinct sections:

1) The years 235-324 C.E. which encompass fifty years of crisis and anarchy in the Roman empire, followed by the process of rehabilitation under Diocletian (284-305 C.E.), and concluding with the first years of Constantine's rule, prior to his ultimate conquest of the Land of Israel;

2) The years 324-425 C.E., i.e. the first stage of Roman-Byzantine rule, characterized primarily by the growing predominance of the Christian Church both on the social fabric in the Land of Israel and on the legal status of the Jews within the empire.

While scholars are divided on the dimensions of the crisis that overtook Rome in the third century,[172] the political anarchy and economic pressures that resulted were clearly felt by the Jews of the Land.[173] In essence, there was a direct link between the political instability and military pressures imposed on Rome, and the ever-growing need to extract more taxes as a means of propping up an over-extended army and empire. Rampant inflation had forced Rome to discard monetary taxation as the major source of income in the provinces, and in its place we encounter an elaborate system of taxes taken out of food, clothing, raw materials, forced labour and billeting of soldiers and administrators. Rabbinic literature is replete with references to all these taxes,[174] and inconveniences such as billeting frequently crop up due to the halakhic questions that were raised.[175]

The general phenomenon of *anachoresis*, wherein members of a city council, or the population as a whole, would simply abandon their homes and flee, was not unheard of in the Land of Israel as well.[176] Hence R. Yohanan, the head of the Tiberian academy, suggests that if one's name has come up as a possible candidate for the local council βουλή 'let the Jordan be your boundary'.[177] Nevertheless, it would be mistaken to deem Roman behaviour towards the Jewish nation as one of persecution. Rather, the difficult times evinced harsh words, but probably no different than what could be heard in other parts of the empire.[178]

Jewish leadership did, however, undergo some changes in the days following Yehuda the Patriarch's death. While his son Rabban Gamliel III remained in Sepphoris, the Sanhedrin – in what may have been a reaction to the strict control and, in addition, the ostentatious lifestyle of the deceased Patriarch – asserted its independence by moving to Tiberias. It is more than noteworthy,

[172] MacMullen, *Response*, 1-23.
[173] Cf. Avi-Yonah, *The Jews*, 89-136.
[174] *P.T. Shev.* 5, 36a for a list of the various taxes; compare *P.T. Pea* 1, 15b.
[175] Cf. *T. Er.* 5:22; *P.T. Er.* 6, 23a; *P.T. Er.* 6, 23c.
[176] *Gen. R.* 24,1 (p. 229); *P.T. Shev.* 9, 38d; *B.T. Bava B.* 8a; and see Sperber, *The Land*, 102-18.
[177] Cf. *P.T. Sanh.* 15, 26b: R. Yohanan's generation frequently refers to the pervasiveness of the Roman tax collector, unavoidable no matter where you go, cf. *B.T. Sanh.* 98b.
[178] Cf. Lieberman, 'Palestine'.

however, that approximately one generation later, the Patriarchate followed in its steps.[179] In general, there is a renewed tension between the Patriarchate of the third century and the Sages of the Tiberian academy, and this frequently created uncomfortable incidents for both sides.[180] While there is no conclusive justification for positing a major decline in the Patriarchate's powers, there clearly developed something of an ideological rift between some Sages and the Patriarch over the precise definition of the office.[181]

The Amoraic period in the Land of Israel produced, alongside the Palestinian Talmud, a vast corpus of aggadic midrash collections, and together with the Talmud these reflect a wide variety of social and cultural developments in the land. It is noteworthy that, in contradistinction, Babylonia, for all the prominence of its rabbinic academies and their monumental achievement – the Babylonian Talmud – did not produce any major midrashic work. This fact has been the source of much speculation. Part of the answer may have been given by a rabbinic Sage in late third century Caesarea, R. Abbahu. In explaining to Christian co-residents of his town why his Babylonian colleague Rav Safra, albeit learned, is not well versed in biblical studies, Abbahu remarks: 'We (in the Land of Israel) live among you, hence we take it upon ourselves to learn'.[182] In fact, by the third century the confrontation between Jews and Christians in the Land of Israel had ceased to be an internal affair, i.e. relating to Jews who embraced a belief in Jesus on a communal level. Now it evolved into an outright confrontation between two distinct communities. Major figures of the Church, such as Origen and Eusebius, resided in Caesarea, and from the third century on the Sages would have to be prepared for ongoing confrontations with their Christian counterparts. These debates are frequently discernible in midrashic literature, and even more fascinating is the real relevance and meaning these rabbinic texts take on, when compared with the contemporary writings of Church Fathers on the same topics of biblical verses.[183]

This relationship, of course, underwent radical changes with the final conquest of the Land of Israel by Constantine in 324 C.E. Scholars have appraised at varying degrees the role played by the first Christian emperor in shaping the attitude of Christian Europe towards the Jews, and in general the degree of anti-Jewish policy that found its way into Roman legislation at the time.[184] What remains certain is that the new legislation went out of its way to limit the legal status of the Jews, or at least to create the impression that the new empire would not encourage Jews to play a major role in society. Protection was granted Jews

---

[179] Cf. Cohen, 'Time and Cause'.
[180] *P.T. Sanh.* 2, 19d-20a; note that by now the Patriarchs have a private guard, to be used against various opponents; *P.T. Sanh.* 9:6, 20c-d; *Gen. R.* 80 (p. 950).
[181] Cf. Kimelman, 'Conflict'.
[182] *B.T. Av. Zar.* 4a. On this Sage and his contacts with *minim* cf. Levine, 'Rabbi Abbahu', 29-30.
[183] This issue has aroused a growing interest in recent scholarship; cf. Urbach, 'Repentance'; *id.* 'Homilies'; *id.* 'Rabbinic Exegesis'; Kimelman, 'Rabbi Yohanan and Origen'.
[184] Cf. Linder, 'Government'.

who abandoned their religion,[185] and gentiles were warned not to join the 'nefarious sect' of Jews.[186] The legislator made the possession of gentile slaves by Jews more difficult, and ultimately forbade it completely, thereby allowing a religious scruple (lest the Jew convert the slave) to play a major economic role.[187]

In terms of communal leadership, legislation at first steered a middle path, limiting some earlier privileges but nevertheless granting a limited exemption from civic duties to Jewish public officials. This situation would become progressively worse as we head towards the late fourth and fifth centuries[188] with the Patriarchate and the synagogue emerging as the two main targets of Roman-Christian legislation.

An interesting respite for Jews under Christian rule came about in the years 361-363 C.E. under Julian. Having assumed an anti-Christian stance and wishing to undermine Christian theology, the emperor proposed rebuilding the Jewish Temple in Jerusalem. The affair ended as abruptly as it began, with Julian's death coming during his campaign against Persia in 363 C.E.[189] There is no hard evidence of major Jewish elation upon hearing of the plan, inasmuch as years of Roman rule – and a succession of failed rebellions – had taught the Jewish community to desist from building hopes on major shifts of policy embraced by lone individuals. Even the Jewish uprising that very likely must have engulfed portions of the Land of Israel in 351 C.E.,[190] as evidenced by various archaeological discoveries,[191] nevertheless seems to have been motivated more by local relations than by a grand plan for removing the yoke of Roman rule.[192]

The Amoraic Period in Babylonia

The roots and early development of the Jewish community of Babylonia remain shrouded to this day, and the paucity of ancient sources on this diaspora is all the more striking in light of the crucial role that the Babylonian Talmud would play in determining subsequent Jewish history and lifestyles. There can be no doubt

---

[185] *Cod. Theod.* 16:8,1; 16:8,5. For the 5th century: 16:8,26.

[186] *Cod. Theod.* 16:8,1.

[187] *Cod. Theod.* 16:9,1; 16:9,2; 16:8,6. All Roman legislation concerning the Jews has been collected by Linder, *Legislation*.

[188] There are, however, definite discrepancies between legislation in the West, where relatively few Jews resided, and in the East where opposition had to be taken into account. Compare *Cod. Theod.* 12:1,99 with 16:8,13 and 12:1,158, all dealing with the requirement, or exemption, of Jews from serving on local councils.

[189] Cf. Avi-Yonah, *The Jews*, 185-207.

[190] *Id.* 176-81.

[191] Cf. Mazar, *Beth Shearim* 1, 26.

[192] Cf. Lieberman, 'Palestine', 341. Inasmuch as the Palestinian Talmud was completed some time between the days of Julian and the abolition of the Patriarchate, attempts have been made to lay the perceived lack of a final redaction at the feet of a difficult political situation for the Jews of 4th and 5th century Christian Palestine. The research of Lieberman has shown that this is not the case, as clear signs of redaction are indeed discernible; cf. Lieberman, *Talmuda shel Kisrin*, 20ff.

that Jews reached certain districts of Babylonia, particularly in the vicinity of Nehar Kebar,[193] by the early sixth century B.C.E.,[194] and following the Babylonian conquest of Judah in 586 B.C.E., the number of Jewish settlers grew considerably. Our information on these early communities, however, as well as on Jewish life under the Persians, derives almost entirely from biblical testimony, with the sole addition of documents from the Murashu archives. These last documents – Akkadian inscriptions of the fifth century B.C.E. discovered at ancient Nippur and apparently belonging to a wealthy family of merchants – suggest an economically and socially acclimatized Jewish community, which nevertheless maintained its ethnic identity, at least as far as the impressive evidence of Jewish names permits us to conclude.[195]

Geographically, two major concentrations of Jews would develop during the Second Temple period east of the Euphrates river. The first community, with roots going back even further than those of Nippur, was situated in northern Mesopotamia and east of the Tigris river, in the lands of Adiabene, Assyria and Media, and Jews here would later identify themselves as descendants of the ten tribes exiled by the Assyrians in the eighth century B.C.E.[196] By the end of the Second Temple period, the city of Nisibis would emerge as the main Jewish center of this northern concentration (parallel to the emergence of Nehardea in the south). Here the Jews would gather yearly contributions destined to be sent to Jerusalem,[197] and by the late Temple period we encounter at Nisibis one of the first Babylonian Sages, R. Yehuda ben Bathyra I.[198] Nisibis would remain prominent in Jewish sources throughout the Tannaic period,[199] but by the third century its centrality in Jewish life seems to substantially diminish. It would appear that the geo-political situation of the city, on the border between Rome and Parthia (and later Sassanian Persia) and frequently caught up in the wars between the two empires, finally took its toll on the Jewish community as well,[200] and added to the military strife is evidence of a growing Christian influence in the city, which seems to have effected a Jewish regression.[201]

---

[193] Cf. Ezek 1:1-3; 3:15, 23; 10:15, 20, 22; 43:3. Nehar Kebar is Nar Kabaru which passes through Nippur, appr. 80 kms. southeast of ancient Babylon.
[194] The early settlement dates to the exile of Yehokakhin in 597 B.C.E.; cf. Zadok, *The Jews in Babylonia*, 34.
[195] Cf. Daiches, 'The Jews in Babylonia'; Ebeling, *Jüdischen Exulanten*. On the Jewish names cf. Coogan, 'Patterns'; Bickerman, 'Generation'.
[196] Cf. Jos., *Ant.* 11:133, and compare *Ag. Ap.* 1:194. On the Jews of Mesopotamia cf. Segal, 'North Mesopotamia'. Talmudic Sages would also attempt to identify their settlements with the sites of the Assyrian exile, cf.*B.T. Kidd.* 72a; *B.T. Yev.* 17a.
[197] *Ant.* 18:312, 379. For the possibility of two cities named Nisibis, with one in the south near Nehardea and on rabbinic Nisibis in general, cf. Oppenheimer, 'The Center in Nisibis'; *id. Babylonia Judaica*, 333-4.
[198] *B.T. Pes.* 3b.
[199] E.g. *B.T. Sanh.* 32b; *P.T. Sanh.* 1, 19a; *P.T. Sanh.* 8, 26b; *Sifrei Deut.* 80 (p. 146).
[200] *B.T. Kidd.* 72a.
[201] Cf. Segal, 'North Mesopotamia', 41f.

The other major Jewish center was to the south, in the vicinity of ancient Babylon and Nippur. The southern territory of present-day Iraq, from the convergence of the Euphrates and Tigris rivers (near modern Baghdad) and towards the Persian Gulf, was to become densely populated by Jews. The famous centers of talmudic Babylonia, beginning with Nehardea – already prominent in the late Second Temple period – and followed by Sura, Pumbeditha, Mahoza etc., are all to be found in this southern portion of Jewish Babylonia.[202]

As noted, our information on Jews under the Babylonian and Achaemenian monarchies is minimal,[203] and this situation will not improve during the Hellenistic and Parthian stages of Jewish life in Babylonia, i.e. until the end of the Second Temple period.[204] The one hard fact known to Josephus about this community is that they are 'countless myriads whose number cannot be ascertained',[205] and this fact is echoed by Philo, who also alludes to a certain military potential which would be noted even by Rome.[206] The importance of the Babylonian community, however, was not only in its size, but in the fact that by late Second Temple times it was the only major Jewish concentration outside the confines of the Roman Empire, and, no less important, beyond the immediate impact of Hellenistic culture and society. Moreover, the nature of the Parthian Empire, which would rule over most of Babylonian Jewry from the second century B.C.E. until the early third century C.E., was akin to that of a feudal state, ruled in principle by a central Parthian monarch of the Arsacid dynasty, but in fact divided into satrapies and ethnic communities afforded a high degree of political and cultural autonomy.[207] The divisions within the Parthian kingdom are apparent even in the two major stories supplied by Josephus that have a bearing on Jews in Parthia in the late Second Temple period: the short-lived state founded by two Jewish brothers near Nehardea,[208] and the conversion to Judaism of the royal family of Adiabene.[209] Both stories not only reflect the weak hold maintained by the king on his empire, but also the potential power that could be gained by a tightly knit ethnic community, willing to support the monarchy in exchange for an enhanced degree of local autonomy. Thus, while we know almost nothing about the inner life of Babylonian Jewry prior to its sudden and impressive appearance on the Jewish scene in the early talmudic period, it need not surprise us that the community apparently

---

[202] One of the first important modern studies of talmudic Babylonia was the attempt to uncover the geographical dispersion of the community: Obermayer, *Landschaft*. For a recent and thorough study of this aspect of Babylonian Jewish history, see Oppenheimer, *Babylonia Judaica*.

[203] For general surveys cf. Klamroth, *Jüdischen Exulanten*; Ackroyd, *Israel under Babylon*.

[204] Cf. Neusner, *History of the Jews*; Stern in *Compendia* I/1, 170-9; Gafni, 'The Jews of Babylonia'.

[205] Jos., *Ant.* 11:133; compare *Ant.* 15:14, 39.

[206] *Leg.* 216, 282; this also explains the fact that the rebels of the Land of Israel prior to the Great War, looked to their Babylonian brethren for military assistance; cf. *War* 1:5; 2:388-9; 6:343.

[207] Cf. Debevoise, *Political History*.

[208] *Ant.* 18:310-79.

[209] *Ant.* 20:17-96; cf. Stern in *Compendia* I/1, 172ff.

was able to develop its particular lifestyle and maintain traditions without the political interference and cultural assimilatory influences so common in the Greco-Roman world.

Following the destruction of the Temple, and even before the talmudic era, Tannaic sources point to a growing awareness of the importance of Babylonian Jewry in rabbinic eyes. The Jews of Babylonia, even before 70 C.E., were specifically singled out in traditions describing the announcements to the diaspora of calendar intercalation,[210] and in the Yavne era we find R. Akiva in Nehardea also for functions related to the calendar, although the precise nature of this mission is unclear.[211]

The aftermath of the Bar Kokhba war finds Babylonia as the obvious refuge for some Sages, but the 'pro-Erets-Israel' orientation of the Tannaic sources clearly takes a stand against the potential flight of Sages to Babylonia, even for purposes of continuing their Tora studies.[212] Nevertheless, the movement of some Sages to Babylonia prior to the third century is an important stage in the history of rabbinic tradition, for it suggests that Babylonia had access to the Oral Tora of the Land of Israel even before the redaction of the Mishna. By the Usha period we begin to note a reverse phenomenon, i.e. the arrival in the Land of Israel of Babylonian Sages who in certain cases assume central positions in the Sanhedrin.[213] Interestingly, a number of patriarchs will henceforth have prominent Babylonians serving alongside them either as major supporters (e.g. Yehuda the Patriarch and R. Hiya) or as heads of the Sanhedrin (Gamliel III, and Yehuda Nesia, with R. Hanina ben Hama). The Sages may have come to realize that only an active participation of Babylonian Jews in the leadership framework would preclude further attempts by Babylonian Sages to assert themselves and effect a break with the Patriarchate, probably perceived as weakened after Bar-Kokhba, and even more so in later years under Roman-Christian rule.

The talmudic era of Babylonian Jewry begins, as in the Land of Israel, in the early third century C.E., and in Babylonia we are confronted with a clear case of political periodization coinciding with an internal, cultural turning point. The Sages of Babylonia considered the return home of the native Babylonian Rav, after years of study in the Land of Israel, as the dawn of a new era for the local Tora establishment.[214] This return took place in 219 C.E.,[215] and only a few years later the Parthian-Arsacide dynasty fell, to be succeeded by the neo-Persian

---

[210] *T. Sanh.* 2:6 and parallels.

[211] *M. Yev.* 16:7; cf. Alon, *The Jews* 1, 240f.; Herr in *Compendia* I/2, 857.

[212] *Sifrei Deut.* 80 (p. 146); cf. also Hananya's attempt at intercalating the calendar following Bar Kokhba, and the Palestinian response, above n. 155.

[213] E.g. R. Natan, *Av-Bet-Din* under Rabban Gamliel II at Usha, *B.T. Hor.* 13b (and cf. n. 154); for a list of Babylonians in the school of R. Yishmael cf. Epstein, *Tannaitic Literature*, 570-2.

[214] E.g. *B.T. Gitt.* 6a: 'We consider ourselves in Babylonia as being in the Land of Israel, from the day Rav came to Babylonia'.

[215] Cf. *Iggeret Rav Sherira Gaon*, 78.

Sassanians. Rav himself frequently alludes to the political ramifications of this change,[216] and it appears that he was largely fearful of the effect it would have on continued autonomous Jewish life in Babylonia. These fears were based on the nature of the new dynasty, which clearly deemed itself a second coming of the grand Persian kingdom of Achaemenian times.[217] Attempts were made at tightening the center's control over the empire, and this was accompanied by a revitalization of the Zoroastrian religion and its clergy.[218]

Jewish fears of the impact these changes would have on the continued unhindered life of the community were not unfounded, and certain talmudic statements about Persian 'persecutions' clearly reflect tenets of the Zoroastrian religion.[219] The activities of the Persian priest Kartir towards the end of the third century, who explicitly mentions persecuting Jews among the other minorities of the land,[220] reflect the potentially worsened position of Babylonian Jewry, particularly when the monarchy was not controlled by strong rulers.

Nevertheless, the worst fears were not realized, and Rav's contemporary and head of the center at Nehardea, Samuel, is credited with achieving a *modus vivendi* with the new Persian government, partly through the formulation of the famous talmudic principle recognizing the legitimacy of foreign rulers in their own lands: דינא דמלכותא דינא 'The law of the regime is considered law'.[221]

In general, the first two centuries of the talmudic era passed without any major persecution or prolonged pressures aimed at the Jewish community. In fact, their position was preferable to that of the Christian minority in Persia, which from the fourth century would be suspected of harbouring pro-Byzantine sentiments.[222] By the middle of the fifth century, however, this situation changed radically, due not only to the zealous religious stand adopted by Persian kings beginning with Yazdagird II (438-457 C.E.), but also by external military pressures that served to weaken the monarchy, thereby enabling the clergy once again to assert itself.[223] Medieval Jewish chronicles describe a series of persecutions and executions of rabbis and exilarchs by the second half of the fifth century.[224] If these accounts can be trusted, what emerges is an interesting parallel to the Land of Israel, in that here too the major talmudic corpus reaches

---

[216] *B.T. Bava K.* 117a; *B.T. Av. Zar.* 10b; cf. also *B.T. Yoma* 10a – where Rav prophesizes the fall of Persia (i.e. the new Sassanian monarchy) to Rome.

[217] For the Sassanian empire cf. Christensen, *L'Iran* (on the Sassanian regime, 97-140); *id.* in *Cambridge Ancient History* 12, 109-37; Frye, *Heritage* ch. 6; *id.* 'Political History'. For Jewish history under the Sassanians cf. Neusner, *History of the Jews* vols. 2-5; Widengren, 'Status'.

[218] Cf. Frye, 'Notes'.

[219] Cf. *B.T. Yev.* 63b; *B.T. Bava B.* 58a; *B.T. Gitt.* 16b-17a. See Beer, 'Three Edicts'. These same issues are dealt with in a masterful article by Rosenthal in *Talmudica Iranica*, 38ff.

[220] Cf. Sprengling, 'Kartir'.

[221] Cf. Neusner, *History of the Jews* 2, 69; Shiloh, *Dina De-Malkhuta Dina*, 6.

[222] Cf. Neusner, 'Babylonian Jewry'.

[223] Cf. Widengren, 'Status', 143-3; compare Neusner, *History of the Jews* 5, 66-72.

[224] See *Iggeret Rav Sherira Gaon*, 96-7; *Seder Tannaim we-Amoraim*, 6; cf. Widengren, 'Status', 143.

its final stages precisely during a period of religiously motivated pressures on the Jewish community.

The unique character of the Babylonian Jewish center is dominated by the two institutions that were to become its cornerstone for centuries: the Exilarchate and the Academies. The roots of the Exilarchate, while it claimed a Davidic lineage, become obscure once we search for signs of its activity more than a generation or two before the talmudic period.[225] One medieval chronicle, *Seder Olam Zutta* (appr. 9th cent. C.E.), went so far as to draw up a geneology of 39 names directly connecting the exilarchs of the talmudic and Geonic periods with Yehoyakhin, the exiled King of Judah.[226] While a tradition of exilarchic antiquity certainly existed among Babylonian Jewry,[227] this list was clearly a fabrication, with names Nos. 1-13, 16 and 18-19 taken directly from the list of names in 1 Chr 3:17-24.[228] The first known Exilarch was Huna, a contemporary of Yehuda the Patriarch, whose body was brought up for burial in the Land of Israel,[229] possibly at Beit Shearim which was not only part of the patriarchal estate but also an international Jewish necropolis.[230]

The Exilarch played a major role in Jewish communal life. His economic functions were varied, and included appointment of market officials[231] as well as reserving the market-place for scholars to sell their produce before others, thereby affording them an opportunity to devote themselves to their spiritual activity.[232] His executive powers were enhanced not only by the fact that his court maintained a judicial body,[233] but also by means of a private body of servants who could physically carry out his bidding.[234] One can also assume that a major function of the Exilarchate was to represent the Jewish community before the monarchy, and at least two talmudic stories allude to the Exilarch's presence before a Persian king.[235]

As for the academies, recent scholarship has raised some interesting questions. Certainly the Geonim provide us with information on their schools, and the tendency has been to assume that these were a direct continuation of the talmudic *yeshivot*. It has been posited, however, that we may be confronted with an anachronistic presentation, inasmuch as the Babylonian Talmud itself does not describe the frameworks of these formal institutions in which academic

---

[225] Cf. Beer, *Exilarchate*, 11-32.
[226] Cf. Neubauer, *Chronicles* 2, 73-5.
[227] Cf. *Iggeret Rav Sherira Gaon*, 74.
[228] Cf. Zunz - Albeck, *Derashot*, 307-9.
[229] *Gen. R.* 33,3 (p. 305); *P.T. Kil.* 9, 32b-c; *P.T. Ket.* 12, 35a.
[230] On the custom of reinterment in the Land of Israel cf. Gafni, 'Reinterment'.
[231] *P.T. Bava B.* 5, 15a-b.
[232] *B.T. Bava B.* 22a. The Exilarch's role in tax-collection remains unclear, cf. Beer, *Exilarchate*, 118ff.
[233] Beer, *ib.* 52-93.
[234] *B.T. Bava K.* 59a-b; *B.T. Gitt.* 67b.
[235] *B.T. Zev.* 19a; *B.T. Av. Zar.* 76b.

work was being conducted.[236] The present author has taken issue with that conclusion, inasmuch as the Talmud does not purport to present historical accounts, and, even more important, does not strive to describe the frameworks in which it was developed, for the obvious reason that these frameworks were known to everyone at the time and place (i.e. talmudic Babylonia). Rather, the Talmud preserved a collection of traditions presented in fixed formulae, containing only that information necessary for understanding the discussion at hand.[237]

And yet, the Talmud does describe formal gatherings around the Sages, which are also known from Geonic times. One such example is the *pirka*, a sermon delivered by the head of the *yeshiva* for the public at large, usually on Sabbath or holidays, and combining halakha and aggada.[238] What is striking at these gatherings is their fixed setting and organization, requiring the presence of all the disciples, although they were prevented from commenting during the discourse itself.

The major conclusion of this author's research[239] is that we must search for developments in the rabbinic world of Babylonia *during* the talmudic era, rather than just for discrepancies between the talmudic and Geonic periods. In this context it would appear that the well known gatherings at the *yeshivot* during two months of the year (Adar and Elul) for study as well as public reading of *responsa* sent to the diaspora, the so-called *kalla* months which are well documented in the Geonic period, probably have their antecedents in the Amoraic age, albeit only in the fourth or fifth centuries.[240] One interesting method of examining the Jewish academies under the Sassanians, is by comparing them to contemporary Christian institutions in the same empire. One such exercise, utilizing the records of the Nestorian schools primarily at Nisibis, has shown some interesting similarities to what is reflected on the *yeshivot* in talmudic literature, and this too may help to lift the stigma of 'anachronism' from the Babylonian academies, at least during the latter part of the Amoraic period.[241]

BIBLIOGRAPHY

The history of the Jewish people during the Second Temple period – and frequently up to the Bar Kokhba war – enjoys a copious bibliography, often

---

[236] Cf. the important work of Goodblatt, *Rabbinic Instruction*.

[237] Cf. the summary and bibliography on this and other issues relating to modern scholarship on talmudic Babylonia in: Gafni, 'Survey'; on the academies *ib.* 15-17.

[238] Cf. Goodblatt, *Rabbinic Instruction*, 175-96; Gafni, *Babylonian Yeshiva*, 108-30. These sermons would ultimately serve as the source of a literary genre of the Geonic period, the *Sheiltot*.

[239] Cf. Gafni, 'Yeshiva and Metivta'; *id.*, *Babylonian Yeshiva*, 205-15; this conclusion is shared by Goodblatt.

[240] Cf. Goodblatt, *Rabbinic Instruction*, 155-70; Gafni, *Babylonian Yeshiva*, 126-48.

[241] Cf. Gafni, 'Nestorian Literature'.

addressing the topic as part of an introduction to early Christianity. Most useful is the revised edition of SCHÜRER, *History*, one advantage here being the updated and comprehensive bibliographies before each chapter. For a political history from Pompey to Diocletian cf. also SMALLWOOD, *The Jews*.

Histories of the Jewish people after the destruction are fewer, due primarily to the unique skills required in dealing with rabbinic literature as a historical source. A major work in the field is ALON, *The Jews*, recently translated from the Hebrew. The work deals primarily with the Mishna period, with major treatment of Yavne and the Bar Kokhba war, but only sporadically with the Amoraic period. Alon's collected articles have been published in Hebrew: *Studies*; a selection of these has been translated into English: *Jews, Judaism*.

The political and social history of the Land of Israel from the post-Bar Kokhba period and until the Arab conquest is surveyed in AVI-YONAH, *The Jews*. For collected articles on social and religious life in the Land of Israel in the late Second Temple period cf. AVI-YONAH - BARAS, *WHJP* 8. Collected surveys of the post-Temple period may be found in: BARAS, *Eretz Israel*.

The early history of the world of the Sages has been examined within the context of studies on the Pharisees, as well as the Jewish background to Christianity. Useful – but widely varying – surveys may be found in: JEREMIAS, *Jerusalem*; MOORE, *Judaism* 1; MARCUS, 'Pharisees'; NEUSNER, *Politics*; FINKEL-STEIN, *Pharisees*. For collected articles on various aspects of the activities of the Sages see SAFRAI, *Erets Yisrael*. For links between the world of the Sages and early Christian thought see SANDERS, *Paul*. The social roots of the early rabbinic world are examined by URBACH, 'Class Status'. For a thematic survey of rabbinic thought see URBACH, *Sages*. The rabbinic statements before 70 C.E. are collected and analyzed by NEUSNER, *Traditions*.

For the history of the Jews in talmudic Babylonia see FUNK, *Juden*; BEER, *Exilarchate*; *id. Babylonian Amoraim*; NEUSNER, *History of the Jews*; OPPENHEI-MER, *Babylonia Judaica*.

Chapter Two

Oral Tora

Shmuel Safrai

Preliminary Questions

The chapters of this work describe the literature of the Sages in its various aspects of form and content, as well as the range of documents in which this literature is preserved. The present chapter is devoted to one general aspect which is essential for understanding many of its characteristic literary features: it is oral tradition literature fixed in writing. This aspect is also central to the understanding which the Sages had of their own literature. They saw it as oral tradition both in literary technique and in essence; it was produced, preserved and transmitted orally, and it was to be understood as oral teaching in contradistinction to the fixed teachings of the Written Tora. This perception of the Sages is expressed in the phrase: Oral Tora.[1]

While, as we shall see, the existence of oral traditions is explicitly documented in various Second Temple writings, the concept of an oral tradition as such, as well as the term 'Oral Tora', are found only in the literature of the Sages. This reflects a marked difference with other Second Temple groups. The idea that Tora teaching should remain oral and not be written down was not accepted in Sadducean circles, nor in the various branches of the Essenes. By implication, Oral Tora as it is referred to in the literature, contained the teachings of the Pharisaic Sages and their successors, the Tannaim and Amoraim. We shall use the term Oral Tora here to indicate the diffuse body of oral tradition literature of the Sages, which was gradually created during the Second Temple period and the period of the Tannaim and Amoraim, and which was finally preserved in the written form in which we know it: rabbinic literature.

Thus, Oral Tora has reached us in the form of the various collections: Mishna, Tosefta, Tannaic midrash collections on the Pentateuch excluding Genesis, Amoraic midrash collections on the Pentateuch as well as on the Five Megillot and on certain of the Prophets and Hagiographa, and the Babylonian and Palestinian Talmudim based on the six orders of the Mishna. To this list

---

[1] We retain the Hebrew *Tora*, rather than use the common translations 'Oral Law' or 'Oral Tradition' which cover the word Tora only partially. On the connotations of *tora* see below.

should be added various individual collections of midrash and aggada, some of them Tannaic, like Avot de-Rabbi Natan, and others Amoraic, such as Seder Eliyahu Rabba, and even much later works like the Pesiktot on the Tora portions and sections from the Prophets. Mention should also be made of additional halakhic collections such as the seven 'minor tractates' and the Tractate Sofrim. The date when these works were written in their present form ranges from the end of the Tannaic period till Geonic times, i.e. tenth-eleventh century. This extended process of fixation in writing reflects the character of Oral Tora as the accumulative creation of generations of Sages.

The teachings of the Sages, according to their own statements, were created and transmitted orally. In what forms they were taught, we can only infer indirectly. It is evident that in the period under review this diffuse body of teachings must have undergone major developments, both in number and in quality, until certain parts of it reached their fixed, written form. How much material remained unwritten and thus disappeared from history, we shall never know; how much was later lost in manuscript form we can only guess from occasional recoveries of forgotten material. Our knowledge of Oral Tora must derive from those rabbinic works that did survive in history, complemented by those reflections of Oral Tora present in the various Jewish writings of the Second Temple period and other literary and non-literary sources. That we operate here in a hermeneutic circle is evident but unavoidable: it is essential that we study rabbinic literature as the final, written form of Oral Tora – but our knowledge of Oral Tora derives mainly from rabbinic literature.

Some other fundamental questions are at stake here. It is clear that the destruction of the Temple and the subsequent take-over of the Pharisees had a stimulating effect on the production, collection and redaction of Oral Tora. One difficult question is, in what quantity and in what forms did Oral Tora exist before the destruction? Traces of early collections contained in the Mishna and the Tosefta and scattered traditions attributed to Second Temple Sages must be added here to the scanty external evidence. The problem is, again, that the bulk of relevant information must be distilled from the later written collections. More certainty can be attained about a related question: What place and influence did Oral Tora have in Second Temple Jewish society? The external evidence, which is more ample here, and the internal evidence, justify the conclusion that the teachings of the Sages embodied the social, cultural and religious traditions adhered to by a majority of Second Temple Jewry. This is not to say that Oral Tora was a monolithic body of teachings – on the contrary, it allowed for a great deal of diversity, as will be shown below. We may point here to another difference with Essene doctrine as documented in the Qumran scrolls. Oral Tora did not have the character of a closed group ideology, but was rather a body of teachings created and supported with varying intensity by large parts of society. It is precisely here that we encounter one consequence of its being oral: It allowed diversity and flexibility within the framework of generally accepted attitudes and concepts. This diversity taken into account, Oral Tora must have had a prominent place in society. If not, the smooth take-over by the Pharisees after the destruction remains hard to explain; on another level, it would also be difficult to understand the wide spread of parallels in Second Temple writings to traditions known from rabbinic documents written down centuries later.

THE SCOPE OF ORAL TORA

The prominent place of Oral Tora in Jewish society corresponds to the wide scope of its material. We can describe its scope from two points of view: the historical and the literary. From a historical viewpoint, Oral Tora covered all practical aspects of public and private life in this period, and it dealt with the widest possible range of theological and religious issues. Thus, Oral Tora may be seen at work in the creation and development of such vital social and religious institutions as the synagogue and community prayer;[2] associations (*havurot*) for the doing of good deeds, study and communal meals;[3] the court system and the established procedures in the Temple.[4] Other influential institutions molded by Oral Tora are the offering of the half shekel,[5] the system of courses serving in the Temple,[6] the House of Study,[7] the charity funds in the cities and in the Temple,[8] the school system, and the institution of community envoys.[9] In political life, the importance of Oral Tora can be seen in the negative attitude among the people towards what was called the 'Evil Kingdom' (*malkhut zadon*), i.e. the Greek and Roman imperiums with their social, cultural and religious impact.[10] Finally, Oral Tora naturally had a pervasive significance in everyday life, in the private and in the public sphere.[11]

From a literary point of view, the scope of Oral Tora is expressed in the various literary genres included. It is customary to identify these as the areas of learning of the Sages and their disciples. In rabbinic literature, a threefold division is common. Thus, R. Elazar ben Azaria and R. Akiva are said to have greatly contributed to organizing and structuring Oral Tora, and in this way to have taught 'Midrash, halakhot and aggadot'.[12] Some Amoraic traditions explicitly refer to Oral Tora in connection with this triad. An anonymous tradition states: 'But this is what God said to Moses: write down the Tora and the

---

[2] See *Compendia* I/2, 908-44.
[3] See Oppenheimer, 'Benevolent Societies'.
[4] See *Compendia* I/1, 377-419; I/2, 865-907; and Safrai, *Wallfahrt*.
[5] See Liver, 'Mahtsit ha-shekel'; Bickermann, 'Héliodore', 14.
[6] Lowy,'Barnabas'.
[7] Hüttenmeister, 'Synagogue and Beth Ha-Midrash'.
[8] *B.T. Sanh.* 17b; *M. Shek.* 5:6.
[9] See *Compendia* I/2, 945-70; I/1, 205f.
[10] Urbach, *Sages*, 649-90.
[11] See *Compendia* I/2, 793-833.
[12] On R. Akiva see *P.T. Shek.* 5, 48c; on R. Elazar see *A.R.N.* a 18 (34a). For this phrase see also *M. Ned.* 4:3.

Prophets and the Writings so that they may be in writing; but let the halakhot, midrash and aggadot be oral.'[13] Likewise, the fourth century Amora R. Yoshua ben Nehemia states: 'Tora is of a threefold nature: Tora, Prophets, Writings. Mishna is of a threefold nature: talmud, halakhot, aggadot.'[14] In this last tradition, 'mishna' stands for the teaching of the Sages, in contradistinction to the Written Tora ('Tora'); 'talmud' here is identical with midrash, as is often the case in Amoraic usage.[15]

With the areas of learning reflected in the three genres of midrash, halakhot and aggadot, the literary scope of Oral Tora is not exhausted. It appears that two other genres must be added, although they were not a part of the regular curriculum in the House of Study: prayer and targum. Both have prominent literary characteristics in common with the other three genres. They show the multiplicity of literary parallels and textual variants typical of rabbinic literature, a phenomenon which is directly related to its oral background, as we shall see.[16] Indeed, regarding these two genres we find an explicit prohibition to write them down: prayers and targumim are to be recited orally and not to be read from a written text.[17]

Both prayer and targum functioned in public liturgy, and in their structure and contents largely reflected the teachings of Oral Tora. The Sages taught the particular requirements of individual and public prayer as followed by a majority of Second Temple Jewry, and by even larger numbers after the destruction. Thus, for example, the number of prayers, their structure, their religious content and the expressions with which God was to be addressed are in line with what we find in rabbinic literature, although, it seems, especially in this area uniformity was strongly disliked by the Sages.[18] A similar situation is found with the translations of the Bible and in particular the Aramaic Targumim. Leaving aside now the questions regarding the chronological relationship between the Targumim and the midrash collections, we can safely say that the Targumim represent another part of the literary creation of the Sages. The very existence of the Targumim reflects the desire of the Sages to teach the people Tora. Moreover, they required that targum be recited as a regular part of the ceremony of the reading of the Tora. Further, the contents of the Targumim reflect the halakhic and aggadic exegesis of the Sages. Mostly, they display the

---

[13] *Exod. R.* 47,7.

[14] *Tanh., Yitro* 10 (95b).

[15] See Bacher, *Terminologie* 1, 34f., 122f., 201-3. The variation in meaning of the terms mishna, talmud, midrash and aggada is characteristic of Tannaic and Amoraic usage.

[16] Cf. the range of variants and the entirely different versions of the prayer texts found in the Cairo Geniza, and the additional versions preserved in various rabbinic works. See Heinemann, *Prayer*; Heinemann-Petuchowsky, *Literature of the Synagogue*. For the Targumim, cf. the varying divergencies between the versions preserved in manuscripts, fragments, and medieval quotations. See Grossfeld, *Bibliography*.

[17] On the prohibition against writing prayers see *T. Shabb.* 13:4; *Lev. R.* 23 (p. 530f.). On targum being considered part of Oral Tora see *P.T. Meg.* 4, 74d; *Tanh., Ki Tissa* 34 (127a); *Pes. R.* 5 (14a-b).

[18] On prayer see n. 2.

general opinion found in rabbinic midrash, or one of several opinions mentioned. Even in those cases where the Targum differs completely from the opinions found in the midrash, it is likely to reflect a divergent or an earlier opinion which for some reason was not preserved in rabbinic literature.

As a part of Oral Tora in the sense described above may also be considered the *Masora*, i.e. the rules governing the reading of the Hebrew Bible. Below, we shall cite various rabbinic sources which mention 'two *Torot*' or 'a Tora in writing and a Tora in the mouth'. These phrases express the conception of a flexible, oral Tora existing side by side with the Written Tora which was fixed in character. But the scope of the Written Tora, in other words: which books were to be read in public worship, as well as which books were to be translated in public and which were not[19] – these matters were set down in customs and rules transmitted orally, in other words: in Oral Tora. This did not necessarily have to be uniform; a Sage would recognize those books which had been passed down as authoritative by his teachers.[20] In this period, moreover, there was no written notation of the vocalization and cantillation of the biblical text; these were likewise taught and transmitted orally.

An aggadic genre of Oral Tora which deserves to be mentioned separately here, is constituted by the mystical traditions which in Second Temple sources are described as מעשה בראשית, i.e. 'The Story of Creation', and מעשה מרכבה, 'The Story of the Chariot'.[21] This genre was not a part of the regular teaching in the House of Study open to the public, nor of the public sermons. It was studied, both in the period before and after the destruction of the Temple, in private and under four eyes.[22] Tannaic traditions inform us about the teaching and creation of mystical traditions among the students of important Sages like Rabban Yohanan ben Zakkai, R. Yoshua and R. Akiva.[23] Accordingly, overt or implicit mystical utterings are found all over the literature of Oral Tora.[24]

Origin and Nature of Oral Tora

THE EXISTENCE OF ORAL TRADITIONS

The explicit conception of a tradition to be kept oral and the use of the term Oral Tora itself are advocated only in rabbinic traditions, the earliest of which

---

[19] See, e.g., *M. Meg.* 3 and 4.
[20] Cf. *B.T. Kidd.* 33a.
[21] Based on exposition of the creation story in Genesis and the chariot vision in Ezekiel.
[22] See *M.Hag.* 2:1; *T.Hag.* 2:1.
[23] *T. Hag.* 2:1-2 and parr. in the Talmudim; *Mekh. de-R. Sh.b.Y.* p. 158. A well-known baraita tells of 'Four who entered paradise': One of them 'uprooted the saplings' i.e. abandoned the world of Jewish tradition, two others 'were stricken' as a result of their mystical speculations, and only R. Akiva 'entered in peace and emerged in peace' (*T. Hag.* 2:2-6 and parr.; *Gen. R.* 2,4 p. 17).
[24] See Scholem, *Jewish Gnosticism*.

are attributed to the first Tannaim. But even in circles where this conception did not exist, or did exist but was not positively adhered, the existence of oral traditions could have been an accepted fact. Such is evidenced not only in many other early Tannaic traditions, but also by writings not preserved in rabbinic tradition: Philo, Josephus and early Christian literature. In the first place, we find here many customs, exegetical comments, beliefs, traditions and legends, which do not follow from the plain meaning of Scripture but for which parallels can be found in rabbinic traditions. This suggests that these authors used, consciously or not, elements from the oral tradition of the Sages. In the second place, these works do mention a conscious distinction being made between Scripture and ancestral or prophetic tradition which was not written.

It is a significant fact, first of all, that Philo's explanation of biblical commandments very often accords with rabbinic tradition. Many of the differences can be explained by the fact that Philo represents the earlier halakha, or a tradition which may have been particular to Alexandrian Jews. But for the most part, Philo's halakha is in accordance with the tradition of the Sages.[25] Secondly, Philo does mention unwritten traditions. He describes the details of the commandments as if they were written in the Tora, but knows of the distinction between the written Law and customs initiated by inspired people.[26] More explicitly, in the beginnning of his work on Moses, he states that he makes recourse to oral traditions: 'I will . . . tell the story of Moses as I have learned it, both from the sacred books, those wonderful monuments of his wisdom which he has left behind him, and from some of the elders of the nation; for I always interwove what is said with what is read.'[27] Likewise, after citing four reasons for the commandment of circumcision at the beginning of *On the Special Laws*, he states: 'These are the explanations handed down to us from the old-time studies of divinely gifted men who made deep research into the writings of Moses.'[28] Similar expressions are found in rabbinic traditions.[29]

Not unlike Philo, Josephus, when discussing Jewish history and customs, combines biblical material with comments and other traditions which do not derive from the Bible. Many of these are in complete accordance with historical and halakhic traditions contained in rabbinic literature, and sometimes they

---

[25] Belkin, *Philo*; Alon, *Jews, Judaism*, 89-137.

[26] *Mig.* 90.

[27] *Mos.* 1:4, literally translating (unlike the Loeb edition) the Greek τὰ γὰρ λεγόμενα τοῖς ἀναγινωσκομένοις ἀεὶ συνύφαινον.

[28] *Spec. leg.* 1:8.

[29] See *P.T. Sanh.* 11, 30a and parr; *M. Yad.* 4:3. The Greek ἄγραφοι νόμοι unwritten laws, which Philo discusses elsewhere (*Spec. leg.* 4:149-50; cf. Wolfson, *Philo*, 191-4) are laws not given by a divine or human legislator, but natural laws; a concept which derives from Greek philosophy. See Heinemann, 'Die Lehre vom ungeschriebenen Gesetz'; Urbach, *Sages*, 290-2.

reflect a minority opinion, or the earlier halakha.[30] Moreover, Josephus also explicitly mentions laws handed down by the Fathers which were not written in the books of Moses. In his historical descriptions of the conflict between the Sadducees and Pharisees, he tells of their respective attitudes to the 'tradition of the Fathers' which is not recorded in the Tora. Precisely this difference, he notes, caused one of their disputes. The implication is that he is referring here to what in rabbinic tradition is called Oral Tora.[31] Josephus goes on: '(The Sadducees) hold that only those regulations should be considered valid which were written down, and that those from the tradition of the Fathers need not be observed.' The translator adds, by way of explanation, 'only those written down *in Scripture*'. But Josephus is only saying that *unwritten* laws were not acceptable to the Sadducees. Rabbinic tradition reports that the Sadducees did maintain a tradition of laws which were not written in the Tora, but were written down in their own 'Book of Decrees'.[32] Thus the Sadducees took legal decisions only according to their own written tradition, while the Pharisaic legal tradition appeared not to have been written at all.[33]

Thirdly, early Christian literature explicitly mentions laws not written in the Tora but preserved by the Pharisees. In the Gospels of Matthew and Mark we read of the 'Tradition of the Elders' which was held by the Pharisees 'and all the Jews'.[34] Similarly, Paul testifies concerning himself that he had been zealous in observing the 'traditions of the Fathers', while elsewhere he declares that he has been living as a Pharisee.[35] In addition we may mention the second century Jewish-Christian writer Hegesippus who, according to Eusebius, used various sources, including the unwritten tradition of the Jews.[36]

It is to be noted that Josephus and the New Testament sources associate the various expressions used for oral traditions with the Pharisees. This fits in with rabbinic traditions about the earliest Tannaim and their predecessors. The Babylonian Talmud preserves a tradition of a dispute between the Pharisees

---

[30] Two examples. In *Ant.* 4:214, the 'constitution' which Moses presented to the people is said to include the rule, 'As rulers let each city have seven men . . . ' Such is not stated in the Tora, but it does fit Second Temple practice as well as the halakha stated in *P.T. Meg.* 3, 74b; *B.T. Meg.* 2a. Similarly, *Ant.* 4:281 states that 'an ox that goreth' must be slaughtered. While the Tora only lays down that it must be guarded, accepted halakha was that it was guarded while 'seen as unguilty'; R. Eliezer, however, who apparently represents older halakha here as elsewhere, states, 'the best guard is the knife' (*M. Bava K.* 4:9; *Mekh., Mishpatim* 10, p. 284). The same is found in the LXX translation of Exod 21:29.

[31] παράδοσις τῶν πατέρων *Ant.* 13:297. Cf. *ib.* 13:408; 18:11; 12:142.

[32] *Meg. Taan., 4 Tammuz*, see Lichtenstein, 'Fastenrolle', 331.

[33] Cf. Urbach, *Sages*, 293.

[34] παράδοσις τῶν πρεσβυτέρων Matt 15:2; cf. Mark 7:3.

[35] τῶν πατρικῶν μου παραδόσεως Gal 1:14. Cf. Phlm 3:5, 'a Pharisee according to the Tora'. And cf. Acts 23:6, 26:5.

[36] *Hist. eccl.* 4:22,8.

and king Yannai (103-76 B.C.E.).[37] Its antiquity is attested by certain elements of early Hebrew (as is also the case in other early segments of rabbinic literature). When the spokesman of the Sadducees urges Yannai to kill the Pharisees for their rebellious attitude, and Yannai objects, 'But what shall happen with the Tora?' – the Sadducee answer is: 'Behold, it is written[38] and deposited!' The implication is that there is no need for the Tora of the Pharisees, which appears to have been transmitted orally; it is enough that there exists a Tora that 'is written and deposited'.[39]

The beginning of the well-known tractate *Avot* expresses the continuous chain of tradition typical of the Sages in their awareness of their own place in this tradition. The evaluation of this section is of great importance to our subject, and we shall return to it several times. One important thing is the terminology used: 'Moses received Tora from Sinai and handed it down to Joshua, Joshua to the Elders, the Elders to the Prophets, and the Prophets handed it down to the Men of the Great Assembly. Shimon the Just . . . used to say . . . Antigonos of Sokho received from Shimon the Just . . .' Without doubt, the expressions 'receive' and 'hand down' do not refer only to the way of reading the Written Tora and briefly commenting to it. They equally refer to the actual transmission from teacher to disciple of other teachings which in some way were linked with the Written Tora. These terms are not frequent in Tannaic literature, but when they do appear, they refer to the transmission of Oral Tora.[40] In fact, the sayings that are recorded in chapter one and part of chapter two of *Avot* (which comprise the initial edition of the tractate) are the specific teachings of the Sages themselves, beginning with Shimon the Just (c. 200 B.C.E.) down to Rabban Yohanan ben Zakkai and his disciples. As we shall see, these teachings, while they are associated with 'Tora', represent a spiritual reality different from that of the Written Tora.

THE CONCEPTION OF ORAL TORA

Before we turn to the phrase Oral Tora, it is necessary to pay attention to the word *tora* itself. In biblical Hebrew, the basic meaning of this word is 'instruc-

---

[37] *B.T. Kidd.* 66a. As is known, there were two traditions regarding the split between the Pharisees and the Hasmoneans. One claims that the division took place as early as the days of John Hyrcanus I, while the other dates it to the days of Yannai. These two traditions are found both in Josephus and in rabbinic literature. The dating to the days of Yannai is preferable. See Alon, *Jews, Judaism*, 7, 23, 26f.

[38] Printed editions: כרוכה ומונחת. This makes no sense and on the basis of *Aggadot ha-Talmud* (Constantinople 1511) and various MSS., Urbach has proven that the correct reading is כתובה ומונחת. See Urbach, 'Derasha', 181 n. 52. On the expression itself, see Lieberman, *Hellenism*, 85f.

[39] This is also the explanation which the Amora R. Nahman ben Yitshak gave to this tradition: had Yannai adhered to Pharisaic tradition, he would have answered: 'And what will be of Oral Tora?' *B.T. Kidd.* 66a.

[40] *T. Ed.* 3:4; *B.T. Kidd.* 71a. Cf. also Hillel's answer to the gentile, p. 44. See Bacher, *Terminologie*, 106f.

tion'. This may have either a specific meaning which also allows a plural (*torot*, teachings, laws), or a more general meaning ('The book of this *tora*', Deut 28:61). Likewise, the prophet Haggai asks of 'the priests *tora*' (Hag 2:11), and this appears to be nothing but instruction of the Sages (at that time, the priests) in matters of ritual purity. Post-biblical Hebrew retained these connotations of *tora*. In addition, however, the word came to denote the Pentateuch, and even the whole Hebrew Bible – in other words, the written 'Tora'. Thus, while the latter had been slowly reaching its fixed form, *tora*, i.e. instruction by the Sages, continued to be created as before. In this multiple sense we encountered the word at the beginning of *Avot*; there it covers not just the written Tora, but also the teachings of the Sages which are quoted in the main body of the tractate.

The same extended meaning of the term is found throughout rabbinic literature, in all its periods. *Mishna Sanhedrin* 11:2 describes in great detail how the representatives of a local court would come before the Great Court in Jerusalem, 'from which *tora* goes forth to all Israel'. The word *tora* here implies a halakhic decision by the Sages as well as their explanation of Scripture, not a law laid down in Scripture which, naturally, would not have required an advice of the Great Court.[41] In a later period, the Amora R. Yohanan states: 'In whom do you find (skill to conquer in) the battle of the *Tora*? Only in one who wields bundles of learning (lit. *mishna*).'[42] Here, *tora* covers *mishna*. Another source states: 'everywhere in the *Tora*, Rav Aha teaches the stringent opinion and Ravina the lenient;'[43] and the reference is clearly to their own halakhic opinions. In an aggadic context we read: 'Beware of Hanina and his *Tora*'[44] – which refers to his erudition as a teacher as well as to his entire personality. We also find the phrase *ben tora*, 'son of Tora',[45] which in rabbinic literature indicates a person who has grown up in the world of the Sages and their Tora. *Tora* is also used in conjunction with ethical concepts like *mitswot* (commandments) and good deeds: 'Our friend Ulla is a colleague in *tora* and good deeds.'[46] Thus, apart from the Written Tora (the Pentateuch), the Prophets and the Hagiographa, *tora* can also denote the teachings of the Sages, whether these relate to the Written Tora or not, and can even include the ethical teaching and the personality of the teacher himself. At the same time, however, a conscious distinction was maintained between the Written Tora and the oral teachings of the Sages. The obvious question is: When did this distinction begin to be made?

The standard term תורה שבעל פה, as used in rabbinic tradition and modern literature, is late. It is found only in the Babylonian Talmud and in Amoraic

---

[41] The word *tora* appears also in the parallel of this tradition in *P.T. Sanh.* 1, 19c. However, in the parallels *T. Sanh.* 7:1 and *T. Hag.* 2:9 we read *halakha*.

[42] *B.T. Sanh.* 42a.

[43] *B.T. Pes.* 74b.

[44] *B.T. Pes.* 112b.

[45] *Tanh., Yitro* 15 (97a); *ib. Teruma* 1 (107a); *Lev. R.* 19,2 (p. 423) *et al.*

[46] *B.T. Av. Zar.* 5b.

midrash collections.[47] In a few instances, the term is ascribed to Tannaim and even to Shammai, but this is not the case in the Tannaic parallels to those passages.[48] While the standard term is relatively late, there are early Tannaic traditions which contain other expressions of the same concept. In *Sifrei* we read: ' "They shall teach . . . Israel Thy Tora"(Deut 33:10). – Two *Torot* were given to Israel, one in the mouth and the other in writing. Thus Agnitus the *hegemon* asked Rabban Gamliel and said to him: How many *Torot* were given to Israel? He answered: Two, one in the mouth and one in writing.'[49] Another version ascribes this event to Agrippa and Yohanan ben Zakkai.[50] It is futile trying to decide on the exact date, since such literary formulas may or may not reflect historical reality. But neither do we need to doubt the more general message of this tradition, that prominent Sages of the generation before and after the destruction of the Temple recognized two *Torot*, one written and one oral, as hinted at in Scripture.

Quite possibly, this perception can even be traced back to the generation of Hillel and Shammai. In a famous story, a gentile asked:[51] 'My master, how many *Torot* have you? [Shammai] said: Two, one in writing and one in the mouth.'[52] When the gentile expressed disbelief, Shammai sent him away, and he went to Hillel. Hillel gave him the same answer, but in addition taught him some Hebrew letters and then asked him how one comes to know them. Thereupon Hillel explained: 'Did not our fathers hand down to us that this is an *alef* and this a *bet* and this a *gimel*? Now just as you received[53] this in faith, thus receive that other one in faith.' Again, we do not claim the historical exactness of this conversation. But it seems not without significance that Tannaic tradition ascribed to those it considered as the 'Fathers of the world', Hillel and Shammai, the conception of two *Torot* in these terms. In addition, Hillel's charmingly pedagogic explanation fits his character as we know it from other reports. We do not attach significance to the fact that the two earliest traditions which explicitly mention Oral Tora are formulated as a response to the question of a gentile. It may well be that rabbinic tradition chose or preserved this formulation because only a non-Jew, as an outsider, would express wonder at the

---

[47] *B.T. Shabb.* 31a; *Pes. de-R. K.* 10 (p. 166); *Tanh. Noah* 3 (12a), *et al.* Pace Bacher, *Terminologie*, 22-4.

[48] On Shammai and Hillel see below. The term is also ascribed to the Tanna R. Yehuda, *Pes. de-R.K. Bahodesh*, ed. Buber 102b. The major versions and parallels, however, read: תורה בכתב ותורה בפה. See ed. Mandelbaum 207; *Cant. R.* 2,5. See also Blidstein, 'History', 496-8, and Urbach's comments *ib.* n. 7.

[49] *Sifrei Deut.* 351 (p. 408). The midrash appears to be reading either the plural תורותי, as do Sam. and Peshitta, or a different punctuation.

[50] *Midr. ha-Gad. Deut.* p. 764.

[51] *A.R.N.* a 15, b 29 (31a-b); *B.T. Shabb.* 31a (see next n.).

[52] In *A.R.N.* a 15, Shammai and Hillel both say אחת בעל פה; in b 29, Shammai says אחת בפה and Hillel אחת בעל פה. *B.T. Shabb.* 31a has Shammai use the Amoraic standard expression תורה שבעל פה.

[53] These terms are significant, see above.

phenomenon of an oral tradition in addition to one which is written, while a Jew would be accustomed to it.

We conclude that the probable existence among the earliest Tannaim of the conception of Oral Tora is corroborated by the testimonies on the unwritten 'tradition of the Fathers' associated with the Pharisees, which are found in non-rabbinic writings of the Second Temple period. For a better understanding of this situation it is now necessary to study the prohibition on writing down this tradition – in other words, the conception of a Tora which is to remain oral, and the reasons behind this conception.

THE PROHIBITION ON WRITING

As we shall see below in detail, the teaching and expounding by the Sages in the House of Study was done orally only. Likewise, prayers were not said from written texts by the leader of the congregation, nor did the interpreter (*meturge-man*) recite his Aramaic targum to the Tora portion from a written text. Teaching, preaching, praying and translating were oral literary activities, and were understood by the Sages as manifestations of Oral Tora which should not be written.

However, the earliest explicit statements to this effect are again found only in the Amoraic period.

> Let our Master teach us! Is he who interprets for the reader of the Tora (into Aramaic) allowed to look at a written text? – Thus our Masters taught: The interpreter may not look at a written text and the Tora-reader may not turn his eye from the Tora. For the Tora was given only in writing, as it is written: "And I will write upon the tables"(Exod 34:1). Thus one who interprets in public is not allowed to look at the Tora. R. Yehuda ben Pazzi said: The verse is full: "Write thou these words"(Exod 34:27) – the Bible that was given in writing; ". . . for after the mouth of these words" (*ib.*) – the translation that was given orally.[54]

In the Babylonian Talmud we find a midrash to the same verse in a more general formulation: 'Things that are written you may not say orally; things that are oral you may not say from writing.'[55] Again, a tradition in the Palestinian Talmud mentions a Sage who protests to a reader who translated from a written text;[56] and a baraita appearing only in the Babylonian Talmud states: ' "[Write thou] these words"– these you write and you do not write halakhot.'[57]

All these are explicit statements from the Amoraic period. Significantly, this was also the time in which the writing down of Oral Tora had started, as we shall see below. It is reasonable to assume that the prohibition on writing Oral Tora,

[54] *Tanh. B., Wayera* 6 (44a-b); *Tanh. Wayera* 5 (26a).
[55] *B.T. Gitt.* 60b.
[56] *P.T. Meg.* 4, 74d.
[57] *B.T. Gitt.* 60b; *B.T. Tem.* 14b.

as cited in these statements, must have been existing for a long time. Thus it is likely that at that time the prohibition was being put to the test, and that this necessitated its explicit reinforcement. This argument is supported by traditions from the Yavne period, and from even before the destruction of the Temple, which contain a prohibition on writing targum and prayer. We read in the Tosefta:[58]

> [Written] benedictions, even if they have letters from the name of God and include many topics from the Tora,[59] are not to be saved [from a fire which broke out on the Sabbath], but are left to burn in their place. Thus [the Masters] said: Those who write benedictions are like those who burn the Tora. There was a case of one who wrote down benedictions, and this was reported to R. Yishmael who went to examine him. When R. Yishmael was coming up the ladder, he felt his presence, took the tome (*tomos*) of benedictions and put them in a bowl of water. Thereupon R. Yishmael spoke to him in this language: The punishment for the last deed is more severe than that for the first!

Not only was it forbidden to destroy written benedictions purposefully, it was forbidden to write benedictions to start with. Apparently, there was a tendency to redact the benedictions in writing, a tendency opposed by R. Yishmael. In the same context, the Tosefta states that books containing targum can be saved from fire on the Sabbath, but must be 'hidden' from public use.[60] Then a story is related:[61]

> It once happened that R. Halafta went to Rabban Gamliel in Tiberias and found him sitting at the table of Yohanan ben Nazif. In his hand was a targum of the book of Job, which he was reading. Said R. Halafta to him: I remember Rabban Gamliel the Elder, your father's father, sitting on the stairs of the Temple, when they brought a targum of the book of Job before him. He spoke to the builder,[62] and they hid it under a row of stones.

From the context and from the parallel versions it appears that the opposition was not to the quality of this particular targum or to the translation, *per se*, of the book of Job, but rather to the use of written texts in Oral Tora, of which targum was felt to be a part. Apparently the only translation which could be used with official recognition and did not have to be hidden was the Greek translation, the Septuagint.[63] Again, this brings us to the early Tannaic period, which reinforces

---

[58] *T. Shabb.* 13:4; cf. *P.T. Shabb.* 16, 15c; *B.T. Shabb.* 115b, 61b; *Sofrim* 15:4 (p. 276) and a similar text in *T. Yad.* 2:12.

[59] Community prayers, which consist of benedictions, include quotations and paraphrases of biblical verses and names of God.

[60] *T. Shabb.* 13:2; cf. *P.T. Shabb.* 16, 15b. Thus *M. Shabb.* 15:1 should be understood, and not as *B.T. Shabb.* 115a explains it.

[61] Thus also in *P.T.* and *B.T. ib.*, and in *Sofrim* 14:2.

[62] MS. Vienna לבניו but in all other versions of the Tosefta as well as in *P.T. ib.* (including a Geniza version) and *B.T. ib.* לבנאי.

[63] See *Sofrim ib.*

46

the evidence reviewed above on the cultivation of oral traditions among the Pharisees. Taking into account that Rabban Gamliel the Elder apparently referred to an accepted rule which did not need explanation, it seems probable that the conception of an Oral Tora which should remain unwritten dates from some generations earlier.

We must now consider the possible motives behind the prohibition on writing. Again, we start from the views of the Amoraim:[64]

> R. Yehuda bar Shalom said: When the Holy One, blessed be He, said to Moses "write thou", Moses requested the Mishna to be written [as well]. However, the Holy One, blessed be He, foresaw that the nations would translate the Tora and read it in Greek and claim: We are Israel![65] And that would hold the scales in balance. Said the Holy One, blessed be He, to the nations: You claim that you are my children; I do not know. However, they who possess my hidden teaching (מיסטורין) are my children. What is this? The Mishna which is given orally.

This midrash reflects the historical circumstances of the third and fourth centuries C.E., but it does not explain the phenomenon of Oral Tora. First, Oral Tora had been in existence for several centuries by then. Second, by this time, Tannaic literature had already been written down. And finally, the fact of its oral transmission is certainly not the reason why Oral Tora did not become part of the Christian canon! In other words, the polemic with Christianity is no serious explanation for the phenomenon of Oral Tora.[66]

As for the reasons behind the prohibition on writing, scholars have sought explanations by comparison with similar phenomena in world literature. It has been noted that after an initial extended period of oral production and transmission, some catastrophe in history would cause a literature to be committed to writing.[67] It is even possible to point out a parallel development within Islam, where an oral tradition expanded and commented on the written canon. These explanations, however, are inadequate in regard to Oral Tora. There is evidence of a long tradition of writing books from the beginning of the Second Temple period. As we shall see below, the authors of the books of Ezra and Nehemiah, and especially Chronicles, had the Pentateuch and the Prophets before them in an edited and written form, and commented on them, in writing, in a way similar to later Oral Tora. During the Second Temple period and after the destruction, Hebrew books continued to be written in Palestine. Some were written in circles far removed from the world of the Sages, such as *Jubilees* and the Qumran writings, while others were from circles very close to the Sages, as for example the *Apocalypse of Ezra*. These works also expound and develop

---

[64] *Tanh., Ki Tisa* 34 (127a); *ib. Wayera* 5 (21a); *Tanh. B., Wayera* 6 (44b); *Pes. R.* 5 (14b). Cf. *P.T. Pea* 2, 17a; *P.T. Hag.* 1, 74d. We follow the *ed. princ.*, see next note.

[65] Printed edition: 'We are also of Israel.' This is a later correction since the Christians claimed to be exclusively Israel. This is also the meaning of the text in *Pes. R.*

[66] Cf., however, Urbach, *Sages*, 305f.

[67] See especially Gands, 'Dawn of Literature'; Gerhardsson, *Memory*.

47

what they accept as established Holy Scriptures – the Pentateuch and the Prophets. However, their authors committed these works to writing, and in their own circles they relate to these works as to written literature.[68] The Sadducees also accepted the Tora and the Prophets as Holy Scriptures, but apparently they kept additional written books, such as their 'Book of Decrees'.[69]

In other words, if we accept the classic division of Second Temple Judaism into Pharisees, Sadducees and Essenes,[70] it appears that the concept of Oral Tora developed only among the Pharisees. There is no justification in asserting that the literary development of the Sadducees and Essenes proceeded quicker to the stage of written and edited works. Moreover, as we shall see below, Oral Tora continued to exist as oral teaching material for hundreds of years even after it had been committed to writing. On the other hand, at the end of the Second Temple period the 'Scroll of Fasts' was composed in Pharisaic circles and it was written down. This work, moreover, is quoted in the Mishna and the Talmud as a written book, in contrast to other rabbinic sources existing at the time: '. . . All that is written in the Scroll of Fasts';[71] 'The Scroll of Fasts that was written and deposited . . .'[72] – We conclude that the conscious persistence in not writing down Oral Tora must be explained from internal motives.

The issue of prayer provides a good starting point. There are many testimonies to the fact that in the Tannaic and even the Amoraic period, there was no set text of the benedictions of communal prayer. Apparently, there were well-established larger structures and traditions in phrasing the beginning and ending of the benedictions, but no fully fixed wording. Thus, there were those who expanded their prayer and others who shortened it. The Sages actually encouraged this phenomenon and attempted to preserve flexibility and pluriformity in prayer.[73] Thus we find R. Eliezer and R. Shimon ben Nataniel complaining about those 'who make their prayer a fixed form'.[74] These plain words militate against the idea of fixed components in prayer as mentioned earlier in the Mishna: 'A man should pray eighteen [benedictions] every day;' or, '. . . the substance of the eighteen'.[75] That opinion was expressed by Rabban Gamliel, but even he is not of the opinion that their wording should be fully fixed. In the same discussion, R. Akiva says: 'If his prayer is fluent in his mouth he should pray eighteen, but if not, the substance of the eighteen.' 'Fluent' prayer, however, does not necessarily imply a fixed text. It is clear that this attitude towards prayer could not bear the writing down of benedictions, which

---

[68] See Baumgarten, 'Unwritten Law'.
[69] See n. 27.
[70] Cf. Flusser, 'Pharisäer'.
[71] *M. Taan.* 2:8.
[72] דכתיבא ומנחה *B.T. Er.* 62b.
[73] See *Compendia* I/2, 922-7.
[74] *M. Ber.* 4:3-4. Cf. *M. Avot* 2:13.
[75] On the various explanations given in the two Talmudim see Ginzberg, *Commentary* 3, 237.

would fix their text more than any amount of routine could do. This is why R. Yishmael made sure to take action against the man who wrote benedictions as we saw above. In other words, the Sages sought to preserve the vitality and the continuous regeneration of prayer, and opposed any attempt to establish a fixed formulation.

This makes it plausible that in the other areas, targum, midrash, halakha and aggada, to maintain a similar fluency of the text necessitated a prohibition on writing. This would imply that the very concept of Oral Tora was generated by the wish of the Sages to preserve the fluidity of their tradition and its openness to change and development. Only the words of God spoken to Moses and the prophets, and laid down in the Pentateuch and the prophetic books of the Bible, were considered as fixed texts by the Sages. These served as the unvarying foundation for the teachings of the Sages which should, in contradistinction, 'be fruitful and multiply': a living instruction – *tora* – which is created, studied and passed on, not in books but in the course of live discussion. Certainly the Sages took care to preserve ancient traditions containing sayings, discussions or decisions, but these always served as the starting point for further discussion and teaching. As we shall see in the chapters on halakha, aggada and midrash, these early traditions were not only augmented with new material, but even their wording and content were not immune to change.[76]

An explicit affirmation of the flexibility of Oral Tora is expressed by R. Yannai, an important Sage from the transition period between Tannaim and Amoraim:

> Had the Tora been given cut and dry, no one could stand on his feet. Why? "And the Lord said unto Moses . . ." – Said Moses unto Him: Lord of the universe, tell me, just how is the halakha? He said unto him: "Turn aside after the majority"(Exod 23:2); if the majority exonerate, the accused is exonerated, but if they convict, he is convicted. Therefore, the Tora must be studied both according to the forty-nine ways to declare impure and according to the forty-nine ways to declare pure.[77]

By what stands in opposition to the 'cut and dry Tora', Oral Tora is meant, since the laws of the Written Tora are accepted as clear-cut and fixed. Thus God hands to Moses, without deciding, the various halakhic options of Oral Tora which are implied in the possibility to interpret the Written Tora in different ways. If necessary, the halakha can be decided by a vote of the Sages. Their *tora* should not be 'cut and dry'; therefore it cannot be written down and is passed on only in the course of oral study and deliberation. The one exception was the Scroll of Fasts, the permanent and established list of holidays of the Second Temple period – it was written down since it would not change any more.

---

[76] The present view basically concurs with Weiss, *Dor-dor we-dorshav*, 92-4.
[77] *P.T. Sanh.* 4, 22a.

THE INNOVATIVE CHARACTER OF ORAL TORA

In the above, we have been referring to the chain of tradition listed at the beginning of the tractate *Avot*. We observed that the terms used there indicate that not only the Written Tora is transmitted, but also Oral Tora along with it. In other words, the editors of the tractate present their teachings and that of their predecessors as additions or comments which accompany the Written Tora. On closer look, however, there is more to say. True, the halakhic and aggadic midrash collections, much of the targum material, and even some purely halakhic texts, can be regarded as extensive Bible commentaries, or, more liberally, as 'creative commentaries'. In that sense the Tannaic view of the simultaneous giving of the Written and the Oral Tora is justified – just as we can understand R. Akiva who sees both as one Tora.[78] But as we shall see, there is much in halakha and in aggada which cannot be viewed as commentary to the Tora. This is most evident in certain halakhic texts.

Very illustrative is an ancient mishna which comments on the relationship between various sets of halakhot and the corresponding parts of the Bible: 'The halakhot of Shabbat, of festival offerings and of sacrilege are as mountains hanging by a hair: Scripture is scanty but the halakhot are many.'[79] In other words, the laws of these three subjects can, despite their great number, still be seen as some broad exposition of those few biblical verses. But the beginning of the mishna states: 'The halakhot of release from vows hover in the air and have nothing to support them' – that is to say, in the Bible. The Bible mentions only the releasing of women from their vows by their fathers or husbands (Num 30). The halakha, however, greatly expanded both the concept and the methods of release from vows.

Indeed, Oral Tora abounds with innovations in all areas of thought and life. We return to the beginning of *Avot*. The first saying, of the Men of the Great Assembly, sets down the requirement that the administration of justice be humanized,[80] that a Sage raise many disciples, and that a 'fence' be made around the Tora. The next saying states that the world is established on three pillars: Tora study,[81] worship, and the doing of good deeds. The third saying formulates the requirement that one serve the Master (God) 'in order not to receive a reward'.[82] None of these views and conceptions are found in the Bible but are innovations of the Sages. Thus the programmatic opening of the tractate *Avot* which states that it was from Moses and the Prophets that *Tora* derives, in content testifies to the measure of creative innovation embodied in the oral *Tora* of the Sages.

---

[78] See below, p. 59.

[79] *M. Hag.* 1:8. On its antiquity see Epstein, *Tannaitic Literature*, 46-52.

[80] This is how the phrase הוו מתונים בדין should be understood.

[81] This is the meaning of על התורה; see Urbach, *Sages*, 814 n. 1.

[82] Printed versions: שלא על מנת לקבל פרס; but in the major versions, and also in the quotation of the saying in *B.T. Av. Zar.* 19a, על מנת שלא לקבל פרס. This correct version was advocated already by R. Shimon ben Tsemah Duran in *Magen Avot*, 6a.

Similar things can be said of halakhic texts which reflect the situation of the Second Temple period. Even where many details are given in the Written Tora, Oral Tora may not only explain and further specify, but also introduce substantial innovations. Deut 26:1-11 gives a detailed description of the commandment of first fruits, or *bikkurim*,[83] a subject which is further elaborated in the Mishna tractate *Bikkurim*, chapters one and three. In fact, however, there is also much new material, such as detailed halakhot stating that *bikkurim* are not to be brought from fields which are under the suspicion of having been stolen,[84] or that although women do not recite the festive declaration (Deut 26:3), they may bring *bikkurim*.[85] It is also stated that proselytes may bring but do not recite because of the formulation '. . . which God swore to our fathers to give unto us' (Deut 26:3).[86] But one Tanna teaches: 'A proselyte . . . may bring and declare. Why? – "And thou [Abraham] shalt be the father of a multitude of nations" (Gen 17:5); formerly you were the father of Aram only, from now on you are the father of all the nations [i.e., gentiles].'[87]

Although the roots of these sayings and halakhot can be pointed out in the Tora and the Prophets, it is evident that they imply a substantial further development. Indeed, in a historical perspective, it appears that Second Temple Judaism, and especially the Pharisees and their predecessors, did humanize the court system, attract a great number of students, make 'fences' around the Tora, etc. Rather than being just a commentary on the Written Tora, Oral Tora in this perspective represents a new creative development which sprang from deep religious sources. It represents the will to fulfil the commission imposed on man, spelled out in ritual or inter-human commandments and in religious and ethical teachings.

Significantly, there is a clear and consistent appreciation in rabbinic literature for the ability to innovate in Tora. Rabban Yohanan ben Zakkai when listing the merits in Tora study of his five students, calls R. Eliezer 'a plastered cistern that loses not a drop', but R. Elazar ben Arakh 'a spring flowing with increasing strength'. According to one opinion, Rabban Yohanan considered the 'spring with increasing strength' as the first among his disciples, and if all the Sages were in one scale of a balance and R. Elazar ben Arakh in the other, 'he would outweigh them all.'[88]

This is clearly borne out in a tradition from the Yavne generation:[89]

> It happened that R. Yohanan ben Beroka and R. Elazar Hisma came from Yavne to Lod to pay honour to R. Yoshua at Pekiin. R. Yoshua asked them: what innovation חידוש was taught today in the House of

---

[83] See also Neh 10:36; Ezek 44:30.

[84] *M. Bikk.* 1:1-2.

[85] *Ib.* 1:5.

[86] *Ib.* 1:4.

[87] *P.T. Bikk.* 1, 64a.

[88] *M. Avot* 2:5.

[89] *T. Sota* 7:9-10; *P.T. Sota* 3, 18d; *P.T. Hag.* 1, 75d; *B.T. Sota* 3a.

Study? They answered: we are your disciples and it is of your water that we drink. He said: the House of Study cannot exist without innovation! [Then the two disciples pass on the *derasha* of R. Elazar ben Azaria, which concludes as follows:] Just as a plant bears fruit and multiplies, so the words of Tora bear fruit and multiply.

In the same vein should be understood the saying of Hillel, of the first Tannaic generation: 'He who increases Tora, increases life;'[90] i.e. he who enlarges and develops his *tora* – not, as is usually interpreted, he who studies and repeats it. This is also the intention of his other saying: 'He who does not increase, makes to cease;'[91] – by which is not meant, as later generations explained, the quantity of study or the amount of hours put into it, but the increase and expansion of Tora itself. He who does not make *Tora* increase, his *tora* will cease. The Tannaic and Amoraic Sages saw themselves as handing down tradition while at the same time addressing new questions which were arising from changing circumstances and developing thought. Precisely so, they considered themselves to be fulfilling the commission of *Tora*. They considered *Tora* to be a living and growing reality which bears fruit to all those who labour and 'turn' in it: 'Turn it and turn in it, for all is in it.'[92]

THE BEGINNINGS OF ORAL TORA

The evidence reviewed above makes clear the existence of oral traditions among the Pharisees, and of the conception of an Oral Tora among the first generations of Tannaim – a Tora which should remain fluid and not be written. We have considered the earliest evidence of the phenomenon known as Oral Tora. The typical contents and methods of Oral Tora, however, can be traced back to an earlier period.

The oldest written documents of Oral Tora date from the beginning of the third century C.E. Source criticism, however, established the existence within the Mishna of remnants of earlier collections of halakhot, descending from the Yavne generation or before.[93] Furthermore, written works of the Second Temple period contain references to halakhot which are known from rabbinic literature but which apparently had already existed for centuries.[94] This makes it probable that in many other cases, where such external evidence is lacking, halakhot in Tannaic or Amoraic collections date from the first Tannaic generations.

Rabbinic literature itself preserves traditions which it ascribes to even earlier periods. The beginning of *Avot*, well-known to us by now, programmatically begins with the sayings of the 'Men of the Great Assembly' and of Shimon the

90 *M. Avot* 2:7.
91 *Ib.* 1:13.
92 *M. Avot* 5:22.
93 See Epstein, *Tannaitic Literature*, 15-58.
94 See below p. 135-46.

Just, who lived at the beginning of the second century B.C.E. Elsewhere, halakhot are cited in the name of Yose ben Yoezer and his associate Yose ben Yohanan of Jerusalem, who lived before the Hasmonean revolt.[95] There are also certain regulations (*takkanot*) ascribed to the 'Men of the Great Assembly'.[96] This brings us as far back as literary ascriptions can bring us.

But a closer look at the content of some of these sayings yields more information which is significant in a larger perspective. As we shall see below, public instruction to small or larger groups was the predominant setting in which Oral Tora was created. Precisely this is what seems implied in the saying of the Men of the Great Assembly: 'Be moderate in judgement, raise up many disciples and make a fence around the Tora.' The word 'fence' may be explained either in a wider sense,[97] or in the more narrow sense of an extra boundary to prevent transgression.[98] In any case, we have a reflection here not only of the typical setting in which halakha was created, but also of the attitude of the Sages towards the Written Tora. Without doubt, the required moderation in judgement was not unrelated to the desire to attract many students; and it may well have been this teaching before such large audiences which provided the opportunity to create 'fences' and tackle other halakhic questions that the Written Tora left open. Something similar is expressed in the saying of Yose ben Yoezer: 'Let your house be a meeting place for the Sages and sit amidst the dust of their feet and drink in their words with thirst.'[99] Those Sages, who were travelling from place to place along dusty roads in order to teach Tora to eager students, were not just passing on established traditions of their teachers, but while teaching, were apparently involved in the process of creating Oral Tora. This saying, dated by tradition to the early second century B.C.E., appears to breathe the same spirit as the words of R. Yoshua of almost three centuries later, which we cited above: The House of Study, where eager students drink in their teacher's Tora, 'cannot exist without innovation.'

Tannaic tradition thus presents us with the possibility that the dynamic, oral tradition of teaching which was later to be called Oral Tora operated as a conscious process of creation already by the end of the third century, and therefore may have originated a century or so before. This possibility finds confirmation in two biblical books from the early Second Temple period, Nehemiah and Chronicles. These works, very much like later Oral Tora, see themselves as being dependent upon the Pentateuch and the Prophets, which they consider to be established and authoritative sacred writings. Correspondingly, their way of presenting their own teaching while commenting on Tora and Prophets resembles very much the literary procedures of Oral Tora. Chapters eight to ten of Nehemiah may be seen as the earliest documentation of

---

[95] *M. Ed.* 8:4; *M. Hag.* 2:2.
[96] *B.T. Ber.* 33a; *B.T. Meg.* 17b; *P.T. Ber.* 2, 4d and parr.
[97] See *A.R.N.* a chs. 1-2 (2a-7b).
[98] *Mekh., Pisha* 6 (p. 19).
[99] *M. Avot* 1:4.

the comprehensive and purposeful creation of halakha, and to a lesser extent also of aggada. The book of Chronicles is one extended example of the creation of aggada and midrash. This information is available to us, of course, by virtue of the one decisive difference with the literature of Oral Tora: both works were composed as written books. Just so, they allow a literary comparison which underlines the probability that the process of Oral Tora originated in the third-fourth century B.C.E.

Chapter eight of Nehemiah opens with the assembly of the people, 'men and women' (8:3), and the reading of 'the book of the Tora of Moses' (8:1). This reading is not just for instructional purposes, but is part of the worship of God: as the people stand, Ezra commences the ceremony with a blessing, and the people bow down with their faces to the ground (8:5-6). Now reading and studying the Tora as a form of worship was a characteristic of the Second Temple period; it is regulated by Pharisaic-rabbinic tradition more than by any other sector of society, and this is our earliest testimony of that form of worship. Another detail of great interest is the presence of women at the ceremony of reading the Tora. In preparation for the revelation of the Tora in Exod 19, the nation and the Elders are mentioned,[100] not women. The men, however, are explicitly commanded to refrain from marital intercourse for three days in order to attend the revelation event. Thus the presence of women in Nehemiah 8 is a novel feature; it became a common phenomenon in the later synagogues, which were led predominantly by the Sages, and in public ceremonies most particularly in the circles of the Sages.[101] Furthermore, the presence of the women at the Sinai event is an expository addition typical of rabbinic midrash.[102] There is another significant detail in the description. The people, upon hearing the words of the Tora, begin to weep and mourn as a sign that they had not previously been observing the Tora. However, when Ezra tells them that this is to be a festive day, they go to 'eat and drink and send portions and make great rejoicing because they had understood the words that were declared to them' (8:12). The acceptance of the teachings of the Tora with a sense of joy was to become another characteristic of the Sages' view of Tora.

Nehemiah 10 describes the signing of the covenant by the leaders, the priests and the Levites. This covenant includes the obligation to 'walk in God's Tora which was given by Moses the servant of God,' and a detailed description of eighteen commandments. None of these commandments, however, appears in the Tora in the same language or form; they all reflect midrash on the Tora. The first commandment concerns the prohibition against intermarriage with gentiles (10:31). The Pentateuch has no such general prohibition, and in fact only

---

[100] Exod 19:4, 15.
[101] See Safrai, 'Women's Gallery'.
[102] *Mekh., Ba-Hodesh* 2 (p. 207): '. . ."To the house of Jacob" (Exod 19:3) – these are the women; ". . . and to the children of Israel" – these are the men.' Thus also *ib.* p. 209. And cf. *Exod. R.* 28,2.

forbids marriage with Canaanites, Ammonites, Edomites and Egyptians.[103] The prohibition in Nehemiah is universally directed against all the 'people of the land'. Second comes a prohibition against purchasing from non-Jews on the Sabbath and on festivals (10:32). The Pentateuch lists no specific prohibition against commercial intercourse on these days; the Prophets do mention a prohibition against transactions connected with the transportation of goods on the Sabbath.[104] In the book of Nehemiah this is expanded to include the purchasing on the Sabbath and festivals of food brought in by non-Jews on their own initiative. This prohibition is in keeping with the early Second Temple tendency to limit secular acts on the Sabbath. The sixth commandment is 'The obligation to charge ourselves yearly with the third part of a shekel for the service of the house of our God . . . the continual burnt offering, the Sabbath and the New Moons' (10:33f.). The Pentateuch mentions the commandment to pay a half shekel (Exod 30:11-16). This was, however, a one-time contribution rooted in the need for atonement: 'When you take the census of the people of Israel . . . that there be no plague among them.' Moreover, this half shekel was not meant to support the offering of sacrifices but 'for the service of the tent of meeting', i.e. the erection of the tabernacle.[105] Similar things can be shown for the rest of the eighteen commandments. In other words, the halakhot issued by Ezra all imply midrash of Tora commandments.

We now turn to the book of Chronicles, a work which relates history from Adam until the beginning of the Second Temple period. The influence of Deuteronomy on Chronicles has been stressed;[106] the author, however, is familiar with both Leviticus and Deuteronomy and uses them in combination. It is likely that he also possessed sources, now lost, on historical, genealogical and geographic matters. But for the most part the historical sections of the book closely follow the corresponding sections in Judges, Samuel and Kings. Significant changes are made, however, and the result is a new historical presentation. According to the book of Kings, even those kings who went in God's ways offered sacrifices in high places until this was abolished by Hezekiah and Josiah, while according to Chronicles, the righteous kings observed the entire Tora, including the demand to centralize worship. Moreover, established practices of the Second Temple period, such as the twenty-four priestly courses or the singing by the Levites, are suggested to have existed already in the First Temple period.[107] In this idealized presentation, David and Solomon are bound to be

---

[103] Exod 34:15f.; Deut 7:3; 23:7. The prohibition against marrying gentiles was renewed in the so-called Eighteen Decrees at the end of the Second Temple period; see *P.T. Shabb.* 1, 3c-d (cf. *B.T. Av. Zar.* 36b).

[104] Amos 8:5; Jer 17:19-27; Isa 58:13.

[105] The 'tax of Moses' during the days of Josiah (2 Chr 24:4-10) was not a tax which had been in existence since Moses' days, but resulted from the necessity to repair the Temple at that time. It was a temporary contribution just as the contribution in the desert for the construction of the tabernacle was temporary.

[106] Von Rad, *Geschichtsbild*; Mazar, 'Divrei ha-Yamim'.

[107] 1 Chr 3:15-24; 4:24, 43; 2 Chr 26:9f. *et al.*

completely righteous and their sons are not mentioned. The same is true for Rehoboam and Abiah who fought against Jeroboam.[108] One device used is the exposition of names, such as in the case of Asa seeking help from a physician instead of from God and Jehoshaphat appointing judges.[109] Likewise, Azariah is constantly called Uzziah; and so it is said: 'And God helped him, . . . for he was marvelously helped, till he was strong'![110]

Contradictions between his biblical sources are explained by the author of Chronicles in a manner similar to the midrash of Oral Tora. We shall limit ourselves to an oft-cited example. In the description of the Passover sacrifice in Exod 12:9 it is stated: 'Do not eat of it raw or boiled ובשל with water, but roasted on fire צלי אש.' But in Deut 16:7 it is said: 'And you shall boil it ובשלת and eat it . . . and in the morning you shall turn and go to your tents.' In his description of the Passover of Josiah, the author of Chronicles solves this contradiction in the following manner: 'And they "boiled" the Passover with fire ויבשלו באש according to the ordinance; and they boiled בשלו the holy offering in pots' (2 Chr 35:13). This solution in fact is similar to the Tannaic midrash: ' "Or boiled ובשל" (Exod 12:9) – this word by itself could mean "roasted", as when it says: "And you shall boil it and eat it" (Deut 16:7). And thus it says: "They boiled the Passover with fire according to the ordinance" (2 Chr 35:13).'[111] The verse in Chronicles is taken here as a confirmation of the explanation of the verb בשל in Deut 16:7 to mean 'prepare', make well-done.

In sum, we can discern in these works the budding elements of Oral Tora: the creation of midrash, aggada and halakha as comments accompanying the Written Tora, yet with their own independent teaching; and this creating is done by way of teaching in a festive public gathering, where women are also present. As stated, it is equally clear that the authors of these works,[112] while showing a close relationship to the atmosphere of later Oral Tora, felt no impediment against writing down their teachings. The actual conception of Oral Tora, implying the prohibition to fix it in writing, was apparently born at a later date – in surroundings which we learn to understand ever better as the world of the Sages.

ORAL TORA 'FROM SINAI'

The emphasis of many Sages on the innovative character of Oral Tora may seem hard to reconcile with the emergence of the idea that Oral Tora was given already at Sinai. We shall see, however, that this idea expresses a sophisticated

[108] Cf. 1 Kgs 14 and 15 on 1 Chr 11 and 13.
[109] 2 Chr 16:12; 2 Chr 19. This appeared quite clearly in scholarly research. See Wellhausen, *Prolegomena*, 199.
[110] 2 Chr 26:7 15. See Friedländer, *Veränderlichkeit*, 35-40.
[111] *Mekh., Pisha* 6 (p. 21). On the midrash in Chronicles see Willi, *Die Chronik*; Seeligmann, 'Beginning of Midrash'.
[112] We do not claim a single authorship for both works, as has been done since Zunz. Various literary features point to different authors.

consciousness of the dialectics involved in the creative interpretation of a fixed, written text. This is typical of the Sages.

The words of Hillel and Shammai to the gentile which we cited above state that two *Torot* were given to Israel and, in Hillel's version, that both must be accepted 'in faith'. It is not said, however, that a fully accomplished Oral Tora was given on Sinai. This expression can even be explained to mean that along with the Written Tora, only certain additional comments were given at Sinai. Something similar is implied in the terms used at the beginning of *Avot*: to 'receive' and to 'hand down' Tora. Apart from the Written Tora, which is here included, Tora was given orally on Sinai – but not 'The Oral Tora' in its entirety. Nor do the words ascribed to Rabban Gamliel, of the generation of the destruction of the Temple, mention anything more specific than the general expression 'two *Torot*'.[113]

A more specific conception is found in an anonymous tradition which may be the continuation of a statement by R. Akiva: '. . . This teaches that the Tora, its halakhot, its details and its explanations, were given by Moses from Sinai.'[114] The unambiguous statement that Oral Tora as such was given at Sinai is found from the early Amoraic period onwards. Two traditions take their cue from the remarkable phrasing of Moses' words in Deut 9:10, which in a somewhat literal translation read: 'And the Lord gave me the two tablets of stone, written with the finger of God, and on them after all the words which the Lord spoke with thee.' – 'Said R. Yoshua ben Levi: [One would expect] "on them", [but it says] "*and* on them"; . . . "all", [but it says] "*after* all"; . . . "words", [but it says] "*the* words". Thus Scripture (*mikra*), mishna, talmud and aggada, even what an advanced student will teach before his master – it was already said to Moses on Sinai.'[115] The Babylonian Talmud preserves R. Yohanan's midrash: ' "And on them after all the words" – this teaches that the Holy One, blessed be He, showed Moses the minutiae of the Tora, the minutiae of the Scribes, and the innovations which the Scribes would make in the future.'[116] Similarly, R. Yohanan's colleague and friend, R. Shimon ben Lakish, states: 'What is the meaning of the verse, "And I will give thee the tables of stone *and* the Tora *and* the commandment which I have written, that thou mayest teach them"? (Exod 24:12) "Tables of stone" – these are the Ten Words. "The Tora" – this is Scripture (*mikra*). "And the commandment" – this is mishna. "Which I have written" – these are the Prophets and the Hagiographa. "That thou mayest teach them" – this is *gemara*. This teaches that all these were given to Moses from Sinai!'[117]

---

[113] On these traditions see above p. 44.
[114] *Sifra, Behukotai* 2 (112c). Cf. *B.T. Nidda* 45a.
[115] *P.T. Pea* 2, 17a; *P.T. Meg.* 4, 74d; *P.T. Hag.* 1, 76d. Cf. *Exod. R.* 47 (beginning); *Lev. R.* 22 (beginning); *Eccl. R.* 1,2; *ib.* 5,8.
[116] *B.T. Meg.* 19b.
[117] *B.T. Ber.* 5a. Cf. *Exod. R.* 28,6.

These very Amoraim, however, were among the greatest innovators in all fields of Oral Tora, and were very active in editing, deciding and specifying the traditions they received. Likewise, R. Akiva made many innovations in the halakhot, midrashim, and aggadic teachings which he received, and he did this deliberately.[118] He was also willing to emend his own mishna: 'R. Elazar be-R. Shimon said: This was the mishna of R. Akiva before he came from Zifrin. But when he came from Zifrin he taught . . .'[119]

The conception that Oral Tora in its entirety was given to Moses on Sinai is not some theory stated long after rabbinic literature had been fixed and written. Nor was it formulated by later pious generations as the doctrinal belief that the words of R. Yohanan and R. Akiva were revealed already to Moses on Sinai. Rather, it was expressed by those Sages themselves, while they were teaching in the House of Study or in a public gathering, and were thus innovating and ever renewing their own learning. Remarkably, not only the teachings of ordained Sages, but even what an advanced student will 'teach' and 'ask' before his master, was 'already said to Moses on Sinai'.[120] In other words, the concentrated and devoted involvement of the Sages and their students with Moses' Tora, their teaching and questioning, brings out its meaning. Oral Tora is seen, as it were, as implicitly present in the teachings which Moses gave before the community. Or, conversely, the teaching Sage himself represents a continuation of the revelation of the Tora to the people at Sinai. Ben Azzai, student and colleague of R. Akiva, said of himself: 'I am but finding parallels in the Tora to expressions in the Prophets and in the Prophets to expressions in the Hagiographa; and the words of the Tora are as joyful as on the day they were given on Sinai!'[121] Ben Azzai's undoubtedly innovative search for parallels (a common midrash form) in his own experience re-enacts the revelation at Sinai.

This experience and this consciousness finds a stunning expression in one of the picturesque aggadot of the Amora Rav, another great innovator of Oral Tora:

> When Moses ascended on high he found the Holy One, blessed be He, engaged in affixing coronets to the letters [of His Tora scroll]. Said Moses: Lord of the universe, who stays Thy hand [in adding such embellishments]? He answered: There will arise a man at the end of many generations, Akiva ben Yosef by name, who will expound upon each hooklet piles and piles of halakhot. Lord of the universe, said Moses, permit me to see him. He replied: Turn thee round. Moses went and sat down behind eight rows [of students listening to the discourses on the Tora]. But he did not understand what they were saying.[122]

---

[118] See below p. 204ff.

[119] *Sifrei Z.* p. 232.

[120] For references see n. 115 above.

[121] *Lev. R.* 16 (p. 354) and parr.

[122] *B.T. Men.* 29b. On the phrase 'Halakha to Moses from Sinai' which, ironically, made Moses calm down, see below p. 180-5.

Again, R. Akiva himself is reported, when discussing rabbinic opinions, to have stressed that 'the entire Tora is halakha given to Moses on Sinai.'[123] Yet when Moses came into his House of Study, he could not follow the halakhic discussion! In other words: the idea, or possibly the belief, that the entire Tora was already given to Moses on Sinai and that he taught it to Israel, in no way restricted the creation of new *Tora*. [124]It did not prevent the Sages from innovating halakhot which regulated the social and religious life of the community. It even permitted them to change and emend traditions they had received.

Certainly, the importance of a 'tradition' שמועה and of a 'testimony' עדות was great, in particular when legal decisions needed to be made,[125] or when the mishna was being ordered and redacted. Even Hillel and Shammai, '. . . The fathers of the world, did not persist in their opinion in the face of a tradition.'[126] The entire tractate *Eduyot* is devoted to the various testimonies which the Sages transmitted, mostly from the Yavne period, but also from earlier and later times. Nevertheless, this did not prevent the Tannaim and Amoraim from continuous innovation, either purposefully, or spontaneously in the course of teaching. The degree of innovation was not the same in every generation and R. Akiva, for instance, was not like a R. Eliezer ben Hyrcanus who stated about himself: 'I never said anything which I did not hear from my master.'[127] Not even R. Eliezer, however, was to be considered only 'a plastered cistern which looses not a drop' or 'a tarred barrel which preserves its wine'. In every generation of Sages we can find reflected the same intensity of study and deeds and ramified literary creativity.

The concept 'Oral Tora from Sinai' appeals to the response which is expected from the recipient of the revelation, i.e., the people. Oral Tora did not simply begin with the traditions which Moses received from Sinai, but in the 'interpretation' which the people are said to have given immediately upon hearing the Ten Words. 'Rabbi says: This is to proclaim the excellence of Israel: when they all stood before Mount Sinai to receive the Tora, they interpreted the divine Word as soon as they heard it. For it is said: "He encompassed him [Israel], He made him understand" – as soon as the Word came out, they interpreted it.'[128] This idea is found in a more detailed form in another midrash: ' "He made him understand" – regarding the Ten Words. This teaches that as every Word came forth from the mouth of the Holy One, blessed be He, Israel looked at it and knew what sanction it entailed, what admonitions, how many

---

[123] Baraita on *B.T. Nidda* 45a, and cf. above. On the phrase see previous note.

[124] See especially *B.T. Er.* 54b.

[125] E.g. *T. Sanh.* 7:2; *M. Ed.* 5:7. See Epstein, *Tannaitic Literature*, 184f.

[126] *M. Ed.* 1:3-4; *T. Ed.* 1:3. The entry שמועה was not dealt with sufficiently by Bacher, *Terminologie* 1, 189f. and *Tradition*, 9ff. He did not fully understand the significance of this term in the transmission process of Oral Tora. It refers to a tradition from an authoritative source: a Sage who presents an accepted and established halakha, or a halakha confirmed by the Great Sanhedrin.

[127] *B.T. Sukka* 28a. Cf. *ib.* 27b; *T. Sukka* 3 end; *B.T. Yoma* 66b.

[128] *Mekh. ba-Hodesh* 9 (p. 235).

lenient and how many stringent rulings, how many analogies could be learned from it, how many laws and how many answers.'[129] In other words, the creative process of Oral Tora began with the very acceptance of the Tora by the community at Mount Sinai – and 'this is the excellence of Israel'.

There is another element, without which Oral Tora could not exist and its ascription to Moses and Israel would be meaningless. This is the consciousness, emphasized in various ways in rabbinic literature, of the continuity in the chain of tradition of the Written Tora along with the Oral. Once more we return to the beginning of *Avot*, this time to stress that it teaches not only the origin of Tora, but also the continuity of its transmission and development. It was common knowledge for the Sages that during the First Temple period a majority of the people engaged in idolatry, adultery and bloodshed.[130] Yet the prophets and their disciples remained true to the Tora and handed it down from generation to generation; thus the beginning of *Avot* teaches.

This stands in striking contrast to the doctrine of the Dead Sea sect, which knew of no such continuity in the knowledge and the observance, much less in the interpretation of Tora. The *Damascus Covenant* declares:[131]

> But David[132] had not read in the sealed book of the Tora which was inside the ark, because it had not been opened in Israel since the day when Eleazar and Joshua and the Elders died, for as much as they worshipped the Ashtoret; and they hid the Revealed until [the son of] Zadok arose.

'The Revealed', i.e., the book of the Tora, was hidden and king David did not know its laws, nor did anyone else, until they were finally revealed by the teacher of the Sect. This 'Searcher of the Tora', or 'Man who searches',[133] was not in possession of a continuous tradition as to how the 'Revealed' could be interpreted, and so expounded it following his own understanding and according to the authority with which he was invested.[134]

Ways of Literary Creation

THE CREATIVE PROCESS IN TEACHING

According to the sources, in ancient Judaism Tora was taught and studied not just in academies but in a variety of situations.[135] These can be summarized as follows: 1) the Sage teaching to a small group of students; 2) *derashot* (homilies) of the Sage in the synagogue or House of Study; 3) the teaching of Tora at

---

[129] *Midr. ha-Gadol Deut.* p. 705. A similar text in *Sifrei Deut.* 313 (p. 355).

[130] *P.T. Yoma* 1, 38c and parr.

[131] CD 5:2-6.

[132] The author of the scroll is attempting to explain why David took more than one wife, for according to the sect it was forbidden to do so. See CD 4:21.

[133] CD 6:7-11; 1QS 8:11f.

[134] Cf. 1QpHab 7:3-5. See Schiffman, *Halakha at Qumran*, 22-76; Herr, 'Continuum'.

[135] See *Compendia* I/2, 960-9.

assemblies and communal meals, at the marketplace or at any other suitable location. These various settings in fact constitute the situations in which Oral Tora was created. In other words, they represent the *Sitz im Leben* of that type of Jewish literature which we term Oral Tora.

Certainly, not every derasha, even of the most prominent Sages, would be an innovation, and without doubt there were many which only repeated or combined well-known material. The same can be said for the master teaching his students; often, he may just have been passing on to his students what he had received from his own teachers, with minor changes. But it should be stressed that apparently the Sages did not sit in isolation setting down their teachings in written books. Their literary creativity took place during the very act of teaching at those manifold locations mentioned above. Thousands of traditions found in all areas of rabbinic literature of our period testify to this fact. They also prove that at least from the Tannaic period onwards, each public gathering, such as a wedding or a funeral service, could occasion the creation of Oral Tora, in the fields of halakha or aggada, or both together.

The Tosefta relates:[136]

> It occurred that R. Tarfon was sitting in the shade of a dovecote [at Yavne][137] on the Sabbath afternoon. They brought before him a bucket of cold water. Said R. Tarfon to his students: Which benediction should be recited by one who drinks water to quench his thirst? They replied: Teach us, master. He said: [Blessed be He] Who creates many living things and [provision for] their needs.

Then three questions are asked regarding the interpretation of biblical verses, and answers are offered. These verses were possibly connected to the portion which was read on that Sabbath. In any event, this meeting of R. Tarfon with his students was an occasion on which halakha and midrash were created. In the continuation, the Tosefta tells that R. Akiva and some of his student-colleagues were sitting in the gate house of R. Yoshua and were discussing one of the subjects touched on by R. Tarfon. He had stated that the tribe of Judah had become worthy of the kingship because its patriarch had confessed the rape of Tamar. This explanation was rejected by R. Akiva with the words: 'Then is reward given for a sin?' Hereupon, other explanations were offered, and finally R. Akiva taught:

> The reason is that this tribe sanctified the name of God. When the tribes went up [from Egypt] and stood on the shores of the sea, each one claimed that he would be the first to descend into the sea, but the tribe of Judah did jump and descend first and thus sanctified the name of God. On this hour it is written: "Save me, O God, for the waters have come up to my neck, I sink in a deep mire!"(Ps. 69:2-3). And further it is stated:

[136] *T. Ber.* 4:14-16.
[137] Thus in the parallel, *Mekh., Wayehi* 5 (p. 106). In *Mekh. de-R. Sh.b.Y.* p. 63: 'in the vineyard of Yavne'.

"When Israel went forth from Egypt, Judah became his sanctity"(Ps. 114:1-2) – Judah sanctified His name at the sea and therefore: "Israel is his [Judah's] dominion"(*ib.*).

The question asked by R. Tarfon was triggered by the bucket of water they placed before him. Often, however, such questions were not provoked by a particular event, but rather by the topic under discussion. Thus we read in the *Mekhilta*:[138]

> Once R. Yishmael, R. Elazar ben Azaria and R. Akiva were walking along the road, followed by Levi the netmaker[139] and Yishmael the son of R. Elazar ben Azaria. And the following question was asked in their presence: Whence do we know that the duty of saving a life supersedes the Sabbath [commandments]?

R. Yishmael, R. Elazar ben Azaria and R. Akiva all gave their response. Then the editor brings in additional explanations from Sages of the same generation, and also from those of two or three generations later. In the generation of R. Yishmael and his colleagues, it was accepted halakha that the commandments of the Sabbath – as all other commandments except the prohibitions of idolatry, adultery and bloodshed[140] – are superseded by the requirement to save a life. These Sages, however, while using the opportunity to study during the long hours of walking, wished to clarify the grounds of this halakha, either from the Bible or from a combination of logic and biblical support.

One of the things stressed by the Sages is the importance of discussing Tora at festive meals,[141] and when important Sages were present at such occasions, new and innovative matters would be discussed which found their way into the tradition of Oral Tora. One tradition relates the words of Tora spoken by R. Eliezer and R. Yoshua at the circumcision ceremony of Elisha ben Avuya in Jerusalem:[142]

> They were sitting and engaged themselves with words of Tora: from the Tora to the Prophets and from the Prophets to the Writings, and fire came down from heaven and encircled them. Said Avuya to them: My masters, did you come to burn down my house? They said to him: Heaven forbid, but we were sitting here and going over the words of the Tora, from the Tora to the Prophets and from the Prophets to the Writings; and the words were as joyful as when they were given from Sinai, for the essence of their being given is – through fire.

These Sages, present at a circumcision ceremony in the house of an important leader of Jerusalem, began a lively discussion on Tora, and this is seen by our story as a continuation of the creation and the giving of Tora at Sinai.

---

[138] *Mekh., Shabta* 1 (p. 340f.); *T. Shabb.* 15:16; *B.T. Yoma* 85a-b.

[139] סרד a netmaker, as in the major versions, and not סדר as in the printed editions of the *Mekhilta* and the Babylonian Talmud.

[140] This is stressed in the continuation in the Tosefta.

[141] E.g. *M. Avot* 3:2-3.

[142] *P.T. Hag.* 2, 77b; *Ruth R.* 6,13; *Eccl. R.* 7,10; *Eccl. Zutta* p. 110.

A LEARNING COMMUNITY

A perusal of rabbinic literature reveals a plurality of opinions in almost every area. The various opinions may be found scattered over different sources, or they may have been edited in the literary format of a *mahloket* (conflict of opinions) of Sages of one generation. Often, a dialogue, a shorter or a more elaborate discussion, is added.[143] On the other hand, it is also possible to point to many basic elements agreed upon by all disputants and schools throughout the generations. Stressing such common elements, halakhic codifiers from the Geonic period onwards have attempted to create, out of the mass of opinions and details in rabbinic literature, a monolithic system of halakha. Naturally, their approach had to be eclectic, choosing only those decisions or opinions which fitted into their systems and ignoring the differences existing within one generation as well as the historical development of halakha through the generations. Modern studies stressing the existence of common features, particularly in the spheres of religious thought and law,[144] tend to be more responsive to historical reality, but here, too, it is possible to point to unjustified generalizations and projections.

These strictures taken into account, the sources permit us to state that the world of the Sages as reflected in their literature shows a basic unity in fundamental religious outlooks, social values and law. First of all, we can point to the authority of the Written Tora and to the creative process of Oral Tora directly connected with it – a conception which must have originated, as we saw, sometime early in the Second Temple period. Likewise, the development of prayer as a form of regular worship is a phenomenon known throughout the period, from the time of Ezra onwards. The kingdom of heaven as an overriding ideal, whether mentioned explicitly or indirectly, recurs in the various bodies of literature of our period. Concepts such as repentance, the People of Israel, the Land of Israel and its holiness, and the expectation of redemption, and socio-ethical values such as the fostering of family life, the institution of charity and social justice, appear throughout the period. To an even larger extent, lasting structural elements are to be found in various areas of halakha. There is, for example, the well-defined set of rules known as the Commandments Dependent upon the Land which cover the cycle of seasons from the initial stages of sowing to the setting aside of heave-offering and tithes – notwithstanding the many controversies about details. Similarly, in spite of unceasing development from the days of Ezra to the Amoraic period, there are many unchanging elements in the laws of 'forbidden labours' on the Sabbath. And although, as stated, one may criticise the theories of the talmudic roots of Jewish Law in many details, the sources confirm that there was a basic consistency in court procedures and jurisprudence in the talmudic period. Sometimes, such unitary

[143] On the *mahloket* as an instrument in the formulation of halakha, see below pp. 168ff.
[144] See in particular the works of A. Gulak in the field of law and of E.E. Urbach on religious thought.

features suddenly appear fully developed throughout rabbinic literature in a certain period; pertinent examples are the laws concerning the financial obligations of a husband to his wife and the four official manners of execution. In such cases, these features must have been in existence long before they appear in the datable sources.

The basic coherence of Pharisaic-rabbinic thought and law as outlined here, however, did not result from the activities of central legislative or educational institutions. It is a unity which grew organically and included diversity and development.[145] The main cause is that it represents the teachings and decisions formulated by generations of Sages on innumerable and varied occasions. It is true that there is evidence of a limited number of halakhic decrees (*takkanot*) issued by the Nasi or head of the Sanhedrin. Usually, however, these decrees officially sanctioned some matter which had been practiced for many generations, such as the binding force of the marriage contract or the possibility of collecting debts after the Sabbatical Year. This coherence of rabbinic law and thought can be traced to the teaching process of the Sages. In the course of this process, informal decisions would gain authority in time and thus become cornerstones for further teachings.

When Shimon the Just taught, 'Upon three things is the world based: upon Tora, upon the [divine] service, and upon the practice of loving-kindness,'[146] no approbation by an academic institution or decision of the Sanhedrin was required. This teaching reflects and creatively summarizes the thought of generations preceding him. The three elements he enumerates were not merely preserved in the traditions of Oral Tora; they were also expressed in many halakhot, concepts, social values and institutions which in effect sought to maintain a balance between these three values: the study of Tora, the worship of God and the doing of good deeds. Likewise, Shemaia, the teacher of Hillel, teaches, 'Love labour and hate lordship.'[147] This saying represents a remarkable innovation in comparison to the accepted, aristocratic view of labour in Greco-Roman society.[148] Not only did this concept acquire great importance in aggada and halakha, it also had much influence on Jewish society at large and the position of the Sages in it. Many of the Sages who contributed to Oral Tora were tradesmen or artisans from among the common people. On the verses in Exod 18:20, 'And you shall teach them the statutes and the decisions and make them know the way they must walk in and the deed they must do,' we find the *derasha* of R. Elazar of Modiim:[149] ' "And make them know" means: make them know

---

[145] See pp. 163-8.

[146] *M. Avot* 1:2.

[147] *M. Avot* 1:10.

[148] Sir 38:33f., too, has a negative attitude towards labourers. However, an appreciation of work is found in other works of the Second Temple period such as the *Testament of Issaschar*, and see Philo, *Spec. leg.* 2:60 and Josephus, *Ag. Ap.* 2:39.

[149] *Mekh., Amalek* 2 (p. 198); *B.T. Bava K.* 99b; *B.T. Bava M.* 30b. The *derasha* is also absorbed in *Tg. Ps-Yon., ad loc.*

how to live [how to earn a living].[150] "The way" refers to visiting the sick. "They must walk" refers to burying the dead. "In" refers to deeds of loving-kindness. "And the deed" refers to the line of strict justice. "They must do"– beyond the line of strict justice.' Not all elements of this *derasha* are new, but taken as a whole it had a fertilizing influence on Jewish society and literature. Sayings like these, then, became basic threads in the fabric of Oral Tora which was being woven in the midst of a developing religion and society.

Nor was the teaching location of any decisive importance. It is true that much teaching was reported to have taken place at official assemblies of the Sages in the Chamber of Hewn Stone or afterwards in the Sanhedrin at Yavne or Usha. There is, for example, the halakha issued by Rabban Shimon ben Gamliel the Elder which caused the price of doves for sacrifices to drop considerably; this happened in the court at the Temple Mount, i.e., the Chamber of Hewn Stone.[151] Similarly, several teachings of R. Elazar ben Azaria are said to have been delivered 'in the Vineyard at Yavne', i.e., the seat of the Sanhedrin; we quoted one of these above.[152] In *Mishna Sota*, a number of *derashot* of R. Akiva and other Sages touching on important halakhic and aggadic matters are preserved, and they were said 'on that very day', at what appears to have been an important assembly of Sages at Yavne or some other place.[153] A last example may be found in *Canticles Rabba* which preserves a number of *derashot* given by important Sages during a gathering at Usha.[154] However, in none of these examples is there any indication that the statements made derived their authority from the location. In no way are they intrinsically more important than such teachings as are reported to have been delivered 'in the shadow of the Temple',[155] 'in the markets of Tiberias',[156] 'under a fig tree', 'under the olive tree' or 'in the opening of the gate'.[157] In other words, there is no distinction between teachings uttered just anywhere in public and those taught in the academy or Sanhedrin. Only in the later Amoraic period does it happen that Sages refrained from the public teaching of a halakha about which they were uncertain.[158] A particular teaching gains authority and becomes part of Oral Tora only by its inherent quality and by its being recognized by the students and the public.

---

[150] Thus Rashi on *B.T. Bava M.* 30b explains, because the word חיים often means a trade through which one makes a living (*B.T. Kidd.* 28b; *B.T. Ket.* 50a (according to the explanation of the *Arukh*); *Eccl. R.* 9,9 *et al.*

[151] *M. Ker.* 1:7.

[152] See p. 51. For a halakha he taught at the same or a similar occasion, see *M. Ket.* 4:6 and *T. Ket.* 4:8.

[153] *M. Sota* 5:2-5. According to *B.T. Ber.* 28a this was the meeting of the Sages at Yavne when Rabban Gamliel the Younger was deposed. This tradition, however, is very indefinite.

[154] *Cant. R.* 2,5. This tradition is preferable to *B.T. Ber.* 63b which has Yavne as the meeting place.

[155] *B.T. Pes.* 26a.

[156] *B.T. Moed K.* 16a.

[157] *M. Yev.* 12:10; *P.T. Ber.* 2, 5c; *Cant. R.* 4,4.

[158] *B.T. Taan.* 26b.

The same is true regarding the authority of the teachers themselves. As is well known, after the destruction of the Temple a strict distinction was introduced between the ordained Sage and the student, by means of the title 'Rabbi'.[159] This title granted the Sage authority to adjudicate in criminal cases and offered him protection in the case of a mistake. Most Sages in the following period bore this title, but there were those who did not, and these included important and creative Sages such as Shimon ben Azzai and Shimon ben Zoma in the Yavne generation and Shmuel in the first generation of Amoraim. The teachings of these 'students'[160] have their place in the tradition of Oral Tora, just as those of 'Rabbis' or heads of academies. Moreover, the Sages acknowledged this, as is expressed by R. Yoshua ben Levi who said that 'even what an advanced student will teach before his master' has the authority of words spoken by Moses at Sinai.[161] Surely, such prominent Sages as Hillel, Rabban Yohanan ben Zakkai or R. Akiva had a far greater influence than most other Sages, but this had nothing to do with their official status. The teachings of these Sages came to constitute a prominent part of Oral Tora mainly because of their quality and their being accepted, and also because of the great number of their students who, naturally, carried on the teaching of their master in his name.

It is also quite clear that no Sage ever claimed authority from a divine vision or prophecy. In the view of the Sages, prophecy had come to an end, and with it the teaching through divine visions. Nor was there a Sage who had been divinely elected to his office. The Sages did believe in the election of the people of Israel and its Sages, as the benediction says: 'Blessed be He who chose them and their teaching.' They did not believe, however, in the election of the individual Sage. On the other hand, a Sage who taught a particular matter, but later changed his mind and taught otherwise, did not think that new Tora had been revealed to him; but rather, that he had taught as one who kept studying and upon further thought, or having heard a different tradition, re-evaluated his opinion.[162] There was, of course, a certain degree of authority to halakhic decisions of the Sages, and to decrees and votes in the court. However, formal decisions were but one factor, and not the major one, in the creative development of Oral Tora – neither in the field of halakha,[163] nor, certainly, in the fields of midrash, exegesis and religious thought.

THE IMPORTANCE OF QUESTIONS

Illuminative of the creative process of Oral Tora is the importance of questions. Asking questions was an essential element in the teaching process, which, as we have seen, is the actual *Sitz im Leben* of the literature of Oral Tora. Questions

---

[159] See *Arukh s.v. Abaye*; *Iggeret Rav Sherira Gaon*, Additions, 128f.
[160] *B.T. Kidd.* 49b; *Sifra, Nedava* 7 (21c).
[161] See n. 115.
[162] Among many other cases: *M. Taan.* 4:4; *Sifrei Num.* 4 (p. 7).
[163] See below p. 163ff.

of all sorts are found in all the various areas of rabbinic literature, not just in the Talmudim and the midrash collections, but even in the Mishna which is known to have gone through a most rigorous process of editing. The very first mishna of the tractate *Berakhot* contains a question asked by the sons of Rabban Gamliel when they came home late at night. Similar questions are found scattered throughout the Mishna. Only in the midrash collections from the end of the Amoraic period does the function of questions seem to be declining in use.

The importance attached to the question as an integral part of the procedures in the House of Study is well illustrated by a very detailed description given in *Tosefta Sanhedrin* 7:7:

> One does not ask while standing . . . One does not respond while standing, nor from a high position, nor from afar, nor from behind the elders. One does ask only over the subject[164] [under discussion] and one does respond only over what is known.[165] Let him not ask more than three halakhot on the subject [under discussion] . . . One who asks over an actual case מעשה must say: I ask over an actual case. If one asks on the subject and another does not, one responds to the one who asks on the subject. He who does not ask on the subject must say: I did not ask on the subject; thus R. Meir. But the Sages say: there is no need, since all of the Tora is really one subject . . . [If one question is over] an actual case and the other is not, the question about the case is dealt with. [If one question is on] halakha and [another on] midrash, halakha is dealt with. [If one is on] midrash and [another on] aggada, midrash is dealt with . . . [If] a Sage and a student [ask a question], [the question of] the Sage is dealt with; a student and an *am ha-arets* – [the question of] the student is dealt with. If both are Sages or both students or both *ammei ha-arets*; or if both [questions are] on halakha; or if two questions, two answers, or two cases were asked, the speaker מתורגמן may decide which is dealt with.

In other words, those who came to ask questions before the Sages could be Sages or students, but also the *am ha-arets*, the uneducated. Their questions could relate to the subject the Sages were just then discussing, but could also bring in other subjects, be it an actual event or a practical matter, or a question arising from study; it could be in the fields of halakha, midrash or aggada. Many of these questions and the answers given, we can imagine, were a matter of routine, but we can also point to questions which served as catalysts to further study and interpretation.

Questions, as a regular part of the proceedings, could play a notable role. We read, for example: 'This was the manner of Rabban Gamliel. When he would enter and say, "Ask", it was known that he bore no ill feeling. But if he entered and did not say "Ask", it was known that there was ill feeling.'[166] As a rule, we

---

[164] Thus MS. Vienna and *ed. princ.*

[165] במודע thus MS. Vienna. *Ed. princ.* במדע; MS. Erfurt במאורע and in Geonic tradition במראה (*Minhat Bikkurim* in the name of R. David Luria).

[166] *Sifrei Deut.* 16 (p. 26).

may assume, Rabban Gamliel would enter the House of Study and invite questions, but if he did not, it was a sign that he wished to reproach someone.[167] Of another sort are the questions at the beginning of some talmudic *sugyot*. These questions, asked by a student or a Sage, might first cause a great consternation but subsequently result in the clarification and creative re-formulation of fundamental issues.[168] Curiously, in the attempt to depose Rabban Shimon ben Gamliel, questions were devised which he would supposedly not be able to answer for lack of preparation and learning.[169] Thus, the head of an academy might react with annoyance to a difficult question which had been asked but had remained unanswered in previous generations; he was prone to consider this as an attempt to embarrass him.[170] It could also happen that questions resulted in a far-reaching discussion on the observance of certain commandments under new conditions.[171]

The asking of questions on Tora was not restricted to the House of Study. There are numerous traditions reporting on questions which Sages and students asked their masters in other locations. We have seen already some of that above. Thus, the Mishna preserved a series of questions asked by R. Akiva of Rabban Gamliel and R. Yoshua at Emmaus when they went to buy an animal for the wedding feast of Rabban Gamliel's son.[172] The many traditions about the travels of the Sages also record questions – sometimes series of questions – asked under way or in remote places, such as those asked of R. Akiva at Ganzak, Media,[173] and of R. Yoshua in Alexandria:[174] 'The men of Alexandria asked R. Yoshua ben Hanania twelve things: three on halakha,[175] three on aggada, three out of ignorance, and three on good manners.' In both examples the halakhic questions included not only actual issues from daily life, but also halakhot no longer in use at the time, such as those relating to the Temple service, i.e., questions arising out of study.

We have stated that the questioner can be either a Sage, a student or anyone – even an illiterate. In addition, many instances can be cited where the questioner was a woman.[176] It could happen, to be sure, that a woman questioned a Sage who was of the opinion that Tora was not to be passed on to women since 'the wisdom of a woman is only in her spindle'.[177] This was not, however, a generally held opinion. Moreover, the continuation of the same story informs us that the woman came before the Sage when he was sitting with his students, and that her

[167] *Ib., ib.* and 1 (p. 3f.).
[168] *P.T. Ber.* 4, 7c; *B.T. Ber.* 27b; *B.T. Bekh.* 36a; *M. Bekh.* 4:4.
[169] *B.T. Hor.* 13b.
[170] *B.T. Bava B.* 81b.
[171] *M. Yad.* 4:4; *Sifrei Num.* 124 (p. 158f.).
[172] *M. Ker.* 3:7-9; cf. *Sifra, Hova* 1 (16b c).
[173] *B.T. Av. Zar.* 34a; *B.T. Taan.* 11a. The version 'R. Akiva' appears in the major versions.
[174] *B.T. Nidda* 69b. The matter is hinted at in *M. Neg.* 14:3 and *T. Neg.* 9:9.
[175] חכמה here, as in some other sources, is to be understood as halakha.
[176] E.g. *B.T. Rosh H.* 17a; *B.T. Nidda* 45a.
[177] *P.T. Sota* 3, 19a and parr.

question was not about a personal matter, but dealt with the explanation of a verse in the Tora – which the students were anxious to hear after she had departed! Similarly, not a few questions were asked by non-Jews, and not necessarily out of ill-will or with polemical intentions, but rather from a desire to understand a particular point of Jewish tradition. Non-Jews often took part as well in questioning the Sages during sessions with students.[178]

Questions were also sent from the diaspora to the House of Study or its head in Palestine. There is evidence of this from the later Tannaic period and especially from the early Amoraic period.[179] Just like in the other instances, these questions were not only about practical issues, but also reflected the wish to study, either halakha or other fields, and this contributed to the growth of Tora.

The above discussion throws light on the background of the genre of midrash called *yelammedenu*. This name derives from the formulaic opening question at the beginning of each section, usually a halakhic question: *Yelammedenu rabbenu*, 'Let our master teach us.' The ensuing *derusha* is structured as a halakhic-aggadic answer to that question. In the course of time, the question in the *yelammedenu* literature became a mere literary device of the redactor and no longer reflected a real question asked by the community. Its origin, however, was in the custom to begin a public gathering with questions from the audience.

COLLECTIVE AUTHORSHIP

The peculiar nature of the Tannaic and Amoraic tradition literature is understandable only if we see it as the creation of a multitude of authors. At this point it is well to recall certain aspirations of the Sages discussed elsewhere in this chapter: to disseminate Tora and raise many disciples, to inspire every person to realize his right and duty 'to make Tora increase', and to encourage the asking of questions. Internal and external evidence indicates that Oral Tora is the creation of thousands of Sages and students who were active in the period which stretches from Ezra and Nehemiah till the last stages of redaction of rabbinic literature.

As of yet there has not been an exact and detailed study of the names of the Tannaim and Amoraim who are mentioned in the various branches of rabbinic literature. Since many names appear in varying forms or corruptions in the various sources, what may appear as different names in reality may refer to one and the same Sage. Conversely, many different Sages had the same name, and it is not always possible to differentiate between them, not even by means of an analysis in depth. The lexica and indices, from the medieval period until the present, either were not intended to include all names, or were not thouroughly

---

[178] *Sifrei Deut.* 321 (p. 408); *Pes. de-R.K., Para* (p. 71) and parr.; *Gen. R.* 17 (p. 116) *et al.*
[179] *B.T. Ket.* 69a (cf. *P.T. Gitt.* 5, 46d); *B.T. Pes.* 103a; *B.T. Hull.* 95b *et al.*

done so that many names were overlooked. This is especially so in the case of Sages who are mentioned only once or twice.

Taking this into account, it is nevertheless possible to ascertain that a few hundred Tannaim and a few thousand Amoraim are mentioned by name. In addition, it is quite likely that a couple of thousand unnamed Sages made their contributions. Most of the names of Tannaim, for example, are from the later Tannaic period, and only a few are from the Temple period. There is more information about the Amoraic period, but here, too, the great majority of names are from a limited number of generations. This situation is not only dependent on the 'quantity' of Tora taught during one particular generation but also very much depends on the progress made in the work of collecting and editing the material in that particular generation or the following one. The names of many Sages responsible but for a single saying were forgotten and their words were transmitted in the name of an important Sage who headed the academy where the sayings were collected; these were perhaps even rephrased and thus transmitted to the students. Often we can assume almost with certainty that a particular statement as it came down to us represents a development over many generations, and only in its final form received the name of one particular Sage attached to it, or in other cases continued to remain anonymous. Long and short anonymous sayings appear in all branches of rabbinic literature. Many of these may be from a Sage whose name is known, but for some reason was not attached to them; but we can be sure that numerous sayings and teachings are from Sages or students whose names have been completely forgotten.

The following tradition may exemplify not only the openness to participation in the creation of Oral Tora, but also the anonymity which befell many of its contributors:[180]

> An *am ha-arets* said to R. Hoshaya: If I tell you a good thing, will you repeat it in public in my name? – What is it, asked he. – All the gifts which the Patriarch Jacob made to Esau, replied he, the heathens will return to the Messiah in the messianic era.What is the proof? "The kings of Tarshish and the isles shall return tribute" (Ps 72:10). It does not say "shall bring" but "shall return". – By your life, he exclaimed, you have said a good thing and I will teach it in your name!

The Sage likes the midrash which the man told him, and repeats it in his public teaching; thus it was preserved to the present day. The irony of this case is, of course, that, in spite of R. Hoshaya's good will, the name of the man was not preserved. We can be certain that events like this, although not necessarily with an *am ha-arets*, were no exception. Oral Tora was created in a process of organic growth. It increased not so much through the decisions of official authorities, nor through the literary work of individual authors, but through the activity of a teaching and learning community.

[180] *Gen. R.* 78 (p. 933).

A comparison with the various Jewish writings of the Second Temple period highlights this peculiar feature of Oral Tora. These writings, such as the narratives, apocalypses, wisdom sayings and historiographies, are the literary creation of a single or just a few authors or editors, and in any case are intended to be understood as such by the reader, either directly or under the disguise of pseudepigraphy. Oral Tora, however, is intended as oral teaching matter, which is not created by one or more writers, but transmits the teachings and insights of any number of teachers, students and laymen. Even a thoroughly edited work such as the Mishna is a stylized selection of traditions and opinions orally taught by a great number of named or anonymous teachers, and it is intended to be taught and studied as such – orally.

REDACTION IN TEACHING

Not only the creation of Oral Tora, but also its redaction is to be situated in the teaching event. The editing of the extant texts, Mishna, Tosefta and both Talmudim, was not done at the desk of an editor, but rather, emerged from instruction and discussion between the Sages and their students. Furthermore, the editing of these texts was not done on one occasion, but took place in a process lasting several generations. Thus, the extant texts contain shorter or longer fragments from collections edited by previous generations, so that it is possible to speak of the layer structure of the Mishna and other rabbinic texts.[181]

A good illustration of the process of editing while teaching is found in the following report.[182] First it is told that R. Akiva was teaching one particular version of a halakhic dispute between Beit Hillel and Beit Shammai. Then it says: 'When R. Akiva was ordering halakhot before his students he said: Let all who have heard an explanation supporting his friend come and say it.' Thereupon R. Shimon cited a different version of the same dispute, but R. Akiva responded: 'Not everyone who jumps forth is praiseworthy, but he who gives the explanation with it. Then R. Shimon said before him: Thus said Beit Hillel to Beit Shammai . . .' – and an explanation for the version he just cited is offered. The report concludes: 'From then on, R. Akiva taught according to R. Shimon.' R. Akiva is found here 'ordering halakhot', or in other words, editing 'his mishna', and he does so in discussion with his students and learning from them. Interestingly, the corresponding part of the Mishna first sets forth the initial version of R. Akiva and then that of R. Shimon without mentioning either name. This implies that this is a section of R. Akiva's mishna which R. Yehuda the Prince embedded in his mishna, i.e., 'the Mishna'.[183]

Editing mishna is done while teaching. This is also borne out by the fact that all the testimonies concerning R. Yehuda the Prince and others 'ordering

---

[181] See below, chap. 4.
[182] T. Zavim 1:4-6.
[183] M. Zavim 1:1. See Epstein, Tannaitic Literature, 73.

halakhot', or in other words editing mishna, involve the phrase 'he taught' (*shana*) and similar expressions. It is recorded that R. Yehuda the Prince 'taught' thirteen versions of one halakha, seven of which to R. Hiya.[184] Sages commenting on the Mishna state, 'Here Rabbi [Yehuda the Prince] taught',[185] or, 'Thus Rabbi taught',[186] or again, 'In every place where Rabbi taught . . .'[187] Likewise, Rabbi himself, when dealing with the final version of the Mishna, relates that he 'taught' the Mishna to R. Yitshak bar Avdimi and that he examined it and thus committed it to him.[188]

These testimonies regarding the editing of Oral Tora during the act of teaching and in discussions with students all refer to the major halakhic texts, Mishna, Tosefta and the Talmudim. It is very likely that the same happened with the other Tannaic collections as well, and, so it seems, also with Targum Onkelos.[189] However, it is not impossible that certain other midrash collections and Targumim did not emerge from such a process in the House of Study, but were the work of literary compilers and editors. This, however, must be decided on the basis of literary analysis, since no direct testimonies were preserved in the sources.

Oral Tora and Rabbinic Literature

ORAL TORA WRITTEN DOWN

At the beginning of our chapter, we discussed the remarkable phenomenon of the oral creation and preservation of the tradition of the Sages. It is this which is remarkable, not the fact that large parts of this tradition were eventually preserved in that form which was universally preferred for its effectiveness in warding off oblivion: writing. When we turn now to this written form, we shall have to be very attentive to the peculiarities connected with its being the written fixation of the oral tradition of the Sages.

First of all, we must distinguish between the editing of rabbinic literature, which, as we saw, was done orally in the course of teaching and study – and its reduction to writing. For central texts such as the Mishna, the Tosefta and the Talmudim, the writing down was only the final step concluding an extended process of creation and redaction. Moreover, it was not seen as causing a decisive change in their character, since, as we shall see below, even then these texts continued to be taught and studied orally.

The priority of the long oral editing process over the actual writing explains, for one thing, the difficulty modern scholarship has in handling the problem of

---

[184] *B.T. Ned.* 41a.
[185] *B.T. Yev.* 41a.
[186] *P.T. Pes.* 3, 30a.
[187] *P.T. Kidd.* 3, 64c.
[188] *P.T. Maas. Sh.* 5, 55d.
[189] See Komlosh, *Bible,* 28f.

dating rabbinic texts, and the lasting necessity to examine the date of every single tradition unit. As far as the collections are concerned, we do have concrete traditions regarding the compilation of some of the more important texts; in some cases we even possess early information on the compilers themselves or their Houses of Study. Thus there are many traditions to the effect that the Mishna was edited by Rabbi Yehuda the Prince approximately 150 years after the destruction of the Temple, i.e., c. 220 C.E. Less clearly, we have internal evidence relating to the process of the editing of the Babylonian and Palestinian Talmudim. There is much controversy among scholars, however, regarding those works lacking clear-cut external or internal evidence regarding the date of editing. The various opinions cite dates often differing by hundreds of years. Thus some date *Seder Eliahu Rabba* to the third-fourth centuries while others place it in the ninth-tenth centuries. As stated, these texts resulted from generations of collective creation and redaction. They are the written form of an oral tradition literature.

Thus far, we have only spoken of the collections, and not of the traditions and remnants of earlier collections contained in them. As we have said before, the Mishna clearly incorporates fragments of earlier 'orderings of halakhot'.[190] The date of redaction of such works serves in fact as the *terminus ad quem* of the traditions contained in them. In many cases, the establishment of a *terminus a quo* for individual rabbinic traditions is impossible. In other cases, there are explicit attributions or other indications assigning traditions to an early date.

The date of writing of the rabbinic documents seems to be closely related to the maturation of the editing process. Such at least is the case with the Mishna, the earliest collection to be written down. Since the Middle Ages, it has been disputed whether or not the Mishna was written down immediately upon its final redaction, and this controversy still continues in talmudic scholarship.[191] Careful examination of the sources, however, proves without doubt that Saadia Gaon and others following him, like Sherira Gaon, were correct in saying that the Mishna was committed to writing in the days of R. Yehuda the Prince, and that, at least from this time onwards, collections of baraitot, aggada and other matters were written down.

Scholars have listed the talmudic sources in which Sages appear to be using written rabbinic texts, and we shall give some of the more clear-cut examples:[192]

1. Two traditions in the Babylonian Talmud quote Rav stating that he found a 'scroll of secret matters' מגילת סתרים hidden in his house or in the House of Study of R. Hiya, and it contained written halakhot or halakhic midrash.[193]

---

[190] Cf. above p. 71.

[191] See Epstein, *Tannaitic Literature*, 692-706; Lieberman, *Hellenism*, 83-93.

[192] The most complete list is found in Epstein, *ib.*, but not all of his proofs are conclusive.

[193] *B.T. Shabb.* 6b; *ib.* 96b; *B.T. Bava M.* 92a.

2. In *P.T. Maasrot* 2, 49d, a baraita is quoted twice, and the second time it is introduced with the words: 'R. Yona said: We found in the booklet of Hilfi that . . .' Thus this booklet contained written baraitot.[194]

3. In *P.T. Demai* 2, 22d R. Yohanan sends someone who had a question to Hanania ben Shemuel 'who taught on this matter'. The answer is, reportedly: 'He did not show me a baraita מתניתא , but told me a tradition שמועה .' The baraita could have been seen as a written text, but only an oral tradition was received.

4. In *B.T. Temura* 14a-b, within a discussion about the prohibition against writing down Oral Tora it is stated: 'R. Yohanan and Resh Lakish used to study a book of aggada on Sabbaths and explained (their attitude) in this manner: (Scripture says) "It is time for the Lord to work, they have made void Thy Tora" (Ps 119:126) – whence they said: It is better that one letter of the Tora be uprooted (i.e. by writing down midrashim) than that the whole Tora should be forgotten. [Another version says: The rabbis trust their version and since things are forgotten they write and put these things down. And when things are forgotten they read the book.]'[195]

5. Certain problems concerning the text of the Mishna and its corruption as dealt with by the Amoraim, do not result from difficulties in oral transmission but rather from mistakes or ambiguities in a written text.[196]

From interpreting all the evidence, it appears that there was a progressive acceptance of written rabbinic texts among the Sages. The first testimonies refer to the writing of halakha. It seems clear that the editing and writing of the Mishna by Rabbi Yehuda the Prince brought about the writing down of more Tannaic material: collections of halakhot (baraitot or *toseftot*) and of (mainly) halakhic midrash. In the second generation of Amoraim we already have evidence regarding the use of written targum, although the Sages continued to oppose the public reading of such works in the synagogue. The redaction of the large Amoraic texts, the Talmudim and the Amoraic midrash collections, marks the end of the talmudic period. It would appear that the last stage of the process was the writing down of prayers. This must have started only after the close of the talmudic period, since apart from the Yavne episode, rabbinic literature does not record any attempt to set down written prayers.

Although certain external causes have undoubtedly had their influence, this progressive appearance of written rabbinic documents can be understood very

---

[194] Cf. *T. Maas. Sh.* 2:3. Booklets of the Sages in which halakha and aggada were listed are mentioned in *B.T. Shabb.* 156a *et al.*

[195] The section in brackets does not appear in the printed versions but is found in many medieval versions; see Epstein, *Tannaitic Literature*, 696 and *id., Amoraitic Literature*, 143. It does not reflect the early Amoraic period in Palestine, when written texts were not checked even in cases of doubt, but the Babylonian situation of the late talmudic and the early Gaonic period. See *Iggeret Rav Sherira Gaon*, 171 and especially Rav Aharon Gaon in the Responsa published by S. Assaf in *Madaei ha-Yahadut* (1926) no. 58.

[196] See Epstein, *Tannaitic Literature*, 704-6.

well from the inherent development of Oral Tora. The creative process of Oral Tora evolved towards its gradual consummation as organically as it had been originating. As we shall discuss below, the final redaction of the Mishna was understood only afterwards as the closing of a period; its reduction to writing did not change that fact. Neither can it be seen as a measure out of necessity. On the contrary: the period of R. Yehuda the Prince was a time of prosperity and peace. It is more appropriate to view the final redaction of the Mishna and its immediate reduction to writing as a sign of cultural strength.

We have sought the reasons behind the remarkable prohibition on writing Oral Tora in its inherent flexibility, as opposed to the permanent fixity of the Written Tora. While the Written Tora was taken to represent the divine Word in its revealed form, Oral Tora, although closely related to it, was seen as a human tradition open to dissension and change. However, the process of collecting and redacting gradually bore fruit. From the end of the Tannaic period onwards, collections of Oral Tora were felt to have been reaching a conclusive stage of redaction. Their being written down indicates that any confusion with the authority of the Written Tora was no longer seen as a danger.

STUDY FROM ORAL TEXTS

The editing of the Mishna resulted in its being written down, and this gradually invited other collections of halakha, midrash and aggada to be written. However, even in the following period the Mishna and other works of the Sages continued to be studied as well as to be created as Oral Tora. Quotations from the Mishna and baraitot, which are found in multiplicity in the Amoraic collections, are brought forth not as obligatory references to a written text, but as texts to be studied. The Sages did not base their teaching on an authoritative written text, but on a tradition of learning.

Nowhere in rabbinic literature is the Mishna examined as a written text when opinions are divided on its exact wording. Typically, the question whether the Mishna in *Maaser Sheni* reads 'A fourth year vineyard' or 'Fourth year's plantings' was not answered by R. Yehuda the Prince by referring the questioner to some written document. Rather, 'He told him to go out and ask R. Yitshak the Great to whom I carefully committed every mishna'.[197] In other words, the text is checked by consulting the *tanna*, the text teacher of R. Yehuda's House of Study, to whom he had orally committed his entire Mishna.

The authority of a mishna or baraita did not rest upon some verified text as such, but rather upon the fact that it was taught in the House of Study: 'Every mishna which was not admitted in the *havura* (group of Sages) is not to be relied on;'[198] or, 'Every mishna which was not taught in the House of Study of R. Hiya

---

[197] *P.T. Maas. Sh.* 5, 55a.
[198] *P.T. Er.* 1, 19b.

and R. Hoshaya is corrupt.'[199] In other words, such a mishna cannot be brought forward as a proof in the deliberations of the following generations.

In the Houses of Study in Palestine and Babylonia there were students chosen to recite from memory the mishnayot and baraitot before the master and his students. During the course of a lesson they presented the text to be studied and they were turned to in order to ascertain the exact wording. In Hebrew these specialized Sages were called *shonim*, 'repeaters', and in Aramaic-Hebrew *tannaim*.[200] In the singular, the Aramaic-Hebrew form *tanna* is the more common; it is found first among the students of R. Akiva.[201] There were *tannaim* who were specialized in the Mishna of a certain House of Study: 'This one would teach (the Mishna of the House of Study) of Bar Kappara and this one of R. Hiya and this one of our holy Rabbi.'[202] However, most of them taught the Mishna (of Yehuda the Prince) and other tannaic collections indiscriminately.

In a passage about conditions acceded by a man to his proposed bride we read: '. . . But if he says to her: (Marry me on the condition that) I am a *tanna*, this is valid only if he has learned halakha (i.e., Mishna), Sifra and Tosefta.'[203] Scattered all over both Talmudim are references to *tannaim* who repeat the mishnayot and baraitot before the heads of the academies. So too, the Church Father Jerome tells of his meeting with one of these *tannaim*: 'I visited Luda, one of the Hebrews whom they call Sage and repeater (*deuterôtês*).'[204] The *tanna*'s major task was to serve, as it were, as a living book. It also happened, however, that they were consulted by the head of the House of Study or that they took part in the discussion on a mishna or baraita.[205] Then again, the understanding of a most reliable *tanna* could be quite limited and one of the Babylonian Sages quotes the popular saying: 'The magician mumbles and knows not what he says, the *tanna* repeats and knows not what he says.'[206]

Memorization was not the responsibility only of the *tannaim*, but also was required of all students and of everyone who studied Tora. The very phrasing of the literature of Oral Tora was designed for memorization. Thus, the language is lively, but the sentences are short and clear. Many longer units are structured in a sequence that will facilitate memorization. Thus tractate *Sheviit* (the Seventh Year) is composed following the seasons of the year, beginning with the eve of the sabbatical year, and leaving the laws concerning remission of

---

[199] *B.T. Hull.* 141a-b. Cf. *B.T. Bava M.* 34a.

[200] In Amoraic usage the term *tannaim* refers to 1) the Sages of the Mishna and the *baraitot*; 2) those who ordered the Mishna; and 3) those who recited the Mishna and *baraitot* and transmitted them orally. See Epstein, *Tannaitic Literature*, 673-81; Lieberman, *Hellenism*, 83-99.

[201] *B.T. Sota* 22a according to the major versions. See Epstein, *Tannaitic Literature*, 674 and Lieberman, *Hellenism*, 88 n. 39.

[202] I.e., R. Yehuda the Prince. *Midrash yelammedenu* in *Yal. Shim., Balak* no. 771.

[203] *B.T. Kidd.* 49b.

[204] *Adivi Liddae quendam de Hebraeis qui sapiens apud illos et* δευτερωτής *vocabantur*' (*Comm. in Hab.* 2:15). This *tanna* is mentioned in both Talmudim: *B.T. Shabb.* 96b; *P.T. Tann.* 4, 67a *et al.*

[205] E.g., *B.T. Nidda* 33b; *B.T. Hull.* 64b.

[206] *B.T. Sota* 22a.

debts for the end of the tractate. Another mnemotechnic is the use of numbers as in the beginning of tractate *Terumot* or chapter five of *Avot*.

Another feature indicative of the oral character of the text is found in the phrasing of quotations within the Mishna. Often, the same mishna appears in different contexts, and sometimes one of these appears to be the more original one. This is clear from the fact that the redactor quotes the mishna in full, without apparent necessity. He may even preserve the connective particles and words, as well as other elements which are understandable only in some other context.[207] Without doubt this way of quoting best facilitates oral recitation, and this is expressed by the saying: 'Mishna does not move from its place.'[208]

Even more important to the Sages was the care they gave to the appropriate methods for oral study.[209] Thus, in various formulations we frequently find the requirement to study aloud and not in silence, so that the text will be ingrained in the memory. A student of R. Eliezer who used to study silently reportedly forgot his learning within three years.[210] Furthermore, the repetition of collections of mishnayot and baraitot was accompanied by a specific rhythmic drone.[211] One version of the story of R. Yohanan ben Zakkai's flight from Jerusalem tells that while he was imprisoned in a Roman cell, he was able to discern the hours of day and night by means of the chapters of mishnayot and other texts which he recited orally in his regular rhythm.[212]

It was also stressed that all recitation and repetition had to be done with full and accurate articulation: 'That the words of the Tora be crisp in your mouth.'[213] However, most important was the requirement that those who would learn, persist in their studies and in the repetition of their learning. It was told regarding R. Yohanan ben Zakkai 'that he was never found sitting in silence, but sitting and studying.'[214] Those traveling on the road would be repeating their learning, either individually or together.[215] From time to time, students and Sages would go over their entire course of study in order that the material which they had learned with great effort would remain at their command.[216]

THE COMPOSITION OF THE COLLECTIONS

Roughly, the various documents of rabbinic literature are compiled following two criteria: the exposition of the material, and the subject. By subject, the

---

[207] Cf. *M. Shev.* 10:8 on *M. Makk.* 2:8, especially the words בו כיוצא.
[208] E.g. *B.T. Yev.* 30a.
[209] Cf. Gerhardsson, *Memory*, 163-70.
[210] E.g. *B.T. Er.* 53b-54a.
[211] *B.T. Meg.* 31b.
[212] *Lam. R.* 1 (34a).
[213] *B.T. Kidd.* 30a-b.
[214] *B.T. Sukka* 28a.
[215] *M. Avot* 3:7; *B.T. Taan.* 10b.
[216] *B.T. Ber.* 32b; *B.T. Pes.* 68b; *M. Avot* 3:8. See the long statement of Elisha ben Avuya in *A.R.N.* a 20 (38b).

Mishna and the Tosefta are collections of halakha, not aggada, and their material is expounded independent of Scripture. To give another example: the Amoraic midrash collections contain aggada, expounded as midrash. However, one of the peculiar features of rabbinic literature is that these criteria are never strictly followed, not even in the most thoroughly edited document, the Mishna. This is another reflection of the oral character of this literature, even in its written form. The typical ways of creating and of studying Oral Tora, and in many instances the way of editing it while teaching, explain the occurrence of many deviations from the general editorial line.

The Mishna is intended to be a collection of halakhot formulated independent of Scripture. However, it does contain purely midrashic sections.[217] Likewise, aggadic sections are found interspersed from beginning till end. In particular, many tractates or smaller collections of mishnayot end with aggadic material, and one tractate, *Avot*, consists wholly of aggada. Furthermore, many chapters of the Mishna are more like a description of life than they are halakha. This is especially true for those chapters dealing with the Temple, such as the entire tractates *Tamid* and *Middot*, and chapters four and five of the tractate *Sukka*. But it can also be said of other sections, such as chapter ten of *Pesahim* which records the order of the Passover meal in the period after the destruction. Similarly, a great many events מעשים are incorporated into the formulation of the halakha. Some are introduced as precedents.[218] Others, however, are simply historical traditions loosely associated with the preceding halakha, such as the tradition about Yohanan the High Priest at the end of *Maaser Sheni* or about Onias the Circle Maker in *Taanit* 3:5. Again, various prayers and blessings are included in the Mishna, whether they have a bearing on the halakha or not.[219]

The Mishna also contains short discussions, responses of certain Sages to the sayings of their colleagues or predecessors and historic traditions which explain the background of a halakha or the results of it. There is not a single tractate or even a single chapter which does not have some of these elements. One example may suffice. We mentioned already the question asked by Rabban Gamliel's sons at the beginning of *Berakhot*. In the same chapter we read the tradition known also from the Passover Haggada:

> We must mention the exodus from Egypt by night. R. Elazar ben Azaria said: I am like a man of seventy, yet I was unable to understand the reason why the exodus from Egypt should be related at night until Ben Zoma deduced it from the verse, "That thou mayest remember the day of thy going forth from the land of Egypt all the days of thy life" (Deut 16:3). "The days of thy life" implies the days only; "all the days of thy life" includes the nights also. But the Sages say, "The days of thy life" would

---

[217] Among other instances: *M. Sota* 5:1-6; *M. Bava M.* 2:5; *M. Sanh.* 4:5.
[218] See below, p. 178ff.
[219] Cf. *M. Ber.* 4:2, 4:4; *Maas. Sh.* 5:13; *Er.* 3:9; *Pes.* 7:1, 10:5-6; *Tam.* 7:3.

imply this life only; "all the days of thy life" includes the days of the Messiah.[220]

All of these elements, but in a greater measure, are also found in the Tosefta, which follows the format of the Mishna. Blessings, prayers, stories, events, aggadot, and historical traditions are all quite liberally interspersed in the Tosefta. This difference remains even if we take into account that the Tosefta is much larger than the Mishna. To a great extent this fits in with the aim of the Tosefta, which is to preserve the 'additional' material not included in the edition of the Mishna. Thus, for example, *M. Shabbat* 6:10 states that according to the Sages one may not go out on the Sabbath, as on other days, with the egg of a locust, the tooth of a fox or a nail from a cross, because they represent 'the ways of the Amorite', i.e., superstitious practice. In the corresponding two chapters (6-8) the Tosefta elaborates on this, mentioning many additional things included in 'the ways of the Amorite', as well as things not included. These chapters in effect present us with a live description of those popular practices frowned upon by the Sages, and of those they grudgingly accepted.[221] Interestingly, this includes stories of Sages themselves being involved in such practices. Likewise, chapters two to fifteen of *Tosefta Sota* are essentially aggadic *derashot*; and so are chapters two to four in the tractate *Sanhedrin*, and many more passages.

Similarly, the so-called 'halakhic midrashim', i.e., the Tannaic midrash collections to Exodus, Leviticus, Numbers and Deuteronomy, contain much aggada. While the phrase 'halakhic midrash' is not found either in Tannaic or Amoraic sources, it is clear that these collections were devised in a halakhic framework. They cover only the legal sections of the Pentateuch, excluding the book of Genesis – for which no trace of a Tannaic midrash collection has been found –and the longer narrative sections such as Exod 1 - 11. Thus we see that the main interest of the editors was with halakha. However, their collections do contain extended sections of purely aggadic material, either occasioned by narrative sections in Scripture or interspersed within purely halakhic midrash portions for other reasons.

The editorial inconsistency stemming from the oral nature of this literature is found to an even greater extent in the two larger collections of Oral Tora: the Palestinian and Babylonian Talmudim. Both are built round the Mishna as a commentary and discussion on each and every mishna in sequence. However, they rarely restrict themselves to just this. Usually, additional subject matter is brought in which may be more or less closely related, but also only vaguely connected to the subject.

This phenomenon can best be illustrated with some examples. The first mishna in *Berakhot* deals with the halakha of the recitation of the evening

---

[220] *M. Ber.* 1:5. Other examples are: *M. Pea* 1:5; *Shabb.* 16:8; and *Yad.* 4:3.

[221] There was an ancient legend that the Ten Tribes found the magic book of the Amorites. See Lieberman's commentary p. 80.

Shema, to which subject are added other things to be done during a certain time in the evening, such as the burning of the fat of the sacrifices. Now the Talmudim greatly elaborate on this mishna and introduce discussion on such topics as the course of the stars at night, the night and the fears it engenders, the study of Tora at night, and the rising of the dawn. These secondary items lead in turn to discussions of even more remote topics, such as, for example, the story of King David's lyre which was played by the wind at night, or the activities of the Sages at night. A similar example is found in the beginning of tractate *Pea*, the comments to which are found in the Palestinian Talmud only. The mention of good deeds and Tora study in the first mishna triggers a long series of traditions more or less closely related to the mishna.

An extreme example is the halakha at the beginning of chapter five of *Mishna Bava Batra* which discusses what things exactly are included in the purchase of a ship. The *sugya* in the Babylonian Talmud[222] begins with stories told by sea-travellers to the Amora Rabba bar Rav Hanna and then continues with the fantastic adventures of this Amora himself during his travels at sea and in the wilderness. Some of these stories have little to do with Jewish tradition while others do have some Jewish elements. See, for example, the story of the Arab merchant who travelled with him and pointed out the huge 'Dead of the wilderness', who lie on their backs and one of whom had a raised knee. Rabba, riding his camel, was able to pass underneath with his spear erect; he cut off a part of the prayer shawl to bring to the House of Study in order to elucidate certain halakhic points – but unfortunately he had to return the garment!

LITERARY PARALLELS

One of the most prominent phenomena in rabbinic literature is the great number and variety of literary parallels. The distribution of parallel versions of a tradition is also quite varied. Thus a particular tradition may be found in the Tosefta, in both Talmudim and in various midrash collections. Alternatively, a saying may be repeated a number of times in one tractate or midrash collection, but then appear only sporadically in other collections. Often, only part of a tradition is cited in one source while a parallel gives it in its entirety. Again, the parallel source may repeat a tradition almost *verbatim* while in other cases there may be smaller or greater deviations. A remarkable phenomenon is the divergency generally found between parallels in Palestinian and Babylonian sources. A story may appear a number of times without much difference in the Palestinian Talmud and in Palestinian midrash collections, while it appears in a quite different form in the Babylonian Talmud.

Although these things are quite common, we will give some examples. There is an early tradition which tells that Shimon the Just was dissatisfied with the institution of the Nazirite, and only once was he sure about the true intentions of a Nazirite, whereupon he exclaimed: 'May there be many like you in Israel

222 *B.T. Bava B.* 73a-75b.

doing the will of God.' This tradition appears in the Tosefta, the Tannaic midrash, the Palestinian and Babylonian Talmudim, and an Amoraic midrash collection.[223] This wide spread may be due to the fact that a saying of one of the earliest teachers of Oral Tora is involved, a saying which, moreover, conveys a profound teaching couched in a beautiful, characteristic language which was preserved almost without change in all those sources. Another example is found in the tradition which enumerates the things which were created before the creation of the world. This tradition appears in its entirety in thirteen sources,[224] and in many additional sources in a more or less fragmentary form. Between the versions of this tradition, there are many differences. As a last example there is the midrash about the well in the desert which sprang forth at Abraham's request that 'a little water be fetched' (Gen 18:4). This tradition appears in twelve parallel sources, showing many divergencies.[225]

The occurrence of parallels is a common phenomenon in ancient literature, both in the Bible and elsewhere. However, in rabbinic literature this phenomenon has unique features which are best explained by the methods of of creating and editing. This literature was formulated and re-formulated orally while teaching or preaching, which often necessitated text adaptation. Naturally, this did not affect all areas equally. We have noted the verbatim quotations from other sections within the Mishna even when this included irrelevant elements – a phenomenon that doubtlessly relates to the importance attached to the exact formulation of this oral document. It is easy to imagine, however, how the form of a midrash could freely be adapted to meet the specific requirements of a given situation. Furthermore, the formulation of this midrash in the subsequent oral transmission process could easily be affected by other midrashim which were transmitted along with it in a larger unit. Moreover, it was possible that more than one Sage or student present at a particular situation preserved the midrash and transmitted it within the framework of a larger unit – hence the origin of parallel but different versions. In a later stage, the redactor of a larger collection of midrashim may have known one of those versions, while the redactor of a similar collection knew another. Finally, both these sets of midrashim may have ended up in the same midrash collection, presenting later generations with two different versions of one tradition. In fact, most midrash collections we know show traces of just such a stratified editing process and contain literary parallels in great number and variety.

---

[223] *T. Naz.* 4:7; *Sifrei Num.* 22 (p. 26); *P.T. Naz.* 1, 53c; *P.T. Ned.* 1, 36d; *B.T. Ned.* 9b; *Num. R.* 10:7.

[224] *Gen. R.* 1 (p. 6); *Sifrei Deut. Ekev* 37 (p. 70); *B.T. Pes.* 54a; *B.T. Ned.* 39b; *Tanh., Naso* 11; *Tanh. B., Naso* 19 (17b); Fragment of a *Yelammedenu Tanhuma* published in *Kovets al Yad* 6 (1966) 9; *Midr. Ps.* 72 (p. 327); *ib.* 90 (p. 391); *ib.* 93 (p. 414); *S.E.R.* 31 (p. 160); *Pirkei de-R. El.* 3; *Midr. Prov.* 8.

[225] *T. Sota* 4:2; *Mekh., Beshallah, Petihta* (p. 81); *Gen. R.* 43 (p. 487); *Lev. R.* 34 (p. 758); *Exod. R.* 25,5; *Num. R.* 14,2; *Tanh., Wayera* 4 (25b); *Tanh. B., Wayera* 5 (43a); *Pes. R.* 14 (57a); *Eccl. R.* 11,1; *S.E.R.* 12 [13] (p. 59).

TANNAIC AND AMORAIC LITERATURE

In the preceding, we have been touching on the difference between Tannaic and Amoraic literature several times. This is an important subject which now deserves a separate treatment. Rabbinic literature itself distinguishes between Tannaic and Amoraic literature, and between the authority of Tannaim and Amoraim. This distinction arose as a consequence of the work of R. Yehuda the Prince, i.e. the editing of the Mishna at the end of the second century and the beginning of the third. It resulted in the editing of those halakhot not contained in the Mishna in the parallel collection called the Tosefta. The chronological span of the Tosefta is somewhat longer than that of the Mishna, and includes many of the contemporaries of R. Yehuda the Prince not mentioned there. Judging by the names of the Sages, it appears that the editing of the Mishna and Tosefta led to the collection of the Tannaic midrashim at approximately the same time. This edited corpus of Tannaic texts eventually came to serve as the demarcation point between two periods: that of the Tannaim and of the Amoraim.

Rabbinic literature does not mention any particular reason for this division. Those Sages who taught and innovated immediately after the collection of the Tannaic material probably were not aware of any difference between two periods. Two or three generations later, however, the distinction was self-evident to the Sages. The clearest expression of this is found in the maxim that Amoraim may not dispute with Tannaic halakha and that if a mishna or baraita can be produced which contradicts the opinion of an Amora, it takes precedence.[226] What, however, is the exact scope of this maxim? Certainly, R. Hiya, who lived in the transitional period between Tannaim and Amoraim, was allowed to disagree with a Tanna. However, even his younger contemporary and nephew, the Amora Rav, was so privileged: 'Rav is (to be considered) a Tanna and may dispute.'[227] In the second generation of Amoraim we still find Amoraim who disagree with a clear-cut mishna[228] or claim that the Mishna does not represent the opinion accepted in practice.[229] It was only later that Tannaim and Tannaic works automatically superseded an Amoraic opinion, although even then the Amoraim did not refrain from explaining, limiting or expanding upon the Tannaic traditions.

The difference between the literature of Tannaim and Amoraim is not restricted to the authority ascribed to them. There are also differences in quality, and one of them is the degree of innovation apparent in both periods. This is not to deny that much of the Amoraic material represents real innovation

---

[226] See refs. next n.

[227] *B.T. Bava M.* 5a; *B.T. Er.* 50b; *B.T. Ket.* 8a *et al.* See also the comments of Hai Gaon brought in the *Arukh s.v. Rav*.

[228] *P.T. Sanh.* 3, 21d: R. Shimon ben Lakish disagrees with the Mishna and the Talmud does not consider this unusual. Cf. *B.T. Sanh.* 30a; *P.T. Bava B.* 3, 14a.

[229] *B.T. Beitsa* 37a; *B.T. Yev.* 43a.

in the spheres of halakha and religious thought. We may point, for example, to the laws of the 'unpaid keeper', which in the Bible and the Mishna effectively defend the keeper's rights;[230] this allowed abuse, however, which was cured by legal specifications of the Amoraim.[231] Another example has to do with the invalidity of the testimony, according to Tannaic halakha, of anyone engaged in robbery[232] or dubious financial activities.[233] Amoraic halakha extends this to include not only the economic transgressor but any wrongdoer, either in the inter-human sphere or in relation to God.[234] A typical Amoraic innovation in the sphere of halakha is the conversion of individual and concrete cases into abstract categories of law. Even the clearest legal principles contained in Tannaic halakha, such as the one defining the nature of forbidden and permitted labours on the Sabbath,[235] always remain tied to concrete events. Not so with the Amoraim: the legal principle called *asmakhta*, 'surety' is known already in Tannaic law,[236] but the Amoraim develop it into a far-reaching abstract category based more on logic rather than on concrete legal considerations, and taking into account decisive differences in the economic situation.[237] Finally, not only in halakha, but also in the sphere of religious thought did the Amoraim introduce many innovations. Sages like R. Hanina, R. Yoshua ben Levi, R. Yohanan, R. Ammi, R. Assi, Rav, Rav Yehuda, Rabba, Rav Nahman, Abaye, Rava and Rav Ashi, as well as outstanding preachers like R. Yitshak, R. Tanhuma and many others, made invaluable contributions to rabbinic tradition.

In an overall evaluation, however, the innovations embodied in Tannaic literature undeniably are not only more numerous but also more fundamental to the development of Jewish culture and society. Here, the basic elements of halakha, jurisdiction, religious life and thought and social institutions, all of which had been taking shape during the periods of the Second Temple and the Tannaim, found their literary expression. Whereas the Amoraim tended and expanded the traditions of the Tannaim – among other things by explaining the Mishna and giving it its final form[238] – the literary foundations were laid by the Tannaim.

---

[230] Exod 22:6-14; *M. Bava M.* 3:1, 7:8.

[231] The keeper who claims that the object was stolen or lost has to swear the additional oath that the object is not in his possession (*B.T. Bava M.* 6a; *B.T. Bava K.* 102b). Even if he pays the restitution to be exempted from the oaths prescribed by the Mishna, the owner may demand that the keeper swear that it is not in his possession (*B.T. Bava M.* 34b; *P.T. ib.* 3, beg.; cf. the commentary of R. Hananael *ad loc.*).

[232] *T. Sanh.* 5:5; *P.T. Sanh.* 3, 21a; *B.T. Sanh.* 25b; *Mekh., Kaspa* 20 (p. 322). (A corrected version of the *Mekhilta* appears in *S.E.R.* 20, p.147.)

[233] *M. Sanh.* 3:3.

[234] *B.T. Sanh.* 27a, with a midrash on Exod 23:1, 'Do not give your hand to the evil one.'

[235] *M. Shabb.* 19 beg., and both Talmudim *ad loc.*

[236] *M. Bava B.* 10:5.

[237] See, e.g., *B.T. Pes.* 168a and 173b; *B.T. Bava M.* 48b and 10a; *B.T. Sanh.* 24b. Cf. De Vries, *Studies*, 142-56, who gives other examples as well.

[238] See Epstein, *Tannaitic Literature*, especially 166ff.

There are also stylistic differences between Tannaic and Amoraic literature. Tannaic literature is usually of a higher literary quality. In Amoraic literature, no texts are to be found equal to *Avot* or *Avot de-Rabbi Natan*. No Amoraic sayings can compare to the concise clarity of chapter four of *Mishna Sanhedrin* which describes the court procedures in monetary and capital cases. Although Amoraic literature does record information on life in Palestine and Babylonia, it contains nothing equivalent to chapter three of *Mishna Bikkurim* which describes the bringing of first fruits to Jerusalem.[239] Amoraic literature does describe discussions between the Sages in the House of Study, but Tannaic descriptions of such discussions are usually on a much higher level both in content and in style.[240]

In Tannaic literature, even the non-halakhic material which is included, e.g. in the Mishna and the Tosefta, is formulated on the same high level of linguistic and literary quality and of religious content. The traditions are carefully worded even in those instances where 'modest' miracle stories are given, as happens particularly in the Tosefta. Tannaic stories are always concise and clear, while Amoraic narratives tend to be complex in character and to indulge in exaggeration. Tannaic aggada is not like folklore, and does not contain spirits and fabulous creatures, in contradistinction to the two Talmudim and other Amoraic literature. Particularly in the Babylonian Talmud, one finds a choice of popular sayings, medicines, amulets, charms against illness or ghosts, dream interpretations and so on.

Another significant difference between Tannaic and Amoraic literature has to do with the languages used. Tannaic literature is almost entirely in Hebrew. There are exceptions, such as *Megillat Taanit*, which in its final form dates from the end of the Second Temple period and is written in Aramaic.[241] Furthermore, there are some very early traditions in which Aramaic is used, such as the testimonies of Yose ben Yoezer,[242] the earliest halakhic traditions dating from before the Hasmonean revolt and some of Hillel's sayings.[243] In addition, most of the contracts preserved within rabbinic literature are in Aramaic.[244] Together, however, these exceptions form only a tiny part of Tannaic literature, which as a whole is in Hebrew – be it in the spheres of halakha, midrash or aggada, either in the main collections or in quotations within Amoraic literature.

By contrast, Amoraic literature is written, both in its halakhic and aggadic parts, partly in Hebrew and partly in Aramaic. While halakhic statements tend to be in Hebrew, particularly when phrased in an authoritative and ordered

---

[239] Cf. the Amoraic description of pilgrimage in *Lam. R.* 1 (40a-41a).
[240] See for example *M. Yad.* 4:3; *Sifrei Num.* 118 (p. 141); *ib.* 24 (p. 158f.) as against *B.T. Bava M.* 84a; *B.T. Kidd.* 70a-b.
[241] See Lichtenstein, 'Fastenrolle'.
[242] *M. Ed.* 8:4.
[243] *M. Ed.* 1:13; *A.R.N.* a 12 and b 27 (28a-b).
[244] E.g. *M. Ket.* 4:9; *T. Ket.* 4:11; *M. Gitt.* 9:3; *T. Yev.* 12:15.

form, the discussions surrounding them are largely in Aramaic. Likewise, tales and discussions of the Sages are mostly in Aramaic, as well as the connective phrases between Tannaic traditions and Amoraic comments. Stories covering both Tannaic and Amoraic events are in both languages and may within one story switch from one language to the other several times. Stories stemming from a Tannaic source appear to be always in Hebrew, and often the consequent use of Hebrew in some parts of one passage and of Aramaic in others allows to differentiate between the Tannaic and the Amoraic layers.[245] There is no significant difference here between the Babylonian and the Palestinian Talmud. While, of course, the Western, Palestinian Aramaic is different from its Eastern, Babylonian counterpart, the proportion of Aramaic used in both Talmudim is about the same.

A genre of Oral Tora in which Hebrew remained the sole language to be used is prayer. All prayers found both in Tannaic and in Amoraic literature, either public prayers or those designed for private use, are entirely in Hebrew, without any trace of Aramaic or Greek.[246] Another genre which, remarkably, maintained the use of Hebrew, is the parable. While it is part of the literary creation both of Tannaim and Amoraim, the main frame of the parable is always, and the component parts practically always, in Hebrew.[247]

In the use of Greek, there is a similar difference, but somewhat vaguer. Greek words describing all kinds of utensils and objects as well as those denoting legal concepts are found all over the literature of Oral Tora,[248] but they are relatively sparse in the Mishna and the Tannaic midrash collections. In the Talmudim, however, they are much more frequent. The Palestinian Talmud is notable for its number of Greek words, particularly the greater tractate *Nezikin* (i.e. *Bava Kamma*, *Bava Metsia* and *Bava Batra*) which appears to have been edited in Caesarea, the Roman administrative and commercial centre in Palestine.[249] Even more frequent are Greek words in the aggadic midrash

---

[245] See, for example, *B.T. Ber.* 27b-28a; *P.T. Ber.* 4, 7c-d; *B.T. Ber.* 63b-64a; *P.T. Sanh.* 1, 19a; *B.T. Hor.* 13b-14a.

[246] There may be words, however, whose roots are Aramaic or Greek. Ginzberg, *Commentary* 3, 235 and 310f. is of the opinion that the word לגיונות in prayers for the 9th of Av (*P.T. Ber.* 4, 8a and parr.) is to be explained in terms of the Greek-Latin root of the word. However, some prayer versions published recently read לגאיונים which means rich and powerful people who seized Jewish lands after the destruction of the Temple.

[247] See Flusser, *Gleichnisse*, 16f.

[248] See Krauss, *Lehnwörter*.

[249] This was pointed out already by Frankel, *Mavo*. See further Lieberman, *Talmuda shel Kisrin*; id., *Greek*.

collections of the Amoraim, not in the last place, without doubt, due to their more popular character.[250]

TANNAIC TRADITIONS PRESERVED IN AMORAIC LITERATURE

As a result of the oral transmission and editing of rabbinic literature, much Tannaic material not found in the Tannaic collections appears in the various collections of Amoraic literature. This is another characteristic of rabbinic literature, which calls for adequate methods of study.

Naturally, the Mishna is quoted many hundreds of times in Amoraic literature. This may be at the beginning or in the course of a halakhic discussion, or at its end with the introduction 'Hence we have learned . . .' The Mishna is also quoted at the beginning of certain aggadic discourses.[251] Usually, these quotations follow the accepted version of the Mishna, with or without minor differences, and occasionally, a different version may be found which contains additional elements or opts for a different halakha; yet this is clearly a different version of the same Mishna. It is different with the other Tannaic texts. While they are often quoted, like the Mishna, with minor variants or according to some other version, at other times it is clear that the Amoraim had before them an altogether different Tosefta or midrash collection than the ones known to us. Sometimes, the arguments adduced by the Amoraim engaged in a particular discussion plainly contradict the Tosefta or Tannaic midrash as we know them, and in such cases it is evident that these were not known to them in their extant form.

Most important for a correct understanding of the development of Oral Tora, however, is the fact that much Tannaic material is only found in Amoraic literature. There is hardly a talmudic *sugya* or midrash section without it. Foremost are the traditions of named Tannaim which are transmitted by Amoraim of the first, second or even the third generation. Amoraim like

---

[250] On Greek in Palestine see further Alon, *Studies* 2, 248-78 (criticism of Lieberman, *Greek*); Lieberman, 'How Much Greek'; Sevenster, *Do You Know Greek?* (dealing with an earlier period but with conclusions touching on Tannaic and Amoraic literature); and cf. Sperber, 'Greek and Latin Words'. Latin is rather rare in rabbinic literature; its use is restricted to some technical terms and implements imported from Latin-speaking areas, usually found also in later Greek; see Lieberman, *Hellenism*, 17-19. Contrasting with the early Second Temple period, the use of Persian in rabbinic literature is practically restricted to some Middle Persian (Pahlavi) words appearing in the Babylonian Talmud. – On the languages of Oral Tora see further the chapter by M. Bar-Asher, to appear in the second part of this volume.

[251] This is a very widespread phenomenon. In *Genesis Rabba*, e.g., tractate *Berakhot* is quoted three times, *Ketubbot* six times and *Sanhedrin* also six times; cf. Albeck, *Introduction*, 54f. Likewise, in *Tanh. B.*, *Hukat* 3 (52a), *M. Para* 2:2 is cited; *ib.* 4 (52a), *M. Neg.* 8:2 and other mishnayot; *ib.* 24 (59b), *M. Para* 1:1; *ib.* 25 (59b) *M. Shek.* 4:2.

Rav,[252] R. Yohanan[253] and R. Abbahu[254] transmit many traditions in the name of Tannaim of the Usha or even the Yavne generations. Often, particularly in the Babylonian Talmud, a Tannaic quotation is announced as such by a quotation formula like תני 'he taught', תניא 'it is taught' or תנו רבנן 'our masters taught'. Quite often, however, we can infer that the Palestinian Talmud and the Amoraic midrash collections, and to a lesser extent the Babylonian Talmud, quote Tannaic material not known to us from elsewhere, either of named teachers or anonymous and without formal introductions. One explanation may be that an Amoraic editor orally taught – or, in a later stage, copied in writing – parts of an earlier Amoraic collection, now lost, along with anonymous Tannaic material found there.

Thus it can happen that traditions which seem to be Amoraic are Tannaic in truth. We can be certain of this when a saying which is attributed to an Amora in one source appears in another source with a chain of tradition leading back to Tannaic times, or with a simple Tannaic attribution. There are many cases where we can prove that an idea which was much developed in Amoraic literature was Tannaic at root.

Some examples may illustrate this. There is a tradition ascribed to the Amora R. Yohanan: 'Jerusalem was destroyed because they judged according to the (written) letter of the Tora' – i.e., out of an attitude of social and religious rigidity.[255] Elsewhere in Amoraic literature, this idea was transferred to the story of Kamtsa and Bar Kamtsa, who were said to have brought about the destruction of Jerusalem on account of their inflexibility and mutual hate.[256] However, the same idea is found in a number of versions of an anonymous baraita and, in addition, in a tradition of the Tanna R. Yohanan ben Torta, a colleague of R. Akiva: 'The First Temple was destroyed because they committed idolatry, adultery and bloodshed. In the time of the Second Temple, we know that they laboured in the Tora and were intent on the commandments and the tithes, and had every good quality – however, they were loving money (*Mammon*) and hating each other with groundless hatred.'[257] A similar case is found in a characteristic midrash about the 'four species' at the Feast of Sukkot, which in the Babylonian Talmud is ascribed to the Amora R. Abbahu and in the

[252] E.g., *B.T. Ber.* 60b; *B.T. Pes.* 3b; *B.T. Moed K.* 18b.

[253] E.g. *B.T. Ber.* 46a; *B.T. Sanh.* 43b; *P.T. Sota* 7 beg.; *P.T. Ter.* 9, 47d.

[254] E.g. *P.T. Yev.* 13, 13c; *Tanh. B. Noah* 16 (26a) – a dispute between Beit Shammai and Beit Hillel!; *P.T. Demai* 7, 26d.

[255] *B.T. Bava M.* 30b.

[256] *B.T. Gitt.* 55b; *Lam. R.* 4, 3.

[257] *P.T. Yoma* 1, 38c; *B.T. Yoma* 9a-b; *Sifrei Deut.* 105 (p. 165); *B.T. Bava M.* 88a; *P.T. Pea* 1, 16c.

Palestinian Talmud to R. Levi, but which in a Tannaic work is attributed to the Tanna Ben Azzai.[258]

Finally, there is much Amoraic material which has no parallels in Tannaic tradition but can be assumed to be pre-Amoraic on the basis of non-rabbinic sources. Not infrequently, such a tradition found in Amoraic literature may have had a long development, as in the following example. In the Midrash to Song of Songs 2:13, the words 'the fig tree put forth her green figs' is explained by a number of Amoraim as referring to the days of the Messiah. A similar messianic *derasha* is certainly the core of the various traditions of a fig tree in the Gospel narratives about Jesus.[259] Thus the messianic midrash of the fig tree was in existence in the Second Temple period in some form, even though in rabbinic literature it emerges only in third-fourth generation Amoraic traditions. Examples like these are indicative of the presence of much unidentified Tannaic material embedded in Amoraic literature.

The Terminology of Oral Tora

During the long history of Oral Tora, hundreds of new concepts, terms and phrases were created which define and structure the tradition of the Sages and their methods of studying. Many terms and concepts were created for the study of Tora and for expressing the connection between the teachings of the Sages and the Written Tora. Likewise, a terminology was devised to denote the various fields of literature and to structure the process of redaction and transmission.

These words either did or did not exist in biblical Hebrew. If they did, they received a specific meaning in the tradition of Oral Tora, either in a wider or in a narrower sense. Thus, for example, the word *daat* in biblical Hebrew has the meaning of 'knowledge'. In Oral Tora it came to denote recognition, differentiation, awareness, understanding and even that self-awareness which is required for appropriate behaviour. As the saying has it: 'A Sage without *daat* is no better than carrion;' or, 'Every man who possesses *daat* – it is as if the Temple was built during his days.'[260] In addition to these aggadic-philosophical meanings, it came to be used even in halakhic contexts. A person is not obligated to

---

[258] Cf. *B.T. Sukka* 35a; *P.T. Sukka* 3, 53d; *Sifra, Emor* 16 (102d). Two other Amoraic works also ascribe it to Ben Azzai; *Lev. R.* 30 (p. 767) and *Pes. de-R.K.* 27 (p. 413). In *B.T. Sukka* 31b, the same tradition appears as an anonymous baraita. Another example is the midrash which connects the benedictions at meals and Tora study with Scripture. Cf. *B.T. Ber.* 21a, where an elaborate *derasha* of Rav Ya d R. Yohanan is given, with the Tannaic traditions in *Mekh. Bo, Pisha* 16 (p. 60f.); *P.T. Ber.* 7, 11a; *B.T. Ber.* 48b.

[259] This *derasha* presents a curious development already as found in the Gospel tradition. There is a messianic saying of Jesus about the fig tree (Matt 21:19-21; Mark 11:12-14), a parable of a fig tree (Luke 13:6-9) and a messianic miracle at Jesus' entrance into Jerusalem (Matt 24:32; Mark 13:28; Luke 21:29).

[260] See next n.

fulfill a commandment if he has no *daat* of it; his vow is not valid if he is not impressed with a degree of *daat* regarding the consequences; and he cannot transfer ownership without *daat* of the transfer.[261] Conversely, a narrower meaning was acquired by the word *tsedaka*. In the Bible it means 'righteousness' which includes an attitude of mercy and grace, but in Oral Tora it became the technical term for charity to the poor; for the wider, biblical sense the word *emet* came to be used.[262] On the other hand, the literature of Oral Tora contains many words not found in the Hebrew Bible or in other post-biblical sources. They are used in the fields of both halakha and aggada, as we shall see below.

The terminology created in Oral Tora relates to a number of subjects which may be divided into five areas: 1. Halakhic and Legal Terms; 2. Religious Concepts; 3. Exegetical and Dialectical Terms; 4. Terms for Literary Genres and Units; 5. Terms for Administrative Functions. In the first two categories we shall enumerate the technical terms in alphabetical order.

HALAKHIC AND LEGAL TERMS

אבות מלאכה *Principal Classes of Labour.* In order to deal with the forbidden 'labours' on the Sabbath, all possible labours or activities were summarized into main categories, following the normal activities of the day or following the work done for the building of the Tabernacle in the biblical narrative.[263] Likewise, there are *Principal (Causes of) Damages* אבות נזיקין[264] and *Principal (Sources of) Impurities* אבות טומאה.[265]

אונס *Compulsion* or force majeure is a concept much discussed both in connection with transgressions against one's fellow-man and against God. It is asked, for example, how valid is a sale or a divorce made under compulsion?; a distinction is made between a compulsory act which yet was premeditated or not; and the difference is discussed between compulsion caused by others or by oneself.[266]

ארוסין *Betrothal*, the act in which a man 'sanctified' a woman while she remained in her father's house, was distinguished from marriage itself נשואין, the state in which she lives with her husband. There are many halakhot dealing with legal matters made problematic by this intermediate state of betrothal, such as divorce and levirate marriage, the financial rights acquired by the woman and, if she is betrothed to a priest, her right to consume *teruma*. There was also a difference between the accepted behaviour of a betrothed couple in

---

[261] See the *sugya* in *B.T. Sanh.* 24b-25b; *Lev. R.* 1 (p. 32) *B.T. Ber.* 33a.
[262] *Tsedaka* in its wider biblical sense appears only in *derashot* which deal with that word in a biblical verse.
[263] *M. Shabb.* chap. 7.
[264] *M. Bava K.* 1:1.
[265] *M. Kel.* 1:1. Cf. Below p. 263f. on the term *avot*.
[266] *M. Ket.* 1:10; *M. Ned.* 3:1; *Sifra, Tsav* 14 (38a).

Judea and in Galilee.[267] At another level, the benedictions to be pronounced at the betrothal ceremony are discussed. The concept of betrothal is also used in non-halakhic contexts, and so can serve as a symbol of God's relation with Israel at Sinai.[268]

אסמכתא *Asmakhta* – a legal term which appears only in the Amoraic period. We have discussed it above.[269]

ביקור חולים *Visiting the sick*. This concept includes the obligation to visit the sick, to link them with the community, to attend to their well-being and to supply their material needs. This is one of the concepts most frequently stressed in utterances of the Sages and in stories about them.[270]

בית כנסת *Synagogue* – a building constructed for the purpose of prayer and the reading of the Tora. This name does not derive from the root כנס, to assemble, but from the phrase כנסת לעדה meaning congregation or community.[271]

ברכות *Benedictions* – the basic component of most prayers. Prayers are in the form of a series of benedictions which end with the formula: 'Blessed art Thou O Lord who (giveth wisdom etc.).' There are also benedictions which open with 'Blessed art Thou' as well. Prayers consist of, and are referred to as, 'Two Benedictions', 'Three Benedictions' (e.g., the priests' prayer at the sacrifice), 'Seven Benedictions' (the Sabbath main prayer), or 'Eighteen Benedictions' (the weekday main prayer).[272]

גיור *Proselytism* – the process by which a non-Jew is accepted into the community of Israel. The word גר, meaning 'proselyte', is found in the Bible, but there indicates a 'sojourner' who simply comes to live in the land. In the literature of the later Second Temple period and in rabbinic literature the conversion process is described as consisting of circumcision (for males), ritual immersion and the offering of a sacrifice.[273]

דמאי *Demai* – the name indicates grain or fruit from which it is uncertain whether its seller has set aside tithes. The word exists in halakha from the time of John Hyrcanus onwards, and appears often because of the many practical problems associated with this matter. An entire Mishna-tractate, *Demai*, is devoted to it. The etymology of the word is not clear.

הכנסת כלה *Escorting the bride* – i.e., the requirement to assist a woman in getting married by participating in her bridal expenses, and by joining in the bridal procession to gladden her and make her more honoured and lovable to her husband.[274]

מפקר *Hefker* – i.e., pronouncing a possession of any kind to be outside the legal

---

[267] *M. Ket.* 1:6, 5:1, 8:1; *M. Yev.* 4:10; *B.T. Yev.* 43a.
[268] *Exod. R.* 15 end; cf. the biblical background in Hos 2.
[269] See p. 83. Cf. *B.T. Buva M.* 73b; *B.T. Sanh.* 24b.
[270] *B.T. Shabb.* 127a; *B.T. Ned.* 39b-40a.
[271] See *Compendia* I/1, 908-44.
[272] E.g. *M. Ber.* 1:4, 4:3; *M. Tam.* 5:1.
[273] *M. Ker.* 2:1; *B.T. Yev.* 46b; *B.T. Ker.* 9a.
[274] *B.T. Shabb.* 127a; *B.T. Meg.* 3b; *B.T. Ket.* 17a; *P.T. Pea* 1, 15d.

state of ownership and personal liability, so that anyone may come and take possession of it. This regards the ownership of such items as tithes, heave-offerings, monies, leavened foodstuff on Pesah, and also of possessions ex-propriated by an act of the court.[275]

טהרה *Purity*. While in the Bible this verbal noun means 'purification' from some actual impurity, in post-biblical usage it turned into a concept which denotes the abstract state of purity in which some object or person may be. Thus this concept took on a spiritual connotation, as appears also from phrases such as God who 'purifies' the people of Israel, or 'one who comes to return in repentance and to be pure'. Likewise, one must return one's soul (at the moment of death) 'in purity' just as it was received 'in purity' at birth.[276]

ידים *Hands*. This word, either in the singular or the plural, took on many connotations: possession, authority, handle, etc. We will deal here only with the more literal meaning which implies the concept of impurity of the hands. This concept was stressed strongly in the halakha. There was a constant care for the hands not to touch defiling objects, but on the other hand the purification of the hands was simplified. Impurity of the hands did not require complete immersion of the body or even of the hands, but only that water be poured on them from a vessel. Hands were considered to be constantly in a state of defilement and always had to be purified before eating, reading or studying the Tora and praying.[277]

כונה *Kawwana*, intent. In various contexts it is discussed to what extent the execution of a commandment or of a legal action requires conscious intent. For example, *M. Ber.* 2:1 questions whether one occupied in studying the Tora who accidentally read the Tora portion for the *shema* at the time required for saying the *shema*, has actually fulfilled the commandment of saying the *shema* or not. Also is discussed whether various commandments, such as those pertaining to prayer, require conscious intent to a different degree or not [278]

כזית *An olive's measure*. The measure of an olive became the standard minimum quantity of food relevant in halakha, such as the quantity of food requiring grace after meals, leavened foodstuff on Passover and certain purity laws.[279]

מוקצה *Muktse*, lit. 'set apart'. This halakhic category denotes objects which may not be carried or handled on the Sabbath, an issue which figures in many Sabbath halakhot.[280]

מכשירין *Makhshirin*, 'predisposers'. The purity laws of the Sages implied that food could not become ritually impure unless it had come in contact with a

---

275 *M. Pea* 1:6, 6:1; *M. Shek.* 1:2; *P.T. Shek.* 1, 46a.

276 *M. Yoma* 5:9; *B.T. Yoma* 38b; *B.T. Shabb.* 152b.

277 *B.T. Ber.* 14b-15a; *B.T. Pes.* 46a. The Mishna tractate *Yadayim* is devoted to these laws.

278 *T. Ber.* 2:2; *B.T. Ber.* 13a; *P.T. Ber.* 2, 5a (for the correct text see Ginzberg, *Commentary* 1, 357); *B.T. Rosh H.* 28b-29a.

279 *M. Ber.* 7:1-2; *M. Beitsa* 1:1; *M. Kel.* 8:6; *Sifra, Shemini* 10 (57a).

280 *B.T. Shabb.* 44a, 45a, 157a.

liquid. Such liquids are thus predisposers for impurity. The word came also to be used in various other fields of halakha related to the purity laws. The Mishna tractate *Makhshirin* deals with this matter; among other things it is stated that the liquid has this function only if it is brought on the food by a deliberate act.[281]

מעילה *Sacrilege*. This term conceptualizes the abuse described in Lev 5:16f., i.e., the illegal, unintended consumption of priestly food of at least a *peruta*'s worth. The pertinent halakhot are formulated in tractate *Meila*. The concept was expanded to include unlawful and treacherous behaviour in other halakhic spheres, such as marriage and monetary matters.[282]

שחיטה *Ritual slaughter* – the obligation to slaughter animals, including fowl, either for sacrificial or non-sacrificial purposes, in the prescibed manner: by severing the oesophagus and trachea. This manner is not laid down in the Bible, and is considered *gemara* or tradition. Tractate *Hullin* deals with the many halakhot for non-sacrificial slaughtering; there are also many halakhot for sacrificial slaughtering.[283]

שיעור *Measurement* – the establishment of measures (size or amount) for the fulfillment of specific commandments. There are also commandments 'without a measurement'.[284] Measurements are mentioned in many halakhic fields such as *pea*, heave-offering and Sabbath.

RELIGIOUS CONCEPTS

אהבה ויראה *Love and Fear*. Both concepts are used already in the Bible for man's attitude towards God, but in the specific usage of the Sages they are alternative ways of serving God on different levels. Serving God out of love is a higher aim than out of fear.[285]

גבורה *Omnipotence*. This is one of the common attributes of God. Paradoxically, it is often used in conjunction with God's immanence or nearness to man, as in the narrative of the Sinai revelation, or in the expression that man's good deeds 'add power to His omnipotence'.[286]

גן עדן, גיהנום *Paradise, Hell*. Paradise or the Garden of Eden is reserved for the just in the world to come; the wicked, however, will suffer punishment in hell or *Gehinnom*. In the course of time, these phrases came to denote the reward as such of the just and the punishment of the wicked. They appear in many contexts, either in conjunction or apart, abstract or in concrete descriptions.[287]

יצר טוב, יצר רע *Good Inclination, Evil Inclination*. These two concepts are

---

[281] *M. Makhsh.* 6:6; *M. Maasr.* 1:8; *M. Para* 11:6.
[282] E.g. *Sifrei Num.* 7 (p.11).
[283] *B.T. Hull.* 27a; *Sifrei Deut.* 75 (p. 140f.).
[284] *M. Pea* 1:1.
[285] *Sifrei Deut.* 32 (p. 54); *M. Sota* 5:5.
[286] *Mekh., Bahodesh* 9 (p. 235); *Pes. de-R.K., Sus asis* p. 469; *ib. Selihot* p. 379f.
[287] *M. Avot* 1:5; *B.T. Hag.* 15a.

found many times in rabbinic literature, both in combination and in opposition. To be sure, the evil inclination does not reside in the body, nor is it to be identified with sin inherent in man's limbs. Neither is the good inclination to be located in the soul; both attributes coexist in man and are equally necessary. Without the evil inclination, mankind would cease to exist. On the other hand, however, man is to struggle and master it through doing good deeds, and thus worship God 'with both his inclinations: with the good and the evil inclination'.[288]

כביכול *'As it were'*. This expression enabled the Sages to state audaciously concrete ideas about God and Israel's attitude towards him without lapsing into crude anthropomorphism. They simply added 'as it were'.[289]

כנסת ישראל *The Assembly of Israel*. Especially in later sources, we find, apart from the name Israel, the expression 'Assembly of Israel', particularly when the Sages wanted to express the intimate relationship between Israel and God. The phrase, therefore, mostly appears in the feminine form and is couched in the imagery of the relationship between the betrothed and her bridegroom.[290]

מידת הדין, מידת הרחמים *The Measure of Justice, The Measure of Mercy*. These are two attributes of God which often appear together in the literature. Characteristically, they are used to explain the names of God: the tetragrammaton *YHWH* implies the attribute of mercy while the name *Elohim* indicates the attribute of justice. In Amoraic usage, these concepts practically develop into divine hypostases, but the Sages remained careful in avoiding any hint of dualism and insisted on the continuous coexistence of both attributes in God's relation to his creatures.[291]

מלכות שמים *The Kingdom of Heaven*. The purpose of the Tora and the commandments is the acceptance of the 'Yoke of the Kingdom of Heaven', 'Heaven' being another appellation of God. The acceptance of the Kingdom of Heaven is fulfilled by the daily recitation of the *shema* (Deut 6:4ff., etc.). To recite it is to depreciate the power of idolatry and to expand the Kingdom of Heaven; to refrain from the recitation is to annul the reality of the Kingdom over oneself – for the time being. The essence of the Kingdom of Heaven is not in the first verse, which proclaims the unity of God (Deut 6:4), but in the continuation: the requirement to love God and to do his commandments. The Kingdom of Heaven is both a reality in which man must live at present and a hoped-for reality in the future, when it will fully unfold in the final redemption.[292]

מצוה, עבירה *Commandment, Transgression*. In the Bible the word commandment primarily appears attached to the name of God (e.g., Num 15:31, Deut 8:6). The singular form does appear in the Bible without the mention of

---

[288] *B.T. Yoma* 69b; *Gen. R.* 9 (p. 72); *M. Ber.* 9:5.
[289] *Sifrei Deut.* 311 (p. 351); *ib.* 346 (p. 404); *Sifrei Num.* 84 (p. 81).
[290] *Sifrei Deut.* 306 (p. 329); naturally, the expression is frequent in *Cant. R.*
[291] *Sifrei Deut.* 26 (p. 41); *Gen. R.* 8 (p. 59f.); *Mekh., Shira* 4 (p. 129f.).
[292] *M. Ber.* 2:2; *Mekh., Shira* 10 (p. 150); *Midr. Ps.* 99 (112a).

God, but always as part of a longer series such as 'The commandment, the statutes and the ordinances' (Deut 6:1). The same usage prevails in Qumran literature. In rabbinic literature, however, the commandment functions as a relatively independent spiritual concept. Moreover, it has an exact opposite, the transgression, which does not appear as such in the Bible. Thus, rabbinic literature can state: 'The reward of a (fulfilled) commandment is a (further) commandment'; and 'The reward for a (committed) transgression is a (further) transgression.' We also hear of 'light' and 'heavy' commandments, and some-one with 'even one commandment in his hand' will not inherit *Gehinnom*.[293]

המקום *The Omnipresent*, lit. 'the place'. This appellation of God is very common in Tannaic literature and begins to appear in the earliest traditions.[294] It does not appear in Aramaic rabbinic texts, nor in Qumran literature, the Apocrypha, the Pseudepigrapha and the New Testament. The Amoraim gave an explanation for it: 'He is the place of his world',[295] but it is doubtful whether this was the original meaning. This name of God is most often associated with his immanence, as in the following expressions: 'The Place has pity on his creatures;' 'The Place gave it him lovingly;' 'They clung to the Place'; and 'The Place rescued him.'[296]

עולם הבא *The world to come*. This phrase has two meanings, both in Tannaic and in Amoraic literature: 1) the hereafter, where the righteous will be rewarded and the wicked will be punished, as in the expressions: 'Tomorrow my lot will be with them (the righteous) in the world to come;' 'Four (transgres-sions) for which one must pay in this world, although the main punishment is reserved for the world to come;'[297] 2) the world to come at the end of days, starting with redemption and the raising of the dead: ' "Let Reuben live and not die" (Deut 33:6). – Is he not already dead? But "and not die" means, in the world to come;' 'Jerusalem of this world is not like Jerusalem in the world to come.'[298] Often it is hard to decide which meaning prevails; indeed many times the word *olam* represents both the spatial cosmos and the temporal aeon, as in the Bible.

צניעות *Modesty*. The requirement 'to walk humbly with thy God' is found in the Bible (Mic 6:8).[299] However, the root verb expanded and took on several meanings, among them: 1) decent behaviour, even in private – 'All of the

---

[293] *M. Avot* 3:2; *M. Kidd.* 1:10; *P.T. Kidd.* 1, 61d.

[294] Thus in the story of Shimon the Just and the Nazirite in all sources (except the Babylonian Talmud): *Sifrei Num.* 22 (p. 20); *T. Naz.* 4:7; *P.T. Naz.* 1, 56c. Likewise, in the words of Shimon ben Shetah in *M. Taan.* 3:8 and other early sources.

[295] *Gen. R.* 68 (p. 777).

[296] *Sifrei Deut.* 192 (p. 233); *Sifrei Z.* p. 263; *Sifrei Deut.* 45 (p. 150); *Mekh., Amalek* 1 (p. 192). Much has been written on this appellation, unfortunately mostly irrelevant and without textual criticism. See, however, Urbach, *Sages*, chap. 4.

[297] *Sifrei Deut.* 307 (p. 346); *P.T. Pea* 1, 15d.

[298] *Sifrei Deut.* 347 (p. 404); *B.T. Bava B.* 75a.

[299] In Prov 11:2, 'With the lowly צנועים is wisdom', there are versions which read נועצים those who take advice.

women dally with the harvesters, but this one (Ruth) maintains her modesty;' 'One is not called modest unless he is also modest in the privy;'[300] 2) modesty as opposed to haughtiness – 'Be modest and patient;' God praises 'a rich man who sets aside his tithes in private בצנעה;' 'Anyone who teaches Tora in public must be modest as a bride.'[301]

קידוש השם *Sanctification of God's Name.* When faced with great difficulties or temptations, man's correct behaviour sanctifies the name of God. Many midrashim emphasize that the patriarchs sanctified God's name in difficult situations: Judah, who plunged first into the Reed Sea;[302] Joseph, who resisted temptation even in private;[303] Judah, who, in another situation, confessed the affair with Tamar.[304] While in Tannaic literature the expression has the wider meaning of doing God's will in difficult situations, in Amoraic literature it began to take on the specific meaning of martyrdom, the sacrifice of one's life for God's sake. This use of the expression is unknown in Tannaic sources; the few passages which seem to prove the opposite have a dubious textual basis.[305]

שמחה של מצוה *The Joy of the Commandment.* This is the requirement that commandments be done out of joy and happiness. We find this expression, and the requirement embodied in it, in various forms in both Tannaic and Amoraic literature. Israel is praised for its joyful acceptance of the Kingdom of Heaven at Sinai;[306] biblical figures joyfully did good deeds without knowing that these would be recorded in the Bible and this teaches 'that one should fulfill a commandment with a joyous heart;'[307] an Amora is praised 'since he is great in Tora and joyful in the commandments'.[308]

תורה לשמה *Tora for its own sake.* This expression arose out of the requirement to occupy oneself with Tora, but not 'as with a shovel to dig with' or 'a crown to glorify with'; in other words, not as a means to human ends, but for its own sake. One of the issues discussed is whether an improper occupation with Tora can develop into Tora for its own sake.[309]

EXEGETICAL AND DIALECTICAL TERMS

The ways of studying peculiar to the Sages implied specific literary techniques which led naturally to the creation of hundreds of new technical terms. Much of Oral Tora is connected in some way to the Bible, and connective or exegetical terms were required to make this explicit. In like manner, the teachings of

[300] *Ruth R.* 4,4; *B.T. Ber.* 62a.
[301] *M. Avot* 6:1; *B.T. Pes.* 113a; *Yal. Shim.* on Cant., nr. 988.
[302] *Mekh., Beshallah* 5 (p. 107); *T. Ber.* 4:16.
[303] *B.T. Sota* 10b.
[304] *Ib.*
[305] See Safrai, 'Kiddush Ha-Shem'.
[306] *Mekh., Ba-hodesh* 5 (p. 219), and frequent in Tannaic midrash.
[307] *Lev. R.* 34 (p. 790).
[308] *B.T. Ber.* 9a.
[309] We deal with this on p. 105f.

earlier Sages served as the basis for later teaching; the preservation and transmission of old and new strata necessitated terms defining the dialectics of this learning tradition. These terms are found in the Mishna itself, in baraitot, and particularly in the discussions in both Talmudim. We shall review some of them, abandoning the alphabetical order followed previously.

As we described earlier, the main way of studying consisted of deliberations of the Sages with their students or among themselves. In these discussions, both scriptural verses and traditions of other Sages are adduced and commented upon. Many of the technical terms structuring the argument are for referring specifically either to Scripture or to traditions of Sages. Others, however, are used to refer to both Scripture and tradition; we shall give two examples.

מידה *Midda*, i.e., measure, rule, may refer to midrash: 'Hillel the Elder taught seven *middot* before the Sons of Bathyra;'[310] R. Yishmael says: through thirteen *middot* is the Tora expounded.'[311] These seven or thirteen 'rules' are only applied in scriptural exegesis. However, the word *midda* as such is used in connection with teachings of Sages as well: 'According to R. Yishmael's *midda* it remains valid, but according to R. Yoshua's *midda* it is invalid' (i.e. the defiled residue of the meal offering);[312] or, 'R. Yishmael applied his *midda* equally' (to two different halakhic cases).[313]

כיצד *How*, is a dialectical term often used in the context of scriptural exegesis. ' "And the children of Israel ate manna for forty years" (Exod 35:16). R. Yoshua says: they ate the manna even for forty days after Moses died. How?' – and he goes on to explain this by bringing in other relevant verses.[314] However, this term is also used very often in expanding or commenting on traditions of Sages. A clear example is *Avot de-R. Natan*, which in several parts begins every comment on the subsequent sayings of *Avot* with this word.[315]

As previously stated, some technical terms were used specifically to refer to teachings of Sages. Terms frequently found in Tannaic literature are:

במה דברים אמורים or אימתי *when does this apply?*;[316]

זאת אומרת *this teaches that*.[317]

In the Talmudim, a number of standard phrases are used to introduce questions and answers to them:

בעא *it was asked*;[318]

---

[310] We deal with this on p. 154.
[311] *Sifra*, beginning. Cf. also the tradition of R. Eliezer the son of R. Yose Hagalili on the 32 rules through which the *haggada* (in the main versions) is expounded; it is found in R. Samson of Chinon's *Sefer Keritut* and appended to the tractate *Berakhot* in editions of the Babylonian Talmud.
[312] *M. Men.* 3:4.
[313] *M. Shek.* 4:7.
[314] *Mekh., Wayisa* 5 (p. 172).
[315] See e.g. version A chaps. 6 (p. 14a) and 7 (18a).
[316] *B.T. Er.* 81b-82a; *B.T. Sanh.* 24b-25a.
[317] *Sifra, Emor* 5 (97c); *B.T. Sanh.*
[318] *P.T. Halla* 1, 57d; *B.T. Ber.* 20a.

איבעיא להו‎ *the problem was posed*;[319]

תיובתא‎ *a refutation*;[320]

תיקו‎ *an unsolvable problem*.[321]

The terminology used specifically in midrash or exegesis is not at all petrified or mechanical, as some would have it, but very versatile, varied and creative. We enumerate here some of the more common expressions connected to the word 'Scripture':

בא הכתוב‎ *Scripture came* – such a personification of Scripture is very common and appears in various forms and contexts;[322]

הכתוב אומר‎ *Scripture states*;[323]

הכתוב אסרם‎ *Scripture forbade*;[324]

גזירת הכתוב‎ *Scripture decreed* – this expression is very common in the Babylonian Talmud but does not appear in Tannaic midrash;[325]

הכתוב מדבר‎ *Scripture refers*;[326]

הגיע הכתוב לסוף‎ *Scripture came to the end of the issue of. . .*;[327]

הוסיף הכתוב‎ *Scripture added*;[328]

הזהיר הכתוב‎ *Scripture warned you*;[329]

החזירו הכתוב‎ *Scripture brought back*;[330]

הטילן הכתוב‎ *Scripture removed*;[331]

הניח הכתוב‎ *Scripture placed*;[332]

העלה הכתוב‎ *Scripture raised*;[333]

הפריש הכתוב‎ *Scripture set aside*;[334]

הקדים הכתוב‎ *Scripture made precede*;[335]

הקיש הכתוב‎ *Scripture considered equal*;[336]

בא הכתוב לחלוק‎ *Scripture came to dispute*.[337]

---

[319] B.T. Bava K. 33a; P.T. Sanh. 3, 21b.

[320] B.T. Ber. 10a.

[321] Lit. let it stand, i.e. the question cannot be answered and therefore remains in its place. B.T. Bava M. 34b; B.T. Hull. 46a.

[322] Sifrei Num. 70 (p. 67); Mekh., Pisha 6 (p. 19).

[323] M. Pea 5:9; M.Taan. 3:8; Mekh., Pisha 13 (p. 43).

[324] Sifrei Deut. 252 (p. 279); Sifra, Nedava 11 (10c).

[325] B.T. Bekh. 5b; B.T. Bava M. 11a.

[326] Mekh., Pisha 17 (p. 63); M. Zev. 11:1.

[327] Sifrei Deut. 84 (p. 149); cf. ib. 220 (p. 253).

[328] Mekh., Pisha 6 (p. 19); Sifra, Metsora 7 (74a).

[329] Also the less personal 'Scripture warned'. Mekh., Nezikin 18 (p. 311); Sifra, Mekhilta de-Milluim 1 (42a).

[330] The eleventh rule of R. Yishmael. Sifra, Nedava 19 (14d).

[331] The fifteenth rule of the thirty-two mentioned above.

[332] Sifra, Ahare Mot 13 (86a); Sifrei Num. 23 (p. 28).

[333] Mekh., Pisha 3 (p.9); M. Avot 3:7.

[334] T. Zev. 11:7; T. Ber. 3:8.

[335] Mekh., Pisha 5 (p. 14).

[336] Mekh., Nezikin 5 (p. 277); Sifrei Num. 39 (p. 42).

[337] Mekh., Nezikin 10 (p. 283); Sifra, Metsora beginning (70a).

With three exceptions, all of the exegetical terms, both in Tannaic and in Amoraic literature, are in Hebrew or Aramaic. Only three are taken from the Greek: סימן σημεῖον - *a sign*; נוטריקון νοταρικόν - *acrostic*; גימטריה γραμματεία *gematria*, i.e., numerical interpretation.[338] Significantly, these three are found only in aggada.

TERMS FOR LITERARY GENRES AND UNITS

It is impossible to determine exactly when the literary genres began to be consciously differentiated. In any event, terms like *miqra*, *mishna*, *midrash*, *aggada* and *halakha* were fully in use since the Yavne period.[339] These are general terms, indicating broadly the various fields or methods of Oral Tora. With the editing of the first collections, further distinctions arose between such terms as *mishna*, *tosefta*, *baraita*, and *gemara*; we also find names for the various collections of Tannaic midrash: *Torat Kohanim*, which is equal to *Sifra*, and *Sifrei*.[340] Distinctions were made between an unambiguous teaching from a verse and a mere זכר *reference*[341] or אסמכתא *secondary support* [342], and between teaching and mere tradition.[343] The term מעשה *event* was introduced;[344] we also find the term משל *parable* early on, in a meaning different from the biblical *mashal*.[345]

We must pay special attention to the categories of פשט *peshat* and דרש *derash*. The verb דרש means to explain, to teach. Although the use for biblical teaching predominates,[346] it is used in reference to Oral Tora as well. Only in Babylonian Amoraic usage from the second generation onwards does the specific term *peshat* appear, indicating the plain meaning of the verse.[347] And only as late as the fourth Amoraic generation do we find the Babylonian use of

---

[338] *Gematria* appears in two forms: the reckoning of the numerical value of the letters (*Gen. R.* 42, p. 416) and of their inversed numerical value (*Pes. R.* 43, 181b).

[339] See *A.R.N.* b 28 (29b); a 14 (29a); *B.T. Sukka* 25a – on R. Yohanan ben Zakkai; *Sifrei Deut.* 344 (p. 401) on Rabban Gamliel the Younger.

[340] The name *Mekhilta* is not found in talmudic sources; the Tannaic midrash collection to Exodus was most likely included in the general term *Sifrei*. Palestinian sources use the name *Torat Kohanim* for the collection which in Babylonian sources is called *Sifra*; see *Cant. R.* 6,9; *B.T. Sanh.* 86a; *B.T. Er.* 96b.

[341] A common expression in Tannaic literature is, 'Although there is no evidence on the subject, there is a reference to it;' *M. Shabb.* 9:4; *Sifrei Num.* 153 (p. 199).

[342] In the Babylonian Talmud, there are various expressions: '[This is a] teaching of the Sages – the scriptural verse is only an additional support' (*B.T. Ber.* 41b); or 'This halakha they learned – the scriptural verse is only an additional support' (*B.T. Pes.* 81b).

[343] *M. Shek.* 6:1; *B.T. Hull.* 63b.

[344] Common in Tannaic and Amoraic literature, and even in traditions from the Temple period. *M. Makhsh.* 1:6; *M. Mikw.* 4:5.

[345] The biblical meaning of the term is a verse with two parallel members; in rabbinic literature it means parable.

[346] *Cant. R.* 6,2; *Lev. R.* 19 (p. 416); *Lam. R.* 4 (77a); see Ginzberg, *Commentary* 2, 250f.

[347] *B.T. Ar.* 8b; *B.T. Hull.* 133a.

the two terms, *peshat* and *derash*, side by side, as indicating the two alternative ways of explaining; curiously enough, this regards a passage from Ben Sira.[348] In this line, the Babylonian Talmud quotes several times the following saying: 'Scripture never loses its plain meaning.' Once, however, we read: 'Although in the entire Tora the scriptural verse does not lose its plain meaning, in this case one must explain it by way of *gezera shawa* which entirely removes it from its plain meaning.'[349] But even in this period the interpretation of Scripture was flexible and there was no fixed rule that every verse should be expounded in terms of *peshat* and *derash*, or, in addition, allegorically.[350]

TERMS FOR ADMINISTRATIVE FUNCTIONS

As we mentioned earlier, much Tora teaching was not done in formal institutions. An ancient saying states: 'Let thy house be a meeting house for the Sages;'[351] in other words, let your house be a welcome meeting place for Tora teachers on their continuous travels. However, the Sages did teach Tora in the Sanhedrin as well, first in the Chamber of Hewn Stone in the Temple compound and, afterwards, in Yavne and the later Galilean locations. At the same time, this Great House of Study served as the judicial, legislative and administrative centre of the nation. Public administration and Tora education were thus united in one institution – a situation which more or less existed already in Temple times, but was enhanced in the period after the destruction. Many specific terms were created in this situation.

The Sanhedrin itself carried many names, such as בית המדרש *The House of Study*,[352] בית הווער *The House of Meeting*,[353] בית דין הגדול *The Great Court*,[354] and, of course, סנהדרין *Sanhedrin*, although this last name was less common after the destruction of the Temple.[355]

The head of the House of Study and of the Sanhedrin was called נשיא *Nasi*, a term which is found in Leviticus and Ezekiel[356] but in post-biblical Judaism was apparently not used until the Bar Kokhba revolt.[357] This title remained in

---

[348] *B.T. Sanh.* 100b.

[349] *B.T. Yev.* 11b; *B.T. Shabb.* 63a; *B.T. Yev.* 24a.

[350] The system of the four-fold sense of Scripture, indicated by the acrostic *Pardes* (i.e. *peshat, remez, derash, sod*) appears only in the Middle Ages, and it is likely that this reflects Christian influence. The opinion of König, *Einleitung*, 516-29 does not comply with these facts, in spite of all the later support it enjoyed. See Bacher, '*Pardes*'.

[351] *M. Avot* 1:4, and see *A.R.N.* a 6 and b 11 (14a).

[352] *T. Sota* 7:9; *B.T. Ber.* 28a; *Sifrei Num.* 116 (p. 133).

[353] *M. Sota* 9:15; *P.T. Ber.* 4, 7c.

[354] *M. Sota* 9:1; *P.T. Sanh.* 3, 21a.

[355] *T. Sanh.* 8:1; *B.T. Rosh H.* 31a.

[356] Lev 4:22; Ezek 44:3, 46:2.

[357] *M. Hag.* 2:2 counts *Nesiim* already among the Pairs, but it appears that this is an addition to the early Mishna, since otherwise this title of the head of the Sanhedrin is in use only from the Bar Kokhba episode onwards, such as Rabban Shimon ben Gamliel ha-Nasi, Rabbi Yehuda ha-Nasi, etc. See, however, Mantel, *Studies*, 1-53.

continuous use until the institution was abolished in the fifth century.

Serving next to the Nasi was the אב בית דין *Head of the Court*.[358] A third functionary in the administration of the Court was called the *Hakham*. This title, however, appears only in the last two Tannaic generations.[359]

Ordained Sages carried the title רבי *Rabbi*. The use of this term as a fixed title preceding the private name is not in evidence before the destruction of the Temple and must have been instituted thereafter. Apart from this title, those ordained were referred to as חכמים *Hakhamim*, Sages.

Students in the House of Study are called תלמידים *Talmidim*, students, or תלמידי חכמים *Talmidei Hakhamim* – the singular of which term apparently was not תלמיד חכם, as in later sources, but תלמיד חכמים *Talmid Hakhamim*, student of the Sages.[360]

The ordination of a Sage is referred to as סמיכה *semikha*, laying on of hands, in Babylonian sources, but as מינוי *minnui*, appointment, in Palestinian sources.[361]

The Nasi and the Sanhedrin could send שליחים *Envoys*, representatives, and in one Amoraic passage such a functionary is decorously referred to as שליח ציון *Envoy of Zion*.[362]

Legislation is referred to as תקנה *Takkana* – ordinance, lit. improvement;[363] or as גזרה *Gezera* – decree, essentially a prohibition, such as the 'Eighteen Decrees' which are all prohibitive ordinances.[364]

The voting procedure is described as נמנו וגמרו *They voted and concluded*.[365]

The sessions in the House of Study were not presided over directly by the Sage but by a functionary called מתורגמן *Meturgeman*, lit. interpreter, or חזן *Hazzan*, overseer; by the end of the Tannaic period he was called אמורא *Amora*, lit. speaker. The task of this functionary was to open and guide the discussion in the name of the Sage and in his presence. This function is not mentioned in traditions from the Temple period and from Rabban Yohanan ben Zakkai's time, but only from Rabban Gamliel's rule onwards. However it is not impossible that it existed earlier.

As previously indicated,[366] the House of study had one or more students who specialized in the exact recitation of halakhot. These were termed תנא *Tanna*, lit. repeater, or, like the functionary just mentioned, *Meturgeman*. This position is not in evidence before the generation of Usha.

[358] *B.T. Hor.* 13b; *T. Sanh.* 8:1.
[359] *B.T. Hor.* 13b; *B.T. Ket.* 103b.
[360] *T. Kidd.* 3:9; *B.T. Kidd.* 49b. The name is common in all types of rabbinic literature.
[361] *P.T. Sanh.* 1, 19a; *B.T. Sanh.* 13b.
[362] *M. Rosh H.* 1:4; *B.T. Beitsa* 25b.
[363] *M. Gitt.* 4:2-10; *M. Rosh H.* 4:1-4; *P.T. Rosh H.* 7, 59b; *B.T. Rosh H.* 31b.
[364] *B.T. Bava B.* 60b; *M. Shabb.* 1:4.
[365] *M. Shabb.* 1:4; *M. Yad.* 1:1-3; *M. Oh.* 18:9.
[366] Above p. 76.

Central Religious Concepts Developed in Oral Tora

In the preceding, we discussed the innovative character of Oral Tora as it appears in its terminology, its relation to the Written Tora, and in the view of Tora cherished by the Sages themselves. In the final section of this chapter we will outline some basic religious concepts which are characteristic of the literature of the Sages. In other words, these concepts may represent the degree of innovation inherent in Oral Tora as a major component of Jewish culture and religion.

In the First Temple period, the majority of the people did not feel responsible for the Tora, whether in the sphere of faith and thought or in the observance of commandments. As evidenced by the vehemence of the prophets, and as confirmed by archeological remains, idolatry and other elements of pagan culture were widely accepted among the Israelites. In other words, the commandments and ideals of the Tora and the prophetic books do not reflect everyday life of the people at large. Rather, they represent the reality and the visions cherished and practiced by a minority with high moral and religious values. By contrast, the rules and ideals of Oral Tora reflect the life situation both of the Sages and teachers and of the common people. The populace no longer engaged in idolatry as they did in the First Temple period.[367] Loyalty to Tora was widespread among the people, as shown not only by their keeping the commandments but also their studying Tora and sending their children to schools. A majority of the nation remained faithful to the Tora even in difficult times,[368] in exile and in the various diaspora locations.[369]

On the other hand, the Sages were fully aware of the realities of their times, not only when teaching concrete halakhot and issuing *takkanot*, but also in formulating moral and social ideals. They do not express such lofty visions as in the words of the prophet, 'and the wolf shall dwell with the lamb . . . and the sucking child shall play on the hole of the asp' (Isa 11:6-8), or 'They shall not hunt nor destroy in all My holy mountain, for the earth shall be full of the knowledge of the Lord as the waters cover the sea' (*ib.* v. 9). Rather, they state the requirements of 'making peace between man and his fellow',[370] and of 'getting early to the House of Study morning and evening'.[371] Nor do the Sages countenance general practice slavishly; they try to guide and correct them step by step, thinking a few steps ahead but never losing touch with reality. While, as we have been emphasizing, Oral Tora embodies revolutionary innovations in

---

[367] According to *M. Sukka* ch. 5, this consciousness was expressed by pilgrims who went to draw water from the well of Shiloah during the festival of Sukkot. Cf also *B.T. Yoma* 69b for an aggadic description of the destruction of the evil inclination to idolatry at the beginning of the Second Temple period.

[368] Josephus *Ant.*, end of bk. 3; *Ag.Ap.* 2:232-5.

[369] Cf. *Compendia* I/1, 184-6.

[370] *M. Pea* 1:1.

[371] *B.T. Shabb.* 127a.

many areas, these changes did not result from lofty and remote visions. Certainly, the Sages could and did speak in elated and apocalyptic terms about messianic redemption as well as about the glorious past. The innovations of Oral Tora, however, did not result from prophetic visions but from generations of instruction, counsel and creative study on the interface between the ever-increasing Tora and the realities of life.

This insight into the social position of Oral Tora enables us to outline some of its characteristic religious concepts. Of course, we cannot deal with all of them. We do not speak now of many important subjects such as Prayer, the Sanctification of the Name, Proselytism, Charity, the Pilgrim Festivals, or the sphere of the family. Nor do we deal with purely aggadic topics such as the Love of God or Redemption, or halakhic topics such as Purity and Impurity, Sabbath, Court Procedures, etc. Some of these items were enumerated above in the section on terminological innovation. Now we deal with some others which embody ideas characteristic of Oral Tora. Full treatment taking into account their development in history is equally impossible. We will give a representative selection, stressing the innovative aspects of four basic religious concepts.

THE STUDY OF TORA

A theme constantly emphasized in all of rabbinic literature is the significance of Tora and of its study.[372] Oral Tora introduced many new aspects into the concept of Tora and its place in the life of the people; this both reflected and influenced the religious consciousness of the people and their way of life. We mentioned before the two sayings with the oldest attribution, preserved at the beginning of *Avot*: the exhortation of the Men of the Great Assembly 'to raise up many disciples' and the saying of Shimon the Just that 'the world is based on three things: the Tora, the divine service (*avoda*) and charity'.[373] In the last saying, it should be noted, Tora is mentioned first, before the (Temple) service. One studies Tora not just to observe commandments and to learn to do good and avoid evil in a social context, but also as a religious experience and an act of worship in itself. This is expressed by the concept that one who studies Tora with others or alone enjoys the company of the divine Presence.[374] Study of Tora is considered as worship of God and the verse 'to worship him (*le-avdo*) with all your heart' (Deut 11:14) can be interpreted to mean Tora study. In the same passage, God's commandment to Adam in the garden of Eden 'to work it (*le-avda*) and guard it' (Gen 2:15) is explained as follows: 'But what work (*avoda*) was there in the past [before the fall and the curse]? Here you learn that "to work it" means study (*talmud*).'[375]

---

[372] On the place of Tora in everyday life see *Compendia* I/2, 945-70.
[373] *M. Avot* 1:1-2.
[374] *M. Avot* 3:2, 3:6; *Mekh., Ba-hodesh* 11 (p. 243); *B.T. Ber.* 6a.
[375] *Sifrei Deut.* 41 (p. 87); *A.R.N.* b 21 (22b).

Tora is the essence of God's covenant with Israel;[376] it is also the 'light' which is their reward.[377] One who studies Tora and discovers new insights and interpretations is like one who 'received it himself on Mount Sinai,'[378] and even hears the words: 'Thus said the Holy One blessed be He'.[379] Thus, as we saw, Ben Azzai said of the burning enthusiasm of his Tora study: 'The words of the Tora are as joyful as the day they were given at Sinai;' he added: 'For the essence of their being given is through fire, because 'the mountain burned with fire into the heart of heaven' (Deut 4:11).'[380] Study of Tora represents one of the most important religious values: 'These are the things the fruits of which a man enjoys in this world but the capital of which remains for him in the world to come: Honouring one's father and mother, deeds of loving-kindness, and making peace between a man and his fellow; but the study of Tora is equal to them all.'[381] Or in another formulation: ' "And its lamps, seven, over it" (Zech 4:12) – this refers to seven specific commandments set down in the Tora: heave-offerings, tithes, sabbatical years, Jubilee years, circumcision, the honouring of one's father and mother, and Tora study which equals them all.'[382] It is even stated that the Tora is 'greater than the priesthood and than royalty'.[383] This throws extra light on the saying of Hillel: 'Be thou of the disciples of Aaron, loving peace and pursuing peace, loving [thy] fellow-creatures and drawing them nigh to the Tora.'[384]

With the giving of the Tora to Israel it was as if God had sold himself to Israel: 'The Holy One blessed be He said to Israel: I sold you my Tora – it is as though I sold Myself with it.'[385] From that moment on, everyone must toil in the labour of Tora for 'man was created for the labour of Tora'.[386] Rabban Yohanan ben Zakkai used to say: 'If you have learned much Tora, ascribe no merit to yourself; for this you were created.'[387] The enigmatic verse, 'At His right hand a fiery law unto them' (Deut 33:2) was applied to the comparison of the Tora with fire: 'Eveyone who came to study Tora saw himself as if he were standing in the fire.'[388] However, it is implied that one must study it out of a feeling of love and joy.[389]

---

[376] B.T. Shabb. 33a; B.T. Ber. 5a.

[377] B.T. Meg. 16b.

[378] Yal. Shim., Tavo no. 938.

[379] S.E.R. 11 (p. 55), according to the version in Yal. Shim., Shofetim no. 49.

[380] Lev. R. 16 (p. 354) and parr. See above on 'Oral Tora from Sinai'.

[381] M. Pea 1:1.

[382] Pes. R. 8 (29b).

[383] M. Avot 6:5.

[384] M. Avot 1:12.

[385] Exod. R. 33,1.

[386] B.T. Sanh. 99b. Cf. Gen. R. 13 (p. 117).

[387] M. Avot 2:8.

[388] Pes. de-R.K., Berakha p. 450. Cf. Sifrei Deut. 343 (p. 399); P.T. Shek. 6, 49d.

[389] Sifrei Deut. 48 (p. 113); B.T. Ar. 11a; S.E.R. 5 (p. 21). Cf. ib. chap. 18.

Tora as dealt with here does not just mean the passing on of theWritten Tora itself along with the oral transmission of its explanation and of the ways of reading it. It implies, as we have set forth above, the requirement to search in it and to 'turn in it',[390] to make it increase and reveal ever new insights and explanations through study and discussion. Let us cite more fully the *derasha* of R. Elazar ben Azaria delivered at Yavne, which the grey R. Yoshua, who could not be present, insisted to hear from the mouth of his students since 'the House of Study cannot exist without innovation':[391]

> "The words of the wise are as goads, and as nails well planted" (Eccl 12:11) – just as the goad directs the ox to bring life into the world, likewise the words ofthe Tora are but life to the world, as it is said, "She is a tree of life" (Prov 3:18). Or, just as the goad can be picked up and taken away, are the words of the Tora likewise? Scripture says: "And as nails well planted". [Or, are they neither decreasing nor increasing? Scripture says, "Planted".][392] Just as a plant bears fruit and multiplies, so the words of the Tora bear fruit and multiply.

The words of the Tora do not bear fruit and multiply by themselves; they must be tended and cultivated in order to bring out their hidden treasures. A similar idea is expressed by the parable which compares the words of the Tora to 'a *kav* of wheat' and 'a bundle of flax' which a king gave to two of his servants. The dull one guarded them without doing anything, but the clever one worked the flax into a nice cloth and the wheat into a loaf of bread, presenting them to the king upon his return.[393]

In concrete terms: halakhot which were forgotten or new questions confronting the people should not be left to be answered through divine intervention: 'It is not in heaven, saying: who shall go up for us to heaven and bring it to us, so that we may hear and do it' (Deut 30:12). Thus, when laws were forgotten 'during the mourning period of Moses' and unprecedented problems arose, and the nation wanted Joshua to seek a divine answer through the Urim and Tummim, he is said to have refused, 'for it is not in heaven'; thereupon Othniel the son of Kenaz 'restored them [the halakhot] through his dialectics'.[394]

The requirement to study Tora is not addressed to any particular class or circle, such as priests or Sages, but to the whole nation: 'Lest you say, let the sons of the Elders study, or the sons of the Prominent or the sons of the Prophets – Scripture says: "Keep them, keeping" (*shamor tishmerun*, Deut 11:22); this

---

[390] *M. Avot* 5:22.

[391] *T. Sota* 7:10; *B.T. Hag.* 3b; *Num. R.* 14,4. See above p. 51. The *derasha* appears in other sources as well, but with the above missing or differing in emphasis.

[392] This sentence is missing in MS. Vienna, but found in *ed. princ.*; MS. Erfurt has a similar version. The idea itself appears in the other parallels.

[393] *S.E.Z.* 2 (p. 171); see p. 183 for a more elaborate treatment.

[394] *B.T. Tem.* 16a. A similar use of the verse is made in the story of R. Eliezer's banning, *P.T. Moed K.* 3, 81d; *B.T. Bava M.* 59b.

teaches that all are equal in Tora.'[395] Another midrash states: ' "And Moses wrote this law and delivered it unto the priests" (Deut 31:9). Said Moses to them: are you willing that a covenant be made that all who wish to study Tora shall not be witheld? They responded: Yes. They stood up and swore that no one is to be prevented from reading the Tora, as it is said: ". . . Unto all Israel saying"(Deut 27:9). Then Moses said to them: "This day thou art become a people" (ib.).'[396] In other words, the people of Israel became a nation only when they swore not to prevent anyone from drawing nigh to the Tora.

The question was, of course, does every member of society have the opportunity to study Tora? In a relatively late source we read: 'Rava said: When a man is led in for judgement he is asked: Did you deal faithfully? Did you fix times for Tora? Did you engage in procreation? Did you hope for salvation? Did you engage in the dialectics of wisdom? Did you understand one thing out of another?'[397] It was expected that one deal faithfully in business and await redemption, and in addition not just set aside time for Tora study, but try to engage in higher wisdom. In other words, the study of Tora, even on advanced levels, was not delegated to professionals; it was everyone's care. In this light should be understood the sayings of Hillel quoted above: 'He who does not increase [Tora] makes [it] to cease', and 'He who multiplies Tora multiplies life'.[398]

The study of Tora is to be done for its own sake, and not for any gain which could be derived from it. This requirement was formulated by Hillel, and reiterated by the early Tanna R. Zadok: 'R. Zadok says: Do not make them [the words of Tora] a crown wherewith to magnify thyself or a spade wherewith to dig. And thus used Hillel to say: He who makes profit of the Crown shall perish.'[399] Another Tannaic source states: ' "To love it [the commandment]" (Deut 11:22) – lest you say, I study Tora in order to be called Sage, in order to be seated at the head of the academy, or in order to lengthen my days – therefore it is written: "To love it".'[400]

Since the days of R. Akiva and his students, the requirement is heard to study 'Tora for its own sake'; he who studies it not for its own sake, 'it were better had he not been born alive'.[401] It is in the Amoraic period that we hear of a more lenient view: 'Rav Yehuda said in the name of Rav: One should always engage oneself in Tora and commandments, even not for its own sake, for from "not for its own sake" one comes to "for its own sake".'[402] This outlook became

---

[395] *Sifrei Deut.* 48 (p. 112).
[396] *Yal. Shim., Tavo* no. 938, from *Deut. Z.*
[397] *B.T. Shabb.* 31a.
[398] *M. Avot* 1:13, 2:7. Above, p. 52.
[399] *M. Avot* 4:5; 1:13. Cf. *A.R.N.* a 12 (28a); b 27 (28b).
[400] *Sifrei Deut.* 48 (p. 113) and in a similar version, 41 (p. 87).
[401] *M. Avot (Kinyan Tora)* 6:1; *Kalla Rabbati* 8, and the commentary in the course of that chapter. Cf. also *Sifrei Deut.* 306 (p. 383); *B.T. Taan.* 7a.
[402] *B.T. Sota* 22b, with many parallels in the Babylonian Talmud. In *Lam. R., petihta* 2 (2b) it is found in the name of Rav Huna.

widespread in Amoraic teaching, and we find it formulated by other Sages.[403] It was also expressed in a personal prayer: 'May it be Thy will, O Lord our God, to establish peace among the celestial household and the earthly household, and among the students who occupy themselves with the Tora, whether for its own sake or not for its own sake, and all those who do it not for its own sake, may it be Thy will that they do it for its own sake.'[404]

Certainly not every person in Israel could indeed have been able to 'multiply Tora' and to deal with it for its own sake. But the teachings and the insights of the Sages not only contributed much to the establishment of Houses of Study, schools, synagogues and other formal or informal places of instruction, but, we may even say, created a learning nation. To judge from the sources, participation in the study of Tora extended to all strata of society, be it much or little, in regular frameworks or not. It was not done only for a few years in school or in the House of Study, but as a way of life and in length of days. All this resulted in the gradual creation of Oral Tora, which we have been describing above as the literary product of a learning community and the expression of a collective authorship.

THE OBSERVANCE OF MITSWOT

The study of Tora represented a supreme value of its own in Oral Tora, and it could be exercised without referring to the observance of commandments in practical life. However, there is no Tora without commandments, or with the Hebrew term we shall use in this section: *mitswot*. One of the prime goals of Tora study is the doing of practical deeds out of knowledge and understanding. This view found its classical expression in the following tradition: 'When R. Tarfon, R. Akiva and R. Yosi ha-Galili were once reclining in the house of Aris in Lydda, this question was asked before them: What is more important, study or deeds? R. Tarfon said: Deeds are more important. R. Akiva said: Study is more important. Then all answered and said: Study is more important, for study leads to deeds.'[405] Study has priority over deeds, but only because it leads to deeds. The same is expressed in a saying: 'The purpose of wisdom – repentance and good deeds,'[406] and in a Tannaic midrash: ' "If you walk in my statutes and observe my commandments and do them" (Lev 26:3) – he who studies to do them [is meant], not he who studies not to do them; for he who studies not to do them, it were better that he had not been born.'[407]

Biblical verses like the one just quoted stress the observance of the *mitswot* and their significance for the fulfilment of the covenant, but in Oral Tora this is expanded and deepened. The people of Israel consider it a mark of distinction

[403] *B.T. Pes.* 50b.
[404] *B.T. Ber.* 16b-17a.
[405] *Sifrei Deut.* 41 (p. 85); *B.T. Kidd.* 40b and parr.
[406] *B.T. Ber.* 17a.
[407] *Sifra, Behukotai* 1 (110c).

that they enlarged the complex of *mitswot* and thus strengthened the bonds of love between themselves and God: ' "New and old which I have laid up for Thee, O my beloved" (Cant 7:14) – said the congregation of Israel to the Holy One, blessed be He: Lord of the universe, I have issued more restrictions (*gezerot*) on myself than Thou hast done, and I have observed them!'[408]

The doing of *mitswot* extends not only to the relation with God and with one's fellow, but includes the care for one's body:[409]

> "The merciful man doeth good to his own soul" (Prov 11:17) – this is Hillel the Elder. Once, Hillel the Elder walked along with his students after their session had been concluded, and they asked him: Master, where are you going? He replied: to perform a *mitswa*. What *mitswa* did Hillel depart for, they asked. He said to them: to wash in the bath-house. Said they: is this a *mitswa*? Yes, he said, it is as with the statues of a king which are erected in their theatres and circuses: they are scoured and washed by the man who is appointed to look after them, and who thereby obtains a salary and an honorable position in the kingdom – how much more we, who have been created in [His] image and likeness, as it is written, "For in the image of God made He man" (Gen 9:6).

The numerous *mitswot* which, as it were, surround the individual's life, including his body, are beloved to him and he rejoices in their observance. To verses like 'And Moses did as the Lord commanded' (e.g. Num 27:22), the Tannaic midrash is wont to add: 'He went and did so joyfully.'[410] The pervasiveness of the *mitswot* can be a joyful physical experience:[411]

> R. Meir says: You cannot find a man person in Israel who is not surrounded with commandments – *tefillin* on his head, *tefillin* on his arms, a *mezuza* on his doorpost, and four *tsitsiot*: these [seven items] surround him and on these David said, "Sevenfold dayly do I praise Thee, because of Thy righteous ordinances" (Ps 119:164). And when David entered the bath-house and saw himself naked he exclaimed: Woe is to me that I stand naked without *mitswot*; but then he was reminded of the circumcision in his flesh and his mind was set at ease.

In the Amoraic period, this idea found expression in the famous midrash of R. Simlai:[412] 'Six hundred and thirteen *mitswot* were communicated to Moses: Three hundred and sixty-five prohibitions, corresponding to the number of days in the solar year, and two hundred and forty-eight positive commandments, corresponding to the number of man's members.' Another midrash states on this basis: 'Every single member of the body says to man: Please, fulfill through

---

[408] *B.T. Er.* 21b.
[409] *Lev. R.* 34 (p. 776). A different version appears in *A.R.N.* b 30 (33b).
[410] *Sifrei Num.* 148 (p. 187) and *Sifrei Z.* p. 322.
[411] *T. Ber.* end; *B.T. Men.* 43b.
[412] *B.T. Makk.* 23b. R. Simlai is of the second Amoraic generation. Any numbering of the commandments mentioned in Tannaic literature is a sure addition which does not appear in the major versions. See Urbach, *Sages*, 343 and 836 n. 1.

me this *mitswa* . . . and every day says to man: Please, do not commit on me this transgression!'[413]

The Halakha set down many details as to the exact observance of the *mitswot*, but did not turn into a system of 'ingrained commandments of men' (Isa 29:13) to be performed thoughtlessly. They should be observed out of love and involve one's whole personality:[414]

> "This day [the Lord commands you]" (Deut 26:16) . . . As though you received them this day from Mount Sinai. . . . R. Yohanan said: He who does Tora in its true intention, it is reckoned as if he made himself, as it is said: "And the Lord commanded . . . statutes and ordinances, for your making them" (Deut 4:14) – it does not say "to do" but "your making [doing] them", and this teaches that it is reckoned as if he made himself.

Doing the *mitswot* shapes a person and creates him, as it were, anew. This makes man, in a way, a partner of God in the act of creation. Scholars have rightly stressed that the concept of observance of the *mitswot* and of the ethical commandments as developed in Oral Tora, is not one of an autonomous ethic, i.e. an ethic rooted in man, but of a theonomy: the basis of all *mitswot* is the divine imperative.[415] Nevertheless, doing the *mitswot* with true devotion not only makes man a partner in the creation of his own personality, but also in the creation of the *mitswot* themselves. Such is the message of R. Yohanan's other midrash, brought in the same context:[416]

> "You observe and you do them" (Deut 26:16) – R. Yohanan said: He who does a *mitswa* with true intention, Scripture reckons it as if he gave[417] it from Mount Sinai, as it is said, "You observe *and* you do"; and why does it state, "You do [= make] them"?[418] To say that everyone who observes the Tora and does it with true intention, it is as if he himself decreed it and gave it from Mount Sinai.

These statements of R. Yohanan can be considered a concluding reformulation of conceptions which existed already in earlier generations, to the effect that man has an active role in the shaping of himself and of the *mitswot*.

REPENTANCE

The idea of repentance is found in all parts of the Bible. The prophet Hosea calls

---

[413] *Pes. de-R. K.* 14 (p. 203).

[414] *Tanh. B., Tavo* 3 (23b); *Tanh., Tavo* 1 (119a). The midrash hinges on both meanings of the verb עשה to make and to do, for which the English does not have one equivalent; thus the grammatical form לעשותכם your doing, which in itself is remarkable, is interpreted as 'your making'.

[415] Thus Cohen, 'Problem', in his critique of Lazarus, *Ethik des Judenthums*; see Urbach, *Sages*, 317ff. who analyzes the rabbinic dicta which might appear to support Lazarus' theory of autonomous ethics.

[416] *Tanh., Tavo* 1 (119a – not in *Tanh. Buber*); a shortened version in *Midr. ha-Gad. Deut.* p. 602.

[417] In the *textus rec.* and ed. Mantua נתונה. This should be read נתנה on the basis of the contents of the midrash (as proposed by Urbach, *Sages*, 828 n. 30) and of *Midr. ha-Gadol*.

[418] Here and in *Midr. ha-Gad.* ועשיתם אותם; in the Masoretic text ועשית אותם.

to Israel: 'Return O Israel, unto the Lord thy God.'[419] Almost the entire book of Jonah is devoted to the theme of repentance. The prophet brings his message to Nineveh, with the result stated at the end: 'And God saw their works, that they turned from their evil way, and God repented of the evil which He said He would do unto them, and He did it not.'[420] However, not only is the abstract concept of *teshuva*, repentance, not found in the Bible, but neither is there an awareness of the 'state' of repentance as a strived-for spiritual attitude, as we find it in the rabbinic saying: 'One hour of repentance and good deeds is more beautiful than the entire world to come.'[421] Or, another example, one who reached the state of repentance is called a *baal teshuva*: 'To one who is a *baal teshuva*, one should not say: remember your former deeds.'[422] The term *teshuva* itself was not an innovation of the Sages. While it is not found in Qumran literature, the word or a Greek equivalent appears a number of times in other Second Temple writings such as Ben Sira, the *Letter of Aristeas* and the Prayer of Manasseh.[423] However, in rabbinic literature the term received a much wider connotation, and it is often mentioned and discussed in depth; thus it represents another concept characteristic of this literature.

Repentance almost replaces the biblical concept of atonement. In the description of the Day of Atonement in Leviticus the sacrificial service is the centre of the process of atonement for sin: 'For on this day shall atonement be made for you to cleanse you; from all your sins shall you be clean before the Lord.'[424] However, the Mishna states: 'Death and the Day of Atonement atone together with repentance [only].'[425] Furthermore, in the baraita it is stated that there are 'four types of atonement' which, as R. Yishmael taught, correlated to the gravity of the transgression; but in all four, repentance is the basis of atonement.[426] The baraita of the four types of atonement was taught after the destruction when sacrifices had ceased, but in the teaching of the Sages repentance was connected with the offerings as well.[427] In addition to a sin offering or a guilt offering it was necessary for a person seeking atonement to confess his sin and confession is in fact a sign of repentance.[428]

The Sages realized very well that the presentation of repentance as the answer to the problem of sin and of atonement, implied a certain circumvention of the biblical laws regarding atonement through sacrifices and of the idea of retribution. Repentance in fact was considered the 'personal' and direct answer

---

[419] Hos 14:2.
[420] Jonah 3:10.
[421] *M. Avot* 4:17.
[422] *M. Bava M.* 4:10.
[423] Sir 17:19(24), 18:20(21); *Arist.* 188; Pr Man 8.
[424] Lev 16:30.
[425] *M. Yoma* 8:3.
[426] *T. Yoma* 4:6 and parr.; see Lieberman *a.l.*
[427] *T. Yoma* 4:8; *Sifra, Emor* 14 (102a); *B.T. Ker.* 7a.
[428] *Sifrei Num.* 2 (p. 6); *Sifra, Behukotai* 8 (112b).

of God to sin beyond the Tora and the Prophets. This thought is beautifully expressed in the words of the Palestinian Amora R. Pinhas:[429]

> It is written, "Good and upright is the Lord, therefore does He instruct sinners in the way" (Ps 25:8). Why is He good if He is upright? They asked the Tora: What is the punishment of the sinner? She answered: "Let him bring his offering and be atoned." They asked Prophecy: what is the punishment of the sinner? She answered: "The soul that sinneth shall die" (Ezek 18:4). They asked David: What is the punishment of the sinner? He ansered: "Let sinners cease out of the earth" (Ps 104:35). They asked Wisdom: What is the punishment of the sinner? She answered: "Evil pursueth sinners" (Prov 13:21). They asked the Holy One, blessed be He: What is the punishment of the sinner? He replied: Let him repent, let him do repentance and I will accept it. Therefore it is written: "Good and upright is the Lord, therefore does He instruct sinners in the way" – to do repentance.

In other words, God's 'goodness' takes precedence over his 'uprightness'. Somewhat earlier, R. Yehuda Nesia associates a similar thought with the Masoretic version *yado* instead of *yedei* in the biblical text: 'What is the meaning of the verse, "And they had the hand (*yado*) of a man under their wings" (Ezek 1:8)? *Yado*, his hand, is written – this is the hand of the Holy One, blessed be He, whose hand is folded under the wings of the beast-angels in order to accept those who repent (*baalei teshuva*) from before the Attribute of Justice.'[430] A similar expression is transmitted by R. Yohanan in the name of the Tanna R. Shimon ben Yohai, and the issue is the legend of King Manasseh's repentance: 'What is the meaning of the verse, "And he prayed unto Him, and an opening was made for him . . . " (2 Chr 33:13)? – This teaches that the Holy One, blessed be He, made a kind of opening in the heavens in order to accept him with his repentance from before the Attribute of Justice.'[431] The divine Attribute of Justice may claim that Manasseh was a sinner who also made others sin and that he deserved his punishment; it is even related that 'the angels sealed the windows in order that his prayer shall not rise up';[432] but repentance has priority over the Attribute of Justice.

The essence of repentance is to leave the path of sin and to decide not to return to it. It is not accompanied by acts of asceticism, and fasting is considered only a means of awakening man to repentance. According to the Mishna, the Elders say to the congregation on the occasion of a public fast: 'Our brethren, it is not said of the people of Nineveh, "And God saw their sackcloth and their fasting," but, "And God saw their works that they returned from their evil way"

---

[429] *P.T. Makk.* 2, 31d according to the Geniza fragment published by S. Wieder, *Tarbiz* 17 (1946) 133; the version of MS. Leiden and *ed. princ.* is fragmented and corrupt.
[430] *B.T. Pes.* 119a.
[431] *B.T. Sanh.* 103a; *P.T. Sanh.* 10, 28c; and parr. in the midrash collections *ad loc.*
[432] *Pal. Talmud* and midrash coll. *ib.*

(Jonah 3:10); and in the Prophecy it says: "Rend your heart and not your garments" (Joel 2:13).'[433]

It appears that under the influence of the book of Jonah, the universal aspect of repentance was stressed. R. Meir says: 'Great is repentance! For on account of one person who repents, the sins of all the world are forgiven, as it is said: "I will heal their backsliding, I will love them freely, for mine anger is turned away from him" (Hos 14:5) – it is not said "from them" but "from him".'[434] Indeed, the Tannaim teach explicitly: 'Thy right hand is extended to all creatures;'[435] God delayed in carrying out the sentence against the generation of the flood in order to allow time for repentance and even performed wondrous deeds to arouse people to repent, which unfortunately they did not. Similarly, God granted respite to the people of the Tower of Babylon and of Sodom and Gomorra.[436] The Amoraim ascribe repentance already to Cain. On the verse, 'And Cain went out' (Gen 4:16) it is commented:[437]

> He went out rejoicing, as where you read, "He goeth out to meet thee, and when he seeth thee, he will be glad in his heart" (Ex 4:14). Adam met him and asked: How did your case go? I repented and am reconciled, replied he. Thereupon Adam began beating his face, crying: So great is the power of repentance, and I did not know! Forthwith he arose and exclaimed: "A psalm, a song for the Sabbath day; It is a good thing to make confession unto the Lord" (Ps 92:1).

Adam did not know the power of repentance, but he could have, since, in Amoraic teaching, repentance was among those things existing before creation.[438]

MAN

Our discussion will centre on the intrinsic value of man and his place in the world and in human society. We will not be dealing with other aspects of rabbinic anthropology, such as body and soul, primordial man or historical man, but in a way be continuing our discussion of the significance of Tora, *mitswot* and repentance: underlying these three topics is a specific concept of man.

Man is the purpose of creation, and in fact its consummation.[439] 'One human being counts more than the entire creation.'[440] Man is a world in itself, a

---

[433] *M. Taan.* 2:1.
[434] *B.T. Yoma* 86b.
[435] *Sifrei Num.* 134 (p. 180); *Mekh., Wayehi* 5 (p. 133) and parr.
[436] *Mekh.* ib. and parr. listed for line 16.
[437] *Gen. R.* 23 (p. 220); *Lev. R.* 10 (p. 206); *Pes. de-R.K. Shuva* (p. 359). The clue to the midrash is in the double meaning which the verb *le-hodot* has in Middle Hebrew: to praise and to confess.
[438] *Gen. R.* 1 (p. 6); *Tanh. B., Naso* 19 (19b); *B.T. Pes.* 54a.
[439] *T. Sanh.* 8:9; *P.T. Sanh.* 4, 22c; *B.T. Sanh.* 38a.
[440] *A.R.N.* a 31 (46a).

microcosm: 'Everything that the Holy One, blessed be He, created on the earth, He created in man.'[441] As the 'great rule in Tora', Ben Azzai considered the verse, 'This is the book of the generations of Adam: When God created Adam He made him in the likeness of God' (Gen 5:1).[442] His friend and teacher – 'R. Akiva used to say: Beloved is man for he was created in the image [of God]; still greater was the love in that it was made known to him that he was created in the image of God, as it is written: "For in the image of God made he man" (Gen 9:6).'[443]

Tannaic literature stresses the uniqueness of every human being: 'This is to proclaim the greatness of the Holy One, blessed be He: Man stamps many coins with one seal and they are all alike, but the King of kings, the Holy One blessed be He, stamped every man with the seal of the first man, yet not one of them resembles his fellow. Therefore everyone must say: for my sake was the world created.'[444] In the same passage, moral and social lessons are drawn from the uniqueness of man and of every individual: 'Therefore man was created as one single person, to teach you that if anyone causes a single soul[445] to perish, Scripture reckons it as if he caused a whole world to perish. And if anyone saves alive a single soul, Scripture reckons it as if he had saved alive a whole world.'

Tannaic and Amoraic literature maintain an optimistic view regarding the creation of man. Beit Hillel agree with Beit Shammai that the world was created only 'to bear fruit and multiply', as it is written, 'He created it not a waste, He formed it to be inhabited' (Isa 45:18).[446] The human body is seen as good and beautiful. We cited in the above the opinion of Hillel, that caring for one's body constitutes the fulfilment of a *mitswa*, a commandment of God, since it implies care for the image of God it represents. Of Hillel's grandson, Rabban Gamliel the Elder, it is related: 'When he was walking on the Temple Mount, he saw a non-Jewish woman and said a benediction over her,'[447] in the manner of reciting a benediction upon seeing one of God's beautiful creatures.

A baraita in the Babylonian Talmud seems to contradict the above: 'Our Masters taught: For two and a half years, there was a dispute between Beit Shammai and Beit Hillel. One party says: It were better, had man not been created; the other says: It is better that he has been created, rather than not. They came to a vote and decided: It were better had he not been created, but now that he has been created, let him examine his actions.'[448] According to this baraita, not only did Beit Shammai originally postulate that man's creation is to

---

[441] *A.R.N. ib.*

[442] *Sifra, Kedoshim* 4 (79b); *P.T. Ned.* 9, 41c.

[443] *M. Avot* 3:14.

[444] *M. Sanh.* 4:5.

[445] The addition מישראל 'from Israel' here and in the next sentence does not appear in the major versions and does not fit the context.

[446] *M. Gitt.* 4:5.

[447] *P.T. Av. Zar.* 1, 40a; *P.T. Ber.* 9, 40a (in a shorter form); *B.T. Av. Zar.* 20a (adding that she was 'an extremely beautiful woman').

[448] *B.T. Er.* 13b.

be regretted, but this opinion was confirmed by a majority in a vote. This sounds hardly authentic, as has been pointed out before.[449] First of all, we never find a decision by vote in such aggadic matters. Secondly, the baraita is found only in this one Babylonian tradition; nor is there a reference to this vote or any trace of its subject elsewhere in rabbinic literature. Third, and this is decisive, this pessimistic view contradicts the opinion prevailing in Tannaic teaching, including that of Beit Shammai itself.

The general opinion of both schools is that 'bearing fruit and multiplying', i.e. procreation and the human beings resulting from it, is 'for the betterment of the world'.[450] He who has a share in the creation of humanity is blessed, for 'there are three partners in [the creation of] man: the Holy One, blessed be He, his father and his mother', and that is why 'the honouring of father and mother is like honouring God.'[451] This is the value of man and his place in the world: 'His soul is from heaven and his body from the earth. Therefore, if he did Tora and did the will of his Father in heaven, he is like the heavenly creatures, as it is said: "I said: ye are Godlike beings and all of you sons of the Most High" (Ps 82:6). But if he did not do Tora and did not do the will of his Father in heaven, he is like the earthly creatures, as it is said: "Nevertheless ye shall die like men" (ib. v. 7).[452] Man is on earth with a heavenly commission: to acquire knowledge and thereby 'edify' himself to be a representative of heaven; 'A man who has knowledge, is it as if the Temple was built in his days.'[453]

This positive evaluation of man's place in the world is matched by the emphasis on the fundamental equality of all human beings. We have been discussing the right and obligation of everyone to participate in the study of Tora. This equality extends to other social and religious areas and to personal status. Communal life during the Second Temple period, and even more so in the first few generations after the destruction of the Temple, reflects a broad social outlook. The High Court in Jerusalem and the later Sanhedrin were conceived as representing the entire Congregation of Israel; communal life was the joint responsibility of all residents; and the synagogue was the 'house of the community'.[454]

Within these frameworks, all were considered equal irrespective of origin or economic position. But there were different views on the election to public office of people not permitted to marry within the community, such as bastards. However, the basic right to participate in city politics and to use communal property pertained to all.[455] According to the biblical commandment, only the priests descending from Aaron officiated at the altar in the Temple. But

[449] See Urbach, *Sages,* 252.
[450] *M. Yev.* 6:6; *M. Gitt.* 4:5.
[451] *Sifra, Kedoshim* 1 (86d); *B.T. Kidd.* 30b; *P.T. Kidd.* 1, 61b; *P.T. Pea* 1, 15c.
[452] *Sifrei Deut.* 306 (p. 431).
[453] *B.T. Ber.* 33a; *B.T. Sanh.* 92a.
[454] Cf. above p. 90; see further *Compendia* I/1, 377-419 and I/2, 865-944.
[455] See *Compendia* I/1, 414-7; Safrai, 'Ha-ir ha-Yehudit'.

Pharisaic-rabbinic tradition created a wide social framework around the Temple which made it almost belong to the people at large. The sacrifices were offered in their name, and their representatives were always present. The fundamental equality of all found its full expression in the synagogue. The divine worship conducted in it was based on the participation of all members and could not take place without the quorum of ten. Everyone could read from the Tora before the congregation or serve as the 'representative of the community' leading the prayers.[456] And everyone was allowed to pray to his Creator, either within the community or alone: 'Abba Yudan of Tsidon said in the name of Rabban Gamliel: Whence do we know that one should not say, I am unworthy to pray for the Temple or for the Land of Israel? We learn it from the verse, "I will surely hear their cry [When My anger burns. . .]" (Exod 22:22f.).'[457] Rabban Gamliel teaches that praying for redemption is not the privilege of Sages and holy men, but that it is everone's right and duty and that he has a responsibility for the redemption of all.

The equality of all was expressed also in the concrete rules for financial damages. An early halakha stated that one who causes embarassment to someone or hurts him must pay him compensation 'according to his honour.' Thus, a rich and prominent man must receive a higher compensation for damages and shame than a poor man. This was opposed by R. Akiva and his ruling was accepted by all as general halakha: 'Even the poor in Israel are recognized as freemen who have lost their possessions, for they are the sons of Abraham, Isaac and Jacob.'[458]

A summary of man's place in society as seen by the Sages may be found in the following saying which considers their own position as Tora teachers and leaders of the community, as compared to that of the simple peasant:[459]

> A pearl in the mouth of the Rabbis of Yavne: I am God's creature and he is God's creature. My work is in the city and his work is in the fields. I rise early for my work, and he rises early for his work. Just as he does not boast in his work, I do not boast in my work. And lest you say, I do much and he does little – we have learnt: "He may do much or he may do little, it is all one, if only he directs his heart towards heaven".

---

[456] See *Compendia* I/2, 865-944.
[457] *Mekh. de-R. Sh.b.Y.* p. 211.
[458] *M. Bava K.* 8:6.
[459] *B.T. Ber.* 17a. The reference is to *M. Men.* 13:11. It is a concept which appears often in rabbinic literature and is found already in Philo's work; see Heinemann, *Philons Bildung*, 69f.

The study of the history of Oral Tora has a long tradition. As early as the Geonic period, many works were written which may be viewed as introductions to the literature of the Sages. Several aspects of the edited form of this literature had been inciting the interest of the learned: The spread over the diverse collections, the alternating of the genres of halakha, midrash and aggada, and the lack of chronological order in the presentation of the opinions of the successive generations of Sages. An additional factor was the prominent place of the literature of Oral Tora in the Houses of Study of the community, which caused many to ask questions about the history of Oral Tora and its eventual writing down, as well as the relation between the various collections and genres of this literature.

One work may be mentioned here, not only because it is exemplary for that earliest period of the study of rabbinic literature, but also because it remains to be one of the most important sources for all successive generations of its students: The Epistle written by Rav Sherira Gaon in 986 c.e. in answer to questions asked by Rav Yaakov ben Rav Nissim of Kairuan (LEWIN, *Iggeret Rav Sherira Gaon*).

It was in the modern period, however, that the study of the history of Oral Tora attained to a great expansion. No volume on Jewish history and culture could afford any longer to neglect it, and especially nineteenth century authors payed much attention to it. We shall refer only to outstanding works which brought real innovation in the understanding of the history of Oral Tora.

Leopold ZUNZ, one of the prominent founders of the *Wissenschaft des Judentums*, first published his *Gottesdienstlichen Vorträge* in 1832. In the Hebrew translation of its second edition (1892), with additional notes by ALBECK, this work (ZUNZ-ALBECK, *Derashot*) remains to be the most comprehensive literary and historical introduction to midrash literature we have.

A description of the formation of Oral Tora in a wide historical perspective was presented by Nahman KROCHMAL, *More nevukhei ha-zeman* (1851).

Abraham GEIGER's *Urschrift* (1857) is essentially an introduction to the literature of Oral Tora in a historical and cultural perspective.

Zacharia FRANKEL, *Darkei ha-Mishna* (1859) is not only an introduction to Tannaic literature, but to Oral Tora in general; it is the first really scientific introduction following clear literary-historical definitions.

The first endeavour to encompass all areas of Oral Tora was Isaac Hirsch WEISS, *Dor-dor we-dorshav* (1871-83). This work describes the history of Oral Tora from its first origins till the expulsion from Spain in 1492 c.e.; till the present day no other systematic work comparable in scope has been written.

A large contribution to scholarship are the works of Wilhelm BACHER. In his series on the Aggada: *Babylonischen Amoräer* (1878), *Tannaiten* (1884-90) and *Palästinensischen Amoräer* (1892-99), each Tanna or Amora is first introduced with a short historical and literary survey, and then the aggadic traditions in his name are quoted by subject. Bacher's *Tradition* (1914) treats the ways of transmission used in the Palestinian and Babylonian academies in order to preserve the traditions of their predecessors. Of particular importance for the study of Oral Tora itself as well as for the analysis of its language and style is his *Terminologie* (1899-1905). Here, Bacher treats the Hebrew terminology used, respectively, by Tannaim and Amoraim in their midrash and exegesis of Scripture.

Lesser in volume but not in quality are the works by Israel LEWY (1841-1917). His researches into Tannaic and Amoraic texts excell in analytical depth and textual criticism, resulting in manifold identifications and explanations, and they serve as an example for researchers and commentators that come after him. We mention: *Fragmente* (1876); *Ein Wort* (1889); and *Mavo u-perush* (1895-1914).

In a period of 48 years of active scholarship (1891-1938), Adolf BÜCHLER published a long series of books and articles (mainly in Hebrew, German and English) on Jewish social and literary history in the periods of the Second Temple and of Mishna and Talmud. While they do not focus on the history of Oral Tora proper, all his works contribute to its understanding and evaluation in some way, elucidating its history and ways of development. Most relevant to our subject are his *Sin and Atonement*, *Synedrion* and *Piety*. A full bibliography of his works was published along with the collection of his articles: *Studies in Jewish History*, xxiii-xxx.

In 1913, Ismar ELBOGEN published his *Jüdische Gottesdienst*. This work mainly deals with prayer as it developed in later periods, but nevertheless contains much of relevance to the history of one important area of Oral Tora. The Hebrew edition, *Ha-tefilla*, contains much additional information by Joseph Heinemann and others.

From the beginning of this century to the year 1945, Louis GINZBERG published a long series of German, Hebrew and, mostly, English works, covering a wide range of aspects of the history of Oral Tora. A full bibliography up to 1945 is to be found in the *Jubilee Volume*, 19-47. Characteristic of all Ginzberg's works is the wide perspective in which he perceives Jewish culture, and his broad erudition in analyzing and commenting or in publishing unknown texts. Works most relevant to our subject are *Haggada bei den Kirchenvätern*; *Legends* (in particular the scholarly notes); and *Commentary*, which, while commenting on *P.T. Berakhot* chaps. 1-5, interweaves a wealth of information and research on the development of Palestinian halakha and aggada. A collection of his articles and papers on halakha and aggada were edited posthumously in Hebrew, *Al halakha we-aggada*.

Among the scholars of the last generation, a special place is taken by Jacob Nahum EPSTEIN. He provided the study of talmudic literature, especially the halakhic sections, with a basis of profound scholarship: philology, linguistics, textual criticism and source criticism. His major accomplishment, *Mavo le-nosah ha-Mishna* (1948), was published during his lifetime. The two volumes of this introduction to the textual and source criticism of the Mishna present an unusually high concentration of penetrating analysis and scrupulous observation. Apart from his many articles, other major publications are his dissertation, *Tohoroth*, and, posthumously, *Tannanitic Literature* and *Amoraitic Literature*, as well as his *Grammar*.

Along with Epstein, Hanokh ALBECK had been teaching and publishing his commentaries and other works, emphasizing the history of halakha and aggada. He completed the work of J. THEODOR on the scientific edition of *Genesis Rabba* (1903-36). While commenting on one of the most important aggadic texts, this work is the broadest exposition of the variegated world of aggada existing to date. Likewise, Albeck re-edited the work of Zunz (see above). Furthermore, Albeck wrote a commentary to the six Orders of the Mishna, *Mishna* (1952-8), the importance of which is that it not necessarily depends on the comments found in the two Talmudim. The vocalization of the text published with this commentary was done by H. YALON, who also published *Vocalization*, an important contribution to our knowledge of the particular character of Mishnaic grammar. The other work accompanying the commentary is Albeck's own *Introduction*. His *Babli and Yerushalmi* reflects much erudition and innovation but cannot really serve as an introduction to the Talmudim.

Four volumes of the writings of G. ALON have been published after his early death in 1950: *Toledot* in two volumes, now translated into English, *The Jews*; and another two of *Studies*, the largest part of which were also translated, *Jews, Judaism*. His works elucidate the world of Oral Tora and its Sages with profound vision and masterly treatment of a range of sources, within a comprehensive view of Jewish history and culture.

Starting in 1929, Saul LIEBERMAN published a long series of books, articles and text editions covering the various areas of talmudic literature. His great contribution to scholarship is in the philological elucidation of the texts and the exact exposition of the sources. His main accomplishment is the text edition and commentary of the Tosefta, *Tosefta ki-Fshutah*, running up to the Order *Nashim* (1955-73); the three *Bavot* of Order *Nezikin* will be published posthumously. It is the most comprehensive scientific commentary on a rabbinic document as a whole which exists. It was preceded by the four volumes of *Tosefet Rishonim*, which collect and comment on the scattered medieval Tosefta quotations. Many of his researches deal with the connections between Jewish life and literature and Greek culture; part of them were collected in *Greek* and *Hellenism*. Several scholars disagreed with him on the extent of Hellenistic influence, and in his later publications, Lieberman himself tended to a more reserved position.

From 1932 onwards, Benjamin DE VRIES wrote a number of articles on talmudic texts and the history of the Halakha. He contributed much to our understanding of major halakhic problems, especially relating to the transition from the Tannaic to the Amoraic period. Most of his articles were collected in the two volumes, *Studies* and *Mehkarim*. For a full bibliography see the *Memorial Volume*.

The history of halakha and aggada, both in their inner development and in their contacts with the Hellenistic and Christian surroundings, is elucidated in tens of articles written by E.E. URBACH. Special mention must be made of his large volume, *Sages*, which treats many aspects of the religious thought of the Sages while incorporating the results of philological and historical scholarship.

A recent general introduction to talmudic literature is MELAMMED, *Introduction*, which gives not a not a full introduction but, as explained in the preface, 'Introductory Chapters' mainly covering technical aspects of the halakhic collections. Of importance is also the most recent edition of STRACK's *Introduction*: STRACK-STEMBERGER, *Einleitung*. It is a reasonably full introduction which covers the main documents, stressing the technical aspects and rich in bibliography up to 1980.

A considerable portion of the Halakha and of talmudic tradition in general is concerned with law and court procedures. Law and jurisdiction were a subject of teaching and literary creation in the Houses of Study. The study of this aspect of rabbinic literature has much developed during the last few generations. One of the founders of the scientific study of talmudic law was Asher GULAK (1881-1940). His more important works are: *Das Urkundenwesen*, a comparative study of contracts and deeds; the four-volume *Yesodei ha-mishpat ha-ivri*; *Le-heker toledot* (on the law of property); and *Toledot ha-mishpat* (on the law of obligation). Other works in this category are COHEN, *Law and Tradition* and *Jewish and Roman Law*; ELON, *Jewish Law*.

Of the auxiliary works, the concordances of H.Y. KASOWSKI must be mentioned first of all: *Otsar leshon ha-Mishna*; *Otsar leshon ha-Tosefta*; and *Otsar leshon ha-Talmud* (on the Babylonian Talmud) in 41 vols. (1954-82), which was finished by B. KASOWSKI. The latter also added *Otsar ha-shemot*, an index of names in the Babylonian Talmud. In addition, he compiled concordances on Tannaic midrash collections: *Otsar leshon ha-Tannaim*, on the *Mechilta*, *Sifra* and *Sifrei*. A concordance to the Palestinian Talmud by M. KOSOVSKY (*Concordance*) has also begun to appear.

The situation with dictionaries is deplorable. Those available were compiled around the turn of the century and do not reflect the important recent developments in philology and textual criticism. Thus we have to do with LEVY, *Wörterbuch* (1876-89); KOHUT, *Arukh* (1926); JASTROW, *Dictionary* (1903); DALMAN, *Handwörterbuch* (1922, 1938). The latter work, unlike the others, does not give references and quotations. A special dictionary for Greek and Latin words is KRAUSS, *Lehnwörter* (1898-99).

Publication of a talmudic encyclopedia was started by M. GUTTMANN, *Mafteah ha-Talmud*. Four volumes appeared (1906-30),and the compilation of the remaining material was completed but it went lost in the Holocaust. BERLIN-ZEVIN, *Entsiklopedia talmudit*, mainly covering halakhic topics, is being published since 1946; so far 17 vols. appeared (up to the letter *het*). While this is a handsome and resourceful encyclopedia, it does not follow any method of critical, philological and historical scholarship.

הֶשֵׁב וְעָשָׂה מְלָאכוֹת הַרְבֵּה בְשַׁבָּתוֹת
הַרְבֵּה אֵינוֹ חַיָּיב חַטָּאת אַחַת חִזֵּר וְיָדַע
עִיקָּר שַׁבָּת וְעָשָׂה מְלָאכוֹת הַרְבֵּה
בְּשַׁבָּתוֹת הַרְבֵּה חַיָּיב עַל כָּל מְלָאכָה
וּמְלָאכָה הָעוֹשֶׂה מְלָאכוֹת הַרְבֵּה
מֵעֵין מְלָאכָה אַחַת אֵינוֹ חַיָּיב אֶלָּא
חַטָּאת אַחַת ב אֲבוֹת מְלָאכוֹת
אַרְבָּעִים חָסֵר אַחַת הַזּוֹרֵעַ שֶׁהוּא זוֹרֵעַ
הַמַּעֲמִיר הַדָּשׁ וְהַזּוֹרֶה הַבּוֹרֵר הַטּוֹחֵן
הַמְרַקֵּד הַלָּשׁ וְהָאוֹפֶה הַגּוֹזֵז אֶת
הַצֶּמֶר הַמְלַבְּנוֹ וְהַמְנַפְּצוֹ וְהַצּוֹבְעוֹ
וְהַטּוֹוֵהוּ הַמֵּסַךְ וְהָעוֹשֶׂה שְׁנֵי בָתֵּי
נִירִים הָאוֹרֵג שְׁנֵי חוּטִים וְהַבּוֹצֵעַ
שְׁנֵי חוּטִים הַקּוֹשֵׁר וְהַמַּתִּיר וְהַתּוֹפֵר
שְׁתֵּי תְפִירוֹת וְהַקּוֹרֵעַ עַל מְנָת לִתְפּוֹר
שְׁתֵּי תְפִירוֹת ג הַצָּד צְבִי הַ
הַשּׁוֹחֲטוֹ וְהַמַּפְשִׁיטוֹ וְהַמּוֹלְחוֹ וְ
וְהַמְעַבְּדוֹ וְהַמְמַחֲקוֹ וְהַמְחַתְּכוֹ הַכּוֹתֵב
שְׁתֵּי אוֹתִיּוֹת וְהַמּוֹחֵק עַל מְנָת לִכְתּוֹב
שְׁתֵּי אוֹתִיּוֹת ד הַבּוֹנֶה וְהַסּוֹתֵר
וְהַמְכַבֶּה וְהַמַּבְעִיר וְהַמַּכֶּה בְפַטִּישׁ
וְהַמּוֹצִיא מֵרְשׁוּת לִרְשׁוּת אֵלּוּ אֲבוֹת
מְלָאכוֹת אַרְבָּעִים חָסֵר אַחַת ה
וְעוֹד כְּלָל אַחֵר אָמְרוּ כָּל הַכָּשֵׁר לְהַצְנִיעַ
יִצְנְעוּ כָּמוֹהוּ הוֹצִיאוֹ בְּשַׁבָּת חַיָּיב
עָלָיו חַטָּאת וְכָל שֶׁאֵינוֹ כָּשֵׁר לְהַצְנִיעַ
יְאֵין מַצְנִיעִין כָּמוֹהוּ הוֹצִיאוֹ בְשַׁבַּת
אֵינוֹ חַיָּיב אֶלָּא לַמַּצְנִיעוֹ ו

הַמּוֹצִיא אֶת הַתֶּבֶן כִּמְלֹא פִי פָרָה עֵצָה
כִּמְלֹא פִי גָמָל עָמִיר כִּמְלֹא פִי טָלֶה
עֲשָׂבִים כִּמְלֹא פִי גְדִי עָלֵי שׁוּם
וְעָלֵי בְצָלִים לַחִים כִּגְרוֹגֶרֶת יְבֵשִׁים
כִּמְלֹא פִי גְדִי אֵינָן מִצְטָרְפִין זֶה
עִם זֶה מִפְּנֵי שֶׁלֹּא שָׁווּ בְּשִׁעוּרֵיהֶם
הַמּוֹצִיא אֱלִים כַּגְרוֹגֶרֶת מִצְטָרְפִין
וְזֶה עִם זֶה מִפְּנֵי שֶׁשָּׁווּ בְּשִׁעוּרֵיהֶם
חוּץ מִקְּלִיפֵּיהֶם וְגַלְעִינֵיהֶם וְעֻקְצֵיהֶן
וְסוּבָּן וּמוּרְסָנָן ר יְהוּדָה אוֹמֵר חוּץ
מִקְּלִיפֵּי עֲדָשִׁים הַמִּתְבַּשְּׁלוֹת עִמָּהֶם
פ ז ה ל ו
הַמּוֹצִיא יַיִן כְּדֵי מְזִיגַת הַכּוֹס חָלָב
כְּדֵי גְמִיעָה וּדְבַשׁ כְּדֵי לִיתֵּן עַל הַכָּתִית
שֶׁמֶן כְּדֵי לָסוּךְ אֵבָר קָטֹן מַיִם כְּדֵי
לָשׁוּף אֶת הַקִּילוֹרִית וּשְׁאָר כָּל הַמַּשְׁקִין
בִּרְבִיעִית וְכָל הַשּׁוֹפָכִים בִּרְבִיעִית
ר שִׁמְעוֹן אוֹמֵר כּוּלָּם בִּרְבִיעִית לֹא
אָמְרוּ כָל הַשִּׁעוּרִים הָאֵלּוּ אֶלָּא
לְמַצְנִיעֵיהֶם ב הַמּוֹצִיא חֶבֶל
כְּדֵי לַעֲשׂוֹת לוֹ אֹזֶן לַקֻּפָּה גֶּמִי כְּדֵי לַעֲשׂוֹת
תְּלִי לְנָפָה וְלִכְבָרָה ר יְהוּדָה אוֹמֵר כְּדֵי
לִיטּוֹל מִמֶּנּוּ מִדַּת מִנְעַל לַקָּטָן נְיָר כְּדֵי
לִכְתּוֹב עָלָיו קֶשֶׁר מוֹכְסִים הַמּוֹצִיא
קֶשֶׁר שֶׁל מוֹכְסִים חַיָּיב נְיָר פָּסוּל
כְּדֵי לִכְרוֹךְ עַל פִּי צְלוֹחִית קְטַנָּה
שֶׁל פְּלַיְטוֹן ג עוֹר כְּדֵי לַעֲשׂוֹת
קָמִיעַ קְלָף כְּדֵי לִכְתּוֹב עָלָיו פָּרָשָׁה

MS. Kaufmann, Mishna *Shabbat* 7:1-8:3 (Budapest, Library of the Hungarian Academy of Sciences, Hebr. MS. A 50).
7:2-4 (traditional division, 7:2) enumerates the thirty-nine 'Principal classes of labour' forbidden on the Sabbath; see p. 156.

Chapter Three

Halakha

Shmuel Safrai

General Characteristics

DEFINITION AND SIGNIFICANCE

One of the most important elements of Jewish literature in the period under discussion is what is known as הלכה halakha, that is to say, the sum total of rules and laws – derived from the Bible, from religious thought and teaching, from jurisprudence and custom – that govern all aspects of Jewish life.

As is the case with with other technical terms, nowhere in rabbinic literature from the talmudic period do we find any attempt to define, or even to interpret, the word *halakha*. It is only in the *Arukh*, the eleventh century talmudic lexicon compiled by R. Natan of Rome, that two definitions are suggested: 'something that goes on (*holekh u-ba*) from beginning to end'; and, 'that in which Israel goes'.[1]

Modern scholars have proposed to trace the word to the Aramaic administrative term הלך *halakh* (Ezra 4:13) or הלכא *halkha*, meaning a (land) tax. Our 'halakha' would then originally have the same meaning as the Latin *regula* (whence the modern 'règle', 'Regel', 'rule') which also could denote a fixed land tax. In effect, the prime meaning of halakha would be 'fixed rule'.[2]

Whatever the original meaning may have been, the wider phenomenon of halakha encompasses both: 'that in which Israel goes', i.e., the ways of life of the Jewish people, and the fixed laws which emerged from the thought and study of the Pharisaic Sages and other circles within Jewish society. Therefore an adequate understanding of the literature of halakha cannot be derived merely from the literary form in which it was eventually fixed and preserved, but requires an insight into the nature and historical development of halakha. The aim of the present survey is to contribute to that insight.

In time, the term came to denote several things: 1) 'a halakha', a law, the smallest unit of a halakhic collection, such as 'a halakha' from the Tosefta –

---

[1] *Arukh completum* 3, 208.
[2] See Lieberman, *Hellenism*, 83 n.3, with references to further literature. The Greek χανών had the same meaning: fixed land tax – at least since the 4th cent. c.e.

involving the plural 'halakhot'; 2) 'the halakha' as the accepted law, where different opinions exist, such as in the usage, 'A says. . . , B says, but the halakha is . . .'; 3) halakha (or 'halakhot') as an object of study and a literary genre, as opposed to aggada (aggadot); 4) 'the Halakha' as the legal aspect of Jewish life and the legal tradition of Judaism, in which one can distinguish, for example, between the halakha of the Sages and the halakha of Qumran.

That halakha occupied a place of prime importance in Jewish literature, as well as in life and thought, in the periods of the Second Temple and the Talmud, we can see from various sources. First of all, there are the halakhic collections which reached final redaction beginning about the end of the second century C.E., and which by their size, literary form and content reflect the great importance attached to them. Furthermore, the great significance of halakha can also be seen in the other genres of rabbinic literature, such as the various midrash collections and the Targumim.[3] We could easily get the impression that preoccupation with halakha was always regarded as the very essence of Oral Tora. That would clearly be an exaggeration, as it would also be exaggerated to assume that among all Pharisaic teachers and their circles (*havurot*) halakha was the most important subject of teaching. However, there can be no doubt that in their circles the study and creation of halakha was a basic object of attention.[4]

This internal evidence of the rabbinic tradition can be augmented with other testimony. Thus we know that even within circles which, to a greater or lesser extent, were quite remote from the world of the Pharisaic Sages, halakha occupied a a substantial place in thought and literature. In the writings of the Dead Sea sect, as well as in related earlier works such as the Book of *Jubilees*, we find many halakhic elements and discussions, and some of these works are in fact primarily halakhic in content.[5] Furthermore, despite their opposition to particular halakhic details, the Gospels, too, contain many elements of halakhic discussion, testifying to the importance of halakha even in the world of earliest Christianity.[6] Finally, the great significance of Halakha is confirmed by sources close to Pharisaic circles. Many halakhic elements can be discerned in the narratives dating from the early Second Temple period, such as Judith and Tobit, or in historical works such as First Maccabees,[7] just as halakhic discussions are to be found in the writings of Philo and Josephus.[8]

[3] Cf. Albeck, 'External Halakha'; Heinemann, 'Early Halakha'.
[4] For some examples illustrating this see *M. Ber.* 8:1; *T. Ed.* 1:1; *T. Sota* 7:21; *A.R.N.* a 27 (41b); *B.T. Tem.* 14a.
[5] In the eyes of the Pharisees, the Dead Sea sect would belong to 'those who write halakhot', but from the historian's point of view, their library gives us invaluable information as to the actual existence of halakhic genres and documents in the middle of the Second Temple period. See the *Temple Scroll*, the *Damascus Covenant* and large parts of the *Community Rule*.
[6] See Matt 5:31-37, 12:1-12; Mark 7:1-22; Luke 6:1-11, 2:21-41.
[7] On Judith and 1 Maccabees see below. On Tobit see Tob 1:6-8; 2:1; 2:9; 7:4 (particularly according to the longer version).
[8] For Josephus, see esp. *Ant.* 4:1; for Philo, e.g., *De spec. leg., passim.*

HALAKHA AND THE BIBLE

The biblical laws found in the Tora, to a lesser degree in the prophets, and also in the Hagiographa, can be said to govern all areas of life. The Tora laws contain not merely rules for religious ceremony, Sabbath and festivals, but also statutes whose purpose is to shape the life of society, including such areas as legal procedure, the position and function of the king, and all of family life. Sometimes these laws are given with great detail in a full discourse which includes the religious concepts behind them, as in the case of the laws of the Sabbatical Year and the Jubilee, the rules of slavery or of the Sabbath. In other areas, the Tora barely indicates such religious ideas, while the commandments which could follow from them are merely hinted at.

Both in regard of those elaborate topics of biblical law and of such as are barely mentioned at all, the Halakha represents a considerable further development. In all areas of halakha, as we find it crystallized in the collections of the Tannaim and Amoraim and, more incidentally, in Jewish writings of the Second Temple period, details and definitions not found in the Tora were added. Two examples from different areas may illustrate this.

The commandment to observe the Sabbath and not to work on that day is found several times in the Tora, both in general terms and in specific prohibitions. In the Ten Commandments, a general rule is given: 'Remember the Sabbath day to keep it holy, six days shalt thou labour . . . but on the seventh day is a Sabbath unto the Lord thy God, in it thou shalt not do any work' (Exod 20:8-10). Elsewhere, the Tora specifies what are forbidden activities, such as 'In ploughing and in harvesting thou shalt rest' (Exod 34:21), and 'Thou shalt kindle no fire' (Exod 35:3). In the prophetic writings and the Hagiographa, other items are added, such as the prohibition to sell (Amos 8:5), to carry from domain to domain (Jer 17:21f.) and other prohibitions (see Neh 13:15f.). In addition, the religious concepts embodied in the Sabbath are made explicit (e.g. Gen 2:1-3; Exod 20:8-11; 31:12-17; Deut 5:13-15). All this makes the Sabbath a relatively elaborate topic in the Bible, although the laws are not very detailed. The halakha of Oral Tora, however, developed a complete system of Sabbath laws that makes the biblical laws seem rudimentary. The Mishna itemizes thirty-nine 'principal classes of labour', eleven of which are concerned with agriculture, thirteen with producing garments, nine with preparing parchment for writing and the writing itself, and five labours involved in the manufacture of utensils; the remaining one is 'carrying from domain to domain'.[9] These 'principal classes of work' or 'main labours' in turn have 'subordinate labours'[10] which resemble or are connected with a principal labour. Additional types of labour were prohibited because of *shevut*, i.e., the principle of 'the day of rest'. This

---

[9] *M. Shabb.* 7ff. See also pp. 89 and 156. It appears that there existed other systems. An allusion to a system of twenty-two labours, according to the number of labours performed in the creation of the world, is found in *Jub.* 2:23.

[10] *P.T. Shabb.* 7, 9d.

prohibition was seen as not founded on the Bible but on the authority of the Sages, though it was also supported by midrash.[11] There is also the category of *muktse*, which implies an object that has been 'put aside' (the literal meaning) and was not ready on Friday for use on the Sabbath and therefore may not be used, moved about or eaten. This prohibition is found as early as in the Book of *Jubilees*, and also in the *Damascus Covenant*.[12] Furthermore, the Tora states in a general way that the Seventh Day is 'a holy Sabbath of solemn rest unto the Lord' (Exod 35:2), and similar expressions. The Sages interpreted these statements as being the basis for the custom and the precept to gather together on Sabbath in order to hear the word of the Lord. Such gatherings were held in official, formal settings, in synagogues, or more informally, in the form of meetings of small groups in houses belonging to a courtyard, or even in a storehouse for straw which had been vacated for that purpose. This we learn from many sources of the Second Temple period and after.[13]

The Sages were cognizant of these multiple and far-reaching innovations. An ancient mishna from the days of the Temple emphasizes that the Sabbath laws as expounded in Oral Tora have but a small basis in Scripture and in that respect are 'as mountains hanging by a hair, for Scripture is scanty and the halakhot are many.'[14]

A second example is concerned with an area of halakha no less important than the Sabbath in Second Temple life, namely, ritual purity. The mishna just quoted also states that 'Purity and impurity . . . have firm foundation.' Indeed, these matters are dealt with in much more detail than the Sabbath laws, appearing as they do in Leviticus in various contexts, and several times in Numbers as well. But even here, the distance between biblical law and Tannaic halakha is vast. The Halakha established a detailed system of 'Main sources of impurity': a person who had contact with a corpse, the eight types of dead 'creeping things', a male or female who had a flux of any type, and anything infected with 'leprosy'. The corpse itself is considered the 'Source of sources of impurity' and as such forms the highest category of impurity. A detailed gradation of the impurity emanating from these sources was established: first, second and third degree defilements. It was also set forth which things could be rendered impure by contact with something impure in the first or second degree, and which things required still other conditions for becoming impure. And most important, finally, the purification procedures corresponding to each of the various categories of impurity were established. All of this is the subject of an entire Order of the Mishna, and not the smallest: *Toharot*.

As seen above, the halakhic areas of Sabbath and purity are clearly represented already in the Tora. There exist, however, broad areas which are merely

---

[11] *Mekh., ki tisa* beginning (p. 340) links the *shevut* category to Scripture.

[12] *Jub.* 50:8; CD 10:22. See also above p. 91.

[13] Some examples: *M. Shabb.* 16:1; 18:1; *M. Er.* 3:5; Acts 15:21; Philo, *Quod omn.* 81; *Mos.* 2:211; Josephus, *Ag. Ap.* 2:175.

[14] *M. Hag.* 1:8. On its antiquity see Epstein, *Tannaitic Literature*, 46ff.

hinted at by a generalized statement in the Tora. For example, the Tora contains almost no detailed laws regarding commerce. What one finds is: 'Thou shalt not steal' (Exod 20:13); or 'If ye sell to your neighbour or buy from your neighbour, thou shalt not wrong one another' (Lev 25:14); and some other scattered verses of a similar nature. The Halakha, however, devised from ancient times legal procedures regarding such matters as sale, commerce, overreaching and voiding of purchase, the writing of contracts, and legal evidence. The Sages were often able to find some support for these sets of halakhot in Scripture, but in other cases they could find nothing but such general verses as 'Thou shalt not wrong one another'.[15]

Another important area of Jewish life not covered in the Tora is the elaborate system of worship which consists of the public reading of the Tora, public and private prayer, the recitation of the *shema*, and benedictions to be said before and after eating, drinking, and any other enjoyment, including the privilege of fulfilling a commandment or studying Tora. None of the halakhot governing this system have any explicit scriptural support and at best constitute a fulfilment of the broad precept to 'love the Lord with all thy heart' or 'to fear the Lord and to love Him'.

The above examples are, like other sets of halakhot, a practical realization of remote scriptural laws in the actual life of the nation. But they are more. As an integral part of Oral Tora, the Halakha was not just an interpretation and actualization of the Written Tora, but a living tradition of learning and teaching, with an unfailing impetus towards new creation and insight. Throughout the period under discussion, the Tora and its commandments were contemplated not only in order to obtain solutions to practical problems, but also out of the desire to study the Tora for its own sake. It is typical of Jewish tradition that this desire brought forth not only new religious insights and concepts, but also new halakhot.

THE SCOPE OF THE HALAKHA

While, as we have said, the biblical laws touch on all areas of life, they leave much to be filled in, not only in the details but also in extensive areas such as community worship and commercial life. It was, in the view of the Sages, Oral Tora which would meet this need, through the learning process leading to practical realization, and concentrated study for its own sake. This process took place to a great extent during the Second Temple period. Certainly, the halakha of the Sages was to pass through still another stage of great development in the Tannaic and Amoraic periods. It was then that the classification, definition and specification of halakhot, likewise the establishment of general principles, came to the fruition which largely gave the Halakha its present shape. Not the least important, it was then that the Halakha found its literary formulation in the

---

[15] See e.g. the discussions in *B.T. Bava M.* 35a; *B.T. Sanh.* 32b.

classical collections in which it was preserved – Mishna, Tosefta and the Talmudim. However, there is no doubt that already many generations before the
destruction of the Second Temple there existed a large number of halakhot and
sets of halakhot encompassing all areas of life – though possibly in other forms
and formulations than those preserved. In the next section we shall study some
of the external evidence which allows us to draw this conclusion.

Thus in the Second Temple era, and even more so in the Tannaic and
Amoraic periods, the halakha of the Sages intended to regulate and govern
human life from the moment of birth, through education and studies, adoles-
cence and marriage, until one's last days, death, burial, and the mourning rites
performed for the deceased. It shaped the activities of man through the whole
day, beginning with the recitation of the *shema* upon arising from sleep, the
conduct of meals, and so on until returning to sleep. It delineated the weekday
and the Sabbath, the festivals and the yearly cycle. Finally, many detailed
halakhot can be found, even from the Second Temple era, regarding public law,
judicial procedures, and the ways of supplying municipal and national services.

This all-embracing scope of the Halakha, as we know it from the various
sources, can be seen to be consonant with the conception of the Sages that no
realm of human life is exempt from the divine commission implied in the Tora.
In the teaching of Sages such as Hillel the Elder, the human body, for example,
is not a negative concept that stands in contrast to man's spirit and soul, but is to
be cared for by commandment of the Creator who created man in His image.[16]
Likewise, a meal is a form of divine worship, and a festive table at which words
of Tora are spoken is comparable to the altar, just as the participants are
regarded as though eating from the divine table.[17] There is an intimate connection between such ordinary human actions and man's divine commission; which
implies that the commandments do not merely serve a purpose of utility. The
labour which a man performs 'for the sake of the habitation of the world' (a
characteristic concept and halakhic principle of the Sages) not only keeps him
from robbery and evil deeds, but is actually seen as a moral-religious value in its
own right and as a means of human perfection.[18] So too, the Land of Israel is not
merely the geographic area where the specific commandments of tithes, heave-
offerings and the Sabbatical year can be performed; it is also the Land of God, a
holy land with its own uniqueness, just as the city of Jerusalem is sanctified and
specifically distinguished from the rest of the Land.[19]

Nor did the Sages of the Second Temple period regard the Tora as directed to
the Jews only, but rather as encompassing all humankind. True, they did not
think or even hope that the nations of the world should join the Jewish people,
or would do so in the future, but neither did they think that all those who do not
accept the yoke of the Tora and all of its commandments would be condemned

[16] See above p. 107.
[17] *M. Avot* 2:13.
[18] See esp. *A.R.N.* a 11 (22b) and b 21 (*ib.*).
[19] See *M. Kelim* 1:6-9.

to perdition. They viewed all inhabitants of the world as being encompassed in man's commission, and accordingly, the Halakha established the minimal demands incumbent upon all mankind for the sake of humanity: the so-called Noahic commandments.[20]

In this overall view, there is an organic connection between halakha and aggada. All the above viewpoints are expressed both in aggadic dicta and homilies on Scripture, and in halakhot and halakhic principles. Throughout the period in which the halakha of the Sages developed, we can point to a mutual dependence between the creation of halakha and of aggada. The Halakha influenced the creation of aggadic tales interpreting the deeds of the Patriarchs and the Bible in general, as well as the creation of stories, parables and ethical dicta.[21] On the other hand, we can point to many halakhot that were formulated under the influence of religious or social ideas current in aggadic literature. For example, beginning in the time of Shemaya (one of the Pairs, c. 50-20 B.C.E.) we have sayings in praise of labour.[22] In the Mishna, this appreciation finds its halakhic expression when it is ruled that men who concern themselves with occupations that do not further 'the habitation of the world' – such as professional dice-players or those gambling with pigeons – are disqualified from serving as judges or legal witnesses.[23] This creative mutuality between halakha and aggada underscores once more the pervasiveness of the Halakha in the life and thought of the nation. Conversely, the nature of halakha and its development can be adequately understood only from the perspective of this correlation with religious thought and aggada.

There was also a marked internal development of legal thought, which left its imprint on the development of the Halakha. The Halakha, as a set of rules governing all of life, had an organic unity which allowed the Sages to transfer concepts, definition and exegetical methods from one halakhic domain to another. Halakhic concepts such as a man's intention and 'acceptance' were transferred from the laws of sale to the sphere of purity and impurity, in order to be able to determine whether a man regards an object as a utensil, which is susceptible of defilement.[24] The application of any concept in a different halakhic area led to the clarification and innovation of many halakhot. As we shall observe below, there were also halakhot which originated in a decree, such as the decree of Shimon ben Shetah (c. 80-50 B.C.E.) establishing the *ketuba*

---

[20] Precisely which commandments and how many in total are included is subject to variation. Later Tannaic tradition fixes it at seven; see *T. Av. Zar.* 8:4-6 and parallels. See Flusser - Safrai, 'Aposteldekret'.

[21] The Halakha forbids the keeping of small cattle because they eat from the fields of others. Accordingly, the stories of the Patriarchs, who were shepherds, were interpreted so as not to contradict the Halakha, even to the extent that the Patriarchs were not shepherds at all, or at least shepherds who did respect the possessions of others. See the Targumim to Gen 25:27 and *Exod. R.* 2,3.

[22] *M. Avot* 1:10.

[23] *M. Sanh.* 3:3; *T. Sanh.* 5:2.

[24] See *M. Kelim* ch. 2ff., and many sugyot in the Talmudim.

(marriage contract)[25] or that of Hillel the Elder (c. 20 B.C.E. - 20 C.E.) who ordained the *prozbul*, an economic measure related to the Sabbatical Year.[26] Such decrees became the foundation for the creation of new halakhot as though they had been written in the Tora, or could serve as a basis for clarification when a legal decision was needed or a difficult problem arose in Tora study.

The wide scope of the Halakha is also expressed in the close connection between the teaching in the academies and the solving of problems which might arise in the life of the community. Almost throughout the period under investigation, the centres of Tora study served at the same time as places of instruction in practical conduct and as lawcourts. Thus, the Book of Judith relates how the people of Bethulia sent to Jerusalem to inquire of the Elders how to act with regard to tithes and heave-offerings during the siege.[27] In a later period, the Alexandrians came before Hillel the Elder to ask questions regarding the *ketuba* and other aspects of marriage.[28] And about one of Hillel's descendants, Rabban Shimon ben Gamliel the Elder (died during the first Roman War), it is reported that he issued a decree from the Great Court in order to bring down the soaring prices of doves, the offerings of the poor.[29] The period following the destruction of the Temple abounds with sources identifying the House of Study as the place to which people came to make enquiries about practical problems and for trials. This situation was an important factor in the development and expansion of the Halakha.

This is not to say that the halakha of the Sages was a monolithic system that allowed no freedom of choice. Despite its pervasiveness and great attention to detail, in almost every area the Halakha left considerable space for the individual to decide according to his own will or inclination, the degree of his piety or his personal and local custom. Thus, in the Halakha frequent allowances are made for the custom of a particular place, and in the Mishna it is occasionally reported that in one place the custom was such, while elsewhere it was otherwise, and no attempt is made to decide between the two. Sometimes these variations in local custom even concerned fundamental halakhic questions.[30]

HALAKHA AND LIFE IN THE TANNAIC PERIOD

The sources dating from the early Second Temple period until the end of the Tannaic era reveal a close relation between the halakha of the Sages and the realities of ordinary human life. In contrast to the message of the prophets, the Halakha was not a vision for the future, with its directions addressed to the king

---

[25] *P.T. Ket.* ch. 8 end.
[26] *M. Shev.* 10:3.
[27] Jdt 11:13f.
[28] *P.T. Ket.* ch. 8 end.
[29] *M. Ker.* 1:7; *T. Ker.* 1:10.
[30] See *M. Pea* 1:2; and esp. *M. Pes.* ch. 4 and *T. Pes.* 2:17-20. See also below, on Beit Shammai and Beit Hillel.

and the leading priests. Nor was the Halakha a theoretical construction imposed upon the community in a 'legalistic' way. Characteristic of the Halakha as taught by the Sages was the desire to improve and sanctify the life of society through practical rules and measures. They expounded the Tora and created halakhot within the actual realities of personal and communal life, and there was a vital correspondence between the teaching of the Sages and the ways of life of society and the problems arising within it (see pp. 63-69). We can perceive a difference here with the Essenes: their way of life as well as their teachings show that their aim was not to edify the life of the community of Israel as a whole. By contrast, the saying of Hillel, which, incidentally, may have been directed against movements such as those of the Essenes, expresses well the attitude of the Sages: 'Do not separate from the community' (*Avot* 2:5).

The tractates *Berakhot* in Mishna and Tosefta which deal with the rules for reciting the *shema*, prayer and the various benedictions, do not give one the impression that these rules are mere theoretical constructions. We find here people reciting the *shema* in various circumstances, and saying grace before and after their meals; we read what benedictions they said over enjoyments derived from seeing wise or beautiful human beings or sights of nature. They recited a special benediction before performing a ritual commandment, out of the awareness that in observing the commandment they were performing a sacred act. Corroboration of these impressions is obtained from other sources, such as reports and narratives scattered throughout Tannaic and Amoraic literature. Various archeological finds, including letters which were discovered recently, confirm many details of the general picture which emerges from the Tannaic sources. While we must take into account that Tannaic halakha as preserved has undergone a great deal of regulating and re-formulating as regards prayers and benedictions, largely the same reality is found reflected in sources from earlier periods, e.g., Josephus and the Jewish stratum of the early Christian sources.

The same can be said for such halakhot as those of *pea* (corner of the field) and *kilayim* (diverse kinds), the sabbatical year, damage laws, and, last but not least, purity rules. Contrary to opinions held in the scholarly world but which are based on a limited view of the sources, the purity rules as taught by the Pharisaic-rabbinic Sages were widely observed in the Second Temple period and for some generations after the destruction of the Temple.[31]

A very important area of halakha in this connection, about which we have much and varied information, is the Sabbatical Year. The halakhot of the Seventh Year were without doubt among the most difficult from an economic point of view. The laws of the Tora are already quite demanding, and added to them were the prohibitions of Oral Tora, such as those against eating wild growths or working the land during the sixth year for the benefit of the seventh. Reviewing the entire system of laws of the sabbatical year, we might find it rather unrealistic and utopian. However, a careful examination of the talmudic

---

[31] See Alon, *Jews, Judaism*, 190-234; Safrai in *Compendia* I/2, 828-32.

and other sources (Maccabees, Philo, Josephus, Bar Kokhba papyri, etc.) lends firm support to the assumption that the picture which emerges from halakhic literature indeed represents actual life in Second Temple and Tannaic times. Certain extraneous factors, e.g., the unwillingness of the Roman government to free the Jews from taxes, caused some breaches in the observance of the Seventh Year. In general, however, the pertinent commandments were observed in all their details. The halakhot of the Seventh Year, we conclude, were not theoretical constructions but were addressed to a wide community of observant Jews.[32]

As we stated with regard to prayer, we should take into account the degree of development which took place as regards application, specification, expansion or contraction of the various halakhot. But those changes that took place should not be perceived as being detached from reality. Both the halakhic teachers of the Halakha and the community which observed it – and of which the teachers were full members in every sense – were concerned with concrete reality and practical problems. The halakhic questions and cases that have been preserved illustrate this. We shall give some examples from the sphere of agriculture, the main economic basis of society.

> If a man sowed two kinds of wheat and made up one threshing-floor, he grants one *pea* (corner of the field left for the poor); but if two threshing-floors, two *peot*. It once happened that R. Shimon of Mitspe sowed his field (in two kinds of wheat) before Rabban Gamliel, and they went up to the Chamber of Hewn Stone to inquire . . .[33]

While the halakha at the beginning of the quotation might create a theoretical and 'legalistic' impression, the case following it shows that it reflects a practical situation from the Second Temple period. Similar examples can be found. There are, for instance, the two cases having to do with the laws of *kilayim* for trees which are reported to have been settled by an itinerant student. In both instances (one was in the region of Ariah and the other in the irrigated field of Sepphoris) he ruled that the trees had to be cut down. The two cases were later brought before the Sages at Yavne, however, and while in the first case it was confirmed that 'that student spoke correctly', his other decision brought forth the question: 'Who was it that came up to you? – He is a disciple of Beit Shammai!'[34]

This affinity of the Halakha to the life of the community is further demonstrated if we take into account those areas of the Halakha which had no relevance to real life. This was a common phenomenon in law systems of that time. However, it may be more conspicuous in the tradition of Oral Tora, which not only preserves laws passed on from generation to generation, but also expounds the

---

[32] See Cohen, 'Eduyot'; Safrai, 'Sabbatical Year'.
[33] M. Pea 2:5-6.
[34] T. Kil. 1:3f.

Written Tora for its own sake, thus also in those areas of biblical law which had no application at that time. This is what is termed 'halakhot for the Messiah'.[35]

Several such 'theoretical' areas of halakha can be pointed out. For instance, there are many halakhot concerning the 'Hebrew bondman and handmaid', although, according to evidence in Tannaic literature itself, these institutions no longer existed during the Second Commonwealth.[36] However, that did not prevent the Sages from studying the relevant biblical laws and all the detailed rules resulting from them.[37] We may also point to the laws of the Jubilee Year (the Fiftieth Year, Lev 25). Unlike those of the Sabbatical Year, the biblical regulations of the Jubilee were not in force. The Sages explicitly mentioned the legal areas of the Jubilee and the Hebrew bondman together, stating that neither was in force in their day.[38] Likewise,while the Order of *Kodashim*, which deals with the Temple worship, in many chapters reflects late Second Temple practice, it also contains many halakhot innovated by the Sages of Yavne and Usha, which could only have been intended for the Temple to be built in the future. Similarly, the tractates *Sanhedrin-Makkot* record laws for capital crimes, many of which may date from the Second Temple period when capital cases were adjudicated. But there are also many halakhot from post-destruction period, when the courts were no longer allowed to do so. Several of these halakhot are even so speculative that they would be difficult to apply in actual court proceedings.[39] For example, the laws of the 'rebellious son' which are laid down in Deut 21:18-21 are so radically limited by Tannaic halakha, that Tannaic tradition itself drew the conclusion: 'The rebellious son never was and never shall be.'[40] A similar evaluation is given of the laws of 'house-leprosy' (Lev 13:33-53) which are taught in Mishna *Negaim,* chapters twelve and thirteen: 'The leprous house never was and never shall be; then why was it written? to teach you: study (the Tora for its own sake) and receive reward.'[41]

These subjects of 'theoretical halakha', however, make up only a part of the totality of the Halakha. By far the greatest part of the Halakha emerged from the realities of everyday life, or from theoretical considerations closely related to them.

Moreover, even those halakhot which were explicitly declared to be no longer in force were more than mere futuristic or utopian halakhot; in many instances, studying them did have an actual significance. Although, for exam-

---

[35] See *B.T. Zev.* 45a; *B.T. Sanh.* 51b.
[36] Urbach, 'Hilkhot avadim' argues that the institution of the Hebrew bondman did exist in the periods of the Second Temple and the Mishna. Our view, however, does not incline in that direction.
[37] *B.T. Gitt.* 65a; *B.T. Kidd.* 69a; *B.T. Ar.* 29a; cf. *P.T. Shevu.* 7, 37c.
[38] *Ib. ib.*
[39] E.g. the halakha that the accused may be sentenced to death only if the witnesses had warned him at the time he was committing the crime, and the accused has confirmed that he had heard the admonition yet persisted in perpetrating the crime; *T. Sanh.* 11:1-4; *P.T. Sanh.* 5, 22d-23a; *B.T. Sanh.* 80b.
[40] *T. Sanh.* 11:6; *B.T. Sanh.* 71a.
[41] *T. Neg.* 6:1.

ple, the Jubilee was not in force, the laws concerning it, as arranged in Scripture and in Oral Tora, had a decided influence on agrarian relationships. None of the land that was consecrated to the Temple remained in the possession of the Temple, but rather was put up for sale, while it was emphasized that the Temple had a primary religious duty to redeem 'the field of possession'.[42] In contrast to temples in other cultures, the Jerusalem Temple did not possess land. Tannaic tradition tells of a custom according to which a man would be disgraced for selling the 'field of his possession', even as a man would be glorified for redeeming his meadow and thus reclaiming it to his field of possession.[43] The Halakha also declares: 'No man is entitled to sell the field of his possession and keep (the money) in his belt . . . even to trade with it; unless he becomes impoverished, if he sold it his sale is invalid.'[44] The great influence of this ruling can be seen from the fact that for generations after the destruction of the Temple most of the land in Palestine remained in the possession of small farmers. Even the *colonatus* laws of the later Roman administration were only introduced in Palestine towards the end of the fourth century, considerably later than was normal in the Roman empire. It was only at that time that the balance of land ownership shifted tothe detriment of the small farmers.[45] Similarly, the 'theoretical' laws of the 'rebellious son' and of capital punishment do reflect, in their strict conditions which made capital punishment practically impossible, the humanization process of the Halakha. In this respect, they continue the tradition that is presented as the beginnings of Oral Tora – the instruction of the Men of the Great Assembly: 'Be moderate in judgement.'[46]

The reciprocal relationship between the Halakha and the life of the community was vital to many of the Sages, and this found expression not only in the content of their enactments, but also in explicit maxims: 'No decree is decreed for the community unless the majority are able to keep it,'[47] or, 'Any decree which a court enacts and most of the community do not accept it, is no decree.'[48] One of the most famous collections of prohibitive decrees are the Eighteen Decrees (see p. 192f.). Later Sages apparently regarded these decrees to be so binding that whereas normally the decree of one court could be abrogated by another, in regard to the Eighteen Decrees it was said that 'Even if Elijah and his court should come (and abrogate them) we would not listen to them.'[49] Nevertheless, in the days of R. Yehuda Nesia (mid-third century C.E.) one of

---

[42] Lev 27:16-24; *M. Ar.* chs. 7-9.

[43] *P.T. Ket.* 2, 26d; *P.T. Kidd.* 1, 60d.

[44] *T. Ar.* 5:6.

[45] See Gulak, *Toledot ha-mishpat*, 35-42, 135-7.

[46] *M. Avot* 1:1. My observations in this section do not agree with the approach of Wacholder, *Messianism and Mishna*.

[47] *T. Sota* 15:10; *B.T. Av. Zar.* 36a; *B.T. Hor.* 3b; *et al.*

[48] *P.T. Av. Zar.* 2, 41d; *P.T. Shabb.* 1, 3d; *B.T. Av. Zar.* 36a.

[49] *P.T. Shabb.* 1, 3d.

the decrees, the ban on gentile oil, was abrogated because, it was reported, the prohibition had not been accepted by the majority of the community.[50]

Origins of the Halakha

In this section, we shall review evidence from Second Temple writings which confirms the antiquity of halakhot preserved in rabbinic literature. The implication of this evidence varies. In some cases, the halakhic practice documented in these early sources is identical with Tannaic halakha. In other cases, it accords with ancient halakha that was later rejected, or with one out of several disputed opinions that are recorded in Tannaic literature. The Book of *Jubilees* even presents us with passages which testify to the antiquity of the halakha of the Sages by rejecting it. In this chapter, we must of necessity be selective. Systematic examination of all available sources will reveal much additional evidence. On the basis of that information, we can presume that many halakhot found in the Mishna and even in later collections in fact have their foundations in some ancient period and only represent a last stage of development.

This should, however, not be exaggerated into a general conclusion about Tannaic halakha. The simple fact is that the Mishna found its final redaction only by the end of the second century c.e., and that much development had taken place in the Tannaic period which preceded. We are entitled to speak of the ancient origins of any halakha contained in rabbinic literature only on the grounds of its contents, phrasing, early attribution, or other internal or external evidence.

It is true that there are such terms as 'Beforetime', or 'Such was the earlier mishna' or 'The earlier Sages used to say . . .' But the implication of these terms has often been overemphasized. For example, the mishnaic halakha, 'All utensils may be handled except for . . . (three exceptions),' receives the following comment in the Tosefta: '*At first* they used to say: Three utensils may be handled on the Sabbath: . . . *Afterwards* they kept adding and adding until they said: All utensils may be handled on the Sabbath except for . . .'[51] The two Talmudim ascribe this 'at first' to 'the days of Nehemiah'.[52] Naively following this attribution and thus exaggerating the meaning of the phrase 'at first', scholars dated this halakha to the early post-exilic period. But this attribution is clearly founded on the biblical account of Nehemiah's zeal for the Sabbath in opposition to prevailing practice. The 'at first' here is simply the previous Halakha which could be earlier by only a few generations, since the Sabbath halakha shows a development towards leniency in the latter part of the Second Temple period. Thus we should beware of hasty conclusions about halakhot from early Second Temple days or still earlier periods.

---

[50] See the Talmudim *ib*.

[51] *M. Shabb.* 17:1; *T. Shabb.* 14:1.

[52] *B.T. Shabb.* 123b; *P.T. Shabb.* 17, 16a.

With that in mind, we shall now turn to the evidence on the ancient origins of a number of rabbinic halakhot.

Talmudic tradition ascribes many halakhot and decrees to such biblical leaders as Moses,[53] Joshua,[54] David,[55] Ezra,[56] and others. It is hard to see in these attributions more than piety or literary creation, even where personalities from the early Second Temple period are concerned. Attributions of Second Temple halakhot to biblical heroes may be founded on interpretations of scriptural passages containing their statements,[57] and certain national institutions may be ascribed to biblical situations on the basis of external similarities.[58] Halakhic traditions with actual ascriptions are found only from the time of the first 'Pair' onwards, in the name of Yose ben Yoezer who lived during the first half of the second century B.C.E.[59] At the most, there may be some substance to the attribution of certain halakhot to Haggai and other early Second Temple prophets.[60]

On the other hand, we do find halakhot in the Mishna and other works which clearly predate the first Pair. In fact we can point to the appearance of halakha – rules based on laws or legal ideas found in the Tora, yet not identical with them – early in the Second Temple period, and sometimes already in the days of the First Temple. We shall give a clear example.

---

[53] Two examples among many: *B.T. Meg.* 32a, 'Moses ordained for Israel that they should ask and expound about the matters of each day: The halakhot of Passover on Passover, the halakhot of the Pentecost on Pentecost etc.' *P.T. Meg.* 4, 75a states: 'Moses ordained for Israel that they should read from the Tora on Sabbaths and festivals and on New Moons and on the intermediate days of festivals.'

[54] To Joshua were attributed in particular halakhot which order the relations between neighbours in the Land of Israel and the rights of the tribes in their territories; *B.T. Bava K.* 81b.

[55] *T. Taan.* 4(3):2 etc.

[56] *B.T. Bava K.* 82a; *B.T. Yev.* 86b etc.

[57] *M. Meg.* ch. 3 end enumerates Tora sections to be read in public on various occasions, concluding with the biblical basis for this injuction: 'For it is written: "And Moses declared unto the children of Israel the set feasts of the Lord" (Lev 23:44) – their respective commandment is to read each one in its set time.' The words 'And Moses declared' are understood to mean that Moses spoke about each festival on that festival itself (see *Sifra, Emor* 17, p. 103b) and on the basis of this interpretation the Mishna concludes that the commandment is to read on each festival the biblical section concerning that festival, and in addition, that it was Moses himself who gave this commandment. Finally, this held not only for the festivals: 'Moses ordained that the Tora should be read on Sabbaths (which are also mentioned in the verse) and on festivals and on New Moons and on the intermediate days of festivals, since it is written: "And Moses declared" etc.'

[58] In Josh 24:25 it says: 'So Joshua made a covenant . . . and set a statute and ordinance . . .' Tradition took these to mean not laws of the Tora but rules drawn up by Joshua himself, governing the relations between the tribes and between neighbours in their settling of the Land. Cf. *B.T. Bava K.* 81b and Nahmanides' commentary on Exod 15:25.

[59] *M. Ed.* 5:4; *M. Hag.* 2:2.

[60] *T. Kelim Bava B.* 2:3; *P.T. Yev.* 1, 3a; *B.T. Yev.* 16a; *B.T. Naz.* 53a *et al.*

The Halakha as formulated in the Mishna obligates every Jew to contribute yearly half a shekel, a contribution that goes toward the financing of the divine worship in the Temple as well as other public functions of the Temple.[61] The Tora, however, refers only to an exceptional command to contribute half a shekel (Exod 30:11-16), the reason being that a census was held and a plague among the people had to be warded off. Somehow, this one time payment was turned into a regular contribution. In 2 Chr 24:6ff., mention is made of the collection by King Joash of 'the tax levied by Moses',[62] and Neh 10:33f. mentions the yearly charge of 'the third part of a shekel for the service of the house of our God, for the showbread . . .'[63] This is basically the commandment of the half-shekel as contained in the Mishna,[64] and as described in various late Second Temple sources.[65] During the Hasmonean period, the donation of the half-shekel became a matter of principle, after a long struggle between Pharisees and Sadducees.[66] Thus we are confronted here with a halakha formulated in the Mishna, which dates back to the early Second or late First Temple period.

Other biblical evidence points in the same direction. We have referred to the fact that the Tora mentions only a few labours prohibited on the Sabbath. The Tora, furthermore, does not mention any specific prohibition of labour on the New Moon or anything that would distinguish the New Moon day, other than its special sacrifice (Num 28:11-15). Now in the prophetic books, especially towards the end of the First Temple period and the beginning of the Second, we find various additional laws. Several times the New Moon and the Sabbath are mentioned together as days when one should refrain from commerce,[67] when people assemble for feasts,[68] and when people gather in the Temple and go to see the prophet.[69] Again this indicates that in addition to what was written in the

---

[61] See *M. Shek.* 1-4.

[62] Similarly, 2 Kgs 12:15ff., without mentioning Moses.

[63] This custom was apparently accepted by the Jews of Elephantine, who donated to their temple 2 shekels apiece. For a more exact reading, see Porten-Greenfield, *Jews of Elephantine*, 134-46.

[64] The difference is that in Chronicles and Kings it is directed towards the upkeep of the Temple (cf. Exod 38:25-28) and it is not stated that it is yearly; whereas in Nehemiah and in the Mishna it is an annual tax to finance the daily offerings and other Temple expenditures.

[65] Josephus *Ant.* 18:312; Philo *Spec. leg.* 1:78; Matt 17:24 *et al.* Even if we agree with those scholars who see no connection between what is related in the *scholion* to *Megillat Taanit* and the Scroll itself which only mentions the dates when 'the daily offering was set up', the existence of the struggle between Pharisees and Sadducees over this question is not in doubt, as evidenced by *B.T. Men.* 65a; *Sifrei Num.* 142 (p. 188); *Sifrei Z. Num.* 28:2 (p. 322) *et al.* The literature on this subject is summarized in Hampel, *Megillat Taanit*, 110-15.

[66] The Pharisee opinion, which won in the end, is that public sacrifices may only be funded from the contributions of the half-shekel and no individual is allowed to volunteer a public sacrifice, as the Sadducees held. See *Meg. Taan.* beginning and the *scholion ad loc.* The Dead Sea sect held that the half-shekel was to be donated only once in a lifetime, see *DJD* 5, 7. For a clarification of the issue and its implications for early Christianity see Liver, *Studies*, 109-30; Flusser, 'Matthew xvii'.

[67] Amos 8:5; Isa 58:13; Neh 10:32, 13:15ff. In a baraita in *B.T. Meg.* 22b it is assumed that no work may be done on the New Moon, or at most only a little work be done on that day.

[68] See 1 Sam 20:18.

[69] 2 Kgs 4:23; cf. Isa 1:13.

Tora, other laws were in force already in First Temple times.

Thus the beginning of the Second Temple period ushered in a period of major development in the Halakha. A source which enables us to observe this in an explicit way is the narrative of Ezra-Nehemiah, which was extensively referred to above (pp. 153-5). As we saw, the contents of the covenant in Neh 8 and 10 show clear traces of a deliberate exposition with further specification and, in effect, augmentation of what is written in the Tora. One of the novel commandments is the general prohibition to marry foreign women, a prohibition which gained great importance in the Halakha and which showed a development through several stages. What is striking here is not so much the quantity of these and other halakhot, but the clear evidence of the creation of halakha by the Sages of that day.

HALAKHA IN JUDITH

The Book of Judith, in our opinion, is a work from the end of the Persian or the beginning of the Hellenistic period.[70] In this work are found many halakhic matters that are not mentioned in the Tora.[71] A milestone in the history of the Halakha might be seen in the story about Achior the Ammonite who, after witnessing the redemption of Israel, underwent circumcision and joined the Jewish people.[72] The halakha behind this event is consistent with the Tannaic halakha, and we mention it because of its novelty. As is well-known, the Tora does not know of proselytism in the sense of a formal religious act that determines the passage from heathendom to Judaism. During the biblical period the *ger*, lit. sojourner, would simply come to dwell with Israel, while in the Second Temple period there is the possibility of a formal transition. Correspondingly, the word *ger* now came to mean 'proselyte'. In the Ezra-Nehemiah story, we hear of no such possibility. There is mention of 'all who for the sake of the Tora of God have kept themselves apart from the foreign population',[73] but no suggestion is raised by Ezra and Nehemiah that foreign women must convert to Judaism so as not to be divorced by their Jewish husbands. The first clear-cut evidence of the change is the story of Achior in Judith; and from then on it appears firmly established in the Halakha for all subsequent generations.[74]

Another example from Judith has to do with that heroine's custom of immersing herself in a spring every morning at dawn before praying. It is conceivable

---

[70] In this respect I agree with Grintz, *Yehudith*. The book is not from the Hasmonean period, as many scholars believe.

[71] The halakhic discussion in Grintz, *Yehudith*, 47-51 is not of great value. The most penetrating study is still Büchler, 'Hearot'.

[72] Jdt 14:10.

[73] Neh 10:29. Cf. Ezra 4:1-2; Zech 8:23; Esth 8:17.

[74] It is not clear when immersion and the sacrifice became required. On this question there was disagreement in the Tannaic era: some demanded both circumcision and immersion, while others said that immersion was not necessary. See *B.T. Yev.* 46b (according to the better MSS.); *P.T. Kidd.* 3, 64d. See Finkelstein, 'Baptism'.

that this immersion was on account of defilement by gentiles, a halakha we hear about in other Second Temple sources.[75] But it is certainly not far-fetched either to explain these immersions as preparation for prayer, a custom we read about in various other sources. In later periods we hear about the washing of the hands prior to prayer – a sort of 'abbreviated' immersion. In fact, immersion of the whole body before prayer was practised by certain Jews for hundreds of years after the Book of Judith.[76]

A last instance is connected with Judith's custom to fast throughout the period of her widowhood except on Fridays, Sabbaths, New Moon eves, New Moons, festivals and days signifying joy for Israel.[77] The custom of taking upon oneself a fast for a limited period is known from various sources throughout the Second Temple period and later.[78] What is important for the history of the Halakha is the emphasis that Judith refrained from fasting not only on Sabbaths and festivals, a custom firmly documented in halakhic tradition, but also on the eves of Sabbaths and festivals. Tannaic halakha only states that on the days listed in the *Scroll of Fasting*, and the day preceding, is it forbidden to fast, but it is permitted to fast on the eves of Sabbaths and festivals.[79] However, there also existed a view that it is forbidden to fast on Fridays, and thus it is reasonable to suppose that the Book of Judith preserved an ancient tradition that later was more or less repressed.[80] Furthermore, it is significant that Judith refrained from fasting not only on the festival days mentioned in the Tora, but in addition on other days of national rejoicing. This reflects a halakha that is in fact the basis of the *Scroll of Fasting*, which was written in Aramaic at the end of the Second Temple era, and which opens with the statement that 'these are the days on which it is forbidden to fast', and then proceeds to list all those days, without counting the Sabbaths and festivals.[81]

HALAKHA IN THE SEPTUAGINT

In a considerable number of places the Septuagint translates in accordance with Tannaic halakha, even though this rendering could not have been arrived at

---

[75] See Alon, *Jews, Judaism*, 146-89.

[76] See Alon, *Jews, Judaism*, 201ff.

[77] Jdt 8:6. There is some divergence among the textual witnesses; we prefer this version on the basis of considered comparison.

[78] See Safrai in *Compendia* I/2, 804-16.

[79] *T. Taan.* 2:6; *P.T. Taan.* 2, 66a; *ib.* 1, 70c; *B.T. Taan.* 17b. The reason is that those festivals which are enumerated in the Tora do not need further strengthening, but the days which were ordained by the Sages do.

[80] See also Ginzberg's remarks in *Ginzei Schechter* 1, 543; Lieberman, *Tosefta ki-Fshutah* 5, 1089-92.

[81] A Palestinian Amora of the late 3d cent. commands the scribes that if a woman should come and ask, they should tell her that she is permitted to fast on all days except Sabbath, festival and New Moons; *P.T. Taan.* 3, 66a.

from the plain meaning of the Hebrew and thus presupposes some hidden source.[82]

Exodus 12:15 reads: 'Seven days shall ye eat unleavened bread; even the first day ye shall remove leaven out of your houses.' – What is meant by 'You shall remove'? The Septuagint translates ἀφανιζεῖτε. This verb is used in the Septuagint to translate twenty-three different Hebrew verbs, including בער, שמד, כחד and כלה, all of which denote elimination and destruction.[83] This explanation concurs with prevalent Tannaic halakha; in Tannaic literature we find widespread use of the expression 'burning of leaven'.[84] In this respect, the Mishna records a difference of opinions:[85] 'R. Yehuda says: Removal of leaven may only be by burning. But the Sages say: It may (even)[86] be crumbled up and scattered to the wind or thrown into the sea.' However we also find a minority opinion that it is permissible to use leaven after the Passover, and there is someone who even rules that it is permissible to eat it,[87] i.e., that it is not necessary to destroy and burn the leaven, but merely to conceal it. The same opinion is found in an Aramaic papyrus from the year 419 B.C.E. in which Hananya writes to the Jews of Elephantine that all leaven should be brought into an inner chamber and hidden there from sundown of the fourteenth of Nisan until the twentieth of that month.[88] The ancient Halakha merely demanded, so it seems, that the leaven be concealed. In later years, this was generally rejected and remained a minority view, while the more widespread opinion demanded that all leaven be destroyed. It is precisely this opinion that is found expressed already in the Septuagint.

Our next example from the Septuagint is of great importance for the history of the Halakha. In Lev 23:11 it is stated: 'And he shall wave the sheaf before the Lord, to be accepted for you: on the morrow after the Sabbath . . .' What does the Tora mean by 'the morrow after the Sabbath'? Is it the day after the first Sabbath following the Passover mentioned in the preceding passage? Or does it refer to the morrow of the first day of the Passover, which the Tora calls 'Sabbath' because it is a day of rest? As is known, the Sadducees and the Pharisees disagreed over this question;[89] furthermore, already the Book of

---

[82] We ignore here the issue of later additions and redactional changes of the text. It is likely that the latest of these predate the Tannaic sources. The most systematic study of the halakhic problems connected with the Septuagint remains Frankel, *Einfluss*. See also Prijs, *Jüdische Tradition*.

[83] See Hatch-Redpath, *Concordance*, 181.

[84] E.g. *M. Tem.* 7:5; *M. Pes.* 1:4. The concept 'burning' is presumed to be at the basis of the teaching of R. Yonatan in *Mekh. Pisha* 8 (p. 28).

[85] *M. Pes.* 2:3; *B.T. Pes.* 27b; *P.T. Pes.* 2, 25c-d; *Mekh. Pisha* 8 (p. 28); *Mekh. de-R. Sh.b.Y.* p. 17.

[86] This is the correct reading; see Epstein, *Nosah*, 1010.

[87] *Sifrei Deut.* 130 (p. 186); *B.T. Pes.* 28b; *P.T. Pes.* 2, 28d; *B.T. Hull.* 4b.

[88] See Cowley, *Aramaic Papyri* no. 21; in the ed. of Porten-Greenfield (1974) p. 28.

[89] See *Meg. Taan.* p. 324f. and 276ff. Since Wellhausen and Geiger, scholars have disagreed as to whether this was actually the intention of *Megillat Taanit* or only of the *scholion*; but the existence of the controversy is certain. For a summary of the literature on this question, see Hampel, *Megillat Taanit*, 115.

Jubilees and other early sources take a stand on this issue.[90] Now the Septuagint translates with emphasis:[91] τῇ ἐπαύριον τῆς πρώτης, clearly intending to harmonize with the Pharisaic halakha.

A last example from the Septuagint in conformity with later accepted halakha: Deut 25:5 states that if one of two or more brothers dies 'and has no son וּבֵן אֵין לוֹ', his widow must undergo a levirate marriage, that is, marry another brother. The Tannaic halakha states unambiguously: ' "And has no son" – in any case'.[92] That is to say: Even if the deceased brother left not a son but a daughter, his wife is not subject to the levirate marriage and the surviving brother is forbidden to marry her. The Septuagint renders: σπέρμα δὲ μὴ ᾖ αὐτῷ 'without leaving seed', i.e. any seed at all, including, apparently, a daughter. Similar views are found in Josephus and the New Testament.[93]

Where the Septuagint translates in consonance with one out of several opinions preserved in the later halakha, it is difficult to know whether this represents a definite tradition or just one of several possible renderings. In Exod 21:10, for example, among the husband's obligations to his wife are listed: שְׁאֵרָהּ כְּסוּתָהּ וְעֹנָתָהּ, which the Septuagint translates as food, clothing and sexual intercourse. This is the interpretation of R. Yoshua in the *Mekhilta*, but there are others.[94] Likewise, in Deut 21:12 it is stipulated with reference to the 'beautiful captive' whom one may marry, that 'she shall shave her head and do עָשְׂתָה her nails.' This verb can be understood either in the sense of paring the nails or of letting them grow long. The Septuagint translates: καὶ ξυρήσεις τὴν κεφαλὴν αὐτῆς καὶ περιονυχιεῖς αὐτὴν i.e. he should pare her nails.[95] This interpretation conforms with R. Eliezer's opinion, while R. Akiva says that she should let her nails grow.[96]

Scholars of the Septuagint and of rabbinic literature have pointed out that in the Septuagint there are also found halakhot that contradict the halakha of the Sages.[97] However, this may have any number of causes, and it is impossible to decide between them. Did the Septuagint translators arrive at these interpretations independently, being unaware of the halakha of the Sages? Or did there not exist any clear halakhic view on the particular issue at that time? Or does their rendering reflect their partial identification with the Hellenistic world they lived in? A fine example is Exod 22:27, 'Thou shalt not revile *Elohim*, nor curse

[90] *Jub.* 15:1; and see Charles, *APOT* 2, 34; Noack, 'Day of Pentecost'. Very important in this respect is the stand of the *Temple Scroll*; see Yadin's introduction in vol. 1, 82-99 (Hebr. ed.).

[91] This is also the translation in *Tg. Onk., Ps.-Yon.* and *Neof.*; and such is the opinion of Philo, *Spec. leg.* 2:62 and Josephus, *Ant.* 3:250.

[92] *Sifrei Deut.* 288 (p. 306); *Midr. Tann.* p. 165; *B.T. Bava B.* 115a, 109a.

[93] *Ant.* 4:254; Matt 22:24f. – John the Baptist condemned Herod Antipas for having married his brother's wife although she had a daughter, Salome. See also Mark 6:17f; Matt 14:3f.; Luke 9:7-9; and cf. *Ant.* 18:135f.

[94] See *Mekh. Mishpatim* 3 (p. 258f.); *Mekh. de-R. Sh.b.Y.* p. 167f.; *B.T. Ket.* 47b-48a.

[95] Such is the rendering in the *Peshitta*, Vulgate and *Tg. Ps.-Yon.*, and in Philo, *Virt.* 111.

[96] *Sifrei Deut.* 212 (p. 245f.); *B.T. Yev.* 48a. R. Akiva's opinion is also reflected in *Tg. Onk.*

[97] Concisely arranged in Albeck, *Introduction*, 13f.

a ruler of thy people.' Tannaic tradition interprets here the word *Elohim* in either of two ways: As a warning against cursing God, or as a prohibition against cursing a judge.[98] The latter interpretation is based on the use of the word elsewhere.[99] The Septuagint translates it here in the plural: θεοὺς οὐ κακολογή-σεις, which implies: It is forbidden to curse the gods of other nations. And indeed, Philo emphasizes a warning against cursing the gods of other peoples.[100] This case is certainly unlike those which preceded, and does not yield information about the antiquity of the Halakha. But neither is it impossible that the translation follows from some ancient midrash which left no trace in rabbinic tradition. In any case, Josephus, too, twice mentions the prohibition against cursing or disparaging other men's gods.[101]

HALAKHA IN JUBILEES

The importance of the Book of *Jubilees* is not merely in that it abounds with halakhic material, nor that it is one of the earlier sources, but principally in the fact that some of its halakhot, including the structure of its calendar, apparently disagree with Pharisaic halakha.[102] During recent years it has become clear how closely this book parallels the Essene halakha, as documented in the Qumran scrolls. Now the *Temple Scroll* has shed even more light on that fact.[103]

As is known, the author of *Jubilees* strives to show that Noah and the Patriarchs observed the commandments as handed down to them orally and in writing. Interestingly, a large portion of the halakhot he mentions do not agree with the halakha of the Sages. It is significant, however, that in some cases the author betrays knowledge of that halakha in the version supposedly existing at his time, yet rejects it. He knows, for example, that 'in the future' there will be those 'who will make observations of the moon' in order to determine the calendar and that 'all the children of Israel will forget, and will not find the path of the years'. Therefore he establishes his own calendar of three hundred and sixty-four days per year.[104] Significantly, the same calendar is found in the Book of *Enoch* [105]and in the *Temple Scroll.*[106]

---

[98] *Mekh. Kaspa* 19 (p. 317f.); *Mekh. de-R. Sh.b.Y.* p. 213; *P.T. Sanh.* 7, 22a; *B.T. Sanh.* 66a; *Exod. R.* ch. 31; and the Targumim.

[99] Cf. Exod 21:6, 22:7, 22:8; 1 Sam 2:25.

[100] *Spec. leg.* 1:53. Cf. *Mos.* 2:205.

[101] *Ant.* 4:207; *Ag. Ap.* 2:237.

[102] See Albeck, *Buch der Jubiläen.*

[103] See Yadin, *Temple Scroll,* introduction, 79f.

[104] *Jub.* 6:32-38. On the calendar of *Jubilees* many studies have been published, especially since the discovery of the Dead Sea scrolls. See Talmon, 'Judaean Sect'; *id.* 'Sect from the Judaean Desert'; Jaubert, 'Calendre des Jubilés'.

[105] *1 Enoch* 75:1-2; 82:4ff. In these formulations there is also a polemic against the prevailing calendar reckoning.

[106] See Yadin, *Temple Scroll,* introduction, 81ff.

Very interesting is the stand of *Jubilees* on the laws of Passover. The author apparently is arguing against several Pharisaic halakhot, and we shall review them all: 1) when the paschal lamb must be slaughtered, 2) for whom it is slaughtered, 3) where the proper place is to consume it, and 4) till when it may be eaten.

The first halakha requires some introductory explanation. There are many scriptural passages that deal with the slaughter of the paschal lamb and they state, among other things: 'And the whole assembly of the congregation of Israel shall kill it in the evening בין הערבים.'[107] The plain meaning is that it should be sacrificed towards evening, 'at twilight'.[108] During the Second Temple period, however, it was apparently decided to slaughter the paschal lamb during the final third of the day. Because of the increase in the number of pilgrims, it must have been impossible to slaughter all the paschal lambs at twilight; thus it was necessary to begin earlier – towards the ninth hour. That this was the actual practice at least during the last Second Temple generations, we know from the combined evidence of the Mishna and Josephus.[109] Accordingly, the Tannaic halakha states: 'The daily (evening) offering is slaughtered at eight and a half hours (2:30 p.m.) and sacrificed at nine and a half hours. On the eve of Passover it is slaughtered at seven and a half hours and sacrificed at eight and a half hours.'[110] In other words, on Passover eve the daily offering is advanced by an hour, evidently in order to be able to slaughter the paschal lamb in time. Apparently even this was considered inadequate, and the principle was laid down that the time of slaughtering was to be 'from the sixth hour and onwards'. This situation is reflected in the exposition of Philo.[111]

However, the Book of *Jubilees* warrants the sacrifice of the Passover offering 'between the evenings, from the third part of the day'. Further, the author immediately specifies this to mean: 'And it is not permissible to slay it during any period of the light, but during the period bordering on the evening.'[112] The author apparently has in mind the halakha assigning an earlier hour during the daytime, which may have been introduced in his day or somewhat earlier, but argues against this innovation and adheres firmly to the older tradition.

The second Passover law regards the age of those allowed to eat the Passover sacrifice. The prevailing Pharisaic halakha, as recorded in Tannaic literature, is that it may be eaten by all members of the household, including women and

---

[107] Exod 12:6; cf. Lev 23:5; Num 9:3, 5. See also Deut 16:6, 'at even at the going down of the sun'; Josh 5:10, 'on the fourteenth day of the month at even'.

[108] The phrase בין הערבים means literally 'between the eventides', rendered in the Targumim בין שמשיא, lit. 'between the sunsets'; the exact English equivalent is 'at twilight'. It is also the plain meaning of Deut 16:6 and Josh 5:10.

[109] *M. Pes.* ch. 5; *War* 6:423.

[110] *M. Pes.* 5:1.

[111] *Mekh. Pisha* 8 (p. 17) and parallels, as against the ancient tradition, held by the school of Shammai, that it must be offered at dusk; Philo, *Spec. leg.* 2:145. See on this whole issue Safrai, *Wallfahrt*, 220-4.

[112] *Jub.* 49:10-12.

children. The rule is even laid down: 'A minor . . . who is able to eat . . . an olive-size portion of roast meat, the Passover sacrifice is slaughtered for his sake.'[113] The author of *Jubilees* rules otherwise, and his opinion, significantly, is found also in the *Temple Scroll*: 'Every man . . . shall eat it . . . from the age of twenty years and upwards.'[114]

The third law is concerned with where the sacrifice may be eaten. Of great significance is the view of *Jubilees*, stated with repeated emphasis: it may be consumed only in the Temple. Again, this opinion is shared by the *Temple Scroll*.[115] The book of Deuteronomy prescribes that certain sacrifices must be eaten 'in the place which the Lord shall choose'. This concerns the second tithe: 'And thou shalt eat there before the Lord thy God' (14:26). It also concerns those sacrifices which are consumed in part by their owners, and which are designated as '(offerings of) minor sanctity' in the Halakha; thus Deuteronomy states: 'There ye shall eat before the Lord your God' (12:7). The Passover offering belongs to this category, and in the chapter on the paschal sacrifice Deuteronomy reiterates: 'And thou shalt roast it and eat it in the place which the Lord thy God shall choose' (16:7). Correspondingly, the biblical books from the later First and early Second Temple era testify that in those days the Passover and other offerings in which the owners partook were consumed only within the Temple precincts.[116] Such was apparently the older Halakha. Now in Tannaic halakha, as far as these sacrifices of minor sanctitiy are concerned, the sanctity of the Temple extends to the whole city of Jerusalem within the walls: 'The first-born, the tithe and the Passover are offerings of minor sanctity; they are slaughtered in any part of the Temple court . . . and may be eaten throughout the city.'[117] That this was the accepted practice, at least in the later part of the Second Temple period, may be learned not only from many halakhot, dicta and stories in rabbinic literature, but also from Philo, Josephus and the New Testament.[118] Again we are apparently able to point to an innovation in the Halakha which the author of *Jubilees* disputes. Adhering vigorously to the older Halakha, he maintains that the Passover be consumed only within the area of the Temple, just as those other offerings may be eaten in the Temple only.[119]

Finally, let us examine the question as to until when the Passover may be eaten. The Tora states: 'And that night they shall eat the flesh . . . And ye shall let nothing of it remain until morning; and that which remaineth of it until morning ye shall burn with fire' (Exod 12:8-10). The obvious question is: what exactly is meant by 'that night'? In the Mishna, this is dealt with along with some other questions about commandments to be performed at night, such as the

---

[113] *T. Hag.* 1:2 and parallels; cf. *Mekh. Pisha* 4 (p. 12).
[114] *Jub.* 19:17; *Temple Scroll* 17:8.
[115] *Jub.* 49:16-20; *Temple Scroll* 17:9.
[116] See Safrai, *Wallfahrt*, 191-3; Büchler, 'Brandopfer'.
[117] *M. Zev.* 5:8.
[118] See listing of sources in Safrai, *ib.*
[119] See also *Jub.* 7:36; 32:10-14.

question as to what is the latest time for saying the evening *shema*. For all of these commandments, the rule is: 'Its proper time is until dawn. And why did they say, "Until midnight"? In order to keep a man far from transgression.'[120] However, the same mishna also records the opinion of R. Eliezer, who was known for his adherence to the older halakha, to the effect that the outer limit for saying the evening *shema* is the end of the first night watch, i.e., the first third of the night. This is certainly also his opinion with regard to consuming the paschal offering.[121] Significantly, this same opinion is also found in *Jubilees*: 'And let them eat it at the time of the evening until the third part of the night.'[122] Again, it is likely that the Book of *Jubilees* – as R. Eliezer, the conservative Shammaite – holds to the older Halakha and emphatically opposes an innovation made in its day.[123]

This concordance between *Jubilees* and R. Eliezer the Shammaite invites us to discuss the attitude of the Book of *Jubilees* towards the Halakha in general. From an overall comparison with Tannaic tradition, it appears that *Jubilees* takes a very strict approach towards the Halakha, much stricter than the Pharisaic halakha, not only according to Beit Hillel, but also according to Beit Shammai. For example, *Jubilees* not only forbids the drawing of water and sexual intercourse on the Sabbath[124] – acts which Tannaic halakha permits – but sanctions this prohibition with the death penalty. Death penalty is also imposed for loading a beast, speaking about business, or fasting[125] on Sabbath. Tannaic halakha also forbids these things on the Sabbath, but could not possibly impose death penalty for them. A similarly strict approach, and an equally wide application of the death penalty, is conspicuous in the *Temple Scroll*. While in some cases this greater severity may be a conservative overreaction towards innovations, it more often seems to be simple adherence to the older Halakha. In this respect, *Jubilees* is a valuable witness. Not only does it prove the antiquity of a large number of halakhot preserved in Tannaic literature, but it also gives a clear insight into the development of the Halakha and into the great influence of the halakha of the Sages during the latter part of the Second Temple period.

---

[120] *M. Ber.* 1:1; *Mekh. Pisha* 6 (p. 19). In the printed editions of the Mishna the words 'the consuming of the Passover offering' do not appear, but they are found in the principal MSS.; see Horowitz's notes in the *Mekhilta ib.* and Epstein, *Nosah*, 76. The words 'until midnight' appear also in *Tg. Ps.-Yon.* on Exod 12:8.

[121] In baraitot in the Babylonian Talmud and in Tannaic midrashim there is mention of R. Eliezer saying that the time is until midnight; however here we should read, as in the parallel versions, R. Elazar (ben Azaria). See Epstein, *Tannaitic Literature*, 331 n. 66; and the emendation of the *Ot Emet* (Saloniki 1565) 4.

[122] *Jub.* 49:12. The translator explains: until 10 p.m. The *Temple Scroll* does not refer to this question.

[123] See Epstein, *ib.*

[124] The Sabbath laws are arranged in the last chapter, ch. 50; see also 2:29f.

[125] *Jub.* 49:13. It may be, however, that the original Hebrew here had וצדו 'and hunts', which would fit the preceding, and not וצמו 'and fasts'; this was suggested by Leszynsky, *Sadduzäer*, 194.

HALAKHA IN THE FIRST BOOK OF MACCABEES

A far different source for the history of the Halakha is the First Book of Maccabees. It shows a close relation to the world of the Pharisees, at least from a halakhic point of view. It is a very useful historical source, giving us much information on early Pharisaic halakha which would otherwise be lacking. One extremely important halakha on which this book informs us, namely, the permission for waging war on the Sabbath, happens to be amply covered by a range of other sources. In this case, we have continuous literary and historical evidence about the history of a halakha, from its origin in the Hellenistic period (documented in 1 Maccabees), through the destruction of the Temple and until its formulation in Tannaic halakha.[126]

According to the account beginning in 1 Macc 2:32, the enemy exploited the fact that those loyal to the Tora of Israel would not fight on the Sabbath, and consequently attacked them precisely on that day. The God-fearing would not even fight in defense, neither hurl stones or close up their hiding-places with rocks. Only later in the campaign did they decide that they were permitted to defend themselves on the Sabbath. This is confirmed by 2 Maccabees, which relates two other cases of enemy exploitation of Jewish piety.[127] It is also confirmed by Josephus, who tells of abstention from war on the Sabbath in the pre-Hasmonean period, citing a non-Jewish Greek source,[128] and again at the beginning of the Hasmonean campaign, until finally it was decided to permit a defensive war on the Sabbath: 'And until the present day we are accustomed to wage war on Sabbaths, whenever necessary.'[129] Elsewhere, Josephus informs us more specifically: 'The Law permits to defend one's self when the enemy opens an offensive and is attacking, but forbids it when they are doing something else.'[130] In other words, a preventive attack or similar initiative is forbidden, but to fight out of self-defense is permitted. Something similar seems implied in another case in 2 Maccabees, where the Jews were not able to prolong their pursuit of the enemy at the approach of the Sabbath.[131]

This same distinction, as well as other similar details, are found reflected in Tannaic halakha. 'Beforetime,' it is reported, people used to leave their weapons during wartime in a house near the wall on account of the Sabbath, which led to a massacre when the enemy attacked on that Sabbath, and 'therefore (the Sages) ordained that everyone bring their weapons to their homes'.[132] In the same context, it is stated that it is permitted and obligatory to defend oneself on the Sabbath, even if this means having to go out against the approaching enemy. As for non-defensive battle, which the Halakha defines as a non-mandatory war

---

[126] See on this issue Herr,'Problem of War'.
[127] 2 Macc 5:25ff.; 6:11.
[128] The Greek author is Agatharcides of Cnidus, see *Ant.* bk. 12 beginning, and *Ag. Ap.* 1:212.
[129] *Ant.* 12:276.
[130] *Ant.* 15:63; *War* 1:146.
[131] 2 Macc 8:25f.
[132] *T. Er.* 3:5-6; *P.T. Er.* 4, 21d; *B.T. Er.* 45a.

מלחמת רשות, it is permitted to continue an offensive on the Sabbath if it was started more than three days earlier. This was taught already by Shammai the Elder, around the turn of the eras, expounding the verse: 'When thou shalt besiege a city for many days . . . until it falls' (Deut 20:19), i.e., carrying on the attack to victory, 'even on the Sabbath'.[133] The Palestinian Talmud comments on the same halakha: 'This refers to a non-mandatory war, but a mandatory war (may be started) even on the Sabbath, since we find that Jericho was taken on the Sabbath itself.'[134]

The Book of *Jubilees*, as could be expected, includes battle, without qualification, among the things prohibited on the Sabbath, evidently preserving the older Halakha.[135] In this perspective, the straightforward report in 1 Macc 2:41 is of great significance for the history of the Halakha: 'On that day they reached this decision: If anyone attacks us on the Sabbath day, let us fight against him and not all die, as our brothers died . . .'

Another interesting halakhic detail is found in 1 Maccabees 4:42-46:

> And (Judah) selected priests without blemish, devoted to the Law, and they purified the Temple, removing to an unclean place the stones which defiled it. They discussed what to do with the altar of burnt-offering which was profaned and rightly decided to demolish it, for fear it might become a standing reproach to them because it had been defiled by the gentiles. They therefore pulled down the altar and stored away the stones in a fitting place on the Temple mount until a prophet should arise who could be consulted about them.

It should be noted in passing that the story is reflected in the Mishna tractate *Tamid*, which was redacted about the time of the destruction of the Temple: 'The North-East – there the Hasmoneans stored away the stones of the altar that had been profaned by the kings of Greece.'[136] Of interest for the history of the Halakha is the fact that Judah selected unblemished ἄμωμος priests to purify the Temple. This reflects a halakha found in the Tosefta, which apparently already existed in some form at that time: 'All may enter (the sanctuary) to build and to repair and to remove impurity. The preferable way is by means of priests . . . who are unblemished. If there are no unblemished ones, blemished ones may enter.'[137]

---

[133] *T. Er.* 3:7; *B.T. Er.* 45a; *P.T. Shabb.* 1, 4a (near end); *Sifrei Deut.* 204 (p. 240); *Midr. Tann.* p. 123. In MS. Erfurt of the Tosefta: 'Hillel the Elder', but in all other versions and in the Bab. Talmud: 'Shammai'. In *Sifrei* the tradition is anonymous, and in *Midr. Tann.* it is cited in the name of a late Tanna.

[134] *P.T. Shabb.* 1, 4a (near end). Jericho's fall on the Sabbath is a common theme, see *S.O.R.* ch. 11; *Gen. R.* 47 (p. 477) and other parallels.

[135] *Jub.* 50:12. The extant Qumran scrolls are silent on this issue.

[136] *M. Tam.* 1:6. This event seems to be reflected as well in *Meg. Taan.* p. 337 (23 Marheshwan). See the comment of Abel, *Maccabées*, 85.

[137] *T. Kelim* 1:11.

Other ancient halakhot can be seen in the gathering called by Judah at Mitspe, a place overlooking the city, before they drew up for battle.[138] The arrangement of the whole ceremony bears many similarities to the rules for a fast set down in the Mishna.[139] A fast was announced and they put on sack-cloth, placed ashes on their heads, read from the Tora and sounded the ram's horn.[140] It is also said that they rent their garments, a gesture prescribed by a baraita in the Babylonian Talmud for one who sees Jerusalem and the Temple in desolation.[141]

The Origin of Independent Halakha

Rabbinic literature records halakha in two principal forms: as 'independent halakha', stated without reference to Scripture, and as statements derived, at least formally, from biblical verses, that is, in the form of *midrash*. A question much debated in modern scholarship is, which form is the older and more original: halakha based on midrash or independent halakha?

The distinction between the two forms is reflected in the collections of rabbinic literature. The Mishna, the primary collection of halakha, and the collections of baraitot are formulated predominantly in the form of independent halakha, and likewise the majority of the halakhic dicta from the Amoraic period. The three halakhot with the most ancient explicit attribution in rabbinic literature, namely to Yose ben Yoezer of Tsereda, a Sage of the first 'Pair',[142] are formulated, at least in their extant form, without reference to any biblical text. The same holds for the first mishna of *Berakhot*, which refers to sacrificial rites in the Temple, and that of the second tractate of the Mishna, *Pea*, which also relates to Second Temple practice. It is true that in the Tannaic midrash collections and particularly in the two Talmudim, a scriptural basis is very often sought and found for halakhot which are taught without such in the Mishna or elsewhere. Or the reverse: in many cases Tannaic midrashim discuss the meaning of a verse and arrive at an interpretation identical with a halakha taught independently elsewhere. Nevertheless, a great number of halakhot have no support of any kind in the Bible.

Halakha formulated in the form of midrash is found first of all in the Tannaic midrash collections. In the second place, it is found in the many baraitot scattered over the two Talmudim which in formulation are very similar to the Tannaic midrashim, though hardly ever identical. Halakhic midrashim are found occasionally also in the Amoraic midrash collections, in formulations which are sometimes close to those found in the Tannaic collections and

---

[138] 1 Macc 3:46-54.
[139] See *M. Taanit* ch. 2.
[140] In the manner of sounding the *shofar* there are minor differences. cf. *M. Rosh H.* 3:4 and *M. Taanit* 3:5.
[141] Cf. *B.T. Moed K.* 26a. There seems to be some support for this usage already in Jer 41:5.
[142] *M. Ed.* 8:4. The title 'rabbi', found in the printed eds. and in some MSS. is not a correct reading.

sometimes quite different, without giving a clue as to an earlier source or its relation to the Tannaic collections.

The Mishna does contain midrashic sections interwoven among the independent halakha.[143] A case in point is chapter two of *Bava Metsia* which deals with the rules for returning lost objects. The halakhot in this chapter are arranged according to a logical order: When is one exempt from announcing the finding of a lost object? When does one have to announce it? How must one care for the object? And finally: How must one return it? The second half of the chapter has many halakhot with the concluding formula, '. . . as it is written . . .', in a greater frequency than is normal in the Mishna.[144] This formula functions as a secondary support from the Bible. However, mishna 5 contains a halakha which is completely built upon a midrash on Deut 22:3 and which appears in almost identical form in the Tannaic midrash.[145] The verse reads: 'Thou shalt not see thy brother's ox or his sheep go astray . . . thou shalt in any case bring them again . . . In like manner shalt thou do with his ass and so shalt thou do with his garment and with all lost things of thy brother's.' The mishna explains:

> The garment could have been understood to be included in all those things (in the verse: "all lost things")? Why is it mentioned separately? – In order to draw an analogy from it and to teach you: Just as the garment is special in that it has identifying marks and it has claimants, so any thing that has identifying marks and has claimants must be announced (when found).

This is, however, an exceptional case in the Mishna; in general, the demarcation between the two forms of halakha is maintained with clarity. In the sources throughout the Tannaic and Amoraic eras, halakha and midrash are emphasized, alongside aggada, as different branches of Oral Tora. The usual order is: midrash, halakha and aggada.[146] The extant Tannaic midrash collections received final editing slightly later than did the Mishna and Tosefta and they are dependent on them. Frequently, at the end of a midrashic discussion a short conclusion is given: 'Hence did they say . . .' and similar phrases, whereupon a halakha is cited from the Mishna or Tosefta. Such citations of a halakha in a set formulation inserted in a midrashic context is especially prominent in collections from the school of R. Akiva, where they can be counted in the hundreds, but to a lesser extent they are also found in those of the school of R. Yishmael.[147]

---

[143] See also above p. 78.

[144] In mishna 7 twice, in 9 once, in 10 twice. In many larger tractates, such as *Shabbat* (24 chaps.), *Kelim* (30 chaps.) and *Ahilut* (18 chaps.), no use is made of this term.

[145] *Sifrei Deut.* 224 (p. 257).

[146] *M. Ned.* 3:3 states that 'midrash, halakhot and aggadot' are not included when someone vows that his fellow shall not receive enjoyment from him. Similarly, *P.T. Shek.* ch. 5 (beg.) says of R. Akiva that he ordained 'midrash, halakhot and aggadot'.

[147] The citation numbers arranged by the various collections and by the various quotation formulas are given by Melammed, *Introduction*, 233-53.

Given this overall differentiation between midrash and halakha, as found in the sources and in the perception of the Sages themselves, the question is: What is the historical relationship between the two forms of halakha? Which came first, midrash or (independent) halakha? This question can be split into two: 1) Did (independent) halakha derive secondarily from midrash, or, the other way around, was midrash created as a secondary support for (independent) halakhot? 2) What was the original framework in which halakha was studied: the formulation of (independent) halakha, as in the later formulation process of the Mishna; or midrash and study following the outlines of Scripture, as reflected in the Tannaic midrash?

With regard to the first question, the discussion has been going on for years; we shall deal with it below. Concerning the second question, however, there has been almost unanimous agreement since the beginning of the modern science of Judaism that midrash was the original framework of the study of halakha. As one scholar formulated it, 'even if it would appear that halakha preceded midrash, there is no difficulty, since (the Sages) studied it and attached it to the Bible, and thus they even attached to the Written Tora halakhot that have no basis at all in Scripture.'[148] This opinion seems to draw its inspiration from Rav Sherira Gaon, the first to give a general introduction to the literature of the Sages, who remarked: '. . . And *Sifra* and *Sifrei* are midrash of scriptural verses, where the halakhot are found hinted at in the verses; and originally, during the days of the Second Temple in the time of the early rabbis, they used to study them according to this manner.'[149]

A 'PERIOD OF THE SCRIBES'?

The position that originally the creation and study of Oral Tora, and of halakha which was part of it, was tied to the Written Tora and only later was detached from it, was fundamentally argued by one of the first modern scholars of Judaism, Nahman KROCHMAL. Krochmal devoted much attention to that early period, which he termed the 'Period of the Scribes (*Sofrim*)'. In it, he said, the Sages occupied themselves 'with the interpretation of the Law, and the entire creation of the Oral Tora and its study were connected to Scripture. This situation lasted until the days of Shimon the Just. Only from his time onwards, after there had been so much study of the Tora in which halakhic principles and specifications had been derived, and newly arisen cases had been dealt with which were not included earlier, either in Scripture or its interpretation by the Scribes, . . . things which were so numerous that they could no longer be memorized along with the recitation of Scripture, . . . they established the form of the abstract dicta . . . calling them halakhot.'[150]

---

[148] Albeck, *Introduction*, 42.
[149] *Iggeret*, 39.
[150] *More nevukhei ha-zeman*, 156.

The great majority of modern scholars accepted this view. They disagreed only over the date of this change from the midrashic way of learning to the studying of independent halakha, and over the literary or political causes behind it. LAUTERBACH, who summarized the arguments of his predecessors, proposed the year 190 B.C.E. as the time of the change-over.[151] The greatest talmudic scholar of the last generation, EPSTEIN, sees the change as having occurred after the persecutions of Antiochus, since the earliest independent halakhot were handed down in the name of Yose ben Yoezer: 'Most certainly, the causes of this change were basically the multiplication of halakhot and their upshots that were connected only loosely to the Tora. . . . From the days of Yose ben Yoezer onwards, the method of *halakha* and *mishna* took priority over the method of *midrash*.'[152]

But in the meantime, it has rightly been pointed out that we have no proof that there ever existed an 'age of the Scribes', an age in which literary creation and study were exclusively connected to Scripture.[153] The statements of Rav Sherira are not founded on ancient tradition from the days of the Second Temple, since he had no such traditions. Tannaic tradition does not allude anywhere to such an age nor does it ascribe anything to 'Scribes' who would have been active after Ezra and before the age of the Tannaim. By contrast, it does ascribe decrees and other activities to the 'Men of the Great Assembly' who had been coming together since the days of Ezra.

It is true that in certain Second Temple writings the Sages are referred to as Scribes, and that the teachings of the early Sages are sometimes designated 'words of the Scribes' in rabbinic sources.[154] However the implications of this are not unequivocal. We also find the appellation 'scribes', alongside that of 'sages', in the speech of Tannaim referring to their own contemporaries. It may suffice to bring in evidence the words of Rabban Gamliel: 'Scribes, leave me be and I shall expound this symbolically.' Admittedly, the identification of these 'Scribes' with 'Sages' does not appear in any version of this tradition, but 'scribes' as referring to the companions of Rabban Gamliel[155] is found in all versions.[156]

In other words, the term 'Scribes' is not a specific reference to Tora teachers during the generations following Ezra. Ezra, it is true, is called 'a skilled *sofer* in the Tora of Moses' (Ezra 7:6), but the men of his company who assist him in inculcating the Tora are not *sofrim* but rather *mevinim*, 'those who cause the

---

[151] Lauterbach, *Essays*, 163-256. Historiographers of Judaism accepted the results of Talmud scholars: Graetz, *Geschichte* 2, 150ff.; Schürer, *Geschichte* 2, 394ff.

[152] Epstein, *Tannaitic Literature*, 509. Cf. *ib.* 501 for a review of previous opinions. For a later view see Melammed, *Introduction*, 166f.

[153] Kaufmann, *Toledot* 4/2, 481-5; Urbach, 'Derasha', 172-4.

[154] *M. Orla* 3:9; *M. Toh.* 4:7, 4:11; and see Schürer, *History* 2, 325 and n. 9.

[155] Some versions read 'Rabban Shimon ben Gamliel', others 'Rabban Gamliel the Elder'.

[156] *B.T. Sota* 15a; *Sifrei Num.* 8 (p. 14); *Numbers R.* 9,31; and cf. *Tanh. Naso* 3 (54b); *Tanh. B. Naso* 5 (14b). Cf. *M. Avot* 6:9, '*hakhamim* and *sofrim*', in the name of a Sage of the Yavne generation.

people to understand' (Neh 8:7-9). Nor are Tora teachers specifically indicated with the term *sofrim* in Second Temple sources in general. It is doubtful whether *sofer* in the Book of Chronicles refers to a Tora scholar; in any case the Tora teachers in 2 Chr 7:7-9 and the judges in 2 Chr 19:1-5 are not so called. In Ben Sira, *sofer* appears only once (38:24), along with terms such as 'master of Tora' תופש תורה (15:1) and 'searcher of Tora' (דורש תורה 35:15).[157] 'Scribes', 'Sages' and 'Elders' are mentioned alongside one another in Apocrypha and Pseudepigrapha, though it is not always possible to determine whether the author was referring to wise men in general or to the Sages of Oral Tora.[158] In the New Testament, the expression 'Scribes' is a common designation for the Sages of the Tora, but other epithets, such as 'Sages' and 'Teachers of the Tora' are also found.[159]

Thus the use of the term 'scribe' does not justify the hypothesis of an 'Age of the Scribes' in early Second Temple days. Still more dubious is the assumption that 'scribes' are specifically involved in the interpretation of Scripture. Apparently too much weight has been given to the statement in the Babylonian Talmud: 'Hence the early ones were called *sofrim* because they would count (hebr. *sofrim*) all the letters in the Tora,'[160] the assumption being that this implied exegesis of Scripture. This late account, found only in the Babylonian Talmud, should not be regarded as more than a sort of homiletic interpretation, one among various other explanations of the epithet *sofrim*. It is no more valid than the following interpretation found in the Palestinian Talmud: ' "The clans of *sofrim* living at Jabez" (1 Chr 2:55). What is meant by *sofrim*? They made the entire Tora into number (*seforot*): "Five should not give heave-offering;" "Five things incur the obligation of dough-offering;" "Four principal causes of damages" etc.'[161] While it is indeed true that ancient mishnayot and collections of them are arranged in a numerical order, this explanation is obviously only another interpretation of the term *sofrim*. But it is significant that even in this explanation the term *sofrim* is not at all connected to scriptural exegesis, but rather to independent halakha.

There is no proof whatsoever that at the beginning of the Second Temple era the study and creation of Oral Tora was primarily connected to Scripture. Of the traditions ascribed in the beginning of *Avot* to the Men of the Great Assembly and to Sages of the Hellenistic era such as Shimon the Just, Antigonos of Sokho and Yose ben Yoezer, none are in the form of midrash. The same

---

[157] All examples are from the Hebrew sections preserved in the Geniza.
[158] In 1 Macc 7:12, 2 Macc 6:18 and *Test. Levi* 8:17 the term used is 'Scribes'; but in 13:7 it is 'Sage'. In Wis 7:24, 4 Ezra 14:46 and *Asc. Mos.* 5:5 the term used is 'Sages', but in Jdt 11.15 it is 'Elders'.
[159] γραμματεῖς in Matt 2:4; 7:29 (and parrallel in Mark 1:22); 9:3 (par. Mark 20:6, Luke 5:21); Mark 2:16 (par. Luke 5:30); 12:28 (par. Luke 20:39); Luke 6:7; John 8:3; Acts 4:5 etc. The term σοφός, a less common and less precise designation of the Sages, is found Matt 11:25, 23:34 (both terms together). Other designations for the Sages are found in Luke 14:3; Acts 5:34, etc.
[160] *B.T. Kidd.* 30a.
[161] *P.T. Shek.* ch. 5 beg.

passage we just quoted from the Palestinian Talmud contains another explanation which, if it were to prove anything, points in a different direction:[162]

"Therefore I will divide him a portion with the great, and he shall divide the spoil with the strong" (Isa 53:12). – This refers to R. Akiva, who ordained midrash, halakhot and aggadot. Some say: This was done by the Men of the Great Assembly. Then what did he ordain? The exegetical method of "generalization and particular".

This statement of the Palestinian Amora R. Yona informs us that at least 'some say' that it was the legendary Men of the Great Assembly who instituted not only midrash, but halakhot and aggadot as well.

We have not yet dealt with the expression 'words of the Scribes' דברי סופרים, so common in Tannaic and Amoraic literature. In fact, this phrase does not refer to the innovations of the early 'Scribes'. It can, for instance, be used also to refer to the teachings of the School of Hillel.[163] In a wider sense, it refers to the whole of Oral Tora, whether in the form of midrash or of independent halakha. We offer some examples.

(A transgression of) the words of the Scribes may be more serious than of the words of the Tora. (How?) – If someone says: "There are no phylacteries" in order to transgress the words of the Tora, he is exempt; (but if he says) "there are five frontlets" in order to add to the words of the Scribes, he is liable.[164]

In other words, the commandment of phylacteries itself is from the Tora, while its interpretation by the Sages to the effect that the phylactery should contain four biblical passages is part of the concept 'words of the Scribes'. Another example: ' "According to the Tora which they shall teach thee" (Deut 17:11). – For (a transgression of) the words of the Tora one may be sentenced to death, but one is not sentenced to death for the words of the Scribes.'[165] Clearly, 'the words of the Scribes' here is a term for the teaching of the Sages as a whole. Again, a baraita which recurs in several places in the Palestinian and Babylonian Talmudim stresses that the Sages found themselves forced to make certain of their innovations more stringent since 'the words of the Tora do not need strengthening' while 'the words of the Scribes need strengthening'. These innovations include festival days which were added during the Second Commonwealth and are enumerated in the *Scroll of Fasting*, as well as laws on sexual relations.[166] Significantly, most of these halakhot are not connected with any interpretation of Scripture.

Against the near-consensus of scholars, an altogether different theory concerning the nature of the 'Scribes' and the function of midrash was offered by

[162] *P.T. Shek.* ch. 5 beg.
[163] A baraita in *P.T. Ber.* 1, 3a.
[164] *M. Sanh.* 11:3.
[165] *Sifrei Deut.* 154 (p. 207).
[166] *P.T. Yev.* 9, 10a; *P.T. Ket.* 11, 34c; *B.T. Rosh H.* 19a; *B.T. Taan.* 17b. These data do not support the theory on the relation between midrash and halakha proposed by Urbach, 'Derasha'; see below.

URBACH. He, too, posits that there was never a period of the Scribes, but he draws other conclusions for the development of the Halakha. He presumes that the earliest halakha originated not in midrash but in the administrative institutions, in other words, in legislation by decree and by court decision. One indication is the anonymity and absence of dispute distinctive of early halakha: 'It was not exegetical dialectics, nor theoretical discussion, that was decisive, but rather authority; and this authority belonged to institutions. For this reason the only Sages to be mentioned [in the earliest period of the Halakha] are the Heads of the Sanhedrin and Presidents of the Courts, to whom those few decrees were attributed.'[167] The class of the 'Scribes' had nothing to do with these decrees nor with the teaching and creation of Oral Tora as such. They were clerks whose task was the writing and copying of the Holy Scriptures, and they should be clearly distinguished from the superior class of the Sages.

It was, according to Urbach, among this class of the Sages, and not the Scribes, that midrash was subsequently born. The first *derashot* would have contained only explanations of difficult words, on the basis of comparisons with parallel passages. At the same time, these *derashot* brought with them solutions to issues that had not been made explicit in the Tora. The halakhot thus resulting from the midrash, however, were recognized only to the extent that they conformed to the established traditions, decrees, testimonies and precedents of the Sages. The acceptance of the *derasha* as a basis of authority of the Halakha was a gradual development which was accelerated by the weakening of the internal governmental structures, the breakdown of order and the loss of powers of the Sanhedrin. In this connection, Urbach accepts the view of GINZBERG, that the founding of the Dead Sea sect was another symptom of this disintegrative process and their midrash-based halakha a sign of new-found independent authority.[168]

Urbach's theory, however, has no more hard evidence to support it than the majority view he is opposing. A seeming corroboration is the well-known tradition of R. Yose, reflected also in the above-quoted words of Rav Sherira, to the effect that in the early generations of Sages there were no disputes, that difficult questions were decided by the Great Sanhedrin and that disputes came into being only with the increase of students 'who did not serve (their masters) sufficiently', thus indicating the decay of authority. The historical value of this tradition, however, must be seriously questioned.[169] It is a highly idealized and schematic picture; it is not confirmed by the ancient sources, and, in addition, the Tannaim maintained other views of their own early history. Nor is the distinction between Sages and Scribes as proposed by Urbach supported by the sources. It is true that in later days – perhaps even shortly following the destruction of the Temple – it was customary to limit usage of the term 'scribe'

---

[167] Urbach, *ib.* 70.
[168] Ginzberg, *Jewish Sect.*
[169] We shall treat this tradition below, p. 171f.

to elementary (Bible) teachers and Bible copyists, as in the statement of R. Eliezer the Great: 'From the day when the Temple was destroyed, the Sages began to be like the Scribes.'[170] There is no justification, however, in projecting this back into an earlier period. When 1 Macc 7:12 reports that there came before Bacchides and Alcimus a delegation of suppliants consisting of a συναγωγή γραμματείων (assembly of scribes), it is clear that these are not copyists or schoolteachers but Tora scholars and Sages, members of the council of elders and the like. Similarly, 2 Macc 6:18 calls Eleazar one of the πρωτευόντων γραμμτέων (foremost Scribes) who by his example inspired others to remain faithful to the Tora, thus clearly presenting him as a leader of the people and not someone from the lower class of clerks and schoolmasters.[171]

MIDRASH AND INDEPENDENT HALAKHA

Let us now return to the question about the relationship between halakha formulated independent of Scripture, and biblical study or midrash. We reiterate that there is no evidence that the midrash form of halakha was the more original, nor that independent halakha enacted by legislative institutions preceded the creation of halakha by way of midrash. Let us review what the available evidence does teach us.

We have already pointed out that the halakhot with the oldest specific attribution are the three halakhot testified to by Yose ben Yoezer.[172] One of these reads: 'He who touches a corpse is defiled.' The commentators to the Mishna, starting with the Amoraim, have always found this statement difficult, inasmuch this is explicitly stated in the Tora (Num 19:11, 16). But Israel LEWY has aptly explained that the meaning is that only one who himself touches a corpse is defiled, not one who touches someone else who was defiled by a corpse. Significantly, this 'independent' halakha is also found in midrash form, and is thus attributed to 'the first elders', who in Tannaic tradition represent a period at least as ancient as that of Yose ben Yoezer:[173]

> "Or if a soul touch any unclean thing" (Lev 5:2) – The First Elders used to say: You might have thought that even if one touched [a man impure through contact with a corpse][174] he would be liable. (This is not so.) Hence Scripture says: "The carcass of an unclean beast, or the carcass of unclean cattle, or the carcass of unclean creeping things" (*ib.*) – in so far

---

[170] *M. Sota* 9:15. This is a baraita added to the Mishna; see Epstein, *Nosah*, 949, 970. *Sofer* in the sense of elementary school teacher is found in *B.T. Bava B.* 21a: ספר מתא (according to the MSS.) and סופר יהודי וסופר גוי.

[171] Indeed, the author of 4 Macc 5:4 portrays him as 'Eleazar, of priestly extraction and knowledgeable in the Law'.

[172] See n. 142.

[173] *Sifra, Hova* 12 (ed. Finkelstein 173). Lewy's explanation is cited by Horowitz, 'Sifre Sutta', 74 n. 5; and see *B.T. Av. Zar.* 37b.

[174] Thus the version of MS. Vatican 30, which seems more authentic than the editions.

as these things are distinguished in that they are Principal Sources of Impurity, we should exclude anything that is not a Principal Source of Impurity.

Halakhot transmitted with attributions by name are quite scarce for the period from Yose ben Yoezer until Hillel and Shammai. Actually, we find such halakhot in increasing numbers only starting with the days of Hillel and Shammai. Beginning from exactly this same time we have evidence of a developed system of midrash! Concerning Hillel it is related: 'Hillel the Elder expounded seven things before the elders of Bathyra by *kal wa-homer* (*a minori*) reasoning, etc.'[175] What we find here is an elaborate system of midrash rules, which must have been developing for generations, Hillel's contribution being to have systematized them, fixing them at seven. In speaking of Hillel's teachers Shemaya and Avtalion, Yehuda ben Dortai, a Sage contemporary with Hillel or slightly later, complains: 'I am amazed at the two foremost men of this generation, Shemaya and Avtalion: Though they are great Sages and great expounders (דרשנים), they did not tell Israel that the pilgrimage offering overrules the Sabbath . . .'[176]

In subsequent generations of Tannaim, until and beyond R. Akiva, there was a similar sort of correlation between the production of halakha and of midrash. Judging by the evidence of the extant collections, we may call the time of R. Akiva and R. Yishmael the period of most intensive creation in the realm of halakha. At the same time, theirs is also the great age of creativity in midrash, marked by the establishment of the two great schools in the field of midrash, those of R. Akiva and R. Yishmael.

A survey of all the sources and research literature only leads us to the conclusion that there is no ground for assuming that the midrash form of halakha preceded the 'independent' mode of study and formulation; nor for the opposite view that the midrash form was secondary. The interpretation that best fits the evidence is that these two forms of study and literary creation developed concomitantly within the very society they were shaping. Admittedly, we have only scanty information on the earliest period and that of the first Pairs. Here, we find only isolated halakhot and midrashim with an attribution by name or other indication of date. Thus for this period we must be careful not to construe too much from the sources. However, it is certain that from the days of Hillel and Shammai onwards – and probably even some generations earlier – halakha and midrash constituted two concurrent modes of literature and study, both in content and in form.

This duality may very well be related to the essence of Oral Tora. From the beginning, the Tora of Moses and the visions of the Prophets must have influenced the creation and development of halakha in two ways: practice and study. The independent mode of halakha seems closer to practice: here, there

[175] *T. Sanh.* ch. 7 end; *Sifra, Wayikra* beg. (ed. Finkelstein 9); *A.R.N.* a 37 (55b).
[176] *B.T. Pes.* 70b.

was a drive towards fulfilling the Tora by creating ways of life, formulating these in rules and thus imparting them to the people, and also by spelling out in concrete halakhot what such generalized commandments imply as 'not to do any labour on the Sabbath', 'to love the Lord with all one's soul', or 'not to wrong one's neighbour'. The second way was through diligent study, interpretation and further elaboration of both form and content of what is written in the Tora; this resulted in the mode of midrash. Obviously, these two ways work together, both with regard to halakhic reasoning and practical decision making; this will be made clear by examples to follow in the next section.

Sources of the Halakha of the Sages

This section will deal with the sources from which the halakha of the Sages developed. The previous section, discussing the origin of 'independent' halakha alongside the midrash form, ended with the conclusion that indeed midrash was one of the ways in which halakha was created. We shall now continue that discussion and treat midrash as one among various other sources of halakha.

MIDRASH AS A SOURCE OF HALAKHA

In order to attain to a balanced apreciation of the evidence, it is necessary to reiterate that this discussion regards only a part of the Halakha. It is undeniable that a goodly portion of it not only was not derived by means of midrash, but was never connected with it in any way. An additional part of the Halakha originated independently, and was only supported by midrash in a later stage. We shall begin our argument by reviewing a number of examples of halakha in which midrash did not function as a source; then we shall investigate the secondary support function of midrash; and finally we shall turn to the evidence attesting to the creative function of midrash.

The oft-quoted mishna *Hagiga* 1:8 states explicitly:
> (The halakhot of) release from vows hover in the air and they have naught to support them; the halakhot about the Sabbath, Festal-offerings, and sacrilege are like mountains hanging by a hair, for (teaching of) Scripture (thereon) is scanty and the halakhot many; (the halakhot of) civil law and the (Temple-)service, of purity and impurity and of incest, they have that which supports them, and it is they that are the substance of Tora.

To this the Tosefta adds:
> In addition to these: (The halakhot of) vows of valuation, vows of prohibition, vows of dedication and of second tithe have that which supports them, for Scripture is ample and the halakhot few. Abba Yose

ben Hanin says: These are the eight branches of Tora, the substance of halakhot.'[177]

Abba Yose ben Hanin was a Jerusalemite who lived at the end of the Second Temple period,[178] and already before him, the list recorded in the Mishna must have been arranged along with the addition in the Tosefta, since he summarizes it as 'the eight branches of halakhot.' A fairly early tradition tells us, then, that there are areas of halakha that have almost no formal basis in the Bible, i.e., they have no serious foundation in any form of midrash. However, even those areas about which it is said that they have much Scripture and few halakhot in fact contain many halakhot which were not derived or corroborated by means of midrash.

When we review tractate after tractate in the Mishna, we encounter a general connection between the Bible and the halakhot in the Mishna. But a detailed examination of the halakhot, or even of their general principles, their arrangement or their larger structure, reveals the frailty of this connection. Even when a halakha is derived from midrash, this concerns only a part of it, or its rough outline. We shall examine only two well-known tractates, *Berakhot* and *Shabbat*. *Berakhot* deals with the halakhot of reciting the *shema*, of prayer, meals and the benedictions said before and after them, and benedictions in general. Each of these fields has some basis in Scripture, and there are *derashot* that seek to find more of it. However, there still remain halakhot – in fact the majority – that have no connection at all with Scripture. To mention only a few: the precise definition of the times for reciting the *shema*; who, and under what circumstances, is exempt from reciting; the various types of benedictions, including the benediction before and after saying the *shema*; and the structure of the benedictions.

Prominent in tractate *Shabbat* is the system of thirty-nine principal classes of labour that are forbidden on the Sabbath (see above p. 89); these are not derived by means of midrash and receive some connection with Scripture only in late midrashim. As is known, Tannaic halakha defined the concept of 'labour' in the form of thirty-nine classes according to the labours that were performed in the Tabernacle, as is reflected in some form in Tannaic midrash.[179] The Mishna, however, categorizes the thirty-nine labours on a completely different basis, namely, the main branches of material labour: work in the fields ('A man who sows . . .'; 'He who harvests . . .'; 'And he who bakes . . .'), in husbandry ('He who shears wool. . .'; 'He who dyes it white . . .'; 'He who rends in order to stitch it back . . .'), in hunting ('He who hunts a deer . . .'; 'He who slaughters it . . .'; 'He who scrapes it [i.e. the hair off its hide] . . .'; 'He who cuts it . . .'), and the various urban crafts ('He who writes two letters or erases in order to write . . .'; 'he who builds . . .'; 'He who strikes with a hammer . . .').

---

[177] *T. Hag.* ch. 1 end; cf. *T. Er.* end.
[178] See *T. Men.* 13:21; *B.T. Pes.* 57a.
[179] *M. Shabb.* 12:3; *T. Shabb.* 11:2, 6. Explicitly, the connection is stated only by the Amoraim, see *B.T. Shabb.* 49b; *P.T. Shabb.* 7, 9b.

It is likely that labour was originally defined according to these trades, and only afterwards, perhaps by R. Akiva,[180] was it connected to the work in the Tabernacle. These thirty-nine 'actual' labours thus are prohibited with support from the Tora, and hence he who transgresses them inadvertently is liable to a sin-offering, and if knowingly, death 'by the hands of Heaven'. In addition, we have seen above, many other activities were prohibited under the concept of *shevut*, which aims to insure complete rest on the Sabbath. It is true that this concept is connected with Scripture.[181] However, what activities are included in it is in no way derived from Scripture.[182]

Thus having set aside that large portion of halakhot which do not have any connection to the midrash, we are still faced with many hundreds that do. The question is: did these halakhot originate in midrash, or alternatively, were they created in some other way and subsequently attached to biblical verses? There is a school of historians of the Halakha who are of the opinion that the midrash did never create halakha, but at most supported it. In an extreme form, this conception is presented by HALEVY. In his opinion, the source of halakha is only to be found in tradition, and the Sages never relied on a midrash, not even the most clear and simple one.[183] EPSTEIN does not go so far as regards the sole authority of tradition, but concerning midrash and halakha he expresses a similar view: 'The midrash supports the Halakha but does not create halakha; (the Sages) bring confirmation for the Halakha from the Bible, but they do not derive or invent halakha on the basis of midrash. Thus, "A man may draw a *gezera shawa* (analogy by similar words) to support the teaching he received, but he may not draw a *gezera shawa* in order to disprove the teaching he received." '[184]

There is no denying that many midrashim of the Amoraim, and to a lesser extent also of the Tannaim, are merely a support for a halakha that was already fixed and accepted. For instance, it is very likely that a good deal of the midrashim concerning the order of sacrifices followed accepted practice in the Temple. Often, the entire scriptural proof of a midrash is founded upon logic, or even upon the very same halakha for which the biblical verse is supposed to be adduced. That is to say: the halakha that preceded the midrash left its imprint upon the interpretation of the biblical text, and subsequently the verse was interpreted according to this halakha. Thus the verse was not produced as a proof, but rather as an indication that it should be thus interpreted. Often, the Tannaic midrash interprets a biblical passage in such a way that it includes one instance and excludes another. Then the question arises: Whence do we include this and exclude that, although it is similar? Could we not have argued the

---

[180] Thus according to MS. Vienna, *T. Shabb.* 11:6.
[181] *Mekh. Pisha* 9 (p. 33), expounding Exod 12:17.
[182] See *M. Beitsa* 5:2 for activities included in *shevut*.
[183] *Dorot ha-Rishonim*, I/3, 292ff.; I/5, 467ff.
[184] *Tannaitic Literature*, 511; the (Amoraic) saying is in *P.T. Pes.* 6, 33a; we deal with it below.

opposite? And the answer is that on the grounds of reason or of the Halakha we decide this way – even though the reasoning and the halakha involved are not stated in the biblical text and sometimes were derived through midrash themselves.[185]

A clear case is the recitation of the *shema* and the question whether it should include the Decalogue. Which passages should be included in the *shema* recitation is derived from the verse, 'And thou shalt teach them diligently unto thy children and shalt talk of them' (Deut 6:7). If it is clear that 'them' indicates words of the Tora itself, it is equally obvious that it is not stated which. Three passages are included, according to the Halakha, two of which (Deut 6:4-9; 11:13-21) refer both to the obligation to 'teach diligently' and to 'bind on the forehead' (i.e. the phylacteries). The third passage (Num 15:37-41) contains neither reference but treats of the fringes on the garment. Now in the midrash on the first *shema* passage,[186] it is objected that the phylacteries, the binding of which is an explicit commandment, should contain four biblical passages, two of which are identical with the first two of the *shema*, and two others (Exod 13:1-10 and 11-16). While the first two mention the 'binding on the forehead' as well as the 'diligent teaching', these other two mention only the 'binding'. Then why are these two not also included in the *shema* recitation, since the third *shema* passage does not contain either of these commandments, yet is included? The simple answer is that 'And thou shalt teach them' is included in the first two passages, but not in the other two! By similar reasoning the question is answered whether the Decalogue should be included in the *shema*. If the third passage is included, which was preceded (in the Tora) by many other commandments, then why are not the Ten Commandments included, which were given first of all? Now, the argument used above is reversed: the two other phylactery passages contain the 'binding' commandment yet are not included in the *shema*; therefore the Decalogue, which does not even contain the 'binding', should not be included either. But then why is the third passage included, since it does not contain either commandment, any more than the Decalogue? The answer: 'Therefore Scripture says: "And thou shalt teach them" – these are included in "teaching diligently", but the Decalogue is not included.'

Obviously, in the Bible there is no indication whatsoever that Num 15:37-41 is referred to in Deut 6:7 and therefore should be included, and even less that the Decalogue is not referred to and should be excluded. Not only this. From Mishna *Tamid* 5:1, with which our midrash must have been familiar, it emerges clearly that in Second Temple days it was customary to recite the Decalogue along with the *shema*. Moreover, both Talmudim inform us that the Decalogue was removed from the service as a reaction to the sectarians who said that only the Ten Commandments were given at Mount Sinai.[187] The midrash, then, must

---

[185] Some examples are given in Albeck, *Introduction*, 59.
[186] *Sifrei Deut.* 34 (p. 60f.).
[187] For further evidence see Safrai, in *Compendia* I/2, 801.

have been aware that at one time it had been customary to recite the Decalogue with the *shema*. But simply because in its time it was no longer recited, and because the third passage was recited, the verse is explained accordingly.

Certain halakhot that were unanimously regarded as having originated in the words of the Sages – some even mentioned by name – were provided with a supporting midrash. Some examples: 'From this (verse) did the Sages find support from the Tora in decreeing *eruvei tavshilin* (fusion of dishes – a legal fiction making it possible to prepare food for the Sabbath on a preceding Festival day)';[188] or 'From this did the Sages find support from the Tora for the decree on the purity of the hands (as separate from the rest of the body);'[189] or again, 'When Hillel decreed the *prozbul* (a circumvention of the literal Tora commandment, allowing debts to be collected after the Sabbatical Year), they supported it on a verse in the Tora.'[190]

The secondary character of the support offered by the midrash is shown most clearly in the following mishna:[191]

> That same day R. Akiva expounded: "And every earthen vessel whereinto any of them (i.e., dead creeping things) falleth, whatsoever is in it shall be unclean" (Lev 11:33). It does not say טמא "is unclean" but יטמא "shall render unclean". This teaches that a loaf of bread suffering second-grade uncleanness renders another unclean in the third grade. Said R. Yoshua: Who will take away the dust from off thine eyes, O Rabban Yohanan ben Zakkai! – for thou didst say that another generation would declare the third (grade unclean) loaf clean, for there is no verse in the Tora to prove that it is clean!

Unambiguously, we are told that there was such an accepted halakha dating at least from the generation before Rabban Yohanan ben Zakkai.[192] Significantly, this is an important halakha which includes many more detailed halakhot. Yohanan expresses the fear that it might be forgotten since it had no scriptural basis. And lo and behold, his disciple's disciple, R. Akiva, with his novel midrash methods, finds corroborating support for it in the Bible. Without this story, it might seem that it was R. Akiva's midrash which created this halakha.

We could also cite examples in which the midrash proves only a part of the argument – which can only be understood to mean that the halakha in question had already been known and accepted, and that the midrash followed only to attach it to a biblical text. One instance relates to the difference made in the Halakha between having something leavened in one's possession and deriving profit from it without actually possessing it. 'Leaven . . . after the Passover had finished, . . . that of a Jew is forbidden for all enjoyment, since it says "Neither shall there be leaven seen with thee" (Exod 13:7).' In fact, the verse offers

---

[188] *B.T. Beitsa* 15b. Cf. the *derash* in *Mekh. Beshallah, Wayasa* (p. 169).

[189] *Sifra Metsora, Zavim* 4 (77a); *B.T. Hull.* 106a.

[190] *P.T. Shev.* 10, 39c.

[191] *M. Sota* 5:2.

[192] Cf. *M. Hag.* 3:2, which is part of an ancient collection of pilgrims' halakhot.

support only for the prohibition to possess leaven during Passover, and not for the prohibition, tacitly accepted by the Mishna, on deriving profit from it in other ways.[193]

Cases could also be cited in which midrash originated only after the halakha in question had been determined.[194]

All this evidence, however, does not exclude the possibility that in certain cases midrash did have a primary function in the creation and decision of halakha. To our mind, there is no ignoring the well-documented arguments of ALBECK and DE VRIES to the effect that midrash served in many cases as a fundamental, authoritative source in the formation of halakha.[195]

In fact it would suffice to analyze one of the fundamental proofs often advanced to argue the opposite, namely, the story of Hillel and the Benei Bathyra, which is related at length in the Tosefta and in both Talmudim.[196] The issue is whether the activities needed for the paschal offering prevail when the fourteenth of Nisan falls on a Sabbath. We are told that Hillel employed various methods of midrash to prove that it does: *hekkesh* (proof by juxtaposition of verses), *kal wa-homer* (argument a minori) and *gezera shawa* (proof by similar wording). Now in the version of the Palestinian Talmud – and this is stressed by those maintaining that midrash did not create halakha – the argument which decided the issue in his favour was not any of these midrashim but tradition: 'Even though he continued to sit and expound to them all day long, they did not accept it from him until he said to them: Let (such and such) befall me! Thus did I hear from Shemaya and Avtalion.' While each of Hillel's midrash arguments were rebutted by his opponents, in one case they said, and this is important: 'As to the *gezera shawa* which you said – a man may not invent his own *gezera shawa*.' The Palestinian Talmud then quotes an Amoraic saying: 'A man may draw a *gezera shawa* in order to support the teaching he received, but he may not draw a *gezera shawa* to disprove the teaching he received.' However, the emphasis that Hillel's midrashim were not accepted until he had recourse to tradition is found only in the Palestinian Talmud, not in the Tosefta and the

---

[193] *M. Pes.* 2:2. The sugya in *B.T. Pes.* 29a also emphasizes that the verse offers no real support, but merely indicates the penalty for transgressing this halakha. The same phenomenon can also be observed for religious concepts. Thus the verse, 'He fashioneth their hearts alike, he considereth all their works' (Ps 23:15) is taken to imply that all inhabitants of the world pass before God in judgment *on New Year's day* (*M. Rosh H.* 1:2). That date, however, is not mentioned in the Bible, nor are the dates of other acts of judgment believed to be passed on other festivals (*ib.*). These were accepted tradition, and the verses function only as an illustration.

[194] Halevy cites a number of such examples. However, many are Amoraic midrashim which use typically Amoraic methods and do not prove that the Tannaim did not have their own scriptural arguments. His examples of Tannaic midrash, too, only prove that in those particular instances the midrash had no primary or creative function.

[195] Albeck, *Introduction*, 40-62; De Vries, *Toledot ha-halakha*, 9-21.

[196] *T. Pes.* ch. 4; *P.T. Pes.* 6, 33a; *B.T. Pes.* 66a. The story is adduced, among others, by Epstein, *Tannaitic Literature*, 511. See n. 196 above.

Babylonian Talmud. Moreover, even in the Palestinian Talmud the objection is not to the authority of midrash *per se*, but only against one specific form of midrash, the *gezera shawa*.[197] With regard to the *kal wa-homer* and the *hekkesh* used by Hillel, the Benei Bathyra raised only specific 'technical' objections. By implication, this proves that all agreed that these other midrash methods are capable of creating and deciding halakha.

We shall cite some more general examples.

The Mishna relates how difficult cases were referred to the Great Court in the Chamber of Hewn Stone in Jerusalem. The representative of the local court would appear in the Great Court and say: 'Thus did I expound דרשתי and thus did my colleagues expound; thus did I teach and thus did my colleagues teach . . .'[198] This implies that the local court had tried to arrive at a decision on the ground of midrash, and it was only when they did not reach a consensus that they came to hear the opinion of the Great Court.

If a certain midrash was found acceptable to all, the Halakha would be decided accordingly. This seems to have been the procedure in capital cases as described in the Tosefta.[199] If the judges felt that the accused was likely to be found guilty, the vote was postponed until the next day: 'And they would discuss a relevant (scriptural) passage throughout the night: if he is accused of murder, they discuss the passage dealing with the murderer; if he is accused of incest they discuss the passage dealing with incest.' Admittedly, this does not say that the verdict was decided according to the midrash learned by the judges, but it is obvious that the verdict was supposed to have influence on it, and thus on the determining of the Halakha in that case. It is hard to know whether these descriptions of the trial process from the Tosefta and the Mishna reflect actual criminal court proceedings in the Second Temple era, but they certainly give us the picture entertained by Tannaic tradition itself.

Another example is related to the issue we just dealt with: the question whether the paschal offering may be sacrificed on a Sabbath which coincides with Passover eve. For the Mishna, the problem had already been solved, and it stipulates that only the paschal sacrifice is offered on the Sabbath, since the Tora emphasizes it must be sacrificed at its 'appointed time', but not the pilgrimage offering (*hagiga*) which accompanies the paschal offering. This point, however, was argued vigorously in Second Temple days, and in this context Yehuda ben Dortai gives the testimony we cited already: 'I am amazed at the two greatest men of their generation, Shemaya and Avtalion: Though they are great Sages and great expounders (דרשנים), they did not tell Israel that the pilgrimage offering overrules the Sabbath . . .'[200] Thus in his eyes it was possible to decide on the grounds of midrash and permit the pilgrimage offering

---

[197] In fact, rabbinic sources emphasize that the use of *gezera shawa* is apt to break all limits of midrashic invention. See *P.T. Pes.* 6, 33a; *B.T. Pes.* 66a.

[198] *M. Sanh.* 11:2.

[199] *T. Sanh.* 9:1.

[200] *B.T. Pes.* 70b.

on the Sabbath. And indeed the sugya in the Babylonian Talmud arrives at the conclusion that the pilgrimage offering is equivalent to the paschal offering.

The Babylonian Talmud records three points of disagreement between the school of R. Yishmael and that of R. Akiva. All three turn on the question whether a certain action mentioned incidentally in the Tora is in fact voluntary, as the school of R. Yishmael hold, or obligatory as is the view of R. Akiva's disciples.[201] It is very unlikely that this consistent disagreement between the two exegetical schools in all three issues is based on halakhic tradition, and has nothing to do with their respective exegetical approach. Although this is not midrash in its fully technical sense, we are here confronted with two halakhic systems dependent on different exegetical approaches. And indeed, the approach of the disciples of R. Yishmael is very similar to that of their master recorded elsewhere:[202] ' "If thou lend money to any of my people" (Exod 22:25) – R. Yishmael says: Every "if" in the Tora is (referring to a) voluntary (action), except for this one and two others.' Clearly, an exegetical rule is stated here for the purpose of deciding halakha.

Certain biblical passages occasioned the collection of sets of halakhot. One of these is Num 27:8-11, three verses which in *Sifrei* to Numbers are the basis for arranging a series of halakhot regarding inheritance. But not it is not only the arrangement of the halakhot which is influenced by these verses. The passage in *Sifrei* concludes with a statement which reveals the value attached to midrash in this context:[203] ' "And this (the preceding three verses) shall be unto the children of Israel a statute of judgement" (Num 27:11) – The Tora gave intelligence[204] to the Sages to expound לדרוש and to say: Whoever is closest in blood relationship takes priority in inheritance.' Similarly, the Babylonian Talmud explains the reason why the Mishna placed a certain halakha before another in the laws of inheritance with the words: 'Since (the Tanna) derived this one by midrash, it is more dear.'[205] The authors of these statements in *Sifrei* and the Babylonian Talmud understood, it would seem correctly, that at least a part of the halakhot of inheritance was created and determined by way of midrash.

Finally, we shall review an example in which a difference in the Halakha appears to be based on a difference in midrash. In Mishna *Terumot* 6:6, R.

---

[201] *B.T. Sota* 3a. The three passages are: Num 5:14, 'And the spirit of jealousy came upon him and he be jealous of his wife'; Lev 21:3, the priest may not be defiled by a corpse, but 'for his kin that is near to him . . . and for his sister, a virgin that is near to him, . . . from her he may be defiled'; Lev 25:46, the Hebrew bondman does not serve perpetually, but 'of the children of the strangers that do sojourn amoung you . . . they shall be your bondmen forever'. The school of R. Akiva holds that it is obligatory, and the school of R. Yishmael that it is voluntary – for the husband to be jealous, for the priest to defile himself on behalf of close relations, and for the master to keep non-Jewish slaves in perpetual bondage.
[202] *Mekh. Nezikin* 19 (p. 315).
[203] *Sifrei Num.* 19 (p. 315).
[204] דעת; in *Yal. Shim.* no. 776 רשות.
[205] *B.T. Bava B.* 108b.

Eliezer and R. Akiva disagree on the substance of the restitution an Israelite should pay in case he ate inadvertently from the heave-offering reserved for the priests:

> R. Eliezer says: One may pay out of one type of produce for another, as long as he pays out of superior produce for inferior produce. But R. Akiva says: One may only pay out of the same sort of produce. . . . From the same verse whence R. Eliezer derives the more lenient ruling, R. Akiva derives the more stringent ruling: It is written, "And shall give it unto the priest *with* the holy thing" (Lev 22:14) – (namely) whatsoever is fit to be holy. Thus R. Eliezer, but R. Akiva says: "And he shall give unto the priest the holy thing" – the same holy thing he consumed.

The meaning of these words appears to be that the basis of the difference in the Halakha between R. Eliezer and R. Akiva lies in their different appreciation of the emphasis in the verse.

Refraining from citing more examples and summing up the evidence, we are justified in asserting that in many cases midrash was not just theoretical exegesis of Scripture, nor a mere corroboration of halakha that had been created in some other way, but an actual source and inspiration of halakha. In other words, the study of Scripture and the desire to fulfill its demands is to be reckoned among the vital sources of the Halakha. In a historical and theological perspective we may even say that without taking into account this function of the Midrash, a correct understanding of the development of ancient Judaism would be impossible.

LEGISLATION AND CASE LAW

The Mishna and other Tannaic sources contain much evidence of legislation by the Sages. The laws that resulted are called either *takkanot* (corrective ordinances) or *gezerot* (prohibitive decrees). They were issued by the Sages who stood at the head of the Sanhedrin or of the Pharisaic Sages. The earliest specific attributions are from the days of the first Pairs, Yose ben Yoezer[206] and Shimon ben Shetah.[207] Further legislation is reported coming from Hillel the Elder and his descendants, down to R. Yehuda the Prince, the redactor of the Mishna,[208] and even his grandson, R. Yehuda Nesia, who is mentioned in additions to the Mishna.[209] The question before us: to what extent is this legislative activity of the Sages – to which may be added their court decisions in specific cases – a source of halakha? Great importance has been ascribed to the legislation of the Sages by URBACH, who, as mentioned above, sees it as essential and, originally,

---

[206] On the first 'Pair', Yose ben Yoezer, see *P.T. Pes.* 1, 27d; *P.T. Shabb.* 1, 3d; *B.T. Shabb.* 14b-15a.

[207] *P.T. Ket.* ch. 8 end; *P.T. Shabb.* 1, 3d; *P.T. Pes.* 1, 27d.

[208] *M. Shev.* 10:3; *M. Gitt.* 4:3; 5:6; *M. Ar.* 9:4.

[209] *M. Av. Zar.* 2:6, etc. See *P.T. Nidda* 3, 50d on his *takkanot*. And see Epstein, *Tannaitic Literature*, 230f.

the exclusive source of halakha. In other words, the Halakha would from the beginning have been an institutional law system imposed by the Great Court and other legal institutions.[210] Before discussing this theory, we shall review the evidence.

In addition to those we mentioned, the Mishna mentions many other decrees and ordinances. Chapters four and five of Tractate *Gittin* record *takkanot* ordained for the 'betterment of the world' תיקון העולם. Thus we read: 'Hillel decreed the *prozbul* for the betterment of the world' (4:3). The *prozbul* is a legal fiction which allows debts to be collected after the Sabbatical year, and it was Hillel's intention thereby to overcome the fear that money-lenders had of loosing their money and so to encourage them to issue loans. We also find the various *takkanot* of Rabban Gamliel the Elder in matters of divorce and the collection of the *ketubba* (4:2-3). Concerning R. Yehuda the Prince, it is related: 'Rabbi convened a court and they voted . . .' (5:6), i.e., he assembled the Sanhedrin for legislation; the issue was the right of an owner to take back land that had been confiscated by the government. Regarding that same session of the court, incidentally, we are informed in detail about the Sages' participation and the order of seating,[211] and even about those who abstained from the vote and for what reasons.[212] Well-known are the Tannaic traditions about the eighteen halakhot over which Beit Shammai and Beit Hillel disagreed, and which were issued after a vote, apparently during the Roman War, with the intention of strengthening the separation between Jews and gentiles.[213] Often we find expressions in the Mishna and in baraitot that apparently refer to decrees and ordinances, such as 'At first they would . . . They decreed התקינו'; 'At first they would . . . When this became common they decreed . . .'[214]

The Mishna and baraitot attest to an additional source of halakha which is important in this context: case law. The 'case' מעשה is a practical problem brought for decision before the Great Court or another court, or before an important Sage. The decision made becomes a precedent, a rule of halakha and a basis for further halakhic creation. Thus we read: 'R. Tsadok testified that if flowing water was more than the dripping water (the whole) was still fit (as flowing water which purifies in whatever quantity).'[215] This testimony is based on a decision by the court, as stated at the end of this mishna: 'Such a case happened at Birat ha-Pilya and when the case came before the Sages they declared it fit.' Likewise, the subsequent mishna reports: 'R. Tsadok testified that if flowing water was led through (a channel made from) foliage of nuts it

[210] Urbach, 'Derasha'.
[211] *P.T. Gitt.* 5, 47b; *B.T. Gitt.* 59a; *B.T. Sanh.* 32a.
[212] *T. Ah.* ch. 18; *P.T. Shev.* 6, 36c; *P.T. Yev.* 7, 8c.
[213] *M. Shabb.* 1:4; *T. Shabb.* 1:16-17; *P.T. Shabb.* 1, 3c.
[214] E.g. *M. Shev.* 4:1; *M. Bikk.* 3:7; *M. Rosh H.* 4:4.
[215] *M. Ed.* 7:3; cf. *M. Mikw.* 5:5 (see next p.). On the 'case see further p. 178ff.

remained fit. Such a case happened at Ahalya, and when the case came before the Sages in the Chamber of Hewn Stone they declared it fit.'

In all, the Mishna and other Tannaic sources preserve more than sixty halakhot which are explicitly identified as decrees or ordinances, either attributed by name or with an anonymous formula such as 'they ordained'. In addition, the halakhot designated as 'cases' come to several dozen. But URBACH correctly claims that the real number of *takkanot* and *gezerot* cannot be limited to those so specifically described. Very likely the tradition concerning the ordinance or court decision regarding a particular halakha was not preserved. We can infer this from examples where in one source only the halakha is preserved, while a parallel source records the circumstances in which it was created. The Mishna merely states: 'For how long must a man proclaim (that he has found something)? Until all his neighbours know of it. So R. Meir. R. Yehuda says: At the three festivals and for seven days after the last festival.'[216] The Tosefta relates the evolution of this halakha: 'At first they used to proclaim it for three festivals and for seven days after the last festival; but when the Temple was destroyed they ordained that one should proclaim it thirty days. And from the "Peril" (the Hadrianic persecutions) onwards, they ordained that one should inform his neighbour, his relations and his townsmen, and that is sufficient.'[217] Similarly, the halakha concerning flowing water with dripping water, which we just cited, is mentioned in another place in the Mishna, but without referring to the case that occurred in Birat ha-Pilya.[218] Thus there is no doubt that it is only by accident that for large numbers of halakhot we possess no evidence of the court cases or the legislation that preceded them.

Nevertheless, it is extremely doubtful whether on the basis of this evidence we are entitled to affirm on the institutional character of the Halakha in general, or even of the early Halakha specifically, as is done by URBACH. Even if the actual number of decrees and case law decisions is hypothetically several times greater, it will still not amount to more than a tiny portion of the halakhic tradition as a whole. If we may enumerate some main areas of halakha, such as the sets of halakhot concerning prayer and benedictions; the basic rules of the synagogue; the structure of the laws of tithes, heave-offerings, and forbidden mixtures (*kilayim*); the thirty-nine classes of labour on the Sabbath; the Temple ritual; the laws of levirate marriage; the four principal classes of damages; the rules of bail; oaths and vows; or the laws of purity and impurity – there is no ground to believe that these, in part or as a whole, were created and formulated through legislation and court decision. No tradition concerning such *takkanot*

---

[216] *M. Bava M.* 2:6.
[217] *T. Bava M.* 2:17.
[218] *M. Mikw.* 5:5.

has been preserved, nor were they attributed to any institution or specific Sage.[219]

Generally, the traditions concerning *takkanot* or case law decisions refer to a specific halakha; at most we find a reference to a number of isolated halakhot. This is very far from being a sufficient basis for the conclusion that the Halakha is essentially the result of institutional legislation and court acts. Even less can this be held in view of the thousands of individual halakhot in the early period, and most certainly not in the later Tannaic and the Amoraic periods.

As we shall demonstrate below, halakhic disputes appear from the very beginning of the history of the Halakha ; disputes are recorded along with the oldest attributed traditions. It even happened that such halakhic controversies persisted through several generations and were not even decided by the time of the redaction of the Mishna or the Talmud. This fact alone testifies that the Halakha is not basically of an institutional nature. Furthermore, many halakhot reported to have been issued as *takkanot* or *gezerot*, are really ancient halakhic traditions known from early literary sources. In these cases, the *takkana* or *gezera* is merely a corroboration or official confirmation of an ancient and accepted halakha.[220] It is also doubtful whether the expressions 'they ordained' or 'when this became common . . . they ordained' and the like always testify to an actual tradition to the effect that the halakha involved was instituted through a court decision. It is not impossible that in many cases this is just a literary device to explain a change that occurred in the Halakha.

One of the prime sources of the Halakha is the opinion expressed by an individual teacher and its subsequent acceptance. Throughout the period under discussion, we find Sages expressing their views about the Halakha; and while at times their halakhot are accepted by their colleagues and general usage, at other times they are rejected. The Tosefta records two ancient halakhot which were rejected by other Sages:[221]

> Hilfeta ben Kavina says: Garlic from Baalbek is subject to defilement, since they sprinkle water on it and afterwards they braid it. Said the Sages: If so, let it be susceptible to uncleanness for Hilfeta ben Kavina, but insusceptible to uncleanness for all Israel.
>
> Yoshua ben Perahia says: Wheat which comes from Alexandria is susceptible to uncleanness because of their ἀνταλία (irrigation wheel). Said the Sages: If so, let it be susceptible to uncleanness for Yoshua ben Perahia and unsusceptible to uncleanness for all Israel.

Yoshua ben Perahia is one of the second Pair, and presumably Hilfeta ben

---

[219] The ordaining of the Eighteen Benedictions was ascribed to the Men of the Great Assembly, 120 elders including many prophets, *P.T. Ber.* 2, 4d and parr.; *Sifrei Deut.* 343 (p. 396). But it is very doubtful whether this is an actual tradition and not rather a homiletical image. See Ginzberg, *Commentary* 1, 230-327.

[220] Thus a large portion of the Eighteen Decrees (*M. Shabb.* 1:4; *P.T. Shabb.* 1, 3c) are actually ancient halakhot. See Alon, *Jews, Judaism*, 156-9, and see *ib.* n. 22 for previous literature.

[221] *T. Makhsh.* 4:3-4.

Kavina, who is mentioned first, lived before him. If so, we have here two of the very oldest halakhot attributed to named Sages, and significantly, they did not result from legislation, but rather are the opinions of individual Sages that were rejected by another Sage, or the majority of colleagues, here designated as 'the Sages'.[222]

In a later period we hear much about opinions of individual Sages that gradually became generally accepted. Earlier we quoted the story of R. Tarfon who, while reclining with his students in the shade of a dovecote on Sabbath afternoon, taught what he thought should be the benediction before drinking water to quench one's thirst: '(Blessed art Thou) Who createst living beings with their wants.'[223] In the Mishna, however, we read: 'If one drinks water to quench his thirst, he should say: . . . by Whose word all things exist. R. Tarfon says: . . . Who createst many living beings.'[224] Only in the days of the last Tannaim was there a sort of compromise reached between the two formulas, so that before drinking the anonymous formulation of the Mishna is recited, while after drinking R. Tarfon's formula is recited.[225] Similarly, we learn that R. Akiva once taught a halakha that was in contradiction to an earlier view:

> "Sick with her impurity" (Lev 15:33) – The first Elders used to say: She (the menstruant woman) shall be in her impurity, she should not apply kohl or rouge until she has immersed herself. Until R. Akiva came and taught: This will lead to hostility and he will wish to divorce her.[226]

R. Akiva did not serve as the head of a court, and his words therefore have no institutional significance. He was merely a Sage teaching his disciples, and as his view was accepted by them, it became current among the academies and thus a part of the Halakha. There are also testimonies to the effect that R. Akiva retracted his original teaching for another view, this later opinion being recorded in the Mishna.[227] In the Mishna, and more often in the Tosefta, we frequently encounter the expression: 'R. Akiva retracted and taught . . .'[228]

In sum, it cannot be denied that to some extent legislation and court decisions caused and influenced the creation of halakha. Certain problems were brought before the Sanhedrin, and it also happened that halakhot were initiated and formulated in the Sanhedrin in Jerusalem, and in the courts that later continued the operations of the Sanhedrin at Yavne and Usha and in the other towns of Galilee.[229] But this is exceptional. Fundamentally, the Halakha did not derive from legislative institutions such as the Sanhedrin, but rather emerged from the

---

[222] See on this phenomenon Epstein, 'Amru Hakhamim'.

[223] Above p. 61.

[224] M. Ber. 6:8.

[225] P.T. Ber. 6, 10b; B.T. Ber. 44b.

[226] Sifra Metsora end.

[227] Cf. Sifrei Z. p. 232 on M. Bava K. 9:12, where R. Akiva's revised opinion is found anonymously. See also above, p. 71.

[228] E.g. M. Taan. 4:4; T. Hull. 5:9; T. Zav. 1:6.

[229] See above p. 65.

small companies of the Sages and their disciples, which in turn were closely connected with society at large. The Halakha is a vital part of Oral Tora which, as demonstrated above, was created and even edited in the teaching situation by generations of Sages. This teaching situation, moreover, was open to questions from 'outsiders' such as the illiterate, women, and even non-Jews, and sometimes these questions brougth new ideas and thus were incorporated in Oral Tora. Just like the other parts of Oral Tora, the Halakha may be seen as the product of a learning community, in which certainly the Sages played a leading role, but not without a close and reciprocal relationship with the people at large.

CONTROVERSIES

As we have noted in passing, one of the foremost positive factors in the creation of halakha was the מחלוקת, controversy, between Sages. This is a fact which has not been sufficiently emphasized in previous research. Before discussing the significance of the phenomenon of halakhic controversies in rabbinic tradition, we shall first outline their nature and scope.

In fact, a conspicuous feature of rabbinic literature, and especially of the Halakha, is the large number of controversies and disputes. For the most part, the differing opinions are cited in the names of two opposing Sages of the same generation. Sometimes, however, the opponents are two academies or schools. This is particularly noticeable in the long series of disputes between Beit Shammai and Beit Hillel, which, in the Mishna and other Tannaic collections, amount to several hundreds. There are also cases involving three or more disputants. Very often we find an anonymous view opposed by the opinion of a named Sage. This anonymous view is sometimes designated with formulas like 'the Sages say' חכמים אומרים, 'but the Sages say' וחכמים אומרים, or 'said the Sages' אמרו חכמים.

Frequently, it happens that an opinion which is presented as anonymous or as that of 'the Sages' in one of the collections, usually the Mishna, appears elsewhere with the name of a specific Sage. A nice example is the first mishna, *Berakhot* 1:1:

> From what time in the evening may the *shema* be recited? From the time when the priests enter to eat of their heave-offering until the end of the first watch; thus R. Eliezer. But the Sages say: Until midnight. Rabban Gamliel says: Until the rise of dawn.

The parallel at the beginning of the Tosefta reads:

> From what time in the evenings may the *shema* be recited? From the time when the people enter to eat their bread on Sabbath eves; thus R. Meir. But the Sages say: From the time when the priests are permitted to eat of their heave-offering.

This shows that the first halakha, which in the Mishna is cited anonymously, was in fact the subject of a controversy. In addition, the Babylonian Talmud contains a baraita which teaches that the anonymous view of 'the Sages' in the

Tosefta is really the opinion of one of the Sages, R. Yoshua, and that there were still other opinions:

> From what time do we begin to recite the *shema* in the evening? From the time when the sanctity of the day begins on Sabbath eves; thus R. Elazar. But R. Yoshua says: From the time when the priests become ritually clean to eat of their heave-offering. R. Meir says: From the time when the priests immerse themselves to eat of the heave-offering. R. Hanina says: From the time when the poor man goes in to eat his bread with salt. . . . R. Aha says: From the time most people go in to dine.[230]

On the basis of this and many other examples, it may be presumed that in many cases we just happen to lack evidence of disagreement or disputed opinions, so that the number of controversies may in fact be much larger than would appear from the extant sources. Yet even if we count only those mentioned, the controversies amount to several thousands. Moreover, they are found in all halakhic collections and other collections which mention halakhic topics. Controversies are found in almost all areas of the Halakha and in all domains of life. Only a few early collections preserved within the Mishna, in particular those which recount realia of the Temple, contain almost no disputes and those which do appear are mostly additions by later Tannaim.

Nevertheless, the halakhic controversy is not a phenomenon that appears only in the later Tannaic period, but is found already in the earliest attributed traditions. The earliest participants in Oral Tora mentioned by name are the members of the first Pair, Yose ben Yoezer and Yose ben Yohanan the Jerusalemite, who lived during the struggle between the hellenizers and the Hasidim in Jerusalem, in the period of Antiochus Epiphanes.[231] Apart from the *takkanot* ascribed to Yose ben Yoezer which we have mentioned, two halakhic traditions are attributed to him. One of these is a dispute with his colleague Yose ben Yohanan in the matter of the laying on of hands on offerings prior to slaughtering them on festival days, a dispute which is reported to have continued throughout the days of the other Pairs.[232] The other tradition attributed to Yose ben Yoezer contains three testimonies, one of which we reviewed above, and to which the Mishna adds: 'And they called him Yose the Permitter'; implying that his halakhot were opposed by his colleagues or by other existing traditions.[233] The second Pair were Yoshua ben Perahia and Nitai the Arbelite. Two halakhic traditions have come down to us from Yoshua ben Perahia, both of which take the form of a dispute. One is about the wheat from Alexandria, the second about the laying on of hands on festivals; both have been mentioned

---

[230] *B.T. Rosh H.* 2b.

[231] Earlier in fact are some halakhic traditions attributed to the prophet Haggai, see above p. 134.

[232] *M. Hag.* 2:2. Scholars have suggested a number of explanations for the term לסמוך; see Albeck, *Mishna*, in his addenda *a.l.* However, the simple meaning is undoubtedly as we have written.

[233] *M. Ed.* 8:4; and see Epstein, *Tannaitic Literature*, 510. On one of these halakhot see above p. 153.

above.[234] The same situation prevails throughout the generations of Tannaim and Amoraim.

Many times, disputes concern details, there being agreement about the main point of the halakha in question. We find this in the dispute about the time for saying the *shema* in the evening, which was referred to earlier. All Sages agree that the *shema* is to be recited at the beginning of the evening; the disagreement is over the exact time. In effect, the differences are not great, as testified in the Palestinian Talmud at the beginning of *Berakhot*: 'Their views come close to being identical.'

There is, however, a number of disputes that touch on halakhic problems of fundamental importance. When we review, for example, the many controversies between Beit Shammai and Beit Hillel, we do find among them disagreements about central halakhic issues, and we can even speak of fundamentally divergent conceptions and attitudes. A disagreement of minor importance again concerns the reading of the *shema*, the question being whether the phrase in the Tora, 'When thou liest down and when thou risest up' (Deut 6:7) refers to the time or to the manner of reciting.[235] Of great significance is their well-known dispute in the matter of divorce: according to Beit Shammai a woman may not be divorced unless there is found in her unchastity (i.e., adultery), while Beit Hillel permit divorce even if she merely 'spoiled his dish for him', that is, any reason is sufficient for divorce. [236]Another very important area of controversy is the Sabbath, which we shall discuss in detail.

We are informed about the disagreement between Beit Shammai and Beit Hillel about the Sabbath in many sources. In Mishna, Tosefta, the two Talmudim and the Tannaic midrash collections, we find a series of disputes that revolve around the question: is it permissible to begin work on Friday if the work will be completed by itself on the Sabbath? For example: 'The School of Shammai say: Ink, dyestuffs or vetches may not be soaked (on Friday) unless there is time for them to get soaked the same day. And the School of Hillel permit it.'[237] In a Tannaic midrash we read:[238]

> "Six days shalt thou labour and do all thy work" (Exod 20:9) – This is what Beit Shammai say: Ink, dyestuffs and vetches may not be soaked unless there is time for them to get soaked the same day; nets may not be spread for wild animals, birds or fishes unless there is time for them to be caught the same day; the beams of the olive-press and the roller of the wine-press may not be moved unless there is time for (the juice and the

---

[234] Pp. 166 and 169. His name is also involved in a tradition about his activities in the sacrifical service (*Sifrei Z*. p. 302) but apparently this is a textual corruption. See Safrai, 'New Research', 204-7.

[235] *M. Ber.* 1:3.

[236] *M. Gitt.* 9:10; *P.T. Gitt.* end; *Sifrei Deut.* 269 (p. 288). Cf. also Matt 19:3-9.

[237] *M. Shabb.* 1:5.

[238] *Mekh. deR. Sh.b.Y.* p. 149. On the differences with other sources see Lieberman, *Tosefta ki-Fshutah* 3, 17-21.

oil) to flow on the same day; water may not be channelled into gardens unless there is time for it to be filled up on the same day; flesh, onions and eggs may not be placed on the fire nor cooked dishes into the oven unless there is time for them to be roasted on the same day. And Beit Hillel permit all these things.

In the continuation, the fundamental difference in attitude between the two schools which lies at the basis of these controversies is also recorded:

Since Beit Shammai say: "Six days shalt thou labour and do all thy work" – meaning that your work shall be completed on Friday. And Beit Hillel say: "Six days shalt thou labour" – you may labour all six days while the remainder of your labour may be performed of itself on the Sabbath; "and have done all your work" – that you may be on the Sabbath like one without work.

Accordingly, Beit Shammai forbid handing any work over to non-Jews willing to do it on the Sabbath: 'The School of Shammai say: One may not sell anything to a gentile or help him to load his beast . . . unless there is time for him to reach a place near by (before the Sabbath). And the School of Hillel permit it.'[239]

Such basic controversies exist in all areas of the Halakha, and they occur throughout the Tannaic period. Thus, in quantity as well as in content, the dispute is a phenomenon of great importance in rabbinic literature. The question before us now is: How was the dispute regarded by the Sages of Oral Tora? Was it not seen as an undermining of the authority of the Halakha? There is one baraita, attributed to R. Yose, which, seemingly, confirms this possibility; we have already referred to it briefly.[240]

In their days (i.e., of the earliest Sages), they disagreed only about the laying on of hands. There were five Pairs. . . . Said R. Yose: At first there were no disputes in Israel. The court of seventy-one sat in the Chamber of Hewn Stone . . . If someone had a question he would go before the court in his town . . . If they had a tradition they would tell them. If not, both would come before the court in the Chamber of Hewn Stone. Even though it has seventy-one, there are not less than twenty-three . . . The halakha was asked. If they possessed a tradition, they told them. If not, they put it to a vote. If the majority declared unclean, it was unclean. If the majority declared clean, it was clean. From there, halakha went forth and prevailed in Israel. But when there were many disciples of Shammai and Hillel who did not serve (their masters) adequately, controversies multiplied in Israel and the result was a Tora divided into two.[241]

---

[239] *M. Shabb.* 1:7. There are additional examples in the Mishna and baraitot.
[240] *T. Hag.* 2:8; *T. Sanh.* ch. 7 beg.; *P.T.Hag.* 2, 77d; *P.T. Sanh.* 1, 19c; *B.T. Sanh.* 88b.
[241] The lament about disciples who did not serve their masters adequately is also voiced in *T. Sota* ch. 14 end. There are versions which read: כשתי תורות; v. Lieberman, *Tosefta ki-Fshutah* 5, 1298; *ib.* 8, 756.

Without going into details, we can state the general message of this tradition: in ideal times there were only a few disputes; any disagreement was ultimately resolved by a vote of the highest halakhic authority, the Sanhedrin. Only with the proliferation of disciples who did not sufficiently respect the authority of tradition and its bearers, did controversies multiply. The baraita remains silent, however, as to why the disciples of Shammai and Hillel did not go up to the Sanhedrin and have their controversies resolved, and why in fact the Sages of that generation permitted the multiplication of disputes and the creation of two *Torot*.[242]

From the few sources we have cited above, it is already clear that the baraita of R. Yose reflects at most only a part of the historical situation. We could point first of all to the controversies which almost unseparably accompany the oldest halakhic traditions transmitted from before Shammai and Hillel. Secondly, it is not true that only Shammai's and Hillel's disciples, 'who did not serve their masters properly', had controversies. Most of the halakhic traditions transmitted in the names of Shammai and Hillel themselves are formulated as controversies between the two.[243] Moreover, how are we to reconcile R. Yose's baraita with the beginning of tractate *Eduyot*, mishna 1-3, where we find Shammai fixing measures in the halakhot of menstrual impurity, dough offerings and ritual baths, while Hillel is setting measures of his own – and the Sages disagree with both of them? Not only this: in mishna 7 and 8, Shammai even disagrees with both Beit Shammai and Beit Hillel; in mishna 10 Shammai disagrees with Beit Shammai, Beit Hillel and other Sages; and in mishna 11 Shammai again disagrees in two halakhot with Beit Shammai and Beit Hillel! And most important: all the Sages known to have been members of the schools of Shammai or Hillel, such as Rabban Yohanan ben Zakkai, R. Eliezer and R. Yoshua, and R. Akiva, are not only among the most prominent of the Tannaim – but are also those most commonly involved in controversies. What would be the point of calling these Sages 'disciples who did not serve their masters adequately'? And if they are not to be called such, then who could be those ill-reputed disciples?

But what is important for our discussion is not our analysis or historical criticism of R. Yose's view of the development of the Halakha, but rather that historiographers of Oral Tora since the days of the Geonim have accepted this view as the foundation of their histories. Is it, however, the same view of history and of the value of controversy as is generally accepted among the Tannaim? Let us consider some other Tannaic views.

---

[242] This question occupied Talmud scholars of all generations. See Albeck, 'Sanhedrin', esp. n. 28.
[243] See the sugya in *B.T. Shabb.* 15a which states that their disagreement was only over three issues, but the sugya in fact brings up five controversies, which make up a majority of the halakhic traditions transmitted in their names.

In a Sabbath homily held by R. Elazar ben Azaria at Yavne, in which he discussed the character of the Tora, he said among other things:[244]

> ["The words of the wise are as goads, and as nails well planted by the masters of assemblies which are given from one shepherd"; Eccl 12:11.] "And as nails well planted" – just as a plant bears fruit and multiplies, so the words of Tora bear fruit and multiply. "Masters of assemblies" – those who go in and seat themselves in groups and declare the unclean unclean and the clean clean, unclean in one place and clean in another place. Lest a man think: Whereas Beit Shammai declare unclean and Beit Hillel declare clean, one man forbids and another permits, why should I learn Tora any more? Therefore it says: "Words", "The words", "These be the words" (Deut 1:1) – "All these words" (Exod 19:1) were given by "One shepherd"; one God created them, one leader gave them; the Lord of all creation, blessed be He, said it.[245] So you too shall fill your heart with chambers and make room for the words of Beit Shammai and the words of Beit Hillel, the words of those who declare unclean and those who declare clean.

The emphasis of this homily is quite different from that of R. Yose's baraita. The controversies, including those of the school of Hillel and of the opposing school of Shammai, are not the result of neglect of studies ('not serving the master sufficiently'). On the contrary, 'One God created them', 'One leader gave them'.

Similarly, the following statement in Mishna *Avot* gives a positive evaluation of the great controversies:[246]

> Any controversy that is for the sake of Heaven shall in the end be of lasting worth, but any that is not for the sake of Heaven shall not in the end be of lasting worth. Which controversy was for the sake of Heaven? Such was the controversy of Hillel and Shammai. And which was not for the sake of Heaven? Such was the controversy of Korah and all his company.

Thus the disputes of Hillel and Shammai are not only for the sake of Heaven, but they are also of lasting value.[247] In the same vein, the two Talmudim in several places, when discussing controversies such as those of Beit Shammai and Beit Hillel, say of the two opposing views: 'These and these are the words of the Living God.'[248]

---

[244] *T. Sota* 7:9-12; *A.R.N.* a 18 (34a); *B.T. Hag.* 3a. Above pp. 51, 104, we quoted other parts of this homily.

[245] אמרו; in the *ed. princ.* אמרן.

[246] *M. Av.* 5:17.

[247] The attempts of medieval and contemporary commentators to harmonize this mishna with R. Yose's baraita are to be rejected as contradicting the plain meaning of both sources. See Albeck, *Mishna a.l.*

[248] *P.T. Ber.* 1, 3b; *P.T. Yev.* 1, 3b; *P.T. Sota* 3, 19a; *P.T. Kidd.* 1, 58d; *B.T. Er.* 13b; *B.T. Gitt.* 6b.

The dispute is not a matter of error or insufficiency, but itself belongs to the 'words of the Living God'. Such is borne out in the Tosefta, where R. Elai, a Sage of the Yavne generation, tells one version of a controversy between Beit Shammai and Beit Hillel, adding that when he came before R. Elazar ben Azaria and told him this version, R. Elazar said: 'By the Tora! Those very things were told to Moses on Sinai!'[249] Similarly, the Babylonian Talmud relates that when the prophet Elijah, being questioned by a Sage, revealed that in heaven they were at that moment studying a certain Tora passage, and when the Sage asked about a certain interpretation disputed among the Sages, the reply is: 'Evyatar my son says this; Yonatan my son says . . .; these and these are the words of the Living God.'[250] The Tora is material for study and meditation, including for the Holy One, blessed be He, and any interpretation or disputation which originates in a sincere striving to understand and to teach the divine Word, and not in self-aggrandizement or over-criticism, is seen as 'words of the Living God'.

In other words, the dispute is seen as an essential factor in the development and creation of the Halakha and of Oral Tora in general. It constitutes a large portion of both, and apparently it is one of the more fruitful elements in the history of halakhic thought throughout the period under discussion.

In the view of the present writer, the positive significance ascribed to controversies is also shown in the fact that even after a halakhic decision has been reached, the minority view is very often recorded along with the majority opinion and thus preserved for later generations. This may take the form of two ascribed opinions, or of one opinion being designated as that of 'the Sages' i.e., that which was accepted and fixed in the academies, while the other opinion is attributed by name. Chapter one of Mishna *Eduyot*, first having given the disputations between Shammai and Hillel, offers several explanations for this phenomenon: 'And why does one record the opinions of Shammai and Hillel when these do not prevail? To teach later generations that none should persist in his opinion, for lo, the Fathers of the World did not persist in their opinion.'[251] 'And why does one record the opinion of the individual against that of the majority, while the Halakha can be only according to the majority opinion? Because then, if (another) court approves the opinion of the individual, it may rely upon him.'[252] In the next mishna, yet another reason is suggested by R. Yehuda: 'Because then, if one shall say "I have received such a tradition", another may answer, "You did hear it as the opinion of such-a-one".'[253] In fact, we do find several instances where Sages belonging to various generations relied, when necessary, on a minority opinion that was rejected but recorded by

---

[249] *T. Pea* 3:2.
[250] *B.T. Gitt.* 6b. In the continuation, this sugya seeks to ease the tension in this dictum; cf, however, *B.T. Meg.* 15b and *B.T. Bava B.* 75b.
[251] *M. Ed.* 1:4.
[252] *M. Ed.* 1:5.
[253] Cf. *P.T. Shev.* 1, 33a.

the Mishna.[254] This last justification for recording the minority opinion was also employed in actual practice.[255]

However, it is doubtful whether these explanations do represent the original reasons for the custom of recording rejected opinions. It is more probable that at the root of this practice lay the conception of the legitimacy and positive significance of the halakhic controversy. The rejected view was preserved because of the fundamental belief that the Sages or the House of Study who advocated it did represent a legitimate element of the Halakha and of the Tora of the Living God.

CUSTOM

Another source of halakha of some importance, and especially so in the field of civil law, is מנהג custom. In early and later sources, many halakhot are said to have originated in popular custom. We also find rules dealing with ritual and with civil law indicated in some sources as 'custom', and elsewhere as established halakha. Conversely, we can surmise that many halakhot not explicitly identified as being derived from the teachings of the Sages, be it by logic, by way of midrash, or as an authoritative decree, in reality originated in popular custom. As a result of their general acceptance, these halakhot can be said to be legal innovations made by the community as a whole.

Except for a few in the domain of civil law, the halakhot attested to have originated in custom are not of central importance. They were not the sort of halakhot that led to the creation of entirely new areas and sets of rules. Of the main halakhic systems, such as those governing agriculture and the ritual commandments pertaining to it, the Sabbath, festivals, prayer and benedictions, purity and impurity, and the penal system, none were ascribed to custom. Those that were, outside the economic sphere, are mainly expansions of existing halakhot or halakhic systems without fundamental significance. This should not, however, lead us to underestimate the power of custom to create halakha.

The creative power of custom, it seems, was understood in two ways: as a determinant in a doubtful case, and as an actual source for new creation. The determining function is formulated in the following dictum: 'Not only this halakha, but every halakha about which the court is not sure, and you do not know its nature – go out and observe how the community behave, and behave accordingly;'[256] or in the Aramaic phrase: 'Go out and observe what is the custom of the people'.[257]

---

[254] See *B.T. Ber.* 9a; *B.T. Shabb.* 45a; *B.T. Er.* 46a; *B.T. Gitt.* 11a; *B.T. Nidda* 6a; *ib.* 9b.
[255] *T. Halla* 1:10.
[256] *P.T. Pea* 1, 20c; *P.T. Maas. Sh.* 5, 56b; *P.T. Yev.* 7, 8a.
[257] *B.T. Ber.* 45a; *B.T. Pes.* 54a.

Custom as a creative factor can be observed in a detail of the following mishna: 'All the land-bound commandments do apply only in the Land (of Israel) . . . except for *orla* (fruit from a young tree, Lev 19:23) and *kilayim* (mixture of diverse kinds, Lev 19:19). R. Eliezer says: Also *hadash* (new produce before bringing the *omer*, Lev 23:14).'[258] Thus as an exception to the general rule, these three land-bound commandments are binding both inside the Land of Israel and outside it. Now the sources of the three commandments are enumerated in another mishna: '*Hadash* is prohibited from the Tora in every place,[259] *orla* by halakha, and *kilayim* from the words of the Scribes.'[260] Thus three sources are discerned: the Tora, the 'words of the Scribes' i.e., a ruling of the Sages, and 'halakha'. Regarding the last source, there is a dispute between Amoraim. R. Yohanan believes that it means a halakha that was accepted through the generations, 'halakha to Moses from Sinai'; Shmuel however thinks that 'halakha' here means the law of the land, the custom of the local community.[261] For our purposes we do not have to decide which was the intention of the Mishna; it suffices that some regarded the validity of the rules of *orla* outside the Land of Israel as being founded on popular custom.

But it was in the area of financial relationships, between individuals or between the individual and the community, that the creative function of custom was most prominent. Here, there was not felt to be any contradiction or even tension between the principles of the Halakha and general custom. In the literature of Oral Tora there was a widespread conception that in monetary arrangements 'a man may stipulate against what is written in the Tora'.[262] Custom was understood as a *de facto* agreement accepted by the entire community, and thus by all sides to these arrangements. For this reason, Tannaic and Amoraic halakha recognizes custom in all laws to do with debt, mutual obligation, purchase and the like, even though they stand in opposition to the rules laid down by the established Halakha. In the same way, deeds are valid, even when not drawn up according to the Halakha, so long as they conform to the custom of the respective lands.[263] The only limitation which we find to the halakhic recognition of custom is in cases where custom contradicts the principles of justice or of individual rights and privacy.[264]

More problematic was the relation between custom and established halakha in other spheres. As we have said, various sources indicate that custom can be the decisive factor in doubtful cases and be the source of new halakhot. The

[258] *M. Kidd.* 1:9.
[259] Lev 23:14 gives an absolute prohibition: 'And ye shall eat neither bread, nor parched corn, nor green ears, until the selfsame day.'
[260] *M. Orla* 3:9.
[261] *B.T. Kidd.* 38b; *P.T. Orla* 3, 63b.
[262] Although other Sages opposed this. See e.g. *M. Ket.* 5:1; *B.T. Ket.* 56b; 83a-b; *P.T. Pea* 5 end, 19d.
[263] *M. Bava B.* 10:1; *B.T. Bava B.* 165a; cf. *B.T. Kidd.* 49a.
[264] See the *Responsa* of R. Shlomo ibn Adret, Vol. 2 no. 168; Elon, *Jewish Law* 2, 764-7.

question is, however, whether custom has validity even where it contradicts the Halakha in areas not governed by the kind of mutual agreement between individuals that obtain in monetary matters. There is a principle that states: 'Custom overrules halakha', and at least in one place it is applied in non-monetary matters. The Tora stipulates that when a man refuses to marry his deceased brother's widow in a levirate marriage, she may protest to the elders of the town: 'Then shall his brother's wife come unto him in the presence of the elders and loose his shoe (נעל) from off his foot' (Deut 25:9). The term נעל is specified by the Mishna to mean a real shoe or a sandal with a heel-piece, not a felt shoe or a sandal without a heel-piece.[265] A stricter interpretation is rejected by the Palestinian Talmud with the words: 'If Elijah will come and say that *halitsa* may be performed with a shoe – we listen to him; that it is not performed with a sandal – we do not listen to him, since the majority were accustomed to perform *halitsa* with a sandal, *and custom overrules halakha.*'[266] Medieval authorities and modern scholars have had great difficulty explaining this pericope and have tried to soften its clear implications, finding it hard to accept that even with regard to matrimonial law, custom has the power to overrule the Halakha.[267] Even if we do not accept these explanations, we should admit, however, that there is no other instance like this outside the realm of monetary law, and it is obvious that in the history of the Halakha this principle or others like it were not used extensively, either in theory or in practice.[268]

These limitations taken into account, the relative importance of custom as a source of halakha must be stressed. It seems to be related to the conception of the Sages that Oral Tora is handed down to the People of Israel which observes the Tora. The community is granted power and authority to create halakha and to decide between conflicting opinions, not only on the presumption that the community strives to fulfill the true intentions of the Tora, but also because a custom or a particular interpretation, by the very fact of its acceptance in the practice of the People which 'does the Tora', constitutes halakha.

This leads us to the fundamental restrictive function of custom in the field of halakha: new halakhot legislated by the supreme authority, the Sanhedrin, do not become halakha unless they are accepted in actual practice by the nation, and any halakha which does not gain such acceptance is not considered to be in force. We shall give three examples. We have been referring above to a halakhic dispute of Hillel's, in which it was finally agreed that the Passover sacrifice is to

---

[265] *M. Yev.* 12:1.
[266] *P.T. Yev.* 12, 12c. When the prophet Elijah returns, one of his missions will be to resolve difficult halakhic questions, but not all of his decisions will be accepted. See *M. Ed.* 8:7; *B.T. Av. Zar.* 36a.
[267] See Lifshits, 'Minhag'.
[268] Another example is from the Gaonic period: Rav Yehudai Gaon (757-761) wrote to the Jews of Palestine that they were not behaving according to the Halakha as regards ritual slaughter and other halakhot, and they replied, according to an opposing Sage, 'Custom overrules halakha'. See *Ginzei Schechter* 2, 560. In general we can say that custom remained to be an important creative factor in the Halakha in the post-talmudic period.

be offered even when the eve of Passover falls on a Sabbath. However, an additional question arose: should it also be permitted to carry the knives (for slaughtering) on the Sabbath? This time, Hillel does not have a clear-cut tradition, but referring to the popular custom of having the sheep carry the knives in their furs, his reply is: 'Leave them (the Israelites) be, the Holy Spirit is upon them. If they are not prophets, they are at least children of the prophets.'[269] Similarly, in tractate *Sofrim*, concerning a controversy on the reading of the *megillot* on festivals, we read: 'And thus was the custom of the people, since no halakha is determined until there is a custom.'[270] Again, when the Sages wished to annul the prohibition of the oil of gentiles – a prohibition not found in the Tora but decreed by the Sages – they based their decision on the fact that the prohibition had not gained acceptance, as testified by actual reports, and a general maxim is quoted: 'Any decree enacted by a court for the community, but which the majority of the community did not accept, is no decree.'[271]

PRECEDENTS

Throughout the Tannaic and Amoraic periods, the precedent or 'case' מעשה functioned as a source for creating or deciding halakha. At the very beginning of the Mishna, *Berakhot* 1:1, a case involving Rabban Gamliel's sons is mentioned: 'Once (lit., a case:) his sons returned from a wedding feast. They said to him: We have not recited the *shema*, etc.' Dozens of such cases are cited in all Orders of Mishna and Tosefta, and in baraitot.[272] In Amoraic literature as well, many cases are introduced, sometimes followed by a conclusion such as: 'Learn from it three things . . .'[273]

In the following example, such a conclusion is drawn, but it is interesting also to study the contents of the decision made. The Babylonian Talmud relates:[274]

> He said: A case עובדא occurred at the house of R. Hiya bar Rabbi – Rav Yosef teaches: R. Oshaia bar Rabbi (was also present); and Rav Safra teaches: R. Oshaia bar R. Hiya (was also present, and the case was brought before these three Sages)[275] – that there came before them[276] a proselyte who had undergone circumcision but not ritual immersion. They said to him: Stay here until tomorrow and we will immerse you (in order to complete his conversion).

From this case the sugya derives three halakhot:

---

[269] *T. Pes.* 4:2; *P.T. Pes.* 6, 33a; *B.T. Pes.* 66a.

[270] *Sofrim* 14:16.

[271] *P.T. Shabb.* 1, 3d; *B.T. Av. Zar.* 36a. This was one of the 'Eighteen Decrees', cf. above.

[272] In the Order *Zeraim* 18 cases are brought, in *Moed* thirty-three. See Wacholder, 'Rabban Gamliel', 143f.

[273] *B.T. Ber.* 27a; *B.T. Shabb.* 40b etc.

[274] *B.T. Yev.* 46b.

[275] See commentaries of Rashi and others.

[276] Principal versions: לקמייהו.

Learn from this that a proselyte requires three (judges constituting the court required for conversion), learn from it that he is not deemed a proselyte until he has undergone both circumcision and immersion, and learn from it that a proselyte is not immersed at night (since a court does not sit by night).

The second halakha derived from this case is in effect a decision in the old Tannaic dispute as to whether circumcision alone suffices or immersion is also required for a proselyte.[277] The other two halakhot are Amoraic innovations from the time of R. Yohanan to the effect that conversion must be administered by a court and hence requires three judges and must be performed by day;[278] these new rules were confirmed or even authorized by the case cited above.

Another example is from late Second Temple times. The Mishna relates:[279]

He (R. Hanina the prefect of the priests) testified also of a little village near by Jerusalem wherein lived a certain old man who used to lend money to all the people of the village and write out (the bond of indebtedness) in his own hand, and the others (the witnesses) signed it; and when the matter came before the Sages they declared it permissible (even though the bonds were not written by the hand of the witnesses, as was the practice at the time). Hence you may conclude that a woman may write out her own bill of divorce and a man his own quittance, for the validity of the document depends only on its signatories.

The latter halakha is mentioned elsewhere without citing the case: 'A woman may write out her own bill of divorce and a man his own quittance, for the validity of a document depends only on its signatories.'[280] This halakha, which, as we learn from the first passage, was preceded by a case, not only was incorporated in the established Halakha, but also became the basis for many subsequent halakhot in the matter of legal documents.[281]

Thus far we have presented examples of precedents which, when brought before a court, resulted in a clear halakhic decision in a case of ambiguity or unclarity about a halakha. Even without such a decision, however, a precedent was able to influence current practice simply by virtue of an individual Sage's own behaviour. In connection with the *halitsa* ceremony we referred to above, the Mishna tells of the biblical passage which is to be recited:[282] 'And she shall answer and say, So shall it be done unto that man that will not build up his brother's house' (Deut 25:9). To which the Mishna adds: 'Thus far one used to recite. But when R. Hyrcanos recited it under the terebinth in Kfar Eitam[283] and completed the (Tora) section, the rule was established to complete the section

---

[277] *P.T. Kidd.* 3, 64d; *B.T. Yev.* 46a-b. On this passage see Alon, *Jews, Judaism*, 172.
[278] *B.T. Yev.* 46b.
[279] *M. Ed.* 2:3.
[280] *M. Gitt.* 2:5.
[281] *B.T. Gitt.* 20a-23b.
[282] *M. Yev.* 12:6.
[283] The reference is to Eitam in Judea south of Bethlehem (cf. 2 Chr 11:6).

(thus including the words): "And his name shall be called in Israel: The house of him that hath his shoe loosened".' R. Hyrcanos's own behaviour in the case of a certain *halitsa* procedure became a new halakhic norm.

Similarly, the Tosefta reports:[284]

> It happened that when our masters gathered in the towns of the Samaritans by the road (leading from Judea to the Galilee), they (the Samaritans) brought before them greens (to eat). R. Akiva jumped up and tithed it as untithed produce (assuming that the Samaritans are considered Jews but do not tithe their produce). Said Rabban Gamliel to him: How is it that your heart impelled you to transgress the words of your colleagues? Or who gave you permission to tithe? He replied to him: Did I establish halakha in Israel? And he said: I did tithe my greens. He said to him: Know that you have established halakha in Israel by tithing your own greens!

The Halakha is bound to actual practice, and a precedent established by a Sage who is recognized for his wisdom and for his practical behaviour in the eyes of most or all of the community has the power to establish and determine halakha.

A good example of the importance of the halakhic precedent is the dispute between Rabban Yohanan ben Zakkai and the Benei Bathyra at Yavne. In the Temple it had been customary to sound the shofar on the New Year even when it fell on a Sabbath, but the shofar was not blown on the Sabbath outside Jerusalem and the Temple. Rabban Yohanan ben Zakkai wished, following the destruction of the Temple, to have the shofar sounded at Yavne – just as it had been in the Temple. Regarding this case we read:[285]

> Our masters taught: Once the New Year fell on Sabbath and all the towns assembled. Rabban Yohanan ben Zakkai said to the Benei Bathyra: We shall sound it. They said to him: Let us discuss it. He said to them: We shall sound and afterwards discuss. After sounding the shofar they said to him: Let us discuss. He said to them: The horn has already been heard at Yavne, and there is no refuting an established case.

It is likely that here we have to do with literary exaggeration, since the Benei Bathyra certainly must have been aware of the decisive importance of a precedent. Notwithstanding, this tradition nicely expresses the place of precedent in the development of the Halakha as viewed by the Sages themselves.

'HALAKHA TO MOSES FROM SINAI'

Three times in the Mishna,[286] as well as a number of times in the Tosefta, Sifra and the two Talmudim, it is said with regard to certain halakhot that they are הלכה למשה מסיני 'a halakha given to Moses from Sinai'.[287] In addition,

---

284 *T. Demai* 5:24.
285 *B.T. Rosh H.* 29b.
286 *M. Pea* 2:6; *Ed.* 8:7; *Yad.* 4:3.
287 In the *Mekhilta, Sifrei Num.* and *Sifrei Deut.* no such halakhot are found.

several baraitot describe halakhot in slightly different terms, such as 'These are the words spoken to Moses from Sinai', or 'These words were spoken from Mount Horeb'.[288] Halakhot are ascribed to Moses from Sinai by Amoraim as well, mainly in Palestine, in the two Talmudim.[289]

Sometimes, a single halakha is ascribed to Moses from Sinai. Such is the case in the tradition part of which was quoted already (the detailed 'chain of transmission' in this tradition will occupy us later):

> It once happened that R. Shimon of Mitspe sowed (his field with two kinds of wheat and the case came) before Rabban Gamliel; and they went to the Chamber of Hewn Stone to inquire. Said Nahum the scrivener: I have a tradition from R. Measha, who received it from his father, who received it from the Pairs, who received it from the Prophets as a halakha given to Moses from Sinai, that if a man sowed his field in two kinds of wheat and made them up into one threshing-floor, he leaves one *pea*; but if two threshing-floors, he must leave two (separate) *peot*.[290]

Similarly, 'The willow branch (which must be taken and waved, apart from the *lulav*, when going around the altar at the Feast of Sukkot) is a halakha to Moses from Sinai.'[291]

It also happens that collections of halakhot are designated as such, like the following from the source called *Tanna de-Bei R. Yishmael*: '("To make a difference . . .) between the beast that may be eaten and the beast that may not be eaten" (Lev 11:47) – these belong to the eighteen *treifot* (meats made unfit for consumption) that were conveyed to Moses from Sinai;'[292] or the words of R. Yohanan: 'All measures – halakha to Moses from Sinai.'[293]

Most of the Geonim and the medieval rabbis saw no problem whatsoever in accepting that a specific halakha or halakhic principle was actually 'revealed to Moses from Sinai', in the sense that the Holy One, blessed be He, delivered it orally to Moses and that it was transmitted in this form through the generations. Indeed, support for this conception could be seen in the chain of transmission in the mishna on the *pea* which we cited above and in the other instances in the Mishna which contain similar detailed chains of transmission.[294]

However, in some cases medieval rabbis felt difficulty in ascribing a halakha to Moses. The outstanding example is the mishna (*M. Yad.* 4:3) stating, as 'halakha to Moses from Sinai', that in Ammon and Moab, second tithes must be separated in the seventh year. Now Ammon and Moab are considered outside the Land of Israel, and according to the accepted Halakha, the Tora dispenses

---

[288] E.g. *T. Pea* 2:2; *T. Halla* 1:6.
[289] Many scholars drew up lists of these halakhot. See Bacher, *Tradition*, 33-46; a fuller list is in Levinger, *Maimonides' Techniques*, 190-205.
[290] *M. Pea* 2:6.
[291] *T. Sukka* 3:1.
[292] *B.T. Hull.* 42a.
[293] *P.T. Shev.* 1, 33b etc.
[294] *M. Yad.* 4:3 and, in shorter form, *Ed.* 8:7.

the lands outside the Land of Israel from the obligation of tithing; it is even stated explicitly that it is only the tradition of the Sages that prescribes such for these lands. Thus, the medieval commentators were forced to explain how it could be that such a halakhic detail which is merely based on the tradition of the Sages could nevertheless be 'a halakha revealed to Moses from Sinai'.[295]

Since the modern period, scholars such as KROCHMAL, GEIGER, FRANKEL, WEISS, LAUTERBACH and ALBECK are naturally much less inclined to accept the attribution of halakhot to Moses from Sinai.[296] In particular this regards such Tannaic traditions as present the idea that 'Elijah will . . . return to remove afar those [families] that were brought nigh by violence and to bring nigh those [families] that were removed afar by violence,'[297] or the revelation on what issues precisely Beit Shammai and Beit Hillel disagreed,[298] as 'halakha to Moses from Sinai'. Most scholars take the expression to mean 'as if it were a halakha to Moses from Sinai', or to refer to 'halakhot which were accepted from days of old' or those for which the Sages could not find a source. Other scholars hypothesized that the expression was used by the Pharisaic Sages in their struggle against the Sadducees who did not accept their oral traditions.

As against these early and later explanations, it may be observed that we do not find a single instance in which a halakha is said to be 'like a halakha given to Moses from Sinai'. The ascriptions to Moses from Sinai are given straightforward, with or without a chain of transmission. Furthermore, it is highly improbable that the Tannaim or the Pharisees preceding them would have ascribed halakhot to Moses for the reason that these had no scriptural support or were contested by the Sadducees. We have seen above that there are many halakhot and halakhic decisions in Tannaic literature without any formal basis in exegesis or in legislation.

As we read in the oft-cited beginning of Avot, the Sages saw the creation of Oral Tora as rooted in the giving of Tora from Sinai and its transmission and explanation by the bearers of Tora throughout the generations: 'Moses received Tora from Sinai and delivered it to Joshua, Joshua to . . . the Elders and the Elders to the Men of the Great Assembly.' But along with its transmission, innovations were introduced, by way of midrash, commentary, decisions and legal institutions, or simply by way of innovation flowing from 'the ever-increasing spring' (M. Avot 2:8). The Sages, as we saw, did not hesitate to describe essential halakhot as 'floating in the air', as far as scriptural support is concerned, and 'having naught to support them'; and others 'as mountains hanging by a hair, for Scripture is scanty and the halakhot many' (M. Hag. 1:8). However, with regard to these halakhot and similar ones which could be added,

---

[295] See the commentary of R. Shimshon me-Sens on M. Yadayim, and Rabbenu Asher in his Hilkhot mikwaot No. 1.
[296] Krochmal, More nevukhei ha-zeman, 211-13; Geiger, Kovets maamarim, 60-70; Weiss, Dor dor we-dorshav 1, 10; Lauterbach, Midrash and Mishnah, 96-128; Albeck, Introduction, 26-28.
[297] M. Ed. 8:7 (cf. the forced explanation of Maimonides ad loc.).
[298] T. Pea 3:2.

the Sages did not care to state that they were 'halakha to Moses from Sinai'. Likewise, in the above we have enumerated a number of halakhot which are in evidence since the earlier Second Temple period. But neither to these nor to any other halakha with similar ancient evidence is this qualification given.

Our explanation is that the Sages in ascribing halakhot and other traditions to Moses on Sinai did not intend to teach us that some specific tradition was revealed to Moses and thus transmitted through the generations. Their intention was to state that, indeed, it is no more than a halakha and a tradition, and such in itself is 'halakha to Moses from Sinai'.

Three important traditions emphasize the aspect of innovation inherent in the creation of Oral Tora; and these very same traditions also state that the words of Oral Tora are spoken on Horeb or given from Mount Sinai.

A midrash in *Seder Eliyahu Zutta* [299] compares the Written Tora to a measure of wheat and a bundle of flax which a king handed to his two servants. The foolish one 'did not do a thing' but the wise servant 'took the flax and wove a cloth; he took the wheat, ground, sieved and winnowed it and kneaded and baked it into a loaf; then he placed it on the table and spread the cloth on it.' Thus the Tora as it is first given is like a principle, a kernel which the wiser servant by himself, knowing the intention of the king, took and worked into something new. The midrash even mentions explicit examples of such elaboration: the order of prayer on the Sabbath and weekdays, the order of reading the Tora, the various benedictions etc. The parable and the examples are intended to teach that Scripture and tradition alike 'are given to us from Mount Sinai', and '*Mikra* (Scripture) and *mishna* (tradition) both are spoken from the Mouth of Omnipotence'. The very formation of Oral Tora is taken as evidence of the fact 'that when the Holy One, blessed be He, gave Israel the Tora, He gave it only in the form of wheat to be worked into flour and flax to be worked into a cloth.'

Likewise, the beautiful aggada in the name of Rav, one of the pillars of the Babylonian Talmud, tells us of the growth of Oral Tora; we have cited it in our previous chapter as well.[300] When Moses arrived on high, the Holy One blessed be He referred him to R. Akiva: '. . . he went and sat down at the end of eight[een][301] rows (of benches), but he did not understand what they were saying. . . until . . . the students asked: Master, whence do you have this? He answered: Halakha to Moses from Sinai.' Moses our Master did not understand a single word of what R. Akiva taught to his students, for R. Akiva went far beyond what was revealed to Moses on Sinai. Moses even did not understand that last 'halakha to Moses on Sinai'! However, all halakhot that R. Akiva teaches are 'halakha ot Moses from Sinai', for all that is created and taught as

---

[299] Chap. 2 (p. 171f.).
[300] *B.T. Men.* 29b.
[301] Thus in all major versions.

halakha has its basis in the Tora of Moses. The words of the Tora contain implicitly what is later created explicitly in the Halakha.

In fact, this is what we hear in a tradition in the name of R. Akiva himself. In a baraita,[302] a decision he made in a halakhic issue appeared to be new in the eyes of his students: 'Behold, the students were looking one at another. He said to them: Why is this difficult in your eyes? . . . just like all of Tora is halakha to Moses from Sinai, so (the halakha he was teaching them) is halakha to Moses from Sinai.' As soon as the Tora was given, Israel started to explain and expand it, and any innovation they made was incorporated into it, and thus 'all of Tora is halakha to Moses from Sinai'. In another passage, R. Akiva says:[303] ' "And the Tora which the Lord gave between himself and the children of Israel from Mount Sinai through the hand of Moses" (Lev 26:45) – this teaches that the Tora, its halakhot, its details and its stipulations were all given through the hand of Moses from Sinai.' R. Akiva, as we shall set forth below (see p. 200-7), was among the greatest innovators in the Halakha; his innovations may even exceed in number those of all of his colleagues; yet he stated that all of Tora is 'halakha to Moses from Sinai'.

In a very picturesque *derasha* attributed to an older contemporary of R. Akiva, R. Elazar ben Azaria,[304] innovation in Tora is compared to the plowing with an ox which must be directed in the right course and, thus directed, brings life into the world so that things 'grow and multiply like plants'. The things that grow and multiply even include matters disputed between Beit Shammai and Beit Hillel, yet 'all these words were given by one Shepherd and One God created them'. This same Sage, R. Elazar ben Azaria, protested against R. Akiva's endeavours to derive certain halakhot from Scripture, saying that such sophisticated midrashim were not justified because these were 'halakha to Moses from Sinai'.[305] The Babylonian *sugya* summarizes the differences between both Sages as follows: 'For R. Akiva: Scripture, for R. Elazar ben Azaria: halakha.'[306]

In the same vein must be understood all those expressions in rabbinic literature which state that what a Sage or a student teaches is like the teaching of Moses himself, and that being witness to this teaching is like being present at Mount Sinai.[307] In fact, this same conception is contained in the tradition attributed to Jesus, that the Scribes and Pharisees 'are seated on the chair of Moses' (Matt 23:2). This is an expression which is also found in a saying of a later Amora; it must be added that teaching was done by a Sage while being

---

[302] *B.T. Nidda* 45a.
[303] *Sifra, Behukotai* 2 (112c).
[304] *T. Sota* chap. 7:9-10; *A.R.N.* a 18 (34b) etc. Cf. above, p. 173.
[305] *Sifra, Tsav* 11 (43b).
[306] *B.T. Nidda*, end.
[307] Cf. Urbach, *Sages*, chap. 12.

seated.[308] The tradition of R. Yoshua ben Levi is widespread in rabbinic literature: 'Even what an accomplished student will teach before his master, it was said already to Moses from Sinai.'[309] That student, however, did not receive this teaching from his master; he is creating a new teaching, setting it forth before his master and only realizing what is potentially present in the words of the Tora.

The 'chains of transmission' which in Tannaic literature attribute a certain halakha to the master and the master's master, and so on, are to be explained as a mere literary expression indicating that it is a reliable halakha which can be associated without scruples with the Tora given to Moses from Sinai.

In sum, we may state that halakhot which are called 'halakha to Moses from Sinai' have nothing special. They are neither ancient traditions nor traditions without an authoritative source. They are a part of Oral Tora which goes hand in hand with the Written Tora; and the latter is seen as given through Moses in his time and thus for the generations.[310]

It seems, however, that from the second or third Amoraic generation onwards Sages started to consider these halakhot as being distinct from the teachings of the Sages.[311]

Stages in the History of Tannaic Halakha

THE CONTROVERSIES BETWEEN BEIT SHAMMAI AND BEIT HILLEL

In the section on the sources of the Halakha, we discussed the important role of controversies in the creation of halakha. These controversies, however, especially the more prominent ones, have other aspects, a knowledge of which is essential for understanding the history of the Halakha. Many of the disputes of the Amoraim and Tannaim have to do with some minor detail in the evaluation of a certain act, such as a measure, etc., and offer no reason to speak of a real difference in religious and social outlooks. But in quite a number of other controversies, especially those among Sages who are regularly involved in disputes, certain general characteristics can be discerned which point to fundamentally different halakhic attitudes of the disputants. Most important are the large group of disputes between the schools of Shammai and Hillel. In fact, the controversies of Beit Shammai and Beit Hillel reveal the existence of two basic currents in the Halakha during a period of great importance, the early Tannaic period or, roughly, the first century C.E.

We mentioned already that we have evidence of only a limited number of controversies between Hillel and Shammai themselves. But Tannaic tradition

---

[308] *Pes. de-R.K.* 1 (p. 12). The relationship between both traditions was pointed out earlier by Bacher, 'Siège de Moïse'; see also Sukenik, 'The Chair of Moses in the Ancient Synagogues'.

[309] *P.T. Pea* 2, 17b; *P.T. Hag.* 1, 76d; *Lev. R.* 22 (p. 492) etc.

[310] For more elaboration see Safrai, 'Halakha le-Moshe mi-Sinai'.

[311] See e.g. the *sugya* in *P.T. Pea* 1, 15b top.

records hundreds of disputes with explicit reference to their schools. To these we must add the controversies between R. Eliezer and R. Yoshua, in which R. Eliezer, who is often named *Shammati* i.e. the Shammaite,[312] expresses the view of Beit Shammai either directly or in some redacted version, while R. Yoshua represents the line of Beit Hillel. Regarding some of these controversies we are told this expressly; with regard to others we are able to infer it with certainty through a comparison of the sources; while for still other cases we can presume it with some degree of probability.

We possess almost no controversies between Beit Shammai and Beit Hillel concerning the order of the sacrificial cult and the priestly service. Nor do we know of disputes between the two schools in matters of the Sanhedrin, the death penalty or corporal punishment. We do know of many controversies in matters of prayer and benedictions, agricultural laws, Sabbath and festival laws, matrimonial law and related financial questions, and purity laws.

A fact which strikes one immediately is that the school of Shammai are the more stringent in halakha. To cite some examples:

> Beit Shammai say: Ink, dye-stuffs and vetches may not be soaked (on Friday before sundown) unless there is time for them to be soaked the same day. And Beit Hillel permit it.[313] In three things Rabban Gamliel gives the more stringent ruling following the opinions of Beit Shammai: Hot food may not be covered up on a festival day for the Sabbath, nor may a candlestick be put together on a festival day; nor may bread be baked into larges loaves, but only into thin cakes.[314]

> In Judea one uses to work until midday on Passover eves. But in Galilee one uses to do nothing at all; in what concern the (preceding) night – Beit Shammai forbid, but Beit Hillel permit it until sunrise.[315]

> Beit Shammai declare an old *sukka* invalid, but Beit Hillel declare it valid.[316]

> The measure of heave-offering: Beit Shammai say, a generous offering is one-thirtieth, average is one-fortieth, and a miserly offering is one-fiftieth; but Beit Hillel say, a generous offering is one-fortieth, average is one-fiftieth, and a miserly offering is one-sixtieth.[317]

> Beit Shammai say: A man may not change his *selas* (of second tithe money) for gold denars. But Beit Hillel permit it.[318]

---

[312] The correct reading is שמתי without a *waw*, as found in *P.T. Beitsa* 4 end, 62d and in Gaonic texts. See *Ginzei Schechter* 2, 151, and especially *Iggeret Rav Sherira Gaon*, 11. The reading שמותי *shammuti* is found *P.T. Shev.* 9, 39a; *P.T. Ter.* 5, 43c; *P.T. Sukka* 2, 53b; *P.T. Beitsa* 1, 60c; *P.T. Yev.* 13, 13d; *P.T. Naz.* 9, 55d top; *B.T. Shabb.* 130b; *B.T. Nidda* 7b. – On R. Eliezer's Shammaite allegiance see below.

[313] *M. Shabb.* 1:5.

[314] *M. Beitsa* 2:6; *M. Ed.* 3:10.

[315] *M. Pes.* 4:5.

[316] *M. Sukka* 1:1.

[317] *M. Ter.* 5:3.

[318] *M. Maas. Sh.* 2:7.

Tannaic tradition also regarded Beit Shammai as the more stringent. This is seen, for example, in Mishna *Eduyot* chapters four and five. The Mishna first enumerates, quoting R. Meir's mishna,[319] twenty-four disputes which are remarkable for the fact that Beit Shammai are the more lenient and Beit Hillel the stricter; then six more are listed from R. Yehuda's Mishna, six from R. Yose, three from R. Shimon and two from R. Eliezer.

A definition of Beit Shammai as the more stringent school, however, does not really explain their basic approach. Certainly, it does not explain the cases listed in Mishna *Eduyot*, where Beit Shammai are the more lenient. Furthermore, often, and especially in matters of interpersonal relationships, the categories of 'strict' and 'lenient' hardly apply. Thus it is no surprise that modern scholarship made several attempts at a more fundamental explanation. Causes for the divergency between Beit Shammai and Beit Hillel have been sought in their exegetical approaches, their world views and the socio-economic classes they belonged to. It is, of course, not feasible here to discuss all of the opinions expressed by scholars and to examine to what degree they are justified by the evidence. One approach, however, gained particular attention and influence, directly or indirectly, and we shall treat it at some length.

It was GINZBERG who first offered the theory that the differences between the two schools originated in their different socio-economic background. In his own words: 'An analytical approach to many of the decisions on which the Schools of Shammai and Hillel disagreed will reveal that, in all their discussions and decisions, the former spoke for the wealthy and patrician class as over against the latter who reflected the needs of the lower social classes. . . . The strictnesses of the School of Shammai and the leniencies of the School of Hillel were based on the differing economic and social status of the two Schools. It is my theory that the adherents of the School of Shammai and the conservatives who preceded them belonged to the upper or middle classes, whereas the adherents of the School of Hillel were mostly of the lower classes; the former assert that the Torah should not be taught to anyone except a man who is wise, modest, *high-born* and *rich*; whereas the latter maintain that it should be taught to everyone, without distinction.'[320] In accordance with this view, Ginzberg explains several disputes in various areas of the Halakha. Let us examine his first two examples.[321]

1) Mishna *Berakhot* 6:5, 'If one pronounces a benediction over the bread, he need not recite one over the side-dishes. . . . Beit Shammai maintain that not even cooked foods are included.' In Ginzberg's view, the dispute may be explained on the grounds '. . . that bread was the main dish of a poor man's meal and, therefore, once he recited a benediction over the bread, he thereby blessed the entire meal; for the rich man, however, who ate meat, fish and all

---

[319] This is not mentioned in the Mishna but stated several times by R. Yohanan; *P.T. Beitsa* 1, 60b; *P.T. Sota* 3, 19b end; *et al.*

[320] Ginzberg, *Law and Lore*, 103. The quotation is from *A.R.N.* a 3 (7b); see below.

[321] Ginzberg *ib*. 104.

kinds of delicacies, bread was not the main dish . . .' Hence the benediction over bread would not suffice for other things.

2) Mishna *Beitsa* 2:6, 'In three things Rabban Gamliel gives the more stringent ruling following the opinion of the School of Shammai: . . . nor may bread be baked into large loaves but only into thin cakes.' Ginzberg explains: '. . . because the rich has no need of coarse bread on holidays . . . whereas the School of Hillel permitted it, because to the poor and the middle class bread . . . was the main dish . . . even on the Sabbath and holidays.'

In response to this theory we must state first of all, that there is no factual evidence that Hillel and his school came from the lower and poorer classes while the followers of Shammai belonged to the wealthy. We have details about the economic statuses of only four adherents of the two schools. About R. Eliezer the *Shammati* it is stated that he was in fact wealthy, as opposed to R. Yoshua ben Hanania, the representative of Beit Hillel, who was extremely poor.[322] However, of the other two, who lived in Second Temple times, the Shammaite R. Yohanan ben he-Horanit was very poor, while R. Tsadok of Beit Hillel was apparently rich; in any case he sent food to R. Yohanan when he heard about his poverty.[323] True, there is a legend about Hillel's humble origins, according to which in his youth he is said to have lived on his daily wages as a labourer; and thus Hillel is called an 'accuser of the poor' meaning one who leaves no one the excuse that he is too poor to study Tora. This legend, however, is found only in the Babylonian tradition and has no historical significance. It is opposed by many early Palestinian traditions; moreover, it contains internal contradictions.[324]

In the second place, the tradition from *Avot de-R. Natan*, version A, which is quoted by Ginzberg as the foundation of his whole theory, is a corrupt textual reading. In fact, Beit Shammai taught that only a man who is 'high-born', that is, of superior morals, and כשר, 'virtuous', should be given instruction. This last word became corrupted in the printed editions of version A, to read עשיר, 'rich'.[325] Thus Ginzberg's whole theory appears to be unfounded; and, as we shall see, those few halakhot which he explains according to his theory are open to other interpretations.

It appears that there are no grounds for seeking a single historical cause behind all the disputes of Beit Shammai and Beit Hillel. There must have been several factors operating in a complex way. In any case, we discern in the greater part of the disputes a common character which, in our view, suggests part of the explanation. The general stringency of Beit Shammai can be seen as rooted in a more simple, rigid and conservative conception of the Halakha. By contrast, Beit Hillel took a more flexible approach, expressing itself in sophisticated halakhic reasoning, and rooted in a more tolerant and humane attitude.

[322] On R. Eliezer see *A.R.N.*a 6 (16a); *Gen. R.* 41 (p. 398). On R. Yoshua see, e.g., *P.T. Ber.* 3, 7d.

[323] *T. Ed.* 2:2; *T. Sukka* 2:3; *B.T. Yev.* 15b.

[324] See Safrai, 'Tales of the Sages', 220-3.

[325] See Safrai, 'Decision', 34.

Let us return to the two examples quoted from Ginzberg's argument. In the view of Beit Hillel, the benediction over the bread may logically be taken as regarding the whole meal, whereas according to Beit Shammai, the benediction over bread is no different from other benedictions and only regards the kind of food mentioned in it. Second, if it is permissible to cook and bake on a festival day, then logically it makes no difference whether the loaf be large or thin. Further, the mishna preceding the one adduced in the latter example, *Beitsa* 2:5, quotes the schools of Shammai and Hillel as disagreeing whether it is permissible to heat water on a festival day when it is not for drinking. Beit Shammai forbid this because of their literal adherence to what is written in the Tora: '. . . But what every one must eat, that only may be prepared by you' (Exod 12:16). The school of Hillel, however, permit heating water for any use whatsoever since the acts of cooking and heating have been permitted in principle.

The same basic difference can be discerned in the first dispute between the two schools which is mentioned in the Mishna:[326]

> Beit Shammai say, In the evening all should recline when they recite (the *shema*) but in the morning they should stand up, for it is written "And when thou liest down and when thou risest up" (Deut 6:6). But Beit Hillel say, They may recite it every one in his own way, for it is written "And when thou walkest by the way" (*ib.*). Then why is it written "And when thou liest down and when thou risest up"? (It means) the time when men usually lie down and the time when men usually rise up.

The Shammaites adhere to the literal meaning of Scripture, implying that the *shema* should be recited in the evening while lying down and in the morning while standing. But the Hillelites see in those expressions concepts of time and not an exact description of the posture of the reciter. Again, we see that the Shammaite attitude is more unsophisticated or conservative, while the more flexible argument of the Hillelites is based on logic.

The interpretation which we are proposing would also explain the instances in which Beit Shammai in effect are the more lenient. One of the well-known controversies is: 'Beit Shammai declare black cumin insusceptible to uncleanness; but the school of Hillel declare it susceptible. So too (they differ) concerning (whether it is liable to) tithes.'[327] According to the Shammaites, cumin does not fall under the definition of 'food', and there is no need to separate heave-offering or tithes from it, nor is it susceptible to uncleanness as is actual food. But the Hillelites, more logically, expand the definition to include both things that are eaten and those that are not, such as spices that are taken with bread. The net result is that the Hillelites are more stringent on the purity and the tithing of cumin.[328]

---

[326] *M. Ber.* 1:3.

[327] *M. Ed.* 5:3.

[328] Cf. Jesus' basically positive attitude on the tithing of cumin, Matt 23:23; Luke 11:42.

This is one of the three instances of Shammaite lenience given by R. Shimon. Another of these also illustrates our interpretation: 'According to Beit Shammai the book of Ecclesiastes does not render the hands unclean (i.e., is not Holy Scripture). But Beit Hillel say: It does render the hands unclean.'[329] As may be well-known, any book which is reckoned among the Holy Scriptures is considered as defiling the hands, and the hands must be washed after holding it. The Shammaites, in their conservative adherence to the plain meaning of the text, were reluctant to include Ecclesiastes, a book which contains teachings hard to reconcile with the Tora. However, the school of Hillel saw no problem in attaching a broader significance to the written text and thus could see in Ecclesiastes an actual part of Holy Writ.[330] Incidentally, this also illustrates why the terms 'stringent' and 'lenient' are not always unambiguous. The more flexible Hillelite approach is able to accept Ecclesiastes as Holy Scripture and therefore decrees, as the more 'stringent' opinion, that hands must be washed after touching the book.

Illuminative of the Shammaite conservative adherence to the literal meaning of Scripture is a tradition of R. Eliezer the *Shammati*, who continues the tradition of Beit Shammai (see below). A halakha found widespread in the Mishna and other Tannaic texts teaches that in cases of bodily assault, the assailant is obligated to pay a series of compensations, and biblical expressions like 'an eye for an eye and a tooth for a tooth' refer to the obligation of monetary compensation.[331] Notwithstanding, R. Eliezer disagrees and says: ' "An eye for an eye" – actually.'[332] This does not necessarily imply that courts in places which followed the tradition of Beit Shammai actually ruled in this way; it is possible that even they would allow the assailant to redeem himself by making monetary compensation. Nonetheless, the basic approach underlying this interpretation of the Bible is very significant.[333]

In line with the preceding, the basic difference between the two schools is well illustrated in a long series of halakhot, most of them purity rules, in which a person's intention plays an important role. In these halakhot, the Shammaites take into account only the evident status of the pertinent object or the evident quality of the pertinent act, and not the intention of the person who handles the object or performs the act. The Hillelites, however, view the intention of the owner of the object or the performer of the act as decisive for the act's purpose

---

[329] *M. Ed.* 5:3; see also *M. Yad.* 3:5. In *M. Ed.* 5:3, the *textus receptus* reads 'R. Yishmael'; but the reading 'R. Shimon' is found in all the principal versions as well as in *T. Ed.* 3:7.

[330] In *M. Yad.* 3:5 (cf. 4:2), Shimon ben Azzai testifies that the Sages of Yavne, 'On the day when they appointed R. Elazar ben Azaria', decided by vote that Ecclesiastes renders the hands unclean.

[331] Exod 21:24; Lev 24:20; Deut 19:21. For the explanation see *M. Bava K.* ch. 8; *B.T. Bava K.* 83b-84a; *Mekh. Nezikin* 8 (p. 277).

[332] *B.T. ib.*; *Mekh. ib.* and see Horowitz's notes there.

[333] The *scholion* to *Meg. Taan.* ch. 4 reports that this was a controversy between the Sadducees and Pharisees. However these remarks should apparently not be treated as a historical testimony, and it is doubtful if they belonged to the text of the scholiast himself. See Belkin, *Philo*, 97; Gilat, *R. Eliezer*, 37f.; Hampel, *Megillat Taanit*, 137-140.

and function or the status of the object. Two examples may suffice to illustrate this.

According to the Halakha food does not become susceptible to defilement unless it comes in contact with water. The expressions in Lev 11:34-38, 'all meat . . . on which water cometh', and 'if water be put upon the seed', were interpreted to mean that only if water was put on the food, and that by a wilful act and not by itself (rain, irrigation etc.), did the food become susceptible to defilement by a source of impurity. The dispute between the two schools hinges on the status of, for example, fruit which was sprinkled with water by a wilful act not intended to sprinkle that fruit – such as if one shakes water off a bundle of herbs and it touches the fruit nearby. In such cases, the Shammaites declare that fruit susceptible, because the water reached it through a purposeful act. The Hillelites, however, extend the concept of intention to include not only the water but the fruit as well. The one who shook the bundle of herbs had no interest in the water touching the fruit, and thus it is declared not susceptible to impurity.[334]

The second example concerns an object, not an act. According to the Halakha only such vessels as are fit for human use are susceptible to defilement, not vessels intended for other purposes. The schools disagree over a scroll wrapper, an object which can be used for wrapping up a book-scroll but also for covering oneself. The school of Shammai declare scroll-wrappers always unclean since they are fit for human use, irrespective of the actual intentions of the owner. But the school of Hillel believe that if figures have been portrayed on them, indicating the purpose for which they are intended for: wrapping scrolls, they are not susceptible, whereas without such they are susceptible. – Thus we are able to see how the Shammaite attitude is the more rigid and simple, while the approach of the Hillelites is more flexible and subtle.

Another aspect of the difference between the two schools concerns their general attitude towards man. At the beginning of this discussion we have referred to a number of cases in which Beit Shammai, following their basic approach, in the final result take the more lenient position. But these are exceptional cases, as Tannaic tradition indicates. In general it is the Hillelites who are the more lenient. This can not be ascribed merely to their sophisticated halakhic reasoning, since by such means one can also arrive at stringent positions, as we have seen. Rather, it must derive from a more positive and liberal attitude towards man.

Here, it is necessary to insist on the relationship between halakha and aggada, which, as we have said earlier, was natural in the framework of the Oral Tora of the Sages. The more tolerant and humane attitude of Beit Hillel is in fact expressed in a number of disputes which the two schools are reported to have had on aggadic and theological issues, such as the creation of the world, the role of man, atonement for sins, punishment in the *gehenna* and one's share

[334] *M. Makhsh.* 1:2-4; *T. Makhsh.* 1:1-4.

in the life in the world-to-come. In the view of Beit Shammai, for example, the heavens were created first and only afterwards the earth, on which man resides, whereas Beit Hillel held that the earth was created first, thus apparently stressing the importance of man.[335] In another midrash we find the view of the Shammaites that sacrifices merely 'suppress' sins, whereas according to Beit Hillel 'they wash the sins clean' and 'make (the sinners) as a year-old infant who is pure from all sin'.[336] Again, in a series of disputes about punishment in the *gehenna* and reward in the world-to-come which were held between the schools or Sages representing them, such as R. Eliezer and R. Yoshua, Beit Shammai are the stricter and Beit Hillel the more liberal.[337]

Prominent in these controversies, including those over halakhic issues, is Beit Shammai's theocentrism or emphasis on the glory of God. Beit Hillel, on the contrary, express a markedly anthropocentric attitude.[338] According to one tradition, it was Hillel who first expressed the view that loving one's neighbour is the very foundation of Tora; according to another version, it was Beit Hillel's great inheritor, R. Akiva.[339] And it was Hillel who saw in the care for the human body a divine commandment.[340]

Among the themes of these disputes we also find that of the relation with non-Jews, in which, again, the Shammaites took a tougher position. We are referring especially to the famous disputation between R. Eliezer and R. Yoshua, in which the first held that 'All gentiles – they have no share in the world-to-come', while the latter maintained that 'there are righteous among the nations who have a share in the world-to-come'.[341]

The Shammaite intransigence towards the gentiles is also seen in the issuing of the Eighteen Decrees: '. . . A vote was taken, and Beit Shammai outnumbered Beit Hillel; eighteen decrees were enacted on that same day.'[342] These eighteen decrees were all, or largely, severe regulations designed to strengthen the separation between Israel and the nations. Some re-enacted ancient prohibitions such as that against gentile bread. But others, such as the ban on accepting gentile donations to the Temple, militated against current practice in the later Second Temple period. It is related that the Shammaites succeeded in passing the eighteen prohibitions by force, since they did not allow anyone who was suspected of belonging to the school of Hillel to enter the chamber to

---

[335] See e.g. *Gen. R.* 1,14 (p. 13); *Lev. R.* 36,1 (p. 833); *P.T. Hag.* 2, 77c; *B.T. Tamid* 32a.

[336] *Pes. de-R.K.* 6 (p. 120).

[337] *T. Sanh.* ch. 13 and parallels in both Talmudim. Incidentally, Rabban Gamliel, the descendant of Hillel, is on the side of the Shammaites, being more stringent regarding minor sons of the wicked of the earth. This is no exception, since he always follows the Shammaite view, either in aggada or in halakha. See Safrai, 'Decision'.

[338] See e.g. *M. Hag.* 1:2.

[339] *B.T. Shabb.* 31a; *A.R.N.* b 26 (27a).

[340] *Lev. R.* 34 (p. 776).

[341] *T. Sanh.* 13:2.

[342] See *M. Shabb.* 1:4; *T. Shabb.* 1:16; *P.T. Shabb.* 1, 3c; *B.T. Shabb.* 17a, 153b.

vote.[343] It is significant that while later (Hillelite) tradition regarded this as 'a day as difficult for Israel as the day on which the golden calf was fashioned', R. Eliezer saw it as a blessed day in which the 'measure was made even'. Here, too, tradition reports of a dispute between both representatives of the schools. In R. Eliezer's eyes, the Eighteen Decrees are analogous to 'a jar full of nuts – the more sesame seeds you add, the more firmly it will hold (the contents)'. In other words: additional decrees strengthen the existing structure. But R. Yoshua saw them as a weakening of Israel's real strength, comparing the event to 'a trough full of honey – if you add pomegranates and nuts, it will spit out (honey)'.[344]

The same attitude towards non-Jews is expressed in the legends about Shammai the Elder's unbending attitude towards prospective proselytes, as opposed to Hillel's friendly and tolerant attitude.[345] Stories like these may or may not illuminate the difference between both Sages themselves, but they certainly are illustrative of the basic attitudes of the schools following them.

It is important to note that there is one area of halakha and social thought in which the positions of the two schools do not readily fit into the general picture above: the legal position of women. This should impress upon us that the discussion so far offers only a partial explanation; there must have been factors at work which are still unknown to us. In any case, it is a remarkable fact that Beit Shammai, as well as R. Eliezer the *Shammati* and Rabban Gamliel, who follows Shammaite views, grant women rights, defend their personal and financial status and award credibility to their legal testimony, more so than do the school of Hillel. In addition, regarding some of these halakhot, it is reported that Beit Hillel eventually accepted the view of the Shammaites. We shall present a few striking examples.

The Mishna states that a woman who testifies that her husband died is believed, even if she is the only witness, but, in the view of Beit Hillel, only if 'she came from the harvest in the same country', since with so many other witnesses around she would be afraid to lie. The legal acceptance of her testimony means that she may remarry and does not have to remain in the deplorable state of an *aguna*, a wife without her husband who may not remarry. Thus Beit Hillel accept her testimony only in one guaranteed case. According to Beit Shammai, however, she is believed in each and every case. In the next mishna, Beit Hillel appear to agree with Beit Shammai in that the woman may remarry upon her own testimony, but she is not allowed to collect her *ketuba* (stating the amount of money to which she is entitled upon dissolution of the marriage) like a normal widow. Again, Beit Shammai grant her this right.

---

[343] For sources see previous note. This is no metaphor, but evidence of a violent situation indicative of the tensions caused by the war against Rome. See Lieberman, *Hayerushalmi Kiphshuto*, 38. To the sources he cites may be added: *Cant. Z.* to 3:8 (p. 26); Margulies, *Hilkhot Erets Yisrael*, 142.
[344] Tosefta and Talmudim *ib.*
[345] *A.R.N.* a 15 and b 29 (31a-b); *B.T. Shabb.* 31a.

Remarkably, in both controversies it is reported: 'Beit Hillel retracted and taught according to the opinion of Beit Shammai.'[346]

Another dispute is about a minor girl who has been given in marriage by her mother or brothers, and the question is whether she may refuse such marriages. Beit Hillel state that the minor girl may refuse but be given in marriage again up to four or five times, but Beit Shammai protest: 'The daughters of Israel are not ownerless property! Rather, she exercises the right of refusal (once) and waits until she is come of age, or she exercises right of refusal and forthwith marries.' Similarly, the well-known Shammaite halakha which prohibits to divorce the wife except in a case of adultery,[347] is, taking into account the social circumstances of that age, in effect a reinforcement of the wife's position.

In another instance, the schools discuss a woman's legal power over property that came into her possession after her betrothal. Beit Shammai grant her more rights than do Beit Hillel, and Rabban Gamliel follows Beit Shammai.[348] Finally, there are four disputes about the credibility of a woman's testimony regarding sexual intercourse and loss of virginity, and in all cases R. Eliezer and Rabban Gamliel think she is to be believed, while R. Yoshua, the faithful disciple of Beit Hillel, states: 'We do not rely on her word.'[349]

THE DECISION IN FAVOUR OF BEIT HILLEL

Many Tannaic sources testify that in the final century of the Second Temple era the Shammaites were in a stronger position. It may be that they were more numerous or more powerful. In this connection, we should recall that extant Tannaic literature emanated from Hillelite tradition: R. Akiva and his pupils, and down to R. Yehuda the Prince. If, nevertheless, reports on the Shammaite superiority have been preserved, this evidence must be reliable. This is confirmed by the sources; we shall mention some examples.

One of the best-known controversies between Hillel and Shammai as well as between their schools has to do with whether, as held by Hillel, hands may be laid on offerings on festival days before slaughtering; and whether on such days only peace offerings may be brought which are consumed by their owners, as is the opinion of Beit Shammai, while Beit Hillel held that also whole-offerings may be brought.[350] From a baraita found in many parallel versions we learn that actual practice in later Second Temple times followed Beit Shammai and that there was an attempt to fix the Halakha accordingly. But Bava ben Buti, a Shammaite, was convinced that Beit Hillel were correct, and he once publicly acted according to their opinion and thus caused the Halakha to be established

[346] *M. Yev.* 15:2-3.
[347] *M. Gitt.* 9:10. And cf. Matt 19:9; Mark 10:11.
[348] *M. Ket.* 8:1. See also *T. Ket.* 8:1; *P.T. Ket.* 8, 32a; *P.T. Pea* 6, 19c; *B.T. Ket.* 75b. And see Lieberman, *Tosefta ki-Fshutah* 6, 306-10.
[349] *M. Ket.* 1:6-9.
[350] *M. Beitsa* 2:4; *M. Hag.* 2:4 and parallels.

correspondingly.[351] The other example is found in Mishna *Pesahim* (8:5): The schools of Shammai and Hillel disagree whether a proselyte who underwent conversion on the eve of Passover is entitled to eat of the paschal offering in the evening. 'The school of Shammai say: . . . He may immerse himself and consume his Passover-offering in the evening. And the school of Hillel say: He that separates himself from the foreskin is as one that separates himself from a grave.' The Tosefta supplies the testimony of R. Eliezer ben Yaakov about soldiers who underwent circumcision and immersion and ate their paschal offerings that same evening.[352] From this we learn that soldiers who were made proselytes in Jerusalem on Passover eve behaved according to Shammaite halakha.[353]

Earlier we cited the tradition which holds that the differences between the two schools led to a situation with 'two *Torot*'. It is reasonable to suppose that this evaluation is not especially exaggerated. Many halakhot that are taught without an ascription to either school may well have emanated from the school of Hillel and at the time have been opposed by the school of Shammai. If we take into account that both schools not only represented different halakhic traditions, but apparently also were characterized by very different basic attitudes – at least in their main representatives – the evaluation 'two *Torot*' is understandable. Another tradition widespread in Tannaic literature, while stressing the existence of good relations between the two schools, also highlights the seriousness of the divergence: 'Even though the school of Shammai disagree with the school of Hillel (in various fundamental issues in marriage law without reaching a compromise) . . . Beit Shammai did not refrain from marrying women from Beit Hillel, but rather followed ways of truth and peace between one another, nor did Beit Hillel refrain from marrying women from Beit Shammai, in order to fulfill what is written: "Love the truth and peace" (Zech 5:19). Despite the fact that (in a great number of cases) these forbid and these permit, they did not refrain from preparing their ritually pure foods together, in order to fulfill what is written: "Every way of a man is pure in his own eyes but the Lord pondereth the hearts" (Prov 21:2).'[354] That good relations existed is confirmed by other traditions recording various visits and friendly social meetings between Sages of the two schools, and of Sages from Beit Hillel sending their sons to study with Beit Shammai, and the like.[355] Yet,

---

[351] *T. Hag.* 2:11; *P.T. Hag.* 2, 78a; *P.T. Beitsa* 2, 61c; *B.T. Beitsa* 20a-b.

[352] *T. Pes.* 7:15.

[353] The *sugya P.T. Pes.* 8 (end), 36b takes the Mishna as dealing with uncircumcised Jews who were circumcised on Passover eve; however this does not appear to be the plain meaning of the text. It is likely that the *sugya* found difficulty in the fact that they behave according to Beit Shammai. See J.N. Epstein's long note in Alon, *Jews, Judaism*, 150f., n. 5; Safrai, *Wallfahrt*, 107f. and notes. Additional examples can be found in Büchler, 'Halakhot le-maase'.

[354] *T. Yev.* 1:10-11; *P.T. Yev.* 1, 3b; *B.T. Yev.* 14b; *P.T. Kidd.* 1, 58d; *M. Yev.* 1:4; *M. Ed.* 4:8.

[355] E.g. *M. Sukka* 5:7; *T. Ed.* 2:2 and parallels.

tensions and violent conflicts, as on the occasion of the issuing of the Eighteen Decrees, indicate that an ongoing struggle for power was being conducted.

After the destruction of the Temple, however, a process leading towards the supremacy of Beit Hillel commences, which eventually results in the acceptance of its halakhic tradition in all academies.

The Mishna and the other Tannaic collections testify in many different places that the Halakha, as preserved mainly in the redaction of R. Akiva and his disciples, is in fact the halakha of Beit Hillel. Alongside many a dispute between the two schools we find a number of mishnayot arranged according to Beit Hillel's view; likewise, at the basis of many other halakhot connected with a disputed subject, the view of Beit Hillel is presumed. Thus, for example, the fourth mishna of *Yevamot* chapter one records that Beit Shammai consider the co-wife of a levir's daughter permitted to the levir, but Beit Hillel consider her forbidden. However, in the preceding mishnayot several halakhot are taught which are all based on the assumption that co-wives are forbidden to the levir and that co-wives in general are exempt from levirate marriage – in line with Beit Hillel. Similarly, there was a controversy between the two schools, as we have seen, over whether the *shema* must be recited in the morning standing and in the evening while lying down, as held by Beit Shammai, or, according to Beit Hillel, in whatever position, morning as well as evening. But from the beginning of tractate *Berakhot*, the mishnayot both before and after this controversy are arranged following the assumption that people recite in any position they choose.

Let us now consider the tradition, widespread in various forms in both Tannaic[356] and Amoraic[357] literature, which states that the Halakha was decided according to Beit Hillel:[358]

> Always, the Halakha is according to Beit Hillel. It was taught: A *bat-kol* (heavenly voice) came out and declared: Both these and these are words of the Living God, but the Halakha is according to Beit Hillel. Where did the *bat-kol* come out? R. Bibi in the name of R. Yohanan: It was at Yavne that the *bat-kol* came out.

First of all, it must be said that mention of the *bat-kol* is found only in the Amoraic sources and is missing in the Tosefta passages. In the second place, talmudic tradition explicitly states that the Halakha is never decided according to a *bat-kol*.[359] But most important is the evidence that there was never a single conclusive decision to fix the Halakha according to Beit Hillel: there were disputes that were still not settled by the end of the Yavne era nor even in the

---

[356] *T. Sukka* 2:3 (principal versions); *T. Yev.* 1:13; *T. Ed.* 2:3; *P.T. Ber.* 1, 3b; *P.T. Yev.* 1, 3b; *P.T. Sota* 3, 19a; *P.T. Kidd.* 1, 58d; *B.T. Er.* 6b; *B.T. Rosh H.* 14b; *B.T. Hull.* 43b.

[357] *P.T.* and *B.T. ib.*; *B.T. Ber.* 10a, 51b etc.

[358] *P.T. ib.*; *B.T. Er.* 6b; *B.T. Rosh H.* 14b; *B.T. Hull.* 43b.

[359] E.g. *B.T. Bava M.* 59a-b; *P.T. Moed K.* 3, 81c-d. On this whole issue see Safrai, 'Decision'.

generation of Usha,[360] just as there remained isolated halakhot that were decided according to Beit Shammai.[361]

Yet in spite of the fact that the maxim 'the Halakha is according to Beit Hillel' is not to be understood as a clear and binding principle, there is no doubt that it is a fair generalization. In the academies and the courts from the Yavne era onwards, the Sages followed the opinion of Beit Hillel. This is witnessed not only by the many anonymous mishnayot that agree with Beit Hillel, but also by the fact that in the Mishna Beit Hillel is found to retract and teach according to Beit Shammai several times, whereas there is not a single instance of Beit Shammai accepting the view of Beit Hillel.[362] This absolute absence cannot be sufficiently explained by the general inflexibility of Beit Shammai. The logic is that there was no point in recording that Beit Shammai accepted the view of Beit Hillel, since in any case the Halakha is according to Beit Hillel. But given this general rule, it makes much sense to mention whenever Beit Hillel retracted to follow Beit Shammai.

It is possible that the process leading to Beit Hillel's supremacy began already in the days of Rabban Yohanan ben Zakkai who re-initiated the teaching and studying of Tora after the destruction of the Temple; but there is no evidence to support this assumption. What is clear is that Rabban Gamliel, who presided over the Sanhedrin after Rabban Yohanan ben Zakkai, certainly did not encourage the establishment of the Halakha according to Beit Hillel, since all his halakhot and decisions are in the tradition and spirit of Beit Shammai.[363]

From the Mishna and other Tannaic collections it can be shown that in particular many teachings of R. Akiva follow Beit Hillel, just as many anonymous mishnayot agree to the view of Beit Hillel as R. Akiva understood it. We shall limit ourselves to two examples.[364] In Mishna *Ohalot* chapter sixteen, the rules for inspecting and cleaning a field suspected of containing a hidden graveyard are discussed. From the parallel passage in the Tosefta, not only is it clear that the method of inspection is as taught by R. Akiva, but also that the

---

[360] E.g. the great dispute of the Yavne generation regarding the 'daughter's co-wife', the account of which is found in the Tosefta and in both Talmudim (*T. Yev.* 1:9; *P.T. Yev.* 1, 3a; *ib.* 3, 4b; *B.T. Yev.* 13b-14a; *ib.* 27a). R. Yohanan ben Nuri tells of a suggested compromise according to which the co-wives would perform *halitsa* and not undergo levirate marriage; however the Sages did not succeed in enacting this as a *takkana* because of the difficult political situation, which we may take to be the Bar Kokhba war. From the continuation of the sugya it appears that the Halakha had not been decided by the time of Rabban Shimon ben Gamliel of the Usha generation.

[361] *T. Ter.* 3:12; *T. Maas. Sh.* 3:15. In *B.T. Ber.* 52b, dealing with *Berakhot* chapter eight which enumerates controversies of both schools, Rav Huna states that in all that chapter the Halakha is according to Beit Hillel except for the one halakha under discussion there. Rav Amram Gaon counts six halakhot in which the Halakha is according to Beit Shammai, most of them following the course of the respective *sugya* (*Siddur Rav Amram*, 15, cited by the Rishonim and others; see Safrai, 'Decision', n. 28).

[362] E.g. *M. Ter.* 8:4; *M. Yev.* 15:2; *M. Gitt.* 4:8; *M. Ed.* 1:12-14 (four halakhot).

[363] See Safrai, 'Decision'.

[364] Most instances are mentioned by Epstein, *Tannaitic Literature*, 71-87.

way of cleaning is according to R. Akiva's interpretation of Beit Hillel's view.[365] Even clearer is the halakha on the selling of leaven to gentiles on Passover eve. While the Mishna teaches anonymously that this is permitted as long as leaven may also be eaten by Jews, a baraita informs us that this was the view of Beit Hillel while Beit Shammai teach that it is permitted only if one is sure it will be consumed before Passover.[366] Thus the Mishna has chosen for Beit Hillel's view. From the Tosefta we learn, however, that this was not based on the legendary decision at Yavne nor on the guidance of a *bat-kol*, but that it was a decision made by R. Akiva:[367]

> At first they used to say: Leaven may not be sold to a gentile and it may not be given as a gift unless he will have time to consume it before the time of burning it; until R. Akiva came and taught that it may be sold or given as a gift even at the very hour of burning. Said R. Yose: These are the words of Beit Shammai and these are the words of Beit Hillel, and R. Akiva decided in support of the words of Beit Hillel.

The approach of Beit Hillel became more and more prevalent in the Halakha. Nevertheless, offshoots of the opinions of Beit Shammai left their impression on many areas of halakha as well as in many academies. In the Yavne generation several Sages, to say the least, inclined towards Beit Shammai. First and foremost among them is R. Eliezer.

R. Eliezer ben Hyrcanos is designated by talmudic tradition as *Shammati*.[368] Significantly, his opinion is worked into statements of Beit Shammai in several baraitot and talmudic *sugyot*.[369] R. Eliezer shares the attitude of Beit Shammai in attaching more importance to deeds than to intentions. Correspondingly, he judges the halakhic status of objects according to their factual situations and not according to the intention of their makers or users. Earlier we cited the controversy over the status of scroll-wrappers as regards their possible impurity; we saw there that R. Eliezer represents Beit Shammai.[370] Incidentally, among the halakhot defining susceptibility to impurity, a much-disputed issue between Beit Shammai and Beit Hillel, we find another example in which the name of R. Eliezer is mentioned along with that of R. Yoshua as the disputants.[371] And

---

[365] Cf. *M. Oh.* 16:3-4 on *T. Ah.* 16:3 and 6.

[366] *M. Pes.* 2:1; *B.T. Pes.* 21a; *B.T. Shabb.* 18b; and see Tosefta cited below.

[367] *T. Pes.* 1:7.

[368] See above n. 312.

[369] E.g. *T. Shek.* 3:16; *T. Ed.* 2:2; *T. Ar.* 4:5; *P.T. Beitsa* 1, 60c and 4, 62d.

[370] We can add that in *M. Kil.* 9:3, contrary to the anonymous teaching, R. Eliezer declares that handkerchiefs, scroll-wrappers and bath-towels come under the laws of *kilayim* (diverse kinds). (Traditional eds. and some MSS.: R. *Elazar*, i.e. ben Shamua, but *P.T. Kil.* 9, 32a and *T. Kil.* 5:17: *Eliezer*; cf. Epstein, *Nosah*, 1177.) The Palestinian Talmud *ib.* explains that this is, just as in the question of their being suceptible to uncleanness, because he considers them all as designed for human use.

[371] In the version of R. Yose, *M. Makhsh.* 1:4.

indeed, several Tosefta passages and baraitot declare: 'R. Eliezer conforms to Beit Shammai and R. Yoshua conforms to Beit Hillel.'[372]

In the method of midrash as well, R. Eliezer is heir to the tradition of Beit Shammai. He may not be as extreme as Beit Shammai in interpreting Scripture according to its plain meaning, but he remains within the domain of the literal and does not tend toward the flexible methods of Beit Hillel and its successors. We quoted already R. Eliezer's exposition, ' "An eye for an eye" – literally' (p. 190). An additional example from halakhic midrash may be given. The verse about the beautiful captive states: 'And she shall bewail her father and her mother a full month, and after that thou shalt go in unto her' (Deut 21:13). R. Eliezer explains thus: 'Her father and mother – literally', while R. Akiva expounds: 'Her father and her mother refers to idolatry, as it is written: "Saying to a stock, Thou art my father, and to a stone, Thou hast brought me forth" (Jer 2:27).' In the continuation, R. Eliezer and R. Akiva again disagree, the latter arriving at the exposition that he must wait three months,[373] as is the rule for divorced or widowed women, in order to distinguish between the seed of the first and the second husband, while R. Eliezer sticks to the plain meaning and says he must wait only one month.[374]

As is well known, R. Eliezer was excommunicated because in one halakha he refused to accept the majority decision. He may have died under the ban, as suggested by several sources, or the excommunication may have been only temporary,[375] but there is no doubt that in spite of the great admiration for him and his erudition, his views were rejected and his colleagues kept their distance from him.[376] In the Mishna, his opinions are often recorded only in order to disagree with them. Nevertheless, R. Eliezer had an influence on the Mishna and on the development of the Halakha in general. In the Mishna, there are several anonymous mishnayot which in fact are from the Mishna of R. Eliezer,[377] just as there are many elements of his teachings in the Tannaic midrash

---

[372] E.g. *T. Shek.* 2:16; *T. Ar.* 4:5.

[373] He expounds the elaborate expression of the verse: 'ירח – that means thirty days, ימים – that makes two months, ואחר כן – this supplies the third (month).'

[374] From some passages it would appear that the ban lasted only for a specific period. In any case, some sources seem to imply that he was banned in the days of Rabban Gamliel and by his order. *P.T. Moed K.* 3, 63a (beg.) has him make halakhic decisions in public in the presence of Rabban Gamliel; see also *ib.* 3, 81d. But cf. Aberbach, 'Rabban Gamliel', 201.

[375] See *T. Halla* 1:10; *A.R.N.* a 25 (40b-41a); *B.T. Sanh.* 68a *et al.*

[376] *Sifrei Deut.* 213 (pp. 246f.); *B.T. Yev* 48a-b; *Semahot* 7:13 (p. 143). The Palestinian Targumim agree with R. Akiva's exposition.

[377] Some examples: *M. Maas. Sh.* 5:12, an anonymous mishna which interprets the verse Deut 26:14, 'nor have I given . . . for the dead' as 'I have not used thereof for a coffin or wrapping for a corpse' – in fact this is R. Eliezer's opinion as contrasted with R. Akiva: *Sifrei Deut.* 303 (p. 322). *M. Orla* 3:9 teaches, anonymously, that the halakha of *hadash* (new produce) may be observed along with those of *orla* (fruit from a new tree) and *kilayim* (diverse kinds). In *M. Kidd.* 1:9, however, this is an addition by R. Eliezer.

collections.[378] In spite of the ban, some of his disciples remained faithful to him. R. Yose ben Durmaskit continued to visit him in Lydda,[379] and through him we possess many traditions of R. Eliezer. Particular mention should be made of his student R. Elai who also continued to visit him, coming to him from the Galilee even on the festival of Sukkot.[380] Many of R. Eliezer's traditions reached us through him and his son, R. Yehuda the pupil of R. Meir, and his grandson, R. Yose be-R. Yehuda.

R. AKIVA

R. Akiva is one of the greatest innovators in the history of the Halakha. In fact, his teaching represents the most important stage in the development of the Halakha between the period of the controversies of Beit Shammai and Beit Hillel and the final crystallization of Tannaic halakha. In other words, it is because of R. Akiva's activities that the later Yavne period (115-132 C.E) is the most influential in the long editing process of Tannaic halakha.

First to be mentioned is R. Akiva's work of classifying and arranging halakha. Earlier halakhic tradition was handed down in various forms. Sometimes it was transmitted in strings of halakhot arranged according to some external feature, such as a certain number or numerical gradation (cf. *Avot* ch. 5). We also find use of mnemonic comparisons: 'There is no difference between this and that except . . .' or, 'Case X is equivalent to case Y in two aspects and to Z in two others'; remnants of these have also been preserved in the Mishna.[381] There was not always a clear separation between halakha, aggada and midrash. That a classification by form and content of Oral Tora, and in particular halakha, was initiated by R. Akiva is emphasized by many Tannaic and Amoraic soures. Thus we learn from the words of the editor of the Mishna, R. Yehuda the Prince, when he recounts the praises of the Sages of the Yavne generation:[382]

> R. Tarfon, call him a heap of stones – some say: a heap of nuts – if one is removed, they all knock about and tumble about each other. Such was R. Tarfon when a student would enter and say to him: Teach me; he would bring Bible, mishna, midrash, halakhot and aggadot. . . . R. Akiva, call him a full treasure-store. To what can R. Akiva be compared? A labourer who took up his box and went outside; if he found wheat he placed it inside, if he found barley he placed it inside, if he found buckwheat he placed it inside, lentils – he placed them inside. When he entered his house he separated the wheat by itself, the barley by itself, the beans by

---

[378] In the Tannaic midrash of the school of R. Yishmael, Abba Hanan frequently cites teachings in R. Eliezer's name: *Mekhilta* (some eight times), *Sifrei Num.* (18 times), the beginning of *Sifrei Deut.*, and *Midrash Tannaim*. Interestingly, almost all Abba Hanan's statements in baraitot in the Babylonian Talmud are in R. Eliezer's name.

[379] *M. Yad.* 4:3; *ib.* 2:16; *B.T. Hag.* 3b.

[380] *T. Pea* 3:2; *T. Halla* 1:6; *T. Sukka* 2:1 and especially *T. Zev.* 2:17.

[381] *Bikk.* ch. 2; *Meg.* 4:5ff.; *Kidd.* 1:6ff., *et al.*

[382] *A.R.N.* a 18 (33b).

200

themselves, the lentils by themselves. Thus did R. Akiva, and he made the entire Tora into coins sorted out separately.[383]

That is to say: R.Akiva fixed the formulation of the traditions that had come down to him and arranged them accordingly. In a different version we read: 'He arranged midrash, Sifra and Sifrei, separately and taught them by themselves, and halakhot by themselves and aggadot by themselves.'[384] Similarly, an Amora who was counted among the foremost Sages of his generation states, expounding a verse, that R. Akiva 'ordained midrash, halakhot and aggadot'.[385]

R. Akiva was not, however, just an editor of the accepted halakha. His work of classifying and arranging went hand in hand with the introduction of halakhic innovations of various sorts, such as general principles, limits and measures, definitions, and legal concepts. We shall give some examples from which may be gathered the far-reaching influence of such innovations.

(1) Mishna *Eduyot* 2:1-3 presents a series of halakhic testimonies in the name of R. Hanina the Prefect of the Priests. This collection is from the mishna of R. Akiva and may well be assumed to have resulted from his editing activities, since to each testimony he adds a comment or draws a conclusion with regard to an analogous halakha. From one of the testimonies in this series is derived a legal principle without an indication as to the identity of its author. The Tosefta cites this same principle in another context,[386] stating that this is the opinion of R. Meir in the name of R. Akiva. Finally, this opinion is brought forward anonymously in Mishna *Gittin* (2:5). The protracted process evolved, then, in the following order: a) Arrangement by R. Akiva of the testimonies of R. Hanina; b) deduction by R. Akiva of a legal principle; c) transfer of this principle, in R. Akiva's name and in opposition to the Sages, to related halakhot in another field; d) incorporation of R. Akiva's opinion as the anonymous halakha in the Mishna.

(2) As is known, there are ritual commandments which, if their appropriate time happens to be on a Sabbath, may be performed even though they entail activities normally forbidden on the Sabbath. These include commandments such as circumcision and the sacrifice of the Passover offering, the performance of which on the Sabbath was accepted in the circles of the Sages without question several generations prior to the destruction of the Temple.[387] There was disagreement, however, about the preparatory work for these commandments. As regards circumcision, R. Eliezer, who was also R. Akiva's teacher, was of the opinion: 'One may cut wood to make charcoal in order to forge an

---

[383] מטבעות מטבעות as in the principal versions.

[384] Thus in Rashi's commentary to *B.T. Gitt.* 77a, apparently his reading in *A.R.N.*

[385] R. Yona, *P.T. Shek.* 5 (beg.), 48c.

[386] *T. Gitt.* 8(6):9.

[387] In Hillel's days there was still disagreement about the Passover sacrifice on the Sabbath, but the question was settled then and we find no evidence that it ever came up again. See *M. Pes.* 5:6 and Tosefta and Talmudim *ad loc.*

iron implement;' and such was the practice in his locality.[388] As against this position, R. Akiva derived a general principle from various related halakhot: 'R. Akiva laid down a general rule: Any act of work that can be done on the eve of the Sabbath does not override the Sabbath (prohibitions), but what cannot be done on the eve of the Sabbath (circumcision which must be on the eighth day) does override the Sabbath.' Now this principle was transferred to other commandments as well: it is mentioned in relation to the offering of the Passover sacrifice and the meal offering if they fall on the Sabbath. Finally, the principle also governed the arrangement of the pertinent Mishna chapters.[389]

(3) The Halakha forbids, anonymously, relatives of suitors to judge or testify in their cases. In the earlier halakha the term 'relatives' was very vague; it was defined only by the general rule: ' "His uncle, his first cousin" (Lev. 25:49), and all that are qualified to be his heirs.' Thus if there was no uncle or first cousin, the right to inheritance passed to some more distant uncle and his children without specification, as long as it was possible to discover any relationship at all. This was, says R. Yose in the Mishna, the 'First Mishna' also with regard to testimony regarding one's relatives. It was R. Akiva who gave a legal definition of the term 'relative' as spelled out in the anonymous halakha which we mentioned: Disqualified for testimony and judgement are those as far as related in the second degree to second degree relatives, either from the mother's or the father's side.[390]

(4) Another limit was set by R. Akiva in the laws of tithing. The accepted halakha in the Tannaic period allowed grain and fruits to be left untithed after harvest time, but no longer than the prescribed time of Removal of tithes, that is, on the eve of the last festival-day of Passover in the fourth and seventh year of each cycle of seven years.[391] The earlier halakha, however, did not specify from what stage in the ripening and harvesting process grain or fruits were liable to tithing, and this was of great importance for the harvest that was not yet in storage when the time of Removal was imminent. Indeed, from two epistles of the Jerusalem Sanhedrin at the end of the Second Temple era we learn that tithes must be separated even from 'five stalks' that were (at Passover!) standing in the field and from oil that is still in the 'olive jar' (at the press, from the last harvest, since at Passover there are as yet no olives on the trees).[392] It appears that in the Second Temple period there was no conception at all that produce became liable to tithes only from a certain stage on. Here, R. Akiva set boundary and measure, as testified by his disciple R. Yehuda, who is apparently referring to messages like those of the Sanhedrin letters: 'Beforetime they used to send to householders in the provinces saying: Hasten and duly tithe your

---

[388] *M. Pes.* 19 (beg.) and Babylonian Talmud *ad loc.*

[389] *M. Shabb.* 19:1; *M. Pes.* 6:2; *M. Men.* 11:3.

[390] *M. Sanh.* 3:4. R. Akiva applied the same definition to the degree of relation in the laws of mourning, see *Semahot* 4:1; *B.T. Moed K.* 20b and *P.T. Moed K.* 3, 83d.

[391] *M. Maas.Sh.* 5:6.

[392] *Midr. Tann.* p. 176.

produce before the time of Removal shall come. Until R. Akiva came and taught that all produce was exempt from Removal if its tithing season was not yet come.'[393] This implies a date set for the tithing, as indeed we find specified for various fruits elsewhere in the Mishna, and which we may infer was another far-reaching innovation of R. Akiva's.[394]

(5) Following the approach of Beit Hillel, R. Akiva further developed the concept of intention. The halakhic status of a person or an object should not be judged only from its factual situation, but also from its potential or intended purpose. Not only the actual function decides, but also whether the person or object is 'fit' for that purpose. A baraita states: 'If a sanhedrin saw a man murder another man, some of its members become witnesses and others judges; thus R. Tarfon. R. Akiva says: They all become witnesses and cannot become judges.'[395] The members of the court that saw the murder have not yet been established as witnesses in actuality, but are merely potential witnesses, and anyone who is regarded as a potential witness is judged as if he were an actual witness and is thereby disqualified as a judge. In several comparable halakhot R. Akiva explains the rulings he gives by the fact that the witness or implement or field must be fit for its function, and he also takes into consideration whether it was fit in the past or will be so in the future.[396]

(6) R. Akiva gave much thought to the concept of awareness, and to the definition of the unintentional act. When is an act really unintentional, when is it due to *force majeure*, and when does it resemble negligence? In the teachings of R. Akiva and his academy, such definitions are repeatedly emphasized in connection with purity rules, as in the following midrash which expounds the emphatic pronoun: ' "That one" (who ate from the sacrifice while impure shall be cut off from his people, Lev. 7:20) – not when he did it by *force majeure*, nor unintentional nor by mistake.'[397] Whereas in capital cases he who acts unintentionally is not liable, R. Akiva derived from Scripture that in case of monetary damage, even he who acts unawares or by mistake is liable.[398] Thus a man who intended to injure another man and by accident injured a pregnant woman, causing her to miscarry, must compensate for the damage (Exod 21:22), but if his ox had caused the damage he would be exempt, even though normally one is held responsible for damage caused by one's ox, since in the case of an ox unintentional acts are not considered like intentional ones.[399] If one had known something and then forgotten it, R. Akiva does not regard this as unintentional, but as verging on the intentional, just as there are cases where he regards an

---

[393] *M. Maas. Sh.* 5:8.
[394] *M. Maasr.* 1:2, 'When do fruits become liable to tithes?. . .' The whole tractate deals with the various aspects of this question.
[395] *B.T. Rosh. H.* 25b; *B.T. Bava K.* 90b; cf. *P.T. Rosh H.* 3, 58d (beg.); *P.T. Sanh.* 1, 18c.
[396] *Ib.*
[397] *Sifra Tsav* 14 (38a) *et passim.*
[398] *T. Shev.* 3:8.
[399] *Mekh. Mishpatim* 10 (p. 283), expounding the verse 'the owner of the ox is free' (Exod 21:28).

unintentional act as verging on compulsion: 'I agree that such a one (who acted on a court decision that was later retracted while he was away) is more nearly not liable than liable (to bring the offering of atonement).'[400] The legal concepts of intentional and unintentional acts were further developed by R. Akiva's disciples, especially R. Shimon ben Yohai and R. Yehuda, and many of their statements are built upon foundations and distinctions developed by their teacher.

Definitions and delimitations like these gave the Halakha a precision and consistency unknown before. They helped to clarify and to innovate many halakhot in various halakhic areas, and they served as the basis for further discussion and new rulings from his main disciples, R. Meir, R. Shimon, R. Yehuda and R. Yose, whose teachings together make up a major part of the halakhic corpus in the various Tannaic collections and the baraitot.

Numerous, but less incisive, are those innovations of R. Akiva's which in fact complement earlier mishnayot, but which nevertheless illustrate his creativity as a teacher. Thus when the Mishna enumerates plants whose hybrids are not accounted 'diverse kinds', R. Akiva, along with his colleagues, adds other kinds: 'Wheat and tares are not accounted diverse kinds . . . R. Akiva added: Garlic and wild garlic, onions and wild onions, lupine and wild lupine are not accounted diverse kinds.'[401] A similar thing happens in a baraita, and here it also indicates that R. Akiva was seen as an important spiritual leader. The baraita enumerates the institutions and services which the citizens of each town must establish and maintain: 'A court of law, . . . a charitable fund, . . . a children's teacher. In the name of R. Akiva they said: Also variety of fruits, for variety of fruits makes the eyes bright.'[402] Similarly, another baraita lists the duties of a father towards his son: 'To have him circumcised, . . . to teach him Tora, to instruct him in a craft, to have him married. R. Akiva says: Also to teach him to swim.'[403]

But R. Akiva's contribution consisted not only of reformulations, expansions and clarifications of existing mishnayot, but also of conscious innovations in explicit opposition to the accepted Halakha. The Sages prior to R. Akiva, as well as his contemporaries, did not alter or rework the mishnayot which they had received from their teachers. They added to them and used them for creating new halakhot, for example, by comparing a new problem with an appropriate accepted halakha. This way of innovating is well illustrated by what R. Akiva himself relates: 'I asked Rabban Gamliel and R. Yoshua in the market of Emmaus . . .'[404] In the continuation, R. Akiva asks a series of questions about specific halakhic cases, to each of which they reply: 'We have heard no tradition about this, but we have heard a tradition about . . .' – whereupon they

---

[400] *M. Hor.* 1:2.
[401] *M. Kil.* 1:3.
[402] *B.T. Sanh.* 17b; *S.E.Z.* 16 (p. 13); cf. *P.T. Kidd.* 4, 66b.
[403] *Mekh. Pisha* 18 (p. 73); *P.T. Kidd.* 1, 61a; cf. *T. Kidd.* 1:11; *B.T. Kidd.* 29a.
[404] *M. Ker.* 3:7-9.

cite a halakha about a similar case and set out to derive a new halakha for the case of R. Akiva's question. To be sure, R. Akiva himself also derived many new halakhot in this way.

What was new was that R. Akiva altered accepted traditions and thus made them what was subsequently called the 'First Mishna'. We shall mention three examples, which illustrate not only R. Akiva's relatively independent stature as a teacher of halakha, but also his humane outlook. We read in a baraita: ' "Her that is sick with her impurity" (Lev 15:33) – The First Elders used to say: She shall be in her impurity and not apply kohl or rouge till the moment when she has again immersed herself. Until R. Akiva came and taught: The matter will lead to enmity and he will wish to divorce her.'[405]

Another direct innovation in the Halakha instituted by R. Akiva concerns theft from non-Jews. It appears that the earlier halakha taught that there is no prohibition against stealing from a gentile. Such is learned from the Tosefta: 'The children of Noah were given seven commandments: . . . the prohibition of robbery, . . . (that is,) a gentile (stealing) from another gentile, or a gentile from an Israelite – forbidden; but an Israelite from a gentile – permitted.'[406] From a story in Tannaic literature it appears that this was the prevalent halakha, except that the Sages of Yavne declared that robbing a gentile is a 'desecration of the name of God',[407] meaning that it was morally prohibited, not legally. R. Akiva, however, ruled that robbery from a gentile is like any other form of robbery: 'R. Shimon said, The following midrash was taught by R. Akiva when he arrived from Zifrin: Whence can we learn that robbing a gentile is forbidden? From what Scripture says . . .'[408] This teaching was continued by his disciple R. Shimon,[409] and it is also expressed in an anonymous baraita.[410] Moreover, it gained currency in Tannaic teaching and became the basis of many halakhot in the area of Jewish-gentile relations.[411]

A last example of an innovation of R. Akiva's in opposition to accepted halakha emphasizes the equality of all classes, as expressed in their right to equal compensation for indignity. The Mishna states that compensation for indignity is paid 'all in accordance with a person's honour'.[412] R. Akiva, however, created a new halakha:

> R. Akiva said: Even the poorest in Israel are looked upon as free men who have lost their possessions, for they are the children of Abraham, Isaac and Jacob. – It once happened that a man unloosened a woman's

---

[405] *Sifra Metsora* end (79c); *P.T. Gitt.* 9 (end), 50d; *B.T. Shabb.* 64b. The *sugya* in the Yerushalmi implies that R. Akiva's view is in line with Beit Hillel.

[406] *T. Av. Zar.* 8(9):4-5; *P.T. Shabb.* 14, 14d (end); *P.T. Av. Zar.* 2, 40d (end); cf. *B.T. Sanh.* 57a.

[407] *P.T. Bava K.* 3, 4b; *Sifrei Deut.* 344 (p. 401); *Midr. Tann.* p. 212; *B.T. Bava K.* 38a.

[408] *B.T. Bava K.* 113a-b. Cf. *P.T. Bava M.* 2, 8c.

[409] *Midr. Tann.* p. 121.

[410] *T. Bava K.* 10:15. Cf. *S.E.R.* 15 (p. 74), 26 (p. 140).

[411] See Alon, *Toledot* 1, 346f.

[412] *M. Bava K.* 8:6.

hair in the street and she came before R. Akiva who condemned him to pay 400 *zuz*. He replied: Rabbi, give us time. And he gave him time. He perceived her standing at the entry of her courtyard and he broke before her a cruse of oil that held an *issar*'s worth of oil. She unloosened her hair, scooped up the oil in her hand and put it on her head. He had set witnesses in readiness against her and he came before R. Akiva and said to him: Rabbi, to such a one should I give 400 *zuz*?! He answered: You have said nothing, since he that wounds himself, even though he has not the right (self-mutilation is forbidden), is not culpable, but if others have wounded him, they are culpable.

In other words: the disgrace she does to herself does not permit others to dishonour her. This belief in human equality was not limited to laws of damages. Continuing this approach, R. Akiva's disciple Shimon ben Yohai teaches that any man may anoint himself on the Sabbath with rose-oil, which the earlier halakha permitted only for 'sons of the kings', i.e. wealthy men of high birth, 'since it is their custom to do so on ordinary days'. But R. Shimon taught: 'All Israelites are kings' children.'[413]

In the foregoing we have given some examples in which not only R. Akiva's ability to innovate in the Halakha is illustrated, but also the prominence of moral values in those innovations. This brings us to another feature of R. Akiva's teaching, with which we close our discussion of his place in the development of the Halakha. Although the phenomenon is not unique to R. Akiva, and is found in some way throughout the period under discussion, his teachings show a conspicuous connection between halakha and aggada. It seems this connection was intentional. While he is a foremost classifier and systematizer of 'midrash, halakhot and aggadot', we often find him giving an aggadic explanation to a halakha or deriving aggadic lessons from it. Thus he explains the reason for the halakha that one who steals cattle must pay only double, while if in addition he slaughters it and sells the meat, he must pay five-fold for cattle and four-fold for sheep: 'Said R. Akiva: Why did they say that if he slaughtered and sold it he must pay back four- and five-fold? Because he became rooted in sin.'[414] In other words, the loss is irreplaceable, and the sinner has no other means to express his repentance except by paying an excessive compensation. A moral lesson is drawn from the halakha that he who derives personal profit from Temple funds deserves death from Heaven: 'R. Akiva says: It happens that a man does his work and thereby is saved from death . . . How? . . . If he were a labourer working on the building of the Temple – although they give him Temple money for his salary and he takes and consumes it, he is saved from death.'[415] The value of human labour is greater than the offence of sacrilege.

---

[413] *M. Shabb.* 14:4.
[414] *T. Bava K.* 7:2.
[415] *A.R.N.* a 11 (22b).

The prominent place of R. Akiva in the development of the Halakha is indicated by the fact that almost all the extant halakhic collections are from the academies of his disciples. We may presume that a large amount of innovations which are not ascribed to R. Akiva but are transmitted anonymously or in the name of his disciples, in fact originated in his teaching. Certainly, the praise of contemporaneous and subsequent Sages reflects his importance as an innovator: 'R. Akiva arose and opened up the Tora;'[416] 'Things that were not revealed to Moses were revealed to R. Akiva.'[417] According to one account, when Moses ascended to heaven the Holy One showed him R. Akiva sitting and expounding all the hidden allusions in the Tora, so that 'Moses our Master did not understand what they were saying'; whereupon Moses wondered why God had not given the Tora through the agency of R. Akiva.[418]

---

[416] *Agg. Shir ha-Sh.* 31,4 (p. 11).
[417] *Pes. R.* 11 (64b).
[418] *B.T. Men.* 29b.

SELECTIVE BIBLIOGRAPHY

Halakha has always been prominent in the study of rabbinic literature. More research is done on halakhic subjects than, for example, on aggada, prayer, or literary aspects of the collections. This phenomenon is in evidence in traditional rabbinic learning from the Gaonic period onwards, and continues to be so even in modern research. Only in the last two or three generations has a change been taking place, attention also focusing on other areas of rabbinic literature.

The prominence of the study of halakha was caused not only by the practical implications, but also by the conception held by scholars for generations and also, largely, in our day, that halakha is a central and essential element of the literature of Oral Tora and of the spiritual heritage of the people of Israel.

Understandably, then, a number of the works mentioned in the following appear as well in our bibliography to the chapter on Oral Tora.

Introductions to rabbinic literature usually pay much attention to the Halakha. The little work called *Seder Tannaim we-Amoraim* (critically ed. by KAHANA), which was written in 884-886 C.E. as the first actual attempt at a historical and methodological introduction to the literature of Oral Tora, is divided into two parts. While the first part sets forth the history of rabbinic literature, the second is devoted to the methodology of deciding the Halakha when Tannaim or Amoraim are divided.

The same situation is largely to be observed in introductions written from the Gaonic period onwards. Many Mishna and Talmud commentators preface their commentary with an introduction to Oral Tora in which the history of the Halakha is central. One such work, which had great influence on Jewish life and learning, is Maimonides' preface to his Mishna commentary (critical ed. with a new translation from the Arabic: QAFIH, *Mishna*); in it, the history of Halakha has a central place.

In the modern period, many works were written on the history of the Halakha, but most are specialized studies. Relatively few can be mentioned which endeavour to deal with the phenomenon of halakha as such, placing the fundamental issues in a larger perspective.

One of the first studies to deal with the nature of halakha as such was KROCHMAL, *More nevukhei ha-zeman*; pp. 189-256 describe the history of the Halakha and its place in Jewish culture. FRANKEL, *Darkei ha-Mishna* is essentially a treatment of the history of the Halakha; the same goes for vol. 1 of WEISS's comprehensive work, *Dor dor we-dorshav*. Mention must also be made of GUTTMANN, *Einleitung*.

More recent attempts at a comprehensive history of halakha are DE VRIES, *Toledot*; BERKOWITZ, *Ha-Halakha*; and, most recently, URBACH, *Ha-Halakha*. A wider picture of the history of halakha is also found in ZILBERG, *Kakh darko shel Talmud*; LAUTERBACH, *Rabbinic Essays*; COHEN, *Law and Ethics*.

Of general importance for an understanding of halakha are GINZBERG, *Al halakha we-aggada*, 13-40 (E.T. 'The Significance of the Halachah for Jewish History', in *Law and Lore*, 77-124); BIALOBLOCKI, 'Ha-perush weha-Halakha', in his collection *Eim la-masoret*, 74-176.

Studies on specific topics:

Halakha in later biblical books and Pseudepigrapha: ALBECK, *Introduction*, 3-39; *id. Jubiläen*.

Halakha in Qumran writings: The augmented English edition of GINZBERG's work, *Jewish Sect*; BAUMGARTEN, *Studies*.

Halakha in the Septuagint: Nothing better has appeared than FRANKEL, *Einfluss*.

Halakha in Philo: RITTER, *Philo*; discussion of some issues in ALON, *Jews, Judaism*, 89-137.

Relation of Halakha and Hellenistic and Roman law: BLAU, *Papyri und Talmud*; COHEN, *Jewish and Roman Law*.

The Sofrim and the relation of midrash and halakha: URBACH, 'Derasha'; EPSTEIN, *Tannaitic Literature*, 501-746.

The halakhic dispute: See list of sources in DISHON, *Tarbut ha-mahloket*.

The importance of custom: ELON, *Jewish Law*, 713-67.

'Halakha to Moses on Sinai': SAFRAI, 'Halakha le-Moshe mi-Sinai'.

Beit Shammai and Beit Hillel: SCHWARTZ, *Controversen*; SONNE, 'Schools'; BÜCHLER, 'Halakhot le-maase'.

The decision according to Beit Hillel: SAFRAI, 'Decision'.

R. Akiva: FINKELSTEIN, *Akiba*; and criticism by ALON, *Studies*, 180-227.

Worth mentioning here are finally the collections of research articles by BÜCH-LER, *Studies in Jewish History*, and ALON, *Jews, Judaism* and *Studies*. While most of them are on history or rabbinic literature, these belong to the best we have on the history of the Halakha.

כלים   פרקין   תלתין
אהילות   פרקין   תמסר
נגעים   פרקין   ארביסר
פרה   פרקין   גריסר
טהרות   פרקין   עשרה
מקוות   פרקין   עשרה
נדה   פרקין   עשרה
מכשירין   פרקין   שיתא
ובים   פרקין   חמשה
טבול יום   פרקין   אפעה
ידים   פרקין
עקצים   פרקין   תלגא

סך פירקין דטהרות
מאה ועשרין ותישׁא

חסלת שיתא סידרי משנה

סכום כל פירקי משנתינו
תתקכג

Mishna, MS. Kaufmann, last folio (Budapest, Library of the Hungarian Academy of Sciences, Hebr. MS. A 50).
The scribe here listed the number of chapters of the tractates in the Order *Toharot*, displaying the tractate arrangement by size; see p. 233.

Chapter Four

The Mishna – A Study Book of Halakha

Abraham Goldberg

Following the destruction of the Second Temple, the amorphous corpus of teaching of the Sages, while remaining oral, began to take on definitive literary form, culminating, after a century and a half of growth and development, into the literary works which go by the name of Tannaic literature. The most important part of this literature, and the first to be edited in accomplished form, is the Mishna. Other Tannaic works are the Tosefta and the Tannaic midrash collections. Since the Mishna serves in many ways as the foundation for these other works, which were also later, it is generally described as the basic work of the Oral Tora.

The Mishna is the carefully worded literary formulation of Pharisaic-rabbinic law as it developed in the late Second Temple period and some generations afterwards. The Sages posited an Oral Tora of equal importance to the Written Tora, and also stemming from Sinai. In their view, Oral Tora embodied, in addition to a wide range of religious custom and practice not explicit in the Written Tora, the key to the correct interpretation of the Written Tora. The Sages emphasized and acknowledged, even during the Temple period, the importance of Synagogue and House of Study alongside Temple worship. For all practical purposes, their tradition was the only one to survive the destruction of the Temple, emerging afterwards into what we know as rabbinic Judaism.

Although other late Second Temple groups had written legal compilations, the oral character of Pharisaic-rabbinic tradition apparently kept it from receiving definite literary form until well after the destruction of the Temple. This is an important point of contrast. Thus the Sadducees, the party primarily of the priestly aristocracy, did not accept the existence of a parallel Oral Tora. Although they most likely also had traditions which were not explicitly biblical, these had the sanction of formal written legal compilations. Pharisaic sources tell us that the Sadducees had their Book of Decrees 'written and deposited'.[1] Of the Essenes, we have in recent times achieved a wealth of writing. The Qumran sect, which most scholars identify with the Essenes, had their own halakhic works, and unlike Pharisaic-rabbinic teaching, these were in writing. The most recently published and probably most important of these writings is

---

[1] *Meg. Taan.* p. 331.

the *Temple Scroll*. Although there are affinities to the related *Book of Jubilees* and the *Community Rule*, the *Temple Scroll* is closest to the *Damascus Covenant* in its detailed exposition of halakhot, having even something of the nature of halakhic midrash.[2]

From the very beginning, a prime distinguishing feature of Pharisaic halakha was its oral character. Later talmudic literature claims to find scriptural support for the prohibition of putting down Oral Tora in writing. Yet it seems that this prohibition was established from the very beginning as an historical necessity, and as the historical situation changed, the prohibition gradually relaxed until it disappeared altogether. Just because the halakha of the Sadducees and the Essenes was in written form, the Pharisees had to strip all authority from anything outside of Scripture itself in written form.[3] Thus, the Book of Decrees referred to by the Sadducees during legal procedures became a meaningless document, as equally all that which was Essene. The claim recently made that Pharisaic tradition was also written, until after the destruction the Sages reverted to the archaic procedure of oral transmission for propaganda purposes, is highly artificial.[4] After the destruction, there was hardly need for such 'propaganda', given the silent disappearance of the other groups, along with their writings (the Qumran scrolls were really hidden for outsiders, until their recent discovery).[5]

If change would come about after the destruction in the handing down of the tradition, it would be in the nature of Oral Tora. During the Second Temple period, it was hardly formalized; it was the essence of an idea, a thought or a halakha that was transmitted from generation to generation during the early period. After the destruction, so it seems, a process of re-formulation started, emphasizing a specific wording or formula of the tradition. In this period, it would not be written, but it would be memorized by the *tannaim*. Eventually, as we shall see later, this memorized form would become transcribed and Oral Tora would turn into written literature.

In this perspective, the Mishna marks a definite turn in the literary form of Oral Tora. Historical necessity here again called for a sure way for the preserva-

---

[2] See on these works Yadin, *Temple Scroll*; Licht, *Rule Scroll*; Schechter, *Fragments*; Ginzberg, *Jewish Sect*.

[3] This was done in part by demanding proper explanation and scriptural basis for Sadducee written law, which the Sadducees were not trained to give. See *Meg. Taan. ib.*

[4] Neusner, 'Written Tradition'; *id.*, *Rabbinic Traditions* 3, 173-5. See critique by Baumgarten, 'Form Criticism'. Neusner's reply, 'Exegesis and the Written Law', simply evades the critique.

[5] Even more extreme is the theory that with the passage of time there was a rapprochement between the Pharisees and the Sadducees, and that parts of Sadducee law found their way into Pharisaic tradition, and even into the Mishna. See Leszynsky, *Sadduzäer*; and the critique by Ginzberg, *Jewish Sect*, 323-34.

tion of Oral Tora in this time of crisis.[6] A process of set formalization began which was to continue for over a century and would result in the Mishna as we have it today. In this there was both gain and loss. The obvious gain was that now the Oral Tora could be memorized by rote and its preservation made easier. The loss would be that in time the outer literary shell would take dominance over the inner meaning. Human language is imperfect and no idea put in a set literary pattern will be understood by everyone everywhere and always in the same way. As long as Oral Tora had been without set formulation, the teacher would be transmitting ideas. Now it would be patterns of words which could often be understood in a variety of ways.[7]

As stated, the Mishna is the rote formulation of Pharisaic-rabbinic halakha.[8] It can, however, be described even more precisely: it is the formulation of a particular tradition in Pharisaic halakha. It is primarily representative of the School of Hillel as against the School of Shammai. This is not immediately apparent to the outsider, for the opinions of Beit Shammai find frequent mention. But wherever the Mishna presents the opinions of both schools, the anonymous follow-up of detailed explanation limits itself to an exposition of the views of the school of Hillel alone.[9] Furthermore, within the Hillelite tradition, the Mishna generally details the teachings of the school of Rabbi Akiva, as we shall demonstrate below. In other words, the Mishna is a very particularized presentation of Pharisaic-rabbinic law.

Since halakha is the prime matter of the Mishna, it is definitely a book of law. The question is, whether it was intended to be a binding code, i.e. a definite compilation of canon law, or whether it was never intended to be more than a text-book of law. Although this question has been raised ever since the modern study of the Mishna began more than a century ago, scholars still remain divided. Two leading scholars of our recent generation take opposing views:

[6] See the beginning of *T. Eduyot*, which gives expression to the post-destruction fear that the tradition might be lost: 'When the Sages assembled in the vineyard at Yavne, they said: There may come a time when one will seek something of the words of the Tora and will not find . . . They said: Let us begin from Hillel and Shammai.'

[7] A parallel may be found in the U.S. constitution and its subsequent interpretation by the Supreme Court. The question is most often not: what did the Founding Fathers have in mind with a particular formulation, but: what can it be made to mean?

[8] The teaching of the Mishna, from the 'Pairs' in the Hasmonean period onwards, is definitely Pharisaic. Sadducean teachings are mentioned only disparagingly (*Er.* 6:2; *Makk.* 1:6; *Nidda* 4:2; *Para* 3:7; *Yad.* 4:6-8). In addition, indirect traces of an anti-Sadducean bias are found, such as in the opening pericopes of the tractates *Shabbat* and *Shekalim*; see Goldberg, *Shabbat*, 3.

[9] One example is the opening section of *Kilayim* ch. 4, which gives the different views of both schools regarding the requisite area of open space in 'a bare vineyard patch' and 'an outer vineyard patch'. However, when the anonymous mishna continues its discussion it ignores the views of the School of Shammai completely.

EPSTEIN lists a number of cogent arguments in support of the view that the Mishna was intended to be a binding code,[10] whereas ALBECK comes to the opposite conclusion.[11]

The fact that the Mishna will quote a difference of opinion in phrases like 'Rabbi so-and-so says thus, but the Sages differ' is proof, argues Epstein, that the intention is to establish the accepted law in accordance with the views of 'the Sages', especially when we learn from a parallel baraita that 'the Sages' are none than another individual Tanna. For why otherwise should the compiler of the Mishna give an individual opinion as a majority point of view? Albeck, however, contends that the editor of the Mishna never was more than a compiler and refrained from expressing his own point of view. The editor drew from various sources, and if a particular source gave the view of an individual Tanna in the name of 'the Sages', so, too, did the editor record it in his compilation, without any intention of implying that such should be binding law. Moreover, there are so many contradictory sources in the Mishna, and many anonymous pericopes in direct opposition to one another, that it would be hard to regard the Mishna other than as a text-book for the study of the halakha, the prevailing law becoming established in accordance with principles outside the Mishna.

Our own point of view agrees with Albeck, but is based on partially different reasoning. As we shall see in the course of our discussion, the Mishna consists of several layers of legal teaching corresponding to consecutive generations of teachers. Later layers often are a presentation of possible interpretations to unspecified teachings given in an earlier layer. The chief aim of the final editor was to present the gamut of possible interpretations, and not to compile a definite canonical code of Pharisaic law. In particular, as we shall see, the editor is interested in presenting the teachings of R. Akiva as they become reflected in the interpretative teachings of his prime pupils.[12]

Although indeed the Mishna is primarily a text-book of law, it is also very definitely a literary work. Definite patters of composition and style are recognizable. Its language, syntax and choice of words have been the primary influence in the molding of the Hebrew language till the present day. Many poetic features are found, such as alliteration,[13] chiasmus,[14] repetition[15] and paralle-

---

[10] Epstein, *Tannaitic Literature*, 255-6.
[11] Albeck, *Introduction*, 106-7, 270-83, giving a detailed rebuttal of all the arguments of those who claim that the editor intended the Mishna to be a code of law.
[12] See Goldberg, 'Purpose and Method'.
[13] E.g. *Pea* 4:10.
[14] E.g. *Pea* 6:8.
[15] E.g. *Men.* 10:3.

lism.[16] Yet for all this the proper delineation of the rules of mishnaic construction, whether in prose or poetry,[17] still awaits detailed research.[18]

Origins and Development

All sources, including the immediate post-mishnaic authorities in both the Palestinian and Babylonian Talmudim, agree that Rabbi Yehuda the Patriarch (generally referred to as 'Rabbi') was the editor, or final editor, of the Mishna.[19] His political leadership and literary activity were within the confines of the last decades of the second century C.E., and at the very latest, the first two of the third. There is also general agreement that he represented the high point of an intense period of specialized literary activity – all in oral transmission – which began with the Sages who assembled at Yavne after the destruction of the Second Temple. The aim was to preserve in a definite literary form the great spiritual heritage of the Second Temple period, especially of its later generations. This heritage had been centered in great measure around the Temple ritual and worship, but perhaps even more in the many schools for the study of both the Written and Oral Tora. Since everything had to be saved and recorded for posterity, there was nothing in late Second Temple ritual and Pharisaic teaching which escaped the attention of the Sages and their disciples who assembled at Yavne for several generations: the description of Temple architecture, the involved and detailed rites of sacrifice, incense-offering and prayer worship at the Temple, holy day celebrations, Sabbath laws, ethical and moral teaching, and a highly developed Pharisaic code of civil and criminal law based on case-law as well as legislative activity.

Yavne, then, marks the beginning of the compilation of the Mishna. This does not mean, however, that mishna-type material did not exist before then. Oral law teachings abounded in late Second Temple days and some of the formulations may have come down to us unchanged. But it was only at Yavne that the process of establishing a fixed literary form for all that had to be

---

[16] E.g. *Shabb.* 2:3.

[17] We even find definitely lyrical passages, especially in the descriptive tractates. Epstein, *Tannaitic Literature*, 28 points to such a passage in *Tam.* 7:3.

[18] In the description of the ascent to Jerusalem with the First Fruits (*Bikk.* 3:3), one almost feels Keat's *Ode to a Grecian Urn*:
   Those that came from near brought figs and grapes
   And those from far, dried fruits.
   The ox for sacrifice led before them,
   Horns gold-covered
   And olive-leaf wreath on his head,
   While the flutes went playing in front.

[19] See Epstein, *Tannaitic Literature*, 200ff. for a detailed listing of the sources. Also, Albeck, *Introduction*, 99ff.; Strack, *Introduction*, 20. The criticism that Albeck 'never challenges the belief that Rabbi was the final editor of the Mishna' (Neusner, ed., *Modern Study*, 224; cf. Strack - Stemberger, *Einleitung*, 128) is entirely theoretical and not supported by any trace of evidence in the sources.

gathered and formulated was begun. While scholars are divided on this issue,[20] they largely agree that the editing of the Mishna was a continuous process. Internal evidence as well as talmudic tradition indicate that some tractates received close to complete form earlier than others. These were the tractates which describe Temple ritual and worship, and which we may call the historical or descriptive tractates. Thus the tractate *Tamid*, which describes in detail the complete Temple morning ritual, is attributed to Shimon of Mitspe, of late Second Temple and early Yavne days.[21] Similarly, *Middot*, which deals with the architecture of the Temple, is attributed to the first R. Eliezer ben Yaakov, of almost the same period.

While Yavne marks the beginning of the literary formulation of the Mishna, the great flowering did not really come until the next generation, that of R. Akiva. It is he who is rightly called the 'Father of the Mishna'.[22] The Sages of the first Yavne generation, R. Yoshua,[23] R. Eliezer[24] and their colleagues, had formulated late Second Temple teachings in what was to become the first layer of the Mishna. They were the editors, one might say, of this first layer; more correctly, the editing of the 'official Mishna' seems to have been the prerogative of the Patriarch, as we learn from various stories about Rabban Gamliel the Younger and his son Shimon.[25] Yet this first generation of teachers had much to teach, both as comment on and extension of what they were formulating as well as what originated with themselves. This could be given official formulation only in the following generation, the generation of the Bar Kokhba uprising.

Thus the primary, but the very shortest, layer of the Mishna in its final form is that comprising late Second Temple teachings as formulated by the first Yavne generation. The second layer comprises the teachings of these teachers themselves as formulated mainly by R. Akiva. The third layer is composed primarily of

---

[20] We largely follow Albeck, *Introduction*, 82ff. An extreme view is taken by Halevy, *Dorot ha-Rishonim* 1/e, 203ff., who ascribes the earliest layer of the Mishna to the Men of the Great Synagogue. More moderate are Hoffman, *Erste Mischna*, and Epstein, *Tannaitic Literature*, 40, 44, who claim origins for the Mishna in the days of Agrippa and offer proof for such from the Mishna itself.

[21] See Ginzberg, 'Tamid', especially the last section which deals with the dating of the treatise.

[22] Cf. Epstein, *Tannaitic Literature*, 71-95; this is the best exposé of R. Akiva's contribution to the Mishna we have. Historical surveys abound, such as Finkelstein, *Akiba*; Alon, *Toledot*; Goldin, 'Profile'; Safrai, *Akiva*.

[23] Prime teacher of R. Akiva. See Hyman, *Toledot*, 624f.; Epstein, *Tannaitic Literature*, 59-65.

[24] On the mishna of this highly individualistic figure see Epstein, *Tannaitic Literature*, 65-70. Neusner, *Eliezer*, offers (249-86) a valuable chapter of summary and critique on previous research literature; yet his own end result is a highly distorted picture. Refusing to accept source traditions about R. Eliezer, the author comes to base himself upon his own conjectures which, sadly, are void of solid evidence. Thus R. Eliezer is presented as an innovator seeking to liberalize Pharisaic law. This is in complete contradiction with the sources, which call R. Eliezer a Shammaite and, when his opinions are compared with those of his contemporaries, show him to be an extreme conservative who does not dare to decide on any issue on which he lacks a decision of his teachers.

[25] For Rabban Gamliel see *B.T.Bekh.* 36a; *B.T. Ber.* 27b. For Shimon, see *B.T. Hor.* 13b.; cf. Epstein, *Tannaitic Literature*, 255f. and *passim*.

the teachings of R. Akiva himself as formulated by Rabban Shimon ben Gamliel and R. Akiva's pupils in the post-Bar Kokhba academy at Usha.[26] The fourth and final layer of the Mishna consists of the teachings of the disciples of R. Akiva, as formulated under the aegis of R. Yehuda the Patriarch.

R. Akiva and his Pupils

The teaching of R. Akiva is predominant in the third layer of the Mishna, and indirectly also in the fourth layer. Literary analysis will show it to be the underlying common denominator of all the Usha discussions, no matter how much difference there may be in detail.

One might object that many contemporaries of R. Akiva, such as R. Yishmael and R. Tarfon, find quite frequent mention in the Mishna. Careful attention, however, to the exact place and manner in which they do occur will show that these opinions in many instances function as a kind of foil to those of R. Akiva himself, much the same way that the Shammaite view is cited to set off the Hillelite opinion.[27] R. Akiva's predominance can be understood from a historical point of view. First of all, he appears to have been the leading spiritual figure in his time, with the upheaval of the Bar Kokhba war. Second, the war itself and its tragic aftermath forced the dispersion of the scholars of the academy. Many established themselves among the prosperous and safe Babylonian Jewish community. When conditions in Palestine became favourable, many did return, but not all. Those who did return to assemble at Usha all happened to be disciples of R. Akiva, as is apparent from the names of those who appear in the Usha discussions.

In the above description, we posited that no editor or group of editors recorded in official formulation the teachings of their own generation, but always those of the previous one. Not only is this the more plausible function of an editor, but the literary evidence points in the same direction. The first, Yavnean, layer records late Second Temple traditions; the last layer, which was edited by Rabbi, has almost nothing of his own generation. Yet the Mishna is rightly called 'Rabbi's Mishna', since even if he did no more than add the final layer, this is indeed the largest one and serves as signature to the Mishna. Below we shall discuss why there was no continuation in a fifth layer which would

[26] The name of R. Akiva occurs more than 250 times in the Mishna, and this is several times more than any of his contemporaries, perhaps more than all combined. Yet there is more. A very great portion of the anonymous Mishna is to be attributed to R. Akiva and is perhaps primary in giving the Mishna its definite *Akivan* tone. See Goldberg, 'Teachings of R. Aqiva', and the introductions to *Shabbat* and *Eruvin*.

[27] An example: The anonymous earlier layer of *Pes.* 10:6 teaches that the Benediction of the Redemption is recited after the second of the four cups of the Passover eve meal. The formulation of this benediction is a matter of dispute in the next layer; the formulation of R. Tarfon which is given first, lends special significance to the more elaborate formulation of R. Akiva. Another example is *Ter.* 9:1-2.

contain the teachings of Rabbi and his generation. Other scholars, notably EPSTEIN, hold that each layer was the product of a contemporary teacher, and that Rabbi's task was primarily one of selection and re-editing.[28]

The fourth layer differs from the others not only in that it is the last and the largest one. It also stresses no single line of teaching, as that of Beit Hillel or that of R. Akiva in previous layers. There are four primary teachers here: R. Meir, R. Yehuda, R. Yose and R. Shimon. They all are disciples of R. Akiva and basically teach his Mishna; their differences are rooted in different approaches and explanations to it. Here each tradition is of equal importance, and the reason why sometimes one takes precedence in Rabbi's selection is, as we shall see, not because it was considered the binding opinion. Occasionally, other pupils of R. Akiva are mentioned, such as R. Elazar or R. Nehemia, but their opinions are usually only very minor variations of one of the four main streams of interpretation.[29]

Now each of these traditions has an individual character of its own, something which has generally gone unnoticed until now. A close study of the opinions of the four prime pupils of R. Akiva in the wide and varied frame of topics in the Mishna will show how each takes a particular, consistent approach to the teachings of his master. Thus, R. Meir always gives a literal interpretation to what R. Akiva teaches, ruling out any external factors which might limit its validity. R. Yehuda, on the other hand, will usually limit R. Akiva's teachings to a specific situation, whether in time or place.[30] R. Yose almost invariably takes a middle position between these two and is therefore known as 'the arbitrator among the Sages'.[31] R. Shimon, like R. Meir, does not limit the generalized teaching of R. Akiva to a particular situation, but tends more to seek a unifying and consistent line than just literal interpretation. In discussion with R. Meir, he is often at a completely opposite point of view.

The Four Layers

Before going on to analyze the layered structure of the Mishna, it may be helpful to state that its appreciation does not depend upon the acceptance of the view that Rabbi's task was limited to the editing of the final layer. Even those

---

[28] See Epstein, *Tannaitic Literature*, 188 and *passim*. In his view, each Sage taught his own mishna which often included citation or discussion with that of his contemporaries, and the work of Rabbi was to select from the various (orally) extant mishnayot, incidentally changing or supplementing them. Our approach is closest to that of Frankel, *Darkei ha-Mishna*; see esp. p. 225. Frankel discerns only three layers, that of R. Akiva, of R. Meir, and of Rabbi; Rabbi would not only have edited the teaching of R. Meir and his colleagues, but have gone back and added to the previous layers what he found had been omitted there, and therefore his final edition is rightly called the 'Mishna of Rabbi'.

[29] See Goldberg, 'Teachings of R. Aqiva'.

[30] R. Yehuda is also known for his affinity to the Shammaite tradition of R. Eliezer; R. Elai, his father, was a disciple of R. Eliezer. Yet, R. Yehuda remains a faithful pupil of R. Akiva. His limitative approach to the teachings of his master aims at bringing both traditions as close as possible.

[31] See Epstein, *Tannaitic Literature*, 126.

who take the view that the entire Mishna was a rewording by Rabbi, agree that mishna or mishnayot existed before Rabbi, and that he preserved its basic literary character as a several-generation compilation. The truth is that the Mishna can be properly understood and interpreted only when the relationship between each layer remains clearly recognizable, as we have consistently aimed to demonstrate in many places.[32] The precise origin of this layer-structure is not terribly important; it is there for us to recognize and exploit.

We have spoken of four layers of the Mishna; yet it is very hard to find a single mishna with all four layers, or even with three. Most mishnayot consist of a single layer only or, less frequently, two layers. As the final layer is by far the largest one, and as single layer mishnayot predominate, it is logical that the majority of mishnayot consist of the teachings of the disciples of R. Akiva alone.

Differences of opinion among the Sages as they find mention in the Mishna are limited, as a rule, to the last three layers, and are almost always located within one layer. The usual pattern is that only two opinions are recorded, the first being given anonymously. Occasionally, we find three different opinions, and here, too, the first one is mostly anonymous. Very rarely, four different opinions are given, and this happens only in the last layer, the four prime pupils of R. Akiva each giving a specific interpretation of a general teaching of their master. Now these specific interpretations are very rarely identified as such, and are for the most part to be inferred. It is as if the editor used this elliptical form in order to emphasize the importance of particularized interpretation.

Despite the great number of differences of opinion recorded in the Mishna, most mishnayot are anonymous. Where the opinion of a single Sage is given, as is most often the case in an anonymous mishna, the varying opinions, where they exist, are generally recorded in the Tosefta or in a baraita. Nor is it difficult to identify the teacher of such anonymous mishnayot.[33]

In order to give as full an illustration as possible of the final and most important layer, we shall select a mishna which mentions four particularized opinions of the pupils of R. Akiva, all mentioned by name, which, as stated, is exceptional. The discussion evolves around the carrying of an object from a house into a joint courtyard on the Sabbath, which can be made permissible by the institution of an *eruv* (a symbolic food partnership) by the dwellers; the

---

[32] See Goldberg, *Shabbat*, *Eruvin* and *Ohaloth*.

[33] The view that an anonymous mishna is a suppressed tradition (Neusner, *Eliezer* 2, 82 and elsewhere) has nothing substantial to base itself on. In the Mishna, one and the same teaching may be given sometimes by name and sometimes anonymously. See, e.g., the teachings of R. Meir and R. Shimon in *Hull*. 5:3 and 6:2. The Palestinian Amora R. Yohanan even taught that the anonymous opinion was purposely intended to indicate the view which the editor accepted as halakha – the very opposite of suppression! In our view, anonymous presentations have nothing to do with suppression, but rather with selection. They serve a literary and pedagogic purpose, as we shall endeavour to demonstrate below.

question is whether the following circumstance would limit the institution of the *eruv*:

> One (whose house opens into a joint courtyard) who leaves his home to spend the Sabbath in another town, whether he be gentile or Israelite, prohibits (the other dwellers of the courtyard from instituting the *eruv*); thus R. Meir. R. Yehuda says: This one does not prohibit. R. Yose says: A gentile prohibits, but not an Israelite, for an Israelite is presumed not to be returning on the Sabbath. R. Shimon says: Even one who left his home only to spend the Sabbath with his daughter in the same town, does not prohibit, since he has removed (the idea of returning on the Sabbath) from his heart. (*M. Eruvin* 8:5)

Here, we have four differing teachings of R. Akiva's pupils, from which we may infer the underlying general teaching of the master. R. Akiva probably taught that a member of the joint courtyard who leaves his home to spend the Sabbath elsewhere, without having made provision to participate in the joint *eruv*, prohibits the other dwellers from instituting such. Now since this general teaching can bear amplification, each one of his prime pupils interprets it in accordance with his own particular approach to R. Akiva's teachings. R. Meir, as usual, gives a very literal interpretation. Since the wording does not specify whether an Israelite who does not travel on the Sabbath is concerned or a gentile who may return, or whether it be an Israelite who leaves for a house in the same town from which he may come back or one who leaves for another town, no such distinctions must be drawn and the prohibition is absolute in all cases. R. Yehuda's basic approach is to limit R. Akiva's teachings to some particular situation, and he explains the prohibition to apply only in the case where the joint occupant leaves for a house in the same town, and thus may return and make invalid an *eruv* instituted by the remaining dwellers. If he leaves for another town – a situation also included in the prohibition of R. Meir – he is not likely to return, and thus is not considered part of the group who dwell in the courtyard over the Sabbath and decide to make an *eruv*; therefore he does not prohibit. R. Yose takes his usual middle position, and – like R. Meir but unlike R. Yehuda – includes the case where the joint occupant leaves for another town, but on the other hand limits this prohibition to the case where he is a gentile, for a gentile may return from the other town, but an Israelite is not likely to do so. R. Shimon, like R. Meir, pays close attention to R. Akiva's wording, but comes to a completely opposite conclusion. Since the idea behind R. Akiva's teaching seems to be that any joint occupant who may return on the Sabbath prohibits, but not one who will not return – as both R. Yehuda and R. Yose also interpret – there is really no reason to differentiate between an Israelite leaving for the same town or for another town, since once the person involved makes up his mind to spend the Sabbath with his daughter, even if it is in the same town, he has no intention to return and is not likely to do so.

Mishnayot containing all four interpretative approaches are very rare, but even those with three differing opinions are not frequent.[34] Most frequent are juxtapositions of two differing opinions,[35] the first usually being anonymous.[36] That does not mean, however, that in those cases no more than two differing opinions existed – only, that they are not cited in the Mishna. In many cases, other opinions can be found in the Tosefta or in baraitot in the Talmudim.[37] Finally, as stated, many mishnayot, mostly anonymous, express only a single opinion; but again, this may represent only one of different opinions existing.[38]

The above example (as well as those indicated in the notes) is of a mishna consisting of one layer only, and only of the final layer.[39] Let us now see a multiple-layer mishna. Again, for our own purposes of full demonstration, we shall choose one of those rare mishnayot with explicit mention of a full complement of named views. Our example has to do with produce which, as long as it is kept outside, may be partaken of even when no tithes have been set aside from it, but once brought in a house or other sheltered structure must be tithed before being consumed. The question is, in what circumstances a sheltered courtyard imposes this restriction on produce brought inside it.

> What courtyard is liable to tithes? R. Yishmael says: A Tyrian type, in which the objects therein are guarded (by a gate watchman). R. Akiva says: Wherever one occupant opens (at will) and another locks (at will), it is not liable. R. Nehemia says: Any (courtyard) in which a man is not ashamed to eat is liable. R. Yose says: Any (courtyard) in which one will enter and none will say to him, 'What are you looking for', is not liable. R. Yehuda says: Two courtyards, one within the other – the inner one is liable and the outer one is not. (*M. Maasrot* 3:5)

R. Yishmael and R. Akiva are of the second Yavne generation; R. Nehemia and R. Yose are both pupils of R. Akiva and belong to the Usha generation. This mishna, then, consists of two layers, the first consisting of the teachings of R. Yishmael and R. Akiva as edited by the next generation at Usha, and the second layer consisting of the teachings of R. Akiva's pupils, R. Nehemia and R. Yose, i.e. the final layer of the Mishna edited by R. Yehuda the Patriarch. R.

---

[34] See, e.g., *Shev.* 3:1 – R. Meir, R. Yehuda and R. Yose.

[35] *Shabb.* 6:10, R. Yose and R. Meir.

[36] *Shabb.* 14:4, anonymous (R. Yehuda) and R. Shimon. *Ib.* 21:1, anonymous (R. Meir) and R. Yehuda.

[37] See Goldberg, 'Teachings of R. Aqiva', where even five differing opinions are inferred from an analysis of Mishna teachings and outside sources.

[38] *Shev.* 1:2 is an anonymous mishna expressing the view of R. Meir, as may be inferred from *T. Shev.* 1:1. There we are also informed that R. Yehuda held the same opinion, but that R. Yose and R. Shimon are opposed. The preceding mishna (1:1) is the teaching of R. Akiva given anonymously, which in this case does not have to be inferred, and to which his four disciples give different interpretations.

[39] An example of an earlier layer with four named opinions (also very rare) is *Ter.* 4:5 where R. Eliezer, R. Yishmael, R. Akiva and R. Tarfon are mentioned, except that there are only three differing views, since R. Akiva and R. Tarfon give the same teaching.

Yishmael gives a positive definition, and R. Akiva a negative one, of a common courtyard which imposes the restriction of tithing. They do not deal with a courtyard belonging to one occupant. That issue is taken up by R. Akiva's pupils, the one again giving a positive definition and the other a negative one; we may assume, although it is not explicit, that both follow and specify a teaching of their master, R. Akiva.

Most mishnayot, even if multi-layered, are anonymous, as we have said. An example of a three-layered one is the opening mishna of tractate *Shabbat*.[40] The first two mishnayot of *Shabbat* chapter eleven consist also of three layers, except that the middle layer has a named difference of opinion (R. Akiva and the Sages, whom Talmudic sources identify as Ben Azzai).[41] An example of a two-layered anonymous mishna is the opening of *Shabbat* chapter seventeen, the first layer being the teaching of R. Akiva and the other the teaching of his pupils.

Principles of Editing

We have seen that the Mishna contains both anonymous and named teachings, but that the anonymous parts in most cases can be identified by name through comparison with outside sources. This raises a question: what induced the editor to give some teachings by name and others not? Another question, even more important, is: why does the editor give a single opinion, and that often anonymously, in those many cases where other opinions are known to exist because they were preserved in the other sources? And again, where he does give more than one point of view, why does he usually limit himself to two, when there may be actually three or four? In other words: what are the editorial principles behind the Mishna as we have it? For lack of an editorial introduction elucidating these principles – as not only modern legal compilations have, but also most medieval halakhic codes – they must be deduced by close scrutiny from the Mishna itself.

Some of these questions seem to receive an easy answer from the theory, to which we have already made reference, that the Mishna is intended as a binding code of halakha. A mishna containing a single anonymous opinion, or an anonymous teaching placed alongside a named one, would reflect the editor's opinion of what is binding law. Such indeed is the answer of FRANKEL to the question which principles guided Rabbi in editing the Mishna: 'He weighed, in his wisdom, the opinion of early Tannaim; and in his Mishna he presented that view which found favour in his eyes either as the first of differing opinions, or as the opinion of the Sages, or as an anonymous unopposed view.'[42] We have pointed out above why we cannot accept this theory.

[40] See Goldberg, *Shabbat*, 4-7.
[41] See Goldberg, *Shabbat*, 217-20.
[42] Frankel, *Darkei ha-Mishna*, 226 and *passim*.

The Mishna presents itself as a textbook of halakha to be studied orally in the academies, and its literary character reflects this aim. The editing of the Mishna was guided by specific pedagogic principles, and below we shall enumerate those which we have uncovered so far. It is an interesting question to what extent these principles reflect the contemporary Hellenistic climate where systematic and well thought-out programs and theories of education played important roles. On the other hand, some of them may seem quite modern. Thus a good textbook of necessity needs to be selective in the presentation of the material, in order to offer the student a maximum of information in a minimum of text. Moreover, it would not have a stereotyped approach to every issue, but rather employ a variety of patterns of presentation, each in that context where it would be most effective. We may add some easily recognized features of a text intended to be studied orally: mnemonic patterns and name patterns governing the arrangement of the material. These are general pedagogic characteristics which we may expect to find in the Mishna. However, a close analysis of its text reveals very specific editorial principles which guided Rabbi in his presentation of the halakha.

1. *The anonymous point of view is usually that which comes closest to the generalized teaching of R. Akiva.*[43] As we have already seen it is R. Meir who teaches his master's doctrine most literally, without limiting it to a specific situation, time or place. For this reason the anonymous mishna is mostly that of R. Meir, as correctly stated by the third-century Palestinian Amora R. Yohanan.[44] Yet occasionally, especially in the transmission of a particular version of controversy between Beit Shammai and Beit Hillel, the version of R. Yehuda will come closer to the generalized teaching of R. Akiva, and Rabbi will set this out.[45]

2. *In an extended discussion, different points of view will be introduced in the course of the discussion.* Sometimes a particular topic will be discussed for a complete chapter or more. In order not to confuse the student by the introduction of all the different points of view at the very beginning of the discussion, these will gradually become clear in the course of the chapter. Thus the apparent juggling with sources in the choice and arrangement of mishnayot becomes purposeful. A few examples will make this clear.

In the course of a description of the Temple festival of the drawing of water on the Feast of Tabernacles, *M. Sukka* 5:4 tells us that the priests blew three

---

[43] For examples, see the following mishnayot of tractate *Shabbat* and my commentary to them (Goldberg, *Shabbat*): 1:2; 1:3; 2:7; 4:1; 5:1; 5:3; 5:4; 6:9; 7:2; 7:3; 8:3; 11:5; 14:3; 15:1; 16:1; 16:6; 16:7; 16:8; 17:1; 17:4; 17:6; 19:1; 19:5; 19:6; 23:1; 24:2.

[44] *B.T. Sanh.* 86a.

[45] See *Shabb.* 3:1 and my commentary (Goldberg, *Shabbat*, 57 n. 3).

trumpet-blasts while standing at the gate on top of the fifteen steps leading down from the Court of the Israelites to the Court of Women, three more on the tenth step, and another three when standing below. The next mishna, however, which enumerates the total number of blasts which would be heard at the Temple on different days, omits mention of the three blasts on the tenth step. In the Babylonian Talmud this contradiction is reduced to the use of different sources by the editor.[46] Mishna five is the view of R. Eliezer ben Yaakov (another pupil of R. Akiva) who agrees on the total number of blasts heard during the ceremony but for the three blown on the tenth step substitutes three others sounded at the time of the water libations on the altar. In the actual description of the water-drawing procession (mishna four) the editor would have found it confusing to introduce a parenthetical note explaining that not all agree on the blasts of the tenth step.

A more elaborate example is found in *Ohalot*, chapters two and three. The pupils of R. Akiva differ as to the exact nature of the controversy between their master and R. Yishmael on the question of whether two half-measures of uncleanness may be considered a full measure (needed to convey uncleanness) when brought together under a common roof. The points of view of all four main pupils of R. Akiva are given in a variety of places in the course of the related discussion. Thus, that of R. Yehuda appears at the beginning of chapter two, that of R. Shimon at its end, and those of R. Meir and R. Yose at the beginning of chapter three. Of all these, only the name of R. Meir is mentioned, the views of the others appearing anonymously but not difficult to identify.[47]

3. *Ease of presentation determines the place where a certain opinion will be introduced.* Such is undoubtedly the case in our last example, where four different views on a particular subject were taught in three different places. The topic taken up at the beginning of chapter two is the question: What things spread uncleanness to persons and things heretofore clean when all find themselves under a commonroof? A sub-topic is the question whether these same things spread uncleanness only when the minimum unit of unclean matter remains undivided, or also when it is divided. In order not to complicate the discussion of a difficult topic, Rabbi prefers to avoid any discussion of sub-topics at the beginning. He introduces as the first point of view that which is the least complicated, in this particular case that of R. Yehuda. The more complicated points of view are brought in as the presentation of the topic unfolds into

---

[46] *B.T. Sukka* 54a.
[47] See Goldberg, 'Teachings of R. Aqiva', 250-4.

sub-topics. Another example of this pedagogic principle of editing is found in *Maasrot* chapters two and three.[48]

4. *A single point of view will be taught where it serves most easily as a starting point from which differing points of view may be apprehended.* Sometimes pedagogic and other reasons apparently require limiting a teaching in the Mishna to one opinion alone, although differing opinions are stated in the Tosefta or baraita. The question then is: Why just this particular point of view? Here the answer lies in how much a certain teaching gives and whether the student can most easily use it as a starting point from which to apprehend the differing opinions. An example will make this clear.

Chapter four of tractate *Taanit* opens as follows: 'Upon three occasions during the year do the priests lift up their hands (to recite the priestly benediction) four times of the day – at the morning prayer, at the additional prayer, at the afternoon prayer and at the closing-of-the-gates prayer – namely: on fast days, at the *maamad* local prayer assemblies and on the Day of Atonement'. This anonymous mishna gives only one opinion, in this case R. Meir's. The baraita however, *B.T. Taanit* 26b, tells us that there are yet two other views: R. Yehuda holds that even on these days there are no more than the regular two morning priestly benedictions (morning and 'additional' prayer), while R. Yose characteristically takes a middle point of view and specifies three. Why did Rabbi select the teaching of R. Meir? Because it is most striking and the easiest of starting points. For R. Yehuda makes no differentiation between priestly benedictions on these days and those on ordinary days (and in effect there is hardly anything to teach from this view), while R. Yose's middle view is not anything different from what generally characterizes his teaching.

---

[48] The issue is whether produce not yet liable for tithing becomes liable by transfer of property such as sale, gift or exchange. In 2:1, the anonymous view (R. Meir) declares that sale of the produce imposes the duty to tithe, but that a gift does not. In 2:2 the anonymous mishna (again R. Meir) limits this to a gift given to one passing through the market, but not to one sitting in a doorway or shop. Here, R. Yehuda disagrees and declares it free. 2:3 records another difference of opinion between these Sages, and here the anonymous first position is that of R. Yehuda, because it is the most striking. 2:4 introduces R. Shimon's view on another single sub-topic, given on this particular place, which incidentally reveals his approach to all the questions raised in the preceding mishnayot to be the most lenient of all. In 3:5, a mishna quoted above in full, two more pupils of R. Akiva appear – R. Nehemia and R. Yose – with regard to the definition of a courtyard which entails the duty to tithe. In a kind of summary, the two extreme opinions are recorded again in 3:8, R. Meir's view being given anonymously and R. Shimon's by name.

A slightly different, but related pattern is that of an anonymous, general mishna which covers most situations but not all, whereupon the Tosefta turns to an unusual situation which mostly involves a difference of opinion.[49]

5. *Topical arrangement of subject matter often calls for a selection from a variety of sources.* This principle of editing may be joined to one of the preceding, especially the last mentioned. To maintain a straight topical line in a chapter devoted to a single topic, it is rare that a single source will suffice. The following elaborate example may make this clear.

Tractate *Shabbat* chapter sixteen enumerates Sabbath violations permitted in the case of fire. For each item, the editor will obviously seek the most striking opinion, in accordance with the previously listed principle. In this chapter it will always be the most permissive view, or the lenient teaching of a Sage who is generally known for his severe approach. The wider the frame of permitted violations thus being listed, the better the chapter will serve the purpose of presenting the most striking opinions as text, from which differing views will not be hard to fathom. Thus, the first mishna presents anonymously the teaching of R. Eliezer, usually of a strict Shammaite point of view, but here lenient in the matter of saving Holy Writ from conflagration on the Sabbath. The second mishna which deals with the saving of food in the case of fire has as the anonymous opinion that of R. Nehemia, who of all the pupils of R. Akiva usually takes a most stringent view. So, too, is the third mishna, which also deals with the saving of food. The fourth mishna gives the anonymous teaching of R. Meir. The editor switches sources here because it is R. Meir who gives the widest latitude in the saving of raiment, the subject of this mishna. The fifth mishna gives first the named teaching of R. Shimon ben Nanas, who is more lenient than the differing opinion of R. Yose, also mentioned, in permitting indirect extinction of a conflagration on the Sabbath. The sixth mishna teaches anonymously that it is permitted to allow a non-Jew to extinguish on his own volition any blaze which may occur among Jews on the Sabbath. This teaching is expressly aimed against certain individuals who would not avail themselves of this permission, as recorded in the Tosefta 13(14):9. The seventh mishna anonymously teaches permission to cover a burning light where something might catch fire. The last mishna of the chapter teaches, anonymously, permission to make use of a light on the Sabbath which a non-Jew lit for his own purposes.[50]

---

[49] One example is in Mishna and Tosefta *Sheviit*. Discussion evolves around the limitation of the setting-up of cattle-fold pens on the fields during the Sabbatical Year, since this leads to fertilization which is prohibited in the Sabbatical Year. *M. Shev*. 3:4 teaches anonymously (R. Meir, in accordance with R. Akiva) that such a pen should be limited to two *sea*'s space. Now *T. Shev*. 2:15 questions: What if the entire field is only two *sea*? Here, R. Meir teaches that 'he should not turn it entirely into a pen' in order not to create the impression that he intended to fertilize his field. R. Yose, however, permits the enclosing of the entire area.

[50] See Goldberg, *Shabbat*, 284-300.

It may be possible to uncover other principles of editing, although perhaps less important than those we have listed. What becomes most apparent from our study is the editor's typical selectivity. His aim in choosing a source is always its pedagogic value for the preparation of an official text of study for the academy, regardless of whether the source chosen is the accepted law or not. The editor does not commit himself to any particular point of view, other than a general acceptance of the Akivan line in the Hillelite tradition, as pointed out above.

Arrangement

The Mishna is divided into six Orders (*sedarim*), each Order being itself divided into tractates (*massekhtot* – ranging from seven to twelve), tractates into chapters (*perakim* – three to thirty) and chapters into mishnayot or pericopes (averaging seven or eight a chapter). In the traditional editions, the total number of tractates of the six Orders is sixty-three. Originally, however, this number was sixty. R. Yitshak Nappaha, a late third century Amora from Palestine, associates this round number with the verse, 'There are threescore queens'.[51]

Each Order deals with a broad area of halakha, whereas the tractates treat specific topics within each main area. The Orders are as follows:

1. *Zeraim* (Seeds) – 11 tractates. Primarily agricultural laws, plus a first tractate dealing with prayer and blessings.
2. *Moed* (Festivals) – 12 tractates. Sabbath, holy day and fast days.
3. *Nashim* (Women) – 7 tractates. Marriage and divorce; the Temple ritual of the suspected adulteress; vows in general and that of the Nazirite in particular.
4. *Nezikin* (Damages) – 7 tractates, the first one being traditionally sub-divided into 3 and the second into 2, making a total of 10. Civil and criminal law; restraints against idolatry; ethical teachings (*Avot*).
5. *Kodashim* (Hallowed Things) – 11 tractates. Temple sacrifices and offerings; laws of animal and bird slaughtering; priestly and Temple privileges; description of the morning sacrificial service; architecture of the Temple.
6. *Toharot* (Purities) – 12 tractates. Euphemistic name for the Order dealing with all matters of ritual impurity and the required purifications.

The foregoing is the commonly accepted sequence of the Orders. It is identical with the one cited by the third century Palestinian Amora R. Shimon ben

---

[51] *Midr. Cant.* 6,9, referring to Cant 6:8.

Lakish as corresponding with a biblical verse.[52] The sequence postulated a century later by R. Tanhuma varies considerably: Women, Seeds, Purities, Festivals, Hallowed Things and Damages. He, too, associates it with a biblical passage, but apparently juggles it somewhat in order to make it fit his accepted sequence.[53] Just as in the case of the Orders, the names of the tractates and their sequence within each Order vary in the sources. Here, however, an original sequence can be determined. The best and most complete discussion of these matters is that of EPSTEIN.[54]

We shall now list the tractates in the sequence found in most manuscripts and printed editions, and briefly describe their contents. At the same time, we shall enumerate the number of chapters in every tractate, a matter of importance in determining the original sequence of the tractates. We shall also refer to the biblical sources of the halakhot involved.

ZERAIM

1. *Berakhot* (Benedictions) – 9 chapters: prayers and benedictions (Deut 6:4-9, 8:10; Ps 45:18; Dan 6:11)
2. *Pea* (Corner of the Field) – 8 chapters: the right of the poor to the corner of the field reserved for them, to gleanings and to 'forgotten sheaves' (Lev 19:9-10, 23:22; Deut 24:19-22, 14:28-29)
3. *Demai* (Uncertain Produce) – 7 chapters: the condition of produce whose tithing is in doubt; how and when it must be tithed again (no biblical source)
4. *Kilayim* (Mixed Kinds) – 9 chapters: the prohibited mixing of diverse seeds in sowing, of diverse animals in breeding or working and of wool and flax in weaving (Lev 19:19; Deut 22:9-11)
5. *Sheviit* (Seventh Year) – 10 chapters: prohibited and permitted field work during the seventh year; release of debts (Exod 23:10-11; Lev 25:1-7; Deut 15:1-3, 9-10)
6. *Terumot* (Heave Offerings) – 11 chapters: the share in the harvest reserved for the priests (Num 18:8, 11-12, 25-32; Deut 18:4)
7. *Maasrot* (Tithes) or *Maaser Rishon* (First Tithe) – 5 chapters: the tithes reserved for the Levites (Num 18:21-24)

---

[52] *B.T. Shabb.* 31a. The verse is Isa 33:6, 'And the faith of thy times shall be strength, salvation, wisdom and knowledge.' 'Faith' corresponds to the Order of Seeds (sowing requires faith in the harvest), 'Times' to Festivals, 'Strength' to Women (a wife is a helpmeet), 'Salvation' to (the repair for) Damages, 'Wisdom' is needed to handle Hallowed Things, and 'Knowledge' required for the transcendent rationality of the purity laws. This midrash is the source for the alternative name for *Nezikin*, namely *Yeshuot* i.e. salvations, remedies. In addition, Daube, 'Civil Law', 358 associates this name with the Roman legal term *remedium*.

[53] *Midr. Teh.* 19,14; the passage is Ps 19:8-10.

[54] Epstein, *Nosah*, 980-1006. See also Strack, *Introduction*, 26-64 and appendices 1-3; Strack-Stemberger, *Einleitung*, 121-5.

8. *Maaser Sheni* (Second Tithe) – 5 chapters: second tithes and fourth-year produce which are taken to Jerusalem to be eaten (Lev 27:30-31, 19:23-28; Deut 14:22-27, 26:12-15)

9. *Halla* (Dough-Offering) – 3 chapters: the dough set aside as a priestly offering when baking (Num 15:17-21)

10. *Orla* (Banned Fruit) – 3 chapters: fruit of any tree prohibited the first three years after planting (Lev 19:23)

11. *Bikkurim* (First Fruits) – 3 chapters: the agricultural offerings of the first fruits brought to the Temple (Exod 23:19, 34:26; Num 18:13; Deut 26:1-11)

MOED

1. *Shabbat* – 24 chapters: prohibited and permitted Sabbath work ('main labours') (Gen 2:1-3; Exod 16:22-26, 29-30, 20:8-11, 23:12, 31:12-17, 34:21, 35:2-3; Lev 19:3, 30, 23:3; Num 15:32-36; Deut 5:12-15; Isa 56:2, 58:13-14; Jer 17:21-22; Ezek 20:12; Amos 8:5; Nch 10:32, 13:15-19)

2. *Eruvin* (lit. Fusion) – 10 chapters: the arrangement for the symbolic fusion or connection of private domains as well as limited walking distances, so that carrying between private domains or walking more than 2,000 cubits past the city limits, otherwise forbidden on the Sabbath, becomes permissible (cf. Exod 16:29-30)

3. *Pesahim* (Passovers) – 10 chapters: the prohibition of leaven during the seven-day Passover holiday; the proper preparation of unleavened bread; the paschal lamb sacrifice at the Temple on the eve of Passover; the second month Passover; the Seder service (Exod 12:1-18, 39, 43-50, 13:3-10, 23:15, 18, 34:18, 25; Lev 23:5-8; Num 9:1-14, 28:17-25; Deut 16:1-8; Josh 5:1-11; 1 Kgs 23:21-23; Ezek 6:19-22; 2 Chr 30:13-22, 35:1-19)

4. *Shekalim* (Shekels) – 8 chapters: the annual shekel tax (or contribution) towards the maintenance of the Temple service (Exod 30:11-16; 2 Kgs 12:5-17; 2 Chr 24:4-14; Neh 10:33-34)

5. *Yoma* (Day of Atonement) – 8 chapters: the Temple ritual on the day of Atonement; fasting and the other 'afflictions' of the day (Lev 16:1-34, 23:26-32; Num 29:7-11)

6. *Sukka* (Booth) – 5 chapters: the booths erected under the open sky for eating and sleeping during the Festival of Booths; the four species and the Temple celebrations (Lev 23:33-34; Num 29:12-35; Deut 16:13-15)

7. *Beitsa* (Egg) or *Yom Tov* (Festival Day) – 5 chapters: prohibited and permitted work on festival days (Exod 12:17)

8. *Rosh Ha-shana* (New Year) – 4 chapters: sanctification of the New Moon day; blowing the *shofar* on the New Year and its special place in the liturgical service of the day (Exod 12:1-2, 23:16; Lev 23:23-25; Num 29:1-6; Ps 81:2-5)

9. *Taanit* (Fast) or *Taaniot* (Fast Days) – 4 chapters: fast days and their liturgical service; prayers for rain (Num 10:9; 1 Kgs 5:35-39; Joel 1:14, 2:16-17; 2 Chr 20:3-4; Zech 7:2-3, 8:19)

10. *Megilla* (Scroll) – 4 chapters: the reading of the scroll of Esther on the Purim holiday; the holiness of the synagogue; scriptural readings in the synagogue on Sabbaths, festival days and other occasions (Esth 9:17-32)

11. *Moed Katan* (Minor Festival Days) or *Maskin* (One may irrigate) – 3 chapters: work prohibited and permitted on the intermediate Passover and Sukkot days; mourning customs as affected by the Sabbath, festivals and their intermediate days (Lev 23:37)

12. *Hagiga* (Festival Sacrifice) – 3 chapters: sacrificial offerings incumbent upon all who are on pilgrimage to the Temple; prohibited public teachings; ritual purity laws connected with Hallowed Things and the festival pilgrimages (Exod 23:14-18, 34:23-24; Deut 16:14-17)

NASHIM

1. *Yevamot* or *Yibmut* (Levirate Marriage) – 16 chapters: prohibited and permitted levirate marriages; prohibited marriages in general; the *halitsa* ceremony (Deut 25:5-10; Ruth 4:5, 8-10)

2. *Ketubot* (Marriage Deeds) – 13 chapters: rights and obligations of married women, divorcees and widows (Exod 22:16-17; Deut 22:13-21, 28-29)

3. *Nedarim* (Vows) – 11 chapters: The making and revoking of vows (Num 30:2-17)

4. *Nazir* (Nazirite) or *Nezirut* (Nazirate) – 9 chapters: the taking of the Nazirite oath; types of Nazirites; the sacrificial offerings and the burning of the hair at the end of the period (Num 6:1-21; Judg 13:2-5, 16:17)

5. *Sota* (Suspected Adulteress) – 9 chapters: the Temple ritual of the suspected adulteress; the historical blessings and curses pronounced at Mt. Ebal and Mt. Gerizim; the priestly blessings; the kingly scriptural reading at the end of the Sabbatical year; the priestly charge before battle; the rite of the heifer whose neck is broken (Num 5:11-31; Deut 20:1-9, 21:1-9, 24:5, 31:10-13)

6. *Gittin* (Bills of Divorce) – 9 chapters: the proper writing of a divorce bill and the proper manner of its delivery; enactments 'for the good of the worldly order' (*takkanot*) (Deut 24:1-4; Isa 50:1; Jer 3:1)

7. *Kiddushin* (Betrothals) – 4 chapters: valid means for the acquisition (betrothal) of a woman, of a bondman (and his release), of cattle and property; betrothal by agency; permitted and prohibited marriages (Deut 24:1)

NEZIKIN

1. *Nezikin* (Damages) – 30 chapters originally, commonly divided into three parts, 10 chapters each:

Bava Kamma (First Gate) deals with torts in general (Exod 21:18-37, 22:3-8; Lev 5:20-26, 24:18-20; Num 8:5-8)

Bava Metsia (Middle Gate) deals with lost and found objects, the laws of bailees, interest, cheating, workers' rights, creditors' rights and limitations, and neighbours' rights (Exod 22:6-14, 20, 25-26, 23:4-5; Lev 25:14, 35-37; Deut 22:1-4, 23:20-21, 25-26, 24:1–18, 25:4)

Bava Batra (Last Gate) treats of ownership of real estate, limitations of property owners, weights and measures, acquisition of property through purchase and inheritance, and preparation and interpretation of legal documents (Lev 19:35-36; Num 27:8-11; Deut 21:16-17)

2. *Sanhedrin* (Great Court) – 14 chapters originally, but commonly divided into two parts:

Sanhedrin – 11 chapters: civil and criminal courts; judgments; interrogation of witnesses; forms of punishment (Exod 23:2; Lev 21:10-12; Num 35:30; Deut 13:13-18, 17:18-20, 21:18-23)

Makkot (Flagellations) – 3 chapters: the punishment of false witnesses; refuge cities; punishment by flagellation (Num 35:9-28, 32; Deut 19:1-13, 15-21, 25:1-3)

3. *Shevuot* (Oaths) – 8 chapters: various types of individual oaths; oaths of testimony; 'deposit' oaths; court oaths; guardianships (Exod 20:7; Lev 5:1-13, 20-26; Num 30:3).

4. *Eduyot* (Testimonies) – 8 chapters; testimonies confirming oral traditions of the early generations of teachers (no specific biblical source)

5. *Avoda Zara* (Idolatry) – 5 chapters: objects of gentile idolatry and the prohibition of all benefit from them; trade with gentiles before and during their festivals; prohibited images; idolatrous libation-wine (Exod 23:13, 24, 32-33, 34:12-16; Deut 7:1-5, 25-26, 12:1-3)

6. *Avot* (Fathers) – 5 chapters: ethical and wisdom teachings of the teachers of Oral Tora in various chronological orders (no biblical source)

7. *Horayot* (Decisions) – 3 chapters: erroneous decisions given by the Sanhedrin or High Priest (Lev 4:1-5, 13-23; Num 15:22-29)

KODASHIM

1. *Zevahim* (Animal Offerings) or *Shehitat Kodashim* (Sacrifice Slaughter) – 14 chapters: the various animal and bird sacrifices; their validity and invalidity; proper and improper place of sacrifice (Lev 1:1-9, 14-17, 3:1-5, 4:27-31, 7:1-5)

2. *Menahot* (Meal Offerings) – 13 chapters: the various types of meal offering; validity and invalidity; proper place of sacrifice; the *omer*, the two Loaves and Showbread offerings (Lev 2:1-13, 6:7-11, 7:9-10)

3. *Hullin* or *Shehitat Hullin* (Non-Sacrificial Slaughtering) – 12 chapters: proper and improper methods of slaughter; *terefa* among animals; the prohibition of slaughtering the dam and its offspring on the same day; covering the blood; prohibition of eating the sinew of the hip; prohibition of cooking and eating meat and milk together; carrion uncleanness; priestly portions of non-sacrificial animals (Gen 32:33; Exod 22:30; Lev 17:13-14, 22:28; Deut 12:20-24, 14:21, 18:3-4, 22:6-7)

4. *Bekhorot* (Firstlings) – 9 chapters: redemption of the first-born; where redemption is unnecessary; blemishes which permit the slaughtering of the animal; definition of first-born; tithes of cattle (Exod 13:2, 11-13, 22:29-29, 34:19-20; Lev 27:26; Num 3:13, 18:15-18; Deut 15:19-23)

5. *Arakhin* (Valuation Vows) – 9 chapters: personal and property vows of dedication to the Temple; who may vow and who may be vowed; the lower and upper levels of valuation; dedication of goods to the Temple; dedication of fields; sale of houses in a walled city (Lev 25:25-34, 27:1-8, 16-24, 28; Num 18:14)

6. *Temura* (Substituted Offering) – 7 chapters: where substitution in animal sacrifice is valid and where not; how individual sacrifices differ from public sacrifices; the born of animal sacrifices; animals not proper for sacrifice; altar and Temple consecrations (Lev 27:9-10, 32-33)

7. *Keritot* (Extirpations) – 6 chapters: transgressions for which extirpation or 'being cut off' is the penalty; atonement by sin-offering and guilt-offering (Exod 12:15; Lev 17:4, 10, 14, 18:29, 20:5, 18, 23:29)

8. *Meila* (Sacrilege) – 6 chapters where the law of sacrilege applies in Holy Things; where it does not; agency in sacrilege (Lev 5:15-16)

9. *Tamid* (Daily Whole-Offering) – 6 chapters: a detailed description of the morning sacrificial service (Exod 30:7-8; Num 28:3-8)

10. *Middot* (Measurements) – 5 chapters: detailed description of the architecture and measurements of the (Second) Temple (Cf. Ezek 43:11)

11. *Kinnim* (Bird Offerings) – 3 chapters: the sacrifice of bird-offerings; offerings of obligation and free-will offerings; where birds of two different types of offering become mixed up (Lev 5:7-10, 12:8)

TOHAROT

1. *Kelim* (Vessels) or *Toharot* (Cleannesses) – 30 chapters: cleanness and uncleanness in vessels: earthenware vessels, metal vessels, wood, skin and bone vessels, glass vessels (Lev 11:29-38, 15:4-6, 9-12, 19-27; Num 19:14-15, 31:19-24)

2. *Ohalot* (Tents) or *Ahilot* (Overshadowings) – 18 chapters: ritual uncleanness by contact with the dead, whether by touch, by carrying, or by overshadowing; various ways of overshadowing; obstructions to the spreading of overshadowing uncleanness (Num 19:11, 14-16, 22)

3. *Negaim* (Leprosies) – 14 chapters: leprosy-signs in humans, in apparel and in houses; skin, head and beard leprosies; the ritual of cleansing from leprosy (Lev 13:1-17, 18-23, 24-28, 29-39, 40-46, 47-59, 14:1-20, 21-32, 33-53; Deut 24:8)

4. *Para* (Heifer) – 12 chapters: the rite of the red heifer, whose ashes are mixed with 'living' water for use in the ritual of cleansing from corpse-uncleanness; the condition of those who participate in the preparation of the ashes and the mixing with the water (Num 19:1-14, 17-21, 31:23)

5. *Toharot* (Cleannesses) – 10 chapters: euphemistic name for a tractate which deals with the ritual impurities of food and drink; of doubtful impurities in a private and public domain; of the impurity of the *am-ha-arets* (no specific biblical source; cf. Lev 11:33-34)

6. *Mikwaot* (Ritual Immersion Pools) – 10 chapters: fit and unfit pools for ritual immersion; doubtful immersions; drawn waters; immersion of vessels (Lev 11:31-32, 36, 15:13, 16; Num 31:23)

7. *Nidda* (Menstruant) – 10 chapters: periods of uncleanness of the regular and irregular menstruant; the uncleanness of childbirth (Lev 12:1-8, 15:19-30, 18:19, 20:8)

8. *Makhshirin* (Predisposers) – 6 chapters: liquids which 'predispose' food for contracting ritual uncleanness; the conditions which influence such predisposing (Lev 11:34, 38)

9. *Zavim* (Flux Sufferers) – 5 chapters: the periods of uncleanness of those suffering from a flux; the conveying of uncleanness in various degrees to persons or objects through direct or indirect contact with a flux (Lev 15:1-15)

10. *Tevul Yom* (One Immersed That Day) – 4 chapters: leniencies regarding a person in an intermediate state, i.e. after immersion but before the sundown which is biblically required for full purity (Lev 11:32, 22:6-7)

11. *Yadayim* (Hands) – 4 chapters: the second-degree ritual uncleanness attributed to unwashed hands; the proper vessels for the ritual washing of hands and the proper water (no biblical source)

12. *Uktsin* (Stalks) – 3 chapters: stalks and parts of fruit serving as a 'handle' which contract and convey uncleanness but do not enter into the measurement of the fruit itself in determining the minimum size for the susceptibility of uncleanness: kernels, shells and encasing leaves (no biblical source)

As can be readily seen, the arrangement of the tractates is not in a strict topical order; nor is it a chronological sequence, for both *Yoma* and *Sukka* precede *Rosh Ha-shana*, although the latter is first in the calendar. The logic of the arrangement is purely external: it is according to the size of the tractates, the largest being first and the smallest last.[55] Thus, where two or more tractates have the same number of chapters, the order is often interchanged, as for instance *Shekalim - Yoma*, both having eight chapters: we also find *Yoma - Shekalim*. The same goes for *Sukka*, *Beitsa*, and *Rosh Ha-shana*, all having five chapters; *Nazir*, *Sota* and *Gittin* with nine chapters; *Avoda Zara* and *Avot* with five; *Toharot*, *Mikwaot* and *Nidda* with ten; and *Tevul Yom* and *Yadayim* with four chapters each.

[55] The first to offer this explanation was apparently Geiger, 'Plan und Anordnung'. It was reiterated by Derenbourg, 'Les sections'; today it is accepted without question. It is to be noted that almost all ancient collections, most noteworthy, the Koran, are arranged according to the same principle. The traditional view, skilfully expounded in Maimonides' *Commentary to the Mishna*, attributes an inner logic in this arrangement of the Mishna; this started already with the Savoraic additions to the Babylonian Talmud (cf. *B.T. Taan.* 2a; *Naz.* 2a; *Sota* 2a; *Makk.* 2a; *Shevu*, 2b, 17b).

The only exception to this principle of arrangement is in the first Order, according to its traditional sequence. Yet even here certain manuscripts preserve a more basic arrangement, as does the Vienna MS. of the Tosefta. Here the arrangement is as follows: *Berakhot* (9 chaps.), *Pea* (8), *Demai* (7), *Terumot* (11), *Sheviit* (10), *Kilayim* (9), *Maasrot* (5), *Maaser Sheni* (5), *Halla* (4), *Orla* (3) and *Bikkurim* (3). In this arrangement there are two distinct frames with a descending order, the second starting with *Terumot*. What we really have, then, are two sub-orders. Indeed, the first three tractates are a unit by themselves, differing from the rest of the Order which deals either with hallowed or with prohibited agricultural products. As the first three tractates could hardly make up an order by themselves, they were placed with no change in their own sequence together with the tractates making up the other 'sub-order'.[56]

The chapter division of the tractates is very ancient, the number of chapters and their order finding occasional mention already in the Talmud.[57] Even names of chapters, derived from their opening words, are to be found.[58] Yet there are also occasional differences in the order of chapters in certain tractates.[59] The chapters, which contain between three and fifteen mishnayot, are not arranged according to the number of mishnayot.[60] The mishnayot themselves vary greatly in length, and a proper study of chapter sizes should depend more on word-counting. Largely, the division and the arrangement of the chapters is by topic, although not quite consistently, since one chapter may deal with more than one subject and a subject taken up at the end of one chapter may even continue into the next.

Thus the first four mishnayot of *Shabbat* chapter nine which each begin with 'whence do we learn', are really a continuation of the last mishna of the preceding chapter. Yet this 'illogical' break[61] is not without reason, for the 'whence do we learn'-series deals with topics not related with the Sabbath, while the last mishna of the preceding chapter does. On the other hand, the list of

---

[56] The sequence of the first Order has vexed many a scholar. Derenbourg, *ib.* 209-10 was the first to discuss it at length and attempt a solution; however, it does not seem satisfactory. Nor does that of Epstein, *Nosah*, 987-8. The solution proposed here is given in more detail in Goldberg, *Shabbat*, introd., n. 3.

[57] See *B.T. Rosh H.* 31b: 'And this is one of the nine enactments of R. Yohanan ben Zakkai, six of this *chapter*, one of the first *chapter*, and the others' etc.; *P.T. Bava K.* 1, 2a: 'The derivatives of (the main cause of injury) "Pit" we teach in the entire *third chapter of Nezikin*'.

[58] *B.T. Bava M.* 35a: 'We were seated before R. Nahman and our chapter was *Hamafkid*' (i.e. the third chapter of *Bava Metsia*).

[59] Chaps. 3 and 4 of *Berakhot* are reversed in Rashi's commentary. In *Eruvin*, some MSS. place chap. 5 before 3, and one MS. places 4 after 7. For a full listing of such variations, see Epstein, *Nosah*, 996-8.

[60] At most some cyclical arrangement according to chapter length seems to be found within larger tractates. *Shabbat* seems to have six or seven such cycles within its 24 chapters, which have the following number of mishnayot: 11, 7, 6, 2, 4, 10, 4, 7, 7, 6, 6, 6, 7, 4, 3, 8, 8, 3, 6, 5, 3, 6, 5, 5. In MS. Kaufman: 15, 7, 5, 2, 4, 10, 6, 7, 7, 6, 7, 6, 7, 4, 3, 9, 8, 3, 6, 5, 4, 6, 5, 5. In smaller tractates there is hardly any logic in chapter size. *Rosh hashana* has 9, 9, 8, 9; in MS. Kaufman 11, 12, 9, 11.

[61] Thus Epstein, *Nosah*, 994.

takkanot in *Gittin* 4:2 - 5:9 really constitute a single topic. The reason for the division into two chapters seems to be simply that a chapter of eighteen mishnayot would be too long. Indeed, the corresponding passage in the Tosefta (printed version) consists of one chapter.

Much more complicated is the division and arrangement of the first six chapters of *Bava Kamma*.[62] The opening mishna, which clearly is very old, as are the next two mishnayot which also give general definitions, announces treatment of the 'Four primary causes of injury'. From 1:4 till 3:7, however, there follows a single unit which really details five primary causes, leaving 'fire', the last of the four mentioned in the first mishna, not treated. From 3:8 till 6:6 we find another detailed discussion, listing four primary causes, this time including 'fire'. The difference between both units seems to be based on the interpretation of an ancient legal term introduced in the opening mishna, which is explicitly discussed by Rav and Shmuel, first generation Amoraim.[63]

This last example is complicated, as, indeed, is the question why the topics it treats begin and end where they do. It enables us to see, however, that a topic can begin in the middle of one chapter and end in the middle of some succeeding chapter. But it should be remembered that this is not the general rule. In most cases, the chapter division coincides with the topical arrangement.

The More Important Teachers

We have already made passing reference to leading teachers of the various generations in the Mishna. For a better perspective of the Mishna, however, it is important to have an overall list of the leading Sages. We can afford to limit ourselves here, since rather full listings appear in the various handbooks.[64]

The total number of Sages mentioned in the Mishna is slightly more than a hundred. These can be roughly classified into two divisions: those before the destruction of the Second Temple and those after. Now the former did not participate in the academy established after the destruction at Yavne, where the formulation of the Mishna as a literary document began. Strictly speaking, therefore, they are not teachers of the Mishna, and are generally not called Tannaim, the Tannaic period beginning only at Yavne. Neither do they carry the title of Rabbi, which was introduced at Yavne; they are designated by name

---

[62] We follow the exposition of Weiss, *Studies*, especially 31-54. Fascinating is Daube, 'Civil Law' which shows that three main elements determined the arrangement of this and related Mishna sections: 'Allegiance to Scripture, historical accidents, and the desire for a modern system' (370). In Daube's view this arrangement does not compare unfavourably with Roman law.

[63] *B.T. Bava K.* 3b. The disputed term is מבעה which Rav interprets as human action, while Shmuel considers it to be the injury caused by the eating of an animal in another's field. This difference in turn influences the meaning given to another primary cause, שור 'ox': Rav takes it as a general term implying damage done by the animal's 'horn', 'tooth' or 'foot', while Shmuel limits it to its 'horn', reserving its 'tooth' and 'foot' for מבעה.

[64] See Albeck, *Introduction*, 216-36; Strack, *Introduction*, 105-118.

alone: Hillel, Shammai, Avtolmos, etc. The one exception are the last Patriarchs, who are given the title Rabban. It is logical, therefore, to exclude pre-Tannaic names from the generation listing of the Mishna teachers.[65]

We start our list, therefore, with the Yavne generation, and we count four generations of Tannaim, beginning with the Patriarch Rabban Gamliel II and ending with Rabbi Yehuda the Patriarch. It is customary to indicate a fifth generation of Tannaim, the one after Rabbi, but their names appear only in the Tosefta, as indeed do the great majority of the generation of Rabbi. We shall give those below in the chapter on the Tosefta.

FIRST GENERATION (at Yavne)

Rabban Gamliel (II), the Patriarch. Succeeded in establishing the hegemony of the School of Hillel at Yavne, but did not succeed in his attempt to make the voice of the Patriarch absolute. For this attempt he was temporarily deposed and replaced by the much younger R. Elazar ben Azaria. He was a prime figure in such measures as the fixation of the main prayer (*M. Ber.* 4:3).

R. Eliezer ben Hyrcanos. Together with R. Yoshua considered to be the chief pupil of R. Yohanan ben Zakkai who was the great leader at the time of the destruction. He followed generally the line of the School of Shammai, and when he refused to accept the hegemony of the School of Hillel in the Yavne generation, he was expelled from the academy.

R. Yoshua ben Hanunya. Outstanding exponent of the School of Hillel at Yavne. He accompanied the Patriarch on several missions to Rome and the diaspora. He was familiar with the special type of philosophy and mathematical exposition of legal matter formulated under Alexandrian influence. Feared any rebellion against the Roman government in Palestine.

R. Eliezer ben Yaakov I. One of the late Second Temple teachers who carried on at Yavne. He is held to be the teacher of the Mishna tractate *Middot.*

R. Elazar ben Azaria. Tenth generation descendant of Ezra and of great wealth. Was appointed to fill the position of Patriarch during the temporary deposition of Rabban Gamliel.

SECOND GENERATION

R. Akiva ben Yosef. Greatest disciple of the Yavne teachers. He supported the rebellion of Bar Kokhba and was cruelly put to death by the Romans. It was he who systematized all the branches of study: mishna, tosefta, halakhic midrash. He gave full development to a system of hermeneutics attributed to Nahum Ish Gamzu in which every 'extra' word in Scripture could be a source for midrashic exposition. The Mishna is essentially the book of R. Akiva, for it is he who gave

---

[65] Many scholars do include late Second Temple names in the first generation Tannaim; see Strack, *Introduction*, 109-111.

substance and literary formulation to the first generation teachings from Yavne, and his own teachings were the base for the fourth and main layer of the Mishna, that of the Usha generation.

R. Yishmael ben Elisha. Completed the development of the thirteen *middot*, i.e. rules of hermeneutic exposition of Scripture which bear his name. The chief opponent of R. Akiva in halakhic controversy. Objected as well to R. Akiva's daring method of scriptural exposition and taught: 'The Tora speaks after the manner of human speech.'

R. Tarfon. Another prime opponent of R. Akiva in halakha. A man of sharp speech but of generous disposition.

R. Elai. Chief pupil of R. Eliezer ben Hyrcanos the Shammaite, carrying on his tradition and not leaving him even after his expulsion from the Yavne academy.

R. Yose ha-Gelili. Carrier of a tradition opposed to that of R. Akiva and R. Tarfon both.

R. Yohanan ben Nuri. Differs primarily with R. Akiva.

R. Yehuda ben Bava. Bearer of some ancient testimonies. Gave ordination to the chief pupils of R. Akiva, even though such was prohibited by the Romans and subsequently he was put to death.

THIRD GENERATION (at Usha)

R. Meir. Prime among the four main pupils of R. Akiva, although he had previously studied under R. Yishmael. Taught R. Akiva's general teaching without limitations or extensions.

R. Yehuda ben Elai. While he is another prominent disciple of R. Akiva, he also preserves the tradition of his father Elai, the prime pupil of R. Eliezer the Shammaite. Aims at reconciliation or limiting the gap between teachings of R. Akiva and R. Eliezer. Limits R. Akiva's teachings to a specific situation, time or place. The chief opponent of R. Meir in halakha.

R. Yose ben Halafta. Through his father an inheritor of the Sepphoris-Galilean tradition. Usually takes a middle position between R. Meir and R. Yehuda and therefore known as the 'arbitrator among the Sages'. He is a master of chronological traditions, and the chronography *Seder Olam* is ascribed to him.

R. Shimon ben Yohai. Like R. Meir, he tends to give a literal interpretation to the unspecified teachings of R. Akiva, but sometimes from an opposite angle. The youngest of the four main pupils of R. Akiva.

R. Elazar ben Shammua. Very close to the general approach of R. Yehuda in expounding R. Akiva's teachings. Often mentioned together with the latter, and where not it may be assumed anyway that his opinion is the same. Differs with R. Yehuda on occasion, but only in the narrowest confines of interpretation where he may take a slightly more stringent point of view.

Abba Shaul. Also generally close to the view of R. Yehuda. Mentioned in the Mishna not too frequently, and usually on points of language alone.

R. Nehemia. Like R. Elazar ben Shammua, very close to R. Yehuda's position, but upon occasion of a more stringent view. Infrequently mentioned in halakhic discussion, since the name of R. Yehuda usually suffices for his teaching approach as well. Differs with R. Yehuda relatively frequently in matters of aggada.

R. Eliezer ben Yaakov II. Generally close to the position of R. Shimon, and usually mentioned only where there is a nuance of difference between the two.

Rabban Shimon ben Gamliel. Patriarch at Usha and most probably responsible for the official editing of the Mishna up until (but not including) his generation. He finds frequent mention in the Mishna, and represents a point of view akin to both R. Yehuda and R. Yose.

FOURTH GENERATION

R. Yehuda the Patriarch, or in short, Rabbi. Editor of the last layer of the Mishna. His own name is mentioned only upon occasion in the Mishna. Where this is not a later addition (as is often the case), his name occurs only in the same plane of reference as that of the pupils of R. Akiva.

R. Yose ben Yehuda. Son of R. Yehuda ben Elai, R. Akiva's disciple. Occasionally mentioned in the Mishna in connection with his father, but, like others of his generation, figuring primarily in the Tosefta.

R. Natan. Head of the Court under Rabban Shimon ben Gamliel and Rabbi Yehuda the Patriarch. Son of the Babylonian exilarch, and apparently the representative of that community at the school of Rabbi; his teaching equally represents Babylonian tradition. Only infrequently mentioned in the Mishna.

R. Elazar ben Shimon. Son of R. Shimon ben Yohai, R. Akiva's pupil. Mentioned only e few times in the Mishna, usually because of his father.

R. Shimon ben Elazar. Pupil of R. Meir and mentioned only a few times in the Mishna.

The fourth generation of Tannaim figures most prominently in the Tosefta, as stated before, and we shall treat it in more detail in the pertinent chapter.

Language

The language of the Mishna is Hebrew as it developed in late Second Temple times and afterwards. In vocabulary and syntax, it has an affinity to the later biblical books, although it is quite distinct from biblical Hebrew as such, especially with its fairly large accretion of foreign words. Some scholars in the last century regarded mishnaic Hebrew as an artificial creation of the academies, somewhat in the nature of medieval Latin.[66] It was only in 1908 that SEGAL demonstrated the falsity of this hypothesis.[67] Conclusive proof that mishnaic

---

[66] For an extreme view see Geiger, *Lehr- und Lesebuch*.
[67] Segal, 'Mishnaic Hebrew'. See also Kutscher, *History*, 115-20.

Hebrew was a vital, living language has come with the discovery of the Bar Kokhba letters and others documents in the Dead Sea area caves.[68]

The distinctive character of mishnaic Hebrew is due, perhaps in greatest measure, to the influence of Aramaic, which was also a spoken language for already several centuries in Palestine, and dominant in the eastern diaspora. The Mishna itself includes several teachings of mostly pre-destruction Sages in the original Aramaic in which they were given.[69] Document formulas are also recorded in the commonly used Aramaic.[70] But these are the exception rather than the rule. Aramaic influence is felt mostly in the loan words, some of which, of course, can already be found in Scripture.[71] The vocabulary of the Mishna remains, however, a mine for the preservation of Hebrew. It contains hundreds of Hebrew words not found in Aramaic but mostly authentic Hebrew words which Scripture had no occasion to use.[72] In addition, the Mishna can use biblical words with new nuances of meaning, usually that to be found in the equivalent Aramaic.[73]

Palestine being part of the Hellenistic milieu, it is not surprising to find a large number of Greek and to a lesser extent Latin words. These could have come directly from Greek and Latin or, more likely, by way of the Aramaic. For the most part, they are words for objects and concepts for which there were no ready Hebrew or Aramaic equivalents. Nor are they always easy to recognize. Often, they are hebraized in such a way that the exact Greek original becomes a problem for scholars.[74]

The internal development of mishnaic Hebrew undoubtedly was influenced by foreign patterns as well. It has three tenses, the active participle having been turned into the present tense, whereas biblical Hebrew has only two, and these limited, respectively, to completed and continuous activity. Personal pronouns differ in several respects form the biblical form. Gender is distinguished only in the third singular, whereas all pronouns of the second and third person are differentiated in gender. The subordinating conjunction אֲשֶׁר of biblical Hebrew becomes shortened to שֶׁ attached to the first word of the subordinate

---

[68] Cf. Milik, in *DJD* 2, 70.

[69] Cf. Yose ben Yoezer's testimony *Ed.* 8:4 and Hillel's maxims, *Av.* 1:13, 2:6, 4:5.

[70] Marriage formulas (*Ket.* 4:7-12; *Yev.* 15:3); R. Yehuda's divorce formulation (*Gitt.* 9:3); lease terms for agricultural land (*Bava M.* 9:3); loan formulas (*Bava B.* 10:2).

[71] For an almost complete list of mishnaic words which are also in Aramaic see Albeck, *Introduction*, 134-52. Unfortunately, Albeck's lists suffer from the fact that they are not based on manuscript readings but on the traditional printed editions; nor do they incorporate all the critical information available.

[72] Albeck, *Introduction*, 152-73.

[73] Albeck, *Introduction*, 173-203.

[74] Albeck, *Introduction*, 203-15 gives a practically complete list of Greek and Latin borrowings. The inclusion of Persian borrowings (such as *etrog*) would have made his list even more helpful. Very helpful is Krauss, *Lehnwörter*, esp. vol. 2 with Löw's corrections. Lieberman, *Greek* and *id.*, *Hellenism* has opened wide new fields of investigation in this area.

clause. There are also many differences in grammatical forms and phonetic features.[75]

Text

The text of the Mishna does not represent a unanimously accepted reading. The traditional printed editions differ often from the manuscripts and early printed editions. We are fortunate that a fair number of Mishna manuscripts exists, in addition to considerable fragments from the Cairo Geniza. It is not too difficult a task, therefore, to recover the prime reading of the text, and the changes which have taken place over the centuries can be easily traced.

The two main textual traditions are what is commonly termed Palestinian and Babylonian renderings. These terms indicate that one group of manuscripts represents versions current in Palestine and known by the Palestinian Talmud, while the other group are readings current in Babylonia and underlie discussions in the Babylonian Talmud. A third type of text is a kind of synthesis between the previous two, in the sense that Babylonian readings are grafted upon a Palestinian base. This mixed type is represented especially by Maimonidean manuscript readings and by the first printed edition which is based on Maimonides' text and commentary, and is generally termed the Spanish or Maimonidean group.[76]

Variant readings are to be found both in the consonantal text and in its vocalization, the latter being either in the form of written texts or of oral traditions preserved by specific Jewish communities. Now vocalized Mishna texts, of which there are not many, are generally suspect, for much of the vocalization seems to be artificially patterned after the more familiar vocalization of the Hebrew Scriptures. More reliable are often the oral vocalization traditions, such as those of the Yemenite Jews and other communities.[77]

The best text existing, universally accepted today as such, is the Kaufmann manuscript preserved in Budapest.[78] This manuscript preserves the original Palestinian readings in a purer form than any other manuscript. It is also

---

[75] The most recent comprehensive presentation of mishnaic Hebrew is Kutscher, *History*, chap. 6, esp. 120-42 where Kutscher discusses in detail the phonology, morphology, syntax, vocabulary and dialects. See also Bendavid, *Leshon*; Albeck, *Introduction*, 130-3; Rabin, in *Compendia* I/2, 1020-1.

[76] The best discussion of this subject is Epstein, *Nosah*, 1207-75.

[77] More than by anyone else, this field was studied by Yalon; see his collected articles in *id.*, *Vocalization*. Of first importance is the Hebrew University Language Traditions Project (HULTP) established in 1960. Complete Mishna readings have been taped of the Yemen, Aleppo, Baghdad and Jerba ethnic groups, as well as selections from those of other communies. See also Morag, *Baghdadi Community* (dealing with phonology) and Katz, *Community of Djerba* (dealing with morphology as well); Eldar, *Medieval Ashkenaz* (phonology and morphology).

[78] Facsimile ed. by G. Beer, Den Haag 1929, repr. Jerusalem 1969. The excellence of this text was firmly established by Kutscher, see esp. his 'Lashon Hazal'. For detailed descriptions of MS. Kaufmann see Goldberg, *Ohaloth*, 10-24 and *id.*, *Shabbat*, 36-41. Epstein gives special attention to its readings, see *Nosah*, 1207-69.

vocalized, but the vocalization is of a much later date, and often conflicts with the text itself. Next in importance to MS. Kaufmann is the Parma Mishna Codex.[79] About half of the text is vocalized, but here again the vocalization has problems of its own. A third good text is the Cambridge manuscript.[80]

A very important source for the Mishna text is the growing accumulation of Cairo Geniza fragments, scattered over the world's leading libraries, through the intervention of special research institutes.[81]

Reduction to Writing

At the beginning of this chapter, we have pointed out our own position that the Mishna was edited as an oral compilation and for several generations was transmitted as such. The literary features discussed above all serve to support that view. However, scholars have been divided on this question for long. Rashi and the medieval French school held that the Mishna was an oral compilation; Maimonides and the Spanish school, on the other hand, thought that Rabbi formulated the Mishna in writing. The classical document on the history of rabbinic literature, the *Letter of Rav Sherira Gaon*, has come down to us in a 'French' recension supporting Rashi's view and a 'Spanish' recension which follows Maimonides. Modern scholarship tends to the latter view.[82]

The one certain fact is that the Mishna was eventually put down in writing. The questions are: why and how and when? What we glean from post-mishnaic sources is that this was a very gradual process and not all Sages acceded to the change at the same time. Even two or three generations after the compilation of the Mishna there was still strong opposition to putting down Oral Tora in writing. The third century Palestinian Amora R. Yohanan bar Nappaha quotes

[79] De Rossi 138, facsimile Jerusalem 1970. See Goldberg, *Ohaloth*, 28f. and *id.*, *Shabbat*, 42f. for characteristics.

[80] Cambridge University Library Add. 470, 1. Published by W.H. Lowe, Cambridge 1883, under the somewhat inaccurate title *The Mishna on which the Palestinian Talmud rests* (repr. Jerusalem 1966). See Goldberg, *Ohaloth*, 29f. For a listing of many other MSS. see Strack, *Introduction*, 79f. Many more have become known since, some edited in facsimile. These are Codex Parma 'B', De Rossi 497, Seder *Toharot* only (Jerusalem 1971), important for its pointing and musical notations (see introduction by M. Bar-Asher *ib.*, 1-20 and Goldberg, *Ohaloth*, 24-8); Codex Parma 'C', De Rossi 984, *Nashim - Nezikin*, with Maimonides' commentary (Jerusalem 1971); and a Yemenite MS. of Seder *Moed*, with Arabic commentary of Maimonides (with introd. by S. Morag, Holon 1975), distinguished for its superlinear (Babylonian) pointing. In addition, MSS. of the Palestinian and Babylonian Talmudim are important, since the Mishna is integral in both; see Talmud chapters below for editions. For full discussion of the MSS. see pp. 252-62.

[81] Special mention deserves the Institute of Photocopies of Hebrew Manuscripts in the Hebrew University and National Library in Jerusalem, and of the Geniza Project of the Israel Academy of Sciences directed by Y. Sussman. For a photocopy edition of all Mishna geniza fragments in the Leningrad library, together with a list of variant readings, See Katsh, *Ginze Mishna*.

[82] The fullest discussion of the question is in Epstein, *Nosah*, 692-706. Cf. also Albeck, *Introduction*, 111-15; Strack, *Introduction*, 12-20. These authors all lean to the view that Rabbi himself put the Mishna to writing. Cf. also Safrai, above, p. 72-75.

the verse 'For by *mouth* of these words have I made a covenant with thee and Israel' (Exod 34:27), to support the prohibition against writing down Oral Tora.[83] Moreover, he specifically teaches that 'those who write down halakhot are like those who burn the Tora'; yet the same R. Yohanan, together with his brother-in-law R. Shimon ben Lakish, would 'peruse a book of aggada on the Sabbath'.[84] From this it appears that by the time of R. Yohanan a distinction was already made in Palestine between writing aggada (which had become permitted) and writing halakhot (which was still prohibited). An older teacher of the same generation is still opposed even to the writing down of aggada: 'Thus taught R. Yoshua ben Levi: This aggada, whoever writes it down does not have any portion (in the world to come), whoever expounds it (from a book) is scorched, and whoever hears it does not receive any reward.'[85] Thus even the writing of aggada was not accepted without a struggle. This is in Palestine. In Babylonia the prohibition held on longer. The Babylonian Amora of half-a-century later, R. Zeira, upon coming to Palestine and finding there written books of aggada, exclaimed: 'These are books of witchcraft.'[86]

Once the aggada became written down, it does not seem to have taken too long before the halakha began to be written down as well. Here, especially, the process was gradual. Certainly, students had been making personal notes to refresh their memories even in the earliest period,[87] although none would dare bring them to the academy or even to quote from them by reading. Eventually, when written aggada became accepted generally, halakha too, could be written down without too much ado. It seems logical to posit, therefore, that in Palestine the Mishna became a written book sometime during the early part of the fourth century. Even so, however, this could be only for private use. At the academy and at all public sessions of discourse no books could be used. Publicly, Oral Tora had to remain oral. Even as late as the Gaonic period we know that all teaching in the academy was oral.[88] This explains in great measure why we do not have today any 'official' version of the Mishna. Any written text of such, by its very being written down, would automatically become 'unofficial'.

---

[83] *B.T. Gitt.* 60b.

[84] *B.T. Tem.* 14b.

[85] *P.T. Shabb.* 16, 15c.

[86] *P.T. Maasrot* 3, 51a. Albeck, who agrees that the Mishna was written from the beginning, notes the opposition in these sources to the writing of aggada, but explains it in the opposite direction. In a lengthy note (*Introduction*, 112 n. 20) he theorizes that the fear of writing aggada was greater than was the case with halakha, because the popular aggada could easily become a vehicle for deviating views. This explanation, however, does not reckon sufficiently with the cronology of the sources.

[87] Rav found a 'hidden scroll' teaching halakhic midrash in the home of his uncle R. Hiya: *B.T. Shabb.* 6b, 96b; *B.T. Bava M.* 92a. The mid-third tcentury Palestinian Amora Ilfa is said to have written baraitot in his note-book: *B.T. Men.* 70a. And R. Yona tells: 'I have found written in the notebook of Ilfa ...' (*P.T. Maasr.* 1, 49d) referring to a teaching equivalent to *T. Maasr.* 2:3. For additional references see Epstein, *Nosah*, 700-1.

[88] Rav Sherira Gaon states that neither the Mishna nor the Talmud were taught other than orally in the academies during the Gaonic period. See *Iggeret Rav Sherira Gaon*, 71 (French recension).

Authority

The literary features of the Mishna, as set forth above, characterize it as a text-book of law rather than a binding code. Nevertheless, already early in the Amoraic period, and first of all in Babylonia, it came to be looked upon in almost complete measure as a book of canon law. This was a natural develop-ment which has parallels elsewhere in legal history.[89] The conflict with the halakha accepted in Babylonia, wherever this occurred, was overcome mostly by giving the Mishna a forced interpretation. Thus, for example, the first generation Amora Shmuel gives a forced interpretation to three different mishnayot in the tractate *Gittin* (2:4, 5; 3:2) in order to make them conform to the opinion of R. Elazar, which he accepted as binding. Yet the simple meaning of these mishnayot, and undoubtedly what Rabbi intended them to mean, is in accordance with the view of R. Meir.[90]

Only a little later in Palestine itself we find R. Yohanan teaching along the following line: Rabbi accepted the view of R. Meir in the case of 'the dam and its young' and taught it as the view of the Sages, but in the case of 'the covering of the blood' that of R. Shimon and taught it in the name of the Sages.[91] So, too, is the general line taken by the Babylonian Talmud. 'Is it not Rabbi who edited the Mishna? Then why with respect to the Sabbath does he give the anonymous view in accordance with R. Shimon, and with respect to the Festival Days according to that of R. Yehuda?'[92]

A less sophisticated way of giving the Mishna a unified presentation and of making it conform to accepted halakha is to emend the wording, frequent in both Talmudim.[93] Although we find occasional emendations by first generation Amoraim in both Palestine and Babylonia, they become more frequent with the passing of the generations.[94]

It is not at all uncharacteristic that one and the same mishna quotes two different sources, often both anonymously, to the effect that its opening and closing sections may contradict one another. In a text-book of law this may be even commendable, but it is jarring in what is taken to be a code. In order to tackle this difficulty, the Babylonian Talmud developed in time a characteristic process of supplying 'missing links' between the two sections so as to make them

[89] Jackson, 'From Dharma to Law', shows how Indian law texts originally written as *dharma*, i.e. merely desirable, eventually became binding law by custom or royal ordinance. As in the case of the Mishna, this is expressed in literary phenomena.

[90] See references and discussion in Goldberg, 'Purpose and Method', 261-2.

[91] *B.T. Hull.* 85a; the reference is, respectively, to *M. Hull.* 5:3 and 6:2.

[92] *B.T. Beitsa* 2b, referring to *M. Shabb.* 24:4 and *M. Beitsa* 4:3. And see below, p. 308ff.

[93] *Pes.* 10:4 formulates as one of the four Seder questions: 'On all other nights we dip only once; on this night twice.' The Palestinian custom of 'dipping' before the meal was unknown in Babylonia, and Rava emends the Mishna to read: 'On all other nights we do *not* dip *even* once; on this night twice.' *B.T. Pes.* 116a.

[94] For a detailed discussion of emendations and emendatory interpretations, from the second Amoraic generation onwards, see Epstein, *Nosah*, 353-404, 439-595.

appear as part of a unified teaching. This process is termed *hasorei mehasra*, 'there is a lacuna in the Mishna'. Its effect is that different sources become plastered over and that the Mishna takes on a more unified character. It is important to note that the Palestinian Talmud knows nothing of this harmonizing method (see below, 332-3).[95]

Viewed as a code of law, the Mishna with its literary characteristics confronted later generations with the task of removing its contradictions, of limiting the number of differing opinions, and of narrowing the gap between them. Despite all this, however, not every teaching of the Mishna could be successfully reinterpreted to conform to accepted halakha, and many explicit rejections of Mishna teachings are recorded in both Talmudim.[96]

Bibliography

COMMENTARIES

From the very beginning, the stylized and concise language of the Mishna, as well as its special selectivity in the arrangement of the Halakha, has called for explanation. In a very special way, the Mishna interprets itself, each layer serving as a commentary on an earlier one. This is true for both individual mishnayot and for larger sections of the Mishna. Thus, as we pointed out above, *Bava Kamma* 1:4 serves as the focal point for the explanation which follows in the entire second chapter of that treatise. In the second place, the Tosefta, a parallel compilation to the Mishna, is primarily a supplement and commentary to it. In much smaller measure, the Tannaic midrash collections contain such commentary. In the third place, the Palestinian and Babylonian Talmudim, despite the diversified areas of discussion in both, remain first and foremost interpretations of the Mishna.

It is important to note that from the start there was no single unified interpretation of the Mishna. Teachers of the second generation will often differ in their understanding of a general teaching of the previous generation.[97] So, too, will teachers of the third generation give different interpretations to general statements of the second, as we have seen above in our discussion on R. Akiva and

---

[95] The only thorough and practically exhaustive analysis of *hasorei mehasra* is in Epstein, *Nosah*, 595-672.

[96] *M. Beitsa* 4:2 teaches that on a Festival day one may bring in wood which lies collected on a field or which lies scattered about in an enclosed storage area. Shmuel (*B.T. Beitsa* 31a) rejects this mishna and teaches, more strictly, that it may be brought in only from the enclosed area and only when it lies collected together. *M. Shev.* 9:6 teaches that leaves both of reeds and of vines cannot be stored in the house on the Sabbatical Year after the time that leaves of such fall from their stems in the field. R. Yohanan, however, does not accept this teaching with regard to reeds, limiting it to vines alone (*P.T. Shev.* 9, 39a).

[97] The early layer of the Mishna in *Pes.* 10:6 states simply that the Seder meal is ended with the Blessing of Redemption. Yet in the formulation of this blessing, R. Akiva and R. Tarfon (second generation) differ.

his pupils. Equally so is the relationship of the fourth to the third or any preceding generation.[98] Moreover, there are often distinct Palestinian and Babylonian traditions in the interpretation of the Mishna.[99] Again, later generations of Amoraim may differ in their interpretation from their predecessors.[100] It is a paradoxical fact that a unified interpretation of the Mishna begins to take shape only with the appearance of what we commonly recognize as commentaries.

The first complete commentary to the Mishna is that of MAIMONIDES, written in Arabic over a period of seven years and completed in 1168. Hebrew translations were not long in coming.[101] Maimonides usually gives but one interpretation to a particular mishna. Almost always he follows the latest teachers in the Babylonian Talmud, and only in a handful of cases gives an independent interpretation. Almost all commentaries written afterwards are based on Maimonides' commentary. This is the reason why the scores of commentaries usually concur in one single interpretation of any mishna. Of special importance is Maimonides' introduction to the Mishna and to Oral Tora in general, as well as his specific introductions to some of the Orders of the Mishna. The great influence of Maimonides' commentary can be gleaned from the fact that it accompanied the first printed edition of the Mishna and appears today, among other places, in almost all editions of the Talmud.

Of the classic commentaries, that of Maimonides is the only one to treat the entire Mishna. Partial commentaries did exist earlier on which left their mark as well. A Gaonic commentary to the Order *Toharot* is the first known commentary in existence, but consists primarily of word interpretation.[102] The same is true for the Palestinian eleventh century commentary of R. NATAN FATHER OF THE ACADEMY, except that it covers most of the Mishna.[103] A very important

---

[98] These differences are recorded almost always in the Tosefta or the baraitot. Thus in *T. Ber.* 1·1, Rabbi and R. Natan differ as to the length of the 'watch' referred to in the very first mishna, R. Natan, as a Babylonian, following the eastern division into three night watches, and Rabbi following the Roman division into four night watches.

[99] See preceding note. Similarly, R. Yohanan the Palestinian will always interpret the Mishna in accordance with the Palestinian baraita of the school of Rabbi, whereas R. Elazar, of Babylonian origin, will give a literal interpretation. In many cases, of course, Babylonian interpretation will follow the Palestinian. See the extended discussion in Epstein, *Nosah*, 47-74 *passim*.

[100] See my discussion of the Babylonian *sugya*, below 337-9.

[101] The first ed. of the Mishna (Naples 1492) is printed with Maimonides' commentary translated in Hebrew, but by different hands of uneven quality. A modern, more exact translation was made by the Yemen-born scholar Yosef Qafih, *Mishna* (1963-8). Previously, J. Derenbourg had made a translation of Maimonides' commentary on Seder *Toharot*, Berlin 1887-89. See Strack, *Introduction*, for other translations.

[102] The critical edition is one of the greatest achievements of modern scholarship: Epstein, *Tohoroth*.

[103] Preserved in the Arabic as copied by a twelfth century Yemenite scholar, a copy which includes additions from other commentaries; the exact contribution of R. Natan himself cannot always be certified. Short introductions are included to the whole Mishna and to several of the tractates. Chapter divisions do not always coincide with the usual. A Hebrew translation was made by Y. Qafih, Jerusalem 1955-58.

commentary is that of R. YITSHAK BEN MALKHI TSEDEK ('RIVMATS') of Siponto in southern Italy in the first half of the twelfth century, covering the Orders *Zeraim* and *Toharot*, the Orders which lack Babylonian Talmud.[104] The prime partial commentary is that of R. SHIMSHON OF SENS in France, in the latter half of the twelfth century. Although it is also limited to *Zeraim* and *Toharot*, it is considered one of the very best in its use of all rabbinic sources.[105] Other partial commentaries are those of R. MEIR OF ROTHENBURG of the early thirteenth century, covering *Toharot*[106] and of R. ASHER BEN YEHIEL ('ROSH') of the early fourteenth century, on *Zeraim* and *Toharot*.[107]

Popular commentaries to the Mishna make their appearance with that of R. OVADYA OF BERTINORO, Italy, in the late fifteenth century.[108] The Renaissance influence of popularization is reflected throughout and to this very day it is the 'inside' page commentary, parallel to the place of Rashi in the Talmud editions, in all traditional editions of the Mishna. Its easy, clear style makes it eminently readable. It makes no claim for originality, basing itself primarily upon Rashi's Talmud commentary and the Mishna commentaries of Maimonides and R. Shimshon of Sens. In turn, the supercommentary of R. YOM TOV HELLER, early seventeenth century, is based on Bertinoro.[109] At about the same time, a Yemenite scholar residing in Hebron, R. SHLOMO HA-ADANI, wrote a full commentary to the Mishna remarkable for its almost modern scientific quality, giving close attention to variant readings and basing itself on the prime sources.[110] The early nineteenth century commentaries of R. ELIYAHU THE GAON of Wilna *(Zeraim, Toharot)* are also noteworthy for their originality and their use of the prime sources.[111] Another very good commentary is that of R. EFRAIM

---

[104] The *Zeraim* part is printed in the Romm Wilna edition of the Talmud and all copies of it. The *Toharot* part is known only through quotations by others. This commentary served as a model to R. Shimshon of Sens in its full use of all Tannaic and Talmudic sources. Difficult words are often translated into the vernacular Greek, the language spoken at the time in southern Italy.

[105] First published in the Venice 1523 Bomberg edition of the Talmud and to this day appears in all Talmud editions alongside Maimonides' commentary.

[106] Only the tractates *Ohalot* and *Negaim* have so far been printed in the newer Talmud editions.

[107] First published in the Talmud editions Amsterdam 1714ff. and Berlin - Frankfurt/O 1715ff.; now in all editions.

[108] First printed Venice 1548-49. Latin translation by Surenhuysen (Surenhusius) Amsterdam 1698-1703.

[109] First edition by author, Prague 1614-17; second edition Cracow 1643-44. It is constantly referred to, although it suffers from the fact that it is based on Bertinoro. It is printed in all traditional editions of the Mishna, taking pride of place on the outside area of the page. A short abstract of both Bertinoro's and Heller's commentaries called *Melo Kaf Nakhat*, by Shneior Feibush ben Yaakov, was published, Offenbach 1737 and republished, Berlin 1832-34, as well as occasionally afterwards.

[110] Despite its recognized importance it remained in the hands of N. Coronel up to 1854 and did not appear in print until the large Romm Wilna edition of the Mishna, 1887 (*Zeraim, Toharot*), 1908ff. (the other Orders). It is unfortunately confined to the end of the volumes except for the first and last Orders.

[111] Called *Shenot Eliyahu* and *Eliyahu Rabba*, respectively, and found at the back of the Romm Wilna edition and all its reprints.

YITSHAK of Premysl.[112]

Truly scientific commentaries are a phenomenon of modern times. The only one which covers the entire Mishna is ALBECK, *Mishna*. Because it aims to be a popular commentary as well (an aim which was achieved, in view of its remarkable sales in Israel), most of the critical writing is confined to the introductions to Orders and tractates, and to the elaborate notes at the end of each volume. The commentary by KAHATI, equally popular, is helpful but not for critical study.[113]

Of prime scientific importance are the full discussion of hundreds of individual mishnayot in EPSTEIN, *Nosah* to which we have often referred in the above. Critical editions of single tractates with German commentary have appeared in the Giessen series, but these mostly do not really have a full apparatus of variants nor does the commentary fulfill most critical requirements.[114] A much better and fuller German commentary, though with no particular pretensions to an exacting critical approach, is HOFFMAN - SAMMTER, *Mischnajoth*.[115] Comprehensive critical commentary, a critical text with a full apparatus of variant readings, and extensive introductions are found in GOLDBERG, *Ohaloth*, *Shabbat* and *Eruvin*. LIEBERMAN'S classic commentary, *Tosefta ki-Fshutah*, contains much scientific commentary to the Mishna.

For the English-reader, there is as yet no truly scientific commentary. BLACKMAN, *Mishnayot* is helpful, as is some rudimentary commentary in I. EPSTEIN, *Talmud*. The twenty-two volumes of NEUSNER, *Law of Purities* contain translations and also scientific commentary to the Order of *Toharot*. Both should be used, however, with caution.[116]

EDITIONS

The first edition of the Mishna, as we pointed out above, was published together with a Hebrew translation of Maimonides' Arabic commentary, Naples 1492. The text is of a Palestinian base on which Babylonian readings have been grafted. The importance of this edition is that it served as the basis for all later printings of the Mishna, although from one printing to the next, more and more Babylonian readings found their way into the text.

A landmark edition is that of Justinian, Venice 1546-50. It is most heavily marked by readings taken from the Mishna text of the Babylonian Talmud. A quarto edition with the commentary of Bertinoro appeared in Venice, 1548ff.

[112] To *Zeraim* (called *Mishna Rishona*) and *Toharot* (*Mishna Aharona*), appearing on the page of the Romm Wilna edition. Other less important commentaries: see Strack, *Introduction*, 148.
[113] Jerusalem 1950ff.
[114] Beer *et al.*, *Mischna*.
[115] For a full listing of foreign-language commentaries (with translation) see Mielziener, *Introduction*, 88 and 302; Strack-Stemberger, *Einleitung*, 145-6. See also below, 'Translations'.
[116] Although stimulating to further research, mistranslations and misrepresentations abound. Cf. my review of Neusner, *Eliezer* in *JSJ* 6 (1975) 108-14 for some of the methodical inaccuracies of his approach.

Later editions, Riva di Trento 1559, Sabbioneta and Mantua 1559-63, and Venice 1606, all follow the Justinian text, and all were published together with Maimonides' commentary in Hebrew and that of Bertinoro. These last were the basis for the editions of Yom Tov Lipman Heller referred to in the above, Prague 1614-17 and Cracow 1642-44. An important early edition of unknown provenance, but close to the time of the first edition, is extant in the first three Orders only; it was recently reproduced in facsimile.[117] Wherever a dispute is mentioned in the Mishna, this edition adds within the text, and in the same square lettering, Maimonides' halakhic decision. Word explanations are given at the end of every chapter in Rashi-type lettering.

Of the modern editions, several were mentioned in the previous section because of the commentary they contain; others will be mentioned in the next section for their translation. A very important edition is being published at present in Jerusalem; so far the Order *Zeraim* has appeared: SACKS, *Mishna*. There is a complete listing not only of manuscript readings,[118] but also of all Mishna quotations in other rabbinic sources as well as in medieval authorities. Geniza fragments are reproduced in clear facsimile.

TRANSLATIONS

The language of the Mishna is often elliptic and literal translation becomes impossible without words of explanation which tend to become commentary. Yet the moment commentary enters into translation, there can be no guarantee of accurate translation of text. Translations, moreover, have usually been undertaken not by prime scholars in the field. For a full listing of translations into Latin and modern European languages up to 1920 see STRACK, *Introduction*, 142f. Since then many new translations have appeared, both of the entire Mishna and of individual tractates. See STRACK-STEMBERGER, *Einleitung*, 145-6; MIELZIENER, *Introduction*, 88, 302. Most of these translations have commentary as well (see above 'Commentaries'). Translations of the Talmud of necessity are translations of the Mishna as well. See MIELZIENER *ib*. 90-2, 302-3; STRACK-STEMBERGER *ib*. 181, 205.

The first and best known translation into English is DANBY, *Mishnah*. It is a monumental work, although mistranslations and inaccuracies of interpretation

---

[117] Under the title *Unknown Edition, Pisaro or Constantinople*, Jerusalem 1970. For discussion of this edition see Epstein, *Nosah*, 1279f.; Friedman, 'Unknown Editions' and the bibliographical references cited there; and most recently Feintuch, 'Versions'.

[118] It is most unfortunate that the approach is not entirely scientific. Instead of choosing a prime text as the base, such as that of the Kaufmann MS., the unreliable text of the traditional printed editions is used. Nor are the variants assembled in any order of 'families'.

abound.[119] is A complete translation together with pointed text is offered by BLACKMAN, *Mishnayot*. Here, too, the translation is helpful but not really scientific, being based on the traditional text and the Bertinoro commentary. The translation of Mishna sections contained in I. EPSTEIN, *Talmud* is probably the best translation into English so far. The notes and glossaries in this edition, as well as its index, are helpful.

A German translation of generally high quality, together with the Hebrew text, is found in HOFFMAN-SAMMTER, *Mishnayot*. A remarkable effort in producing text and translation is the Giessen series: BEER *et al.*, *Mischna*. Very good is the translation, containing some commentary as well, contained in GOLD-SCHMIDT, *Babylonische Talmud*. It is based not on the traditional text, but on the Venice 1520-23 edition and a fair array of variant readings.

Italian translations are those published in Trieste 1893-1933 and Rome 1962. A French edition is being prepared under the editorship of Ernest GUGENHEIM; a few tractates have appeared so far (Paris, 1968 -). There is, of course, translation of the Mishna in SCHWAB, *Talmud de Jérusalem*. A Dutch translation by S. HAMMELBURG appeared in Amsterdam, 1939.

INTRODUCTIONS

The best handbook in English up until recently was STRACK, *Introduction*, which translation is based on the author's revised copy of the fifth German edition. Although outdated in many respects, nothing really better in any language other than Hebrew was to be found. The scholarly world is today most fortunate in having an up-to-date revision of this work in STRACK-STEMBERGER, *Einleitung*. It is most complete, containing references to almost all relevant publications in book form or in periodicals up to 1976. Its only drawback, perhaps, is that like in all handbooks the excellent and the mediocre in many cases are lumped together, there being little room for real critical judgment.

Though not basically as good, worth mentioning is MIELZIENER, *Introduction*, with a new bibliography by A. GUTTMAN covering the years 1925-67. It is this bibliography, and perhaps even more the additional notes and corrections by BLOCH and FINKELSTEIN which give this book its present value. One must not overlook the introduction in DANBY, *Mishnah*. It is written with very good taste

---

[119] One example among many. The rule that when the 14th of Nissan falls on the Sabbath the leaven does not have to be removed until its appointed time (*M. Pes.* 3:6), receives the following comment: 'The burning of the *hametz* overrides the Sabbath; (...) to burn ordinary food would deprive most men of food on the Sabbath' (p. 139, n. 13). This comment betrays a decisive lack of understanding. No Mishna teacher would permit burning of leaven on the Sabbath. What is meant is that leaven may be kept till the appointed hour on the Sabbath and then disposed of in ways which do not violate the Sabbath (as possibly indicated by *M. Pes.* 2:1). Where not disposed of, it must be covered and may not be burned either on the Sabbath or on the next day which is a festival holy day, but only on the second day of Passover, which is a 'profane festival day'. Unfortunately, Danby while in Jerusalem did not consult with really knowledgeable scholars. It is no exaggeration to state that almost on every page there is at least one inaccuracy.

and considerable skill, encompassing within thirty pages much of the relevant background material for Mishna study. LIEBERMAN, *Hellenism* has some bearing on Mishna background, especially the chapter on 'The Publication of the Mishna'. GERHARDSSON, *Memory* deals also with the problems concerning the methods of transmission of both the Written and Oral Tora in the mishnaic period.

NEUSNER, *Modern Study* is a collection of seminar papers on leading representatives of critical Mishna study since it began about a century and a half ago. Unfortunately, the papers are very uneven, and have the undigested quality of seminar papers in general. More serious is the unfounded pretension expressed throughout, that no truly critical study of the Mishna existed before the Neusner era. It is indeed embarrassing to read Neusner's dilettante disparagement of the great pioneers. Those who studied their works know that almost all of them have already dealt with what are here presented as 'new questions'. Even where today we cannot accept their conclusions, their work has certainly made it easier for others to find the right paths in critical study.

For already more than a century and a half, the best work in critical Mishna study has been written in Hebrew.[120] The most popular of these works, which was also translated into German, is ALBECK, *Introduction*. It treats the Oral Tora as background of the Mishna, traces its earliest beginnings and development, and deals with the organization of the Mishna and its language. There is also a succinct chapter on the history and teachings of the more important Sages. A very good chapter is the one on the commentaries to the Mishna. The critique of preceding theories on the origins of the Mishna is excellent, although his own approach is not one we can entirely accept. There is a certain dogmatism in Albeck's work which detracts from its quality. Nor are his theories, although carefully documented, such as to stand up in all detail. Nevertheless, for a modern general study this is perhaps the best we have so far. The introductions to single tractates in Albeck's commentary, with their gem-like clarity and precision, would add meaning when read together with this *Introduction*.

The greatest achievement in modern Mishna scholarship is without doubt EPSTEIN, *Nosah*; it is a work which will last through generations. Not only does it trace the history of the formulation of the Mishna and the influences which worked upon it, but it shows as well how the interpretation of the Mishna developed over the generations. It is unequalled in its demonstration of the importance of the study of variant readings in the frame of Mishna-interpretation. Keen analysis of all the sources, complete mastery of critical method and unusually gifted insights serve to uncover the prime meaning of many a difficult mishna.

EPSTEIN, *Tannaitic Literature* contains a lengthy general introduction to the Mishna. Published posthumously, it lacks the finished quality of the previous

---

[120] For a complete listing of early and later critical introductions in Hebrew (Brüll, Frankel) and other languages see Mielziener, *Introduction*, 84, 301; Strack-Stemberger, *Einleitung*, 111-2.

work, but is still a very important help in any study of the Mishna. Its main emphasis is on the history of the sources until the final editing of the Mishna and on the contributions to its development made by individual Sages of the subsequent Tannaic generations.

The present writer's introductions to the critical tractate editions, *Ohaloth*, *Shabbat* and *Eruvin*, contain much which can serve as part of a general introduction to the Mishna as well.

An important aid to all Mishna study is the concordance: KASOWSKI, *Otsar leshon ha-Mishna*.

Manuscripts of the Mishna

(by *Michael Krupp*)

The Mishna is oral tradition committed to writing, and not originally the work of an individual. It was a collection accumulated over centuries to which new collections were constantly added. It was edited about 200 c.e. by Yehuda the Patriarch (Rabbi) and his pupils. Several editions were probably made of it not long after Rabbi's and these in their basic elements go back to various redactions of Rabbi's work.

Two main recensions can be clearly distinguished. They do not run, however, uniformly parallel. They display only two main currents: the Mishna text as read in Palestine, and the Mishna text as recognized in Babylonia.

The Mishna texts originally used by the Babylonian and Palestinian Talmudim have not been preserved in their entirety. The extant Talmud manuscripts usually give the whole Mishna text by chapter at the beginning of the Gemara. But the copyists apparently derived this text from other sources, and it was a mixed text deriving from both above-mentioned recensions. This is true of both the Babylonian and the Palestinian Talmud. The former originally contained the Mishna text, either entirely or in large parts, in the so-called *piskaot* spread over the Gemara, while the latter seems originally to have given none of the Mishna. The Mishna text used by the Palestinian Amoraim can only be deduced from the discussions in the Gemara.

If one accepts the notion of two original recensions, the MSS. of the Mishna may be divided into at least four families:
a) text as given at the beginning of each chapter in the Palestinian Talmud; so the complete Parma MS. (see below) at least in some tractates;
b) the Mishna text of the complete manuscripts, especially the Codex Kaufmann and the Cambridge codex (see below) and the fragments from the Cairo Geniza;
c) the Mishna text as found at the beginning of each chapter in the old Talmud MSS.;
d) the Mishna text which can be reconstructed from the *piskaot* of the Talmud manuscripts and fragments; this text is contained piece-meal as Mishna text in some Geniza Talmud fragments.
Texts a) and b) belong to the Palestinian version, the others to the Babylonian. None of the four traditions is found in printed editions of the Mishna, all of which go back to the Naples printing of 1492, presumably the first impression of the whole Mishna. At least, no full copy of earlier date has been found. The Naples edition gives the Mishna along with Maimonides' commentary (translated into Hebrew), which displays a special textual tradition, a mixed text between types b) and c).

The text of this first printed edition was further mutilated by Christian censorship from the middle of the 16th century on. Wherever, for instance, the various Hebrew words for stranger, non-Jew, Samaritan and so on appear, they have been rendered as 'adorers of stars and constellations'. At the beginning of the twentieth century, with censorship finally eliminated – last of all in Russia, where the *editiones majores* of rabbinical literature, including Mishna and Talmud, had been published – an effort was made to restore the original of the censured texts. But this was often done without recourse to older impressions, much less older MSS. The result is a particularly corrupt text.

In view of this state of the text, the surviving MSS. must be consulted.

THE THREE COMPLETE MISHNA MANUSCRIPTS

MS. KAUFMANN. Hungarian Academy of Sciences, Budapest, MS. A 50, formerly in the possession of David Kaufmann; facsimile edition first published by G. BEER, The Hague 1929; reprint in smaller format, Jerusalem 1968.

The MS. probably comes from Palestine and was written in the tenth or at the latest the eleventh century. Script and form of letters closely resemble certain MSS. of the Bible of eastern origin, written in the tenth or eleventh century.

The MS. contains comments, mostly emendations of the text, contributed by several hands. The emendations of one particular hand are constant and form the majority. The same hand also vocalized the codex. This vocalization was not inserted by the original scribe but was done probably some centuries later, when it was transferred from a vocalized copy which offered a text differing much from the Kaufmann codex. The punctator inserted these variations into the Kaufmann codex. The pointing and the emendations from the punctator display a second MS. belonging to another recension.

The peculiarities of the Kaufmann MS. are more numerous than in any other, including most of the Geniza fragments. It has kept older forms of the Palestinian type of text and it often reflects the spoken language of second century Palestine. The Kaufmann codex is undoubtedly the oldest complete Mishna text and contains the best readings, even though it does not seem as faithful as the Cambridge codex in preserving the Palestinian recension. Hence the Kaufmann codex must now be regarded as the basic text of all scientific editions.

MS. PARMA (DE ROSSI 138). Parma, Bibliotheca Palatina no. 3173 (J.B. DE ROSSI, *MSS. codices hebraici*, Parma 1803, no. 138) contains the whole Mishna. Published in facsimile impression under the title of *Mishna Codex Parma (de Rossi 138)*, Jerusalem 1970. The first half of the MS. and some odd pages later are vocalized. This was done by a later hand, as appears especially from a comparison with the few words vocalized in a different fashion throughout the codex, not by the first copyist but by someone using the general vocalization.

The manuscript is from several hands. When it is compared with the Codex Hebr. Vaticanus 31 (published Jerusalem 1972 as *Torath Cohanim [Sifra]; Seder Eliyahu Rabba and Zutta; Codex Vaticanus 31*), it appears that the Parma codex and Vatican 31 stem from the same school or family of scribes.[121] According to the colophon, Vatican 31 was written in 1073. This provides a set dating for the Parma codex. Like the Kaufmann codex, the Parma was written either in Palestine or Italy, or, as suggested by the marginal glosses, Southern Italy, where it was to be found in any case soon after it was completed.

In keeping with its oriental character, the Parma codex is a fair copy with few scribal errors and few *homoioteleuta*, many of which were corrected by the same hand, while others had perhaps been in the prototype. Like the Kaufmann codex, the Parma preserves very faithfully the external signs of the Palestinian type of text.

The vocalization added by the second hand goes back to ancient traditions, which do not sharply distinguish *kamets* and *patach* or *segol* and *tsere*. Pausal forms are frequent. The use of the *rafe*-line even over consonants not belonging to the בגדכפת group is remarkable. There are also punctuation signs in the vocalized parts. The punctuation at the end of a Mishna (the paragraphs) comes from the first copyist and is also found throughout the non-vocalized parts.

Close though the Parma is to the Kaufmann in script and handwriting, it does not belong to the same recension. It shows affinities with the Mishna text of some Talmud MSS. which give the Mishna always at the start of a chapter. It is particularly close to the Mishna text as given at the beginning of each chapter of the Palestinian Talmud in the Leiden MS.

MS. CAMBRIDGE (LOWE). Cambridge, University Library Add. 470 (II) contains the whole Mishna. The manuscript was published as *The Mishna on which the Palestinian Talmud Rests* by W.R. Lowe, Cambridge 1883. This is not a facsimile impression but an exact line by line reproduction which tries to copy in print line-fillers, slips of the pen, corrections and so on. The types used are of the Rashi style, to keep as close as possible to the features of Spanish cursive. Apart from a few misreadings and misprints the offprint is correct. This offprint and not the original manuscript was reprinted in Jerusalem 1967, without any alterations.

The script is rabbinical 'with cursive elements from a Sephardic hand of the 14th to 15th century'. The script features overlengthening of letters which rise or descend above the line. The letters are often written in cursive.

The scribe was very hasty, as is particularly clear from the many *homoioteleuta*, which often disguise completely the meaning of a text. Omission of single words, however, is rare, while slips of the pen are frequent. The Cambridge codex is the most consistent in writing the final *mem* in the plural.

The Cambridge codex offers far fewer original forms even in script and grammar than the two codices described above. But no one questions that it belongs to the Palestinian recension and is in many traits freer from corruption than the Kaufmann codex.

---

[121] See Krupp, 'Relation'.

OTHER MISHNA MANUSCRIPTS AND FRAGMENTS

Manuscripts containing only the Mishna are extremely rare, and it seems that they all derive from Palestine or Italy, possibly even from Egypt. The Mishna is so bulky a book that it is not surprising that there are only three manuscripts with the whole text. But it is strange that there are hardly any partial manuscripts. Here is a list of the few that have been preserved:

MS. PARMA (DE ROSSI 497). Facsimile edition *Mishna Codex Parma B*, ed. M. BAR-ASHER, Jerusalem 1971. The codex contains the whole of the Sixth Order, and was written in North Africa, perhaps Egypt, in the 12th or 13th century. The manuscript is completely vocalized, done probably by the copyist himself, which makes it probably the Mishna MS. with the oldest vocalization. The manuscript also contains accents throughout, to mark divisions of sentences. In longer sentences there can be up to four accents, found elsewhere only in some Geniza fragments. These features alone suffice to make this manuscript particularly important.

The text is that of the old Mishna manuscripts and is particularly close to Parma 138. The script is however strongly influenced by the Babylonian, much more than in the three complete manuscripts.

MS. NEW YORK (JTS RAB 1622). This fragment, sixteen pages in all, contains tractates from the Orders *Moed* and *Nashim*. The manuscript is vocalized and comes probably from Italy or Palestine, 12th century. In outward form it resembles Parma 138, but is surely later. In its writing traits, it belongs to the ancient MSS. type.

MS. OXFORD 366. This is a Talmud MS. containing the tractates *Berakhot* to *Shekalim*. It is listed here among Mishna manuscripts because it contains the whole first Order for which, apart from the tractate *Berakhot*, there is no Babylonian gemara. Hence the text of these tractates, like *Shekalim*, which also has no Babylonian Talmud, is a Mishna text. The manuscript seems to have been written in Spain in the 12th or 13th century. The character of the Mishna text in this manuscript needs to be studied further. Apparently it does not belong to the type of the old Mishna manuscripts.

YEMENITE MSS. In the Jewish Theological Seminary, New York, there are two manuscripts containing the Orders *Nezikin* to *Toharot* (*Rab. 31*). They contain only Mishna text and are from Yemen, probably 17th century. Samples showed that they probably depend on early printed books, which were, however, uncensored. The Yemen MS. of the 17th or 18th century, with vocalization (now in Jerusalem, *National Library, quarto 1336*; Orders *Nezikin* to *Toharot* with Bartenora's commentary, facsimile, Jerusalem 1970) is certainly derived from a printed book and merits attention only by reason of its vocalization.

255

Finally, MS. *Enelow 270*, Jewish Theological Seminary, New York, seems to have an interest of its own. It contains the tractates *Berakhot, Sofrim, Megilla, Pesahim* and *Beitsa*, the Order *Nashim* and tractate *Ohalot*, with some commentaries. There are also three Talmud tractates, on which see chapter 8 below. The manuscript is from the 18th century.

THE CAIRO GENIZA. Thousands of fragments of the Mishna were discovered in the Cairo Geniza. There is no tractate without at least a few fragments preserved. There are dozens or even hundreds of fragments of much read tractates, such as *Avot*, the best known and most frequently studied of all. The age of these fragments ranges from the 9th to the 18th century, with the main body of the fragments from the 11th to 13th century, that is, from the same time as the three complete manuscripts of the Mishna. The ancient material is of immense importance for the reconstruction of the original versions of the Mishna. This is true not only of the fragments containing only the Mishna text (often better preserved in the Palestinian recension than in the three complete manuscripts). It is also true of the Talmud fragments, which have preserved, in many cases alone, the ancient Babylonian version even in the Mishna chapters (and not only in the *piskaot*) the quotations of the Mishna in the Gemara.

Though it is nearly ninety years since the material was discovered, there has been no effort to arrange the whole according to individual manuscripts and tractates. A corpus of the whole material or at least the most ancient will have to be available before the significance of the Geniza for the study of the text of the Mishna can be estimated in full. A first step in this direction was taken by Paul KAHLE in the thirties, who brought together (in *HUCA*) four manuscripts, the longest of which, twenty-eight pages, contained the Orders *Nashim* to *Toharot*. Others imitated him, adding to the material. Special mention must be made of three Israeli publications, one of which comprises the main fragments of the Antonin collection in Leningrad, containing the longest Mishna fragment, almost the whole Order *Toharot* (fragment 262).[122] But on the whole, systematic work on the material has hardly begun. A general list of contents is announced by the Hebrew University, Jerusalem.

MISHNA WITH MAIMONIDES' ARABIC COMMENTARY

AUTOGRAPH. *MSS. Sassoon nos. 72 and 73* (now in the National Library in Jerusalem) and Oxford, Bodleian Library (Poc. 295, Uri 182, cat. no. 404) contain, with small gaps, the first five Orders of the Mishna. Published in exemplary facsimile edition by D. SASSOON, *Maimonidis Commentarius in Mishna* 1-3 (Copenhagen 1956-66). These three MSS. are the last copies of the Mishna commentary in his own hand. According to the preface they were finished in 1168. The script is the Spanish cursive of the time.

---

[122] See Krupp, 'Discussion'.

Each tractate is given a title, *Massekhet* NN, but not a colophon. Titles of chapters are *Perek sheni* etc. The mishnayot are not numbered. Maimonides undoubtedly had before him the mishnayot divisions of the manuscripts and very rarely departed from them. But he often takes two or more mishnayot together, either because he does not discuss a section (as directly intelligible) or provides a summary comment. The divisions of the mishnayot in the other Arabic manuscript of the commentary are the same as in the autographs. Some words are vocalized, either to make them clearer or to avoid a misunderstanding. Vocalization is practically never complete. It is the popular vocalization of Tiberias. That *kamets katan* is substituted by *kibbuts* is remarkable. The vocalization of proper names is also interesting.

Maimonides writes in his introduction to the commentary that he adopted the custom of quoting the Mishna section to be commented upon throughout. Thus the autograph contains the whole text of the Mishna, following which nearly all manuscripts with the Arabic commentary of Maimonides and all with the Hebrew translation of the commentary do likewise. Closer examination of several tractates of the autograph Mishna text show that Maimonides composed an eclectic text from the two main recensions, the Babylonian and the Palestinian. He gives preference at times to the Palestinian, again to the Babylonian. As this varies greatly from tractate to tractate, sometimes very basically, preference for a particular text is most probably to be explained by the vicissitudes of his existence. The commentary was begun in Spain and finished in Egypt, and at certain times he may have had only one text at his disposition. Where he could have recourse to both traditions his eclectic procedure and his effort to establish a new intelligible text are particularly clear. In spite of its age, the text in Maimonides' commentary, even that of the autographs, is far less important for textual criticism of the Mishna than the Mishna texts adduced hitherto.

OTHER MSS. Maimonides' commentary, even while he was still alive, gained such importance that from then on, in the East, the Mishna was only transmitted along with his commentary. Dozens of manuscripts have been preserved, far beyond all other early rabbinical texts. In Yemen, from which ninety per cent of the manuscripts come, the commentary was copied along with the text of the Mishna down to the twentieth century. The oldest surviving manuscripts are from a time shortly after the death of Maimonides. A special feature of nearly all these manuscripts is that they render their prototype particularly exactly. According to the colophon, some of these manuscripts were copied from the original, first in Egypt and later in Syria, or were compared with it. These manuscripts are of particular importance where the autograph copy of the Mishna shows a gap, i.e. in the sixth Order which is missing and the lacunae in the other Orders. Among these manuscripts, *Oxford 394-399* stand out, forming as they do one manuscript and containing nearly the whole Mishna. The MSS. *Berlin 93-101* and *London 447-462* are also very valuable. The largest collection of Yemenite Mishna manuscripts is kept at the Jewish Theological Seminary, New York.

Appended is a list of this category of Mishna manuscripts (p. 260-2).

MISHNA WITH HEBREW TRANSLATION OF MAIMONIDES' COMMENTARY

MANUSCRIPTS. The oldest manuscripts with the Hebrew translation of Maimonides' commentary are from the 14th century, probably from Northern Spain, the homeland of the translator:

London 463, containing the Order Moed.

Parma de Rossi 984, containing the Orders Nashim and Nezikin (facsimile edition Jerusalem 1971).

Most of the other manuscripts are from North Italy and were written in the 14th century, unless otherwise stated:

Paris, Bibliothèque Nationale cat. no. 330, containing the Mishna from Pesahim 5:5.

Paris 328/329, containing all six Orders (facsimile edition Jerusalem 1973).

Florence, Bibliotheca Nazionale Centrale 22, 4, containing the Orders Kodashim and Toharot, from the same hand as Paris 328/329.

Berlin 24, containing Orders Moed and Nezikin.

Hamburg 156, with the Orders Zeraim to Nashim, written in 1410.

Oxford 1272, containing the Order Nezikin.

Bologna, University Library 3574d, containing the Order Zeraim.

Oxford, Bodleian Library, cat. no. 409, containing the Orders Kodashim and Zeraim and the tractate Avot, from the second half of the 15th century.

Oxford 2662, containing the Order Moed.

Oxford, cat. no. 408, containing the Mishna from Nezikin on, German cursive, c. 1500.

Cambridge 1020-1021, containing the whole Mishna, 1557.

CHARACTERISTICS. This translation was the joint work of scholars living in Christian Spain and Provence in the 13th century.

As stated, all manuscripts of the Arabic commentary of Maimonides show one single, eclectic type of Mishna text. Similarly, all manuscripts of the Hebrew translation of the commentary have their own eclectic type of text, which however is basically different from that of the Arabic commentary and so cannot be from Maimonides' pen. The simplest explanation of the difference is that the copy before the translators did not provide a full text of the Mishna but, like *Paris MS. 579*, only the openings of the Mishna sections. No texts of this time from Northern Spain have been preserved. It is probable, however, that the Spanish copies did not give the Mishna in full, as the translator of the third Order, Yaakov Abasi, affirms in his preface. Or perhaps the Mishna text of the Arabic original did not satisfy the team of translators, or rather was not consistent with the text of the Mishna in use in the West. Possibly, in the renaissance of Talmud and Mishna studies at the end of the 13th century, also the date of the Hebrew translation, efforts were being made to have a correct text of the Mishna.

The outcome was the text of this translation, which is a classical mixed text. The Mishna text of the Parma MS. (which the translators need not have known) and the text of the Talmud manuscripts (putting the Mishna text at the beginning of each chapter) were especially favoured. The translators also used manuscripts containing the Palestinian type of text, though not in the best tradition. Here, too, there are variations from tractate to tractate. In any case, the Mishna manuscripts with the Hebrew translation are still less important for textual criticism than those with the Arabic commentary.

FIRST PRINTED MISHNA. It was in 1492 that the Mishna was first printed in full, along with the Hebrew translation of Maimonides' commentary, in Naples. A.M. HABERMANN published a facsimile edition, Jerusalem 1970.

The manuscripts used must have been those of the Mishna with the Hebrew version of Maimonides' commentary. But for the text of the Mishna the printers also drew on other texts, such as manuscripts with the Arabic commentary and also texts with the Palestinian recension, as is also found in the Kaufmann codex and the Geniza fragments. Thus the first printed Mishna is, like the Maimonides texts in general, a mixed text with definite leaning to the Palestinian type. It is of no great importance for textual criticism. Nevertheless, it was the master-copy for all later printed Mishnayot right down to the present day, and so has a definite historical significance. It has also escaped the Christian censor.

Mishna MSS. with Maimonides' Arabic Commentary

Explanation of sigla: * = MS. does not contain the complete Order indicated; ↓ = MS. is continued; ↑ = MS. is continuation of above.

Zeraim	Oxford 393 ↓ (autograph)	Oxford 394* ↓ (Or.; c. 1225)	Oxford 400 (Or.; 1222) Berlin 93 (Yemen c. 1300) NY Rab 1606 (Yem. 1317) NY Rab 226* (Yem. 14th cent.) London 447 (Yem. 14th cent.) NY Rab 2320* (Yem. c.1400) London 448* (Yem. 15th cent.) London 449* (Yem. 15th cent.) NY Rab 216* (Yem. 15th cent.) NY Rab 225 (Yem. 15th cent.)
Moed	↑ Sassoon 72 ↓ (autograph)	↑ Oxford 395* ↓ (c. 1225)	Oxford 401 (Yem. 14th cent.) Berlin 94a (Yem. c. 1300) Oxford 402 (Or.; c. 1400) NY Rab 1184 (Yem. 14th cent.) NY Rab 223 (Yem. c. 1400) NY Rab 228 (Yem. c. 1400) NY Rab 234 (Ycm. c. 1400) London 450 (Yem. 15th cent.) Oxford 2662* (Spain 15th cent.) NY Rab 235* (Yem. 15th cent.) London 451 (Yem. 16th cent.) London 452 (Yem. 1513)

			Holon (facs. 1975)
			(Yem. c. 1500)
			NY Rab 222
			(Yem. 16th cent.)
Nashim	↑ Sassoon 73 ↓		Oxford 403
	(autograph)		(Or.; c. 1300)
			Berlin 94b
			(Yem. 14th cent.)
			Paris 578
			(Granada 1391)
			London 454
			(Saana 1401)
			London 455
			(Yem. c. 1400)
			Kapach 90
			(Yem. 16th cent.)
Nezikin	↑ Oxford 404 ↓	↑ Oxford 396* ↓	Berlin 95*
	(autograph)		(Yem. 1222)
			NY Rab 220/1
			(Yem. c. 1400)
			London 456*
			(Yem. 15th cent.)
		Paris 579 ↓	
		(1469)	
			London 457*
			(Yem. 15th cent.)
			Aloni 51
			(Yem. 15th cent.)
			Kapach 65
			(Yem. 15th cent.)
			NY Mic 5523
			(Yem. 15th cent.)
			NY Rab 221
			(Yem. 15th cent.)
			Berlin 96
			(Yem. 16th cent.)
Kodashim	↑ Oxford 404	↑ Oxford 397* ↓	Berlin 97
	(autograph)		(Yem. 1386)
			Berlin 98*
			(Yem. 14th cent.)
			London 460*
			(c. 1400)
			Oxford 405
			(Or.; c. 1400)
			NY Lehm. 309*
			(Yem. c. 1400)
			Kapach 60*
			(Yem. c. 1400)

↑ Paris 579 ↓
London 459
(Yem. 1414)
London 461*
(Yem. 1490)

Toharot   ↑ Oxford 398-399   Paris 580*
(Or.; 13th cent.)
↑ Paris 597
Berlin 100*
(Or.; 14th cent.)
NY Rab 38
(Yem. c. 1400)
Oxford 406
(Yem. 15th cent.)
Kapach
(Yem. 15th cent.)
Berlin 101*
(Saana 1497)
Berlin 99
(Yem. 1499)
London 462
(Yem. c. 1500)
NY Rab 194
(Yem. c. 1500)

Chapter Five

The Tractate Avot

M.B. Lerner

Name

Avot, which has been traditionally translated 'fathers',[1] is actually one of the sixty-three tractates of the Mishna. It is located towards the end of *Nezikin*, the fourth Order of the Mishna, and originally contained five chapters.[2]

Owing to the fact that in contradistinction to all the other tractates, *Avot* does not contain any halakhic material whatsoever,[3] it has usually been classified under the rubric of ethical or aggadic literature. Such a classification is entirely justified for, in essence, *Avot* contains short pithy words of wisdom and aphorisms, similar to the γνώμη and *sententiae* of Greek and Latin literature. They derive from some 63 mishnaic Sages, certainly the largest number of Tannaim in a single tractate;[4] several of these are not found elsewhere in the Mishna.[5]

The title *Avot* is usually explained as a shortened form of *avot ha-olam* (the fathers of the universe), an appellation applied in talmudic literature to some of the leading authorities of the Mishna;[6] or as *avot ha-rishonim* (the first fathers),[7] referring to the 'early authorities', which should be understood as an inference to the earliest transmitters of Oral Tora enumerated in the first two chapters of *Avot*. On the other hand, it is also quite possible that the title *Avot* derives from the biblical *av* אב which denotes 'a major authority' or 'an important personage'.[8] Thus, R. Yohanan b. Zakkai is dubbed *av le-hokhma* and *av le-dorot*, i.e., 'a major authority for wisdom' and 'an important authority for generations' [of scholars].[9] Indeed, practically all of the prominent Sages of the Tannaic

---

[1] See below.

[2] The theory advanced by Finkelstein, *Mabo*, 104-11 (= Summary, xvii-xxii) concerning the structure of the Mishna and the place of *Avot* within this structure is pure conjecture.

[3] Even when a certain saying supposedly contains a halakhic ruling, it was not considered binding, cf. 'Judge not alone, for there is none save One who judgeth alone' (*Avot* 4:8) with *B.T. Sanh.* 5a and *Tosafot ib. s.v.* אנא בגון. See, however Ha-Kohen, *Avot ba-halakha*; Adler, 'Aboth'.

[4] Albeck, *Introduction*, 216-36 lists some 156 mishnaic authorities.

[5] Cf. Meiri, *Beit ha-behira* to *Avot*, Introduction, ed. Prag, 37.

[6] See *M. Ed.* 1:4; *P.T. Hag.* 2:1, 77d; *P.T. Shek.* 3:1, 47b and cf. the caption to Sir 44.

[7] See *T. Tev. Y.* 1:10.

[8] E.g. Jdg 17:10; Gen 45:8.

[9] *P.T. Ned.* 5:7, 39b.

period are mentioned in *Avot*.[10]

An alternative solution, offered by R. Menahem ha-Meiri, relates to the teachings themselves: 'Things which are fundamental principles (*Avot*), essentials and roots and sources for all Tora wisdom and precepts, and a pathway to all perfection'.[11] In view of the prevalent usage of *avot* in the Mishna *per se*,[12] this explanation of Ha-meiri, which has not been considered heretofore, seems the most sound. It is therefore suggested here that the name of the tractate be accordingly translated: 'Essentials' or 'First Principles'.

Contents and Structure

The name of this tractate is referred to in the Talmud as the source whose teachings are to be fulfilled in order to attain piety.[13] However, due to its immense popularity and separate circulation, mainly as part of the prayer-book or as an independent tract, *Avot* came to be known popularly as *Pirkei Avot* (The Chapters of *Avot*). This title was already used by Raymund Martini, *Pugio Fidei* (c. 1278).[14] One may surmise that this is a shortened version of the Aramaic possessive form *Pirkei de-Avot*.[15] It is thus logical to assume that the title *Pirkei Avot* replaced the original rubric of this tractate (*Massekhet Avot*), in order to denote the expanded tractate, which contains a sixth chapter, as well as additions to chapter five.[16]

Chapter one is essentially an ancient document summarizing the Oral Tora from Moses on Sinai through the biblical period, and the period of the Second Commonwealth, extending from the 'Men of the Great Synagogue' אנשי כנסת הגדולה until the beginning of the first century c.e. It is significant to note that the role of the priests in the transmission of the Tora has been completely eliminated from this document, which nevertheless stresses the principle of continuity. This may be a reaction to the teachings of the Dead Sea sect.[17]

The teachings of the Great Synagogue are followed by those of Shimon the Just, one of their last surviving members, and from that point on, the Mishna presents the names of successive eminent teachers and their words of wisdom

---

[10] The most notable exception seems to be Rabban Gamliel II of Yavne, whose absence is most difficult to explain; cf. Hoffman, *Ha-Mishna ha-rishona*, 29, n. 26. However, there is remote possibility that the teachings of Rabban Gamliel in 1:15 actually belong to the Sage in question, since Rabban Gamliel I is ordinarily referred to as *ha-zaken* (the Elder); see Albeck, *Mishna*, 4, 349. If so, R. Gamliel the Elder is not represented in *Avot*. This conclusion alleviates the situation somewhat but nevertheless arouses chronological problems; see below.

[11] *Beit ha-behira* to *Avot*, Introduction, ed. Prag, 10

[12] See M. *Bava K.* 1:1, *avot nezikin* (major categories of damages); M. *Shabb.* 7:2, *avot melakhot* (major classes of labours); M. *Kel.* 1:1, *avot ha-tumot* (major sources of impurity). Cf. p. 89.

[13] *B.T. Bava K.* 30a, adduced by Ha-Meiri *ib.*

[14] Herford, *Aboth*, Introduction, 4.

[15] See R. Elazar of Worms, *Sefer ha-rokeah* par. 329, 227. Cf. also 'Pirkei de-R. Eliezer'; 'Pirkei de-Hasidei', an Aramaic rubric for *B.T. Taan.* chap. 3.

[16] Cf. the caption to *Mahzor Vitry*, 461 in comparison to the colophon *ib.* 549.

[17] See Herr, 'Continuum'.

and counsel. This list is outstanding in that it includes the five pairs (the patriarch and chief justice), active during the second and first centuries B.C.E. ending with Hillel[18] and Shammai.

The last three mishnayot of chapter one (1:16-18) contain the maxims of Rabban Gamliel, his son, Shimon, and Rabban Shimon ben Gamliel. This is obviously a collection of teachings deriving from the patriarchal descendants of Hillel, although their exact identity is somewhat uncertain.[19]

Chapter two which is evidently a continuation of the collection of maxims of the patriarchs,[20] begins with the sayings of R. Yehuda the Patriarch and his son, Rabban Gamliel III (2:1-4), who is apparently not mentioned elsewhere in the Mishna.[21] The ensuing paragraphs of the Mishna adduce several teachings in the name of Hillel (2:4-7). Scholars are divided over the question whether this is a reversion back to Hillel the Elder, in order to continue the chain of tradition with Rabban Yohanan ben Zakkai, the disciple of Hillel (2:8), or whether the Sage mentioned is R. Hillel, the grandson of R. Yehuda the Patriarch.[22] Whatever conclusion one may reach, it is obvious that *Avot* contains the teachings of the earliest mishnaic Sages almost side-by-side with those of some of the latest authorities quoted in the Mishna.

The latter half of chapter two continues the chronological chain, which was interrupted by the collection of maxims of the patriarchs, with the teachings of Rabban Yohanan ben Zakkai and his five major disciples (2:8-14), while the chapter concludes with those of R. Tarfon (2:15-16), who should likewise be considered a disciple of Rabban Yohanan.[23] It is interesting to note that in the academy of Rabban Yohanan ben Zakkai, the curriculum apparently included philosophical investigations.[24]

The first section of chapter three (3:1-10) which commences with the counsel of Akavia ben Mahalalel, intending to prevent one from falling into sin (3:1), is a seemingly disorganised collection of maxims without any chronological basis. However, closer inspection reveals that the first two (Akavia and R. Hanan, the deputy of the priests) and the last two Sages (R. Hanina ben Dosa and R. Dosa ben Harkinos) were active towards the end of the Second Temple period.[25] The

---

[18] It may not be irrelevant to note that the teachings of Hillel (1:12-14) are much more numerous than those of the other Sages.

[19] See above, n. 10.

[20] Cf. *A.R.N.* b 32 (35b-36a).

[21] The reading '. . . The son of R. Yehuda the Prince' in conjunction with Rabban Gamliel is found in all important versions of the Mishna. However, the parallel in *A.R.N. ib.* reads: 'Rabban Gamliel', whereas the quotation in *Eccl. R.* 7:11 (= *Eccl. Zutta*, p. 111) possibly indicates an anonymous source.

[22] Cf. Albeck, *Mishna* 4, 349-5-; Epstein, *Nosah*, 1182-3; Urbach, *Hazal* 3rd ed., 713 (to p. 522, n. 51).

[23] This is clearly evident from *T. Hag.* 3:33.

[24] See 2:9; *Pes. de-R.K.* 4,10 (p. 76); Goldin, 'R. Johanan b. Zakkai'.

[25] Finkelstein, *Mabo*, 52ff. (= xv-xvi), has traced the structure of this section by virtue of a comparison with *A.R.N.* He has also endeavoured to show that these four Sages were Shammaites.

additional teachings adduced in the intermediate paragraphs (3:2-8), are possibly due to the process of association and mnemonics whereby similarity of names of various Sages influenced their juxtaposition, e.g.: Hanania, R. Hanania ben Tardyon (3:2), R. Hanina ben Hakinai (3:4), R. Nehunia ben ha-Kana (3:5), R. Halafta of Kefar Hanania (3:6), R. Dostai ben Yannai (3:8), R. Hanina ben Dosa (3:9-10), R. Dosa ben Harkinas (3:10).[26] Nevertheless, it should be stressed that such an explanation is unable to account for all the Sages mentioned. Suffice it to say that practically all of the teachings in this section relate to the importance of diligent Tora study.

The mishna of R. Elazar ha-Modai (3:11), in the continuation of this chapter, may possibly relate back to the disciples of R. Yohanan ben Zakkai in chapter two.[27] The latter half of chapter three (3:12-17), contains the maxims of the leading Sages of the third generation of Tannaim in Yavne: R. Yishmael (3:12); R. Akiva (3:13-16) and R. Elazar ben Azaria (3:17), while the continuation of the Mishna (3:18-4:4) includes the teachings of additional Sages of that generation.

The middle of chapter four features the teachings of the disciples of R. Akiva and R. Yishmael, who should be classified as the fourth generation of Tannaim: R. Yose (4:6); R. Yonatan (4:9); R. Meir (4:10) and others (4:11-17). This chapter also includes the maxims of several Sages of the fifth generation: R. Yishmael ben R. Yose (4:7-8); R. Shimon ben Elazar (4:18) and R. Yehuda the Patriarch (4:20), concluding with the ornate poetic meditation on human destiny and divine justice and retribution of their contemporary, R. Elazar ha-Kappar (4:21-22). Special note should be taken of Elisha ben Avuya, who in spite of his heresy was granted recognition by the editor of the Mishna by including his semi-autobiographical teaching towards the end of this chapter (4:20).

Chapter five commences with various anonymous statements based on numerical teachings, e.g. 'By ten sayings the world was created . . . Ten generations from Adam to Noah . . . With ten trials was Abraham our father tried . . . Ten wonders were wrought for our ancestors in the Holy Temple . . . Seven qualities characterise the clod, and seven the wise man . . . Seven kinds of calamity come upon the world for seven classes of transgression . . . There are four types of men . . . four types of dispositions. . . four types of disciples . . .' (5:1-15). Following is a series of four statements each introduced by the mnemonic formula: 'Every . . . which is . . .' (5:16-19). The chapter and the entire tractate originally ended with the teachings of R. Yehuda ben Tema (5:20) and an appropriate concluding formula, which is actually a prayer for the rebuilding of the Temple and the attainment of Tora wisdom. Most versions of *Avot* contain several additional teachings which form the end of chapter 5: The

---

[26] Another apparent mnemonic device is the usage of the introductory כל in various maxims; see 3:5; 8-10, and see below on the end of chap. 5.

[27] Cf. *B.T. Bava B.* 10b.

fourteen stages of life from the age of 5-100, attributed to R. Yehuda ben Tema (5:21) and the Aramaic maxims of Ben Bag-Bag and Ben He-He, who are considered to be disciples (or, if this is the same person, the disciple) of Hillel (5:22-23). However, some manuscripts contain a completely different text.[28]

It may be concluded that the first four chapters of *Avot* represent a complete chronological panorama of the mishnaic period. Aside from two major deviations (1:16-2:7 and 3:1-10), which have their own *raison d'être*, and some insignificant minor ones,[29] Tannaic chronology is more of less carefully observed. However, it should be pointed out that direct chronological references which clearly indicate the 'chain of tradition', culminate with the five disciples of R. Yohanan ben Zakkai (2:14). This leads us to the obvious conclusion that the major part of the first two chapters represents the oldest stratum and core of this tractate.

The opening section of chapter five which is composed of aggadic material associated with the number ten (5:1-5), is arranged according to biblical chronology. On the other hand, the material in the continuation of this chapter which is also associated with numbers in a declining sequence, does not have any clear-cut message. However, the teachings associated with the number four (5:10-15), which are based on ethical and pedagogical principles, seem to be the crux of the entire chapter, and this may be the reason for the inclusion of this chapter.

Literary Characteristics

The collection of maxims and teachings in *Massekhet Avot* may be viewed as an important further development of Hebrew wisdom literature. Incidentally, not all of the maxims attributed to the various Sages are original, personal statements, but traditional wisdom sayings. Shmuel the Small is reported to have said: 'Rejoice not when your enemy falls . . . Lest the Lord see it . . .' (4:19), which obviously is a verbatim quotation from Prov 24:17-18. Another Sage (4:14) made similar use of Prov. 3:5 ('And do not rely on your own understanding'). The maxim of R. Levitas of Yavne 'Be exceedingly humble, for the hope of mortal man is the worm' (4:4), seems to be a direct adaptation from Sir 7:17, 'Humble (thy) pride greatly, for the expectation of man is decay'. Numerous other parallels are evident in both works.[30] On the other hand, a relatively large number of teachings in *Avot* have been shown to be stemming from the personal teaching of the Sage in question.[31]

---

[28] See Herford, *Aboth*, 143; 146-7; Taylor, *Sayings*, 23; Sharvit, 'Custom', 185-6. See also below p. 278.

[29] E.g. R. Tsadok (4:5); R. Yishmael be-R. Yohanan ben Beroka (4:5); and R. Yishmael be-R. Yose (4:7). The last two are clearly due to a father-son linkage.

[30] See Segal, *Ben Sira*, indices, p. 371a-b; Zunz-Albeck, *Derashot*, 281, n. 30.

[31] See Melammed, 'La vie des Tannaim'.

Compared to the older wisdom literature, the teachings of *Avot* evince a remarkable development of religious experience and feeling. Teachings such as the following have no parallel in books like Proverbs or Ben Sira: 'Be not like slaves who serve the master on condition of receiving the measured allowance, but be like slaves who serve the master without the condition of receiving the measured allowance' (1:3);[32] 'All is foreseen,[33] but freedom of choice is granted; and the world is judged by grace, but *not* according to the majority of deeds (3:15).[34]

The style of expression of the teachings in *Avot* is usually extremely terse and lapidary: An entire philosophical outlook or *Weltanschauung* may be concentrated in one brief statement or in several concise phrases. In this respect, too, *Avot* is far removed from Proverbs and Ben Sira whose style, moreover, is based on biblical parallelism and repetition. However, the frequent usage of the second person and the direct approach in offering words of advice and guidance are reminiscent of wisdom literature.

In spite of the fact that the teachings of *Avot* are usually epigrammatic, axiomatic, and apodictic in both form and content – undoubtedly characteristic features of wisdom literature – there is no denying the conclusion that many of them derive from Scripture. A cursory glance at the original five chapters of this tractate reveals the exegesis of some twenty-nine different verses in thirteen mishnayot.[35] It is interesting to note that an unusually large segment of these is concentrated in chap. 3:2-8, which may possibly be indicative of the supplementary nature of 3:1-10, alluded to above. Especially noteworthy is the threefold teaching of R. Akiva[36] (3:14) which is based on three verses:[37]

> He used to say: Beloved is man in that he was created in the image (of God). Greater love: it was made known to him that he was created in the image of God, as it is said (Gen 9:6): "In the image of God made He man".
>
> Beloved are Israel in that they are called sons of God. Greater love: it was made known to them that they were called sons of God, as it is said (Deut 14:1): "Sons are ye to the Lord your God".
>
> Beloved are Israel in that there was given to them a precious instrument. Greater love: it was made known to them that there was given to them the precious instrument whereby the world was created, as it is said (Prov 4:2): "For good doctrine I give you, forsake not my Tora".

---

[32] See Bickerman, 'Maxim'. Cf. also 2:4; 4:16.
[33] Early Mishna commentaries explain the statement הכל צפוי to mean: everything is seen (= visible to the Almighty), cf. Urbach, *Sages*, 256, 802 n. 11.
[34] See Safrai, 'Majority of Deeds'.
[35] These are readily evident in the edition of Albeck which lists the biblical sources in the margins.
[36] Cf. however, below, n. 61.
[37] Cf. however, below, n. 40.

Relatively speaking, the prevalence of almost thirty prooftexts in a tractate of minor proportions as *Avot* (five chapters) speaks for itself.[38] Notwithstanding the fact that several of these prooftexts are most likely later additions, as proven by reliable manuscripts and early commentaries[39] – including the above-mentioned threefold quotation from 3:14[40] – there is no denying the fact that the biblical verses in question actually form the basis for these teachings.[41] One might also add that the biblical antecedents for numerous other apodictic teachings in *Avot* are adduced in *Avot de-R. Natan* and other talmudic and midrashic works.[42] The full implications of this phenomenon will become visible only after an exhaustive study of all the sources has been made.

Another characteristic feature of wisdom literature is the usage of numerical groupings.[43] Specific usage of this in *Avot* is evinced by such teachings as: 'Shimon the Just . . . used to say, upon three things (= pillars) the world standeth: upon Tora, upon worship, and upon deeds of loving kindness' (1:2); 'R. Shimon said, there are three crowns, the crown of Tora, the crown of the priesthood, and the crown of kingship . . . ' (4:13); 'R. Elazar ha-Kappar said, Envy, desire, and ambition drive a man out of the world' (4:21) As a matter of fact, the grouping together of three statements of a particular Sage is quite popular throughout the tractate, and almost paramount in chapter one, which, as shown above, contains the teachings of the earliest Sages.[44]

Even though *Avot* is far removed from the language and techniques of the biblical *parallelismus membrorum*, there is, nevertheless, prolific usage of positive and negative statements, which are reminiscent of certain types of biblical parallelism in wisdom literature;[45] e.g., 'R. Nehunya ben ha-Kana said, One who receives upon himself the yoke of Tora, they remove from him the yoke of the kingdom (i.e., taxation etc.) and the yoke of worldly occupation. But one who casts off the yoke of Tora, they place upon him the yoke of the kingdom and the yoke of worldly occupation' (3:5); 'R. Yonatan said, He who fulfils (the teachings of) the Tora in poverty, will eventually fulfil them in affluence. And he who nullifies (the teachings of) the Tora in affluence, will eventually nullify them in poverty' (4:9).[46]

---

[38] The only other tractates competing with *Avot* in the number of verses cited are *Sota* (nine chapters) and *Sanhedrin* (eleven chapters). This is also corroborated by the chance listing of Rosenblatt, *Bible in the Mishna*, 65-6, n. 55-6.

[39] Melammed, 'Nosah', 142-3.

[40] *Ib.* 143, par. 7.

[41] Concerning *M. Avot* 3:14, see *A.R.N.* a 39 (59b); cf. b 44 (62b).

[42] E.g. 2:1 – *Midr. Prov.* 5:21 (p. 53); 3:1 – *P.T. Sota* 3, 18a; 4:2 – *Tanh., Ki Tetsei* 1 (17a); 4:3 – *A.R.N.* a 23 (38b); 4:9 – *Midr. ha-Gad. Deut.* 28:47-8 (p. 619); 4:12 – *A.R.N.* a 27 (42b-43a); b 34 (38b)

[43] E.g. Prov 30:20; Eccl 6:16; Sin 26:5.

[44] Melammed, 'Nosah', 144-50.

[45] E.g. Prov 10-15.

[46] Melammed, 'Nosah', 152-3.

MELAMMED has demonstrated that the teachings of the Sages in *Avot* bear special affinity to biblical literature in their usage of poetic structure and language. Numerous teachings of *Avot* have been shown to contain cadences and rhythmic patterns, which are quite similar to those employed in biblical metrics.[47] Certain linguistic expressions and grammatical forms are also carry-overs from biblical Hebrew.[48]

However, for all intents and purposes, *Avot* is a product of the mishnaic Sages and written in the Hebrew of that period, which is commonly referred to as *Leshon Hakhamim A*,[49] although for some unexplained reason, several of the teachings of Hillel are given in the vernacular Aramaic.[50] A number of expressive apothegms are unique in their usage of repetitive formulae, *jeux de mots* and *jeux d'esprit*, which are strongly felt even in translation, as evinced by the following examples: 'Make His will thy will, so that He may make thy will His will; make naught thy will before His will, so that He make naught the will of others before thy will' (2:4); '. . . Because thou drownedst, they drowned thee; and in the end, they that drowned thee shall be drowned' (2:6);[51] 'Give to Him of what is His, for thou and thine are His' (3:7).

Massekhet *Avot* excels in the usage of picturesque language and metaphors. Tora study and fulfillment are ordinarily depicted as 'work' and its students as 'day labourers', while the Almighty is the 'Employer', as in the delightful metaphoric teaching of R. Tarfon: 'The day is short and the work is great, and the labourers are sluggish, and the wages are high, and the employer is pressing' (2:15).[52] R. Akiva likens the reward and punishment meted out to an individual for his worldly actions to one who engages in credit-shopping: '. . . The shop is open and the storekeeper gives credit, and the account-book is open and the hand writes, and every one who would borrow, let him come and borrow; and the collectors make the rounds continually every day and exact payment from a man with or without his knowledge . . . and the judgment is a judgment of truth, and all is made ready for the banquet (of the righteous in the hereafter)' (3:16). The idea of this world as a vestibule (πρόθυρον) and the world-to-come as a huge banquet-hall (*triclinium*) is further heightened by the teaching of R. Yaakov (4:16). Allusions to classical Greek terminology are also employed in the advocate-accuser[53] concept of the precepts expressed by R. Eliezer ben

---

[47] *Ib.* 154-8.

[48] *Ib.* 159; Melammed, 'Leshona'.

[49] Kutscher, 'Mishnaic Hebrew', 40-7.

[50] 1:13 (see Goitein, 'Spruch'); 2:7; 4:5 (see below); and cf. 5:22-23; *A.R.N.* a 12 and b 27 (28a). Version b 27 (28b) states that Hillel the Elder was accustomed to reciting five of his dicta 'in the tongue of the Babylonians' בלשון הבבליים. Could this possibly infer that these dicta were originally pronounced by Hillel in Babylonia during his early years, prior to his immigration to Erets Yisrael (cf. *P.T. Pes.* 6, 33a; *B.T. Pes.* 66a), or soon after his arrival (cf. *Sifra, Tazria* [67a])?

[51] Additional onomatopoeic and rhythmic teachings of Hillel are found in 2:4 (end) and 2:7.

[52] Cf. also 2:14; 2:16.

[53] פרקליט = παράκλητος; קטיגור = κατήγορος.

Yaakov (4:11).[54]

Moreover, it is important to note that *Avot* also contains some straightforward parables. These include the parable of the 'tree whose branches are many and its roots few etc.' describing the relationship between wisdom and deeds (3:17), and the likening of the difference between studying while old or young with 'ink written on new paper' or on 'erased paper', by Elisha ben Avuya (4:20).

In contradistinction to all other Tannaic sources, *Avot* contains at least one specimen of extended allegorical speech: 'Avtalyon said, Ye wise, take heed of your words, lest ye incur the punishment of exile, and ye be exiled to a place of *evil waters*, and the disciples that come after you drink and die, and the name of Heaven be profaned' (1:11). These 'evil waters' have posed a vexing problem to all commentaries, beginning with *Avot de-R. Natan*[55] and down to modern times.[56] The generally accepted explanation is that the 'evil waters' allude to some sort of heresy,[57] but there is no denying the fact that the *raison d'être* for such allegoristic usage remains most perplexing.

Another unique feature of *Avot* is the reworking of ideas. Novel teachings have been grafted on to traditional forms, thus giving vent to new conceptions which adopt accepted proverbial expressions as their base. The opening and closing teachings of chapter one provide an illuminating example for this phenomenon.[58] Similarly, the opening formulae of the words of advice of Akavia ben Mahalalel, 'Keep in view three things and thou wilt not come into the power of sin . . .' (3:1), was utilized by R. Yehuda the Patriarch in his parallel teaching (2:1). R. Yoshua's adage concerning 'the evil eye, the evil inclination, and the hatred of mankind' which 'drive a man out of the world' (2:11) was rephrased in the above-mentioned teaching of R. Elazar ha-Kappar (4:21).

In this respect, special attention should be paid to the following dicta of R. Tsadok:

> Do not make them (the words of the Tora) a crown wherewith to magnify thyself nor a spade wherewith to dig; and thus Hillel used to say: "And he who makes worldly use of the crown shall perish". Hence thou mayest deduce that anyone who receives profit from the words of the Tora, removes his life from the world. (4:5)

---

[54] Cf. also the picturesque expressions of R. Eliezer following his first three dicta in 2:10. Concerning these, see Melammed, 'Nosah', 218.

[55] *A.R.N.* a 11 (24b); b 22 (24a).

[56] Albeck, *Mishna* 4, 494.

[57] Cf. the expression of R. Shimon ben Menasia in *Sifrei Deut.* 48 (p. 110): ואל תשתה מים עכורים ותמשך עם דברי מינים '. . . and do not drink of turbid waters and turn to heretic teachings'.

[58] Cf. the teaching of Shimon the Just (1:2) with that of Rabban Shimon ben Gamliel (1:18).

In this mishna, R. Tsadok has actually rephrased and elaborated upon one of the original Aramaic proverbs of Hillel (1:13), which is even quoted here verbatim.[59]

One of the crucial problems of *Avot*, which has heretofore not received sufficient attention, is the identification of the various tradents. In spite of the fact that talmudic literature is most insistent on the careful rendering of traditions,[60] numerous variants are extant in parallel texts – *Avot de-R.Natan* and other works of talmudic literature.[61] Suffice it to say that, from a methodological standpoint, studies devoted to the teachings of specific Sages, which base themselves on the name recorded in the Mishna *per se*, and which fail to take into account the traditions of parallel sources, are actually lacking in perspective.

Due to its immense popularity and mass circulation, many of the original readings in the text of this tractate have become corrupted. The lack of a critical edition assembling all textual variants and testimonial evidence is still a major pitfall. No other Mishna tractate evinces such a prolific number of manuscripts, Geniza fragments, and commentaries. In spite of the progress made in the textual and linguistic study of *Avot* during the past few decades, much remains to be done (see p. 280f.).

It is interesting to note that scholars have deduced that the chain of tradition in the first chapter of *Avot* originally contained fourteen links, a number bearing important significance in both Jewish and Christian chronological tradition.[62] In addition, it has recently been shown that the chain of tradition in the first mishna parallels a literary pattern found in classical Greco-Roman literature.[63]

Unlike other tractates of the Mishna, the material has not been systematically fused into topical and conceptual units. The editor or editors of this tractate have chosen to preserve the chronological order of most of the words of wisdom and the maxims of the mishnaic Sages, although, as stated, the inclusion of most of chapter five defies a logical explanation.

Aim

A question usually raised in conjunction with *Avot* relates to the aim of the redactor of the Mishna in compiling this tractate. It has often been suggested

---

[59] Herford, *Ethics*, 101.

[60] *Sifrei Num.* 157 end (p. 213); M. *Avot* 6:6.

[61] Some examples: Hillel (M. Avot 2:5) = R. Akiva (A.R.N. b 33 [36b]; cf. however Sifrei Z. p. 307); R.Tarfon (M. Avot 2:16) = R. Yishmael (A.R.N. a 27 [42b]); Hillel (M. Avot 2:6) = R. Yoshua (A.R.N. b 27 [28b]); R. Hanina ben Dosa (M. Avot 3:10) = R. Akiva (T. Ber. 3:3); R. Akiva (M. Avot 3:14) = R. Meir (A.R.N. a 39 [59b]) = R. Eliezer son of R. Yose ha-Galili (A.R.N. b 44 [62b]).

[62] Cf. Finkelstein, *Mabo* chap. 3, 5-10 (= x-xi); Liver, *House of David*, 33-4. See Matt 1:17.

[63] See Fischel, 'Sorites'. Fischel refers to the mishnayot in *Avot* as 'transmissional sorites'.

that *Avot* is actually an introduction to Oral Tora, with the aim of presenting the chronology and history of tradition from time immemorial until the close of the mishnaic period. However, if that were so, one should have expected that this tractate be placed at the beginning of the Mishna. Moreover, as observed above, the specific chronological references cease towards the end of chapter two. On the other extreme, HERFORD has offered the theory that the tractate, placed close to the end of the fourth Order, was originally composed as an epilogue to the entire Mishna.[64] Taking into account the non-halakhic aspects and the numerous ethical considerations of this tractate, which may be defined as purely aggadic, there may be something to this theory. However, it should be stressed that *Avot* is not the final tractate in *Nezikin*, since in extant manuscripts and editions of the Mishna, it is followed by the tractate *Horayot*.

The inclusion of *Avot* within the framework of the fourth Order has prompted Maimonides to describe and define this tractate as a sort of moral and spiritual guide for magistrates.[65] The Order of *Nezikin* includes several tractates dealing with the judiciary process, and the inclusion of a tractate which enshrines the *esprit de loi* as well as the major tenets of ethical behaviour has been construed as a natural addition to the legal contents of this order. Just as a magistrate is in need of a proper code of laws, so too is he in need of a manual of general ethical principles and teachings, and prudent counsel in judicial matters. Indeed, *Avot* excels in words of practical advice directed specifically at judges and magistrates, such as: 'Be deliberate in judgment' (1:1); or, 'Do not play the part of the *arche-judex* (chief justice); and when there are litigants standing before you, look upon them as innocent men, once they have accepted the sentence' (1:8; cf. also 4:8, 5:8, etc.).

Taken as a whole, it may be said that the teachings of *Avot* provide the student with an appreciation of the essence of Oral Tora, and a proper orientation towards study and fulfillment of the Tora. The centrality of the Tora permeates the entire tractate, while on the practical side, profound wards of counsel direct one to proper religious practice and ethical behaviour, both in regard to human relations and to one's attitude towards the Divinity. On the philosophic side, this tractate offers basic concepts regarding the nature and destiny of man and the doctrines of reward and punishment. To this very day, *Avot* is one of the most important documents for any study dealing with rabbinic teachings and theology.

Perek Kinyan Tora

As already noted, *Avot* originally contained five chapters. A sixth chapter entitled *Kinyan Tora*, 'On the Acquisition of Tora', which consists of numerous teachings in praise of the Tora and those who study it, was added to this tractate

---

[64] Herford, *Aboth*, Introduction, 10-12.
[65] Maimonides, *Introduction*, *Zeraim*, ed. Qafih, 29-31.

later on. This appellation is probably due to the list of 48 virtues which lead to the acquisition of Tora.[66] The addition of the sixth chapter probably took place during the Geonic Period when it was customary to study 'Avot and *Kinyan Tora*' in the synagogue between the Sabbath afternoon and nighttime services.[67] The additional chapter facilitated the recital of a single chapter on each of the Sabbaths between Passover and Shavuot,[68] which suggests a possible anti-Karaite motive. Such a motivation seems to be alluded to by the blessing of the Sages in the caption to this chapter, which also declares its character as an appendix: 'The Sages have taught in the language of the Mishna – Blessed be He who has chosen them and their Mishna . . .' (6:1).

According to the above caption, the teachings of *Kinyan Tora* are supposedly Tannaic and indeed many early authorities regard it as a baraita. However, the inclusion (6:2) of an aggadic teaching attributed to R. Yoshua ben Levi, one of the early Amoraic Sages, and a very popular legendary hero of later sources, would seem to indicate that the material in this chapter is of considerably later vintage. Nevertheless, the contents themselves appear to reflect third (or possibly fourth) century views,[69] and so one cannot postulate too late a date for this short treatise.

In any event, it is important to note the almost complete parallel in *Pirkei Derekh Erets*,[70] the parallels to 6:4-6 in *Midrash Proverbs*,[71] and the appearance of *Perek Kinyan Tora* as one of the component elements of *Massekhet Kalla Rabbati*.[72]

A close examination of the extant sources seems to indicate that *Kinyan Tora* is an independent chapter, and takes its place alongside numerous other *perakim* of midrashic literature.[73] It was also known as *Perek de- (Pirko shel) R. Meir*,[74] in view of the opening statement of that Sage (6:1). Each of the above-mentioned parallel sources apparently utilized *Kinyan Tora* for its own pur-

---

[66] 6:5-6. See also 6:10 where the word *kinyan* (acquisition, possession) appears.

[67] Harkavy, *Responsen der Geonim, Shaarei Teshuva*, no. 220, p. 21d. Cf. Albeck, *Mishna* 4, 351; Sharvit, 'Custom'. It is interesting to note that *Avot* was frequently circulated together with *Perek Kinyan Tora* and *Massekhet Yirath Het* (see below: *Derekh Erets Zutta*) as evinced by Geniza fragments, e.g. MS. Oxford-Bodleian 2669 (see Higger, *Treatises*, 19-20); *Ginzei Kaufman*, no. 17. However, it is quite possible that this arrangement is the result of a custom adduced by Rav Saadya Gaon; cf. *Siddur R. Saadya Gaon*, 123.

[68] A seventh chapter seems to have been included for those instances when there were seven such Sabbaths. By nature, this possibility exists only in the Land of Israel, cf. Sharvit, 'Custom'.

[69] Cf. Lieberman, *Hellenism*, 69-71.

[70] Chap. 2, pp. 15-20 (= *S.E.Z.* chap. 17).

[71] Note that in *Kinyan Tora* these are anonymous teachings, whereas in *Midr. Prov.* 19:17-18 (p. 85) they are adduced in the name of R. Yishmael. Nevertheless, the latter text, which shows signs of editorial adaptation, is undoubtedly the later one.

[72] See below. In ed. Coronel it appears as chap. 8 (7) (14a-16b) and in ed. Higger as chap. 5 (273-98).

[73] Cf. Wertheimer, *Batei Midrashot* 2, 125; Urbach, 'Pirkei R. Yoshia', 83.

[74] R. Yosef ben Yehuda, *Sefer Musar*, 179; Ha-Meiri, *Beit ha-behira*, 9; 104; MS. Adler 2237, cf. Higger, 'Perek Kinyan Tora', 286.

poses,[75] whilst the general impression is that the preservation of this brief treatise *in toto* is to be found in the sixth chapter of *Avot*.

Many Yemenite prayer books were found to contain alternate versions of *Kinyan Tora* with numerous additions and deletions. However, due to the fact that the additional material deals primarily with purely ethical matters, it is self-evident that they do not derive from *Kinyan Tora* which is devoted almost exclusively to topics concerning the study of *Tora*.

BIBLIOGRAPHY

By far and large no other tractate of the Mishna or Talmud has such an abundance of traditional commentaries as *Avot*. Several of the classical commentaries have been discussed by TAYLOR in his *Appendix*. See also BACHER, 'Zwei alte Abothkommentare'. A complete, up-to-date list of the classical commentaries is found in KASHER-MANDELBAUM, *Sarei Ha-Elef*, 305-13, 623-4. See also SHMIDMAN, 'Excerpt', 315 36. The commentary attributed to R. NATAN AV HA-YESHIVA, edited by M.Y.L. SACHS, is appended to the edition of the Mishna published by *El ha-mekorot*, Jerusalem 1955. For other basic commentaries, see below, n. 84. A comprehensive listing of commentaries (mainly post-classical) is offered by KOHN, 'Otsar', 96-111. For an historical-geographical survey of the prolific commentaries to *Avot* throughout the ages, see COHEN, 'Sayings of the Fathers'.

The commentary of R. NOAH HAYIM BEN MOSHE of Kobrin, *Massekhet Avot im Talmud Babli we-Yerushalmi*, Warsaw 1868 (reprinted Tel-Aviv 1955) deserves special attention. This commentary adduces parallels and related material to *Avot* from the main body of talmudic and midrashic literature and represents a most important study aid to this tractate.

Recent modern Hebrew commentaries include the excellent work of ALBECK, as part of his complete Commentary to the Mishna; and DINUR, *Massekhet Avot*, which (abortively) endeavours to comment on the teachings of *Avot* from historical perspective.

Important introductory material concerning the structure of *Avot* is found in FRANKEL, 'Zum Traktat Abot'; ADLER, 'Aboth'; HOFFMAN, First Mishna, 45-64 (= Ha-Mishna ha-rishona, 28-40); EPSTEIN, *Tannaim*, 232-3; FINKELSTEIN, *Mabo*; *idem*, 'Introductory Study'; ALBECK, *Mishna* 4, 347-51. See also the introductions of HERFORD, STRACK et al.; LIFSHITZ, 'Mavo'; REINES, *Tora u-musar*, 217-27. The recent study of SALDARINI, *Scholastic Rabbinism*, exten-

---

[75] Thus *Pirkei Derekh Erets*, p. 15 mentions R. Eliezer instead of R. Meir; cf. Flusser-Safrai, 'Essene Doctrine', 47, n. 2. For a similar substitution in this work, see *ib.* 14 and n. 55. Thus there is no basis for the Palestinian (= Eliezer) – Babylonian (= Meir) theory advanced by Horowitz, *Iggeret Petuha*, 8.

sively treats the themes and the literary structure of *Avot* and their reflection in both versions of *Avot de-R. Natan*.

The linguistic characteristics of *Avot* are dealt with by MELAMMED, 'Leshona'. FISCHEL, 'Sorites', adduces numerous literary parallels from classical literature, some of them pertaining to the form and structure of teachings in *Avot*. KAMINKA, *Mehkarim*, 42ff. compares rabbinic maxims with Greek and Latin apophthegms.

The chronology and historical meaning of chapters 1-2 are discussed by ROTH, 'Historical Implications'. The article of MEVAREK, 'Seder' is based on pure fantasy. Similarly, LOEB, 'Notes' is totally unreliable, due to its hypercritical approach. The recent work of VIVIANO, *Study as Worship* places great emphasis on the ideal of Tora study in *Avot*.

HA-KOHEN, 'Massekhet Avot', claims halakhic validity for the teachings of *Avot*, while MELAMMED, 'La Vie des Tannaim', discusses the biographical aspects of some of its teachings.

A number of studies are devoted to the clarification of individual teachings in *Avot*, especially those related to the pre-Maccabean era, e.g.: BICKERMAN, 'Chaine'; *id.*, 'Maxim'; HERR, 'Continuum'; FINKELSTEIN, 'Maxim'; STEIN, 'Concept'; GOLDIN, 'End of Ecclesiastes'; *id.* 'Three Pillars'; *id.* 'The First Pair'; *id.* 'Mashehu'; GOITEIN, 'Spruch'. Historical and linguistic interpretations to individual sections are offered by WEISS, 'Bikoret sefarim', 122-5; URBACH, *Sages*, passim, see index; TORCZYNER, 'Gilla panim', 270-1; SAFRAI, 'Majority of Deeds'.

Translations and commentaries in German are found in the editions of STRACK, *Väter* and MARTI-BEER, *Abot* (in BEER *et al.*, *Mischna*). There are translations into almost every other modern language within the framework of the traditional prayer book. On Yiddish translations and midrashic commentaries, see the re-edition of LEVI, *An Old Yiddish Midrash*. On Ladino, see SCHWARZWALD, 'Traductions'. English translations as well as commentaries are provided by TAYLOR, *Sayings*; DANBY, *Mishnah*; HERFORD, *Ethics*; GOLDIN, *Living Talmud*.

PEREK KINYAN TORA. Manuscript versions of *Perek Kinyan Tora* were published by HIGGER, 'Avot', 129-31; and KATSH, *Ginzei Mishna*, 124-7.

Alternative versions and additions to this chapter in the Yemenite prayer books, all of similar scope, have been published by MARGOLIOUTH, 'Yemenite Liturgy', 689-703; HIGGER, 'Perek Kinyan Tora'; HAKOHEN, 'Perek'. (Higger was apparently unaware of Margoliouth's edition, and Hakohen of Higger's.)

Most translations and post-classical commentaries to *Avot* also deal with *Kinyan Tora*. See also the discussions of SHARVIT, 'Custom' and of FRIEDMAN, *Pseudo Seder Eliahu Zutta*, 15-17, and EPSTEIN, *Nosah*, 978, concerning the additions to *Avot*.

The various customs of studying *Avot* and *Kinyan Tora* on the Sabbath are dealt with by SHARVIT, 'Custom'.

The Textual Criticism of Tractate Avot

(by S. Sharvit)

Tractate *Avot* presents a very special case for the textual criticism of the Mishna. Often, introductions to scholarly editions of rabbinic texts apologize for having been able to use only two or three manuscripts and printed editions. In *Avot* we are confronted with a very different situation. It has undergone more alterations and distortions than any other mishnaic tractate, both in scope (the object of 'high criticism') and in textual variants ('low criticism').[76]

We discern two basic reasons. First, *Avot* is unique in content, form and style in the Mishna,[77] and in this quality it became one of the most intensely studied and copied books of Judaism. Obviously, the latter fact did not help it being read and copied in strict loyalty to the text.

The second reason for the high amount of textual divergencies is that *Avot* has been transmitted in two different literary frameworks: in a halakhic framework, as a part of the Mishna, and in a liturgical framework, as a part of the prayer books. The former is known to be quite punctilious in textual tradition, but the latter is inherently flexible. *Avot* of the prayer books – usually called *Pirkei Avot*, i.e. Sayings, or Chapters, of the Fathers[78] – changed substantially in scope and in text from generation to generation. Moreover, these changes varied from congregation to congregation in accordance with local rites. Initially, a great disparity existed between the Mishna text of *Avot* and that of the prayer books. However, little by little the students and copyists adapted the mishnaic version to conform to that of the prayer books in which they were fluent. By the fifteenth century, there was almost no difference between the two versions.

TEXTUAL AUTHORITIES

The critical study of the text of *Avot* should be based on four sources: a) manuscripts of the Mishna; b) manuscripts of the prayer books; c) the quota-

---

[76] Many sayings are missing entirely or in part in certain MSS.; others are added. The literary structure and metrics too have been corrupted through scribal errors. See details in Melammed, 'Nosah', 152-60.

[77] The proximity of *Avot* to biblical wisdom literature is evident both in contents and form. Although vocabulary and grammar are mishnaic, the language still preserves more biblical elements than any other Mishna tractate. Moreover, only *Avot* employs some sort of parallelism and other stylistic means reminiscent of biblical wisdom literature. See Sharvit, *Variants*, 4-24.

[78] See above p. 263.

tions by early commentators on *Avot*; d) *Avot de-Rabbi Natan*. We shall give a short description of these sources and discuss their value for the text of *Avot* and its study. Then we shall examine the modern editions, and finally propose a method for a new critical edition.

MANUSCRIPTS OF THE MISHNA. The manuscripts of the Mishna all place *Avot* at the end of *Seder Nezikin*. In addition, there exists a large number of manuscripts of *Avot* alone or in combination with certain extra-mishnaic tractates. A third kind of manuscript material is represented by the fragments from the Cairo Geniza. We have collected more than two hundred and thirty (!) fragments.[79] Only a minor part of these manuscripts have some kind of colophon, from which we learn details as to the date and place of copying. Vocalized manuscripts are also quite rare.

Although the manuscripts are from very different places and ages, most of them share a large number of features. The two most important are that, except for three texts,[80] they all contain five chapters only, and that the saying 5:21 is lacking ('He used to say: At five years old [one is fit] for Scripture . . .').

MANUSCRIPTS OF THE PRAYER BOOK. The presence of *Avot* in the prayer books is a result of by the custom, wide-spread since the period of the Geonim, to read *Avot* on the Sabbath.[81] Hundreds of manuscripts have reached us, ranging from Yemen in the East to Morocco and Spain in the West. Most of them are vocalized and have colophons indicating date and place of copying. Even those which have no colophon can be identified, however, from the rite of prayers and palaeographic criteria. This enables us to classify *Avot* manuscripts into six families according to the main Jewish community centres: Yemen, Spain, Ashkenaz (central Europe), Italy, Balkan (Greece and Rumania) and 'Orient' (Arabic spoken lands: North Africa, Palestine, Syria, etc.). In addition, we can discern the influence of the two large Jewish centres in the previous period: Palestine and Babylonia, and of the version of Maimonides, an eclectic text found in his Mishna autograph. We can summarize the various relations in the following graph:

---

[79] A full catalogue of all these MSS. is given in Sharvit, *Variants*, 251-86.

[80] MS. Paris 327-8 (Mishna) Italy 1399-1401; MS. Munich 95 (Babylonian Talmud) Germany 1343; Mishna Napoli 1492, the first printed edition.

[81] Several of the Geonic *responsa* attribute this custom to Sar Shalom Gaon, head of the Sura academy in the ninth cent., and associate it with the tradition about the death of Moses on Sabbath afternoon. See Sharvit, 'Custom', 169-75.

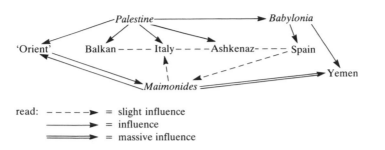

read: – – – – –▶ = slight influence
————▶ = influence
═════▶ = massive influence

All prayer book versions, except for the early Yemenite manuscripts, have a sixth chapter: *Kinyan Tora* (see above). Three of them, Ashkenazic, Balkan and Oriental, end the fifth chapter with a collection of short baraitot. A fourth version, the Spanish, designates this collection as the sixth chapter and *Kinyan Tora* as the seventh (!). The Oriental manuscripts add two chapters from the *Derekh Erets* texts, *Yirat Het* (The Fear of Sin) and *Derekh Erets* (Proper Manners), which are related to *Avot* in contents and style (see below chap. 9). The voluntary reading of these chapters at the end of *Avot* on the Sabbath is first testified in the prayer book of Saadya Gaon.[82]

COMMENTARIES. In addition to the commentaries to the Mishna as a whole, we know of more than two hundred separate commentaries on *Avot*, which were written during the ages in various countries. Most of these do not pay attention to textual variants or linguistic matters. But a dozen of them do, offering citations of other variants, comparisons between their Mishna versions of *Avot* and those of their prayer books, as well as explanations for textual divergencies such as emendations made by earlier copyists. It is not always possible to decide which is the more original: a textual tradition of some saying, or its explanatory rendering.[83] Nevertheless, in combination with the versions of the prayer books, these testimonies are very helpful for the typology of variants according to place and age. The commentary attributed to Rabbenu Natan Av ha-Yeshiva (Land of Israel, 11th cent.) deserves special mention. It contains a literal translation of the Mishna into Arabic which, when re-translated into Hebrew, yields many unique readings and enables us to tell the scope of his version of *Avot*.[84]

---

[82] For full details see Sharvit, 'Custom', 176-87.
[83] See for instance שסופו להשמע/וסופו להשמע(*Avot*3:11);or המגלה פנים בתורה [שלאכהלכה]
(*Avot* 2:4). See details in Sharvit, 'Traditions'.
[84] Other commentaries may be mentioned: The one in *Mahzor Vitry*, attributed to Rashi but written by Rabbenu Yaakov ben Shimshon, France, 11th-12th cent.; *Magen Avot* by Shimon ben Tsemah Duran, Spain, 14th cent.; *Midrash Shmuel* by Shmuel de-Utseda, Land of Israel, 16th cent.; and *Melekhet Shlomo* by Shlomo Adani, Land of Israel, 17th cent. For a full list with further details see Sharvit, *Variants*, 233-45.

AVOT DE-R. NATAN. *Avot* has no companion in the Tosefta or in the Talmudim. Commentaries and elaborations to it were preserved in *Avot de-Rabbi Natan*, a tractate extant in two different versions which may possibly revert to two schools;[85] their relation to *Avot* and to each other is disputed.[86] Nevertheless, the text of *Avot de-Rabbi Natan* is obviously a most important source for reconstructing the early form of *Avot* and for studying its textual variants. A major desideratum, therefore, is a new critical edition of *Avot de-Rabbi Natan*. Treating, as SCHECHTER did, both versions as independent texts with their own apparatus of variants, this new edition should take into account more recent manuscript material and avoid some methodical setbacks found in his pioneering edition of almost a century ago.[87]

CRITICAL EDITIONS OF AVOT

Since the end of the nineteenth century, three attempts were made at a critical edition of *Avot*. In 1877, TAYLOR published a text based on the Cambridge manuscript.[88] Several years later he prepared a descriptive catalogue of manuscripts and a corpus of textual variants. The catalogue is rich; 140 manuscripts from eight libraries, classified accordingly, are included, most of them prayer books and commentaries to *Avot*. However, no Geniza versions are included. The description of the manuscripts varies in length (no. 19 covers fourteen pages, but no. 6 only two lines) and in method; generally, the rite of prayers involved is not mentioned. Taylor's 'prefatory note'[89] makes it clear that he intended his catalogue as a tentative publication and that he was still in search of more material. As to the 'Notes on the Text', i.e. the corpus of textual variants,[90] here too we find sporadic variants and notes without any clear policy. Nevertheless, Taylor's endeavours have laid the foundation for a scholarly edition of *Avot*.

A second edition was made by STRACK (1915). It was in fact a textbook for students which included a vocabulary, and not intended to be a critical edition. It is an eclectic text, based on the major Mishna manuscripts, and vocalized mainly according to the printed prayer books used in Europe. A short apparatus for textual variants from seven Mishna manuscripts and prayer books was added.[91]

---

[85] Cf. Schechter's introduction in his edition, xx-xxiii.
[86] Finkelstein, *Mabo*, 4-5 thinks an earlier version of *Avot* served as the basis of *A.R.N.* See also Lerner, below chap. 9.
[87] Schechter did not hesitate to emend the *A.R.N.* text in accordance with the printed edition of *Avot*. See, for example, version B, p. 62a, where he notes that he added two words to conform with *Avot* 3:16, כותבת [פתוחה והיד] והפנקס and cf. his note to version A, p. 59a.
[88] MS. Cambridge Add. 470.1, which was later published integrally by W. Lowe.
[89] Taylor, *Appendix*, 5f.
[90] Taylor, *Appendix*, 131-73.
[91] Cf. review by Marx, 'Strack's Abot'.

A third edition was published in 1927 by MARTI and BEER, in the Giessen Mishna series. The text is almost identical with that of Strack, including the vocalization, but the apparatus is much wider and more systematic. The editors utilized Taylor's work and added some new material, but no Geniza fragments. There is no distinction between the various sources used and the policy behind the apparatus is not clear. However, this is another important step towards a critical edition of *Avot*.

RABBINOVICZ, who projected a volume on *Avot de-Rabbi Natan* and the Minor Tractates which unfortunately never appeared, warned that mentioning all variants without distinction or comment 'will only cause confusion and obscurity'.[92] Indeed, an indiscriminately inflated apparatus of variants seems rather pointless and even misleading.

In our opinion, two distinctive apparatuses should be employed. The first should present variants from Mishna manuscripts and Geniza fragments. By a pre-selection based on previous studies of Mishna manuscripts, the number of variants can be limited. This apparatus will provide the most faithful text.

A second apparatus should offer a selective presentation of variants from prayer books and other sources. As shown above, the prayer book versions can be classified into six main families, and each of these can be sufficiently represented by some of its best manuscripts. In addition, all the testimonia of the commentators should be given. This apparatus will largely reflect the later form of *Avot*, in scope and in textual tradition. Nevertheless, it will be a valuable aid towards tracing the subsequent history of textual transmission and its ramifications throughout the generations. In this respect, *Avot* again represents a unique phenomenon.[93]

SELECTED BIBLIOGRAPHY

Editions:
TAYLOR, *Sayings*; STRACK, *Väter*; MARTI-BEER *Abot*.
SHARVIT, *Variants* offers a critical edition of *Avot* chap. 1.
HIGGER, 'Avot' gives an edition of MS. Oxford Bodl. 896.

Discussion and further research:
SCHECHTER, introduction to his *Aboth de Rabbi Nathan*; TAYLOR, *Appendix*; MARX, 'Strack's Abot'; FINKELSTEIN, *Mabo*; MELAMMED, 'Nosah'; SHARVIT, *Variants*; *id*. 'Custom'; *id*. 'Traditions'.

---

[92] Rabbinovicz, *Dikdukei Sofrim, Nezikin*, 8.
[93] Sharvit, *Variants*, 287-300 presents an edition of the first chapter of *Avot* according to the method proposed here. A special method is followed by Goldberg, *Shabbat* and *Eruvin*, who gives two parallel texts (MS. Kaufmann and *ed. princ.*) with two separate apparatuses: one for the 'Palestinian' textual tradition and the other for the 'Babylonian' and 'Spanish' MSS. and the printed editions.

Chapter Six

The Tosefta - Companion to the Mishna

Abraham Goldberg

Character and Date

The name *Tosefta* means 'addition', and this is what it is: an addition, a complement to the Mishna.[1] It serves this function in more than one way. First of all, as we shall show below, it is the prime commentary or 'talmud' to the Mishna for the first generations of Amoraim. In this sense it is an 'addition' which gives explanation and illustration to the Mishna. However, it is definitely more, serving as well as a supplementary and companion volume to the Mishna. It will often give a fuller elaboration of mishnaic halakha. Where the Mishna may give only one or two opinions on a particular topic, and often anonymously, the Tosefta is apt to provide us with a greater gamut of opinion in addition to an identification of the Tanna of the anonymous opinion.

In yet another sense, the Tosefta continues the Mishna. It records the teachings of the last Tannaic generations which, in the main, were not included in the Mishna, i.e. the generation of the compiler of the Mishna itself, Rabbi Yehuda the Patriarch, and the one following. Thus while the Tosefta has the same layer structure as the Mishna – each layer corresponding to a generation of Tannaic teachers – it has two more layers. The two layers, however, which make up the greater part of the Tosefta, are the one that parallels the main layer of the Mishna, i.e. the teachings of the pupils of R. Akiva, and the following one which supplies the teachings of the generation of Rabbi.[2]

The Tosefta is also at least three times as large as the Mishna. This is to be expected in a work which combines commentary, supplement and continuation. As such, the Tosefta not only can be seen as the first 'talmud' to the Mishna, but together with the Mishna came to be the very foundation for the teaching of the generations following, which resulted in the Palestinian and Babylonian Talmudim.[3]

---

[1] תוספתא *tosefta* is the Aramaic form of the Hebrew תוספת *tosefet*. The plural forms are תוספתא *tosefata* and תוספות *tosefot*.

[2] See Introduction to Goldberg, *Eruvin*.

[3] The Tosefta is introduced in the Babylonian Talmud, as are baraitot not found in the extant Tosefta, with the redactional terms: תנו רבנן *tannu Rabbanan* (our Masters taught), תניא *tanya* (it was taught) and תנא *tena* (he taught). In the Palestinian Talmud the introductory term is תני *tenei* (which eqals *tena*) but very frequently there is no introductory term at all.

In the following, it will be shown that the text of the Tosefta is very closely interwoven with that of the Mishna, to such an extent that they may almost be considered one literary work. In addition, their language and style are so similar that only one well-trained in the perception of the most delicate literary nuances would be able to tell one from the other when taken out of context. For this reason it seems most irrational to try to search out differences between the two. Nor can any hypothesis which posits artificial distinctions between them, such as the Mishna being oral and the Tosefta written, really hold. Moreover, there is nothing substantial in a theory – and hardly worthwhile the effort – which posits different sources for different tractates of the Tosefta.[4] If there are seeming differences, this is because every individual tractate of the Tosefta relates to its parallel in the Mishna in a particular way.[5] Likewise, differences in order and arrangement have their proper explanations, as will be set forth below. Nor in any way may it be said that the Mishna is Tannaic and the Tosefta Amoraic.[6]

The character of the Tosefta gives away its dating. It is so close to the Mishna and so natural a continuation of it that its editing cannot have been much later. All signs point to a difference of, largely, one generation, i.e. to a date around 220-30 C.E. It is certain that the compilation of the Tosefta preceded that of the Tannaic midrash collections, since the latter often quote it verbatim. This is the generally accepted view today; in the past, however, various scholars regarded the Tosefta as a post-Talmudic compilation which drew upon the baraita material already found in the Talmud.[7]

Arrangement and Contents

Like the Mishna, the Tosefta is divided into tractates, tractates into chapters and chapters into halakhot. Clearly, the arrangement of the Tosefta material parallels that of the Mishna. There are three tractates, however, which have no corresponding Tosefta tractate: *Tamid, Middot* and *Kinnim*. *Avot* has no Tosefta either, but we can consider *Avot de-Rabbi Natan* as such. Again, as stated before, the number of chapters in each tractate does not always correspond; and the number of halakhot in each chapter of the Tosefta is usually more than double the number of mishnayot in the corresponding Mishna chapter. Yet the most marked difference between these parallel compilations of Tannaic literature is in the ordering of the halakhot.

While the order of the halakhot in the Tosefta largely parallels that of the mishnayot, the exceptions are so numerous that they call for an explanation.

---

[4] Thus, apparently, Strack-Stemberger, *Einleitung*, 155.

[5] Thus the Tosefta mostly gives only the supplementary layer to a full three-layer discussion in the Mishna; and where the Mishna limits itself to the teaching of R. Akiva, the Tosefta will supplement those of his pupils. See below.

[6] Strack-Stemberger, *Einleitung*, 157.

[7] Especially, Dünner, *Tosephta*; and, remarkably, even the noted contemporary scholar, Albeck, *Babli and Yerushalmi*, 51-8. Albeck's position will be dealt with in detail below.

Many scholars claim that the Tosefta does not follow the order of the extant Mishna, but of an earlier recension of it.[8] This is solving a literary problem with an undocumented hypothesis, while a close literary analysis may make such forced remedies unnecessary. Thus it can be shown that the Tosefta had no other order of the halakhot before it than that in our Mishna. Where there is digression, this is premeditated and is made primarily for pedagogic reasons.[9] A change in order indeed can sometimes make it easier to present the frame of comment and supplement of the Tosefta. Sometimes it is an external link between phrase and phrase which provokes the change in order. At other times, the consideration is to mark the chronological order of the generations. Other considerations may enter as well, for it must be remembered that even though the Tosefta is primarily a supplement to the Mishna, it remains, nevertheless, an independent literary work with its own patterns of order and arrangement.

Being a supplement and companion, the contents of the Tosefta parallel those of the Mishna. Like the Mishna, it also contains aggadic sections, though these may be distributed differently. It has been remarked that there is more aggada in the Tosefta than in the Mishna. This is only true insofar as the Tosefta is much larger than the Mishna; generally speaking, the proportion of aggada is equal in both.

Aggada is mostly used in the same way as in the Mishna: as a kind of signature to a topic. This is a general phenomenon which is also found in the Talmudim. For example, the Mishna tractate *Kiddushin*, wich deals with the topic of marriage, practically consists of two main sections. The first chapter deals with the validity of methods of acquisition of persons and things, which includes betrothal, while the second chapter is almost exclusively devoted to marriage. Now to mark the transition from the general topic of acquisition to that of marriage proper, the last mishna consists of aggada. Similarly, the last section of the parallel first chapter in the Tosefta is also aggadic, but more extensive.

The Structural Layers

We have pointed out that a prime characteristic of the Tosefta is that it is a continuation of the Mishna. The main difference is, in fact, chronological. Although the Tosefta does preserve layers which are earlier than the last layer in the Mishna, these always come to explain a layer in the Mishna at least one generation earlier. It follows, therefore, that the first layer of the Tosefta cannot have been formulated before the second layer of the Mishna, and is

---

[8] Epstein, *Tannaitic Literature*, 256-60 is one of the foremost exponents of this theory. Moreover, he finds the earlier order of the Mishna which the Tosefta follows far superior to that of the present Mishna.

[9] In my commentaries, *Shabbat* and *Eruvin*, I have shown that the order of the Tosefta really depends upon that of our present Mishna which is highly logical. I hope to demonstrate the same for other tractates where seemingly the order of the Tosefta has very little relationship to that of the Mishna.

indeed parallel to this second layer. Chronologically, the formulation of the second layer of the Tosefta parallels the third layer in the Mishna, and so on. The literary formulation of the Tosefta which starts a generation after the Mishna continues for a generation or two following the completion of the Mishna. We have shown in our discussion of the Mishna that it had its beginnings as a nascent literary document at Yavne following the destruction of the Second Temple in the year 70 C.E. This is the generation of Rabban Gamliel II. The beginnings of the literary formulation of the Tosefta, then, can be assigned to the next generation, that of R. Akiva. And just as the first layer of the Mishna concerns itself with late Second Temple teaching, so does the first layer of the Tosefta concern itself with the teachings of the first generation of Yavne.

What is the difference between the first layer of the Tosefta and its parallel, the second layer of the Mishna? In truth, there is no difference, and in each case one has to learn what is Mishna and what Tosefta. For the second layer of the Mishna itself serves often as an amplification and continuation of the first layer, in a similar way as the Tosefta. So, too, is the relationship between the second layer of the Tosefta and the third layer of the Mishna. Both are 'tosefta' to the second layer of the Mishna. The main difference is that one is included in the prime collection of Tannaic teaching and the other is not. This difference, moreover, is only external. Both Talmudim, especially the Palestinian, give equal status to Mishna and Tosefta. It would not be wrong to conclude, therefore, that every layer of the Mishna had two 'toseftot' – one in the next layer of the Mishna and another in the Tosefta. Obviously, this does not include the last layer of the Mishna.

In our chapter on the Mishna we have already seen how the heading of the first mishna of tractate *Shabbat* (which represents the first Mishna layer) has two parallel 'toseftot', one in the following layer of the Mishna in the same context and another in the Tosefta. Let us now take an example where an early Mishna layer has Tosefta only outside it. *M. Middot* 2:3, speaking of the gates of the Second Temple, states: 'All the gates that were there were changed [and overlaid] with gold, except for the Nicanor Gates, because a miracle had happened with them. And some say, because their bronze shone like gold.' The Mishna does not tell us what miracle happened to the Nicanor Gates. This is left to the Tosefta. Since *Middot* is one of the very few tractates which do not have a corresponding Tosefta tractate, the appropriate Tosefta is to be found elsewhere, in *T. Yoma (Kippurim)* 2:4. After quoting the appropriate section from Mishna *Middot*, the Tosefta there continues:

> R. Eliezer ben Yaakov says, the bronze [of the Nicanor Gates] was Corinthian and was as beautiful as gold. What was the miracle that happened to them? They said: When Nicanor was bringing them from Alexandria, a sea wave came over them to drown them. They took one of them and threw it in the sea. They wanted to throw the second one as well, but Nicanor did not let them. He said to them: If you throw the second, throw me in with it. He was grieved until he reached the port of

Jaffa. As soon as he reached the port of Jaffa, [the first Gate] came up from underneath the boat. Some say: A sea monster had swallowed it, and when Nicanor reached the port of Jaffa it spewed it out and threw it up on dry land. To him the tradition of the verse would apply, 'The beams of our houses are cedars, and our panels are cypresses.'[10]

Sometimes, a first 'tosefta' will be in the Mishna itself and a later tosefta to that mishnaic 'tosefta' in the Tosefta proper. In *M. Yoma* 2:1-2 we have a description of how the priests would compete for the privilege of clearing the Altar of ashes:

Beforetime, whosoever was minded to clear the Altar of ashes did so. If they were many, they would run up the [Altar-]Ramp, and he that reached the top four cubits first gained the privilege. If two were equal, the appointed officer would say to them: Raise your fingers . . .

It once happened that two were equal running up the Ramp and one pushed his fellow and broke his leg. When the Court saw that danger was being incurred, they ordained that the Altar should not be cleared except by lot. There were four lots. This was the first lot.

These mishnayot from *Yoma*, however, are themselves a comment on *M. Tamid* 1:2 and 4: 'The appointed officer came and knocked . . . He said to them: He who has immersed himself may come and participate in the casting of lots. They cast lots. He who won, won . . . He who gained the privilege of clearing the Altar of ashes, went to clear the Altar of ashes.'

In fact, the greatest part of the Mishna tractate *Yoma* is a 'tosefta' to Mishna *Tamid*, this tractate again being one of the very few without a corresponding Tosefta tractate. While *M. Tamid*, which as a whole belongs to the early layers of the Mishna, describes the procedures of the Temple during its very last years, *M. Yoma* fills out the picture by telling what the situation was in former days. This in itself is a characteristic feature of Mishna and Tosefta. While an earlier layer may be still interested only in current practice, the later layer may come to describe the situation of more ancient days.

Now the 'tosefta' in *M. Yoma* 1:1-2 which we quoted, in turn has its own tosefta in *T. Yoma* 1:10. First of all, it tells us how the casting of the lots took place:

How did they cast lots? They (i.e. the priests) enter the Chamber of Hewn Stones and form a snail-shaped circle. The appointed officer comes and takes the mitre of one of them as a sign that the counting begins with him. They would not put out two fingers, but only one. Isolated individuals would put out two, but the extra finger would not be counted.

Secondly, the Tosefta (1:12) supplements the story about the breaking of the leg with a more tragic case:

It once happened that two priests came even running up the Ramp. One pushed his fellow when they reached the top four cubits. He took a knife

---

[10] Cant 1:17, reading ברושים (cypresses) for ברית ים (sea monsters).

and put it in his heart. Came R. Tsadok and stood on the steps of the Porch and said: Hear me my brothers, O House of Israel. Behold it is said: 'If one be found slain in the land . . . and it be not known who had smitten him; then thy elders and thy judges shall come forth and they shall measure unto the cities which are round about . . . and it shall be, that the city which is nearest unto the slain man, even the elders of that city shall take a heifer of the herd' (Deut 21:1-3). Let us measure, who is here required to bring the heifer: the Holy of Holies or the Courts of the Temple? – They all burst out after him in tears.

We have seen how the Tosefta fits into the redactional structure of the Mishna as almost integral to it. The question before us now is: Why should one of two parallel 'tosefta' layers become Mishna and another Tosefta? Why were not both included in the Mishna? This question, however, can at this moment be answered only in a general way, for it is still in need of much detailed research.

It seems that the very nature of the Mishna requires it to have a limited scope and to include only part of what could possibly fit in. Furthermore, there seems to be a difference between tractates where early layers predominate and those where later layers are the rule. A predominance of early layers is to be found primarily among the 'historical' tractates, i.e. those which preserve historical descriptions and traditions of later Second Temple times, such as the tractates *Middot* and *Tamid* we have just quoted. In these tractates, the 'tosefta' is apt to be found preserved in later layers of the Mishna itself, either in the same tractate or in another one close in topic (such as the 'tosefta' to *Tamid* which we found in *M. Yoma*). On the other hand, where later layers make up the substance of the tractate, the tosefta is likely to be outside the Mishna, for there the tosefta element is quite large, usually much larger than what apparently could be contained in the Mishna.

In this connection, it is interesting to compare the number of chapters in Mishna and Tosefta among the various tractates. We find that the 'historical' tractates have more chapters in the Mishna than in the Tosefta. *Yoma*, for example, has eight chapters Mishna and four chapters Tosefta. *Sukka* has eight chapters of Mishna and only three of Tosefta; *Rosh ha-Shana*, five of Mishna and two Tosefta. All these have large parts of historical detail. On the other hand, 'non-historical' tractates have more chapters in Tosefta than in Mishna. The thirty chapters of Mishna *Nezikin* (i.e., *Bava Kamma*, *Bava Metsia* and *Bava Batra*) are paralleled by thirty-three chapters Tosefta; *Sanhedrin-Makkot*, fourteen Mishna and nineteen Tosefta; *Gittin*, nine Mishna, seven Tosefta; *Beitsa*, five Mishna, four Tosefta.

Thus the 'tosefta' of the historical tractates is mostly in the Mishna; that of the non-historical ones in the Tosefta. It is well to note exceptions to this rule. *Pea* for example, a non-historical tractate, has eight chapters Mishna and only four in the Tosefta. This is explained by the fact that what would ordinarily constitute tosefta has been incorporated in large measure in the Mishna. There is no

288

Tosefta, for example, to *Pea* 3:5-8; all the teachings of the pupils of R. Akiva here have found their place in the Mishna. On the other hand, chapter four has three early layers and no room for the last layer containing the teachings of the pupils of R. Akiva. Of necessity, therefore, they are carried over to the Tosefta.

There seems to be some definite system of maintaining a relative proportion between mishnayot and 'toseftot'. In effect, meanwhile, almost all Tosefta chapters are much longer than the average Mishna chapter. It may be that external considerations played a greater role than we know in determining what Tannaic teaching would be included in the Mishna and what in the Tosefta. As stated, all these questions require much further investigation.

Commentary and Supplement to the Mishna

The Tosefta serves as commentary and supplement to the Mishna in various ways. The examples given in the previous section illustrate some of these, but they were chosen from historical tractates with the aim to demonstrate how the Tosefta is a natural continuation of the Mishna. Now we want to spell out a number of characteristics as to the commentary and supplementary function of the Tosefta.

1. Sometimes the commentary character of the Tosefta is obvious and stated explicitly. *M. Shabbat* 2:1-2, for example, tells us that 'heave-offering oil (which has become ritually unclean and) must be burnt', may not be used for lighting either the Sabbath or Festival lamps. But the Mishna does not state why. *T. Shabbat* 2:1 explicitly comes to fill this gap: 'Why have they said that heave-offering oil which must be burnt may not be used for the Festival lighting? Because neither heave-offerings (which have become ritually unclean) nor sacrificial offerings (which have become unfit) nor leaven (which is prohibited on Passover) may be burnt on the Festival-day (and certainly not on the Sabbath).'

2. In other cases, the commentary is interwoven with the language of the Mishna which is quoted, or appended to it. The first mishna of *Eruvin* begins as follows: 'Where the crossbeam of the alley-entry is higher than twenty cubits, it must be lowered' (in order to mark the symbolic closing of the entry so that it may be considered a private domain and thus permit carrying on the Sabbath). The corresponding passage at the beginning of the Tosefta reads: 'Where the cross-beam of the alley-entry is higher than twenty cubits, *which is more than the height of the Temple Sanctuary opening*, it must be lowered.' By inserting the phrase here italicized into the Mishna quotation, the Tosefta explains the measure given in the Mishna. An example of comment appended at the end of a Mishna quotation relates to *M. Shabbat* 17:5, which teaches that fragments of broken utensils may be handled on the Sabbath provided they have some use. R. Yehuda is quoted to be stipulating among other things: 'And of glass, (those fragments are allowed to be handled) which can have oil poured into them.'

T. Shabbat 14(15):6 comments and specifies by subtly adding one word in the Hebrew: 'And of glass, (those fragments are allowed to be handled) which can have oil poured in them *for (anointing) an infant.*'

3. The Tosefta will upon occasion quote a mishna, or part of it, from another chapter or another treatise, when this helps to understand a particular mishna or its sources. Thus, *T. Yoma* 5:13 comments on *M. Yoma* 2:3, which is really a kind of 'tosefta', to *M. Tamid* 3:1. To indicate this, the Tosefta quotes the source mishna in *Tamid* word for word.[11] Again, *T. Shabbat* 14(15):5-6, which comments on chapter 18 in the Mishna, quotes two mishnayot from two other chapters in the tractate to illustrate the topic of the chapter, namely, objects which may be handled on the Sabbath because they are considered 'fit' for use. Thus it brings the last part of *M. Shabbat* 21:1, 'It is permitted to take out the one part of Heave-offering that is fallen into another hundred parts of common produce' (in order to permit the common produce to be eaten on the Sabbath). And it follows with the middle part of 17:5, '(It is permitted to handle) fragments of a kneading-trough for the purpose of covering (the mouth of) a jar; and of glass for the purpose of covering (the mouth of) a cruse.'

4. The Tosefta often supplements the Mishna by teaching, with regard to any particular topic, what may be permitted, where the Mishna teaches what is prohibited, and vice versa. Thus with reference to the Sabbath lamp, *M. Shabbat* 2:4 teaches that 'one may not pierce an egg-shell and fill it with oil and put it on the opening of the lamp' so that the lamp will have an extra reserve of oil. *T. Shabbat* 2:7 teaches what may be done: 'It is permitted to put clay and burned clay under the lamp on the eve of the Sabbath before dark so that it will burn more slowly and last into the Sabbath night. It is permitted to place a grain of salt or a bean on the opening of the lamp on the eve of the Sabbath so that it will burn more slowly and last into the Sabbath night.'

5. The Tosefta will also supplement the Mishna by adding the reverse of items listed in the Mishna to fill out any particular topic. *M. Shabbat* 12:5 teaches that one is not considered culpable for writing two or more letters on the Sabbath where his intention was to write the letter *het*, but instead wrote two separate *zayins* (which when joined form a *het*). The Tosefta 11(12):12 adds that neither is one considered culpable where the actual intention was to write two letters (which when performed would be culpable), but these came out as one.

6. Of quite different nature is the supplementary function of the Tosefta when it discusses topics almost entirely left out in the Mishna. Thus the entire fifth and sixth chapters of *T. Shabbat* are almost like a special treatise on superstitious practices (almost all prohibited) which is an independent take-off from the casual phrase 'ways of the Amorites' at the end of chapter six of the Mishna.

As stated, one of the main two layers of the Tosefta parallels the last and largest layer of the Mishna (i.e. the teachings of R. Akiva's pupils), while the other

---

[11] See Goldberg, 'Tosefta to the Treatise Tamid', 24.

covers the teachings of the following generation. This offers us a general explanation not only of the close interrelation of both works, but also of the complementary function of the Tosefta. A deeper understanding of this interesting and important matter would require detailed analysis, which is impossible in this context. It was given due attention in the course of our recent commentary to tractate *Eruvin*.[12] Drawing on that material, we shall here list a number of instances where the second main layer of the Tosefta indeed supplements the Mishna in that tractate, stating only the type of supplement and the page indication in our commentary. Some of the items are congruent with the types of supplement illustrated in the above, but here we focus on the complementary function of the second main layer of the Tosefta.

Thus the Tosefta explains the controversy between R. Meir and R. Yehuda (123); it adds to the teaching of a single Tanna in the Mishna, R. Yehuda (28); it teaches how one makes a conditional *eruv* (93), and how one 'squares' the permitted limits of the Sabbath boundary (136); and it will give the general point of view of Tannaim which makes for particularized differences in their teachings in the Mishna (87, 127).

Lists in the Mishna may be added on by the Tosefta, as to what may be included in the definition of city limits and what may not be (136), and what may be considered 'as if' leniences (15, 36, 136). The Tosefta will often add limitations to a general teaching of the Mishna (86, 107).

The area of Mishna teaching will be broadened by the Tosefta by discussing topics or cases not taken up in the Mishna (11, 27, 36, 150, 196, 216, 244). The Tosefta will also indicate a case where one of the disputants in the Mishna will agree with the other (75), or a case where the law of the Mishna would change (202).

Often, the Tosefta will amplify topics taken up in the Mishna (52, 89, 119); it will continue a dispute in the Mishna (255); it will indicate additional cases of things permitted and prohibited in Mishna discussions (171, 290). Where the Mishna teaches only the permitted side, the Tosefta will often add the prohibited (303). The Tosefta will frequently give the exact teaching of the Mishna, changing only a positive presentation to a negative one (136, 154, 262). The Tosefta will indicate a differing opinion where the Mishna may have only an anonymous single teaching (144, 241), or a third differing opinion where the Mishna has two (175), or even a fourth to three in the Mishna (303).

Something made invalid in the Mishna may be shown in the Tosefta to be liable to rectification (196, 199). Finally, the Tosefta will add scriptural proof (101), background (106), or reason (143) to Mishna teaching.

All of this once more demonstrates the intimate interrelation of Tosefta and Mishna, making both, as observed before, almost into a single work. Nevertheless, the Tosefta is an independent literary compilation, which will approach the

---

12 Goldberg, *Eruvin*.

teachings of the Mishna in a great variety of ways – all for the purpose of giving the most comprehensive 'completion' to the Mishna.

The Tosefta and the Baraitot in the Talmudim

Scholars have noted that baraitot in the Talmudim which parallel the Tosefta frequently differ in wording and sometimes even in content. The questions asked are: How do these baraitot relate to their parallels in the Tosefta? Are they really derived from the Tosefta? Or are they perhaps to be attributed to a differing Tannaic source? Or alternatively, do they both derive from a single common ancestor before having gone their separate ways? It has also been noted that the parallel baraitot in the Palestinian Talmud in language and content are much closer, and usually identical, than those in the Babylonian Talmud.

This matter is tied up with the theories about the editing of the Tosefta which we shall review below. Regarding the present issue, EPSTEIN maintains that once there was an 'ancient' Tosefta from which two branches developed.[13] The one is that of our Tosefta and the almost identical baraitot in the Palestinian Talmud; the other is that characterized by the Babylonian baraitot. This view seems to be most favoured by leading scholars today. ALBECK, on the other hand, does not believe that the baraitot of the Talmudim derive directly from the Tosefta. At the very most, these may have come from sources also known to the Tosefta, which itself, according to Albeck, is merely a late Amoraic collection. One of his proofs for that theory is that seemingly many Tosefta teachings were not known to the Amoraim.

Our discussions in the present volume allow some observations to be made on this issue. We have seen that the Tosefta is closely interwoven with the Mishna, and, as its commentary and supplement, it certainly did not derive from something more 'ancient'. It also follows that its editing must have been very close to that of the Mishna itself. That some Tosefta sections would seem not to have been known to the Amoraim, is a problem touching on the nature of the talmudic *sugya*, rather than on the Tosefta itself. The only important criterion for determining the nature of the Tosefta is comparison with the Mishna.

As for the talmudic baraitot themselves, these in the main derive from the Tosefta and the Tannaic midrash collections. In certain cases, baraitot otherwise unknown may be the creation of Amoraim, especially so in the Babylonian Talmud.

We have noted already that the Tosefta is quoted much more exactly in the Palestinian Talmud than in the Babylonian. This is because the latter often will intentionally paraphrase the Tosefta in order to make explicit something which may not be entirely clear out of context. The Babylonian Talmud also quite

[13] *Tannaitic Literature*, 246.

frequently interpolates explanatory phrases, even where otherwise it quotes the Tosefta word for word. This is a literary phenomenon which is really no different from what we have already observed for the Tosefta's own relation to the Mishna.[14]

This supplementary relation of the Talmudim to the Tosefta can also be observed in other ways. The Palestinian Talmud especially may continue a debate between Tannaim in the Tosefta, exactly as does the Tosefta to a debate in the Mishna.[15] Similarly, discussion of a special situation not discussed in the Tosefta may be taken up in the Talmudim.[16] These and comparable literary phenomena will be discussed in detail in our chapters on the Palestinian and Babylonian Talmudim.

Editing

Many theories have been expounded as to the manner of compilation and editing of the Tosefta. Since the Amora R. Yohanan speaks of R. Nehemia (pupil of R. Akiva) as being the author of the anonymous opinion in the Tosefta,[17] there have been some who would regard R. Nehemia as the editor as well. This opinion is rejected, however, by almost all scholars as far as the present Tosefta is concerned. Yet many scholars do not wish to exclude R. Nehemia entirely as a candidate for the editorship of the Tosefta, as for example EPSTEIN who writes: 'And, indeed, our Tosefta undoubtedly made use of the "Tosefta" of R. Nehemia. Sufficient proof of such is that the name of R. Nehemia, which occurs so infrequently in the Mishna, is found with great frequency in the Tosefta.'[18] In addition, Epstein continues, our Tosefta made use of many other halakhic compilations, early and late, and this explains the seemingly confused arrangement of the Tosefta.

It was A. SCHWARTZ who first broached the theory that the Tosefta of R. Nehemia is no more than a compilation of the disconnected parts of the Mishna of R. Akiva which his pupil R. Meir excluded from his Mishna, as well as of baraitot dating from earlier periods. This first Tosefta was supplemented later, according to Schwartz, by what R. Yehuda the Patriarch excluded from the compilation he made from the Mishna of R. Meir, and which was compiled by the pupil of R. Yehuda the Patriarch, R. Hiya.[19] The artificiality of this construction is only too apparent. An even more fanciful theory as to the nature of the Tosefta and its origins had been offered at an earlier date by ZUCKERMAN-DEL. The Tosefta, he claimed, is in reality the Mishna of the Palestinian

---

[14] See for example Goldberg, *Eruvin*, 124 n. 54.
[15] Goldberg, *Eruvin*, 255.
[16] Goldberg, *Eruvin*, 11, 25, 29, 35, 127.
[17] *B.T. Sanh.* 86a.
[18] Epstein, *Tannaitic Literature*, 256.
[19] Schwartz, *Nezikin, Baba Kamma* iv, vii.

Talmud. Our own Mishna is a compilation extracted from the Tosefta by the Babylonian Sages.[20] Because of the daring of this approach, it found many adherents at the time, but it is not held by any serious scholar today.

Still another view is the one held by ALBECK which we met already. He considers the Tosefta as a compilation which did not appear before the last days of the Talmud. It did not serve as a source of the baraitot quoted in the Talmud; at the most, sources common to both documents can be supposed.[21] Indeed, contrary to the opinion of other scholars that many Amoraic teachings in reality derive from the Tosefta, Albeck holds that in many instances it was the Tosefta that drew upon these Amoraic teachings. Meanwhile, Albeck does not doubt the essential characteristic of the Tosefta as being a commentary and supplement to the Mishna, although it contains much which finds little mention in the Mishna.[22]

As against Albeck's theory, the close literary relationship between Mishna and Tosefta must again be stressed, which makes it most improbable that the Tosefta achieved compilation only by the end of the Talmudic period. Its literary character stamps it as a Tannaic compilation of the same nature and style as the Mishna, which could hardly have been compiled at more than a generation or two after the Mishna. Let us examine, then, the list of possible editors of the Tosefta, in view of its literary relationship to the Mishna.

Those scholars who rightfully claim that the Tosefta was compiled shortly after the Mishna point out three names of possible editors: Bar Kappara, R. Hiya and R. Hoshaya. Of the ancient traditions, a very few hold Bar Kappara to be the editor. The most respected, that of Rav Sherira Gaon, holds to R. Hiya.[23] Others say R. Hoshaya, and still others both R. Hiya and R. Hoshaya. Indeed, Talmudic tradition records all three as being compilers of *mishnayot gedolot*, i.e. large mishna collections.[24]

It is easy to rule out Bar Kappara. Although a kind of pupil of Rabbi, he was of too independent a mind, and in addition a carrier of the tradition of the South as opposed to that of Galilee, to be considered the one Rabbi would mark for the carrying on of his work. More than once he was in conflict with Rabbi.

R. Hiya, however, was Rabbi's prime pupil, and the logical inheritor of his literary legacy. Although political leadership was handed down by Rabbi to his son, Rabban Gamliel be-Rabbi, not so with respect to the spiritual heritage.

---

[20] See bibliography of his writings in Strack, *Introduction*, 272 n. 11. Zuckermandel saw the Tosefta as the original Mishna edited by Rabbi; with relevant parts of the extant Mishna, it constituted the Mishna of the Palestinian Talmud which shows a greater closeness to the Tosefta than to the Mishna. Our Mishna is the work of Babylonian Amoraim who took the Tosefta, i.e. the Mishna of Rabbi, shortened it and arranged it according to Babylonian halakha and custom. The critique of Schwartz to Zuckermandel's theory is quoted by Strack, *Introduction*, 76. Other critiques worth mentioning are Albeck, *Babli and Yerushalmi*, 58 and Epstein, *Tannaitic Literature*, 250.

[21] *Babli and Yerushalmi*, 57.

[22] *Ib.* 73-5.

[23] *Iggeret Rav Sherira Gaon*, 34ff.

[24] *P.T. Hor.* 3, 48c; *Cant. R.* 8,1.

Here it was the quality of the man which counted, and it was found in R. Hiya. As we have fully detailed in our discussion on the Mishna, the accumulated teachings of the generation of Rabbi could find official editing only in the generation afterwards. But because the official editorship was no longer in the hands of the Patriarch, these teachings could not be incorporated in an 'official' Mishna, but had to be a continuation of the parallel work, the eventual Tosefta. It is this continuation of the Mishna in the Tosefta which most logically should be assigned to R. Hiya. Earlier Tosefta layers parallel to the Mishna were probably not edited by R. Hiya, but already had been existing as a separate compilation. It is very probable that even Rabbi himself had a hand in the earlier-layer compilation of the Tosefta. But what comes immediately after Rabbi, is almost undoubtedly the editing of R. Hiya.

The chief pupil of R. Hiya was R. Hoshaya, and there is logic in ascribing the editing of the Tosefta to him as well. For the continuation of the Mishna in the Tosefta consists of more than one layer. It is most likely that R. Hoshaya edited that Tosefta layer which consists of the teachings of R. Hiya and his generation. For all practical purposes, this second layer after the Mishna may be considered the last layer of the Tosefta. Yet here and there, teachings of R. Hoshaya himself found their way into the Tosefta, and we may therefore discern a very abbreviated third additional layer in the Tosefta whose editor may have been Rav, nephew of R. Hiya.

Tannaim Prominent in the Tosefta

In those Tosefta layers which parallel the Mishna, the same names of Tannaim appear as in the Mishna and approximately in the same frequency. We have listed the prime names of every generation of the Mishna period in the previous chapter. Here we shall enumerate those most prominent in the two Tosefta layers which continue the Mishna. We start with the fourth generation in our counting, that of R. Yehuda the Patriarch which figures to a limited extent already in the Mishna. While there will be some overlappings here, we are stressing now what is important for the Tosefta.

FOURTH GENERATION

R. Yehuda the Patriarch. Although editor of the Mishna, his own teachings are primarily in the Tosefta and the Tannaic midrash collections. His name occurs more than two hundred times in the Tosefta.

R. Natan. His teachings represent a Babylonian Tannaic point of view. They are found almost exclusively in the Tosefta, and, to a greater extent, in the Tannaic midrash collections, particularly in those of the school of R. Yishmael. According to one tradition, the anonymous baraita follows R. Natan.[25] He seems to be a slightly older contemporary of Rabbi, for he already figures as Head of the Court under the patriarch Rabban Shimon ben Gamliel. He is the carrier of a tradition attributing several differences of opinion between the schools of Shammai and Hillel.

R. Yose be-R. Yehuda. As an older contemporary of Rabbi, his name does find mention several times in the Mishna. It is, however, primarily in the Tosefta that he is mentioned, more than eighty times. Generally, he follows the line of his father, R. Yehuda ben Elai. Differences of opinion are mentioned between himself and Rabbi, as well as with R. Elazar be-R. Shimon.

R. Elazar be-R. Shimon. Although hardly mentioned by name in the Mishna, several anonymous mishnayot are said to be according to his opinion.[26] In the Tosefta his name is to be found close to sixty times. He is generally close to the teachings of his father, R. Shimon ben Yohai.

R. Elazar be-R. Yose. Son of R. Yose ben Halafta. Several anonymous mishnayot are said to be according to his opinion.[27] In the Tosefta he is mentioned close to thirty times.

R. Yose ben ha-Meshullam. Together with R. Shimon ben Menasia, he represents the group known as 'The Holy Congregation in Jerusalem'.[28] His name is to be found in the Mishna three times, and several anonymous mishnayot follow his opinion.[29] His name occurs with more frequency in the Tosefta.

R. Shimon ben Elazar. While he is mentioned a very few times in the Mishna, his name occurs more than 150 times in the Tosefta. He is considered to be the prime pupil of R. Meir, whose opinions he follows.

R. Menahem be-R. Yose. Another son of R. Yose ben Halafta. Several anonymous mishnayot are said to be according to his teaching. Like his brother, he is mentioned close to thirty times in the Tosefta.

It is clear that Rabbi and his contemporaries find their primary mention in the Tosefta, but occasionally do appear in the Mishna. Where they do, they may be considered in a sense as being part of the previous generation as well, i.e. of the pupils of R. Akiva.[30] There are, however, also younger contemporaries of Rabbi who are never mentioned in the Mishna, such as the two following.

R. Yishmael be-R. Yose. Brother of R. Elazar and R. Menahem. Member of Rabbi's council. He transmitted many traditions in the name of R. Yose, his father. He is never mentioned in the Mishna, but quite frequently in the Tosefta.

---

[25] According to the version of *B.T. Sanh.* 86a quoted *ib.* by Rashi and some other sources.
[26] Epstein, *Tannaitic Literature*, 174f.
[27] Epstein, *Tannaitic Literature*, 178f.
[28] Cf. Safrai, 'Holy Congregation'.
[29] Epstein, *Tannaitic Literature*, 183.
[30] See Goldberg, 'Tannaitic Teachers', esp. 88.

R. Shimon ben Menasia. Member of Rabbi's council. The other of the two known members of the 'Holy Assembly of Jerusalem' (see on R. Yose ben ha-Meshullam). He is quoted occasionally by Rabbi himself. His name occurs more than a score of times in the Tosefta. The one place where he appears in the Mishna (*Hag.* 1:7) is a later addition from the Tosefta.

FIFTH GENERATION

The second additional layer of Tannaic teaching, which may be considered the last layer of the Tosefta, is very small and contains the teachings of several of the fifth generation (our numbering), i.e. the last of the Tannaim.[31]

R. Hiya. Often known as Hiya the Elder. Originally from Kafri near Sura in Babylonia, he came to Palestine and became the prime pupil of Rabbi. It may well be that he played a part in the academy of Rabbi analogous to that of R. Natan, also a Babylonian, in the academy of Rabban Shimon ben Gamliel in the preceding generation. He, and not any of Rabbi's sons, is the spiritual heir of Rabbi. Ancient testimony, as well as the well-reasoned opinion of many scholars, attribute to him the editing of the Tosefta. While earlier layers may have been existing in edited form before him, in our view he is certainly the editor of the first additional layer not parallel to the Mishna. In a sense this is the most important layer, since it contains the teachings of Rabbi and his generation. He is mentioned twice in the Tosefta, and these teachings belong to the second additional layer of the Tosefta, edited, in all probability, by his pupil R. Hoshaya. In addition, several anonymous teachings in the Tosefta correspond to baraitot which are brought in the Talmudim in his name. As an older pupil of Rabbi, we find him occasionally discussing a topic on the same level as his teacher, and even disagreeing with him.[32] Most of his discussions and differences of opinion, however, are with those of his own generation.

Bar Kappara. A native of the South of Palestine, later a member of Rabbi's academy in Sepphoris, Galilee. The attribution to him of the editing of the Tosefta is very unlikely, for his general opinion was often not in harmony with that of Rabbi. He is never mentioned by name in the Tosefta, but two or three anonymous teachings in the Tosefta are recorded in the Talmud as being those of Bar Kappara.

Rabban Gamliel be-Rabbi. Elder son of Rabbi who succeeded him as Patriarch. He is mentioned only once in the Tosefta (*Sota* 6:8) in an aggadic frame, and once in the addition to the Mishna, *Avot* 2:2.

R. Shimon be-Rabbi. Appointed by his father to be the *hakham* in the academy.

---

[31] Many scholars do not consider these Sages as as real Tannaim but as semi-Tannaim belonging to a transition generation. See Strack, *Introduction*, 118. Because of his late dating of the Tosefta, Albeck, *Babli and Yerushalmi*, 144ff. does not give them even this status but relegates them to the early grouping of the first generation Palestinian Amoraim.

[32] See Albeck, *Babli and Yerushalmi, ib.*

He is not mentioned in the Tosefta, although his name does appear in the addition to the Mishna, *Makkot* 3:15. He received intense instruction in the Mishna which Rabbi compiled and apparently was close to his father in many aspects of its compilation and revision. He was especially familiar with the Tannaic midrash and even taught that on Leviticus to pupils of his father.[33] He is found differing rather frequently with R. Hiya on various matters of halakha and aggada.

R. Shimon ben Halafta. Mentioned in the addition to the Mishna at the end of *Uktsin*, as well as several times in *Sifrei*, but not in the Tosefta.

R. Simai. Mentioned once in *T. Shabb.* 12(13):14, once in *Sifrei* and several times in a baraita in the Talmud.

Bibliography

EDITIONS

For the manuscripts see below.

The first edition was printed as an appendix to Alfasi's compendium to the Talmud, Venice 1521-22. Additional printings followed frequently; see STRACK, *Introduction*, 272. Until this day the Tosefta is almost always printed in Talmud editions which include Alfasi, and since the Wilna 1880 edition with numerous commentaries.

ZUCKERMANDEL published his one-volume text of the Tosefta based on the Erfurt MS., 1877-82. Unfortunately, the Erfurt MS. is marred more than the others by adaptations to the Babylonian Talmud.

A fully scientific, annotated edition of the Tosefta was undertaken by LIEBER-MAN, *The Tosefta*. It is based on the superior Vienna MS., with variant readings from the first edition which is of almost equal quality, from the Erfurt and London MSS., and from the presently-known Geniza fragments. The first complete three Orders have appeared (see below); the first three tractates of the fourth Order are forthcoming, posthumously.

COMMENTARIES AND TRANSLATIONS

Unlike the Mishna and the Talmud, very few commentaries have been written on the Tosefta. It is true that early commentators to the Mishna and Talmud drew heavily on the Tosefta and incorporated it in very good measure in their commentaries, often digressing to explain the Tosefta itself. Thus R. SHIMSHON OF SENS (Provence, early 13th cent.) in his classic commentary to the Mishna Orders *Zeraim* and *Toharot* incorporates almost the entire Tosefta to these Orders. In this he was a follower of R. YITSHAK BEN MALKHI TSEDEK of Siponto

---

[33] *B.T. Kidd.* 33a.

(12th cent.) who quotes much of the Tosefta in the extant parts of his commentary to the same two Mishna Orders.

The first complete commentary which was preserved, as well as the most extensive, is that of R. DAVID PARDO. Three volumes were published in Leghorn (Livorno) 1776-90 and Jerusalem 1890, and reprinted Jerusalem 1971; the last three volumes, all on the Order of *Toharot*, appeared in Jerusalem 1970-77. Short sections of this commentary, not truly satisfactory, were also published in the Romm Wilna edition of the Talmud together with the Text of the Tosefta. The excellence of Pardo's commentary is universally recognized for its erudition as well as for the clear, logical explanations, and will always remain the prime traditional commentary to the Tosefta.

Almost all commentaries since Pardo have been partial ones, many, however, of excellent quality. Such is that of R. YONA BEN GERSHON to the Order *Zeraim*, Wilna 1809. Approximately half a century later R. Shemuel AVIGDOR published commentaries to the Orders *Zeraim, Moed* and *Kodashim* (Wilna 1855ff.), entitled *Minhat Bikkurim* and *Tosefot Ittur Bikkurim*. R. Yitshak SCHWADRON published a commentary to the Order *Zeraim*, Jerusalem 1910 and to the single tractate *Shabbat*, Jerusalem 1914. R. Yehezkel ABRAMSKY is an almost contemporary commentator to the Tosefta; his commentary *Hazon Yehezkel* to the Orders *Zeraim* (Wilna 1925) and *Moed* (Jerusalem 1934-55), as well as to various individual tractates from other Orders (detailed in Strack-Stemberger, *Einleitung*, 161), have been well received. Two commentaries which may be dismissed as of no importance are those of Shlomo PERLMUTTER and Arye (Adolph) SCHWARTZ, both late 19th century. A very important commentary to the Order *Moed* is that of R. Menahem NAHUM of Tchawess (Sklow 1819), in many respects surpassing that of David Pardo.

Matchless in their unusual combination of deep traditional learning and high-quality scientific method are the commentaries written by Saul LIEBERMAN. More than anyone else, he made the Tosefta a truly living book again, after a long period of neglect almost up to our time. His first commentary to the complete Tosefta, *Tosefet Rishonim* (Jerusalem 1937-39), emphasizes textual corrections based upon manuscripts and early editions as well as quotations in early authorities. Somewhat supplementary to this is his *Tashlum Tosefta*, published as an introductory chapter to the reprint of Zuckermandel's edition (Jerusalem 1937); it deals with Tosefta quotations in early authorities but not found in the extant text.

All this was preparatory to his crowning achievement, the new text edition (discussed above) which also includes a short commentary of explanatory notes on the page, and a parallel separate extensive commentary called *Tosefta ki-Fshutah*. Four volumes of text edition and eight volumes of commentary of this unprecedented life-work in the area of Jewish commentary appeared (New York 1955-73), covering the first three Orders. The first three tractates of the fourth Order are forthcoming posthumously. The great contribution of this commentary is its modern relevance, explaining Tannaic texts against the background of Hellenistic culture in an unequalled way. In addition, not only does it explain the Tosefta, but the Mishna, Palestinian and Babylonian Talmudim, as well as much of later Gaonic and medieval literature, come in for extensive discussion.

A Latin translation of the first, second and fifth Orders was made by Biagio UGOLINO in his *Thesaurus antiquitatum sacrarum*, Venice 1755-57.[34] The Hebrew text appears in a parallel column.

A German translation with commentary known as the RENGSTORF edition after the name of one of the general editors has been appearing since 1953 in Stuttgart. Not all of these tractates, however, have been published with the text. This edition gives attention to the readings of the Erfurt and Vienna MSS. and those of the *editio princeps*, as well as other MSS. and Geniza fragment readings where they exist. No general introduction has yet appeared, other than short prefaces. None of these, however, deal with the literary history of the Tosefta. The commentaries are not all of the same quality. In addition to the elucidation of the text of the Tosefta itself, the attempt is made to describe the relationship to the Mishna and Tannaic Midrash, as well as what might possibly relate (mostly formal linguistic) to Philo and early Christian literature. Lieberman's commentary is occasionally referred to.

Other German and English translations, which include isolated volumes, have been appearing, mostly in the first part of this century and most of doubtful quality.[35] A new English six-volume translation appeared under the general editorship of NEUSNER, *The Tosefta*. These translations however, which of necessity include commentary as well, must be used with care.

INTRODUCTIONS AND RESEARCH

There are not many handbooks which can tell us much about the Tosefta. MIELZIENER, *Introduction*, 17 gives half a page on the Tosefta (see also Additional Notes by FINKELSTEIN and BLOCH, *ib*. 282-3). In contrast to his wide coverage of the Mishna, STRACK, *Introduction* has only two pages of text and two of notes on the Tosefta (75, 273-5). This lacuna has been filled in the seventh edition, STRACK-STEMBERGER, *Einleitung*, 150-62, which gives general information and recent bibliography. While it gives satisfactory treatment of the various theories on the editing of the Tosefta, its relation to the Mishna and other issues, it, wisely, does not attempt to find new solutions to these questions. The one apparent attempt to resolve the problem of origin (157-8) comes far from what we have written here.

There is little on the Tosefta in general literature. It has been a work long neglected and has not really come into its own until the modern Hebrew

---

[34] See Strack, *Introduction*, 272.
[35] See list in Strack-Stemberger, *Einleitung*, 160f.

scholarly and critical renaissance in Palestine fifty years ago. It was LIEBERMAN, more than any other scholar, who gave renewed impetus to Tosefta study. His commentaries (see above) do have introductions, but these deal primarily with the history of Tosefta study and textual tradition. However, the commentary has many excursory observations which, when collected, would make much of an introduction.

The nearest we have to a general introduction is EPSTEIN'S 'Introduction to the Tosefta' published in his *Tannaitic Literature*, 241-62, which discusses the sources of the Tosefta, its editing, compilation, relationship to Mishna and Talmud as well as general characteristics of its teaching. To this we can add ALBECK'S Tosefta chapter in his *Babli and Yerushalmi*, 51-78, which reflects much of his earlier *Mehkarim*. Much in Albeck's writing, however, is coloured by his view of the Tosefta as a late Amoraic compilation.

Earlier scholarly writing, such as DÜNNER, *Tosephta*, is given mention in Strack, *Introduction*, 272. To these could be added SPANIER, *Toseftaperiode*, which advances the theory that the Tosefta originated from marginal notes appended to the Mishna. He also wrote *Mischnah und Tosefta*. Merely a curiosum in this connection is GUTTMAN, *Mischna und Tosephta*, which proposes the theory that the origin of the Tosefta is not in marginal notes, as held Spanier, but in modern-type card notations which, before being copied down, became disarranged; and this would account for the 'lack of order' in the Tosefta!

Very important and helpful in every Tosefta study is the six-volume concordance *Otsar leshon ha-Tosefta* by KASOWKSI.

The Tosefta Manuscripts

(by *Michael Krupp*)

The Tosefta forms a sort of margin to the Mishna: giving variants of it, collecting material left out of the Mishna and finally commenting on it. The first major collection of non-mishnaic material was given its final form shortly after the conclusion of the major work, perhaps as soon as a generation after. Appearing as a sort of step-sister of a great personage, the Tosefta made its way only with difficulty – which it surmounted to survive in three manuscripts. Only one of these is complete and another contains only one Order. In the Geniza fragments too it is far less frequent than the Mishna and the Talmudim.

MS. VIENNA Heb. 20 is the only complete manuscript, written in the thirteenth century, one column a page. It has the correctness which is a general feature in Spanish manuscripts. In spite of its Spanish origin, it retained the characteristics of the ancient Palestinian scripts. It belongs to the same family of texts as the first printed edition, which does not depend on it, however. So too it is very much akin to many Geniza fragments. This, and the completeness of the manuscript is why LIEBERMAN chose it as the text for his edition.

301

The second Tosefta manuscript, MS. ERFURT (now Berlin, Preussischer Kultur-besitz), is older, probably written in the twelfth century. A mark signifying a pledge or pawn transaction mentions the year 1260, but the MS. is certainly a hundred years older. ZUCKERMANDEL (*Erfurter Handschrift*) held that it was written in Italy, while M. LUTZKI (in Lieberman, *The Tosefta* 1) argues for Germany. But both agree that it is very ancient. Though the MS. can be proved to have been at Erfurt since the thirteenth century, it is probably rather of Italian origin. It is so like oriental manuscripts that Palestine cannot be excluded. The script is half-rabbinical. The MS. breaks off after the first chapter of *Zevahim*, either because the master copy ended here or because the scribe was prevented from going on. The MS. is conscientious like the Vienna; it contains more ancient, Palestinian types of writing than the Vienna. In some places the vocalization is ancient and unusual. MS. Erfurt represents another type of text than that of the printed edition, Vienna and the Geniza fragments, and hence is particularly valuable. Where available, ZUCKERMANDEL chose its text as the basis of his critical edition.

The third manuscript, MS. LONDON 445, is the latest. It is fifteenth century and in Spanish rabbinical script. It contains *Hullin* and the Order *Zeraim*, in a text differing from the previous ones. It often agrees with the Spanish (as in the Vienna printed edition and Geniza) but supporting variant readings in the Erfurt MS. It often goes its own way but the right one. These variants are printed in Lieberman's edition.

The GENIZA FRAGMENTS which, frequently, render intelligible corrupt places in all existing witnesses, are particularly important. They were exploited in Lieberman's edition, as also in the preliminary edition of Lieberman's *Tosefet Rishonim*, though very incompletely. But as Lieberman's edition only covered the first half of the Tosefta, a whole series of fragments is as yet unpublished and has not been drawn on for textual criticism of the Tosefta.

Chapter Seven

The Palestinian Talmud

Abraham Goldberg

Tannaim and Amoraim

The literary formulation and exposition of Oral Tora as expressed in the corpus of Tannaic literature reached culmination in the mid-third century C.E. The final editing of the Mishna, Toscfta and Tannaic midrash collections marked the end of a period. It was followed by two-and-a-half centuries of specialized commentary to the Tannaic corpus: the period of the Talmud. The literal meaning of the word *talmud* is 'teaching', and indeed the talmudic period is marked by intense commentary to, and extended teaching of, all that went before it.

The period of the Talmud is also known as the Amoraic period, after the teachers of this period who are designated *Amoraim*. This term derives from the verb אמר *amar* which means 'to say'. The Amora 'says' or 'explains', and his teachings are called ממרא *memra*, 'saying'. Thus this period is differentiated from the previous period whose teachers do not 'say' but 'teach' and are called Tannaim (from the Aramaic תנא *tana*, to teach); their teachings are called *matnita*, 'teaching', in Aramaic, or in the Hebrew parallel: *mishna*. The Tanna 'teaches'; the Amora 'says'. The distinction between Tanna and Amora is clearly made in the Talmud itself. Thus Rav Papa refers to 'two Tannaim or two Amoraim who differ with one another'.[1]

Yet despite these distinctions, the transition from the Tannaic to the Amoraic period is not clearly marked. The first generation of Babylonian Amoraim, for example, resemble in many ways the last generations of Palestinian Tannaim such as R. Hiya and R. Hoshaya, and their teachings are often indicated in the

---

[1] *B.T. Sanh.* 33a. A more specific use of the title Amora is to be found in *B.T. Sanh.* 17b, where it seems to indicate teachers of later generations. Thus Rav Huna and Rav Hisda, both of the second generation (250-300 C.E.) are designated סבי *Sabei*, 'elders', of Sura, whereas Rabba and Rav Yosef of the following generation, are called 'Amoraim of Pumbedita' and Rav Hama is called 'Amora of Nehardea'. A third, and very different, meaning of the term *Amora* is implied in its use to indicate the *meturgeman* who interprets in loud voice the soft-spoken words of the Sage in the academy or synagogue.

same way as Tannaic traditions.[2] Of the first-century Babylonian Amora Rav it is stated explicitly: 'Rav is a Tanna and may dispute a mishna or baraita.'[3] In other respects too, the Talmud is not just commentary to the Mishna which itself belongs to a clearly different period, but also an extension of the Mishna. In the course of its commentary on the Mishna it brings in almost every relevant Tannaic teaching, whether it be found in the extant Tannaic collections or in baraitot otherwise unknown. Regarding the last category, both Talmudim are very important sources for our knowledge of Tannaic teaching. Furthermore, the prime aim, especially of the Palestinian Talmud, is a further discussion of mishnayot in relation to other Tannaic halakhot, and in doing so it keeps very close to the direct meaning of the Mishna text.[4]

Palestinian and Babylonian Talmud

The Talmud is an extension of Tannaic teaching not only in time, but also in place. Simultaneously, two parallel processes of post-mishnaic teaching began, in Palestine and in Babylonia. While the Palestinian Talmud had its final editing at the end of the fourth century, the Babylonian Talmud was to grow for another century. Both Talmudim contain the edited discussions and halakhic decisions of the Sages of the various academies in Palestine and in Babylonia.

Although the two Talmudim emerged from two independent teaching traditions, these did not remain separate. They drew upon one another and have much material in common.[5] Thus many a completely Babylonian discussion will be included in the Palestinian Talmud, and, to a much greater extent, Palestinian teaching is found in the Babylonian Talmud, albeit often with characteris-

---

[2] Both Rav and Shmuel, and their schools, teach baraitot which originate with them. Thus we find: 'The *matnita* (= baraita) of Rav differs with him' (*P.T. Ber.* 2, 4c); 'Said R. Zeira, it has been taught (= a baraita) in *Ketuvot* of the school of Rav . . .' (*P.T. Ket.* 2, 26c). The phrase 'Shmuel taught' occurs scores of times (e.g. *B.T. Yoma* 70a; *Sukka* 56b). The verb used in this expression, *teni* in the Palestin Talmud and *tena* in the Babylonian, indicates a Tannaic teaching or baraita. Moreover, the very common 'the school of R. Yishmael taught' is very often a corruption of 'the school of Shmuel taught', as Epstein, *Nosah*, 213 pointed out. On the other hand, late Palestinian Tannaim such as R. Hiya and R. Hoshaya are often indicated as belonging to a 'transition generation'. Albeck, *Babli and Yerushalmi*, 144-63 even lists them as the first generation of Palestinian Amoraim.

[3] E.g. *B.T. Er.* 3b. This is not said explicitly of Shmuel, but his authority against a mishna or baraita is hardly less.

[4] Cf. Frankel, *Mavo ha-Yerushalmi*, 28b-31a.

[5] E.g. the leniencies of Palestinian Amoraim, and of their Babylonian colleagues, regarding work forbidden on intermediate festival days: compare *P.T. Moed K.* 2, 81b and *B.T. Moed K.* 12a-b. Again, Rav's exposition of the anonymous position and that of R. Yehuda in *M. Er.* 1:1, is found in both Talmudim (*P.T. Er.* 1, 18b; *B.T. Er.* 2a) and the parallel sugyot have many literary features in common.

tic changes.[6] The dependence of the Babylonian Talmud upon Palestinian teachings is especially marked in topics belonging to the Orders *Zeraim* and *Toharot*.[7] These close relations between both Talmudim are explained in part by the interchange of Sages between Palestine and Babylonia. In almost every generation, some of the greatest Palestinian Sages were Babylonians who had come to Palestine to study.[8] Most brought their own traditions with them and undoubtedly influenced the tone of Palestinian teaching.[9] At the same time, many Palestinian scholars for one reason or another left for Babylonia. A famous name in the early period is Ulla.[10] The causes for this exodus of Sages may not have been the disastrous outcome of an anti-Roman revolt in the mid-fourth century, as was supposed by historians following Graetz, but rather the difficult economic situation and the deteriorating position of the Patriarchate.[11]

In addition, in all periods special emissaries were appointed by the Palestinian academies to bring Palestinian teachings to their Babylonian colleagues. These emissaries were known as *nehutai*, 'those going down', i.e. from Palestine to Babylonia. In addition to Ulla, who also functioned as such an emissary, other important names are the early fourth-century Babylonian Amoraim Rav Dimi, Rav Abin, Rav Shmuel bar Yehuda and Rav Yitshak bar Yosef.[12]

Yet for all the similarity between the two Talmudim, a world of difference remains. This is reflected both in external form and in content. Externally, the language and the form of editing differ considerably. The non-Hebrew portions of the Palestinian Talmud are in the western Aramaic dialect, whereas in the Babylonian Talmud these are in Eastern Aramaic. Greek words appear quite frequently in the Palestinian Talmud, in contrast to the Persian often found in its Babylonian counterpart. As for editing, the Babylonian Talmud underwent

---

[6] For example, many differences of opinion between the first generation Amoraim R. Yohanan and R. Shimon ben Lakish as recorded in the Palestinian Talmud are reversed in the Babylonian. Even individual statements in the name of R. Yohanan (e.g. *P.T. Ket.* 8, 32b) are ascribed to R. Shimon ben Lakish (*B.T. Ket.* 82a). The exigencies of the Babylonian *sugya* may often make far-reaching changes in the content of the Palestinian tradition.

[7] See Sussman, *Babylonian Sugyot*, who argues forcefully that in all cases where topics from *Zeraim* or *Toharot* are discussed, the Babylonian Talmud bases itself upon a primary Palestinian discussion.

[8] R. Hiya, a Babylonian, studied at Rabbi's academy; so did Rav, but he returned to Babylonia. The outstanding pupil of R. Yohanan was the Babylonian R. Elazar ben Pedat. So were the great scholars of the next generation, R. Yirmeyahu and R. Zeira.

[9] In this respect, R. Zeira stands out. See Goldberg, 'R. Zeira'.

[10] Rav Hisda (2nd half 3d cent.) refers to him as 'our teacher who came down from Palestine', *B.T. Ber.* 38b.

[11] Lieberman, 'Palestine', having thoroughly examined the talmudic and other sources, states that there is no evidence for a Jewish rebellion in the 3rd or 4th cents. The abolition of the Patriarchate in the early 5th cent. was probably the main cause for the 'completion' of the Palestinian Talmud (thus, among others, G. Stemberger in a public lecture, Hebrew University, January 1987; see below n. 44).

[12] These find mention in the Palestinian Talmud as well, except that Rav Dimi goes by the name Rav Avdimi (Abduma) *nahuta* (*P.T. Er.* 1, 19b *et al.*). The phrase 'when Rav Dimi came' (and brought a Palestinian teaching) occurs several hundred times in the Babylonian Talmud, most frequently together with Rav Abin, both bringing variant traditions from Palestine (e.g. *B.T. Shabb.* 72a, 134a, 147a). All four are mentioned together in *B.T. Av.* 73a.

a post-talmudic re-editing which gave it its polished and consistent literary form. It also included additional discussions by the Sages living between the talmudic and Gaonic periods who are known by the name of Savoraim. Compared with this highly developed form, the Palestinian Talmud is much simpler. Differences of content are also quite extensive, although, as stated, both Talmudim have much in common. One of these differences is in the interpretation of the Tannaic sources on which both Talmudim rely. This is related not only to differences in the traditions of interpretation, but also reflects a range of differences in the political, cultural and economic conditions peculiar to each country.[13]

Another difference between both Talmudim is in the aggada they contain. It accounts for about one-sixth of the Palestinian Talmud; the Babylonian Talmud has almost a third. The aggada is often interwoven with the halakha, or may serve as a signature to extended halakhic discussions. Thus it does much to reveal the deep spirituality of seemingly dry halakha. Taken as a literary device, it serves as a variation from the purely intellectual halakhic style. This material goes by the name aggada which is, as Louis GINZBERG wrote, 'a very comprehensive term which includes theology and religious philosophy, folklore and history, mathematics and astronomy, medicine and natural science, and many other subjects.' In this respect, however, there is not only a difference in proportion of material between both Talmudim. Angelology and demonology figure prominently in the Babylonian Talmud, but are almost entirely absent in the Palestinian. Angels, with the exception of Michael and Gabriel who are already mentioned in the Bible, are rarely mentioned, nor do those which appear have names, individuality and specific spheres of activity as they do in the Babylonian Talmud. There is also comparatively little of sorcery, magic, astrology and other popular beliefs in the Palestinian Talmud.[14]

There are differences as well in coverage of the Mishna. There is no Babylonian Talmud to the first Order, *Zeraim*, except for the special first tractate, *Berakhot*. The Palestinian Talmud, however, covers the whole Order of *Zeraim*. Conversely, there is no Palestinian Talmud to the fifth Order, *Kodashim*, while there is Babylonian Talmud to it, except for the tractates *Middot* and *Kinnim*. As for the last Order, *Toharot*, both Talmudim are equal: they have only the tractate *Nidda*. The Babylonian Talmud, furthermore, has no coverage of tractate *Shekalim* in the Order of *Moed*; the Talmud tractate printed in traditional Babylonian Talmud editions in reality is taken from the Palestinian

---

[13] See Ginzberg, *Commentary*, 23-36 for a list of such differences reflected in Babylonian and Palestinian halakha.

[14] Ginzberg, *Commentary*, 34-6, although the absence of these matters from the Palestinian Talmud is somewhat exaggerated.

Talmud. Again, both Talmudim are equal in not covering tractates *Avot* and *Eduyot*; these, as we saw above, have a special character.[15]

Importance of the Palestinian Talmud

It is not because the Palestinian Talmud came first, that we begin our discussion with it. The literary creation process out of which the Talmudim emerged, started simultaneously in Palestine and in Babylonia. The Palestinian Talmud, however, does have a primacy in that it is closest in literary tradition and material conditions to Tannaic literature, which was created almost exclusively in Palestine. This is also what its name implies: the Talmud of those in Palestine.[16] This is the one reason why the Tosefta and Tannaic midrashim are quoted in the Palestinian Talmud almost without change in wording, whereas the Babylonian Talmud often introduces major or minor changes.[17] For the understanding of Tannaic literature, therefore, the Palestinian Talmud is of prime importance. The same is reflected in the difference between Babylonian and Palestinian versions of the same narrative. In most cases, the Palestinian version should be given historical priority.[18]

The distinctive literary unit created in the talmudic discussion and characterizing it, is called the *sugya* (lit. course, lesson). It is a unique arrangement of sources and comments. As we shall see in the next chapter, it attains a fully developed literary form in the Babylonian Talmud, to such an extent that sometimes the literary brilliance obscures the sources on which it is based. In the Palestinian Talmud, the sugya is much simpler; this is another reason why it is much truer to the Tannaic sources. The Palestinian sugya is usually short and concise, with scarce editorial introductions and connections, often to the point of being enigmatic. It may consist of no more than the juxtaposition of a Tannaic text in seeming variance with a mishna, and a reconciliation of the two. Or it may begin with an Amoraic statement to which Tannaic sources or other Amoraic statements are found to relate either in support or in opposition; if the latter, there may be an attempt to smooth out the differences.[19]

---

[15] The question why certain Orders and tractates lack Talmud has occupied many scholars. Especially intriguing is *Kodashim* which has Babylonian Talmud but no Palestinian. Moreover, many believed that even as late as the Middle Ages, Palestinian Talmud to *Kodashim* was still extant. The best discussion of the entire question, including a full critique of all previous writing on the subject, is Sussman, *Babylonian Sugyot*. See also the discussion of the missing tractates, and especially of the Order *Kodashim*, in Strack-Stemberger, *Einleitung*, 165-8; Bokser, 'Guide', 165-8.

[16] While the current Hebrew designation is *Talmud Yerushalmi* (descending from the medieval practice of naming the main city for the land) it is known among early authorities as תלמודא דארץ ישראל 'Talmud of the Land of Israel', תלמוד דמערבא 'Talmud of the West' and the like. See Strack, *Introduction*, 65; Bokser, 'Guide', 149-51.

[17] Epstein, *Tannaitic Literature*, 246; Frankel, *Mavo ha-Yerushalmi*, 22a-23a.

[18] Cf. Safrai, 'Tales of the Sages'.

[19] Cf. Frankel, *Mavo ha-Yerushalmi*, 31a-37a.

The Palestinian Talmud represents a literary creation process of close to two centuries, during which development in literary form was inevitable. This development, however, is but modest when compared to that of the Babylonian Talmud which, even apart from its post-talmudic re-editing, lasted for at least a century after the completion of the Palestinian. A comparison of those sugyot in which only the early generations of Babylonian Sages figure will show that the Babylonian sugya at this time was not substantially different from the Palestinian one.[20] Moreover, development of the sugya in the Palestinian Talmud is especially marked in its later generations of Amoraim, who correspond in time to the middle generations of Amoraim in Babylonia (350-400 C.E.). Thus it is understandable that we find Babylonian sugyot in the Palestinian Talmud.[21] Less surprising is, that the Babylonian Talmud contains many Palestinian sugyot.[22]

In this respect, the special value of the Palestinian Talmud, with all its enigmatic brevity, comes out once again. The sugya is a literary form which develops from generation to generation, and some sugyot reveal the contributions of all the generations. The sugya then becomes a chain of several links, usually independent of one another. Often, however, the chain was shortened in the final editing, the middle link or links being eliminated, and the sugya in its present form retaining only the first and last links of the chain. Where such a sugya from the Babylonian Talmud appears in the Palestinian as well, the chain will end somewhere parallel to the middle of the Babylonian chain, in accordance with the earlier completion date. In these cases, the Palestinian sugya helps us to reconstruct the missing middle links of the Babylonian sugya.[23]

The Palestinian Amoraim and the Mishna

We now address ourselves to the question of how the Palestinian Amoraim related to the Mishna. Did they accept all its teachings, or did they differ with it; or, alternatively, did they try to emend its text? Here, however, we come up to a serious methodical problem.

As we pointed out in our chapter on the Mishna, the Mishna of the Palestinian Talmud is not always identical with that of the Babylonian; there is little doubt that it is closer to the version edited by Rabbi Yehuda the Patriarch. We are referring here, however, to the Mishna text which the Palestinian Talmud itself presupposes. The version which appears chapter by chapter as the heading of each respective Talmud chapter does not always correspond with the text on which the Palestinian *sugya* seems to have been based. It was appended by the printers from available manuscripts which were already influenced by Babylo-

---

[20] See Klein, 'Gemara and Sebara'; 'Gemara Quotations'; 'Some Methods'; 'Significance'.
[21] Epstein, *Tannaitic Literature*, 312-4; Frankel, *Mavo ha-Yerushalmi*, 40a-45a.
[22] Frankel, *Mavo ha-Yerushalmi*, 41a-b.
[23] For examples see Goldberg, *Eruvin*, 44 n. 23; 102 and n. 16; 287 n. 17.

nian textual traditions. It is only the careful study of the Palestinian Talmud itself which can determine the exact Mishna reading which the Palestinian Amoraim had before them.[24]

The leading Sage of the first generation of Amoraim in Palestine, i.e. middle third century c.e., and indeed the most important figure in the entire Palestinian Talmud, is R. Yohanan.[25] His long life spanned the last Tannaic generation and three of the Amoraim. His prime teacher was R. Yannai, a pupil of R. Yehuda the Patriarch, but he also learned from several others of that generation: Hizkia, R. Hanina, R. Hoshaya and R. Shimon ben Yehotsadak. He was most familiar with the baraitot, i.e. the 'extraneous' halakhot not incorporated in the Mishna, and he himself was a *tanna* whose task it was to recite the baraitot in the sessions of the academy.[26]

R. Yohanan regarded the Mishna as a halakhic code rather than a text-book of halakha. However, while he usually follows its teaching, he does not necessarily do so always.[27] He saw the Tosefta and other baraitot as the prime source for a proper understanding of the Mishna, and he almost invariably interpreted the Mishna in harmony with them, even if that implied forcing the meaning of the Mishna.[28] Very remarkable, and almost modern, is his awareness of conflicting opinions within anonymous mishnayot, and he did not attempt to reconcile them even where this seemed most natural.[29] Other Amoraim would try to explain contradictions between different anonymous mishnayot, or even within a single mishna, by positing different situations. But here, R. Yohanan was not prepared to harmonize and preferred to assume different sources, following the principle laid down by his great teacher R. Hoshaya: 'He who taught this (anonymous section) did not teach that one.'[30] In another formulation this

---

[24] Schachter, *Babylonian and Jerusalem Mishnah*, deals with this problem but not in a sufficiently scientific way. The book covers only a selection of less than 150 mishnayot; the author's tendency to accept the Babylonian Mishna readings as primary is entirely unacceptable. Truly critical and of much value is Feintuch, 'Mishna of the MS. Leiden'. A comprehensive and fully detailed treatment of the whole problem is a prior aim of Epstein's main work, *Nosah*.

[25] Outstanding in scope and depth is the discussion of R. Yohanan's attitude to the Mishna and his contribution to the formulation of the Palestinian Talmud in Epstein, *Nosah*, 234-85.

[26] The set phrase תני ר' יוחנן 'R. Yohanan taught' (e.g. *P.T. Kidd.* 1, 58c; *B.T. Pes.* 118a) refers to his teaching a baraita. So does the phrase 'I teach' (*B.T. Shabb.* 66b) and forms of the verb שנה. See Epstein, *Nosah*, 239f.

[27] Cf. his phrase: 'I have only the Mishna to go by', *P.T. Ter.* 2, 41c. Occasionally, he rejects an anonymous teaching with the phrase, 'This is no (authoritative) mishna (being an individual opinion)' (*B.T. Yev.* 43a with reference to *M. Kel.* 13:8). See Epstein, *Nosah*, 241-4, 262-73.

[28] See Epstein, *Nosah*, 47, 68, 160, 223, 244f. In accordance with a baraita he interprets, e.g., the 'dough prepared for dogs' (*M. Halla* 1:6) as being prepared in amorphous form (*P.T. Halla* 1, 58a), even though the Mishna itself seems to define it in terms of quality: 'as long as shepherds can eat of it'.

[29] The first half of *M. Bava M.* 3:9 he takes as giving the view of R. Yishmael and the second as that of R. Akiva, stating: 'Anyone who will explain to me (this mishna of) "jug" according to only one Tanna, I shall be willing to carry his clothes after him to the bath-house.' Other Amoraim, however, offer harmonizing explanations by positing different situations (*B.T. Bava M.* 41a).

[30] His approach is well-put in *B.T. Sanh.* 62b: 'R. Yohanan does not explain the first part (of a mishna) by one situation and the last part by another.' See Epstein, *Nosah*, 241f.

maxim reads: 'Two different teachers taught here.'[31] Viewing the Mishna as a halakhic code, he established the important principle that its editor gave the anonymous opinion or that of 'the Sages' as the accepted halakha.[32] Thus one mishna will teach the opinion of one Sage anonymously and another will give the differing view of another Sage, also anonymously, even though the underlying principle in both mishnayot seems to be the same.[33]

The great contemporary of R. Yohanan was his friend (in the Babylonian aggada, his brother-in-law)[34] R. Shimon ben Lakish.[35] Originally from the South of Palestine, he was attracted, like many from his area, to the Galilee, the greatest center of learning as well as the seat of the Patriarch. Yet he never gave up the traditions of his native area.[36] He is the chief opponent of R. Yohanan in halakhic discussions, differing with him not only on particular questions but in general principles as well.

Whereas R. Yohanan interpreted the Mishna on the basis of the baraita, R. Shimon ben Lakish insisted that the Mishna be interpreted only on what could be inferred from the Mishna itself. He had almost a contempt for the extra-mishnaic collections: 'If Rabbi did not teach such (in his Mishna), how could R. Hiya (Rabbi's chief pupil and compiler of baraitot) know it?'[37] On the contrary, it is only the Mishna which can be used to confirm the teachings of the baraita: 'This is likewhat Rabbi taught . . .'[38] Wherever possible, he preferred to explain away seeming contradictions within a mishna by positing different situations as necessitating different rules.[39] Yet he, too, upon occasion would not accept an anonymous teaching as binding, arguing, as sometimes did R. Yohanan himself, that the anonymous teaching in various mishnayot was only an individual point of view.[40]

The chief pupil of R. Yohanan and the leading scholar of the next generation in Palestine (later third century C.E.) was a Babylonian by birth, R. Elazar ben Pedat.[41] He followed R. Yohanan's general approach to the Mishna, but also brought with him elements of Babylonian teaching. With the passing of the generations, much Babylonian teaching was taken over in Palestine, especially

---

[31] *P.T. Halla* 1, 58a.

[32] See *P.T. Yev.* 4, 6b; *B.T. Shabb.* 46a.

[33] E.g. *B.T. Hull.* 85a.

[34] Cf. Safrai, 'Tales of the Sages', 229-32.

[35] See Epstein, *Nosah*, 285-92.

[36] His first teachers were in Judea: In Lydda, Bar Kappara whom he quotes frequently (*P.T. Pes.* 1, 28a *et al.*); in Caesarea, R. Hoshaya whom he asks for a teaching (*B.T. Yev.* 57a) and whose teachings he quotes (*B.T. Pes.* 34b *et al.*). Of him it is said that he 'went into exile to study' (*P.T. Kil.* 9, 32d) from his native Judea to Galilee.

[37] *B.T. Nidda* 62b.

[38] *B.T. Yev.* 41a.

[39] It is he who remarks with reference to R. Yannai's 'forced' interpretation of *M. Kidd.* 3:6, 'We give a forced explanation, positing different situations, rather than posit different sources' (*B.T. Kidd.* 63b).

[40] *B.T. Yoma* 81a *et al.* See Epstein, *Nosah*, 287f.

[41] See Epstein, *Nosah*, 292-307.

since many of the leading scholars in almost every generation were Babylonian in origin. In this respect the name of R. Zeira is outstanding, for he cleverly tried to show (what he probably believed honestly) that the great Palestinian Sage, R. Yohanan, really taught Babylonian halakha![42]

Five generations of Sages, counting the generation of R. Yohanan and R. Shimon ben Lakish as the first, make their appearance in the Palestinian Talmud.[43] Many scholars date the decline of the Palestinian academies from 351 C.E., when the three important cities Tiberias, Sepphoris and Lydda, seats of the academies, are believed to have suffered greatly in the outbreaks against the Roman commander Ursicinus.[44] Many of the Sages emigrated to Babylonia. The extinction of the Patriarchate in 425 C.E. marks as well a final date for the Palestinian Talmud.[45]

Relationship to Mishna, Tosefta and Baraitot

After the Tosefta, the Palestinian Talmud is considered the most important source in all that concerns a basic interpretation of the Mishna. As we have pointed out above, the *sugya* of the Palestinian Talmud, unlike that of the Babylonian, is in most cases very brief, and it is also closely related to the Tosefta. Very characteristic is the opening of a *sugya* on the Mishna with a quotation from the Tosefta, either with the introductory term *teni* or without.

The Tosefta, as we have already observed in our previous chapter, is for the most part quoted literally in the Palestinian Talmud, and if there are occasional changes, they are minor. In many ways the Palestinian Talmud is a kind of extension of the Tosefta, as the Tosefta is of the Mishna. It will continue debates of the Tannaim begun in the Tosefta.[46] Again, just as the Tosefta will add to a topic taken up in the Mishna by a discussion of situations not brought up in the Mishna, so, too, will the Palestinian Talmud discuss situations not brought up in the Tosefta.[47]

The Tosefta serves the Palestinian Talmud as the prime source for the interpretation of the Mishna, and its interpretations of the Mishna are much closer, therefore, than those in the Babylonian Talmud; and although the latter

[42] See Goldberg, 'R. Zeira'.
[43] A full list of Palestinian Amoraim, arranged alphabetically, and commented upon, is given by Frankel, *Mavo ha-Yerushalmi*, 53-132. An even better presentation, according to the generations, is found in Albeck, *Babli and Yerushalmi*, 144-451.
[44] See Ginzberg, *Commentary*, 38; Marx - Margolis, *History*, 229.
[45] See Marx - Margolis, *History*, 230. Epstein, *Amoraitic Literature*, 274 points out that two generations of Amoraim (those of R. Mana and R. Yose be-R. Bun and of R. Shmuel be-R. Yose be-R. Bun) find mention after the generation contemporary with Ursicinus (that of R. Yona and R. Yose), and he estimates this to be a period of about fifty years. The end of the Palestinian Talmud he places, therefore, at 410-420 C.E.
[46] See e.g. Goldberg, *Eruvin*, 255.
[47] Goldberg, *Eruvin*, 11, 25, 35, 60, 127.

does make use of the Tosefta, it is not to the same extent.[48] Questions in the Palestinian Talmud are often resolved by recourse to the Tosefta.[49]

Occasionally, however, the Palestinian Talmud will differ with the Tosefta[50] and may even 'correct' the language of the Tosefta in accordance with its own interpretation of the Mishna.[51]

The Palestinian Talmud also shows an attitude of relative independence in its interpretation of the Mishna. This is indicated in several ways: a correction given to the Mishna without recourse to the Tosefta;[52] independent interpretations to seemingly redundant language in the Mishna;[53] limitations to the teaching in the Mishna;[54] or independent definitions.[55]

The Tosefta, of course, is not the only source of extra-mishnaic Tannaic teaching in the Palestinian Talmud. The Tannaic midrash is quoted extensively, as it is in the Babylonian Talmud.[56] So, too, are collections of baraitot, attributed to the School of Rabbi, Bar Kappara, R. Hiya, R. Oshaya, the School of R. Yishmael, the School of R. Akiva and the School of R. Shmuel (first generation Babylonian Amora). Most baraitot, even if their source can be determined, are quoted anonymously. A listing of baraitot of R. Hiya and those of R. Oshaya is given by the late American scholar Michael HIGGER, who collected and classified all the baraitot in both Talmudim.[57]

The question of a baraita being quoted sometimes as an Amoraic dictum will be taken up in our discussion of the Babylonian Talmud.

Editing

Four great centers of learning existed during the Amoraic period in Palestine: Tiberias and Sepphoris in Galilee, Lydda and Caesarea in the South. All of these figure to some extent in the Tannaic period.[58]

---

[48] *Ib.* 189, 221, 282.
[49] *Ib.* 196.
[50] *Ib.* 31.
[51] *Ib.* 124.
[52] *Ib.* 155.
[53] *Ib.* 198.
[54] *Ib.* 230.
[55] *Ib.* 239.
[56] The question of relationship will be taken up in our chapter on the Tannaic midrash collections.
[57] *Otsar ha-Baraitot* 2, 141f.; 204f.
[58] Two of these were prime centres at the end of the Tannaic period: Sepphoris and Lydda. The centre at Lydda is generally referred to as 'the South', as in the phrases: 'a *matnita* of Bar Kappara from the South' (*P.T. Shev.* 4, 35d *et al.*); 'our Masters in the South' (*B.T. Er.* 66b; *P.T. Er.* 6, 23c); 'the elders of the South' (*B.T. Hull.* 132b). Sepphoris had long been established as the spiritual centre of the Galilee, leadership of which was handed down from father to son: R. Halafta (a contemporary of R. Akiva), R. Yose (R. Akiva's well-known pupil) and R. Yishmael (a contemporary of Rabbi).

The oldest part of the Palestinian Talmud was edited in Caesarea, the seat of the Roman government in Palestine, in the middle of the fourth century.[59] This 'oldest' Talmud consists of short comments, of almost exclusively halakhic content, to the first three tractates of *Nezikin*. Not only in its brevity does it differ from the rest of the Talmud, but also in style and terminology.[60] Although the differences in place and time of compilation have left their imprint, it is conceivable that the Talmud which at the same time was taught at Tiberias might have resembled in many ways the 'primitive' character of this oldest section.

This oldest part, *Bava Kamma*, *Bava Metsia* and *Bava Batra*, goes now by the name *Talmuda shel Kisrin*, the Talmud of Caesarea, as LIEBERMAN termed it, in contrast to the later editing of the Palestinian Talmud which he called 'The Talmud of Tiberias'.[61] In many ways, it represents the tradition of Judea, as opposed to that of Galilee, and the names of the Amoraim which appear are primarily of the early generations.[62] There are special affinities to the Babylonian Talmud, which in general seems to be closer to Judean than to Galilean tradition.[63]

This theory found confirmation in the Palestinian Talmud contained in the Escorial MS., one of the most fascinating discoveries made recently by the late E. S. ROSENTHAL (see below). This superior manuscript (the Geniza fragments included) preserves the Palestinian Aramaic more closely than the Leiden MS. which is already influenced by the Babylonian Talmud; Greek words are much less mutilated. The Escorial MS. confirms Lieberman's theory of the Caesarean redaction, although some details now require revision. It can be shown, for example, that terms which he took to be uniquely characteristic of the Caesarean edition are only variations in the textual tradition.

The rest of the Palestinian Talmud – namely, the first three Orders and the remaining tractates of the Fourth plus *Nidda* of the Fifth – were edited at Tiberias. Some scholars see the Palestinian Talmud as simply a jotting down of

---

[59] Here we follow Lieberman, *Talmuda shel Kisrin*. Epstein, *Amoraitic Literature*, 279-86 does recognize the strong Caesarean influence in the first three tractates of *Nezikin*, but strongly rejects Lieberman's theory of the prior editing of these tractates. In the 1968 re-capitulation of his *Talmuda shel Kisrin*, 125-36, Lieberman rebuts Epstein's arguments.

[60] The otherwise common phrase עבידא היו 'how can it happen', for example, does not occur here. On the other hand, terms otherwise unknown in the Palestinian Talmud occur, such as והיכי 'and how', i.e. in which situation; and דאמרין כן ואינון, 'and those say thusly', introducing a Babylonian teaching, instead of the usual אמרין תמן 'there they say'. See Lieberman, *Talmuda shel Kisrin*, 7f.

[61] *Talmuda shel Kisrin*, viif.

[62] E.g. 'The school of Levi', which is mentioned four times in these tractates, but not once elsewhere in the Palestinian Talmud (but 'The school of Levi taught' does appear in the Babylonian Talmud). On the other hand, the names of later Amoraim hardly occur. See Lieberman, *Talmuda shel Kisrin*, 6. *Ib*. 9-10, Lieberman gives a list of Amoraim born in Caesarea or otherwise connected with it.

[63] See especially the traditions ascribed to 'The rabbis of Caesarea'. Goldberg, *Shabbat*, 22, 182 emphasizes this parallel.

academic discussion without organization or final reworking.[64] However, it should be emphasized that there was a conscious editing, expressed among other things in a definite plan and arrangement, although it is certainly true that it did not reach the degree of perfection of the Babylonian Talmud. Those attuned to the latter do not often fully appreciate the individual character of the Palestinian Talmud.

Although the greater part of the Palestinian Talmud was edited in Tiberias, it is not the work of one school. Frequent references are made to the scholars of Sepphoris, and to those of Lydda and Caesarea, although the last-mentioned occur somewhat less frequently. The Tiberian editors, of course, incorporated in their work the three treatises of the Caesarean Talmud. And, as we have pointed out in detail, many discussions of the Babylonian academies are introduced as well.

Authority

The Palestinian Talmud remained the Talmud of the Jews in Palestine for a great many years after the editing of the Babylonian Talmud, even though the latter was superior in range and literary quality. The same situation prevailed in adjacent Egypt; and in Kairwan and even as far as Southern Italy, the Palestinian Talmud was of great influence. A work from the mid-seventh century which was discovered fairly recently among the Cairo Geniza fragments, *Sefer ha-Maasim*,[65] indicates that in its day Palestinian Jewry still had one Talmud, i.e. the Palestinian.

This was the situation until the establishment of the caliphate in Baghdad in the eighth century, when Abassid Babylonia became the center not only of Arabic but also of Jewish culture. From then on, the influence of the Babylonian Talmud began to suppress the Palestinian Talmud. However, in Kairwan it continued to be studied; R. Nissim ibn Shahin and R. Hananael maintained it in the curriculum at an equal place with the Babylonian Talmud. Alfasi, the eleventh century scholar from Northern Africa who became the leading authority of Spanish Jewry, incorporated much Palestinian material in his digest of the Babylonian Talmud, most of it as it was already found in the commentary to the Babylonian Talmud of his great teacher, R. Hananael. Even Maimonides, two generations later, used the Palestinian Talmud for his commentary to the Mishna,[66] and occasionally, when deciding contrary to the Babylonian Talmud, in his Code;[67] he even composed a digest to the Palestinian Talmud on the

---

[64] See Strack-Stemberger, *Einleitung*,169f.
[65] See below, pp. 405-7.
[66] Especially to the Order *Zeraim*, to which there is no Babylonian Talmud apart from *Berakhot*.
[67] Again, the seventh book of his Code, *Sefer Zeraim* relies heavily on the Palestinian Talmud.

pattern of Alfasi's digest to the Babylonian.[68] Although students from the Byzantine empire and from all parts of Europe – Italy, Spain, Provence – came to study in the Babylonian center in Baghdad, and subsequently brought its Talmud back home with them, the Palestinian Talmud was not entirely displaced. It continued to be well known in Spain and the Provence, and the first known commentary, now lost, to the Palestinian Talmud was by R. Yitshak ha-Kohen, a younger contemporary of Maimonides from the Provence. Although Rashi in eleventh century France knew it only second hand in all probability, the spreading influence of R. Hananael's commentary and his frequent mention of the Palestine Talmud, brought with it a desire to know the original. The French Tosafists of the twelfth and thirteenth centuries as well as their contemporaries in Germany had a thorough familiarity with it.[69]

It is paradoxical that Alfasi, who did incorporate much from the Palestinian Talmud in his halakhic compendium, was in a way responsible for its later decline. Following a Gaonic tradition, he laid down the rule that where the two Talmudim are in conflict decisions are to be made in accordance with the Babylonian. The Babylonian Talmud is to be considered authoritative, he wrote, since it was later, and its Sages undoubtedly knew of the Palestinian teaching, yet were convinced that their own point of view was the more correct one.[70]

The sufferings and persecutions of Jews in Europe during the fourteenth and fifteenth centuries made Talmud study difficult. It was hard enough to hold to even one Talmud, and the study of another one of lesser authority seemed too much of a luxury for those times. The one exception was in Spain where the Palestinian Talmud continued to be studied. It is not surprising, therefore, that our first extant commentary to the Palestinian Talmud was written by R. Shlomo Syrileio, a native of Spain who emigrated to Palestine after the expulsion of 1492, where he composed his commentary to the Order of *Zeraim* and tractate *Shekalim* in the first third of the sixteenth century.

---

[68] Two fragments are extant, one to *Berakhot* chs. 1-6 (published by Ginzberg in *Yerushalmi Fragments*, 29-36) and another to sections of *Ketubot* chs. 1-8 (published in *Tarbiz* 3 [1931] 21-36). These have been republished with introduction and full commentary by Lieberman, *Hilkhot Ha-Yerushalmi*. Lieberman points to the definite pattern of this digest. Maimonides omits all laws already found in the Babylonian Talmud, and for the most part those which contradict the conclusions of the latter, except for certain cases where the Palestinian discussion can also shed light on the accepted Babylonian halakha.

[69] Two of the latter are R. Eliezer ben Natan of Mayence (1090-1170) and R. Eliezer ben R. Yoel Halevi (1140-1220). As for Italy, the most important figure who has reference to the Palestinian Talmud is R. Natan author of the prime dictionary, the *Arukh*, in the twelfth century.

[70] Alfasi, end of *Eruvin*, 104b. An extensive discussion of the vicissitudes of the Palestinian Talmud and its influence over the generations is to be found in Ginzberg, *Commentary*, introd., 41-50.

Bibliography

COMMENTARIES

There is nothing for the Palestinian Talmud comparable to the Babylonian Talmud commentaries of Rashi and the Tosafists. We have just made mention of the first extant commentary to the Order *Zeraim* and Tractate *Shekalim* written by R. SHLOMO SYRILEIO. Only one really full commentary exists, however, and that is the eighteenth century double commentary *Penei Moshe* and *Mare ha-Penim* by R. MOSHE MARGOLIOT, incorporated fully for the first time in the Zhitomir edition, 1860-67. A brief and rather fragmentary commentary to the entire Palestinian Talmud, written by R. DAVID DARSHAN, had already appeared in the Cracow edition of 1609 and was reprinted later in the Krotoshin edition.[71] Next in importance to the *Penei Moshe* is the *Korban ha-Eda* (with a supplement entitled *Sheyarei Korban*) of R. DAVID FRAENKEL of Berlin (1704-62) on the Orders of *Moed*, *Nashim* and part of *Nezikin*. This commentary was intended in a way to supplement the commentary of R. ELIYAHU FULDA, which was limited to fifteen tractates.[72] Another important commentary is that of R. YOSHUA BENVENISTE on eighteen tractates.[73]

Although all these larger commentaries undoubtedly help much in understanding the Palestinian Talmud, they all suffer from a Babylonian bias in their interpretation. Where the two Talmudim differ, a reconciliation is often attempted, usually without success. It is only in relatively modern times that the principle has been established that each Talmud should be explained in terms of its own individuality.

Perhaps the greatest impetus to the renewed interest in the Palestinian Talmud during the last two centuries was the work of R. ELIYAHU GAON of Wilna (1720-97). Indeed, the most intensive study of the Palestinian Talmud during the nineteenth century was carried out by his pupils. R. Eliyahu's commentary to Order *Zeraim* was published, however, only in the 1926 Wilna edition. Of almost equal importance in this connection is his commentary to the Mishna Order *Zeraim*, called *Shenot Eliyahu*, which is based primarily on the Palestinian Talmud. His commentary to the *Shulhan Arukh* contains as well many explanations of passages in the Palestinian Talmud.

---

[71] This author was identified only in recent years. For a listing of existing commentaries see Strack, *Introduction*, 70f.; Strack-Stemberger, *Einleitung*, 182-4; Ginzberg, *Commentary*, introd. 51-64; Frankel, *Mavo ha-Yerushalmi*, 132-6. Full discussion of the early commentaries is given by Lieberman, 'The Old Commentators'. See especially Bokser, 'Guide', 225-50.

[72] This commentary appeared in different places: Tractate *Shekalim* in Frankfurt, 1689; the entire Order *Zeraim* in the 1710 Amsterdam edition; tractates *Bava Kamma* and *Bava Metsia*, Offenbach 1725; *Bava Batra*, Frankfurt 1742.

[73] Called *Sedei Yehoshua*, in three volumes, Constantinople 1662, 1749.

A really critical approach basing itself upon philological-historical method is less than a century old. It really begins with ISRAEL LEWY'S commentary to the first six chapters of the treatise *Bava Kamma*.[74] The twentieth century has seen the publication of GINZBERG'S four-volume *Commentary*, covering the first five chapters of *Berakhot*. In spite of its limited span in actual commentary to the Palestinian Talmud, it is of great importance because of its wide philological and historical interests.

The greatest modern-day authority on the Palestinian Talmud is the late LIEBERMAN, whose *Hayerushalmi Kiphshuto* covering tractates *Shabbat, Eruvin* and *Pesahim* is outstanding. It is not a full running commentary but elucidates a great number of *sugyot* in the three tractates. Important is also his *Hilkhot Ha-Yerushalmi*; while it relates especially to Maimonides (see above), its prime importance is the insight it gives into the sections of the Palestinian Talmud it covers. Yet, and again, most of his contributions to the establishment of correct readings and interpretations to the Palestinian Talmud are scattered throughout the monumental *Tosefta ki-Fshutah* and *Talmuda shel Kisrin*. Noteworthy is his essay 'The Old Commentators' in which he gives detailed discussion of the early commentaries down to the sixteenth century.

A focus of new and intensified critical study of the Palestinian Talmud has recently emerged in Jerusalem. Outstanding are SUSSMAN, *Babylonian Sugyot*; ASSIS, *Parallel Sugyot*, and *id.* '*Yerushalmi Sanhedrin*'.

TEXT

On the manuscripts see below.

In addition to the extant manuscripts, a valuable source for the textual criticism is the mosaic inscription found in 1974 at Tel-Rehov. In fact it represents the most ancient extant copy of rabbinic literature. Its content closely parallels *P.T. Dem.* 2, 22c-d and *P.T Shev.* 7, 36c. Despite the deviations it is clear that the text of the Palestinian Talmud served as the prototype for the inscription. See the penetrating analysis by SUSSMAN, 'Halakhic Inscription'; *id.* Additional Notes'; *id.* 'Boundaries'. See also LIEBERMAN, 'Halakhic Inscription'; Z. SAFRAI, 'Rehov Inscription', and below p. 408.

Important for the establishment of correct readings is RATNER, *Ahavat Tsion* which culls variant readings and explanations of early authorities to all tractates of the first two Orders except *Eruvin*.

While parts of the Babylonian Talmud began to appear in print since 1482 (Portugal) and 1484 (Italy), the Palestinian Talmud had to wait until 1522-23. Bomberg in Venice, after completing his edition of the Babylonian Talmud, did the same for the entire Palestinian Talmud, basing his edition in the main upon the poor Leiden MS. This text was further corrupted by the editor of the printed

---

[74] Published in the Year Book of the Breslau Seminary, 1895-1914, and now reproduced in book form, Jerusalem 1974.

text, who claimed to have had three additional manuscripts, but made many incorrect changes. The Venice edition was reprinted in facsimile in Berlin (1925) and this reprint was re-published in a smaller format.

A poor reprint of the Venice edition was made in Cracow 1609, with the addition of the small marginal commentary of R. David Darshan; it was followed in both respects by the Krotoschin 1886 edition.

A landmark edition was that printed in Zhitomir 1860-67. It contains on the page the commentaries of R. David Fraenkel and R. Moses Margoliot (see above) which subsequently became 'standard'.

The Petrokow edition of 1900-02 set the tone for the high quality of all future editions. It included many shorter commentaries in addition to the 'standard' Zhitomir commentaries. The most comprehensive edition is that published in Wilna 1922 which contains many new and relatively new commentaries as well as selections of variant readings; it serves as the source for all reproductions since.

There have been many editions of single Orders, such as *Zeraim* in the Amsterdam 1710 edition, which contains the commentary of R. Eliyahu Fulda (see above), as well as of single tractates, such as that of *Beitsa* with the first printing from manuscript of the commentary of R. Elazar Azcari together with introduction and critical notes by Israel Francus, New York 1967.[75]

TRANSLATIONS

Translations of the Palestinian Talmud have been very few and not helpful. The only full translation so far is the French by SCHWAB, *Talmud de Jérusalem*; it is very undependable. A Latin translation to twenty tractates was given by B. UGOLINO, in his *Thesaurus antiquitatum sacrum* vols. 17-30, Venice 1755-65. For translations on individual tractates into English and German and further itemized listing see BOKSER, 'Guide', 164-5; STRACK-STEMBERGER, *Einleitung*, 181.

A complete English translation was undertaken by NEUSNER, *Talmud of the Land of Israel*. As was decidedly pointed out by LIEBERMAN in one of his last written works, 'A Tragedy or a Comedy?', this translation is devoid of any value for scholarship and shockingly demonstrates the translator's ignorance of the textual criticism, languages, idiom and subject matter of the Palestinian Talmud. The German translation appearing under the editorship of HENGEL *et al.*, *Übersetzung*, is quite reliable.

INTRODUCTIONS AND AUXILIARY WORKS

The first real introduction is FRANKEL, *Mavo ha-Yerushalmi* (1870), which is still of importance today. A very readable and quite full introduction is given by

---

[75] For further references on editions see the exhaustive and detailed chapter on the Palestinian Talmud by Haberman in his re-edition of Rabbinovicz, *Maamar*, 203-222. Ginzberg, *Commentary*, introd. 51-64 is important for his critique of editions and commentaries. See also Bokser, 'Guide', 151-3; Strack-Stemberger, *Einleitung*, 180f.

GINZBERG in his *Commentary*, both in English and, more fully, in Hebrew.

Of unequalled importance are LIEBERMAN'S various books on the Palestinian Talmud and related literature. *Talmuda shel Kisrin* establishes the special nature of the first three tractates of Order *Nezikin* and on the redaction of the Palestinian Talmud in general. His important essay 'Al ha-Yerushalmi' deals with the criteria of the establishment of a correct text, with the importance of readings found in early authorities, and describes the attitude of the latter to the Palestinian Talmud as such.

EPSTEIN, *Amoraitic Literature* gives full attention to the Palestinian Talmud, including a general introduction and a collection of variant readings to the first Order. ALBECK, *Babli and Yerushalmi* is devoted to both Talmudim, though more so to the Babylonian. Yet no other book so far contains so succinct and complete a listing of Palestinian (and Babylonian) Amoraim and so helpful a guide to their characteristic teachings.

A most valuable bibliography is BOKSER, 'Guide'. It refers to almost everything written on the Palestinian Talmud, either directly or indirectly, including such aids to the study as geography, inscriptions, legal studies and liturgical works. While one may sometimes disagree on the value of a particular work, his judgment in general is fair and to the point. More limited and without discrimination between the good and the mediocre is the bibliography in STRACK-STEMBERGER, *Einleitung*, 163 and in the course of the chapter on the Palestinian Talmud which follows. This chapter, incidentally, is very helpful and one of the best in the book.

A great help in the study of the Palestinian Talmud will be KOSOVSKY, *Concordance*, a computer-produced production appearing under the auspices of the Israel Academy of Sciences and Humanities and the Jewish Theological Seminary of America. Upon completion it will have three sections: a thesaurus of the language with citations from all relevant passages; a thesaurus of names of persons and localities; and a thesaurus of midrash parallels, containing also all scriptural verses referred to. The concordance is based upon the Venice 1524 edition; a supplement will very likely be published containing textual variants from the various MSS.

Manuscripts of the Palestinian Talmud

(by *Michael Krupp*)

The title *Talmud Yerushalmi*, i.e. 'of Jerusalem', has been current since the first printing, but it was never taught in Jerusalem or edited there. It was taught in the schools of Galilee and Caesarea. Only the first four Orders and part of the tractate *Nidda* of the Mishna were commented upon in the Yerushalmi. The fifth and sixth Orders – in spite of medieval affirmations – were not lost, but never existed there (at least in writing). In contrast to the first four Orders, no fragments of nos. 5 and 6 were found in the Cairo Geniza.

Unlike the Bavli (Babylonian Talmud), the Yerushalmi did not originally contain the successive Mishna sections in full. It was inserted later from other sources, as the numerous Geniza fragments show.

When the Bavli was acknowledged as authoritative in North Africa and Spain in the tenth century, the Yerushalmi lost its importance and was probably transmitted and respected only in Italy and Ashkenaz, classically lands depending on Palestine, even though the Bavli was the supreme authority here. It is somewhat miraculous that under these circumstances the Yerushalmi survived at all: there was only one complete manuscript of it (MS. Leiden), which was then used as a basis for the first printed edition, Venice 1523-25.

MS. LEIDEN, Scalinger no. 3. It was published in a poor facsimile edition (Jerusalem 1971) with an introduction by LIEBERMANN and a list of variants from the Venice printing. The manuscript was the work of Yehiel ben Yekutiel ben Benyamin ha-Rofe, 1289, also well known as scholar, poet and copyist, and especially as author of a book of piety, *Maalot ha-Middot*. He lived in Rome in the 13th century, and the manuscript may have been written there.

The script is rabbinical, very legible, in one column. There is no commentary. In the colophon, the copyist complains that his prototype is corrupt and frequently unintelligible, and says that he had to emend it at times. But Lieberman says in his introduction that this verdict is rather to be referred to the inexperience of the copyist, unacquainted with the Yerushalmi. The prototype was better than the copyist judged it, whose emendations were unimportant and did no damage elsewhere. The real damage was done by the 'improvements' and arbitrary changes, additions and omissions of the compositor of the Bomberg edition, who had even less idea of the special traits of the Yerushalmi. The compositor put some of these emendations into the manuscript in handwriting, mostly on his own initiative and not, as he claimed in the colophon, on the basis of other manuscripts. There may well have been no complete manuscript of the Yerushalmi at the time of printing, apart from the Leiden.

MS. VATICAN 133, published in facsimile, Jerusalem 1970. It contains *Sota* and the Order *Zeraim* minus *Bikkurim*. The manuscript is from several hands, probably from Italy in the 13th century, two columns a page till nearly the end, without a commentary. The manuscript is very corrupt and has, according to Lieberman, hardly a line without several faults. On the other hand, the manuscript offers some good readings, up to sixty according to Lieberman, which show understanding of difficult texts which in the Leiden version are unintelligible. The Mishna text in *Sota* is prefixed chapter by chapter to the Gemara, as in the Leiden manuscript. The tractates of the Order *Zeraim* contain no complete Mishna text but only short *piskaot* at best, as in the Geniza fragments.

MS. ESCORIAL G-1-3 had been known for decades as a MS. of the Babylonian Talmud; it was listed by P. Blanco in 'Los manuscritos hebreos de la Bibliotheca de El-escorial', 1926. It was the late E.S. ROSENTHAL who first discovered, in the seventies, that the almost illegible small script in the upper margin of the first three tractates of *Nezikin* contains practically all of the Palestinian Talmud to that part. It is close to the Kokovtsev Geniza fragment containing five middle chaps. of *Bava Kamma* (GINZBERG, *Yerushalmi Fragments*, 240-53). After Rosenthal's death, the text was published by LIEBERMAN, Jerusalem 1983, not in facsimile, which was inadvisable on account of the difficulties of deciphering the text. The introduction to the MS. was compiled from Rosenthal's notes by his sons A. and D. Rosenthal.

This is the only manuscript of the Yerushalmi from Spain. It is in rabbinical script of the 15th century and displays all the advantages of Spanish correctness. It contains hundreds of readings which are the only key to certain parts of *Nezikin*, a particularly difficult tractate. Apart from its being more exact and complete than the Leiden MS. – it provides the text in the 23 lacunae of the Leiden MS. its importance consists in its representing another type of text than the Leiden, displaying major departures from the known text. This Escorial text has affinities with some of the oldest Geniza fragments, but is more correct than most of them. The division into chapters is uneven. It partly follows through all the thirty chapters of the whole tractate *Nezikin*, partly displays some *Bavot* numbers and often has both enumerations. In *Bava Kama*, and to some extent in *Bava Metsia*, the Mishna is given in full within the Gemara, where it is divided into parts of unequal length. Some parts occur in abbreviated form as *piska*, as in the printed editions of the Babylonian Talmud, while further on only short *piskaot* are found or no Mishna at all, like most of the Geniza fragments.

The manuscripts with the commentary of Solomon SYRILEIO must be numbered among the Yerushalmi MSS. His text of the Yerushalmi rests mainly on manuscripts and contains, along with additions from the Bavli and the midrashim, some valuable variants. Two versions must be distinguished, the first in MS. Paris 1389 and the other in the London 403 to 405, which are regarded as autograph. At least in the second, Syrileio had the printed edition before him in the beginning of the 16th century. The texts comprise the whole Order *Zeraim* and the tractate *Shekalim*.

The Yerushalmi *Shekalim* is also found in the MUNICH codex 95, which contains the whole Babylonian Talmud. As there is no Bavli on *Shekalim*, the scribe copied the Yerushalmi here, but assimilated to the Bavli in idioms. The Yerushalmi *Shekalim* is also given in the Babylonian Talmud MSS. Oxford 366 and 370 (with the commentary of R. Meshulam).

Doubtless, the GENIZA FRAGMENTS are once more a great help for study of the Yerushalmi, representing as they do its text in numerous samples. This is especially true where the Leiden MS. is the only witness. A collection of the

Geniza fragments was published by GINZBERG, *Yerushalmi Fragments*. Many further fragments have since been published, more have been discovered, and a complete edition is awaited.

אני יחיאל ביר יקותיאל ביר בנימן הרופא נבתיוא כתבתי זה הספר ירושלמי
מסדר נשיס וסדר ישועות לר מנחס ביר בנימן ביר מנחס והעתקתי
מספר משובש וטועה הרבה עד מאד ומה שיכולתי להבין ולהשכיל
הגהתי בו כפי עביות דעתי ויורע אני שלא היגעתי לתכלית
השיבושיס והטעיות אשר מצאתי מדעתן היוו ואפיק
לחייים לפיכך הקורא בספר הזה וימצא בו שיבושיס
וטעיות ידינני לכות ואל יתלה כולס עלי · ויהיו
בר תמיין יסלח זרוכי ויעקיני משגיאותיי כמה שנ
שגיאות מי יבין מנסתרות נקיב · הרחמן
יזכה ל מנחס ביר בנימן ביר מנחס להגות
בו הוא וזרעו וזרע זרעו עד סוף כל
הדורות · ויקייס עליו ועל זרעו ועל
זרע זרעו מיקרא שכת לא ימוט
ספר התורה הזה מפיך והגית
בו יומיס ולילה למען תשמ
לעצות כל הכתוב בו כי
אז תצליח את דרכיך
ואז תשכיל ·

ונשלם בכה ימיס לחורש אדר הראשון שלשעת חמישת
אלפים ותשעה וארבעיס לבריאת עול

MS. Leiden, Palestinian Talmud, last folio (Leiden, Bibliotheek der Rijksuniversiteit, MS. Or. 4720).
This is the second colophon, closing the Orders *Nashim* and *Yeshuot* (= *Nezikin*), and giving the date of 25 Adar 5049 (1289 C.E.). See p. 320.

Venice ed. of the Babylonian Talmud (1520-23), *Bava Metsia* fol. 86a.
Lines 2-3 read: 'Rabbi and R. Natan are the end of Mishna; Rav Ashi and Ravina are the end of Teaching' (see p. 341). In the last 3 lines, two terms typical of Babylonian Mishna comment are found: 'What does this come to add?', and 'The Mishna is lacking' (see p. 332).

Chapter Eight

The Babylonian Talmud

Abraham Goldberg

No literary work has been so misunderstood as has the Babylonian Talmud. It has had many detractors as well as many learned admirers,[1] but few have been gifted with the insight to appreciate its high literary quality. Because of its intricate composition, the beauty of its architectural structure can be gleaned only after long familiarity with it. Thus even those who have been appreciative of its universality and its idealism, its concern with the prosaics of daily human living, and the beauty of its popular idiom, as well as its felicitous turn of thought and phrase, have for the most part not been truly aware of its special and even unique literary quality. Again, the Babylonian Talmud has been described as an unsystematic and almost haphazard recording of the discussions of the academies, full of digressions on unrelated matter. Needless to say, this is only a testimony to ignorance. The study of the literary character of the Babylonian Talmud, which has become in a way one of the prime concerns of the age in current talmudic scholarly research, definitely shows refined selectivity in its editing, an intricate but highly systematic pattern of presentation, and a wonderful integration of seemingly different topics. It has literary beauty in depth. But just as a strong literary discipline is needed to appreciate the involved beauty of, say, Milton's page-long sentences, so, too, only one who has acquired the ability to see the patterns of an extended *sugya*[2] in a bird's eye view can begin to appreciate the literary quality of the Babylonian Talmud.[3]

The Halakhic Tradition in Babylonia

Midrashic tradition places the beginnings of Jewish learning in Babylonia as early as the exile of Jehoiachin, eleven years before the destruction of the First

---

[1] See Mielziener, *Introduction*, 103-114 for a listing of positive and negative things said, in particular by Christian scholars, about the Talmud, especially the Babylonian. See also Strack, *Introduction*, 87-89 and Abrahams, 'Talmud'.

[2] Technical term for the basic literary unit which contains a (shorter or longer) discussion of a limited topic. See below.

[3] Of interest is Jacobs, *The Talmudic Argument*; the title does not convey the important thrust of its literary analysis. It analyses 19 different Babylonian *sugyot*, showing the definite literary structure, artificially selective but beautifully developed, of each *sugya*, the ultimate purpose of which is to reach a determined point of view on the basis of elimination.

Temple, explaining the 'craftsmen and the smiths' carried away into exile (2 Kgs 24:14) as referring to the great men of learning.[4] Likewise, the Geonim place the founding of the great Babylonian academies already before the destruction of the First Temple.[5]

Undoubtedly, this Babylonian tradition has some kernel of truth, and indeed the spiritual rejuvenation of the early Second Temple period was in large measure a product of the exiles returning from Babylonia, exemplified in particular in the activity of Ezra and Nehemia. Yet once the new Jewish state became firmly established, the Palestinian influence upon the Babylonian community is obvious. The pilgrimages which every year brought thousands to Jerusalem left their mark on those who returned to Babylonia, having participated not only in the Temple rituals of the priesthood but in the popular dissertations of the Pharisaic teachers as well. In other words, it was Palestinian learning which set the tone for Babylonia as well.

This influence continued even after the destruction of the Second Temple and especially during the time of the Hadrianic persecutions after the Bar Kokhba war. It was then that the leading teachers of Palestine fled abroad. Most found their way to Babylonia, and many remained there even after the persecutions ceased. Here, they established the Palestinian tradition of their age. Most famous among these scholars was R. Hananya, nephew of R. Yoshua ben Hananya, who settled in Nehar Pekod and there took upon himself the Palestinian prerogative of intercalating the calendar and fixing the dates of the new moon. Indeed, it was not without a struggle that the Sages returning later succeeded in retrieving this prerogative for Palestine. Another Babylonian center for Palestinian scholars was established at Huzal in central Babylonia, where the pupils of R. Yishmael had fled. Those of R. Akiva had gone further North to Nisibis, where even in Temple times the scholarly family of Yehuda ben Bathyra had close ties with Palestine.

The pupils of R. Akiva returned to Palestine, establishing the famous center at Usha and ensuring for Palestine the hegemony of the developing tradition of R. Akiva. The pupils of R. Yishmael for the most part did not return. And it was they who in largest measure determined the Babylonian halakhic tradition as we see it in various aspects in later Tannaic literature and in the Babylonian Talmud. All evidence in the various sources points in the direction of a pre-Akivan tradition as having taken roots in Babylonia. This was a conservative tradition, and while the dynamic influence of R. Akiva continued to develop among his pupils who had returned to Palestine, Babylonian tradition remained relatively static. When we speak, therefore, of a Babylonian versus a Palestinian tradition with regard to the later Tannaic and the entire Amoraic period, we really are referring to an earlier Palestinian tradition which remained as it

---

[4] B.T. Gitt. 88a; *B.T. Sanh.* 30a.
[5] Reflected in the addition to *Tanh. Noah*, 3 (13a).

was in Babylonia, over against a Palestinian tradition which had been further developing.

This 'early' Palestinian strand dominating Babylonian halakhic tradition is found especially in the Tannaic midrash collections of the school of R. Yishmael, as the *Mekhilta* and *Sifrei to Numbers*, where native-born Babylonian Tannaim such as Ahai be-R. Yoshiya and Issi ben Yehuda find mention. During the Amoraic period, this tradition carries on especially in central Babylonia, the Nehardea-Pumbeditha area, as exemplified in the teachings of Shmuel and his pupils.

Yet even in the Amoraic period, Palestinian influence continued to find its way to Babylonia. This began early on in the third century, with the return of Rav, nephew of R. Hiya, to Babylonia after an extended period of study in the academy of the Patriarch, R. Yehuda. Rav established an academy at Sura in the South of Babylonia, rivalling Shmuel's central Babylonian academy. It was in Sura, that Palestinian influence and custom prevailed, not only in the Amoraic period, but throughout the Gaonic period.

The Babylonian Academies and Generations of Sages

Just as in Palestine, where several centers of learning existed over the generations, so, too, Babylonia had more than one center. During the Tannaic period these had been Nisibis in the far North and Nehardea and Huzal in the central area. In the Amoraic period they were concentrated in the heavily settled Jewish areas in Nehardea-Pumbeditha in the central part and Sura-Matha Mehasya in the South. Additional centers which flourished for a time were Mahoza, which was situated between these two areas, and in the later period Naresh, further South of Sura. All during the Amoraic period, there were at least two academies in these various areas, and sometimes more, which were functioning simultaneously. Their discussions and interpretations on the Mishna as well as on other Tannaic literature, together with the addition of their own teachings and case history recordings, make up the halakhic part, which amounts to two-thirds of the Babylonian Talmud.

The prime Babylonian tradition found expression in the academy of Nehardea, which after the destruction of the town in 259 c.e. moved to neighbouring Pumbeditha. This tradition, as we have already pointed out, was often closest to pre-Akivan Palestinian teaching, and one of the problems of the teachers of this academy was how to adjust Babylonian tradition to the universally accepted Mishna of R. Yehuda the Patriarch which was definitely Akivan. As we pointed out in previous chapters, the Mishna was treated as a halakhic code in Babylonia with more reverence than in Palestine itself, and this necessitated an interpretation of the Mishna that would not contradict Babylonian tradition. Such interpretations, obviously, were often forced. Where two opinions would be found among the Palestinian teachers, the tendency would be to interpret the anonymous mishna in accordance with the position accepted as law, even where this was opposed to the simple meaning of the mishna.[6] Differences in the interpretation of the Mishna between the Palestinian and Babylonian Talmudim run into the hundreds, but, significantly, the vast majority are between the Palestinian tradition and the Nehardea-Pumbeditha academies.

Mar Shmuel was the leading first-generation Amora in Nehardea. His contemporary *Abba Arikha*, known almost always by the simple designation of *Rav* (a contraction of 'Rabbi Abba'), upon his return from Palestine founded a rival academy at Sura, as we have seen. Sura had heretofore not had any tradition, or even much learning, of its own, and it was easy for Rav to ignore the prevailing Babylonian tradition and plant here the Akivan tradition which he had made his own.

Shmuel died in 254 C.E. and his chief pupil, *Rav Yehuda*, re-established the academy in Pumbeditha following the destruction of Nehardea. Rav was succeeded, following his decease in 247, by his pupil *Rav Huna*, a scholar related to the family of the exilarch. This gave Sura the hegemony over Pumbeditha at the time.[7] Rav Huna's academy was renowned for the great number of pupils it attracted, having a permanent student body of 800 and requiring thirteen *amoraim* (i.e. speakers) to carry the discourses of the head of the academy. According to legend, a heavy dust-cloud could be seen in Palestine as a sign that Rav Huna had ended the session and his pupils were shaking out their garments.[8]

The hegemony of Sura was eclipsed for a long period following the demise of *Rav Hisda* (flor. 299-309), Rav Huna's successor, not to achieve importance again until the time of Rav Ashi towards the end of the Amoraic period.

The third-generation heads in Pumbeditha were *Rabba bar Nahmani* (309-330) and *Rav Yosef bar Hiya* (330-333).

Their chief pupils were *Abaye* and *Rava*, whose activities made the fourth Amoraic generation perhaps the most important in the creation of the Babylonian Talmud. Abaye (333-338) carried on the strong Babylonian tradition in Pumbeditha. Yet when Rava acceded to headship, he removed the academy to Mahoza where he taught for a long period (338-352). It was here that the tradition of Sura made inroads, for Rava himself became the son-in-law of Rav Hisda of Sura. Moreover, he was considered as well a pupil of Rav Nahman bar Yaakov of Mahoza, whose tradition was closer to that of Sura than to that of Pumbeditha.

Rava's pupils were the leading figures of the next generation. One, *Rav Nahman bar Yitshak* (352-356) moved back to Pumbeditha, where the original

---

[6] See Goldberg, 'Purpose and Method', for forced interpretations given to three anonymous mishnayot in *Gittin* by the Amora Shmuel in order to make them conform to accepted halakha.

[7] *Iggeret Rav Sherira Gaon*, 84 informs us that Rav Yehuda and his pupils would appear at the academy of Rav Huna in Sura from time to time as a sign of their subservience to the 'leading' academy.

[8] *B.T. Ket.* 106a.

strong Babylonian tradition continued to prosper. Another, *Rav Pappa* (359-371) established a rival academy at Naresh, not far South from Sura. At Naresh, too, the Sura tradition remained supreme.

Rav Ashi succeeded Rav Pappa and returned the academy to Sura. His long reign (376-427) permitted an extensive review of all that had been achieved by the previous generations in Babylonia and he it was who began the final redaction of the Talmud.

Two more generations of Amoraim are counted in Babylonia, but the contributions of these were probably more in the nature of editing than in novel teachings.

The Babylonian Talmud, however, did not receive final form even then. The Savoraim who followed the Amoraim added many of the literary features of the Babylonian Talmud and much of what is anonymous may stem from this period. The length of the Savoraic period is a matter of dispute, but some bring it up to the last quarter of the seventh century.

The Babylonian Approach to the Mishna

The general approach of the early Babylonian Amoraim to the Mishna is quite close to what we find in the Palestinian Talmud. The school of Rav in Sura was of Palestinian-Akivan character to start with, but in spite of the non-Akivan tradition carried on by the central Babylonian school of Shmuel, the treatment of Tannaic sources as a whole does not vary greatly. What we recognize as specific characteristics of the Babylonian Talmud stem from later developments. They are reflected in a dialectical refinement of all possible interpretations which somehow may fit a particular Tannaic source.

1. *New meanings found in the Mishna.* Often new interpretations of the Mishna arise which were not known to the earlier generations of Amoraim either in Palestine or in Babylonia. These new interpretations often bring about an emendation in the phrasing of the Mishna. An example will make this clear. *M. Shabbat* 17:1 teaches that 'doors' of household objects may be handled on the Sabbath 'even though they became detached on the Sabbath', in contrast to house-doors which may not be handled because they were not fashioned to be moved about. The Palestinian Talmud correctly infers that the Mishna wishes to emphasize the distinction between doors of household objects (utensils) and house-doors. Doors of household objects may be handled in the same way as the utensils themselves even when these doors become detached on the Sabbath, there being no question that such handling would certainly be permitted had they become detached before the Sabbath. The Babylonian Talmud, however, finds it more logical to permit the handling of utensil doors which became detached on the Sabbath, precisely because they may be considered as being 'fit for handling as part of the whole utensil itself', which would not be the

case had they become detached before the Sabbath. According to such reasoning, however, the Mishna teaching that 'all utensils may be handled on the Sabbath and their doors with them *even though* they became detached on the Sabbath' is not logical. Abaye interprets the Mishna to mean, therefore, that even though they became detached *on a weekday*, they may still be handled on the Sabbath. Thus the 'even though' of the Mishna would find proper meaning. An easier way than Abaye's forced interpretation is simply to omit the phrase 'on the Sabbath' at the end. Exactly this is what we find in the Mishna reading in the Babylonian Talmud in later manuscripts and printed editions![9] More often, however, a change in meaning of the Mishna could be managed without such forced interpretation resulting in textual emendation.

2. *Manipulation of Tannaic controversies.* A very common feature of late Babylonian Amoraic Mishna interpretation is the tendency to limit the area of Tannaic controversy. *M. Eruvin* 2:1 teaches that a well in a public domain may be 'enclosed' by setting up eight single boards around it to form right-angle corner pieces, thus transforming the area into a halakhically private domain and permitting to draw water on the Sabbath. This is the view of R. Yehuda. R. Meir holds that in addition, single boards must be set up in the open area between the corner-pieces on all four sides, making a total of twelve boards. Moreover, R. Meir limits the open space to ten cubits, whereas R. Yehuda permits up to thirteen-and-a-third cubits. Thus there is a double controversy here, as understood by the Palestinian Talmud and apparently also by the earlier Babylonian Amoraim. But Rav Papa finds a way of changing this into a single, limited controversy, stating: 'There is no controversy at all with regards to a well which has sides of only eight cubits, where no additional single boards are required. Nor is there any difference of opinion where the sides are twelve cubits, all agreeing that additional single boards are required. The area of controversy is limited to wells which have sides ranging between eight and twelve cubits. It is only in this situation that R. Meir requires four additional single boards between the corner-pieces and R. Yehuda does not.'[10]

Such an interpretation is possible, but hardly necessary. Being possible, however, it becomes almost compulsory in the light of developing Amoraic interpretation.[11] The Babylonian Talmud is even able to dig up a supporting baraita, of which Rav Pappa has no knowledge.[12]

There is also the reverse phenomenon of widening the scope of Tannaic controversy, with the aim to bring out every possible existing view. An example

---

[9] See Goldberg, *Shabbat*, 303f.

[10] *B.T. Er.* 19b.

[11] A similar development towards limiting earlier controversies had already taken place in later Tannaic teaching, notably those between Beit Shammai and Beit Hillel and between R. Eliezer and R. Yoshua as interpreted among the various pupils of R. Akiva. Cf. *M. Beitsa* 1:6 on *T. Beitsa* 1:12; and cf. *M. Tem.* 3:1, *M. Ker.* 4:2 and *M. Toh.* 9:3.

[12] *B.T. Er.* 19b. See Goldberg, *Eruvin*, 37-8.

is the controversy between R. Eliezer and the Sages in *M. Shabbat* 17:7 on whether a window may be shut on the Sabbath with an unattached window-shutter. The Palestinian Talmud sees only two points of view, but the Babylonian interpretation discerns two separate conditions in the opposing view and concludes on three different points of view. Here, again, the Babylonian interpretation is possible but hardly compulsive.[13]

3. *Re-interpretation of Tannaic terms.* The Babylonian Talmud also has the characteristic of extending Tannaic terms and giving them a new use. Thus the Tannaic שמא *shema* i.e. 'lest', 'perhaps', is turned into גזרה שמא *gezera shema* i.e. 'an enactment lest'. This term occurs frequently in the Mishna, as for example in *M. Terumot* 9:2, 'R. Tarfon says: Only priesthood poor may pick (heave-offering produce which has been sown) *lest* they (i.e. non-priests who are not so diligent on heave-offering laws) forget and put into their mouths.' The meaning here is simple and uncomplicated. The Babylonian extension of the term, however, is something complex. It has the function of linking a rabbinic prohibition with a scriptural one, and is encountered especially in the area of Sabbath and Festival law. Thus when *M. Shabbat* 14:3 prohibits the eating of Greek hyssop on the Sabbath 'since it is not the food of them that are in health,' the reason is, according to the Palestinian Talmud, 'that one should not do on the Sabbath as in the manner of week-days.'[14] Eating food which has medical qualities is considered inappropriate for the Sabbath, as is all medicine when one is not really sick, and the entire prohibition is simply to enhance the character of the Sabbath day. The Babylonian Talmud, however, finds a way of connecting this prohibition with a violation of the Sabbath of scriptural stringency. The explanation given is: 'An enactment to safeguard (the prohibition against) the grinding of ingredients (in the preparation of medicine).'[15] 'Grinding' is one of the thirty-nine prohibited 'principal labours'.[16]

4. *Schematic arrangement of Tannaic opinions.* An element in the literary development of the Babylonian Talmud is the tendency to find a schematic pattern in the basic sources, as well as in the elements making up these sources. This is well seen in the discussion on *M. Yevamot* 10:1. The issue here is the case of a woman who remarries in the belief that her husband has died, but then finds that he still is alive. The anonymous mishna teaches that subsequently she suffers thirteen legal restrictions. Regarding the latter, however, three differing opinions are recorded of named Sages: R. Yose, R. Elazar and R. Shimon.

---

[13] See Goldberg, *Shabbat* 314f.

[14] *P.T. Shabb.* 14, 14c.

[15] *B.T. Shabb.* 53b; and see Goldberg, *Shabbat*, 266f.

[16] Cf. above p. 156. For additional instances of the use of this term see Goldberg, *Shabbat*, 11, 38, 46, 56, 59, 63, 64, 74, 99, 105, 113, 114, 300, 313, 382, 392, 400; *id., Eruvin*, 144, 162, 248, 254, 256, 284. The term is hardly met with in the Palestinian Talmud, and then only in the mouth of late Babylonian Amoraim.

Both Talmudim take up the question what is the relationship among these differing opinions.

The Babylonian Talmud[17] gives two diametrically opposed approaches, one in the name of the Babylonian Amora Rav Huna and another in the name of the Palestinian Amora R. Yohanan. According to Rav Huna, the arrangement of the opinions is the clue to their relationship: each Sage agrees only with the opinions following him. Thus R. Yose who is mentioned first, agrees with both R. Elazar and R. Shimon; R. Elazar agrees only with R. Shimon; but R. Shimon agrees with no one else. R. Yohanan, however, teaches more or less the opposite: R. Shimon agrees with both others, R. Elazar agrees with R. Shimon but not with R. Yose, and R. Yose agrees with neither. The Talmud also gives explanations for each point of view, some of which are not without strain.

A comparison with the Palestinian Talmud[18] brings out the artificiality of this symmetric arrangement of two opposing interpretations. Here, we find no logical structure: R. Yose differs only on one point, and R. Elazar would agree on this, but R. Yose would not agree with R. Elazar's point; R. Shimon, finally, agrees with neither, although both others would agree with his point. The explanations offered here are simpler and more convincing, and it is obvious that the Palestinian version is primary, and that the Babylonian Talmud reflects a later development.[19]

5. *Abstraction and systematization of Tannaic law.* Related to the tendency towards schematization and unified patterns is the derivation and further development of abstract concepts and legal principles from concrete Mishnaic halakha. Thus we meet a term like מוקצה *muktse*, lit. 'set aside'. In Tannaic literature it is used to designate a place for drying figs or storing wood and the like.[20] In Babylonian usage it was broadened into an abstract halakhic category, mostly used in connection with Sabbath law to indicate things automatically 'set aside' and not to be handled on the Sabbath.

Another example is ברירה *berera*, lit. 'choice', a word unknown in Tannaic literature and rarely used in the Palestinian Talmud as a Babylonian derivative. It is a term, used widely in judicial and ritual areas, to refer to the retrospective definition of the position or status of a thing which was previously unknown. Characteristically, Tannaic differences of opinion are often explained in the Babylonian Talmud on the basis of the supposed acceptance or denial of this option; an entirely artificial construction of Tannaic sources.[21]

A third example is the term חזקה *hazaka*, lit. 'taking hold'. The Tannaim use it primarily for concrete matters of possession and usucaption. Occasionally,

---

[17] *B.T. Yev.* 91a.
[18] *P.T. Yev.* 10, 10d.
[19] See Goldberg, 'Sources and Development', for a detailed exposition.
[20] Cf. above pp. 91, 124.
[21] For a fuller analysis of the use of *berera* in the Babylonian Talmud see Goldberg, *Eruvin*, 82 and n. 65, 223 and n. 3.

however, it is used in an abstract way to indicate a legal status or condition which is supposed to exist or to continue until evidence is brought to the contrary.[22] Precisely this usage has become standard in the Babylonian Talmud.[23]

The use of such abstract concepts and categories indicates a process of unification and systematization. Many different halakhot, often from areas wide apart, are brought together and explained with the help of these categories.[24] Needless to say, this does not always do justice to the prime meaning of Tannaic halakha. Beginnings of this process may be discerned already in the teachings of early Palestinian and Babylonian Amoraim, but it reached full development only in later Babylonian Amoraic teaching. An interesting parallel to this process may be found in the development of Roman law from the classical to the post-classical period.[25]

6. *Legal exegesis of mishnaic idiom.* In seeking new meaning and additional understanding of the Mishna, the Babylonian Talmud comes to approach the language of the Mishna as if it were Scripture. One of the outstanding phenomena is the exegesis of seemingly unnecessary wording and tautology, an approach entirely unknown in the Palestinian Talmud. Almost always, where the Mishna has a general statement followed by a particularized itemization, the Babylonian Talmud will suppose a new and specific teaching. An example will make this clear.

In *M. Eruvin* 1:4, R. Yehuda teaches that the cross-beam symbolically closing the alley-entry and turning it into a private domain, has to be wide enough, but not strong enough, to hold a half-brick of a handbreadth-and-a-half. The next mishna specifies: if it was of straw or reeds, it is considered as if made of metal, etc. This addition on the face of it is found entirely superfluous in the Babylonian Talmud, and it is asked what the Tanna wants to teach here. The answer is that mention is made of a cross-beam made of straw for a specific reason: one might think that R. Yehuda permits a weak beam made of material such as wood, which can sometimes be strong, but never of straw, which is never strong. Therefore R. Yehuda's teaching that the cross-beam may be even of straw is necessary.[26]

The same procedure is followed where the Mishna has a general rule summarizing a number of preceding halakhot, indicated for example with the expres-

---

[22] This is indicated by the use of the construct form; see *M. Naz.* 9:2 for a clear example.

[23] See *B.T. Hull.* 9a for an example.

[24] The abstract principle מלאכה שאינה צריכה לגופה 'work not at all necessary for the action taken', for example, is used to explain many different specific Sabbath halakhot; see Goldberg, *Shabbat,* 180, 207, 218, 253, 263, 316, 351f., 365, 370.

[25] B.S. Jackson has called my attention to this phenomenon. For Roman law, see Schulz, *History.* It is of additional interest that the parallel development of both legal systems is almost exactly contemporaneous.

[26] *B.T. Er.* 14a.

sion זה הכלל 'This is the general rule: . . .' Here, the Babylonian Talmud almost always will ask: לאתויי מאי 'What does this come to add?' An example is found in *M. Bava Kamma* 9:1 which teaches a number of halakhot each answering in a specific case the question what restitution a thief should pay for stolen goods from which he has meanwhile derived profit. The concluding part reads: 'This is the general rule: All thieves make restitution according to the value at the time of theft.' Here, the Babylonian Talmud asks its usual question and after its manner derives an additional legal situation which results in an entirely new halakha![27]

A phenomenon closely related is the derivation of a new teaching from a number heading followed by a list of particular items. Thus *M. Shabbat* 7:2 opens: 'Principal labours (forbidden on the Sabbath) number forty-less-one', and then goes on to outline all thirty-nine categories in detail. The Babylonian Talmud here starts with the question: 'Why the number?', implying that the reader of the Mishna can do his own counting. This type of question will never be asked in the Palestinian Talmud.

'The Mishna is Lacking and thus the Tanna teaches'

A remarkable literary technique created by the Babylonian Amoraim in explaining the Mishna, which in a sense encompasses all other distinguishing features and therefore deserves separate treatment, is the use of the novel expression חסורי מחסרא והכי קתני 'the Mishna is lacking and thus the Tanna teaches'. It is usually indicated with the first two Hebrew words *hasorei mehasra*. We find it first being used, though sparingly, by the early fourth-century Amora Rava. Later, it became a routine feature in any discussion where it could possibly fit. It is entirely unknown in the Palestinian Talmud, and in this respect differs from other Babylonian features which, as we saw, are sometimes quoted from Babylonian sources in later parts of the Palestinian Talmud.

One of the prime uses of the phrase is where an illustrative story in the Mishna seems to contradict the abstract halakha which it follows. In *M. Pesahim* 7:2, for example, the Mishna reads: 'The Paschal lamb may not be roasted on a (metal) spit nor on a grill. Said R. Tsadok: It happened that Rabban Gamliel said to his servant Tavi, Go and roast the Paschal lamb for us on the grill.' Here, the Babylonian Talmud asks: Is this not a contradictory story? And the answer comes: 'The Mishna is lacking and thus the Tanna teaches: "One may not roast the Paschal lamb on a spit nor on a grill, but if the grill was a perforated one, it is permissable." '[28] Thus the contradiction is resolved. The Palestinian Talmud, however, takes it clearly that the story is brought in to indicate the contrary

---

[27] *B.T. Bava K.* 96b. Rav Ilaa derives the rule that when a 'change' (*shinnui*) occurred, as when a lamb became a ram or a calf an ox, this gives the thief possession of the animal and he is now free to slaughter and sell it. For further examples and discussion see Goldberg, *Shabbat*, 132, 238, 267, 278.
[28] *B.T. Pes.* 75a; see MS. readings as noted in Epstein, *Nosah*, 599.

opinion of Rabban Gamliel who permits roasting on any kind of a grill.[29] It is interesting that even where the Babylonian Talmud recognizes a story as being brought in to present a conflicting opinion, it will still, almost out of habit, use the phrase *hasorei mehasra*.[30]

Not all uses of *hasorei mehasra* are connected with stories. It is often employed to make a connection between two apparently unrelated parts of a mishna, as in *M. Nazir* 1:2. '[If one said:] "I will be like Samson", "like the son of Manoah" (. . .) he becomes a Nazirite the like of Samson. How does a lifelong Nazirite differ from a Nazirite the like of Samson? A lifelong Nazirite whose hair becomes heavy may lighten it with a razor, etc.' The Babylonian Talmud asks: 'A lifelong Nazirite – who has mentioned it (previously in this mishna?). The Mishna is lacking and this is how the Tanna teaches: One who says, "I am a lifelong Nazirite", becomes a lifelong Nazirite. How does a lifelong Nazirite differ from a Nazirite the like of Samson etc.'[31]

There are many more uses of *hasorei mehasra* which our limited exposé does not permit us to clarify. A large and most comprehensive study of this literary technique is given by EPSTEIN.[32] The interested reader will see here how it is also used to remove a contradiction between two parts of an anonymous mishna,[33] or between a mishna and a baraita;[34] to answer a question of an Amora on the Mishna, or the reverse.[35] *Hasorei mehasra* is a daring and remarkable innovation. Its use enables the Babylonian Amoraim to introduce into the interpretation of the Mishna concepts unknown before. Sometimes these concepts are substantiated by a later Babylonian midrash which will find a particular explanation of *hasorei mehasra* inherent in the 'proper' interpretation of a scriptural verse. This purely artificial construction is mostly unhelpful and even confusing for a proper understanding of the Mishna. However, it is of immense importance for an appreciation of the literary development of the Babylonian Talmud.

Relationship to Tosefta, Baraitot and Palestinian Talmud

The foregoing section, though not exhaustive, gives us a fair conception of the great measure of independence towards the Mishna which is shown by the Babylonian Talmud in its full development. The same can be said with regard to its approach to the Tosefta, the baraitot and the Palestinian Talmud.

In previous chapters we have already noted that the Babylonian Talmud quotes the Tosefta in a free manner. Sometimes a quotation from the Tosefta

---

[29] *P.T. Pes.* 7, 34b.
[30] For an example see *B.T. Sukka* 28b on *M. Sukka* 2:8.
[31] *B.T. Naz.* 4a.
[32] Epstein, *Nosah*, 596-672.
[33] Cf. *B.T. Bava B.* 130a.
[34] Cf. *B.T. Er.* 97a-b.
[35] Cf. *B.T. Shabb.* 149a-b; *B.T. Er.* 75a; *B.T. Ket.* 89a.

has undergone so much change that it seems to have come from a source other than the Tosefta. Indeed, this is the view of some scholars. EPSTEIN, as we have written, posits an 'early' Tosefta which came down in two different branches: a Palestinian one which remained close in language and style to the original 'early' Tosefta, and a Babylonian one which differed considerably.

We do not deem it necessary to posit the existence of an 'early' Tosefta – something which will be difficult to prove scientifically anyway. It is sufficient to assume that the Palestinian Talmud takes few liberties with the one Tosefta which we know, while the Babylonian Talmud treats the Tosefta as is does almost all other sources – manipulating it wherever necessary for the literary purposes of the *sugya*. One might say that the Babylonian Talmud is only an extreme expression of a general tendency of later sources to incorporate explanation and even change in a quotation of an earlier source. Thus Tosefta *Eruvin* 2:12 reads: 'Where one gives (the *eruv*) to a monkey to bring (to the one who is to receive it) or places it upon an animal, the *eruv* is valid.' But the baraita in the Babylonian Talmud, *Eruvin* 31a, reads: 'The *eruv* is not valid, yet if he said to another to receive it (from the monkey or animal) the *eruv* is valid.' This is not a baraita from a different source, but a paraphrase of the Tosefta, with the explanation inserted: the Tosefta does not consider the *eruv* valid unless another is to receive it. The Palestinian Talmud (*Eruvin* 3, 20d) has a slightly different interpretation of the Tosefta.

One must be very circumspect before assigning baraitot parallel to the Tosefta to a 'different source'. Just as the Tosefta will quote the Mishna with added words or phrases of explanation, or even in a paraphrase, as we have shown in the relevant chapter above, so, too, will the Babylonian Talmud continue this process – but because of the exigencies of the *sugya* in a more radical way.

This brings us to the problem of many a Tannaic teaching from the Tosefta or Tannaic midrash collections being quoted in the Babylonian Talmud (in particular) in the name of an Amora. Scholars have tried hard to solve this problem,[36] yet never conclusively. In our view the answer is in the manner of quoting. A Tannaic quotation in the mouth of an Amora is hardly ever verbatim. It usually contains a word or phrase of interpretation inserted by the Amora. In this situation it would be wrong to quote it as a Tannaic source. It is that source with the particular explanation of the Amora, sometimes expressing disagreement. The only way the editor could bring this Tannaic source with the particular Amoraic explanation is to quote it in the name of the Amora. The Amora, so to speak, acquires the Tannaic teaching as his own by adding to it.[37]

A slightly more difficult problem to solve is the reverse situation, where a *memra* may turn into a baraita. Every baraita in the Babylonian Talmud which does not find a parallel in Tannaic sources or in the Palestinian Talmud is in a

---

[36] Cf. Strack-Stemberger, *Einleitung*, 192.
[37] For an example of a *memra* (see above p. 303) tied to an explanation of the Tosefta, see my *Eruvin*, 154 n. 19; for a *memra* paraphrasing the Tosefta, *ib.* 267.

way suspect. Undoubtedly, the Babylonian Talmud does preserve authentic Tannaic teachings which may not be found elsewhere. But where a baraita is quoted by a Sage from the middle or late Amoraic period, the probability is that it is of Babylonian manufacture, in many cases based upon a *memra*.[38]

The question of the relationship between the Palestinian and Babylonian Talmudim has occupied teachers and scholars since the time of the Geonim. The traditional view is that the Babylonian Talmud knew the Palestinian one. Modern scholars do not accept this without limitation. Some assume that even where there is implied knowledge of the Palestinian Talmud, it is not always in the form extant today.

On the surface, differences between the two Talmudim sometimes seem vast. But when we keep in mind how each developed we can, in most cases, point to a common origin – as long as Palestinian teaching is concerned as preserved in the Palestinian Talmud. Often, however, the literary exigencies of the *sugya* brought the Babylonian Talmud so far away from its Palestinian source that any connection seems far-fetched.

What must be remembered is that the roots of all the varied facets of Babylonian Amoraic teaching are essentially Palestinian. We have already pointed out that the Palestinian tradition which took root in central Babylonia was pre-Akivan and close to that of the School of R. Yishmael. When Rav set up his academy in Sura, he brought with him, with very slight modification, the contemporary post-Akivan Palestinian tradition. This tradition made certain inroads even in the central Babylonian academies. I have shown elsewhere that with the passing of time Palestinian custom succeeded in modifying Babylonian as far as outer form was concerned, but not essential inner content.[39] Thus the Palestinian custom of reciting the *kiddush* before the *havdala* when a holiday fell upon the outgoing of the Sabbath, and of reciting three sorts of 'distinctions' in the *havdala* blessing, came to be accepted in all of Babylonia. These were matters of 'form'. Nevertheless, the concluding formula which summarizes the essence of the blessing remained Babylonian and thus took over even in Sura. So that, unlike Palestine where one general formula served as the conclusion of all kinds of blessings, including that of the *havdala*: '. . . Who sanctifiest Israel' – in Babylonia there was a specific concluding formula for the *havdala* blessing: '. . . Who maketh a distinction between the sacred and the profane'.

During the Gaonic period and after, attempts were made to explain passages in the Babylonian Talmud in accordance with what was found in the Palestinian one.[40]

---

[38] See Jacobs, 'Fictitious Baraitot'. For a particularized discussion of examples see my *Eruvin*, 3-4 and n. 8, 63 nn. 21, 22.
[39] Goldberg, 'Palestinian Law'.
[40] See below n. 64.

The Aggada in the Babylonian Tamud

The percentage of aggada in the Babylonian Talmud, as we have already pointed out, is much higher than in the Palestinian Talmud. Almost a third is aggada. This may be explained as being due to the fact that there were no separate aggadic compilations in Babylonia as there were in Palestine. Thus a full midrash on the book of Esther is to be found at the end of the first chapter of tractate *Megilla* (10b-17a), entirely unrelated to the preceding discussion of the Talmud. It should be noted, however, that this is not native Babylonian midrash but a mere incorporation of Palestinian midrash, as indicated by the proem introductions and the names of the Sages quoted. So, too, is the long aggadic digression on the destruction of Jerusalem in *Gittin* 55a-58a Palestinian in essence. An important question, which we merely indicate here, is whether most of such Palestinian aggadic sections are not later additions to the Babylonian Talmud.[41]

Thus while the Babylonian Talmud contains a much larger proportion of aggada than the Palestinian Talmud, a good part of it, paradoxically, is Palestinian in origin. There is no doubt, however, that much of the Palestinian aggada is put into characteristic Babylonian mold. In our discussion of the Palestinian Talmud we have already pointed out that the typically Babylonian beliefs in sorcery, magic, astrology, angelology and the like are lacking there or found to a much lesser degagree. These, however, often found their way in Babylonian retellings of Palestinian aggada.

Meanwhile, it would be entirely wrong to dismiss the importance of native Babylonian aggada. Much of it, including, undoubtedly, the prominence of 'popular' beliefs, reflects conditions of the time. Take, for example, this seemingly innocent Babylonian description of Pharaoh: 'Pharaoh the contemporary of Moses was (a puny fellow), a cubit (in height) with a beard a cubit long and his shock of hair a cubit and a span.'[42] What we have here is a description of the fighting appearance of the Parthians or Persians of the time, which was especially meant to put fear in their opponents in battle. Writers of the time have made reference to this aspect of Persian battle.[43]

The use of aggada in the Babylonian Talmud is not dissimilar to that in the Palestinian. In addition to its reflection of the life of the period, it is often interwoven with the halakha, which was a vital part of Jewish living. It serves especially to highlight the ethical quality in the halakha.[44] It also serves impor-

---

[41] It is of note that MS. Vatican no. 134 has the phrase גמרא סליק 'end of gemara' between the preceding talmudic discussion and the beginning of the Esther midrash. See now especially Dimitrovsky, *S'ridei Bavli*, a publication of Spanish Talmud MSS. which definitely show that there is no exact correlation either in readings or in arrangement between Spanish and Ashkenazi traditions regarding the aggada in the Babylonian Talmud – a further indication that such aggada is a later addition.

[42] *B.T. Moed K.* 18a, by Avitol the hair-dresser in the name of Rav.

[43] See the Soncino edition (translator, N.M. Lazarus), especially p. 114 n. 8 and p. 115 n.1.

[44] See Goldin, *The Living Talmud*, 28f.

tant literary purposes, firstly, as a kind of relief from the intellectual pressure of exacting halakhic discourse, and secondly, as a signature marking the end of discussion of a particular topic.

The Sugya

The basic literary unit of the Babylonian Talmud is the *sugya*, which literally means 'course', 'lesson'. We must now turn our attention to it, since, as we stated above, an understanding of the structure and dynamics of the sugya is essential for a true appreciation of the Babylonian Talmud. We have dealt with a number of characteristic ways in which the Babylonian Talmud treats the Mishna and other Tannaic literature, and this certainly gives us a picture of its literary character, but it is not a synthetic one. This can be arrived at best by a study of the Babylonian sugya. The sugya is an extended discussion of a particular topic which incorporates many of the Tannaic and other sources connected with it, and it is in this framework that the sophisticated literary techniques we discussed above come to full fruition.

The construction and form of the sugya, as well as the inner development of its dialectics, are determined by specific aims and principles. Once we gain insight into these principles, we can begin to understand the reasons behind the impression of artificiality and strained logic which at times is inescapable, as well as of the forced interpretation of Tannaic sources which we analyzed above. Another feature which may be added here is the frequent and almost conscious transformation of dicta of early Amoraim when introduced in the discussion; a feature which is equally related to the structural dynamics of the Babylonian sugya.[45]

The artificiality of the sugya as a literary creation is often recognized by the Amoraim themselves, and for this reason they will hesitate to draw halakhic conclusions on the basis of what emerges from the sugya.[46] There is, for example, a lengthy sugya about the possible violation or continued validity of a marital relationship, a weighty question indeed. The issue is about a woman who remarried on the basis of oral testimony that her first husband died in some remote place, but who then returned alive: the second marriage now is void, but may she return to live with her first husband? The sugya comes to the conclusion that she may, on the ground of the principle, 'what could she have done?' Many Tannaic sources, however, which are introduced in the course of the discussion and seem to teach otherwise, are cleverly interpreted to conform to this principle. On this basis, Rav Papa was ready to decide accordingly in an actual case brought before him. To which Rav Huna be-R. Yoshua replies: 'And on the

---

[45] Very important in this connection are the later chapters of Albeck, *Babli and Yerushalmi*, which deal with the Talmud in general but primarily with the Babylonian. Pp. 452-522 deal with the transformation of early Amoraic dicta; 523-56 with differences of opinion as to the meaning of earlier dicta; 557-75 with the sources of the Talmud; 576-96 with the editing of the earlier Babylonian sugyot.

[46] See Albeck *ib.* 545-56.

basis of the resolution (of such conflicting sources) shall we depend (for deciding actual halakha)!?'[47] Incidentally, it is this line which is generally taken by post-talmudic authorities, and this accounts for the many decisions given by the Geonim, by Alfasi, Rashi, Maimonides and others which seem to be in conflict with the Talmud.

The sugya, therefore, as it reaches full development in the Babylonian Talmud must be recognized for what it is: a distinct literary creation. It had early origins, and in our discussion of the Palestinian Talmud we noted its elementary form as it existed both in Palestine and in Babylonia. The subsequent development of the sugya is typical of Babylonian teaching; it continued after the close of the Amoraic era into the Savoraic period. Detailed study of the literary character of the sugya has occupied the attention of several important modern scholars. Abraham WEISS is perhaps the forerunner of them all.[48] The most original contributions, however, have been made in a series of studies by Hyman KLEIN.[49] These have opened new vistas and proved fertile for continued research.[50] A short exposition of his understanding of the sugya will be of prime interest.

Klein made it very clear that the sugya consists of two parts. There is a basic part, which he calls the *gemara*, and an interpretative discussion which he calls *sevara*.[51] The *gemara* is the core of the Talmudic discussion, while the *sevara* is everything built around it in the sugya, including the connecting links between the different parts of the core. It is obvious that the *gemara* is earlier than the *sevara*, although it is not impossible that the *sevara* of one sugya may be earlier than the *gemara* of another. *Gemara* as a rule consists of the bare statement of an Amora, whereas the reason for his statement or its special interpretation is *sevara*. Klein developed a number of objective criteria for distinguishing between the *gemara* and *sevara* of a sugya, such as the use of Hebrew for the *gemara* part and Aramaic in the *sevara*.

One of Klein's innovations is his study of the technical expressions, in Aramaic, which govern the course of the discussion and the outer form of the sugya. Others have dealt with these expressions as they occur in the various sugyot, but Klein was the first to seek a unified solution for all places where the same term occurs. The sugya has an outer literary frame consisting of a question

---

[47] B.T. Yev. 91b. Similarly, Abaye dissuades Rava from issuing a decision on the basis of 'answers' given in the course of the sugya, B.T. Bava B. 135a.

[48] See especially his *Le-heker ha-Talmud*; also *Ha-yetsira ha-sifrutit*. A full presentation of Weiss' contribution to Talmudic research is Feldblum, 'Abraham Weiss'.

[49] Klein, 'Gemara and Sebara'; 'Gemara Quotations'; 'Some Methods'; 'Significance'. These articles appear also in Klein, *Collected Writings*.

[50] Notably Friedman, 'Critical Study'. On a different line, but also important, is Jacobs, *Talmudic Logic*, part II. Goodblatt, 'Babylonian Talmud', 293-318 discusses at length the contributions of such scholars as Kaplan, Weiss and Klein to form and redaction criticism, but does not sufficiently emphasize the importance of Klein.

[51] These terms should here be understood as defined by Klein. In his usage, *sevara* does not necessarily denote a product of the Savoraic period, although it may be such.

with subsequent discussion about a Tannaic text or an Amoraic dictum. This literary frame clearly belongs to the *sevara* part of the sugya and it is reflected in the various Aramaic expressions which were developed by the compilers of the *sevara*. The very common expressions מיתיבי 'they raise objection' and לימא מסייע ליה 'can we bring corroboration', for example, are not part of the primitive core but belong to the *sevara* frame.[52]

The literary craft of the *sevara* reveals itself in many ways. Different Amoraic comments on a single Tannaic text may be carefully connected by the *sevara* in such a way that they appear as a unified discussion. An Amoraic statement to a single Tannaic text may automatically be connected by the *sevara* to all possible Talmudic sources to which it may have application. Or again, the *sevara* shows how an important text may expand in different ways simply by placing the basic elements in different juxtapositions; thus alternative versions are usually a product of the *sevara*.

Perhaps the greatest contribution of Klein's approach is that it proves almost conclusively that both *gemara* and *sevara* are selective. The Babylonian Talmud is neither a stenographic recording of the discussions in the academy nor an exhaustive treatment of the various topics. It is more of an independent literary creation than just a compilation. Of necessity, it is selective. Certainly, it never loses its basic character as a commentary to the Mishna and other Tannaic works. Nevertheless, in the refined literary form of its final editing the prime sources upon which it serves as commentary become in great measure building blocks for its own literary structure.

The Savoraim

The distinction between *gemara* and *sevara* brings us to a discussion of the Savoraim and to the question of how much of the *sevara* may be attributed to their activity. Certainly, the Savoraic period is very important for understanding the literary character of the Babylonian Talmud, but scholars disagree as to just how important. Nor is there agreement on the length of this period. There is logic, however, in dating its beginning with the abolition of the Babylonian exilarchate by the Persians in 500 and its ending with the Arab conquest in 657 c.e., marking the beginning of the Gaonic period.[53]

---

[52] Some other of these expressions dealt with by Klein are: איבעיא להו 'this was asked by them'; איכא דרמי לה מירמא 'some place one source against another'; לאו בפירוש איתמר אלא 'this was not taught explicitly but was derived from a general inference' (these in 'Some Methods'); אלא אי איתמר הכי איתמר 'but if it were taught, it was taught thusly' (in 'Significance').

[53] The primary sources for this period are Rav Sherira Gaon's *Iggeret*; Abraham ibn Daud's *Sefer ha-kabbala* (ed. G.D. Cohen 1967) and *Seder Tannaim we-Amoraim* (ed. K. Kahana 1935). The most important modern works on this period are Lewin, *Rabbanan Savoraei we-talmudam*; Weiss, *Ha-yetsira shel ha-Savoraim*. A very important study dealing especially with the terminology of the Savoraim is Spiegel, *Rabbanan Savoraei*. A resumé and careful critique of all previous theory as well as a new original exposition is Ephrati, *Savoraic Period*.

All scholars agree that the Savoraim made additions to the Babylonian Talmud, but consider these mostly external. EPSTEIN writes: '[The Savoraim] primarily devoted themselves to the external arrangement without changing anything, other than additions and linking phrases between dicta and sugyot, linkings, however, which often change the whole sugya and all its sources. They transferred sugyot from place to place, giving completeness by adding from one to another and tried to conciliate their differences.'[54] While limiting their activity to the 'external arrangement without changing anything', Epstein clearly recognizes the decisive bearing this sometimes had on the meaning of the text. Other scholars give even a wider range to the activity of the Savoraim.

Rav Sherira Gaon mentions the fact that the opening sugya in Tractate *Kiddushin* (2a-3b) is a completely Savoraic creation.[55] This has been extended by WEISS who showed that almost in all tractates the opening sugyot are Savoraic.[56] These serve as a kind of 'introductory lecture' to the tractate in which a plethora of sources are introduced. Moreover, extended 'lectures' may appear again at the opening of chapters or before beginning a new topic.

Many of the distinctive features of the Babylonian Talmud enumerated above seem definitely Savoraic in origin. Thus the attempt to derive new laws from tautologies in Tannaic texts is a main feature of Savoraic activity. So too, is the term צריכותא 'a necessary element', introduced wherever the same halakha will be given in more than one way, or where more than one proof-verse will be quoted on any particular topic. The same holds for a number of other terms found frequently.[57] Again, the rules for deciding the authoritative halakha where there is a difference of opinion among the Amoraim in large measure seem to be of Savoraic origin. KLEIN, when developing his thesis differentiating between *gemara* and *sevara*, did not want to make it depend necessarily on Savoraic activity. For his purposes, it did not matter even if it were assumed that the *sevara* part had its origins in Amoraic times, as undoubtedly some of it did. Nevertheless, major elements of what he classifies as *sevara* actually were the product of Savoraic literary creation.

Redaction

How the Babylonian Talmud was edited is a problem which has occupied

---

[54] *Amoraitic Literature*, 12.

[55] *Iggeret*, 71.

[56] *Le-heker ha-Talmud*, 11-17.

[57] E.g. היכי דמי 'for example'; למימרא 'shall we say'; אליבא דר' פלוני לא תיבעי 'there is no question as far as this teacher is concerned, but according to the other . . .'; לך כי תיבעי לך אליבא . . . ; ודאי 'certainly'; ולא היא 'but it is not so'; ולאו מילתא היא 'but this is not relevant'; הלכך 'therefore'; ותו לא מידי 'and nothing more on the subject'; פשט, 'he resolved'; והלכתא 'and the halakha is . . .'

scholars of all ages and which still is not definitely solved.[58] The same talmudic tradition which call 'Rabbi and R. Natan end of Mishna' places Rav Ashi (d. 427 C.E. and Ravina as 'end of (talmudic) teaching'.[59] Ravina is taken here by many authorities and scholars to refer not to the colleague of Rav Ashi who bore the same same and was survived by Rav Ashi, but to Ravina bar Rav Huna (d. 499). The question is, however: what is the meaning of the term הוראה 'teaching'? It is hard to believe that Rav Ashi was a final editor, for many names of those who lived after him occur. Moreover his task as an editor would have been the assembling of what had gone before him and not the recording of his own contributions. Yet his name occurs so frequently and his role seems so active that one must assume that all this was a part of a later recording.[60]

The problem begins to lend itself to a kind of solution once we realize that we cannot speak of a single editing. The editing of the Babylonian Talmud must have had its beginning long before Rav Ashi and its final form was reached long after him. The question then remains: how do we deal with the talmudic tradition which ascribes to Rav Ashi 'end of teaching'? Similar to the editing process of the Mishna we studied above, there seems to have been from the start an 'official' layer of teaching (gemara)[61] which was the matter of study in the academies and which was added to from generation to generation. Of necessity, it was selective, and a hint of such is to be found in the statement that a certain teaching of the Amora Shmuel had been 'constituted as part of the gemara'.[62] Not everything said or taught in one generation would become part of the official study matter of later generations. The growth of a sugya – at least in the literary frame in which it was put by the final editors – can cover a period of several generations. Such a sugya could have layer after layer of accretions incorporated in its final form.

Now as one surveys the immense number of sugyot in the Babylonian Talmud, he is struck by the fact that the final notations are very frequently given in

---

[58] For a summary of prominent theories see Kaplan, *Redaction*, 3-27; for his own views *ib.* 289ff. More comprehensive but not offering any contribution of its own is Neusner, *Formation of the Babylonian Talmud*. This collection of student seminar papers offers summary and critique of leading theories in the last hundred years, not all equally relevant, the section on Ginzberg being simply an analysis of his study on Mishna *Tamid*. Helpful in giving a general picture of teaching and study in Babylonia are Goodblatt, *Rabbinic Instruction*; Gafni, *The Babylonian Yeshiva*. A good summary of the history of redaction criticism is found in Goodblatt, 'Babylonian Talmud', 304-18.

[59] *B.T. Bava M.* 86a.

[60] Kaplan, *Redaction*, 289ff. regards Rav Ashi as the compiler of the central '*gemara* distillation of previous *talmud*'. Gemara in his usage is the concise conclusion resulting from the lengthy and often complex discussions termed *talmud*. As such, *talmud* precedes *gemara* in time, but it was last to be written down since the prohibition on writing rabbinic literature extended to *talmud* but not to Mishna and *gemara*. Thus the *talmud* parts were redacted only by the Savoraim, while the concise *gemara* parts were compiled by the Amoraim and given final editing by Rav Ashi. For other modern scholarly interpretations, see Goodblatt, 'Babylonian Talmud', 304-18.

[61] Assuming the usage of Klein, see above.

[62] *B.T. Er.* 32b, Rav Nahman, third generation Amora.

the names of Ravina or Rav Ashi. In this sense Rav Ashi may indeed be the 'end of teaching', not as editor, but as one whose name usually marks the end of a sugya covering the contributions of several generations. In other words, the great majority of extensive sugyot end with the contributions of Rav Ashi or Ravina or of both. This has nothing to do with marking the end of the Babylonian Talmud. In fact, there are contributions from Amoraim at least two generations after Rav Ashi, but these are as a rule not incorporated in the structure of the sugya. Rav Ashi is the 'end' – of the sugya. This explanation, incidentally, will also permit us to assume that the Ravina who is mentioned together with Rav Ashi may indeed be the Ravina who was his contemporary.

All this refers, of course, to the *gemara* parts of the sugya, or in other words, the bricks used for its construction. The connecting elements, the *sevara* parts which we might call the 'mortar', must of necessity be later than Rav Ashi and Ravina since, just as in the Mishna, one does not record the teaching of his own generation in the official compilation. Moreover, as we have seen, the finishing literary touches peculiar to the Babylonian Talmud are in very great measure the work of the Savoraim which lasted for several generations after the Amoraic period. Even during the subsequent Gaonic period, lasting till the twelfth century, many 'unofficial' additions found their way into the Babylonian Talmud as we have it today.

Authority

The continuous development of the literary features typical of the Babylonian Talmud long after the final editing of the Palestinian Talmud is undoubtedly one of the prime reasons for its supremacy in later Jewish tradition. Intrinsically, it is the greater literary work, and, as a corollary of such, the one which would draw the gifts of great commentators. With the passing of time, it would become *the* Talmud for general study.

From this point of view it is wrong to attribute the leading position of the Babylonian Talmud to the strong polemic in its favour by the Geonim and other leaders of Babylonian Jewry.[63] True, the fact that Babylonia became the center of Arabic culture under the Abassids automatically raised the prestige of Jewish culture emanating from that center, especially when most Jews at the time lived in Islam-dominated countries. Yet this in itself would not have had a lasting influence and it would eventually have won out even on its own as being the larger and more highly developed of the two.

Nothing perhaps highlights this more than the fact that the two greatest commentators and codifiers of Kairwan and of North Africa in general in the eleventh century, Hananel ben Hushiel and Alfasi, are known especially for their sympathy for the Palestinian Talmud yet gave supremacy to the Babylo-

[63] As does Ginzberg, *Commentary*, introd. 41-46.

nian.[64] Egypt and North Africa were under strong influence of the Palestinian center, although Kairwan had its ties with Babylonia as well, and Palestinian law prevailed here for a considerable period. Yet it was Alfasi who established the rule that the Palestinian Talmud is authoritative equally where it does no more than supplement the Babylonian, but loses that authority where it is contradicted by the Babylonian.

Bibliography

Full bibliographical references are to be found in GOODBLATT, 'Babylonian Talmud', STRACK-STEMBERGER, *Einleitung*, 185ff. An obvious danger of exhaustive bibliographies is lack of discrimination. We shall be selective and mention the important works only. An attempt at evaluation regarding introductions and auxiliary works was made by Goodblatt, *ib.*, 324-6; Strack-Stemberger (which appeared later) should be added to the list there.

The following introductory works should also be mentioned: JACOBS, *The Talmudic Argument*; KAPLAN, *Redaction*; KLEIN, *Collected Writings*; MIELZIENER, *Introduction*; NEUSNER, *Formation of the Babylonian Talmud*.

TEXT AND EDITIONS

For manuscripts see below.

The first complete edition of the Babylonian Talmud was published in Venice by BOMBERG 1520-23. Previously, single tractates appeared in Portugal (1494), Soncino, Barco, Pesaro (1488-1519) and Fez (1494). Not all of these texts are extant. Fragments are being published in a most energetic way by DIMITROVSKY; his first issue is *S'ridei Bavli*. A somewhat better edition was that of JUSTINIAN, Venice 1546-51. Many editions followed. Of note is the Basle edition (1578-81), the first to be officially censored.

The basis of the present 'traditonal' editions is that of Frankfurt/M. 1720-22. The best known of the modern editions is that published in Wilna during the second half of the 19th cent. by the ROMM family. This edition has been extensively reproduced in our own day, especially in Israel, by photographic process with occasional additions of new commentaries.

A critical edition of the tractate *Taanit* was published by H. MALTER, (1928) repr. Philadelphia 1967 and Jerusalem 1973. M.S. FELDBLUM published a critical edition of *Gittin* following the pattern of *Dikdukei Sofrim* with improvements, New York 1966. The first three volumes of the Order *Nezikin* with Hebrew translation and listing of important variants have appeared under the editorship

---

[64] R. Hananael in particular strains to interpret the Babylonian Talmud wherever possible in harmony with the Palestinian. This seems to have been a tendency of some of the later Geonim as well. Examples of such are to be found in my commentaries, *Shabbat*, 22, 64, 80 (n. 3), 137, 151 (n. 96), 166 (n. 10), 199 (n. 4), 239 (n. 14); *Eruvin*, 113-114 and n.32, 128.

of J.N. EPSTEIN: *Bava Kamma* (by E.Z. MELAMMED) Jerusalem 1952; *Bava Metsia* (by M.N. ZOBEL and H.Z. DIMITROVSKY) Tel Aviv - Jerusalem 1960; *Bava Batra* (by S. ABRAMSON) Jerusalem 1952. A critical edition is being published by the Institute for the Complete Israeli Talmud. So far two tractates have been issued, *Ketubot* (two vols. 1972-77) and *Sota* (two vols. 1977-79). A very popular edition with vocalization and punctuation, together with a short modern Hebrew commentary, is being edited by the Israel Institute for Talmudic Publications under the editorship of Adin STEINSALTZ; more than ten volumes have appeared so far, including the tractates *Berakhot* and *Sanhedrin* and several tractates of Order *Moed*.

An informative resumé of the various editions is STRACK, *Introduction*, 83-86; cf. STRACK-STEMBERGER, *Einleitung*, 203-5. Much shorter is MIELZIENER, *Introduction*, 78-80. See also GOODBLATT, 'Babylonian Talmud', 267-8, 270-1.

The very best introduction to the various MSS. and editions, including a detailed description of all those known to him, is given by RABBINOVICZ in various prefaces to the 16 vols. of his *Dikdukei Sofrim*. His famous *Maamar* on the history of the printing of the Talmud has been republished in separate book form with corrections and additions by HABERMAN. It contains a full listing of all the printings following the Wilna edition, including as well a complete list of single tractates.

COMMENTARIES AND TRANSLATIONS

No work of the Jewish spirit has inspired more commentaries than has the Babylonian Talmud. A full list of these up to 1905, running into the hundreds, is given in the *Jewish Encyclopedia*, vol. 12, 28-32. A very good summary of all the prime commentaries is given by MIELZIENER, *Introduction*, 65-68. Most helpful are the summaries in STRACK-STEMBERGER, *Einleitung*, 206-11; GOODBLATT, 'Babylonische Talmud', 326-7.

Many of the translations give some commentary and explanation, especially those of single tractates. The most notable is the German translation given with Hebrew text, by Lazarus GOLDSCHMIDT, Berlin 1897-1933. A very poor abridged translation is that of M.I. RODKINSON in 20 volumes,1896-1903. A very serious translation of the entire Talmud is that of the Soncino Press with I. EPSTEIN as editor, 34 vols. plus index vol., London 1935-52; a small edition appeared in 1959. A modern Hebrew translation of the first three tractates of Order *Nezikin* under the editorship of J.N. EPSTEIN appeared in Jerusalem, 1952ff. (see end of previous section). A modern French translation of several volumes is being done in France under the editorship of E. MUNK. So, too, in Buenos Aires several volumes have appeared in Spanish translation by A.J. WEISS and M. CALÉS. For a detailed listing see STRACK-STEMBERGER, *Einleitung*, 205.

Many single tractates have been translated, usually with commentary. A list of such up to his time is found in Strack, *Introduction* 154-9. A very full up-to-date bibliography of texts and translations is TOWNSEND, 'Rabbinic Sources'.

See also the itemized listing by language in GOODBLATT, 'Babylonian Talmud', 321-2 and comments 328-9.

CONCORDANCE

A word concordance to the Babylonian Talmud was begun by Haim Y. KA-SOWSKI and completed after his decease by his son Biniamin (now also decea-sed): *Otsar leshon ha-Talmud* in 41 vols. The latter also compiled a name concordance, *Otsar ha-shemot*. This monumental project of necessity was limited to the text of the current editions, yet its helpfulness is inestimable.

Manuscripts of the Babylonian Talmud

(by *Michael Krupp*)

The Babylonian Talmud is about a hundred years later than the Palestinian, closing with the last of the Amoraim at the beginning of the sixth century. But that the Talmud as we know it was more or less identical with that of the sixth century is more than doubtful. It was still being worked upon centuries later, in the time of the Savoraim. It is only in the eigth century that the Babylonian Talmud appears as a more or less fixed quantity. By this time it was probably in written form. Maimonides says in his *Mishne Tora* (*Malwe melowe* 15:2) that he had before him a manuscript which was 500 years old and was written on a roll. Jewish historians of about 1000 in Spain speak of manuscripts produced in Spain in the 8th or 9th century from memory. The fact that the Babylonian Talmud was winning recognition beyond the frontiers of Babylonia may have been ultimately the occasion for its being committed to writing. No manuscripts from such early times have survived, but some of the oldest fragments from the Cairo Geniza may go back to the 9th century, not long after the book was first committed to writing.

Distribution of the Mishna within the Gemara is not uniform. It is mainly of two sorts: a) with the Mishna put as a block at the beginning of each chapter; within the Gemara, it is repeated only in longer or shorter citations which never contain more than an abbreviated Mishna text; b) with the Mishna distributed in parts throughout the Gemara, as in the printed editions; in addition, there are *piskaot*, mostly abbreviated citations from the Mishna. The first type is the commonest. It is displayed in nearly all Spanish manuscripts and in most Ashkenazic where there is no commentary, while all Yemenite manuscripts and most Ashkenazic with commentary show the second. The Ashkenazic manuscripts with commentary provided the master copies for the printed editions, where this type predominated.

It seems that originally the Mishna in the manuscripts was distributed in small sections throughout the Gemara. That this gave the complete Mishna within the Gemara is not quite clear but it is very likely, judging from some Geniza fragments. As the Mishna was subjected to more and more abbreviation, the custom established itself of giving the whole Mishna text at the beginning of each chapter, so that the complete Mishna would be transmitted in any case. This introductory Mishna came from another source, as is seen from the way it differs from the text in the *piskaot*. The latter is in any case that of the Babylonian recension as it was read by the Amoraim; this is the text discussed in the Gemara. Some Geniza fragments give this text even in mishnayot distributed within the Gemara, while the later manuscripts, even when giving the text of the Mishna within the Gemara, no longer preserved it.

The Babylonian Talmud is extant in its entirety in only one manuscript. In spite of this, it does not share the fate of the Yerushalmi. This may be because the great size of the Bavli has meant that it was not copied as a whole but by single tractate or a couple of tractates (as in the East) or at most by separate Order (as by Ashkenazim). Along with the complete Talmud manuscript therefore each whole tractate (except *Horayot*) has at least one witness, with as many as nine for much learned tractates (e.g. *Pesahim*). Ordinarily each tractate is represented by four witnesses. Then there are the numerous Geniza fragments, with each tractate represented by at least some witnesses, many by more than a hundred. These fragments, however, are mostly very short and it is improbable that a complete text of any tractate can be reconstructed from them, unlike the Mishna.

The Bavli manuscripts may be divided into groups distinguishable by their place of origin. This process of grouping the manuscripts has only just begun but one can say that the groups are distinguished by their scripts and also by minor differences of content. In comparison with the Midrash collections the differences are slight, especially in the halakhic parts. They are more important in the aggada. Some variants are to be explained by changes in the text in late Amoraic times, which did not find their way into all traditions and therefore into all manuscripts. But such differences are the exception. A more frequent source of variants was erroneous tradition and corruptions in a common prototype. One of the commonest reasons for variants is emendation undertaken by great scholars, or their marginal glosses which in time were worked into the Talmud text itself.

In general it may be said that the majority of manuscripts are from the West. As distinct from that, the second largest group is from Spain; the smallest comes from the East. This is in contrast to some extent with the general picture of rabbinical literature, but is probably to be explained by the fact that the Talmud was studied more frequently in the West than in the East. In the East, it was overshadowed by other works, as especially the work of Alfasi in North Africa, the Mishna with Maimonides' commentary or the *Mishne Tora* of Maimonides in Yemen.

Here is a brief characterization of each group.

SPANISH MANUSCRIPTS. After the Gaonic period, the centre of gravity of Jewish learning shifted from Babylonia to Spain. But Spain had already been in constant contact, via North Africa, with Babylonia. The golden age of Spanish Jewry and the patronage accorded it in the 10th and 11th centuries enabled scriptoriums to be set up in Spain where among other things the Babylonian Talmud was frequently copied. These scriptoriums were famous in the world of Jewry for their exactness and faithfulness to tradition. In France too, as well as in Germany, and in Italy, the second centre of Talmudic learning, Spanish manuscripts were particularly esteemed. In contrast to the Ashkenazic MSS., the Spanish are free from the corrections and emendations of scholars. Slips due to hurried writing are rare. Few or scarcely any abbreviations are used, these being a frequent source of error in the Ashkenazic MSS.

The oldest extant manuscripts from Spain which can be dated confirm this general opinion. An exemplary manuscript of the Spanish tradition is Hamburg 165, written in Gerona in 1184 and containing the three *Bavot* of the tractate *Nezikin*. And the oldest datable manuscript of the Talmud anywhere was written in Spain (Oxford 2673,8) though unfortunately surviving only in a fragmentary state. It was found in the Cairo Geniza.

Other important Spanish MSS. are: the *Avoda Zara* MS., belonging to the Jewish Theological Seminary in New York, which was written in 1290 and was acquired about 1900 in Spain; the three Munich MSS. nos. 6, 140 and 141; the Göttingen MS.; London no. 400; Oxford 366 containing Orders *Zeraim* and *Moed*; Paris 1337; Vatican 108 and finally the Madrid Escorial which became particularly famous because giving in the margins the Yerushalmi on the three *Bavot*.

The Spanish manuscript tradition gives mainly the second and fourth Orders. If we leave aside the complete Talmud, i.e. Munich MS. 95, many tractates are represented only by Spanish MSS. In the third Order only the tractate *Yevamot* is preserved with special care, while the fifth is almost entirely missing. The only exception is the Geniza fragment, Oxford 2673,8, already mentioned.

Almost without exception, the Spanish MSS. give the complete Mishna at the beginning of each chapter. Most manuscripts are in square script, especially the most ancient ones. Single-column manuscripts far outnumber the double-column.

In the Gemara section, mishnayot and *piskaot* are distinguished as a rule by having various introductions such as 'מתני and 'פיסק or by the introductory 'מתני contrasted with the absence of introduction.

ASHKENAZIC MANUSCRIPTS. Two groups can be clearly distinguished in the Ashkenazic MSS., which form the major part of Talmud witnesses. There is an older group, which I should like to see called Italo-Ashkenazic since part of this group was apparently written in Italy. And there is a later group which clearly displays the characteristic script of Franco-German tradition. More than external features mark off the groups. There is also the weight of internal evidence. These features, though numerous, are slight in themselves: common additions, omissions, idioms or the like, but frequent enough to allow of division into two groups.

The Italo-Ashkenazic MSS. are the stronger group, with uniform external criteria. They are in square script, two-columned, always without commentary, and the complete Mishna chapter by chapter precedes the Gemara. The *piskaot* frequently only have spaces to mark them off from the Gemara, though often introduced by 'מתני. As a rule they are more carefully copied, with fewer mistakes than the second Ashkenazic group.

The latter has as external bond only the common Franco-German script. There are manuscripts in rabbinical as well as in square script, commentary or commentaries in rabbinical. Mishna and Gemara are mostly in a single column in the middle of the page, commentary or commentaries in the margins. Munich 95 is unique, with the Mishna in the margin and in large square script, while the Gemara is on the main part of the page and in rabbinical script.

Both groups provide a well-balanced choice of tractates from all Orders of the Talmud. But the marked preference in both groups for the fifth Order is notable. It is transmitted almost exclusively in Ashkenazic MSS., so much so that, in an overall view, this Order is the most strongly represented after the Order *Moed*. *Moed* is remarkably neglected in the Ashkenazic MSS.

The most important manuscripts of the first group are from Florence. And Florence 7 is also the oldest dated manuscript of this group (1177). Taken together, the Florence MSS. contain more than a third of the Talmud. The Vatican MS. (nos. 110, 111 and 130 form one MS.) is also extensive, giving the whole of the Order *Nashim*, and also *Nidda* which often appears together with the tractates of the third Order. Other important manuscripts of this group are Vatican 134, which contains most of the Order *Moed*, the Vatican MS. comprising nos. 118 and 119 with most of the Order *Kodashim*, London 402 with tractates from the same Order and the Karlsruhe MS. which belonged to Reuchlin. Far and away the most important manuscript of the second group is Munich 95 containing the whole Talmud and, in addition, the minor tractates. Then there are the Oxford MSS. 367 and 370 with commentaries and the Vatican MS. comprising nos. 122 and 121, giving the whole Order *Kodashim*; also Vatican 115 to 117 with the *Bavot* of the tractate *Nezikin*.

EASTERN MANUSCRIPTS. None of the six eastern manuscripts contains more than one tractate (including Firkow. I 187, a combination of two different fragments). They are all in one column, square, rabbinical and cursive, without commentary. As a rule, the Mishna is given chapter by chapter at the beginning of the Gemara, but is also subject to sub-divisions. The two oldest manuscripts of this group, Vatican 125 with *Pesahim* and Oxford 2678 with *Beitsa*, display the extremes in each case. In some eastern manuscripts which give the Mishna at the beginning of the Gemara, the divisions of the mishnayot are marked with Hebrew numbers as in the most ancient manuscripts. The text of these manuscripts has so far been too little examined for anything to be said here about it. In addition to the manuscripts of this group already mentioned there are Hamburg 169, Oxford 2675 and Paris 671,4.

YEMENITE MANUSCRIPTS. Two of the six Yemenite MSS. are dated, 1540 and 1608. Those without a date would be still later. This is therefore the latest group of manuscripts. No other manuscripts from this late period are dealt with here, because they were copied from printed editions. This is not true, however, of the Yemenite Talmud manuscripts. They represent an absolutely independent text, which has as yet hardly been examined. KARA, *Babylonian Aramaic* deals only, as the title suggests, with grammatical peculiarities. Why there are only

16th and 17th century manuscripts of the Talmud, none earlier or later, is an enigma. E.S. ROSENTHAL (in *Sefer Hanokh Yalon*, Jerusalem 1963) examined the text of the two manuscripts with the tractate *Pesahim* and came to the conclusion that the prototypes came from Babylonia and were of the time of the Geonim, being among the most genuine of the manuscripts of the Babylonian Talmud.

All manuscripts are in rabbinical script, in one column and mostly without commentary. The Mishna always appears in sections throughout the Gemara and *piskaot* are signalled by 'מתני or 'פיסק or by 'מתני and spaces. A feature of these texts is that they are frequently so badly corrupt that they are unintelligible. The manuscript at the Yad Rav Herzog Talmud institute in Jerusalem is an exception. Nonetheless, the genuineness of the text of these manuscripts makes them one of the most important sources in the investigation of the Talmud.

Along with these manuscripts, there are two others of this type: Colombia, Enelow 271, and Oxford 2677 from the Geniza.

There follow two listings of Babylonian Talmud manuscripts, one arranged by library and another by tractate.

List of MSS. by Library

Arras 889
> Gittin (from 14b with lacunae)
> 14th cent.
> Ashkenazic, square and rabbinical
> Mishna divided over the Gemara
> Contains several commentaries

Remarks: As a rule, Mishna and Gemara are in the centre in square handwriting with the commentaries of Rashi and the Tosafists on both sides. Sometimes the text of the Mishna is set off from the Gemara as well.

Literature: Guesnon, Talmud et Machzor

Cambridge Add. 3207
> Yevamot (35b-58b)
> 13th cent.
> Spanish, square, in one column
> Mishna mostly at chapter beginnings, but in some chaps. divided over the Gemara as well
> Mishna is divided by gaps
> Piskaot introduced with מתני' or marked by gaps

Columbia X893-T141
> Megilla, Moed Katan, Zevahim
> Date: 1540
> Yemenite, rabbinical, in one column
> Mishna divided over the Gemara
> Piskaot introduced with מתני' or marked by gaps

Remarks: According to the colophon, it was written in Saana in the year אתתכא. This is the oldest dated Talmud MS. from Yemen. It contains numerous glosses in the margins and between the lines.

Literature: Kara, Babylonian Aramaic

Columbia X893-T14a
> Beitsa, Pesahim
> 17th cent.
> Yemenite, rabbinical, in one column
> Mishna divided over the Gemara

Piskaot introduced with מתני' or marked by gaps

Literature: Kara, Babylonian Aramaic

Florence 7
> Berakhot, Bekhorot, Temura, Keritot, Tamid, Middot, Meila and Kinnim
> Date: 1177
> Italo-Ashkenazic, square, in two columns
> Mishna at the beginning of each chap.

Remarks: This is the oldest extant larger Talmud MS. Tractate Berakhot was written by another hand and was later bound together with the tractates of the 5th Order. The MS. contains numerous marginal glosses.

Publication: Makor, Jerusalem 1972

Florence 8
> Bava Kamma, Bava Metsia
> 12th cent.
> Italo-Ashkenazic, square, in two columns
> Mishna at the beginning of each chap.

Remarks: Nos. 8 and 9 are one MS. It was owned by Christians early on, as indicated by the Latin translations of many sections in the margin. The selection of the translated parts reflects Christian polemic interests in the Talmud in the 13th/14th cent.

Publication: Makor, Jerusalem 1972

Florence 9
> Bava Batra (73a-140a missing), Sanhedrin, Shevuot
> 12th cent.
> Italo-Ashkenazic, square, in two columns
> Mishna at the beginning of each chap.

Publication: Makor, Jerusalem 1972

Göttingen 3
> Taanit (from 25a), Megilla, Hagiga, Beitsa, Moed Katan (till 10b)
> 13th cent.
> Spanish, square, in one column
> Mishna at the beginning of each chap.
> Piskaot introduced with מתני' or marked by gaps

Remarks: On the title page, a Latin dedication to a retired Lutheran minister, written in the year 1792.

Hamburg 165
> Bava Kamma, Bava Metsia, Bava Batra
> Date: 1184
> Spanish, square, in one column
> Mishna at the beginning of each chap.

Remarks: The handwriting and the correctness of the contents make this MS. an exemplary representative of the Spanish MS. tradition.

Hamburg 169
> Hullin
> 13th cent.
> Oriental, square, in one column
> Mishna at the beginning of each chap.

Publication: Makor, Jerusalem 1972

Jerus. Yad R. Herzog, MS. Maimon
> Sanhedrin, Makkot, Taanit (till 25b)
> 17th cent.
> Yemenite, rabbinical, in one column
> Mishna within the Gemara

Remarks: Unlike the other Yemenite Talmud MS., this text is not corrupt.

Literature: Kara, Babylonian Aramaic.

Karlsruhe 9, Reuchlin 2
>Sanhedrin (from 11b with lacunae)
>13th cent.
>Italo-Ashkenazic, square, in two columns
>Mishna at the beginning of each chap.
>Piskaot set off by gaps

Remarks: The MS. was in Reuchlin's library. Some Latin glosses may be his, but probably not so the incorrect title 'Thalmud hierosolymitanus in libris Sanhedrin . . .'

Leningr. Firkow. I 187
>Ketubbot (from 17b), Gittin
>13th/15th cent.
>Oriental, cursive, in one column
>Mishna mostly at chapter beginnings, but in some chaps. divided over the Gemara as well

Remarks: Two different hands. In the first, the Mishna is at the beginning of each chap., in the second it is divided over the Gemara.

London 400, Harley 5508
>Rosh Hashana (beginning and end missing), Yoma (end missing), Hagiga, Beitsa, Megilla, Sukka, Moed Katan, Taanit (end missing)
>13th cent.
>Spanish, square, in one column
>Mishna at the beginning of each chap.
>Piskaot introduced with מתני' or the like

London 402, Add. 25,717
>Bekhorot, Arakhin, Keritot
>13th cent.
>Italo-Ashkenazic, square, in two columns
>Mishna at the beginning of each chap.

Madrid Esc. G-I-3
>Bava Kamma (beginning missing), Bava Metsia, Bava Batra
>15th cent.
>Spanish, cursive, in two columns
>Mishna at the beginning of each chap.

Remarks: The Yerushalmi is given in the margins of the Bavli.
Publication: ed. Lieberman, Jerusalem 1983, with introd. by E.S. Rosenthal

Moscow Ginsburg 1134
>Nedarim, Nazir
>13th cent.
>Ashkenazic, cursive, in two columns
>Mishna at the beginning of each chap.
>Piskaot set off by gaps

Moscow Lenin 594
>Yevamot
>15th cent.
>Spanish, rabbinical
>Mishna at the beginning of each chap.
>Contains several commentaries

Literature: Ha-Talmud ha-Yisraeli ha-Shalem (1983) with illustr.

Munich 6

Pesahim (from 9b), Yoma, Hagiga (till 26a)
12th/13th cent.
Spanish, square, in one column
Mishna at the beginning of each chap.
Mishna divided by gaps
Piskaot introduced with מתני' or marked by gaps
Remarks: Pesahim is divided up in פסח ראשון (chaps. 1-4) and פסח שני (chaps. 5-10). Many Spanish-cursive glosses.

Munich 95

Entire Talmud
Date: 1342
Ashkenazic, square, rabbinical
Remarks: As it contains the entire Talmud, this is certainly the most important Talmud MS. In a *get* contained at the end, Paris is mentioned, which suggests that the MS. was written in France. The beautiful handwriting notwithstanding, the MS. is full of slips of the pen and omissions. The Mishna is written separately in the margin in square script, the Gemara in a very small rabbinical script.
Publication: Strack, Leiden 1912; repr. Makor, Jerusalem 1970

Munich 140

Moed Katan (from 19), Rosh Hashana, Sukka, Taanit, Megilla (till 28)
13th cent.
Spanish, square, in one column
Mishna at the beginning of each chap. and divided by gaps
Piskaot introduced with מתני' or marked by gaps
The lines contain 25-32 resp. 47-67 letters.
Remarks: The MS. was written by several hands. This explains the inequalility of the lines. One hand is very similar to the copyist of Munich No. 6, which is close to this MS. in other respects as well. Among other features, the marginal glosses seem to be from the same hand.

Munich 141

Yevamot (from 48b)
13th cent.
Spanish, square, in one column
Mishna at the beginning of each chap.
Mishna divided by gaps
Piskaot introduced with מתני' or marked by gaps
The lines contain 27 or 47 letters
Remarks: Somewhat later and from a different hand than MS. Munich 140.

New York JTS Adler 850, Mic 9017

Pesahim (part), Rosh Hashana (with lacunae), Sukka (with lacunae)
12th cent.
Spanish, square, in one column
Mishna at the beginning of each chap.
Piskaot introduced with מתני' or marked by gaps
Remarks: Towards the end, only fragments of single pages containing isolated bits of text are extant.

New York JTS Enelow 270, Rab 218/1
>Yoma, Sukka, Rosh Hashana (till 18a)
>Date: 1608-1615
>Yemenite, rabbinical
>Mishna within the Gemara
>Piskaot introduced with מתני' or marked by gaps
>Contains several commentaries

Remarks: In part, the MS. contains commentaries in the margin, which are entitled טירת כסף and שלטי הזהב. It also contains Mishna tractates with commentaries.
Literature: Kara, Babylonian Aramaic

New York JTS Enelow 271
>Pesahim, Yoma
>Beg. 17th cent.
>Yemenite, rabbinical, in one column
>Mishna within the Gemara
>Piskaot introduced with מתני' or the like
>The lines contain 33 or 60 letters
Literature: Kara, Babylonian Aramaic

New York JTS 44830
>Avoda Zara
>Date: 1290
>Spanish, square, rabbinical, in one column
>Mishna at the beginning of each chap.
>Piskaot introduced with מתני' or פסקא or the like
Publication: Abramson, New York 1957

Oxford 366
>Berakhot, Shabbat, Eruvin, Pesahim, Yoma, Rosh Hashana, Sukka, Hagiga, Beitsa, Moed Katan, Taanit, Megilla
>13th cent.
>Spanish, square, in two columns
>Mishna at the beginning of each chap.
Remarks: A note gives Cairo 1557 as date of purchase.

Oxford 367, MS. Opp. 248
>Yevamot (end missing), Kiddushin (with lacunae)
>14th cent.
>Ashkenazic, square, rabbinical
>Mishna within the Gemara, but in some chaps. also at the beginning of the Gemara
>Contains several commentaries
Remarks: Yevamot has a different chapter division than the editions. As a rule, the Mishna is set off from the Gemara in the margin, but sometimes is given with the Gemara in the middle, with side commentaries in margins.

Oxford 368, MS. Opp. 38
>Gittin (7b-86a with lacunae)
>14th cent.
>Ashkenazic, square, rabbinical
>Mishna at the beginning of each chap.
>Piskaot introduced with מתני' or marked by gaps
>Contains one commentary

Oxford 369
>Bava Batra (9b-79a)
>14th cent.
>Ashkenazic, rabbinical
>Mishna within the Gemara
>Piskaot set off by gaps
>Contains one commentary

Remarks: The end is from another hand.

Oxford 370
>Tamid, Middot, Meila, Arakhin
>14th cent.
>Ashkenazic, rabbinical
>Mishna within the Gemara
>Contains one commentary

Oxford 2673,8, Heb. b 1
>Keritot (with lacunae)
>Date: 1123
>Spanish, square, in one column
>Mishna at the beginning of each chap.
>Mishna division is marked by Hebrew letters
>Piskaot introduced with מתני' or the like
>Found in the Cairo Geniza
>Lines contain 33 or 68 letters

Remarks: This fragment is the oldest dated Talmud MS.
Publication: Schechter, Cambridge 1896

Oxford 2675,1, Heb. d 20
>Yevamot (till 23b)
>13th cent.
>Oriental, rabbinical, in one column
>Mishna at the beginning of each chap.
>Mishna division is marked by Hebrew letters
>Piskaot introduced with מתני' or marked by gaps
>Found in the Cairo Geniza

Remarks: Some pages are very fragmentary.

Oxford 2675,2
>Sota (fragments)
>13th cent.
>Spanish, cursive, in one column
>Mishna within the Gemara
>Piskaot introduced with מתני' or the like
>Found in the Cairo Geniza

Oxford 2677, Heb. e 51
>Sukka (beginning missing)
>16th/17th cent.
>Yemenite, rabbinical, in one column
>Mishna within the Gemara
>Found in the Cairo Geniza
>Lines contain 22 resp. 29 letters

Literature: Kara, Babylonian Aramaic

Oxford 2678, Heb. e 51
> Beitsa (from 28b)
> 12th cent.
> Oriental, rabbinical, in one column
> Mishna within the Gemara

Paris 671,4
> Berakhot
> 15th cent.
> Oriental, rabbinical, in one column
> Mishna at the beginning of each chap.
> Mishna division is marked by Hebrew letters

Paris 1337
> Bava Batra, Avoda Zara, Horayot
> Beg. 14th cent.
> Spanish, square, in one column
> Mishna at the beginning of each chap.

Paris A.I.U. II 147a
> Zevahim (from 22a), Menahot (with lacunae), Meila (fragments), Temura (till 22b)
> 13th cent.
> Ashkenazic, square, in two columns
> Mishna at the beginning of each chap., and divided by gaps
> Piskaot introduced with מתני׳ or marked by gaps

Sassoon 594
> Pesahim (till 113b)
> 16th cent.
> Spanish, square, in one column
> Mishna at the beginning of each chap.
> Piskaot introduced with מתני׳ or the like

Remarks: Many glosses are found in the margin. Scriptural verses are usually vocalized. The chapter division conforms to the older MSS.

Vatican 108
> Shabbat (from 47b), Moed Katan
> 13th cent.
> Spanish, square, in one column
> Mishna mostly at chapter beginnings, but in some chaps. divided over the Gemara as well

Publication: Makor, Jerusalem 1972

Vatican 109
> Eruvin (beginning and end missing), Pesahim, Beitsa
> 14th cent.
> Italo-Ashkenazic, square, in two columns
> Mishna at the beginning of each chap.

Remarks: The ends of Pesahim and Beitsa are from another hand. Pesahim chap. 10 comes after chap. 4.

Publication: Makor, Jerusalem 1972 (without Pesahim)

Vatican 110
>Sota, Nedarim, Nazir
>14th cent.
>Italo-Ashkenazic, square, in two columns
>Mishna at the beginning of each chap.

Remarks: Before the present binding was done, the order must have been Nedarim, Nazir, Sota. Cf. Vatican 111.
Publication: Makor, Jerusalem 1972

Vatican 111
>Yevamot, Kiddushin, Nidda
>Date: 1384
>Italo-Ashkenazic, square, in two columns
>Mishna at the beginning of each chap.

Remarks: The MS. is the continuation of Vatican 110. It has the same scribal features and custos decorations. Vatican 130 is part of the same MS.; it must originally have contained the entire Order Nashim as well as Nidda which is often considered part of it.
Publication: Makor, Jerusalem 1974

Vatican 112
>Ketubbot (till 52a)
>13th/14th cent.
>Italo-Ashkenazic, square, in two columns
>Mishna at the beginning of each chap.

Publication: Makor, Jerusalem 1974

Vatican 113
>Ketubbot (with lacunae), Nidda (till 50a)
>12th/13 cent.
>Italo-Ashkenazic, square, in two columns
>Mishna at the beginning of each chap.
>Piskaot set off by gaps

Remarks: The MS. was written by two copyists, probably from the same school (Italy?). The change is on fol. 30a in the middle of the text.

Vatican 115
>Bava Kamma (last page only), Bava Metsia (incomplete), Bava Batra
>14th cent.
>Ashkenazic, square, in two columns
>Mishna within the Gemara, but in some chaps. given at the beginning of the Gemara

Vatican 116
>Bava Kamma
>14th cent.
>Ashkenazic, rabbinical, in two columns
>Mishna at the beginning of each chap.
>Mishna set off by gaps
>Piskaot set off by gaps

Vatican 117

> Bava Metsia
> 14th cent.
> Ashkenazic, rabbinical, in two columns
> Mishna at the beginning of each chap.

Remarks: The MS. has a colophon, but the date is illegible.

Vatican 118

> Zevahim, Menahot (till 94a)
> 13th cent.
> Italo-Ashkenazic, square, in two columns
> Mishna at the beginning of each chap.

Remarks: The beginning of Zevahim was bound together with MS. Vatican 119 by mistake. Vatican 118 and 119 are one MS., as appears from identical scribal features and custos decorations.
Publication: Makor, Jerusalem 1974

Vatican 119

> Temura, Arakhin, Bekhorot, Meila, Keritot (till 22b)
> 13th cent.
> Italo-Ashkenazic, square, in two columns
> Mishna mostly at chapter beginnings, but in some chaps. divided over the Gemara as well

Publication: Makor, Jerusalem 1974

Vatican 120

> Menahot, Bekhorot, Keritot, Meila, Tamid, Kinnim, Arakhin, Temura, Middot
> 14th cent.
> Ashkenazic, square, in two columns
> Mishna mostly at chapter beginnings, but in some chaps. divided over the Gemara as well

Vatican 121

> Zevahim, Hullin
> 14th cent.
> Ashkenazic, square, in two columns
> Mishna mostly at chapter beginnings, but in some chaps. divided over the Gemara as well
> Mishna divided by gaps
> Piskaot set off by gaps

Remarks: This MS. is the first part of Vatican 120. This appears not only from the identical handwriting and custoses, but also by the note: סדר קדשי' חצי שלי. The MS. seems to have been divided in a heritage partition.

Vatican 122

> Hullin
> 13th cent.
> Ashkenazic, square, in two columns
> Mishna at the beginning of each chap.

Vatican 123

> Hullin (several fragments)
> 14th cent.
> Ashkenazic, rabbinical

Remarks: Two fragments with large segments of Hullin. In one, the Mishna mostly comes first, while it is divided up in the other. One is in one column, the other in two.

Vatican 125
>   Pesahim (beginning and end missing)
>   12th cent.
>   Oriental, square, in one column
>   Mishna at the beginning of each chap.
>   Piskaot introduced with מתני' or marked by gaps

Remarks: The order of chapters differs from the editions. Though the Mishna is given entirely at chapter beginnings in part of the MS., it is also given, practically complete, within the Gemara. Apart from these mishnayot within the Gemara, there are also piskaot.

Vatican 127
>   Eruvin (I + II), Shevuot (I + II), Gittin (till 17a), Nidda (I + II)
>   14th cent.
>   Ashkenazic, square
>   Mishna mostly at chapter beginnings, but in some chaps. divided over the Gemara as well
>   Piskaot introduced with מתני' or marked by gaps
>   Contains a commentary

Remarks: The Mishna is at the beginning of each chapter till Shevuot, where it stands apart and is divided over the Gemara. Elsewhere, Mishna and Gemara are always in the middle, with Rashi's commentary on the sides, often in a special geometric pattern. In Nidda, the Mishna is partly given twice, once at chapter beginnings and again in the course of the Gemara.

Vatican 130
>   Gittin, Ketubbot
>   13th cent.
>   Italo-Ashkenazic, square, in two columns
>   Mishna at the beginning of each chap.

Remarks: The MS. belongs together with Vatrican 110 and 111. Cf. remarks on the latter.
Publication: Makor, Jerusalem 1972

Vatican 134
>   Pesahim, Yoma (till 26b, and 64a-71a), Rosh Hashana (from 28b), Taanit, Sukka, Beitsa,
>   Megilla, Hagiga, Moed Katan
>   13th cent.
>   Italo-Ashkenazic, square, in two columns
>   Mishna at the beginning of each chap.

Remarks: According to Assemani, the MS. once belonged to the Hamburg community. The first part of Pesahim was lacking and was filled in by an Ashkenazic copyist in the 16th cent.
Publication: Makor, Jerusalem 1972 without Pesahim

Vatican 140
>   Gittin, Shevuot
>   14th cent.
>   Ashkenazic, square
>   Mishna within the Gemara, in some chaps. also at the beginning of the Gemara
>   Piskaot introduced with מתני' or marked by gaps
>   Contains a commentary

Vatican 156
>   Shevuot (till 30b)
>   14th cent.
>   Ashkenazic, square
>   Mishna at the beginning of each chap.

Vatican 171,34

Hagiga
Date: 1493
Ashkenazic, rabbinical, in one column
Mishna within the Gemara, in some chaps. also at the beginning of the Gemara
Piskaot introduced with מתני' or פסקא or the like

Vatican 487,11

Ketubbot (9b-95a)
13th/14th cent.
Spanish, rabbinical
Mishna at the beginning of each chap.

List of MSS. by Tractate

Preliminary: MS. Munich 95 which covers the entire Babylonian Talmud is not referred to in this list.

Order Zeraim

Berakhot
Florence 7	1177	Ital.-Ask.
Oxford 366	13th cent.	Span.
Paris 671,4	15th cent.	Orient.

Order Moed

Shabbat
Oxford 366	13th cent.	Span.	
Vatican 108	13th cent.	Span.	from 47b
Vatican 127	14th cent.	Ashk.	I + II

Eruvin
Oxford 366	13th cent.	Span.	
Vatican 127	14th cent.	Ashk.	I + II
Vatican 109	14th cent.	Ital.-Ashk.	beg. and end missing

Pesahim
NY JTS Adler 850	12th cent.	Span.	part
Vatican 125	12th cent.	Orient.	beg. and end missing
Munich 6	12/13th cent.	Span.	from 9b
Vatican 134	13th cent.	Ital.-Ashk.	
Oxford 366	13th cent.	Span.	
Vatican 109	14th cent.	Ital.-Ashk.	
Sassoon 594	16th cent.	Span.	till 113b
NY JTS Enelow 271	beg.17th cent.	Yem.	
Columbia X893-T14a	17th cent.	Yem.	

Yoma
Munich 6	12/13th cent.	Span.	
Vatican 134	13th cent.	Ital.-Ashk.	2a-26b, 64a-71a
Oxford 366	13th cent.	Span.	
London 400	13th cent.	Span.	end missing
NY JTS Enelow 270	1608-1615	Yem.	
NY JTS Enelow 271	beg.17th cent.	Yem.	

Sukka
NY JTS Adler 850	12th cent.	Span.	with lacunae
Vatican 134	13th cent.	Ital.-Ashk.	
London 400	13th cent.	Span.	
Oxford 366	13th cent.	Span.	
Munich 140	13th cent.	Span.	
Oxford 2677	16/17th cent.	Yem.	beg. missing
NY JTS Enelow 270	1608-1615	Yem.	

Beitsa

Oxford 2678	12th cent.	Orient.	from 28b
Vatican 134	13th cent.	Ital.-Ashk.	
Götingen 3	13th cent.	Span.	
Oxford 366	13th cent	Span.	
London 400	13th cent.	Span.	
Vatican 109	14th cent.	Ital.-Ashk.	
Columbia X893-T14a	17th cent.	Yem.	

Rosh Hashana

NY JTS Adler 850	12th cent.	Span	with lacunae
Vatican 134	13th cent.	Ital.-Ashk.	from 28b
Munich 140	13th cent.	Span.	
Oxford 366	13th cent.	Span.	
London 400	13th cent.	Span.	beg. and end missing
NY JTS Enelow 270	1608-1615	Yem.	til 18a

Taanit

Vatican 134	13th cent.	Ital.-Ashk.	
Göttingen	13th cent.	Span.	from 25a
Munich 140	13th cent.	Span.	
Oxford 366	13th cent.	Span.	
London 400	13th cent.	Span.	end missing
Jerus. Yad R.Herzog	17th cent.	Yem.	till 25b

Megilla

Vatican 134	13th cent.	Ital.-Ashk.	
London 400	13th cent.	Span.	till 28
Munich 140	13th cent.	Span.	
Oxford 366	13th cent.	Span.	
Göttingen 3	13th cent. Span.	Span.	
Columbia X893-T141	1540	Yem.	

Moed Katan

Vatican 134	13th cent.	Ital.-Ashk.	
London 400	13th cent.	Span.	
Vatican 108	13th cent.	Span.	
Oxford 366	13th cent.	Span.	
Göttingen 3	13th cent Span.	till 10b	till 10b
Columbia X893-T141	1540	Yem.	

Hagiga

Munich 6	12/13th cent.	Span.	till 26a
Vatican 134	13th cent.	Ital.Ashk.	
Oxford 366	13th cent.	Span.	
London 400	13th cent.	Span.	
Göttingen 3	13th cent.	Span.	
Vatican 171,34	1493	Ashk.	

Order Nashim

Yevamot

Munich 141	13th cent.	Span.	from 48b
Cambridge Add 3207	13th cent.	Span.	35b-58b
Oxford 2675,1	13th cent.	Orient.	till 23b
Vatican 111	1384	Ital.-Ashk.	
Oxford 367	14th cent.	Ashk.	end missing
Moscow Lenin 594	15th cent.	Span.	

Ketubbot

Vatican 113	12/13th cent.	Ital. Ashk.	lacunae
Vatican 130	13th cent.	Ital.-Ashk.	
Lening.Firko.I 187	13/15th cent.	Orient.	from 17b
Vatican 112	13/14th cent.	Ital.-Ashk.	till 52a
Vatican 487,11	13/14th cent.	Span.	9b-95a

Nedarim

Moscow Ginsb. 1134	13th cent.	Ashk.	
Vatican 110	14th cent.	Ital.-Ashk.	

Nazir

Moscow Ginsb. 1134	13th cent.	Ashk.	
Vatican 110	14th cent.	Ital.-Ashk.	

Gittin

Vatican 130	13th cent.	Ital.-Ashk.	
Lening.Firko.I 187	13/15th cent.	Orient.	
Arras 889	14th cent.	Ashk.	from 14b, lacunae
Oxford 368	14th cent.	Ashk.	7b-86a, lacunae
Vatican 127	14th cent.	Ashk.	till 17a
Vatican 140	14th cent.	Ashk.	

Sota

Oxford 2675,2	13th cent.	Span.	lacunae
Vatican 110	14th cent.	Ital.-Ashk.	

Kiddushin

Vatican 111	1384	Ital.-Ashk.	
Oxford 367	14th cent.	Ashk.	lacunae

Order Nezikin

Bava Kamma

Hamburg 165	1184	Span.	
Florence 8	12th cent.	Ital.-Ashk.	
Vatican 116	14th cent.	Ashk.	
Madrid Esc. G-I-3	15th cent.	Span.	beg. missing

Bava Metsia

Hamburg 165	1184	Span.	
Florence 8	12th cent.	Ital.-Ashk.	
Vatican 115	14th cent.	Ashk.	incomplete
Vatican 117	14th cent.	Ashk.	
Madrid Esc. G-I-3	15th cent.	Span.	

Bava Batra
Hamburg 165	1184	Span.	
Florence 9	12th cent.	Ital.Ashk.	73a-140a missing
Paris 1337	beg.14th cent.	Span.	
Oxford 369	14th cent.	Ashk.	
Vatican 115	14th cent.	Ashk.	
Madrid Esc. G-I-3	15th cent.	Span.	

Sanhedrin
Florence 9	12th cent.	Ital.-Ashk.	
Karlsruhe 9	13th cent.	Ital.-Ashk.	from 11b, lacunae
Jerus.Yad R.Herzog	17th cent.	Yem.	

Makkot
Munich 140	13th cent.	Span.	from 19
Jerus.Yad R.Herzog	17th cent.	Yem.	

Shevuot
Florence 9	12th cent.	Ital.-Ashk.	
Vatican 156	14th cent.	Ashk.	till 30b
Vatican 140	14th cent.	Ashk.	

Avoda Zara
NY JTS 44830	1290	Span.	
Paris 1337	beg.14th cent.	Span.	

Horayot
Paris 1337	beg.14th cent.	Span.	

Order Kodashim

Zevahim
Paris AIU II 147a	13th cent.	Ashk.	from 22a
Vatican 118	13th cent.	Ital.-Ashk.	
Vatican 121	14th cent.	Ashk.	
Columbia X893-T141	1540	Yem.	

Menahot
Paris AIU II 147a	13th cent.	Ashk.	lacunae
Vatican 118	13th cent.	Ital.-Ashk.	till 94a
Vatican 120	14th cent.	Ashk.	

Hullin
Vatican 122	13th cent.	Ashk.	
Hamburg 169	13th cent.	Orient.	
Vatican 123	14th cent.	Ashk.	fragments
Vatican 121	14th cent.	Ashk.	

Bekhorot
Florence 7	1177	Ital.-Ashk.	
London 402	13th cent.	Ital.-Ashk.	
Vatican 119	13th cent.	Ital.-Ashk.	
Vatican 120	14th cent.	Ashk.	

Arakhin
London 402	13th cent.	Ital.-Ashk.	
Vatican 119	13th cent.	Ital.-Ashk.	
Oxford 370	14th cent.	Ashk.	
Vatican 120	14th cent.	Ashk.	

Temura
Florence 7	1177	Ital.-Ashk.	
Paris AIU II 147a	13th cent.	Ashk.	till 22b
Vatican 119	13th cent.	Ital.-Ashk.	
Vatican 120	14th cent.	Ashk.	

Keritot
Oxford 2673,8	1123	Span.	lacunae
Florence 7	1177	Ital.-Ashk.	
London 402	13th cent.	Ital.-Ashk.	
Vatican 119	13th cent.	Ital.-Ashk.	till 22b
Vatican 120	14th cent.	Ashk.	

Meila
Florence 7	1177	Ital.-Ashk.	
Paris AIU II 147a	13th cent.	Ashk.	fragment
Vatican 119	13th cent.	Ital.-Ashk.	
Oxford 370	14th cent.	Ashk.	
Vatican 120	14th cent.	Ashk.	

Tamid
Florence 7	1177	Ital.-Ashk.	
Oxford 370	14th cent.	Ashk.	
Vatican 120	14th cent.	Ashk.	

Middot
Florence 7	1177	Ital.-Ashk.	
Oxford 370	14th cent.	Ashk.	
Vatican 120	14th cent.	Ashk.	

Kinnim
Florence 7	1177	Ital.-Ashk.	
Vatican 120	14th cent.	Ashk.	

Order Toharot

Nidda
Vatican 113	12/13th cent.	Ital.-Ashk.	till 50a
Vatican 111	1384	Ital.-Ashk.	
Vatican 127	14th cent.	Ashk.	I + II

Chapter Nine

The External Tractates

M.B. Lerner

From the Amoraic period onwards, there is evidence that numerous tractates of tradition literature circulated independently of the recognized literary units, i.e. Mishna, Tosefta, Talmud and Tannaic Midrashim. These included the aggadic midrashim, later edited in what we know as the Amoraic midrash collections, and the external or 'minor' tractates which are dealt with here.

The fact that these tractates, some of which are certainly not smaller than the everage Tannaic tractate, were not incorporated in the main body of talmudic literature caused them to be referred to as *ketanot* (i.e. small, minor);[1] *toseftot* (i.e. supplementary, additional),[2] or *sefarim hitsoniim* (i.e. external tractates).[3] Even though they do not seem to have been held in high esteem in Gaonic circles,[4] later authorities nevertheless occasionally utilized them for halakhic rulings.[5]

From a literary standpoint, it is important to note that most of these tractates are original independent compilations, and that much of their subject matter is not found in any other extant source. On the other hand, there is no denying the fact that the largest of them, *Avot de-R. Natan*, is a companion text to *Massekhet Avot*, following it closely and elaborating upon it. Furthermore, the enigmatic *Kalla Rabbati* is actually a pseudo-talmudic elaboration of tractates *Kalla, Derekh Erets*, and *Perek Kinyan Tora*.

There is no consistency in regard to subject matter. *Avot de-R. Natan* is purely aggadic, while most of the smaller tracts, e.g. *Sefer Tora, Mezuza* etc., are purely halakhic. Other large tractates, such as *Semahot, Sofrim* and *Kalla*, are ostensibly halakhic in content, but numerous aggadic teachings and episodes may also be discerned in them. The tractates comprising *derekh erets*

---

[1] Harkavy, *Responsen*, no. 15, pp. 6-7; no. 248, pp. 124-5; *Iggeret Rav Sherira Gaon*, 47 (French rec.).

[2] Maimonides, introd. to *Mishne Tora* (ed. Lieberman), 9. Individual tractates were thus sometimes referred to as Tosefta, cf. Higger, *Semachot*, introd., 10; *id*. 'Ketanot', 92-5.

[3] *B.T. Ber.* 18a, *Tosafot s.v.* למחר; R. Eliezer ben Yoel ha-Levi, *Sefer Rabiah* (ed. Aptowitzer) 2, 333. R. Asher ben Yehiel, *Responsa, kelal* III, no. 7. Cf. Higger, *Semachot*, 11-12; also Harkavy, *Responsen*, no. 218, p. 103. Note that this appellation is also used to denote mystic (*Hekhalot*) tracts, see *Sefer Rabiah* 2, 196; *Mahzor Vitry*, 655.

[4] See sources above, n. 1, also Harkavy, *Responsen*, no. 380, p. 197.

[5] See sources above, n. 3; I. Ratzabi in: Kasher, *Tora Shelema* 29, 99.

literature are decidedly of ethical content, but here too, one frequently finds an admixture of halakhic and aggadic traditions.

The exact dimensions of this literature are also uncertain. No official tabulation or complete collection of the various works is extant. A medieval tradition of 'seven minor tractates' apparently included the smallest halakhic tractates but here too, the tractates in this compilation do not seem to have been universally recognized. An alternative tradition of 'nine external tractates' which included *Semahot* and *Kalla*, may also be noted.[6] This situation seems to be summed up ironically by the homily on Cant 6:8, '. . . "And damsels without number" – this is the external mishna'.[7] One should therefore not be surprised over the fact that traditional talmudic study has more or less neglected most of these tractates, and that during the course of time, some of them have fallen into oblivion.

It is somewhat surprising that no clear-cut criteria for determining the date of these compositions have been offered by zunz and his followers.[8] While *Avot de-R. Natan* has come to be recognized as an ancient text, bearing very close affinity to the Tannaic period, many of the other tractates have been relegated to the early Gaonic era, i.e. the eight and ninth centuries.[9] A proper approach demands that each of these texts be subjected to a searching analysis in order to attempt to define its formative period. Suffice it to say, as a sort of preliminary remark, that many novel conclusions may arise from such an analysis.

Owing to the fact that some of these tracts contain halakhic material, they sometimes circulated together with the Talmud.[10] As a matter of fact, three of these tractates, *Semahot, Kalla* and *Sofrim*, were printed together with the first edition of the Babylonian Talmud, Venice 1523. In the third Venetian printing (1550), three more tractates were added: *Derekh Erets Rabba*; *Derekh Erets Zutta* and *Avot de-R. Natan*. In the subsequent complete Talmud editions, the minor tractates were placed at the end of the fourth Order following *Massekhet Avot*, since the largest of these tractates, *Avot de-R. Natan*, relates directly to *Avot*. The remaining tractates (*Kalla Rabbati*; Seven Minor Tracts) were added to the Talmud by the publishers of the Romm edition, Wilna 1883.

It is most fortunate that all of the minor tractates have been subjected to critical editions, which, in spite of their inadequacies, are vital for scholarly study. schechter's edition of *Avot de-R. Natan* (Vienna 1887) was actually the first rabbinic text to be edited on the basis of all existing manuscripts. Special mention should be made of the indefatigable efforts of Michael higger (1898-1952), who within the course of nine years (1929-1937) published six scholarly

---

[6] R. Jacob Sikily in the Introduction to *Yalkut Talmud Tora*, see Higger, *Semachot*, introd. 12.

[7] *Num. R.* 18:21 and parallels, see Higger, *Semachot*, introd., 9.

[8] See Zunz-Albeck, *Derashot*, 45 and notes.

[9] Cf. the remarks of Assaf, *Tekufat ha-Geonim*, 174.

[10] MS. Munich 95 includes the *Derekh Erets* tractates and *Massekhet Kalla*. The latter is also part of the talmudic collection *Extractiones de Talmud* in MS. Paris 16558; see Merchavia, *The Church*, 293, 418.

volumes which cover all of the other texts and in addition include lengthy introductory studies.

Two of Higger's texts (*Massekhtot Ketanot, Massekhet Derekh Erets*) are accompanied by a liberal English translation. A complete translation of all the minor tractates published in the talmudic corpus appeared in two volumes, London 1965 as an addition to the Soncino translation of the Talmud.

Avot de-R. Natan

NAME AND CHARACTERS

The name of this tractate is usually translated 'The Fathers According to R. Natan'.[11] In view of the interpretation offered above,[12] it may be postulated that 'the fundamental principles' of R. Natan are actually implied. This tractate is a companion volume to *Massekhet Avot* and relates directly to it in most of its sections. Owing to the fact that *Avot* is one of the few mishnaic tracts which do not have a parallel tractate in the collection of extraneous teachings (baraitot) within the framework of the *Tosefta*, it has been logically assumed that *Avot de-R. Natan* is actually the 'Tosefta' to *Avot*. This is probably the reason why many early authorities refer to this tractate as a baraita[13] or 'tosefta'.[14] Others occasionally quoted it as '*Mishnat* (i.e. the Mishna of) *R. Natan*',[15] or simply as 'aggada'.[16]

The usage of such variegated epithets seems to heighten the question as to the actual nature of *Avot de-R. Natan*: a) Does it represent the teachings collected by a single authority (R. Natan)? b) Is it a collection of external Tannaic teachings (baraita) relating to the Mishna? c) According to its subject matter, should it not be classified as a work of aggadic and midrashic literature? All of these questions must be answered in the affirmative and this is a sure sign of the composite nature of the tractate. On the one hand, there is no denying its direct relationship to *Massekhet Avot*, but on the other hand, one should be aware of the fact that *Avot de-R. Natan* contains a host of aggadic material not directly related to the Mishna but reminiscent of an aggadic midrash.[17]

---

[11] This is actually a liberal translation employed by Goldin. Technically, one should translate '. . . of R. Natan', cf. Finkelstein, *Mabo*.

[12] See above, p. 264.

[13] R. Yaakov be-R. Shimshon; R. Yosef Bekhor Shor; R. Yehuda ben Kalonymos; R. Menahem ha-Meiri *et al.*; see Schechter, introd., ix-xiii.

[14] *Tosafot* to B.T. *Bava K.* 25a, *s.v.* ק"ו; R. Yosef ben Yehuda, *Sefer Musar* (ed. Bacher) introd. xiii (end). See Zunz-Albeck, *Derashot*, 286 n. 62.

[15] E.g. R. Yaakov be-R. Shimshon, Commentary to *Avot*, *Mahzor Vitry*, 536-7; 544-5.

[16] E.g. R. Yehiel be-R. Yekutiel of Rome, *Maalot ha-middot* (Jerusalem 1968) 24, 71, 256.

[17] E.g. the story of Moses' death, *A.R.N.* a 12 (25a-26a); b 25 (26a-b); also appendix 2 (= MS. Vatican 44) 156-7.

The name of R. Natan in the title of this work is also most unclear. The problems concerning the title were already formulated by R. Yaakov be-R. Shimshon, a twelfth century rabbi, in his commentary to *Avot*:[18]

> This baraita is entitled *Avot de-R. Natan*, and I do not know the reason why. If this refers to this Sage's being mentioned at the beginning of the tractate,[19] it is clearly not the reason, since R. Yose ha-Gelili is the first Sage mentioned, R. Akiva the second, and R. Natan is only the third . . .[20] As a possible answer, we might propound that R. Natan was the redactor of this collection, and this was the tradition of the ancients, much like the 'Mishna of R. Hiya and R. Oshaya . . .'[21] and this work should therefore be identified with the 'Mishna of R. Natan', which is mentioned in Midrash Kohelet . . .

This mention of the 'Mishna of R. Natan'[22] is reminiscent of the early Amoraic tradition which speaks of R. Yehuda the Patriarch and R. Natan as 'the end (i.e. final authorities?) of the mishnaic era'.[23] However, it is difficult to explain the mention of R. Natan, who was actually a predecessor of R. Yehuda the Patriarch, and who was mainly active during the fourth generation of Tannaim (c. 140-175 C.E.), as a 'final authority' of the Mishna. Nevertheless, it is quite possible that the real meaning of the above statements is that R. Natan was the final editor of a collection of teachings,[24] which existed alongside the collection(s) edited by R. Yehuda the Patriarch. This may very well be an allusion to the tractate *Avot de-R. Natan* in some form.

At this point in our discussion, it must be stated that *Avot de-R. Natan* is extant in two different versions, termed version A and version B.[24a] These versions are largely parallel but far from identical. The implications of this situation will be discussed below; here it suffices to state that apparently R. Natan's collection was transmitted in two parallel versions.

At any rate, in view of the above, we may assume that *Avot de-R. Natan* was so called due to the fact that it was based on a recension of *Massekhet Avot* edited by R. Natan the Babylonian. Indeed, scholars have long noted the fact that *Avot de-R. Natan* is based on a version of the Mishna which preceded the

---

[18] R. Yaakov be-R. Shimshon, Commentary to *Avot* 1:1, *Mahzor Vitry*, 463-4.

[19] Several midrashic works derive their names from Sages mentioned in the opening passages, cf. e.g. *Bereshit [de-R. Oshaya] Rabba*; *Pirkei de-R. Eliezer*; *Mishnato shel R. Eliezer, et al.*

[20] See *A.R.N.* a 1 (1a). In version B, there is no mention whatsoever of R. Natan.

[21] *Cant. R.* 8,2. Cf. *Lam. R.* proem 23 (p. 18).

[22] *Eccl. R.* 5,8,2 (see also *Lev. R.* 22,1 [p. 496] l. 4 of the variants) speaks of the 'Tosefot' (= additions) of R. Yehuda the Prince and R. Natan (*Lev. R.* MS. Munich: 'Tosefet of R. Yonatan') which seems to refer to a collection of baraitot, cf. below.

[23] *B.T. Bava M.* 86a.

[24] According to *Iggeret Rav Sherira Gaon*, 41 the 'Babylonian' collections of baraitot were referred to as 'Mishnat R. Natan'. See also Epstein, *Tannaitic Literature*, 169.

[24a] The references given in this volume are with a lower case a or b, with the chapter no. and the folio in parentheses, as in *ARN* a 5 (13b). However, in the course of this discussion we use a capital A or B for typographical reasons: version A, chap. 5; or, A:5, 13b.

extant text of the tractate *Avot*, ordinarily attributed to R. Yehuda the Patriarch.[25] If this assumption is correct, one may hypothesize that the underlying mishnaic portion of *Avot de-R. Natan*, and possibly some additional Tannaic teachings appended to it as well, reflect the redaction of R. Natan. This would probably include the mishnaic material in the first segment (version A, chap. 1-17 and version B, chap. 1-30) and the basic numerical aggadic portions of the final segment (version A, chap. 31ff. and version B, chap. 36ff.). Some of the latter are quoted in ancient Palestinian texts as baraitot of R. Natan,[26] which supports this hypothesis.

On the other hand, it would be most difficult to attribute the redaction of the entire tractate to R. Natan. Such a conclusion would be most difficult since numerous contemporaries and Sages who lived after R. Natan are quoted, and he himself is also mentioned several times.[27] Suffice it to say that in spite of the fact that *Avot de-R. Natan* obviously underwent numerous later redactions, with a considerable amount of interpretative material, teachings, exempla and homilies being added to the rather modest basic corpus, the original title of this work[28] remained the same throughout the ages.[29]

STRUCTURE AND CONTENTS

The fact that the initial segment of *Avot de-R. Natan* corresponds to the first two chapters of the tractate *Avot,* although based on an early redaction of it, also accounts for some distinctive characteristics. This segment represents an elaboration and commentary on the underlying mishnayot, explaining and developing them, in many cases by the adduction of alternative explanations, scriptural antecedents, and Tannaic exempla. On the basis of various halakhic elements, FINKELSTEIN has endeavoured to show that the first section (version A, chap. 1-11; version B, chap. 1-22) originated in the academy of Beit Shammai.[30] Without going into details, it may readily be said that there is no real basis for this conclusion.[31]

The intermediary segment (version A, chap. 14-30; version B, chap. 32-35, corresponding to chap. 3-4 of the Mishna) is of a completely different nature, being mainly a loose collection of teachings of various Sages without additional

---

[25] Hoffman, *First Mishna*, 45ff.; Epstein, *Tannaitic Literature*, 232-3.

[26] See Epstein, *Nosah*, 50.

[27] See Schechter, Introduction, xxxvi, *s.v.* R. Natan.

[28] See however n. 15 above. However, the appellation 'Mishnat R. Natan' may very well be due to the conceptual approach of R. Yaakov be-R. Shimshon; see above n. 18. The only real exception to the attribution of this tractate to R. Natan is evinced by a Westminster College Geniza fragment whose colophon reads 'Avot de-R. Yonatan'; see Bregman, 'Early Fragment', 220, no. 5. However, this may very well be the mistake of a copyist. Cf. also n. 22 above.

[29] The earliest authority to quote our tractate by name is R. Nissim ben Yaakov ibn Shahin of Kairwan (fl. first half of 11th cent.); see his *Sefer ha-mafteah* to *B.T. Shabb.* 112b.

[30] Finkelstein, *Mabo*, 18-39 (xii-xiii).

[31] Cf. Dinary, 'Impurity Customs', 307 n. 40.

elaboration[32] or a systematic organization of the material. Some of the early elements prevalent in this section may also stem from the editorial activities of R. Natan. FINKELSTEIN observed that version A, chaps. 19-22[33] each begin with the maxims of Shammaitic scholars who were active during the last period of the Second Commonwealth.[34] Furthermore, version A, chaps. 23-36 each discuss the sayings of the group of four scholars 'who entered the orchard' (pardes, i.e. mystic experience):[35] Ben Zoma, Elisha ben Avuya,[36] Ben Azzai and R. Akiva.[37] On the basis of these observations,[38] Finkelstein concluded that certain fixed principles have guided the editor. However, this is far from convincing. It is most likely that the editor based his arrangement mainly on chronological considerations and not necessarily on academic alignment.

It is interesting to note that between the first and second segments, version A contains an interpolated chapter, apparently of later vintage:[39] chap. 18, which enumerates the individual distinctions and praises of the Sages active during the third and fourth generations of Tannaim. This is an obvious sequel to the similar praises of R. Yohanan ben Zakkai regarding his disciples.[40] Similarly, the corresponding chapter in version B (i.e. chap. 31) seems to present supplementary material to previous chapters.[41]

The third and final segment of Avot de-R. Natan[42] which parallels chapter five of Massekhet Avot, is a collection of aggadic teachings based on numbers, descending from ten to three. These usually summarize some aggadic principle, e.g. 'Ten people prophesied and did not know that they were prophesying' (B:43, 59b); 'There are seven created things, one superior to the other' (A:37, 54b). As stated above, this section is part of the oldest stratum of Avot de-R. Natan and such ancient works as the Palestinian Talmud and Genesis Rabba seem to have recognized it as a work composed by R. Natan.[43]

Aside from being a collection of the teachings of individual Sages and commentaries, Avot de-R. Natan is replete with aggadic material, including some of the more well-known biographical anecdotes of the Sages. These 'exempla' are usually adduced in order to provide concrete real-life evidence for the educatio-

---

[32] Cf. however A.R.N. a 20-21 (35b-37b).

[33] Cf. A.R.N. b 32; 34.

[34] Finkelstein, Mabo, 52-60 (xv-xvi): R. Nehunya ben ha-Kana; Akavya ben Mahalalel; R. Dosa ben Harkinas; R. Hanina ben Dosa; R. Hanina, the deputy of the High Priest.

[35] Cf. A.R.N. b 33 (36a-b); 35.

[36] Note that in version A, all of chap. 24 is devoted to the teachings of this renegade scholar. See also A.R.N. b 35 (39a).

[37] Finkelstein, Mabo, 74-81 (xvi-xvii).

[38] Note that one of the teachings of Ben Zoma (and possibly the first maxim of Ben Azzai) in A.R.N. b 33 (36b) is directly related to the pardes incident (unnoticed by Finkelstein!). Cf. Lieberman, Tosefta ki-Fshutah 5, 1291.

[39] Vid. Schechter, Introduction, xxi; Zunz-Albeck, Derashot, 51; 286 n. 63.

[40] M. Avot 2:8; A.R.N. a 14 (29b); b 29 (29b-30a).

[41] Specifically to chap. 28 (29b) (most limited in scope), and to the teachings of Hillel (chap. 24-27).

[42] A.R.N. a 31-41; b 36-48.

[43] P.T. Kil. 1, 27b; Gen. R. 5,7 (p. 38).

nal and the moral teachings of the tractate. We may mention some: the defection of the Sadducees and the Boethusians (A:5, B:10, 13b); the patience of Hillel (A:15, B:29, 30b-31a); Hillel, Shammai and the proselytes (A:15, B:29, 31a-b, also B:26, 26b); the siege of Jerusalem and the escape of R. Yohanan ben Zakkai and his disciples (A:4, 11b-13a; B:6-7, 10a-11a); R. Yohanan and the daughter of Nakdimon ben Guryon (A:17, 33a); R. Yohanan mourns the death of his son (A:14, 29b-30a); R. Yohanan on his deathbed (A:25, 39b-40a); the ass of R. Hanina ben Dosa (A:8, 19b); R. Yoshua and the ignorant priest (B:27, 28b-29a; A:12, 28b); R. Yoshua with the captive maiden, and with the beautiful matron (B:19, 21a-b); how R. Eliezer began to study Tora (A:6, B:13, 15b-17a); R. Eliezer on his deathbed (A:25, 40a-b); the martyrdom of R. Shimon and R. Yishmael (A:38, B:41, 57b-58a); how R. Akiva began to study Tora (A:6, B:12, 14b-15b); R. Akiva and the proselyte (B:26, 57a); R. Akiva and his students (A:21, 37b); R. Yehuda and the bride (A:4, 9b-10a; B:8, 11b); R. Shimon and the sick man (A:41, 65b); R. Shimon ben Elazar and the ugly man (A:41, 66a); Benyamin the righteous (A:3, 9a).

Although some of the above-mentioned exempla are known from other sources and may possibly derive from them,[44] many of the biographical tales are unique to Avot de-R. Natan. Several original anonymous exempla are also included, e.g. the poor woman and the greedy landowner (A:38, 57a-b); judging a person's acts in a favourable light (B:19, 20b); the pious and the redemption of captives (A:8, 19a); begrudging a fellow disciple (A:16, 31b).

We also find lengthy digressions on biblical passages. Most outstanding are: the creation of Adam and Eve, according to Ps 139:5 (B:8, 11b-12b); Adam, Eve and the serpent (A:1, B:1, 2b-4b; cf. B:42, 58b-59a); Israel at the shore of the Red Sea (A:33, 48b-49b); the punishment of Miriam (A:9, 20a-21a); the deaths of Aaron and Moses (A:12, B:8, 25a-26b); Moses and Joshua (A:17, 33a); homilies on Isa 58.7-14 (B:14, 37b); id. on Cant 1:6 (A:20, 36b-37a); id. on Eccl. 10:8 (B:3, 7b) and ib. 11:6 (A:3, B:4, 8a-b).

The topics dealt with in Avot de-R. Natan are similar to those discussed in Avot. It goes without saying that special stress is placed on the study of Tora and proper ethical conduct. Sometimes a single pithy saying recorded in the Mishna serves as the catalyst for a lengthy discussion of several pages, covering the topic from almost every possible angle; e.g. 'Love work' (A:11, B:21, 22b-23b); 'make a hedge around the Tora' (A:1-2, B:1-2, 1b-7b).

In spite of the fact that Avot de-R. Natan is an aggadic work par excellence, certain halakhic topics are enumerated. These include the strictures concerning the menstruate wife (A:2, 4b-5a; B:2, 6b), the night-time shema (A:2, B:2, 7b) and the unique halakhic status of Jerusalem (A:35, 52b; B:39, 54a-b). Special attention is called to the halakhic and aggadic implications of certain peculiarities in the Massoretic text (A:34, 50a-51a).

---

[44] Cf. below, notes 73 and 76.

VERSIONS A AND B

As already noted, *Avot de-R. Natan* is extant in two distinctly different versions. Version A is the traditional version of this tractate which was utilized in manuscript by most of the medieval authorities. This version was first printed as one of the supplementary tractates to the Babylonian Talmud, Venice 1550. Version B seems to have had a most limited circulation. In the commentary to *Avot* ascribed to Rashi, mention is made of a certain explanation in a copy of the tractate '*Avot de-R. Natan* which derives from the Land of Israel'[45] as opposed to the explanation offered in the traditional text 'current among the Sages of France'.[46] Notwithstanding the explanations of HOROWITZ and SCHECHTER,[47] this seems to be an indication that pseudo-Rashi to *Avot* was familiar with both versions.[48] Among the limited number of medieval authorities who made use of version B, mention may be made of R. Moshe ha-Darshan (Provence);[49] R. Yehiel ben Yekutiel (Italy);[50] R. Yisrael al-Nakawa (Spain) and R. Shimon ben Tsemah Duran (North Africa).[51]

The existence of an alternate version of *Avot de-R. Natan* was first noted by TAUSSIG who in 1872 published numerous excerpts deriving from this version according to MS. Munich 222.[52] He claimed that these excerpts represent the Palestinian version mentioned by pseudo-Rashi. Fifteen years later, the entire text became known to the scholarly world due to the indefatigable efforts of Solomon SCHECHTER. Basing himself on all known manuscripts of the text and of published and unpublished citations in medieval literature, he single-handedly edited both versions of *Avot de-R. Natan*. Till this very day, Schechter's edition of the two versions in parallel columns remains a model for the industry and erudition demanded of a scholar engaged in the preparation of a classical rabbinic text.

Schechter based his text of version B on MS. Vatican 303 which is divided into 48 chapters, while MS. Parma 327 has 49 chapters. The colophon of a recently discovered Geniza fragment evinces a division of 50 chapters.[53] Even though version A contains only 41 chapters, version B is by far the shorter one. The more concentrated subdivision of version B into smaller units is most evident in the early chapters of the work; individual teachings of a certain Sage in a single mishna, are presented in separate chapters. At times there is even a discrepancy of fourteen chapters between the two versions.

---

[45] I.e., the MS. was brought to Europe from Palestine.
[46] Rashi to *M. Avot* 1:5.
[47] Horowitz, *Beth Eked,* 2-4; Schechter, Introduction, viii; xvii-xx.
[48] See Ginzberg, in *Ginzei Schechter* 1, 244-5; 238; *A.R.N.* a 7 (18a).
[49] *Gen. Rabbati,* introd. 24-25.
[50] In his ethical tract *Maalot ha-Middot, passim.*
[51] Schechter, Introduction, xiii.
[52] *Neve Shalom,* 1-2; 12-47.
[53] Vid. Bregman, 'Early Fragment', 220, no. 15.

Regarding the origin of the two versions, SCHECHTER was of the opinion that both stem from the original *Avot de-R. Natan* which went lost. He claimed that version B, which is not altogether free of errors and omissions, is in a much better state of preservation than version A, which has undergone a greater deal of editorial change and textual corruption due to the activities of scribes and copyists. It is thus logical to assume that he considered version B the more ancient and major version of this work, a conclusion which has heretofore been misinterpreted by most scholars.[54] FINKELSTEIN, who originally contemplated the preparation of a more modern scholarly edition of the work, maintains that the two versions represent the parallel developments of two different schools. In his estimation, the material was transmitted orally, and the tradents took great liberties regarding the inclusion and exclusion of material and the literary style of the text; therefore early and late sources were included in each work.[55] GOLDIN has called attention to what he terms 'a very interesting thematic difference' between versions A and B, namely that version A is primarily concerned with the study of Tora, while version B underlines 'good works' or 'good deeds'.[56] However, even though there may be some basis for Goldin's analysis,[57] he himself admits that it is merely based on observations of emphasis and inflection, and that both versions essentially agree that Tora and 'good deeds' are important tenets of Judaism. In a subsequent study, Goldin has focused attention on certain exegetical terms indigenous with version A but not found even once in version B. In his estimation, this usage is indicative of a separate academy with its own unique terminology, thereby lending some support to Finkelstein's theory.[58] In a posthumous publication, GINZBERG incidentally suggested a rather interesting delineation between both versions, which seems to contradict the basic thesis of Goldin, viz. that version A is an ethical work designed for popular consumption, whereas version B was composed specifically for scholars.[59]

It is somewhat amazing that during the course of a whole century since the publication of Schechter's erudite edition, no attempt has been made at a comparative literary-structural analysis of both versions.[60] It is this writer's firm conviction that despite the major formal discrepancies between the two versions and other literary pitfalls involved, it will nevertheless be possible to

---

[54] Schechter, Introduction, xx-xxiv. See Mandel, *Midrash Eicha*, *100, n. 114. Accordingly, correct Schechter *loc. cit.* chap. 5, ll. 3-4 to read: נוסחא ב'. . . נוסחא א'.

[55] Finkelstein, *Mabo*, xxvi; *id.* 'Pirke Abot', 17 n.9.

[56] Goldin, 'Two Versions', esp. 98f. Note that the interrogatory terminus כיצד is a commonplace of Tannaic literature. The limited list in Bacher, *Terminologie* 1, 77, should be supplemented by the vast material now available in the concordances of Kasowski to *Mekhilta, Sifra* and *Sifrei*.

[57] It is interesting to note that even though version B acknowledges the supremacy of Tora study (cf. b 8 [11b]), here too, great emphasis is placed on acts of loving kindness.

[58] Goldin, 'Reflections', 59-61.

[59] Ginzberg, *Commentary* 4, 21; cf. *Derekh Erets*, below. See however Goldin, 'Two Versions', 99 n. 6.

[60] Cf. Saldarini, *The Fathers*, introd. 3-4.

formulate definite conclusions concerning their relationship. It will appear that, in general, version B represents the original version of *Avot de-R. Natan*, while version A reflects a later development. In dealing with the date of this tractate, it will thus be necessary to treat each version as a distinct literary unit.

DATE OF REDACTION OF VERSIONS A AND B

The common basis for both versions is apparently Tannaic. As mentioned above, the tractate is largely based on an ancient mishnaic text, and much of that material seems to date back to the Tannaic period. In any event, it is most significant that not even a single Amora is mentioned in any of the versions.[61]

The original character of version B is attested to by a more proper arrangement of the subject matter. SCHECHTER himself noted that the sayings of Shammai precede those of Hillel,[62] which is the accepted order in all of talmudic literature.[63] One also receives the impression that in comparison with the sequential order of version A, version B is based on a much more logical arrangement of the subject matter. This version has also preserved the term חבירינו (*haverenu*, 'comrades') an archaic expression apparently used by the head of the Academy when addressing his disciples.[64] Other picturesque expressions also seem to be unique with this version.[65] There seems to be concrete evidence that parts of version B were utilized by Rav Ahai of Shabha, the editor of *Sheiltot*, the mid-eighth century Gaonic compilation of halakha and aggada,[66] and by the editors of *Pirkei de-R. Eliezer*[67] and *Midrash Proverbs*.[68]

Compared to the exempla in version A, the stories in version B exhibit a more logical arrangement and are decisively much clearer in content.[69] Nevertheless, in spite of the Tannaic origin of this work, some of the exempla exhibit signs of later development. The tale of the execution of Shimon and Yishmael found in *Mekhilta de-R. Yishmael*[70] has been amplified and expanded into a dramatic tale

---

[61] The name of R. Yoshua ben Levi (1st gen. Amora) in the printed version of version A chap. 35 was shown by Schechter, p. 105 n. 19 to be a mistake. Saldarini's comment (*The Fathers*, introd. 5, n. 8) that 'only three Amoraim are cited in ARNB', is unfounded since there are sufficient grounds to assume that all of them are Tannaim.

[62] *A.R.N.* b 23 (24a-b); see remarks by Schechter *ad loc.*

[63] Cf. *B.T. Er.* 13b.

[64] See *A.R.N.* b 6 (10a); and cf. Rabinovitz, *Ginzé Midrash*, 227, l. 37; *A.R.N.* b 28 (29b – R. Yohanan ben Zakkai); b 19 (21a – R. Yoshua, twice); b 8 (11b – R. Yehuda).

[65] Cf. Elbaum, 'Shisha inyenei lashon', 175-7.

[66] Vid. Saldarini, *The Fathers*, 13 and n. 34 (correct *ib.*: 'ed. Mirsky, . . . pp. 17-18'); Elbaum, in *KS* 52 (1977), 807, n.6 (correct *ib.*: 'ed. Mirsky, p. 121'). The comment of Schiffman, *AJSR* 9 (1984) 117 is methodologically correct, but need not be heeded in this instance, cf. below.

[67] Cf. Kagan, 'Divergent Tendencies', 168, n. 11 (end).

[68] Ed. Buber, introd. 14. Note that *all* of the citations are from version B (the quotation in 1:7 is not from this tractate!). See also Alon, *Jews, Judaism*, 296. Concerning *Semahot* 8:8, see below n. 160.

[69] Safrai, 'Hasidim', 136-7.

[70] *Mishpatim* 18 (p. 313).

of martyrdom which includes numerous embellishments.[71] This would seem to indicate that the final redaction of *Avot de-R. Natan*, version B took place in the Land of Israel in Amoraic times,[72] probably towards the end of the third century. However, the bulk of the material is of decidedly earlier vintage.

Compared to version B, the contents of version A are much more cumbersome. In many cases, the editorial techniques of the editor are a far cry from perfection. In spite of the efforts of GOLDIN to justify the editorial arrangement of version A, chap. 3, there is no denying the fact that the editor has assembled diversified material from various sources while dealing with the subject of charity, which is completely irrelevant in this location. He has appended to the text selections from the Mishna and Talmud,[73] the first such quotation being introduced by the bizarre declaration that 'there was once a certain man who transgressed the words of R. Akiva'.[74] This effect is further heightened by a festive declaration attributed to the same Sage: 'Blessed be God . . . who hath chosen the teachings of the Tora and the teachings of the Sages . . .'[75] The juxtaposition of this extraneous material from talmudic sources and the special stress on rabbinic teachings may very well reflect anti-Karaite polemics. Incidentally, several additional instances of direct borrowing of exempla from the Babylonian Talmud are evinced by version A.[76] Even some of the parallel exempla have been shown to be pale and diluted versions of the classical tales as they appear in the talmudic sources.[77]

In general, it may be said that the language of version A lacks the polish and originality of expression which characterizes version B. ZUNZ has focused attention on an expression reminiscent of the rhetorical style of *Seder Eliahu* and on the heroic description of Moses' death, which appear to have been adopted from later-day midrashic texts.[78]

The recent discovery of a fragment of *Avot de-R. Natan* written in the form of a scroll – probably the earliest fragment of rabbinic literature so far published – sheds new light on the editorial process of version A. This fragment, possibly dating from the sixth/seventh century, contains parts of chapters 36 and 38 in juxtaposed order and evinces major editorial and textual variations.[79] It seems to represent a previous recension of version A, and presents us with proof positive that during the above-mentioned period this version was still in the process of being formulated. It thus seems reasonable to assume that the final redaction of version A took place somewhat later on. Taking the above-

---

[71] *A.R.N.* b 41 (57b-58a). See also Fraenkel, 'Remarkable Phenomena', 67f.

[72] Cf. Schiffman, *AJSR* 9 (1984) 118.

[73] Cf. *M. Bava K.* 8:6; *B.T. Ber.* 18b; *B.T. Bava B.* 11a; see also *B.T. Yev.* 121a.

[74] *A.R.N.* a 3 (8a); cf. *M. Bava K.* 8:6.

[75] *A.R.N.* a 3 (9a); cf. *M Avot* 6:1.

[76] E.g. a 6 (16b) = *B.T. Taan.* 19b; a 17 (33a) = *B.T. Ket.* 66b; a 25 (40a-b) = *B.T. Ber.* 28b; a 25 (40b) = *B.T. Sanh.* 68a; a 41 (66a) = *B.T. Taan.* 20a.

[77] Fraenkel, 'Remarkable Phenomena', 67.

[78] Zunz-Albeck, *Derashot*, 286 n. 68.

[79] Bregman, 'Early Fragment'.

mentioned literary findings into account, it may be entirely possible to conclude that the basis for the extant arrangement of version A is a product of the latter half of the seventh or the early eighth century, although most of its component material dates back to a much earlier period, i.e. close to Tannaic times.

BIBLIOGRAPHY

The *editio princeps* (being version A) of *Avot de-R. Natan* (Venice 1550) has been reprinted in subsequent editions of the Babylonian Talmud. The critical comments and glosses printed in the collection of works entitled *Tumat Yesharim*, Venice 1622, IV, fol. 61a-66d, and incorporated into the Wilna (Romm) standard edition of the Talmud, are an important textual aid. The critical edition of SCHECHTER, Vienna 1887 is based on the *editio princeps* and two MSS. (See recensions of D. KAUFMANN, *MGWJ* 36 [1887] 374-83; A. NEUBAUER, *REJ* 14 [1887] 293-4; N. BRÜLL, *Jahrbücher* 9 [1889] 133-9.) Addenda derived from MS. Vatican 44 are provided in Appendix 2. Many additional MS. readings are adduced by FINKELSTEIN, *Mabo*. An ancient recension of version A has recently been published by BREGMAN, 'Early Fragment'.

There are numerous commentaries on version A; see the list drawn up by SCHECHTER in his Introduction, xxvii-xxviii.

Version A was translated into Latin by TAYLOR, *Tractatus* and into German by POLLAK, *Rabbi Nathan's System*. GOLDIN's translation into idiomatic English, *The Fathers*, contains copious notes, including many oral communications by LIEBERMAN, and indices. The Soncino translation of the Minor Tractates which appeared in London 1965, represents an independent rendering of this tractate. The recent French translation by SMILÉVITCH-DUPUY, *Leçons*, should be used with caution as this is an 'integrated' edition.

Selections from version B according to MS. Munich 222 were published by TAUSSIG, *Neve Shalom*, 1-2; 12-47. SCHECHTER's edition of this version was based on MS. Vatican 303, and variants from MS. Parma 327 are provided in Appendix 3. See also HOROWITZ, *Beth Eked*, 34-36.

The only translation of version B is the sometimes awkward effort of SALDARINI, *The Fathers* (see critical recension of ELBAUM, *KS* 52 [1977] 806-15). Additional manuscript material relating to both versions, especially of Geniza fragments, is listed by FINKELSTEIN, *Mabo*, 1-3; BREGMAN, 'Early Fragment', 219-22.

Studies dealing with this tractate include: ZUNZ-ALBECK, *Derashot*, 51-2 and 286-7; SCHECHTER, Introduction; HOROWITZ, *Beth Eked*, 2-4; EPSTEIN, *Nosah*, 50; FINKELSTEIN, 'Introductory Study'; *id. Mabo*; and the introductions of GOLDIN and SALDARINI to their translations. The recent study of SALDARINI, *Scholastic Rabbinism* deals with many literary and historical aspects of *Massekhet Avot* and *Avot de-R. Natan* (see recension of SCHIFFMAN, *AJSR* 9 [1984] 116-9).

Geniza fragment of a post-talmudic Palestinian halakhic notebook (Cambridge University Library, T-S N.S. 252.1a, leaf 6 recto and verso).
See p. 406. The halakhot contained in this fragment deal with the *halitsa* ceremony (see Margulies, *Hilkhot Erets Yisrael*, 50).

The Rehov inscription (Jerusalem; by courtesy of the Israel Department of Antiquities and Museums).
Inscription found on the floor of the entrance of a synagogue excavated at Tel-Rehov, Beit Shean valley. While paraphrasing halakhic portions of the Palestinian Talmud (see pp. 317, 408), it is the oldest extant textual witness of the literature of the Sages (6th cent. C.E.).

GOLDIN has devoted numerous articles to the scholarly analysis of this tractate, among them: 'Two Versions'; 'The Third Chapter'; and 'Reflections' (see also below).

Linguistic matters and idiomatic expressions in *Avot de-R. Natan* are dealt with by FINKELSTEIN, *Mabo, passim*; *id.*, 'Phraseology'; TUR-SINAI, 'Language and Phraseology'; ELBAUM, 'Shisha inyenei lashon'.

Some of the biographical exempla of the Sages are analyzed in the articles of SAFRAI, 'Tales of the Sages', 223-9; *id.* 'Hasidim', 136-7; FRAENKEL, 'Remarkable Phenomena', 67-8; ELBAUM, 'Models'. Elbaum's study also contains many valuable comparisons between the statements attributed to the Sages in both versions.

Studies and comments devoted to specific subjects in the tractate include: GINZBERG, *Commentary* 4, 20-21; GOLDIN, 'First Chapter', 278-80; *id.*, 'Reflections'; DINARY, 'Impurity Customs'; FINKELSTEIN, 'Ancient Tradition'; *id.*, 'The Halakhot Applied to Jerusalem'; KAHANA, 'Le-havanat ha baraita'. See also the articles of GOLDIN *et al.* in the bibliography to *Avot* (above) and URBACH, *Sages, passim* (index, p. 1035).

The Tractates Derekh Erets

The Hebrew expression *derekh erets*, which is literally translated 'the way of the land', alludes to proper behaviour and deportment. The tractates bearing this title deal primarily with the ethics and morals which prevent a person from indulging in sin, as well as with the rules of etiquette and polite behaviour. Needless to say, rabbinic teachings placed great stress on the combination of Tora study and erudition with good deeds and 'the fear of sin'. In some instances, they even granted priority to personal ethics and designated these as the true sign of a bona-fide Tora scholar.[80]

Similar to the teachings of *Avot* and *Avot de-R. Natan*, the *derekh erets* tractates usually have the form of short pithy sayings and words of wisdom and counsel. In this respect, they may thus be considered as another continuation of the wisdom tradition of Proverbs and Ben Sira. Indeed, several direct parallels between the *derekh erets* tracts and the Hebrew Ben Sira have been adduced.[81]

The printed versions of the two tractates bearing the rubric *derekh erets*, i.e. *Derekh Erets Rabba* (i.e. major) and *Derekh Erets Zutta* (i.e. minor), are somewhat heterogeneous in their composition, and actually contain several constituent elements. A detailed analysis of each of these tractates and their literary components is vital for a proper appreciation of this literature.

The two tractates mentioned are not larger and shorter versions of an identical treatise,[82] but rather independent compositions, each of an entirely different

---

[80] See *M. Avot* 2:2; 3:9-10, 17; *A.R.N.* a 22 (37b-38a); a 24 (39a); b 34 (38a-b); *M. Ed.* 5:6.
[81] Higger, *Zeirot* (introd.) 8-18.
[82] Cf. *Eccl. Rabba* and *Eccl. Zutta*; *Sifrei Zutta*.

nature, whose common denominator is the subject matter of proper conduct. The theory that *Derekh Erets Zutta* represents the rules and regulations practised in scholarly circles, whereas *Derekh Erets Rabba* was meant for the general public,[83] is most unfounded. Both of these tractates were basically geared towards 'the disciple of the Sages', while anybody wishing to study and practise these directives was certainly encouraged to do so.[84]

Oral tracts dealing with the subject of *derekh erets*, although not considered integral parts of the Mishna, were already in existence during the second century. The fourth generation Tanna, R. Yehuda ben Elai, is said to have encouraged his disciples to engage in the study of *hilkhot derekh erets* when in a state of bodily impurity.[85] It appears that these tracts were studied during the students' study breaks, travels etc., and not as a part of the regular curriculum in the Academy.[86]

Recent studies have shown that the two basic tracts of this literature dealing with moral behaviour, viz. *Massekhet Yirat Het* and *Massekhet Derekh Erets Zeira*, reflect the teachings of the pious circles of the Tannaic period. These Sages, who are described as Hasidim – not to be confused with the modern usage of this term – placed extreme stress on self-deprival and the performance of good deeds and acts of loving kindness in lieu of pure academic 'ivory tower' scholarship. It is thus not surprising that most of the material in these tracts has been quoted in *Seder Eliyahu Rabba* and *Zutta*, which exhibit similar tendencies.[87]

An unusually prolific number of manuscripts, Geniza fragments and other versions containing the *derekh erets* tracts has remained extant. HIGGER, the indefatigable editor of these texts, has offered the following classification of the various manuscripts, according to their origin and contents.[88]

CLASS A – The earliest version of *derekh erets* literature, typified by MS. Adler 428, contains: a) *Perek Yirat Het* (= *Massekhet Yirat Het* chaps. 1-3, see below); b) *Perek Talmidei Hakhamim* (= part of *Yirat Het* chap. 4 and all of chap. 5); c) *Derekh Erets* (= *Derekh Erets Zeira*, see below). Higger has entitled this class as 'The Gaonic Version'.

CLASS B – This class, referred to as the French Version, is based on MS. Oxford - Bodleian 1098. It includes: a) *Derekh Erets Zutta* chaps. 1-9; b) *Pirkei Ben Azzai* chaps. 1-7 (= *Derekh Erets Rabba* chaps. 3-9, see below).

CLASS C – In addition to the elements enumerated in the previous class, class C, dubbed by Higger as 'The Spanish Version', contains the two additional chapters at the end of *Derekh Erets Rabba* (chaps. 10-11).

---

[83] Krauss, 'Derech Ereç', 39-41.
[84] Cf. *M. Kidd.* 1:10; *A.R.N.* b 35 (44a). See also *Lev. R.* 9,3 (p. 176-8).
[85] *B.T. Ber.* 22a. It is interesting to note that the chapters from *Derekh Erets Zutta* in *Kalla Rabbati* 3:1 (p. 212) are prefaced by the name of R. Yehuda.
[86] Cf. Also *Kalla Rabbati* 5:4 (p. 287).
[87] Vid. Safrai, 'Mishnat Hasidim', 147 (= 'Pietists', 27-8); *id.* 'Hasidim', 149-51.
[88] See Higger, *Zeirot*, 7-8; *id. Derekh Erets*, English introd., 20-32.

CLASS D – This class, exemplified by MS. Oxford-Bodleian 2339, is composed of: a) *Derekh Erets Rabba* (chaps. 1-11); b) *Derekh Erets Zutta* chaps. 1-4; 9-11 (= *Massekhet Yirat Het; Perek R. Shimon; Perek ha-Shalom*).[89] MS. Adler 2237 also contains *Derekh Erets Zeira* following *Perek R. Shimon*, thus approximating the ordinary printed editions.

MASSEKHET DEREKH ERETS ZUTTA

In the printed editions of the Babylonian Talmud, *Massekhet Derekh Erets Zutta* contains ten chapters, as well as a supplementary chapter entitled *Perek ha-Shalom*, i.e. 'The Chapter of Peace'. However, on the basis of manuscripts and early versions it is readily evident that this tractate is actually a combination of two distinctly different tracts of similar content, while chapter 10 is probably taken from yet an additional source. In the ensuing discussion, the individual components will be treated separately.

MASSEKHET YIRAT HET. *Yirat Het* which literally means 'the fear of sin' includes chapters 1-4 and 9 of *Derekh Erets Zutta*. The existence of such a tract numbering five chapters is evinced by numerous manuscripts as well as by the *editio princeps* which was printed together with the Babylonian Talmud, Venice 1550. This title is already mentioned in the prayer-book of Rav Saadya Gaon (d. 942 C.E.)[90] and in the writings of his contemporary, Yaakov al-Kirkisani,[91] who was obviously one of Saadya's literary opponents. Alternative titles which add some confusion to the identification of this tract include: *Perek Derekh Erets Rabba;*[92] *Derekh Erets Rabbati*[93] and *Derekh Erets de-Rabbanan,*[94] or *Massekhet Derekh Erets (Rabba).*[95]

The opening paragraph of *Massekhet Yirat Het* deals with 'the characteristics of a student of the wise' (*talmid hakham*), and enumerates some fourteen traits, most of them of a moral nature. Its subsequent teachings preach humility, suffering and self-denial bordering on asceticism. One of the most favourite expressions is: 'Be like a doorstep on which everyone treads, and like a low peg on which all hang their things'.[96]

Yirat Het is mainly a collection of pithy disconnected maxims and exhortations, several of them built in dialectical style.[97] Chapters four and five are

---

[89] Sperber, *Derech Eretz*, Appendix 8, 178 refers to class D as 'The Italian Version'. However, this is pure conjecture, since class D is clearly a *Spanish* version; cf. Higger, *Zeirot*, 65-6.
[90] *Siddur R. Saadya Gaon*, 123.
[91] See Higger, *Additions*, 7, par. 2.
[92] *Halakhot Gedolot*, 647.
[93] MS. Oxford-Bodleian 2833 (Higger, *Treatises*, introd., 16).
[94] R. Yosef ben Yehuda, *Sefer Musar*, 139.
[95] *Massekhet Derekh Erets* in numerous manuscripts, see Higger, *Treatises,* introd.; R. Yehiel ben Yekutiel, *Maalot ha-Middot*, 296-9 and *passim*, who sometimes adds 'Rabba'.
[96] Higger, *Treatises* 1:2 (p. 58); 1:25 (p. 77); 2:9 (p. 96).
[97] See *ib.* 1:24 (p. 76); 1:29 (p. 82-4); 3:3-4 (p. 98-102).

distinguished by three series of negative and positive admonitions and words of advice based on repetitive formulae: 'Say not . . .' ('Let not . . .' 'Be not . . .'); 'Love . . .' ('Be happy . . .'); 'If . . .'. It is interesting to note that each formula is repeated 11, 12 and 13 times, respectively and that the forceful style employed is direct and extremely personal.[98] It is also important to note that five of these negative ethical teachings concerning the body limbs are quoted in midrashic and aggadic works as deriving from a Tannaic source.[99] Several aggadic teachings at the end of chapter one, which do not seem to have any intrinsic relation to the subject matter of the tractate, may possibly be later additions.[100] However, it should be noted that this material is found in almost all of the important manuscripts and early versions, as well as in the parallel chapter in *Massekhet Kalla Rabbati*.[101]

The material in chapters 1-4, with a single exception,[102] is anonymous, and all the Sages mentioned in chap. 9 (= 5) are Tannaim. Many of the anonymous teachings in chapters 1-4 are identical with dicta in *Avot* and *Avot de-R. Natan*[103] and several of them also appear in the BabylonianTalmud.[104] This has prompted most scholars to assume that these chapters of *Yirat Het* are to be considered Tannaic and were already known to the Babylonian Amoraim.[105]

However, a simple perusal of the contents of this tract with its numerous repetitions[106] and disorderly arrangement immediately discounts such a conclusion. The anonymous mishnaic and talmudic statements should be construed as extracts compiled from Tannaic and Amoraic sources. Significantly, this tract includes an obviously anti-Karaitic declaration adopted from the Talmud: 'He who occupies himself solely with the study of Scripture is but of indifferent merit; with Mishna – he is meritorious and rewarded for it; with Talmud – there

---

[98] Cf. the end of chap. 4(3), p. 111: 'These are the items that I have seen fit to present before you. You may act as you like, but do not say "I was not warned".'

[99] *Eccl. Z.* 7:19 (p. 115), apparently quoting *Yirat Het* 4 (Higger, *Zeirot* 78, ll. 13-17; *id. Treatises* 3:6, p. 103-5) using the term דתני ordinarily referring to a mishna in the Babylonian Talmud. Cf. also *Pirkei Derekh Erets* 1 (= *S.E.Z.* 16) p. 1-2.

[100] 1:16-18 (p. 65-70).

[101] *Kalla Rabbati* 3:21-23 (p. 242-9). Note, however, that MS. Adler 418 (*Zeirot*, 83, ll. 6-7) does not contain these aggadic teachings.

[102] The divergent language of R. Hidka, a Tanna of the second century c.e. mentioned in 1:11 (p. 63). In this respect, it may be of some import to note that *Midr. ha-Gad.* to Gen. 26:10 (p. 450) contains a lengthy quotation from chap. 2 (= 1:28-29, pp. 81-5) adduced as a baraita in the name of R. Hidka, which forms part of an unknown homily attributed to R. Eliezer.

[103] See Krauss, 'Traité talmudique', 41-2; Higger, *Zeirot*, introd., 16-19; 34-6.

[104] Cf. Higger, *Zeirot* 2, p. 75 (= *Treatises*, 1:23, p. 134) and *B.T. Ned.* 62b; *ib.* 3, p. 76 (= 3:1, p. 88) and *B.T. Ber.* 4a; *ib.* 4, p. 78 (= 3:6, p. 103-4); and *B.T. Ket.* 5b. See the discussion of Higger, *Zeirot*, 28 and also below, n. 24.

[105] Ginzberg, 'Derek Erez', 530; Higger, *Treatises*, introd., 19; Sperber, *Derech Eretz*, 179.

[106] Cf. Tawrogi, *Tractat*, ii n. 2; Romanov, in *Horev* 4 (1937) 213.

can be no one more meritorious . . .'.[107] Thus it would seem more safe to assume that the final redaction of *Massekhet Yirat Het* took place during the initial stages of the Karaite schism, i.e., during the second half of the eighth century. Nevertheless, it is apparent that the first three chapters[108] of this tract represent an earlier segment, since these alone are dealt with in chapters 3-4 of *Massekhet Kalla Rabbati*.

MASSEKHET DEREKH ERETS ZEIRA. The Aramaic word *zeira* means diminutive, small and, indeed, the four chapters of *Massekhet Derekh Erets Zeira* are less than one half the size of *Yirat Het*. This tract which forms chaps. 5-8 of *Derekh Erets Zutta*, was combined with *Massekhet Yirat Het* beginning with the Frankfurt/Main edition of the Babylonian Talmud (1720-1723), from a manuscript of *Mahzor Vitry*. It is interesting to note that the separate origin of chaps. 5-8 is still indicated in the current printed editions of the Talmud. On the other hand, these two tracts have already been integrated together in the so-called French manuscript tradition (class B) of the treatises *derekh erets*.[109] The medieval Tosafists sometimes refer to this tract as *Hilkhot Derekh Erets*,[110] whereas Nahmanides apparently called it *Pirkei Derekh Erets*.[111]

Like its counterpart, *Derekh Erets Zeira* contains numerous pithy statements, almost all of them anonymous,[112] concerning the proper conduct and traits becoming a 'student of the Sages'. However, this tract also includes several 'practical' instructions relating to table manners and conduct in the bath house, which are most likely adopted from *Pirkei Ben Azzai* (see below).

At the end of chapter four, much stress is laid on what seem to be anti-Karaitic pronouncements such as: 'Whoever makes light of a single point of the Tora is liable to the punishment of *karet* (i.e. divine punishment by premature death).[113] 'Whoever transgresses the words of the Sages deserves death . . .'[114] These would seem to indicate that *Derekh Erets Zeira*, which is definitely later than *Yirat Het*, played an important part in the polemical attack of the rabbis against Karaism. Its final redaction should probably be placed during the ninth century.

PEREK R. SHIMON. Chapter ten of *Massekhet Derekh Erets Zutta* adduces several talmudic traditions concerning the messianic age, the first of which is quoted in

---

[107] Higger, *Zeirot* 4, p. 77, l. 20-21 (= *Treatises*, 3:2, p. 97), from *B.T. Bava M.* 33a. This teaching is obviously an addition as it really does not have much to do with ethics or proper behaviour. See also the criticism of Al-Kirkisani quoted by Bacher, 'Qirqisani', 697-8. In this respect, the additions in MS. Ginzberg (*Zeirot*, 164, l. 21) are most elucidating.

[108] *Zeirot*, p. 73-7 (= *Treatises*, 55-93).

[109] Higger, *Treatises*, introd., 21.

[110] *Tosafot* to *B.T. Meg.* 29a *s.v.* מבטלין; *id.* to *B.T. Bekh.* 44a *s.v.* ואין.

[111] Commentary to Num 15:31 (ed. Chavel, 253).

[112] Noteworthy exceptions are found in *Zeirot* chap. 3, end p. 90 (= *Treatises* 6:4, p. 124) and chap. 4, p. 91 (= 7:10, p. 131).

[113] *Zeirot* cap. 4, p. 90; p. 91 (= *Treatises* 7:7, p. 128); cf. also Nahmanides *ib.* (n. 28).

[114] *Ibid*, p. 91, l. 10-18 (= *ib.* 7:10, p. 131-3).

the name of R. Shimon ben Yohai, hence the name of this chapter. After some additional talmudic traditions of assorted nature, one of them most likely anti-Karaitic,[115] the chapter reverts to a few moral and ethical themes. The closing paragraph is obviously a grand finale and serves as the motto of the entire tractate: '. . . He who possesses both wisdom and fear [of sin][116] is thoroughly righteous.'[117] This chapter is found only in the so-called class D manuscripts of *Derekh Erets Zutta*, and it was obviously added at a relatively late date. Its inclusion was probably due to the ideal combination of 'the fear of sin' and wisdom which is mentioned towards the end of this chapter.[118] Without sufficient grounds, HIGGER[119] classified it under the heading 'Tosefta Derekh Erets' (see below, p. 387).

PEREK HA-SHALOM. All printed editions of the Talmud contain a supplementary chapter devoted to the extolling of 'Peace', immediately following *Derekh Erets Zutta*. This chapter, which is usually found in the class D manuscripts, is a completely independent and unattached composition and was probably appended to the tractate in order to fulfill the customary practice of 'concluding with peace'.[120] Almost all of the teachings in this chapter, which begin with the opening formula 'Great is peace . . .', are culled from midrashic sources.[121] On the basis of a single manuscript, HIGGER entitled this chapter *Perek Shalom*. He also classified it with the 'Tosefta Derekh Erets' (see below). In reality it is a separate entity, which should be viewed as one of the numerous individual *perakim* (= chapters) of aggadic literature.[122]

MASSEKHET DEREKH ERETS RABBA

In the regular printed editions of the Babylonian Talmud, *Derekh Erets Rabba* encompasses eleven chapters. On the basis of the manuscripts, it is quite evident that this tractate is not a homogeneous whole. As in the case with *Derekh Erets Zutta*, we must deal with each of the component elements separately.

PEREK ARAYOT, 'The Chapter of Prohibited Marriages'. Chapter one of *Massekhet Derekh Erets Rabba* deals mainly with illicit marriages and intercourse. Nineteen of the twenty-two paragraphs of this brief treatise contain halakhic

---

[115] Higger, *Treatises*, 10:8, p. 247.
[116] In lieu of the name of the first tract, this is obviously the correct translation. The previous translations render: [of God].
[117] Higger, *Treatises* 10:9, p. 248.
[118] 10:7, 9, p. 247-8.
[119] *Treatises*, 243-8.
[120] Cf. *Lev. R.* 9,9 end (p. 194-5). Incidentally, the subject is also dealt with towards the end of *Yirat Het*, see Higger, *Zeirot* p. 80, l. 18ff.
[121] Esp. *Lev. R.* 9,9 (p. 187-95). Cf. Higger, *Zeirot*, introd., 38-39.
[122] Cf. Urbach, 'Pirkei R. Yoshiah', 83; Sperber, *Derech Eretz*, 181.

rulings, several of which are found quoted in the Talmud, verbatim or with certain differences, as Tannaic baraitot.[123] All the Sages mentioned in the main body of this chapter are Tannaim, its language is reminiscent of mishnaic Hebrew, and the only Amoraic statement seems to be a sort of closing formula, which could very well have been added on at a later date. In addition, some medieval authorities quote from this chapter as if it were of Tannaic origin.[124]

The contents of *Perek Arayot* deal mainly with private law and marriage, subjects found in the third order of the Mishna. Its affinity to the Mishna is attested to by MS. Kaufmann A 50 which appends this chapter to the end of *Seder Nashim*,[125] giving it the appearance of a tractate. Indeed, at least one medieval authority referred to this chapter as *Massekhet Arayot*.[126] However, this external impression is most misleading and there does not seem to be any real valid reason to postulate a Tannaic origin for *Perek Arayot*. A close examination of the text reveals that it is mainly a collection of talmudic sources, and the supposedly 'original' material is actually of an artificial nature.[127]

In his version of the minor tractates (Shklow 1804) R. ELIYAHU GAON of Wilna included *Perek Arayot* as the second chapter of tractate *Kalla*, which in the printed editions precedes *Derekh Erets Rabba*.[128] However, there is no manuscript or other evidence to support this decision, and in spite of the fact that it has been approved of by some modern scholars,[129] it must be taken as pure conjecture.

Perek Arayot should thus be viewed as a post-talmudic collection of Tannaic teachings which mainly circulated as an independent chapter. The inclusion of this chapter within the framework of *derekh erets* literature[130] may be due to the ethical teachings at the close of the chapter, which also give the impression of later additions.[131] Again, HIGGER has classified it as a chapter of 'Tosefta Derekh Erets', without justification (see p. 387).

PEREK HA-MINIM, 'The Chapter of the Heretics'. The first twelve halakhot of *Derekh Erets Rabba*, chap. two, mention various categories of the wicked which evoke appropriate scriptural invectives, while halakhot 13-24 extol the truly righteous and their virtues, together with congratulatory biblical verses.

---

[123] Higger, *Zeirot*, introd. 21-22, 31.
[124] Cf. *Halakhot gedolot* (ed. Traub) 81b; R. Tuvia ben Eliezer, *Lekah Tov* to Lev 18:23 (ed. Buber) 103.
[125] Ed. Beer, 252-4.
[126] *Lekah Tov ib.*
[127] See Higger, *Treatises* 1:4, 6 (p. 267-8) and the comments of Higger to l. 24. Note also Ginzberg, 'Derek Erez', 527a bottom.
[128] It may be interesting to note that par. 13 (p. 275-7) actually has exact parallels in *Massekhet Kalla* 1:8 (p. 132-4) and 1:17 (p. 149-50).
[129] Krauss, 'Traité talmudique', 32 (n. 5) 34; Ginzberg, 'Derek Erez', 527a; *ib*. Reiffman, 'Kuntras', 84 has raised an alternative suggestion, most likely based on the reasoning of the Wilna Gaon.
[130] In class D manuscripts only.
[131] Cf. above n. 186 on 1:8.

Then follow several traditions concerning the sins that caused calamities. The closing dictum, which speaks of the kingdom of God situated in the '390 firmaments', is actually a homily to Deut 32:1.[132] Its relationship to this chapter is most enigmatic and defies a logical explanation.

In MS. Adler 1745, the title of this chapter reads *Perek Maasim* i.e. Deeds.[133] At least one medieval Rabbi referred to it as a 'baraita'.[134] Here too, HIGGER saw a chapter of 'Tosefta Derekh Erets' whereas R. ELIYAHU THE GAON[135] included it as chapter three of *Massekhet Kalla*. In all likelihood, however, *Perek ha-Minim* represents another independent chapter which, in class D manuscripts, was incorporated into *Massekhet Derekh Erets Rabba*.

PIRKEI BEN AZZAI, 'The Chapters of Ben Azzai'. Chapters three to eleven which, in the wake of the statement of Shimon ben Azzai which opens chapter three, are entitled *Pirkei Ben Azzai*, represent the major corpus of *Derekh Erets Rabba*. However, chapter three itself, which contains moral reflections on the origin and destiny of man, as well as the teachings of R. Elazar ben Azarya on his death-bed, is definitely of later origin; the entire chapter is probably adapted from *Avot de-R. Natan*.[136]

Chapters four and five discuss the proper rules of conduct for the Sage and his disciples in public, while chapters six to nine deal with correct social behaviour and table etiquette, as well as proper privy manners.[137] Chapter ten is devoted to the correct behaviour to be observed in the bath house, while chapter eleven enumerates various practices which are bound to endanger one's life or lead to economic failure. The tractate ends with three personal prayers to be recited before sleep, before entering the privy, and before embarking on one's daily activities.

Various exempla are interspersed between the different rules of conduct, especially in chapters 4-7:9. These are biographical episodes relating to several of the major Tannaim,[138] some of which are not found in ancient sources.[139] Chapter four contains important midrashic material on the angels who came to visit Abraham and Lot.[140]

---

[132] See *Pitron Tora*, ed. Urbach, 322.

[133] Higger, *Zeirot*, 96.

[134] R. Elazar of Worms, *Sefer ha-rokeah*, 277.

[135] See above.

[136] However, the chapter heading there is 'Akavya ben Mahalalel'. In this connection it may be of interest to note the reading in the Epstein manuscripts of *Derekh Erets Rabba*: 'R. Natan', a possible allusion to *Avot de-R. Natan*.

[137] The famous baraita 'How does one dance before a bride . . .' (see also *B.T. Ket.* 17a) found in 6:4 (p. 208-10) is probably adduced because of the ethical instruction. 'The disposition of man should always be pleasant with people'.

[138] E.g. Hillel; R. Yohanan ben Zakkai; R. Yoshua; R. Akiva.

[139] E.g. the Patriarch and the Sages and their meeting with the Jewish philosopher in Rome (3:2, p. 184-8); R. Yoshua and R. Shimon ben Antipatris (4:1, p. 193-200).

[140] 4:2 (p. 173-9).

Chapters four to eleven of *Derekh Erets Rabba* (= *Pirkei Ben Azzai* 2-9) probably represent the oldest stratum of *derekh erets* literature. In this section, the style is rhythmic and the teachings give the impression of having been organized in a more or less systematic fashion, although with the passing of time, it is logical to assume that certain additions and alterations were made in the text. In passing, one might mention several expressions and accentuations in chapter eleven which may very well reflect anti-Karaitic polemics.[141] In any event, it is important to note that the only explicit quote from *derekh erets* literature in the Talmud and Midrash is apparently quoted from *Pirkei Ben Azzai*:[142] 'One puts the right shoe on first and then the left shoe. But in taking them off one removes the left shoe first and then the right shoe'.[143]

Alternative titles for *Pirkei Ben Azzai* in manuscripts and in the quotations of early authorities are: *Middat Derekh Erets*, *Massekhet Derekh Erets*, and *Hilkhot Derekh Erets*.[144] The latter is reminiscent of the collection of teachings of that name mentioned by the disciples of R. Yehuda ben Elai.[145] This may be an additional indication of the antiquity of these chapters. There exists an unpublished fragment from the Cairo Geniza which contains part of a chapter of Tannaic rulings similar to those found in chapters 4, 6 and 7 of *Derekh Erets Rabba*. The fragment may very likely represent a very early recension of our text, which approximates somewhat one of the chapters of *Hilkhot Derekh Erets*, and may have been in existence since Tannaic times. The main body of the extant tractate may thus very likely be a product of the third century.

On the basis of the fact that the so-called class B manuscripts conclude with chapter nine and of the fact that there exists a single quotation by a medieval rabbi,[146] HIGGER has reconstructed what he calls 'Tosefta Derekh Erets'. In addition to the four chapters mentioned above, he relegated chapters eight and nine of *Pirkei Ben Azzai* to this enigmatic unit, without any manuscript support. However, the fact that these two chapters basically form a continuation of *Pirkei Ben Azzai* in *Massekhet Kalla Rabbati*,[147] is proof positive of their basic relationship to the former. The solemn closing formula at the end of *Pirkei Ben Azzai* may also be an indication that this chapter represents the closing section of an extensive work.[148]

---

[141] Cf. 9:13 (p.313) 'he who hates Sages and their disciples'; 9:14 (p.314-6) in comparison with *A.R.N.* a 36 (55a).

[142] 8:1 (p. 298-9) with minor stylistic differences.

[143] *P.T. Shabb.* 6, 8a end.

[144] Higger, *Treatises*, introd. 31-3, 40.

[145] *B.T. Ber.* 22a; see above: 'The Tractates Derekh Erets'.

[146] R. David ben Levi of Narbonne, Ha-Mikhtam, ed. Schreiber, 328 (to *B.T. Moed K.* 22b).

[147] *Kalla Rabbati* 9:13-19 (p. 336-40, = chap. 8); *ib.* 20-23 (p. 340-4; a small segment of chap. 9).

[148] 9:18 (p. 320). This formula which speaks of 'the rejoicing of Jerusalem and its consolation' may possibly relate to p. 310 par. 10 ('one who does work on the ninth of Av').

BIBLIOGRAPHY

TRACTATES DEREKH ERETS. Comprehensive studies devoted to the *derekh erets* tractates have been written by ZUNZ, *Vorträge*, 116-9; KRAUSS, 'Traité talmudique'; BACHER, 'Observations'; FRIEDMANN, *Pseudo-Seder Eliahu Zuta* (introd.) 1-13; HIGGER, *Zeirot* (introd.) 1-69.

In the latter publication, Higger edited some of the shorter selections from *derekh erets* literature. A complete critical edition of all the texts, together with an English translation, was offered in HIGGER, *Treatises*. (See reviews of PREISS-HOREV in *KS* 12 [1935-6] 174-5; and ROMANOV in *Horev* 4 [1937] 207-14.)

The affinity of these tracts to the teachings of the pious Sages of the Tannaic period and *Seder Eliyahu* literature has been dealt with by SAFRAI, 'Mishnat Hasidim'; 'Pietists'; 'Hasidim'.

DEREKH ERETS ZUTTA. The nine chapters of *Derekh Erets Zutta* were first edited in 1885 in a critical edition together with a German translation by TAWROGI, *Tractat*.

In his *Zeirot*, HIGGER has published (1929) separate versions of *Yirat Het, Derekh Erets Zeira* and *Perek ha-Shalom* from class A manuscripts together with variants, and these have been prefaced with a detailed scholarly introduction. *Additions* to the same appeared in 1935. These tracts were once again edited according to MS. Oxford-Bodleian 1098 with variants from class B, C and D manuscripts in HIGGER, *Treatises*, together with an English introduction and translation. The Hebrew introduction provides a detailed summary of the numerous manuscripts. It is important to note that the internal division of the chapters is not identical with HIGGER's *Zeirot* or with the ordinary printed editions of the Talmud.

A detailed scientific commentary, as well as a survey of important scholarly information and bibliography concerning this tractate, have been appended to the second edition of SPERBER, *Derech Eretz*. A commentary on *Perek ha-Shalom* is offered in SPERBER, *Great is Peace*. Note that the editor has completely revamped the order of the various teachings.

Studies relating to manuscripts and the division of the tractate have been authored by EPSTEIN, *Mi-Kadmoniot ha-Yehudim*, 104-6; ABRAHAMS, 'Bodleian MSS.' 72-5; *id.* 'Fear of Sin', 660-1. See also GINZBERG, *Derek Erez*.

DEREKH ERETS RABBA. Manuscript versions and explanations to *Perek Arayot* and *Perek ha-Minim* are offered by HIGGER, *Zeirot*, 92-8, 143-6. These texts as well as the rest of the tractate were re-edited in HIGGER, *Treatises*, which is based on the above-mentioned Oxford MS. In this edition, chapters one to two and ten to eleven appear as a separate independent section of the tractate and designated as 'Tosefta Derekh Erets' (see *ib.* p. 265-320) and the internal paragraphs renumbered. A previous, incomplete edition of *Derekh Erets Rabba* chapters 3-6 (= *Pirkei Ben Azzai* 1-4) was issued by GOLDBERG, 'Traktat'.

The Geniza fragment, which seems to be an ancient version of *Hilkhot Derekh Erets*, is being readied for publication by the present author. The introductions to HIGGER's publications provide numerous details. See also GINZBERG, 'Derek Erez'; and the comprehensive studies mentioned above.

The Treatises Semahot

Within the framework of Mishna and Tosefta, there is no special tractate devoted to the laws and customs pertaining to the deceased (burial, mourning *et al.*).[149] These were relegated to a separate tractate which bore the name *Evel*, 'Mourning'. The Talmud itself quotes from such a tractate entitled *Evel Rabbati*,[150] i.e. major, which probably indicates the existence of at least one additional (minor) tractate devoted to these subjects during the talmudic period. The existence of two such tractates is confirmed by the Gaonic tradition which speaks of 'a large tractate *Evel* and a smaller one.'[151] This may be a reference to the two extant tractates, one halakhic and one basically aggadic, which, from the medieval period onward, have usually been euphemistically entitled *Massekhet Semahot*, 'Rejoicings' and *Massekhet Semahot de-R. Hiya*, respectively. Even so, there is concrete evidence attesting to the existence of at least one additional halakhic treatise, and so some uncertainty does exist as to the identification of the Gaonic tradition.[152]

MASSEKHET SEMAHOT

As evinced by the numerous citations of medieval rabbis, this tractate was originally known by the title *Evel Rabbati* (or: *Rabta*).[153] Its fourteen chapters include numerous halakhot relating to all aspects of death: the funeral, burial, mourning and the burial of the bones, with much additional subject matter. Several of the halakhot and customs are of most ancient practice, which were no longer in vogue during the Middle Ages.[154] In addition, numerous halakhot are unique with this tractate and are not found anywhere else in rabbinic literature.[155]

Some of the topics dealt with are: the legal status of a dying man and the moment of death (1:1-7); burial rites in extraordinary cases such as of suicides,

---

[149] Several of these laws are found in *M. Moed K.* 3:5-9 and elaborate details are adduced in the parallel talmudic discussions.

[150] *B.T. Moed K.* 24a, 26b; *Ket.* 28a. This tractate is apparently no longer extant in its original form.

[151] Assaf, *Responsa*, 176 no. 164.

[152] See also R. Simha in *Mahzor Vitri*, 249 l. 2.

[153] Yet, it is not identical with the tractate mentioned in the Talmud, cf. above n. 66. Cf. also the source cited in n. 68.

[154] Cf. Higger, *Semachot*, introd. 73-85; Zlotnick, *Tractate*, introd. 11-17. Zimmer, 'Atifa' discusses the custom of muffling the head with a scarf and its vicissitudes.

[155] Cf. the list in Higger, *ib.* 59.

apostates, those lost at sea (2:1-11) and in the case of infants and children (3:1-5); the defilement of priests (4:1-18); things prohibited during the seven days of mourning, such as working, having one's hair cut, wearing shoes and phylacteries, studying, greeting (5:1-6:7); the Sabbath and festivals as part of the mourning period, and laws concerning the 'thirty days' (7:1-25); proper procedure and usage of the cemetery, tombs and burial practices, and the behaviour towards the mourner after the first week (13:3-14:15).

It must be noted that, although the treatise deals with most practical issues, the material is often arranged in an inexpedient fashion, and that much material of slight relevance is interspersed. A study of the redactional aspects of this tractate remains a major desideratum.

The printed edition as well as some manuscripts of *Massekhet Semahot* begin the tractate with the midrash based on Exod 12:29 and Num 8:17, describing the agony of the Egyptian first-born during the tenth plague. This seems to be a later addition,[156] designed to serve as a cheerful introduction to the tractate whose opening note is set by the last moments before dying of an Israelite.[157] A similar addition is the final halakha of the tractate which closes on the hopeful note of 'miracles wrought for Israel'.[158]

Special attention should be focused on the latter part of chapter eight whose contents are almost completely aggadic. Mention of the death of Shmuel the Small and the prophecy relating to the death of prominent Sages serve as an introduction to numerous martyrological traditions and teachings. Included are stories of the martyrdom of Shimon and Yishmael (8:8), R. Hananya ben Tardyon (8:12), and Pappus and Julianus (8:15), which are arranged in a sort of literary cycle which also alludes to the martyrdom of R. Akiva and R. Yehuda ben Bava (8:8-9). These are interspersed by various reactions, homilies and parables, mainly of the above-mentioned Sages (8:8-11). The only halakha in this section declares that the study of Tora is not to be interrupted until the soul departs from the dying man (8:13). However, this is only an excuse to introduce the story of R. Akiva's extraordinary conduct during the course of his son's demise and the ensuing funeral, including the lengthy eulogy and discourse that he delivered on that occasion (8:13-16). Another aggadic passage, describing the eulogies for the brigand son of R. Hananya ben Tardyon is appended to the end of chapter 13.

It has been postulated that the middle of the eighth century was the date of the final redaction of *Massekhet Semahot*. However, recent research conducted by ZLOTNICK has shown that there is no decisive evidence for such a late date. On the basis of latest Sages mentioned (R. Yehuda the Prince and his contemporaries), the language (mishnaic Hebrew), style and structure (reminiscent of the Tannaim), he has come to the conclusion that an early date is preferable, i.e. the

---

[156] Adopted from *Pes. R.* 17 (87a-b).
[157] Cf. Zlotnick, *Tractate*, Introd., 9-11.
[158] From *M. Ber.* 9:1. See Lieberman, *Tosefta ki-Fshutah* 1, 103, l. 10.

end of the third century. This implies that, for all intents and purposes, *Massek-het Semahot* is to be considered of Tannaic vintage, and thus defined as a collection of baraitot. It is interesting to note that this conclusion concurs with that of Rav Natronai Gaon[159] who described our tractate as *mishna*. Nevertheless, the employment of certain editorial techniques, especially as far as the insertion of aggadic passages is concerned, does not preclude a somewhat later date.[160]

SEMAHOT DE-R. HIYA

Semahot de-R. Hiya, which has never been printed together with the Babylonian Talmud, is one of the more neglected works of talmudic literature. The name of this tractate is based on the quotations by medieval authorities who lived in Italy, although one of these, R. Tsedekia ben Abraham, refers to it by the double appellation: *Semahot Zutarti de-R. Hiya*. It is thus quite possible that this tractate was also entitled *Semahot Zutarti* (i.e. minor). In any event, the identification of the minor tract as that of R. Hiya is confirmed by an earlier Italian rabbi.[161] However, Nahmanides and other Spanish rabbis refer to this tractate as *Massekhet Semahot* or *Evel Rabbati*, sometimes even equating the two.[162] This may be an indication that, at one time, *Semahot de-R. Hiya* formed a part of *Massekhet Semahot*.

Even though the opening section of *Semahot de-R. Hiya* contains several important halakhot concerning the proper attitude towards a learned person on his deathbed, and the requirement of the sick to confess their sins, the essence of the tractate is basically aggadic in content. Chapters two to four may be regarded as an ethical tract whose professed purpose is to encourage one to repent and in this world make the proper preparations for life in the hereafter. It may be conjectured that this section was compiled as a manual to be studied and recited by a person on his deathbed. As such, it is one of the most beautiful and inspiring works of aggadic literature, containing a host of teachings, homilies and parables, and rich in metaphor and philosophical insight. Some of these are not found in other works of talmudic literature. The topics dealt with include repentance and good deeds before death, birth and death; the paths of the evil and the righteous in this world, and their reward and punishment in the world-to-come.

---

[159] Assaf, *Responsa*, 176 no. 164. However in *Arukh s.v.* אבל the word *mishna* is lacking.

[160] Note the following difficulties concerning the historicity of 8:8: a) the usage of the title 'R.' for Shimon and Yishmael (see Lieberman, 'Persecution', 227-8); b) the inclusion of an alternative literary tradition, *A.R.N.* b 41 (57b), as 'some who say'; c) 'They girded their loins with sackcloth' a biblical practice apparently not in vogue during the mishnaic period; d) a Hebrew adaptation of the Aramaic prophecy of Shmuel the Small (cf. 8:7, p. 153).

[161] Shlomo ben ha-Yatom, *Kommentar*, xxiii, par. 9.

[162] See Nahmanides, *Torat ha-Adam* 2, 46; *ib.* 16; R. Yisrael al-Nakawa, *Menorat ha-Maor* 3, 555.

391

Semahot de-R. Hiya is written in classical mishnaic Hebrew, in the style of Tannaic teachings.[163] It is important to note that unpublished Geniza fragments of this tract evince the presence of several controversies of a philosophical nature between the schools of Hillel and Shammai. Two of these are unknown from any other rabbinic source. Since R. Yehuda the Prince and some of his contemporaries are the latest Sages mentioned, it may be concluded that *Semahot de-R. Hiya* is a product of the early third century. The tradition attributing it to R. Hiya, a disciple of R. Yehuda the Prince, may thus be considered quite accurate.

AN ALTERNATIVE VERSION OF MASSEKHET SEMAHOT

In his lengthy treatise on the laws of mourning and burial called *Torat ha-Adam*, Nahmanides occasionally adduces halakhot from a certain *Mekhilta Ahariti de-Evel* or *Nusha Aharina be-Evel Rabbati*. This implies that he utilized a parallel tractate or alternative version of *Massekhet Semahot*. As observed by HIGGER,[164] these quotations generally contain material identical with the laws and traditions of *Massekhet Semahot*, and differ only as to language and style.[165]

The last folio of this elusive tractate has recently been discovered in a Cambridge manuscript from the Cairo Geniza. This fragment, whose colophon contains the title *Massekhta de-Semahot*, indicates that the tractate does indeed contain material very similar to the extant *Massekhet Semahot*. A preliminary study of this folio, which has preserved part of chapter 15 and all of chapters 16-17, reveals that the basic material roughly parallels chapters 10-13 of the extant tractate and that several narrative traditions from earlier chapters of *Semahot* have been juxtaposed in an entirely different fashion. The closing section of this tractate contains the aggadic account of R. Hiya visiting R. Yehuda the Prince on his deathbed,[166] and the homily of R. Hanina ben Antigonos[167] presented anonymously. These give the impression of being editorial additions.

It is quite possible that numerous quotations which medieval authors ascribe to *Massekhet Semahot*, *Evel*, and other titles, but which are not found in these works in their extant form, have their source in this tractate.[168]

BIBLIOGRAPHY

MASSEKHET SEMAHOT. A critical edition of the first four chapters with a German translation was published in 1890 by KLOTZ, *Ebel Rabbati*. The first critical

---

[163] E.g. the unique usage of זו משנת רבי עקיבה (1:4, p. 213); cf. *M. Sanh.* 3:4; *T. Maas. Sh.* 2:1.
[164] Higger, *Semachot*, introd. 19, 54.
[165] Cf. however Nahmanides *ib.* 109.
[166] Cf. *B.T. Ket.* 103b.
[167] *Semahot de-R. Hiya* 2:2 (p. 217).
[168] If so, Higger's observation (*Semachot*, introd. 19) has to be modified.

edition of the entire text, based on four complete manuscripts and the Venice 1547 printing together with a lengthy introduction, was issued in 1931 by HIGGER, *Semachot* (see limited critique by LIEBERMAN in *KS* 9 [1932] 53-56); additional notes *id.*, 'Ketanot', 92-6; 165-9. An English translation, as well as a vocalized edition of MS. Oxford, Bodleian 370:6, prepared by KUTSCHER, together with an introduction and copious notes, several of these based on the oral comments of LIEBERMAN, purporting to utilize all available manuscripts, has been published by ZLOTNICK, *Tractate* (see review by GOLDBERG in *KS* 42 [1967] 459-63). A linguistic critique of the Hebrew text is offered by SARFATTI, *'Texts'*.

The pioneering study of BRÜLL, 'Talmudischen Traktate', has, on the main, been incorporated into the introduction and edition of Higger.

MASSEKHET SEMAHOT DE-R. HIYA was first published from manuscripts, together with an introduction and explanations, by HOROWITZ, *Uralte Tosefta's*, 2-3, 1-8, 28-40. A second edition containing variants from the same two manuscripts used by Horowitz, MS. Parma - De Rossi 1420 and MS. Vatican 44, including some additional material, has been appended to HIGGER, *Semachot*, 59-72, 86-7, 211-29, 250-2. Additional notes *id.*, 'Ketanot', 169-70. Two Geniza fragments, containing some important new material, are being readied for publication by the present author.

ALTERNATIVE VERSION OF MASSEKHET SEMAHOT. The quotations from Nahmanides and the medieval authors have been collected by HIGGER, *Semachot*, 230-50. Additional notes *id.*, 'Ketanot', 170. These should be supplemented by additional material available from subsequent publications. The Geniza fragment containing the last chapter of the alternative version of *Massekhet Semahot* is being readied for publication by the present author.

The Tractates Kalla

The tractates bearing the name *Kalla*, whose simple translation is 'A Bride', ostensibly deal with marriage and sex laws. The *massekhet kalla* (or: *massekhta de-kalla*) which is mentioned several times in the Babylonian Talmud,[169] apparently has no connection with the minor tractates under discussion and obviously refers to the tractate studied during the famous *kalla* sessions in the Babylonian academies.[170]

MASSEKHET KALLA

This minor tractate derives its name from the opening paragraph: 'A Bride is forbidden to her husband without the marriage benediction . . .' In the ensuing

---

[169] *B.T. Taan.* 10b; *Kidd.* 49b; *Shabb.* 114a (see *Dikdukei Sofrim ad loc.*).
[170] See Higger, *Kalla*, introd. 13-21; Aptowitzer, 'Traité', 239-42. On the *Kalla* sessions, see Goodblatt, *Rabbinic Instruction*, 155-70; Gafni, *Babylonian Jewry*, 96-8.

paragraphs, various laws concerning the chastity of the marriage festivities,[171] and additional warnings to males against unchaste behaviour towards females are discussed.[172] Some intimate rulings concerning sexual intercourse between husband and wife are followed by several very negative declarations against virile masturbation.[173] In the final section of the tractate, various answers are provided to the questions 'For what sin do a man's children die young?'[174] and 'What should a man do so that his children grow rich and flourish?' In answer to the latter, it is stated: 'Let him fulfill the will of God and the wishes of his wife.'[175] These are explained as the free distribution of money to the poor and the maintenance of a captivating atmosphere during the performance of conjugal relations. The closing paragraph deals with the proper attitude of the disciple towards his master. Several biographical episodes, all related to Tannaim, are appended to some of the halakhic and ethical rulings.[176]

In its present form, this brief tractate is composed of a single chapter, which the editor of the critical edition has divided into 24 paragraphs. The appellation *Perek Kalla* found in the writings of several early authorities, apparently confirms this.[177] However, the tractate *Kalla Rabbati*, which is an elaboration in talmudic style on *Massekhet Kalla* and other sources, divides the tractate into two chapters,[178] whereas the Geniza fragment published by WERTHEIMER evinces a division of at least three chapters.

Much of the material in *Massekhet Kalla* seems to be derived from baraitot and Amoraic teachings in the Babylonian Talmud, which, in certain cases, have undergone re-editing.[179] A comparison of the parallel texts reveals certain revisions in conjunction with the study of the Bible, and these may very well be anti-Karaitic glosses.[180] This may also be the reason for the rather harsh pronouncement against the disciple 'who opposes the teachings of his master's academy'.[181] A unique, unheard-of benediction mentioning 'the God of our

---

[171] Especially rulings concerning the cup of benediction and the recital of biblical verses from Canticles.

[172] Par. 3-8 (Higger p. 126ff).

[173] Par. 9-19 (p. 135ff.).

[174] Par. 20 (p. 155ff.).

[175] Par. 21 (p. 156ff.).

[176] Par. 16 (p. 146-9); par. 21 (p. 157-60); par. 23 (p. 161-3, in the critical apparatus).

[177] Cf. R. Yehuda Albargheloni, *Sefer ha-Ittim*, ed. Schorr, 246; R. Menahem ha-Meiri, Introduction to *Avot*, ed. Prag, 44 (= R. Yitshak de Lattes, *Schaarei Zion*, ed. Buber, 26).

[178] See below. Two chapters also in *Sefer ha-Aguda* of R. Alexander Zuslin ha-Kohen (Cracow 1571) 225a, but not identical with *Kalla Rabbati*.

[179] Cf. par. 12 (p. 141) with *B.T. Gitt.* 70a; par. 13 (p. 143-4) and *B.T. Ber.* 40a; par. 10 (p. 137ff.) and *B.T. Ned.* 20a-b.

[180] The talmudic source in *B.T. Sanh.* 101a speaks of a) 'students of Bible', b) 'students of Mishna' and c) 'students of Talmud'; whereas par. 4 (p.128) mentions 'a disciple of the Sages' (= b, c) and 'an illiterate person' (= a). See also par. 24 (p. 164) in comparison with *T. Bava M.* 2:29 and *B.T. Bava M.* 33a.

[181] Par. 24 (p. 163); cf. *B.T. Ber.* 27b top; *B.T. Sanh.* 110a.

forefathers, the God of Abraham . . . Isaac . . . Jacob and the God of R. Akiva who has revealed His secret to Akiva ben Yosef',[182] may best be understood against the background of the Rabbanite attacks against Karaism.

Massekhet Kalla may definitely be viewed as a post-talmudic compilation of the early Gaonic Period. There is no basis for the hypothesis of HIGGER that the basic tractate was compiled by a disciple of R. Eliezer ben Hyrcanus.

MASSEKHET KALLA RABBATI

The literary character of the tractate known as *Kalla Rabbati* is reminiscent of the Talmud. It is written in Aramaic and elaborates on the text before it, in the same manner that the Gemara elaborates on the Mishna. In this case, the underlying texts include:[183] chaps. 1-2, *Massekhet Kalla*; chaps. 3-4, *Massekhet Yirat Het* 1-3;[184] chap. 5, *Perek Kinyan Tora* (= *Avot*, chap. 6);[185] chaps. 6-9, *Pirkei Ben Azzai* 1-9 (= *Derekh Erets Rabba* 3-11). The arrangement of material in these texts is more or less the same as in the original tracts, although there are marked discrepancies between the basic text of *Pirkei Ben Azzai* chaps. 3-9 and *Kalla Rabbati* 7:4 till end.

In form and contents, too, *Kalla Rabbati* bears some affinity to the structure of the Babylonian Talmud. Each excerpt (or 'baraita') from the underlying text is commented on by a dialectical discussion, usually quite brief, which utilizes the terminology and method of the talmudic *sugya*.[186] Tannaic sources are quoted and elucidated.[187] There are even two unknown quotations from Ben Sira, one of them in rhymed verse.[188] Numerous Amoraim are mentioned, most of them of Babylonian extraction. Rava, whose explanations are recorded approximately twenty-five times, is by far and large the major authority mentioned.[189] In certain instances there are cross-references from one chapter to another.[190] Since most of the material in the underlying texts is of an ethical nature, the tractate itself contains much aggadic material.

The title *Kalla Rabbati* first appears in the Romm edition of the Babylonian Talmud, where it was appended to the minor tractates (1883). This edition was based on CORONEL's edition (1864). The title *Kalla Rabbati* was actually un-

---

[182] Par. 16 (p. 149) according to the Geniza manuscript published by Wertheimer, *Batei Midrashot* 1, 231.

[183] According to the order of MS. Parma-De Rossi 327 (= ed. Higger). In the MS. published by Coronel, section 3 appears in the middle of section 4. Higger has compiled a chart of the chapter arrangements of the different editions: *Kalla*, introd. 54-5.

[184] Higger, *Zeirot*, 77 l. 9; Higger, *Treatises* 2:7 (p. 93); and see above.

[185] See above, *Avot*.

[186] De Vries, 'Date', 132 has focused attention on the fact that the terminology employed is characteristic of 'the special tractates' (*Nedarim, Nazir et al.*).

[187] A listing of these is found in Epstein, *Nosah*, 866.

[188] See Schechter, 'Quotations', 685, 696-7.

[189] Cf. Higger, *Kalla*, introd. 59-61.

[190] See 4:7 (p. 256), 4:19 (p. 267), 9:13 (p. 337).

known to the medieval rabbis. The sixteenth century cabbalist, R. Eliyahu de Vidas was apparently the first (and only?) authority to employ it.[191] Most of the early authorities refer to it as *Massekhet Kalla, Baraita de-Massekhet Kalla* or simply as *Baraitot*.[192] One medieval rabbi sometimes termed it 'a Midrash', whereas R. Yaakov Sikily consistently referred to the sections connected with *derekh erets* literature as *Gemar* i.e. Gemara, Talmud to *Derekh Erets*.[193] It is thus most plausible that *Kalla Rabbati* is actually a misnomer.[194]

Scholars have long been divided over the date of this tractate. ISH-SHALOM has suggested that it originated towards the close of the Amoraic period,[195] and DE VRIES justified this conclusion on the basis of talmudical terminology.[196] On the other hand, APTOWITZER has raised the possibility that the Rava referred to in *Kalla Rabbati* is the eighth century disciple of Rav Yehudai Gaon,[197] while HIGGER conjectured that he may have been Rava, the Gaon of Pumbeditha, who lived a hundred years earlier.[198]

Whatever the case may be, there does not seem to be any basis for the assumption that this tractate, which has no direct relationship to the Talmud and, on the basis of extant evidence, apparently never circulated as part of it, is a product of the Amoraic Period. In spite of its external resemblance to the Babylonian Talmud, it is at the most a rough imitation of the talmudic discussion and argumentation,[199] which does not seem to have been sanctioned by Gaonic authorities.[200] The possibility that this combined 'gemara' to four separate tracts is artificial and pseudonymous, much like some midrashic texts of the Gaonic Period,[201] should not be ruled out.

BIBLIOGRAPHY

MASSEKHET KALLA. A critical edition based on MS. Munich 95, including variants from six additional manuscripts and various printed editions, was published by HIGGER, *Kalla* (see critique of LIEBERMAN in *KS* 13 [1936-7] 185-7). The Geniza text published by WERTHEIMER in *Batei Midrashot* 1, 227-33; 222; 405-6 which contains many superior readings, has been collated in Higger's edition.

---

191 See Higger, *Kalla*, introd. 101, par. 27. Note well that in four other instances, this title is not used.
192 The Coronel edition is entitled: *Massekhet Kalla weha-Beraita.*
193 Higger, *Kalla*, introd. 92-3.
194 On the usage of 'Kalla Rabbati' in conjunction with the 'Kalla' sessions, which is probably the origin of this phrase, see Goodblatt, *Rabbinic Instruction*, 157 and n. 7.
195 *Pseudo-Seder Eliahu Zuta*, introd. 18.
196 De Vries, 'Date', 132.
197 Aptowitzer, 'Traité', 248. See also Epstein, *Nosah*, 320; *id. Grammar*, 16.
198 Higger, *Kalla*, introd. 113.
199 Already recognized by S.D. Luzzatto and R. Kircheim. Cf. Schechter, 'Quotations', 684. See also the remarks of Aptowitzer, 'Traité', end of n. 3.
200 Higger, *Kalla*, introd. 87-9.
201 E.g. *Midrash Prov.*; *Pirkei de-R. Eliezer et al.* Cf. Zunz-Albeck, *Derashot*, 157.

The supposed 'talmudic' origin of the tractate has been dealt with by APTOWIT-ZER, 'Traité', 239-43.

KALLA RABBATI. A critical edition, based on MS. Parma - De Rossi 327:15, with a lengthy introduction and notes was issued by HIGGER, *Kalla*. Higger also colla-ted the MS. which formed the basis of the *editio princeps* published by CORONEL, *Commentaries*, which contains many superior readings. (See also the critique of LIEBERMAN in *KS* 13 [1936-7] 186-7.)

The first chapter of *Kalla Rabbati* (which also includes the underlying text of *Massekhet Kalla*) is so far the only minor tractate to have an extant commentary by a medieval authority. The commentary of R. Avraham ben Natan ha-Yarhi was edited by B. TOLEDANO (Tiberias 1906, supplemented by HIGGER, 'Yarhi', 340-1) second edition Ramat-Gan 1970.

Important studies on this tractate have been written by FRIEDMANN (ISH-SHALOM), *Pseudo-Seder Eliahu zuta*, introd. 13-19; APTOWITZER, 'Traité',243-4; 248; DE VRIES, 'Date'. For a recent elaboration of 2:6, see BÖHL, 'Paränetische Kettenreihe'.

Sofrim and the Seven Minor Tracts

An additional branch of the minor tractates deals with the Holy Scriptures. These tractates contain practical instructions for scribes concerning the copying of the Tora scroll and the various biblical books, the materials to be used, *et al.* It should be noted that again there is no specific mishnaic tractate devoted to these laws and customs.

MASSEKHET SOFRIM

The word *sofrim* used in the titles of this and the following works alludes to the 'scribes' or copyists of holy writ.[202] However, the accepted title of this tractate, *Massekhet Sofrim* or 'The Tractate of Scribes', is most likely a misnomer. In view of readings in Gaonic responsa[203] and an eleventh[204] or twelfth[205] century rabbinic text which contains numerous quotations from a work entitled *Baraita de-Sefarim* or *Massekhta de-Sefarim*, it is quite apparent that the original title of this tractate was *Sefarim*, i.e. the Holy Scriptures. This is confirmed by the contents of *Massekhet Sofrim* which not only deal with the laws concerning the copying of biblical texts, but also with the occasions of their being read in the

---

[202] Cf. the modern Hebrew usage *Sofer SeTaM* סת"ם סופר which is an abbreviation referring to the copyist of Holy Scriptures, phylacteries, and mezuzot. In mishnaic Hebrew *sofrim* ordinarily refers to the art of elementary school teaching, see *M. Kidd.* 4:13; *Lam. R.* proem 2 (p. 2).

[203] Harkavy, *Responsen*, 3 no. 3; Lewin, *Otzar, Shabbat*, 102 no. 312.

[204] See Adler, *Ginze Mizrayim, passim*; Higger, *Seven Minor Treatises*, introd. 12-15; id. *Sofrim*, 37-9.

[205] See Abramson, 'Hilkhot Sefer Tora' (1).

synagogue, as well as with numerous other synagogue practices and customs.

Following is a general division of the tractate: Chaps. 1-5 contain laws concerning the writing of the Tora Scroll (Pentateuch) with special attention to the writing of the divine names, individual sections of the Pentateuch, and the combination of Tora, *Neviim* (Prophets) and *Ketuvim* (Hagiographa). Three disassociated texts, all found in the Babylonian Talmud as well as the section dealing with the sanctity of certain divine epithets in Canticles and Daniel at the end of chapter five,[206] are probably later additions. It should be noted that this section bears very close affinity with the other extant minor tracts concerned with the writing of the Tora scroll, *Sofrim B* and *Massekhet Sefer Tora* (see below).

The second section of *Massekhet Sofrim* (chaps. 6-9) deals mainly with the exactitudes of the Massoretic text, including 'defective' and 'plene' spelling and the various rules for the reading (*keri*) and writing (*ketiv*) of various words and expressions throughout the Bible. Towards the end of chapter nine, there is a discussion of laws concerning the public reading and translation of certain biblical passages of a sensitive nature, which parallels *M. Meg.* 4:9-10 and includes explanations adopted from the Palestinian Talmud. One may note a rather close relationship between *Sofrim* and the Mishna and Yerushalmi to tractate *Megilla* in most of the ensuing chapters, which accounts for much of the contents of this tractate.[207]

Chapters 11-12 are mainly devoted to the public reading of the Tora scroll. It may be noted in passing that almost all of chapter twelve is based on *P.T. Meg.* 3, 74b.

The beginning of chapter thirteen contains some rules concerning the copying of the Scroll of Esther taken from *P.T. Megilla*,[208] although the continuation of this chapter and the beginning of chapter fourteen deal mainly with the blessings pronounced before and after the public reading of the Tora scroll, the *haftara*, the Five Scrolls, and the Hagiographa, respectively, with special attention to the Scroll of Esther. In the continuation of this chapter, there is a detailed account of the synagogue services after the reading of the *haftara*, and the participation of minors and others in the services, while the closing section reverts back to the Five Scrolls and the time of their appointed readings.

Chapter fifteen commences with the permission to translate the Bible into Greek based on *M. Meg.* 1:8 and adduces several halakhic rulings concerning the Holy Scriptures from *P.T. Shabb.* 16:1. This is followed by various quotations from talmudic lore dealing with the relative importance of Bible, Mishna and Talmud and the importance of the Oral Tora and the study of Tora in general, which are continued in chapter sixteen. The author seems to have

---

[206] 5:17-21 (p. 161-4).

[207] E.g. *Sofrim* 9:9-12 = *Megilla* 4:9-10; 10:6 = 4:3; 11:1 = 4:4; 14:4; cf. 4:5; 14:14 = 2:4; 15:1 = 1:8; 14:12 and 16:9; cf. 4:6; 17:1-2 = 3:4.

[208] 13:1 = 1:1, 70a; 13:2-4 = 3:7, 74b end.

adopted a most harsh attitude towards the circulation of the aggada in written form.[209]

Chapter seventeen reverts back to the public reading of the Tora scroll, on the various holidays and special occasions, while chapter eighteen lays down regulations for the daily and Festival Psalms (not found elsewhere) and while dwelling on the Psalms for the ninth of Av, continues to discuss the ritual connected with this fast day.

Chapter nineteen deals with the holiday prayers and contains a special section devoted to the unique ritual and ceremony for the celebration of the New Moon, while chaps. 20-21 are devoted to the rabbinically ordained celebrations of Hanukka and Purim, respectively.

Most versions of *Massekhet Sofrim* also contain five short aggadic passages which appear as a continuation of chap. 21. HIGGER has printed these aggadot in the form of an appendix, entitled 'Midrash', since they are apparently not related to the tractate *per se*.[210] It is interesting to note that this aggadic material includes legends of a somewhat bizarre content not found in any other sources, such as the astounding proportions of Abraham and Eliezer and the method whereby Jacob deduced that Joseph was alive.

As already propounded by medieval authorities,[211] *Massekhet Sofrim* is definitely of post-talmudic vintage, although certain segments, particularly chaps. 1-5, are clearly of a much earlier origin (see below). It may therefore be safe to assume that the final redaction of this tractate took place during the Gaonic Period.

The prevailing scholarly opinion is that *Massekhet Sofrim* was composed in the Land of Israel.[212] As previously noted, this tractate has made prolific usage of the Palestinian Talmud, and it may be added that many of its rulings and practices are contradicted by halakhic decisions rendered by the Babylonian Geonim who actually do not allude to this tractate.[213] Nevertheless, there are several factors which seem to discount a Palestinian origin, *viz.* the Diaspora custom of a two-day festival,[214] and the reference to the Palestinian authorities as 'Our Masters in the West' or 'Our Masters in Palestine'.[215] To these we might add a direct quote from the Babylonian Talmud and the author's usage of Babylonian Aramaic.[216] However, one need not postulate that either the final recension of this work was composed on Babylonian soil, or that the Diaspora references are later additions. It is entirely possible that *Massekhet Sofrim* was produced in an area which maintained strong Palestinian leanings, but was

---

[209] See 16:2 (p. 284); 16:8 (p. 291-4); 16:10 (p. 296-7).
[210] Cf. however p. 365 l. 1 with p. 292 l. 55; and p. 368 l. 26 with p. 333 l. 53.
[211] E.g. R. Asher ben Yehiel, *Halakhot ketanot, Hilkhot Sefer Tora* 13, 113d.
[212] Higger, *Sofrim*, introd. 80. See also Gartner, 'Mourners of Zion'.
[213] Higger, *Sofrim,* introd. 41f.
[214] 14:16 (p. 270).
[215] 10:6 (p. 214); 17:3 (p. 299); 21:1 (p. 352).
[216] 18:6 (p. 318); 13:9(p. 246).

nevertheless governed by Diaspora law. Southern Italy would seem to fit this definition, but such a thesis awaits more definite proof.

During the Middle Ages, *Massekhet Sofrim* was generally considered a reliable source, and most codifiers accepted its halakhic rulings, although some authorities did refuse to follow this tractate where it bluntly contradicted talmudic law.[217]

The existence of an alternate version of *Massekhet Sofrim* is attested to by the quotations in the Geniza manuscript known as *Hilkhot Sefer Tora*.[218]

MASSEKHET SOFRIM B

This work, which contains 39 halakhot divided into two chapters, was originally published under the title *Massekhet Sefarim*.[219] It roughly parallels the first three chapters of *Massekhet Sofrim*, and may be defined as a somewhat limited and much improved version of that tractate. This allows one to assume a later recension and there is no necessity to subscribe to the thesis of HIGGER, i.e. that version B represents a Babylonian redaction of earlier vintage. There is some possibility that this text, which is based on a *unicum*, is incomplete. Higger has postulated that several quotations from *Baraita de-Hilkhot Sefarim* and *Baraita de-Sefarim* by medieval authorities, derive from missing sections of this tract. On the other hand, version B may represent nothing more than an arbitrary abridgement and adaptation of *Massekhet Sofrim A*, its textual significance thus being of a most limited nature.

Massekhet Sefer Tora. This tract, which in fact may be the oldest of the *Sofrim* Tractates, will be dealt with in connection with the 'Seven Minor Tracts' below.

THE SEVEN MINOR TRACTS

During the Middle Ages, it was customary to group the smallest of the minor tractates together in a literary formation known as *sheva massekhtot ketanot* (The Seven Minor Tracts)[220] which included the following *massekhtot*: *Sefer Tora*[221], *Mezuza, Tefillin, Tsitsit, Avadim, Kutim* and *Gerim*. Each of these will

[217] Higger, *ib*. 69-71. Cf. Ratzabi in Kasher, *Torah Shelemah* 29, 99.
[218] Abramson, 'Hilkhot Sefer Tora' (2), esp. 6-12. Abramson assigns this text to the twelfth century Rav Yosef, Rosh ha-Seder, a contemporary of Maimonides, and not to R. Yehuda ben Bargilai *et al.*, as proposed by various scholars (Adler, 'Introduction'). See also Abramson, 'Hilkhot Sefer Tora' (1).
[219] According to the testimony of Higger, *Seven Minor Treatises*, introd. 10, the MS. title reads 'Sofrim' and not 'Sefarim'!
[220] E.g. Nahmanides, *Torat ha-Adam*, 100; 258.
[221] Nahmanides, *ib*. 258 apparently included *Massekhet Sofrim A* among the Seven Minor Tracts, thereby eliminating *Massekhet Sefer Tora* from that collection.

be discussed in some detail further on. Such a grouping probably reflected the desire to prevent the loss of these miniature tracts.[222]

Significantly, the tracts *Tsitsit*, *Tefillin*, *Mezuza* and *Gerim* apparently are mentioned in early midrashic literature,[223] which is an indication of their data of origin. Another such indication is the observation that they are all written in classical mishnaic Hebrew. Moreover, all the Sages mentioned are Tannaim.[224] Coupled with the fact that numerous halakhot included in these works are not found elsewhere in rabbinic literature, it is logical to assume that the Seven Minor Tracts are actually products of the Tannaic Period. In view of these observations, it is here proposed that they should be classified as baraita or 'extraneous Mishna'.

MASSEKHET SEFER TORA, 'Tora Scroll'. This tract which is composed of five chapters, forms an exact parallel to the first section of *Massekhet Sofrim* (chaps. 1-5) and is almost identical with it. The additional halakhot found in *Massekhet Sofrim* are clearly interpolations, being later-day halakhot[225] and baraitot, whose source is most likely the Babylonian Talmud.[226] It is thus logical to assume that *Sefer Tora* represents the most ancient version of the *Sofrim* tractates.

MASSEKHET MEZUZA, 'Doorposts'. The two chapters of this tract deal with the laws concerning the *mezuza* scroll: Proper materials; doorposts requiring a *mezuza* and those exempt from such; its proper location; the time limits for affixing the *mezuza*; and its re-inspection.

MASSEKHET TEFILLIN, 'Phylacteries'. This tract contains a single chapter which in HIGGER's edition is divided into 21 halakhot. It treats almost exclusively with the laws concerning the phylacteries: The writing of the parchments; those obligated to wear them and the duration for such; the correct method for wearing the phylacteries and the proper respect towards them.

MASSEKHET TSITSIT, 'Fringes'. This tract also contains only one chapter which deals with the biblical law of 'fringes' (Num 15:38-40). Among the topics discussed are: Who is obligated by this law; garments exempted from the fringes; the method of tying them; the blue thread etc.

---

[222] Cf. *B.T. Bava B.* 14b concerning the Twelve Minor Prophets.

[223] Cf. *Lev. R.* 22,1 (p. 496) and variants to l. 4 *ib.*; *Ruth R.* 2,22 (p. 76); Epstein, *Nosah*, 50.

[224] One exception to the rule proves the rule. In *Massekhet Sefer Tora* 1:5 (p. 22) we read: 'R. Shimon ben Lakish in the name of R. Meir'. However, the parallel text in *Massekhet Sofrim* 1:6 (p. 100) reads: 'R. Shimon ben Elazar . . .' and this identical tradent is even found further on in *Sefer Tora* 2:13 (p. 28).

[225] E.g. *Sofrim* 2:11 (p. 116-7; cf. Higger, introd. 41-2); *ib.* 3:6 (p. 125) contains an usually unnoticed halakha which differentiates between the writing of a scroll and a codex דיפתר, a later-day development. See Bregman, 'Early Fragment', 202-4.

[226] E.g. 3:5 (p. 124; = *B.T. Bava B.* 13b); 3:13 (p. 128; = *B.T. Meg.* 32a); 3:23 (p. 136 = *ib.*).

MASSEKHET AVADIM, 'Slaves'. The first two chapters of this tract deal with the laws of the Hebrew bondman and bondwoman (Exod 21:2-11; Deut 15:12-18), especially concerning their sale and redemption, and the working conditions and parting gifts of the Hebrew bondman. The first part of chapter three deals with the Hebrew bondman who opts to continue his servitude after six years, while the latter section lays down the rules for the acquisition and liberation of a gentile slave.

MASSEKHET KUTIM, 'Samaritans'. The two chapters of this tract, which in some manuscripts is entitled *Kutiim*, deal with the religious status of the Samaritans and the regulation of their relationship with Jews in all religious and secular matters.

MASSEKHET GERIM, 'Proselytes'. Chapter one of this tract deals with the procedure for accepting proselytes; the proselytizing ceremony, and the regulation of various matters relating to the proselyte's former status (wine in his possession, loans etc.). In chapter two, the formal aspects of proselytism as well as the question of divine retribution towards the proselyte are discussed. Chapter three treats the 'resident proselyte' (*ger toshav*), as well as the consanguinity laws relating to the proselyte, and the fate of his assets after death, whereas chapter four is actually a *paean* to the proselytes.

BIBLIOGRAPHY

MASSEKHET SOFRIM has been edited, explained, and translated into German by MÜLLER, *Soferim* (1878). Although he based his text on a manuscript, Müller's rendition is not free of errors. HIGGER, *Sofrim* is an edition based on seven MSS. and early authorities with copious notes and a lengthy introduction. However, the arbitrariness of his textual emendations is to be condemned (cf. critique by LIEBERMAN in *KS* 15 [1938-9] 56-60).

MASSEKHET SOFRIM B was first published (1872) by SCHÖNBLUM, in *Shelosha sefarim niftahim* fol. 6a-13a. Two subsequent editions based on the same MS. were issued by HIGGER in his *Seven Minor Treatises* 81-7 including an introduction, *ib*. 10-16, and in his *Sofrim* 375-82.

The SEVEN MINOR TRACTS were first published collectively by KIRCHEIM, *Septem libri*, from a manuscript, owned by E. Carmoly, accompanied by short explanations (1851; *Gerim, Avadim* and *Kutim* had been previously published). See also the remarks of BUBER, 'Hearot'. A critical edition based on MS. Adler 2237, together with variants from MS. Epstein and MS. Carmoly, as well as individual manuscripts of *Kutim* and *Gerim*, including an English translation, was issued by HIGGER, *Seven Minor Treatises*. It should be noted that the internal division of the individual paragraphs is based on the arbitrary decision of the editor.

402

Additional comments are included in an appendix to *id.*, *Semachot*, 265-72; *id.*, 'Ketanot', 171-2.

For German translations of *Kutim, Avadim* and *Gerim*, together with comments, see GULKOWITSCH, 'Samaritaner'; *id.* 'Sklaven'; POLSTER, 'Proselyten'.

Post-Talmudic Halakhic Literature in the Land of Israel

(by *Zeev Safrai*)

Until sixty years ago, it was commonly thought that halakhic teaching and creation in the Land of Israel came to an end with the completion of the Palestinian Talmud in the fourth century. This description was based on the supposed non-existence of any Palestinian halakhic literature from this time and, in addition, on the polemics of an early Babylonian Gaon. In a work entitled *Pirkoi Ben Baboi*,[227] he claimed that religious educational institutions continued to exist only in Babylonia, and that, consequently, Palestinian halakhic tradition was not reliable. Interestingly enough, the fact that between the fifth and eighth centuries a large midrashic corpus was composed in Palestine was not considered to be relevant to the question of halakhic literature.[228]

The discovery of the Cairo Geniza revealed a great number of Palestinian halakhic works and fragments. While it is often difficult to date them and to define their literary nature, most of these fragments have now been examined by talmudic scholars. This resulted in a much better understanding of post-talmudic Palestinian halakhic activity. Fragments of a number of works can now be identified, as is outlined below; we refer to the Hebrew titles used by their editors.

Another document from the same period which is relevant in this context is the Rehov inscription.

PEREK ARAYOT (Chapter on 'Incestuous Relations').

This work is found in MS. Kaufmann of the Mishna at the end of Tractate *Kiddushin* and in certain manuscripts of Tractate *Derekh Erets* as chapter one (cf. above p. 384-5). The work is written in Hebrew and its style and format are similar to the Mishna. It reflects Palestinian halakha, not Babylonian. The work has not been conclusively dated.

HILKHOT ARAYOT (Laws of 'Incestuous Relations').[229]

This work is based on the previous document. According to MARGULIES, it was written during the Byzantine period, the main argument being that it contains a Greek word not found in Amoraic literature. But this argument is far from conclusive. We cannot exclude the possibility that this word derives from an Amoraic work which has not survived; on the other hand, many inhabitants of Palestine continued to speak Greek during the early period of Muslim rule in Palestine. What seems certain is that the work does not reflect in any way the

---

[227] Ginzberg, in *Ginzei Schechter*, 504-73.
[228] Jewish settlement at the end of the Byzantine period has not been extensively examined in modern times. For a recent short survey see Dan, *Ha-ir*, 40-48; see also Z. Safrai, *Ha-Galil*, 15-22; Klein, *Toledot*, 14-44. On the early Muslim period in Palestine see Gil, *Erets Yisrael*, 9-61.
[229] Margulies, *Hilkhot Erets Yisrael*, 56-67.

period of Muslim rule, and therefore should not be dated later than the early Muslim period.

The section that we possess seems to be a collection of responsa. This type of literature was not usual during the Talmud period, but became very common from the Gaonic period onwards. This work then represents the earliest collection of responsa that we possess.

The responsa basically deal with matters pertaining to women (levirate marriage, *halitsa*, betrothal, etc.).

This is the only one of these fragments which is written in Aramaic.

SEFER HA-SHTAROT (Book of Contracts).[230]

This is a collection of legal deeds, one of which[231] is a deed of manumission dated to as late as 826 C.E. The formulas used in the contracts, however, are for the most part early, as MARGULIES has shown from various usages of language and Byzantine idiom in the documents. There are individual documents in this collection which can be dated as late as the ninth or tenth centuries, beyond the purview of our study.

SEFER HA-HILUKIM BEIN BENEI ERETS YISRAEL U-BENEI BAVEL (Book of the Distinctions between the Residents of the Land of Israel and the Residents of Babylonia).[232]

While the book itself is rather late (after the eighth century), it contains a summary of the distinctions between Palestinian and Babylonian halakhic practice most of which are already found in talmudic literature. The book has a lexicographic format, a format popular in Christian literature in the late Byzantine and early medieval periods.

TESHUVOT, SEFER MAASIM (Responsa, A Book of Cases).

This is a category of loosely related fragments. At this point it is still not possible to determine how many different compositions they represent. The only attempt at a classification was undertaken by MARGULIES,[233] but his efforts were not always conclusive.

All of these collections and fragments have a similar literary format. Most begin with the word *maase* ('deed'), meaning a halakhic decision. Some other fragments contain, apparently, answers to halakhic questions and, therefore, begin with the phrase 'and as you asked . . .'

The fragments are in Hebrew and contain dry halakhic decisions with very little 'talmudic' deliberation. The material presented is rarely new or innovative and is usually based on material known from Mishna and Talmud; most of it

---

230. Margulies, *Hilkhot Erets Yisrael*, 27-31.
231. *Ib.* 27.
232. Margulies, *Hilukim*; Levin, *Otsar*.
233. Margulies, *Hilkhot Erets Yisrael*, 72-5.

deals with the laws of adultery and a number of times cite shaving off hair as a punishment. Quite a few halakhot deal with apostasy, one particular halakha on this subject recurring in a number of collections. These issues occupied halakhists throughout the generations and it is hard to draw historical conclusions based on the limited amount of material which we possess.

Roughly, we can speak of the following compositions:

HILKHOT ERETS YISRAEL (Laws of the Land of Israel), several fragments.[234] There is a degree overlapping in these fragments and it is possible that they are all based on the same source. They do not reflect the least trace of Babylonian tradition. Thus they seem to reflect the later Byzantine or the early Muslim period in Palestine, before Babylonian practice became prevalent.

KITSUR HILKHOT ERETS YISRAEL (Summary of Laws of the Land of Israel), an abbreviated form of the previous item.[235] One fragment was first published by MANN, and a continuation of it was published by LEWIN. The section published by FRIEDMAN likewise belongs to this type of literature. All fragments reflect Babylonian halakha and, therefore, represent a rather later period, when the Jewish community in Palestine had declined and Babylonian traditions had begun to penetrate.

PINKAS HALAKHA ERETS-YISRAELI (Halakhic Notebook of the Land of Israel). This is a chance collection of halakhot compiled, it would seem, for personal use. A rather large fragment of this work was published by MARGULIES[236] and re-published by RABINOWITZ;[237] another fragment was published by LEWIN.[238] It is clear now that the fragments of Lewin and Margulies are not identical, but that they largely overlap. Thus one seems to be based on the other, or perhaps both are based on an earlier work.

Another fragment published by LEWIN[239] as well as its partial parallel published by FRIEDMAN[240] should be added to this type of literature. Some fragments published by MARGULIES[241] form another partial parallel. The relationship between these fragments is similar to those mentioned above.

None of these fragments reflect Babylonian halakha. It should be noted that the section published by Margulies mentions a priest 'captured by the Ishmaelites'. This section, which does not appear in the fragment published by Lewin, postdates the Arab conquest.

---

[234] Epstein, 'Maasim', 39-42; *id.*, 'Lore', 319-21; Friedman, 'Shenei ketaim', 17, 19.
[235] Lewin, 'Geniza Fragments', 409; Mann, 'Sefer ha-maasim', 13; Friedman, 'Shenei ketaim', 21-23.
[236] *Hilkhot Erets Yisrael*, 41-53.
[237] 'Sepher Ha-Ma'asim'.
[238] 'Maasim', 91-8.
[239] *Ib.* 99-100.
[240] 'Shenei ketaim', 21-23.
[241] *Hilkhot Erets Yisrael*, 50-51.

In sum: The prototype of this composition must be an unknown work from the beginning of the Muslim period in Palestine.

KITSUR SEFER HAMAASIM (Abbreviated Book of Cases).[242] Some of the responsa of the Geonim also belong here. The major characteristic of this type of literature is the grafting of Babylonian material on a Palestinian core. The Palestinian material probably derives from a *sefer maasim* or a similar type of composition. The collection that we possess is undoubtedly late, although some of the material included appears to be much earlier.

Regarding the relevant responsa in Gaonic literature, it is quite possible that not all have been discovered. Of those which have, it is usually impossible to date them. They have often been elaborated on and incorporated into Babylonian halakhic works.

To sum up the situation, the relationship between all these fragments is far from clear. At this point it is possible to state that there must have been one original *Sefer Maasim*, or perhaps a number of such works which have not yet been discovered. The collections which we do possess were all edited following different criteria and it is extremely difficult, if not impossible, to determine whether the author of one collection utilized another. Some of the collections make use of Babylonian material and these collections are most likely late. It is important also to remember that it is not only necessary to study the halakhic content and the historical background of these works, but also to examine the selection of topics, since this provides a glimpse into the fields of interest of the various anonymous collators.

HILKHOT TREIFOT (Laws of Forbidden Meat).[243]

We possess two fragments of this work which is divided into chapters and halakhot. They represent the first known attempt at a systematic arrangement of all halakhot pertaining to a particular subject. Perhaps the section that we possess is only part of a larger work written in this vein. The fragment reflects Palestinian halakha, not Babylonian. It is difficult to date it; the few Greek words found offer no clue, as we have seen above.

SIDDUR HALAKHA.

A very interesting discovery from the Cairo Geniza are the fragments of a Palestinian *siddur* or prayer book.[244]

The *siddur* is written in Hebrew with various introductions and explanations in Judaeo-Arabic. The material which we possess includes blessings of mourning, prayers recited upon awakening in the morning and going to synagogue, the laws of the synagogue, versions of prayers, customs relating to festivals and

---

[242] Margulies, *ib.* 79-89; Lewin, 'Geniza Fragments', 407-8; Mann, 'Sefer ha-maasim', 5-10.

[243] Epstein, 'Lore', 308-11; Margulies, *Hilkhot Erets Yisrael* 95-117.

[244] Margulies, *Hilkhot Erets Yisrael*, 127-52.

pilgrimage, additions to the *amida* prayer on fast days and *piyutim* to be recited at the conclusion of prayers.

The *siddur* also contains a 'Scroll of Fasts' mentioning the earthquake which occurred in 746/747 c.e.[245] If so, the Scroll postdates the earthquake and the *siddur* must be from the end of the eight century or later. Even so, it does not contain Babylonian material, and the versions of prayer included in it, at least those without parallels, are for the most part Palestinian.

Siddurim are a specific type of halakhic literature which only became common since the Gaonic period in Babylonia (9th-10th centuries) and, later, in Europe. These unique fragments then represent the earliest known composition of this type. They also point to the fact that this type of literature originated in Palestine.

THE REHOV INSCRIPTION.[246]

This is a large mosaic inscription found in the narthex of the synagogue near Tell Rehov. It contains halakhic selections, related to the 'Commandments Dependent upon the Land', and reflecting an agricultural and geographic interest. Most are selections from the Palestinian Talmud, with occasional halakhic decisions inserted in matters deliberated by the Amoraim. Interesting are also several geographic references which do not appear in the Palestinian Talmud.

Most scholars maintain that the inscription dates from the sixth to seventh centuries and recently this has been confirmed by archeological evidence.

The inscription proves that the halakhic decision making process continued in Palestine in the post-talmudic period. In particular, it informs us of the halakhic decision that during this period certain villages in Samaria were released from the requirements of the Commandments Dependent upon the Land, a daring innovation indeed. Similar halakhic innovations, in other halakhic areas, were greeted with much hesitation during the Mishna and Talmud periods. The interesting conclusion is that authoritative and courageous halakhic institutions continued to exist in post-talmudic Palestine.

CONCLUSIONS. The Palestinian halakhic literature from this period is small in quantity and does not reflect a high degree of creativity. For the most part it represents collections, summaries of earlier material and halakhic decisions. Nonetheless, the material does indicate that halakhic activity and decision making continued in the Land of Israel, and occasionally instigated new pathways.

---

[245] *Ib.* 121-2. This scroll will be dealt with in the second part of this volume.
[246] Sussmann, 'Halakhic Inscription'; *id.* 'Inscription in the Synagogue'; Z. Safrai, 'Rehov Inscription'. For the archeological remains see most recently *Hadashot Archeologiot* 74/5 (1985) 7-8 (Hebr.).

From a literary viewpoint this material is of great interest. It reveals halakhic literary forms not previously known to have existed in this period: responsa literature, the listing of halakhic decisions, halakhic codification and the *siddur*. These literary forms did not exist in the talmudic period and would fully develop only in the Gaonic period in Babylonia (9th-10th centuries).

We do not possess Babylonian parallels from the 5th-7th centuries. It is likely that these literary forms were developed in Palestine and from there were transferred to Babylonia and further developed. Thus, the accepted image of Babylonian cultural supremacy may be right regarding the Gaonic period, but is nowhere certain regarding the preceding period.

Abbreviations

1. *Source Indications*

Names of biblical books, Apocrypha, Pseudepigrapha and Qumran writings are abbreviated according to the usage of the Journal of Biblical Literature (see *JBL*, 95 [1976] 334f.). For Philo's works the usage of the Loeb edition is followed. For rabbinic literature see following list:

Ah.	Ahilut
Ar.	Arakhin
A.R.N. a/b	Avot de-Rabbi Natan, version A/B
Av. Zar.	Avoda Zara
Bava K./M./B.	Bava Kamma/Metsia/Batra
Bekh.	Bekhorot
Ber.	Berakhot
Bikk.	Bikkurim
B.T.	Babylonian Talmud
Cant. R.	Canticles Rabba
Dem.	Demai
Deut. R.	Deuteronomy Rabba
Eccl. R.	Ecclesiastes Rabba
Ed.	Eduyot
Er.	Eruvin
Exod. R.	Exodus Rabba
Gen. R.	Genesis Rabba
Gitt.	Gittin
Hag.	Hagiga
Hor.	Horayot
Hull.	Hullin
Kel.	Kelim
Ker.	Keritot
Ket.	Ketubbot
Kidd.	Kiddushin
Kil.	Kilayim

Kinn.	Kinnim
Lam. R.	Lamentations Rabba
Lev. R.	Leviticus Rabba
M.	Mishna
Maasr.	Maasrot
Maas. Sh.	Maaser Sheni
Makhsh.	Makhshirin
Makk.	Makkot
Meg.	Megilla
Meg. Taan.	Megillat Taanit
Mekh.	Mekhilta (de-R. Yishmael)
Mekh. de-R. Sh.b.Y.	Mekhilta de-R. Shimon ben Yohai
Men.	Menahot
Midr. ha-Gad.	Midrash ha-Gadol
Midr. Prov.	Midrash Proverbs
Midr. Ps.	Midrash Psalms (Shohar Tov)
Midr. Tann.	Midrash Tannaim
Mikw.	Mikwaot
Moed K.	Moed Katan
Naz.	Nazir
Ned.	Nedarim
Neg.	Negaim
Num. R.	Numbers Rabba
Oh.	Ohalot
Pes.	Pesahim
Pes. R.	Pesikta Rabbati
Pes. de-R.K.	Pesikta de-Rav Kahana
Pirkei de-R. El.	Pirkei de-R. Eliezer
P.T.	Palestinian Talmud
Rosh H.	Rosh ha-Shana
S.E.R.	Seder Eliyahu Rabba
S.E.Z.	Seder Eliyahu Zutta
Sanh.	Sanhedrin
Shabb.	Shabbat
Shek.	Shekalim
Shev.	Sheviit
Shevu.	Shevuot
Sifrei Deut.	Sifrei Deuteronomy
Sifrei Num.	Sifrei Numbers
Sifrei Z.	Sifrei Zutta
S.O.(R.)	Seder Olam (Rabba)
T.	Tosefta
Taan.	Taanit
Tam.	Tamid

Tanh.	Tanhuma
Tanh. B.	Tanhuma ed. Buber
Tem.	Temura
Ter.	Terumot
Tev. Y.	Tevul Yom
Tg. Onk.	Targum Onkelos
Tg. Ps.-Yon.	Targum Pseudo-Yonatan
Ukts.	Uktsin
Yal. Shim.	Yalkut Shimoni
Yad.	Yadayim
Yev.	Yevamot
Zav.	Zavim
Zev.	Zevahim

2. Names of Periodicals and Series

AIPHOS	Annuaire de l'Institut de philologie et d'histoire orientales
AJCL	American Journal of Comparative Law
AJSLL	American Journal of Semitic Languages and Literature
AJSR	Association for Jewish Studies, Review
ANRW	Aufstieg und Niedergang der römischen Welt (Temporini - Haase)
APOT	Apocrypha and Pseudepigrapha of the Old Testament (Charles)
ASTI	Annual, Swedish Theological Institute
BA	The Biblical Archaeologist
CII	Corpus Inscriptionum Iudaicarum (Frey)
CPJ	Corpus Papyrorum Judaicarum (Tcherikover et al.)
Compendia	Compendia Rerum Iudaicarum ad Novum Testamentum: I/1-2 (Safrai - Stern), II/2 (Stone)
E.T.	English Translation
G.T.	German Translation
H.T.	Hebrew Translation
HTR	Harvard Theological Review
HUCA	Hebrew Union College Annual
HULTP	Hebrew University Language Traditions Project
JAOS	Journal of the American Oriental Society
JBL	Journal of Biblical Literature
JCP	Jews' College Publications
JE	Jewish Encyclopedia 1-12. New York 1901-5
JJS	Journal of Jewish Studies
JQR	Jewish Quarterly Review
JR	Journal of Religion

JRS	Journal of Roman Studies
JSJ	Journal for the Study of Judaism
JTS	Journal of Theological Studies
KS	Kirjath Sepher
MGWJ	Monatsschrift für Geschichte und Wissenschaft des Judentums
MJGL	Magazin für jüdische Geschichte und Literatur
n.s.	New series
NWUJS	Newsletter, World Union of Jewish Studies
PAAJR	Proceedings, American Association for Jewish Research
PIASH	Proceedings, Israel Academy of Sciences and Humanities
PWCJS	Proceedings, World Congress of Jewish Studies
RB	Revue biblique
REJ	Revue des études juives
Scripta	Scripta Hierosolymitana
TLR	Tulane Law Review
VT	Vetus Testamentum
WHJP	World History of the Jewish People. 8: Avi-Yona - Baras, Society and Religion
ZAW	Zeitschrift für die alttestamentliche Wissenschaft

Accumulative Bibliography

Works by the same author(s) or editor(s) are listed alphabetically by first noun.

Transliteration of Hebrew personal names follows most usual form; variations are indicated at the specific entry. Titles of works in Hebrew are given according to non-Hebrew title page, if available, transliterations included. Otherwise, our own transliteration system is used.

Indications of year of publication following the Jewish counting are given here according to the common era; deviations due to the partial overlap could not be eliminated.

1. Editions of Gaonic and Medieval Sources

Following is a limited list of post-talmudic rabbinic source editions. Standard editions of rabbinic literature used in this work are mentioned in the source index below and in the chapter bibliographies.

ADLER, E.N. (ed.) *Ginzei Mitsrayim. Hilkhot Sefer Tora*. Meiuhas le-R. Yehuda Albartseloni. An Eleventh Century Introduction to the Bible (Oxford 1897) repr. Jerusalem 1970

APTOWITZER, A. *et al.* (eds.) *Sefer Rabiah*. Piskei dinim, hiddushim u-sheelot u-teshuvot le-kol ha-Shas, le-R. Eliezer be-R. Yoel ha-Levi. 1-4. Jerusalem 1964-5

ASSAF, S. (ed.) *Gaonic Responsa from Geniza MSS*. [Teshuvot ha-Geonim] Jerusalem 1928 (Hebr.)

CHAJES, (ed.) R. Shlomo ben ha-Yatom, *Kommentar zu Masquin. Perush le-Massekhet Mashkin*. Berlin 1909

CHAVEL, CH. D. (ed.) *Perushei ha-Tora le-R. Moshe ben Nahman (Ramban)* 1-2. Jerusalem 1959-60 and repr.

– [Nahmanides] *Torat ha-adam*. In: *Kitvei rabbenu Moshe ben Nahman* 2. Jerusalem 1964

COHEN, G. D. (ed.) *Sefer ha-Qabbala. The Book of Tradition*. By Abraham ibn Daud. Philadelphia 1967

DAVIDSON, I. - ASSAF, S. - JOEL, B. I. (eds.) *Siddur R. Saadja Gaon*. 4th pr. Jerusalem 1978

ENELOWE, H. G. (ed.) *Sefer menorat ha-maor*. Le-R. Yisrael al-Nakawa. 1-4. New York 1924-34

EPSTEIN, J. N. *Der gaonäische Kommentar zur Ordnung Tohoroth*. Eine kritische Einleitung zu dem R. Hai zugeschriebenen Kommentar (Diss.) Berlin 1915 (2nd improved Hebr. ed. by E. Z. Melammed, with introd. transl. by Z. Epstein. Jerusalem 1982)

HARKAVY, A. *Responsen der Geonim ...nebst Anmerkungen und Einleitung* (Berlin 1887) repr. Jerusalem 1966

HILDESHEIMER, E. *Sefer halakhot gedolot* (Ad fidem codicum edidit; prolegomenis et notis instruxit) 1-2. Jerusalem 1971-80

HOROWITZ, S. H. (ed.) *Mahzor Vitry*. Le-R. Simha, ehad mi-talmidei Rashi. Jerusalem 1963

KAHANA, K. (ed.) *Seder Tannaim we-Amoraim*. Frankfurt 1935

KOHUT, A. (ed.) *Aruch completum* 1-8; and *Additamenta ad Aruch Completum* (ed. S. Krauss). Vienna 1878-1937

LEWIN, B. M. (ed.) *Iggeret Rav Sherira Gaon*. Nusah Sefarad we-nusah Tsorfat im hilufei ha-girsaot (Haifa 1921) repr. Jerusalem 1972

– *Otzar ha-Geonim. Thesaurus of the Geonic Responsa and Commentaries, Following the Order of the Talmudic Tractates* 1-13. Haifa - Jerusalem 1928-42

NEUBAUER, A. (ed.) *Mediaeval Jewish Chronicles* 1-2. Oxford 1887-95

QAFIII, Y. (trans.) *Mishna im perush rabbeinu Moshe ben Maimon*. Makoi we-tirgum. 1-7. Jerusalem 1963-68 (with transl. only: 1-3. Jerusalem 1963)

[RASHBA] *Sheelot u-teshuvot. R. Shlomo ben Adret*. Repr. in 3 vols. Jerusalem 1976

[ROSH] *Sheelot u-teshuvot. R. Asher ben Yehiel*. New York 1954

SCHNIURSOHN, B. S. (ed.) *Sefer ha-rokeah ha-gadol*. Jerusalem 1967

SCHORR, Y. (ed.) *Sefer ha-ittim*. Le-R. Yehuda bar Barzilai al-Bargheloni. Krakow 1903, repr. n.d.

[MAALOT HA-MIDDOT] *Sefer maalot ha-middot*. Le-R. Yehiel be-R. Yekutiel be-R. Benyamin ha-Rofe. Repr. Jerusalem 1978

SCHREIBER [SOFER], A. *et al.* (eds.) *Beit ha-Behira*. Le-R. Menahem ha-Meiri. 1-13. Jerusalem 1965-70

TRAUB, A. S. (ed.) *Sefer halakhot gedolot*. Repr. Tel Aviv 1962

2. Secondary Literature

ABRAMSON, S. 'Hilkhot Sefer Tora ("Ginzei Mizrayim")' [1]. *Sinai* 95 (1984) 197-208; [2] *Sinai* 98 (1986) 1-21

ABRAHAMS, I. 'The Bodleian MSS. Entitled "The Fear of Sin"', in *Festschrift Moritz Steinschneider*. Leipzig 1896, 72-5

– 'The "Fear of Sin"'. *JQR* o.s. 10 (1898) 660-1

– 'Talmud', in J. Hastings (ed.) *Encycl. of Religion and Ethics* 12 (1926) 185-7

ACKROYD, P. R. *Israel under Babylon and Persia*. Oxford 1970

ADLER, E. N. *An Eleventh Century Introduction to the Hebrew Bible*. Oxford 1897

ADLER, L. 'Zum Traktat Aboth'. *MGWJ* 8 (1859) 200-1

ADMONIT, Z. (ed.) *Kovets Shemitta. Hegut u-mehkar*. Jerusalem 1973

ALBECK, H. [CH.] *Das Buch der Jubiläen und die Halacha*. Berlin 1930

– 'External Halakhah in the Palestinian Targumim and in the Aggadah', in *B.M. Lewin Jubilee Vol.* Jerusalem 1940, 93ff. (Hebr.)

– *Introduction to the Mishna*. Jerusalem - Tel Aviv 1959 (Hebr.; G.T. *Einführung in die Mischna*. Berlin - New York 1971)

– *Introduction to the Talmud, Babli and Yerushalmi*. Jerusalem 1969 (Hebr.)

– *Mehkarim ba-baraita we-Tosefta we-yahsan la-Talmud*. Jerusalem 1944

– 'The Sanhedrin and its President'. *Zion* 8 (1942-3) 165-78 (Hebr.)

– '*Semikha* and *Minnui* and *Bet Din*'. *Zion* 8 (1942-3) 92ff. (Hebr.)

– *Shisha Sidrei Mishna* 1-6. Jerusalem - Tel Aviv 1952-8 and repr.

– *Untersuchungen über die Redaktion der Mischna*. Berlin 1923

ALON, G. *Jews, Judaism and the Classical World. Studies in Jewish History in the Times of the Second Temple and the Talmud* (selection of *Studies*) Jerusalem 1977

– *The Jews in Their Land in the Talmudic Age* 1-2. Jerusalem 1980-4

– *In Memory of G. Alon. Essays in Jewish History and Philology*. Ed. by M. Dorman, S. Safrai and M. Stern. Jerusalem 1970 (Hebr.)

– *Studies in Jewish History in the Times of the Second Temple, the Mishna and the Talmud* 1-2. Tel

Aviv 1958 (Hebr.; E.T. see *Jews, Judaism*)
– *Toledot ha-Yehudim be-erets Yisrael bi-tekufat ha-Mishna weha-Talmud* 1-2. Tel Aviv 1958 (Hebr.; E.T. see *id., The Jews*)
APTOWITZER, A. 'Le traité de "Kalla"'. *REJ* 57 (1909) 239-43
ASSAF, S. *Tekufat ha-Geonim we-sifruta.* Jerusalem 1955
ASSIS, M. 'A Fragment of *Yerushalmi Sanhedrin*'. *Tarbiz* 46 (1976-7) 29-90; 326-9 (Hebr.)
– *Parallel Sugyot in the Jerusalem Talmud* (In the Tractates Shabbat, Sotah, Makkoth and Niddah) Diss. Jerusalem 1976 (Hebr.)
AVI-YONAH, M. *The Jews of Palestine.* New York 1976 (re-ed. *The Jews under Roman and Byzantine Rule.* Jerusalem 1984)
AVI-YONAH, M. - BARAS, Z. (eds.) *Society and Religion in the Second Temple Period* (WHJP 8) Jerusalem - New Brunswick 1977
AVI-YONAH, M. - SAFRAI, S. *Carta's Atlas of the Period of the Second Temple and the Mishna and Talmud.* 2nd ed. 1974 (Hebr.)
BACHER, W. 'Zwei alte Abothkommentare'. *MGWJ* 49 (1905) 541-666
– *Die Agada der babylonischen Amoräer.* 2nd ed. (Frankfurt/M 1913) repr. Hildesheim 1967
– *Die Agada der palästinensischen Amoräer* 1-3 (Strassburg 1892-99) repr. Hildesheim 1965
– *Die Agada der Tannaiten* 1-2 (Strassburg 1884-90; 2nd ed. vol. 1, 1903) repr. Berlin 1965
– *Die Exegetische Terminologie der jüdischen Traditionsliteratur* 1-2 (1899-1905) repr. in 1 vol. Darmstadt 1965
– 'Das Merkwort *pardes* in der jüdischen Bibelexegese'. *ZAW* 13 (1893) 294-305
– 'Observations sur la liste des rabbins mentionnés dans le Traité Derech Ereç'. *REJ* 37 (1898) 299-303
– 'Qirqisani, the Karaite, and his Work on Jewish Sects'. *JQR* o.s. 7 (1895) 687-710
– 'La siège de Moïse'. *REJ* 34 (1892) 299-301
Tradition und Tradenten in den Schulen Palästinas und Babyloniens (1914) repr. Berlin 1966
BAER, Y. [F.] *Memorial Volume.* Jerusalem 1981
BAMBERGER, B. 'A Messianic Document of the Seventh Century'. *HUCA* 15 (1940) 425ff.
BARAS, Z. *et al.* (eds.) *Eretz Israel from the Destruction of the Second Temple to the Muslim Conquest* 1. Jerusalem 1982 (Hebr.)
BARON, S. W. *Jubilee Volume* 1-3. Ed. by S. Lieberman. Jerusalem 1974-5
– *A Social and Religious History of the Jews* 1-16. 2nd ed. New York 1952-76
BAUMGARTEN, A. I. 'The Akiban Opposition'. *HUCA* 50 (1979) 179-97
BAUMGARTEN, J. M. 'Form Criticism and the Oral Law'. *JSJ* 5 (1974) 34-40
– *Studies in Qumran Law.* Leiden 1977
– 'The Unwritten Law in the Pre-Rabbinic Period'. *JSJ* 3 (1972) 7-29 (also in *Studies in Qumran Law*, 1977, 13-35)
BEER, G. *Faksimile-Ausgabe des Mischnacodex Kaufmann A 50.* Den Haag 1929
BEER, G. *et al.* (eds.) *Die Mischna: Text, Übersetzung und ausführliche Erklärung.* Berlin 1912-
BEER, M. *The Babylonian Amoraim. Aspects of Economic Life.* Ramat-Gan 1974 (Hebr.)
– *The Babylonian Exilarchate in the Arsacide and Sassanian Periods.* Tel Aviv 1970 (Hebr.)
– 'Notes on Three Edicts against the Jews of Babylonia in the Third Century C.E.', in S. Shaked (ed.) *Irano-Judaica.* Jerusalem 1982, 25-37
BELKIN, S. *Philo and the Oral Law.* Cambridge MA 1940
BENDAVID, A. *Leshon Mikra u-leshon Hakhamim* 1-2. Tel Aviv 1967
BERKOWITZ, E. *Ha-Halakha, koha we-tafkida.* Jerusalem 1981
BERLIN, M. - ZEVIN, S. J. (eds.) *Entsiklopedia talmudit* 1-. Jerusalem 1946-
BIALOBLOCKI, S. *Eim la-masoret* (collected articles) Tel Aviv 1971
BICKERMAN[N], E. 'La chaine de la tradition Pharisienne'. *RB* 59 (1951) 153-65
– 'The Generation of Ezra and Nehemiah'. *PAAJR* 45 (1978) 1-28
– 'Héliodore au temple de Jérusalem'. *AIPHOS* 7 (1939-44) 5-40
– 'The Maxim of the Anshe Keneset Ha-Gedolah'. *JBL* 59 (1940) 455-69
BLACKMAN, P. *Mishnayoth* 1-6 (London 1951-56) 2nd ed. with index vol. New York 1964-65

BLAU, L. *Papyri und Talmud*. Leipzig 1913

BLIDSTEIN, G. 'A Note On the History of the Term Torah She-Beal Peh'. *Tarbiz* 42 (1972-3) 496-8 (Hebr.)

BÖHL, F. 'Kalla Rabbati II,6 – eine paränetische Kettenreihe der Ursprung der sündhaften Handlung'. *Judaica* 34 (1978) 53-60

BOKSER, B. M. 'An Annotated Bibliographical Guide to the Study of the Palestinian Talmud', in *ANRW* II/19.2, 139-256

– 'The Wall Separating God and Israel'. *JQR* 73 (1982/3) 349-74

BREGMAN, M. 'An Early Fragment of Avot de Rabbi Natan from a Scroll'. *Tarbiz* 52 (1982-3) 201-22 (Hebr.)

BRÜLL, N. 'Die talmudischen Traktate über Trauer um Verstorbene'. *Jahrbücher* 1 (1874) 1-57

BUBER, S. 'Hearot we-haggahot le-sheva masekhtot ketanot yerushalmiot'. *Megged yerachim* 4 (1857) 58-9

BÜCHLER, A. 'Das Brandopfer neben dem Passach in II Chron. xxx 15 und xxxv 12, 14, 16'. *ZAW* 25 (1905) 1-46

– 'Halakhot le-maase ke-Beit Shammai bi-zeman ha-Bait', in *Festschrift M. Bloch* 2. Budapest 1905, 21-30

– 'Hearot we-haarot al matsav ha-isha be-Sefer Yehudit', in *Festschrift Blau*. Budapest 1926, 42-56 (also in *Studies in Jewish History*, 45-77)

– *The Political and Social Leaders of the Jewish Community of Sepphoris in the Second and Third Centuries*. [London] n.d.

– *Studies in Jewish History*. Oxford 1956

– *Studies in Sin and Atonement in the First Century*. London 1928

– *Das Synedrion in Jerusalem*. Vienna 1902

– *Types of Jewish-Palestinian Piety*. London 1922

CHARLES, R. H. (ed.) *Apocrypha and Pseudepigrapha of the Old Testament* 1-2. Oxford 1913 and repr.

CHARLESWORTH, J. H. (ed.) *The Old Testament Pseudepigrapha* 1. New York 1983

CHRISTENSEN, A. *L'Iran sous les Sasanides*. (1936, repr. 2nd. ed. Copenhagen 1944) repr. Osnabrück 1971

COHEN, B. *Jewish and Roman Law* 1-2. New York 1966

– *Law and Ethics in the Light of Jewish Tradition*. New York 1957

– *Law and Tradition in Judaism*. New York 1959

COHEN, H. 'Das Problem der jüdischen Sittenlehre. Eine Kritik von Lazarus' Ethik des Judenthums.' *MGWJ* 43 (1899) 385-400, 433-49

COHEN, J. J. 'The "Sayings of the Fathers", its Commentaries and Translations'. *KS* 40 (1964-5) 104-117; 277-85 (Hebr.)

COHEN, S. J. D. 'Parallel Tradition in Josephus and Rabbinic Literature', in *PWCJS* 9 (1986) 11f.

– 'Patriarchs and Scholars'. *PAAJR* 48 (1981) 57-85

– 'The Significance of Yavneh. Pharisees, Rabbis and the End of Sectarianism'. *HUCA* 55 (1984) 27ff.

COHEN, Y. 'Eduyot al kiyum mitswot sheviit bi-yemei Beit Sheni', in Admonit, *Kovets*, 98-116

– 'The Time and Cause of the Transferal of the Patriarchate to Tiberias'. *Zion* 39 (1974) 114-22 (Hebr.)

COOGAN, M. D. 'Life in the Diaspora; Jews at Nippur in the Fifth Century BC'. *BA* 37 (1974) 6-12

– 'Patterns in Jewish Personal Names in the Babylonian Diaspora'. *JSJ* 4 (1973) 183-91

CORONEL, N. *Commentaries quinque (Hamisha kuntrasim)*. Vienna 1864

DAICHES, S. 'The Jews in Babylonia in the Time of Ezra and Nehemiah according to Babylonian Inscriptions'. *JCP* 2 (1910) 1-36

DALMAN, G. H. *Aramäisch-neuhebräisches Handwörterbuch zu Targum, Talmud und Midrasch* (1922) 2nd. improved ed. Göttingen 1938, repr. Hildesheim 1967

DAN, Y. *Hayei ha-ir be-Erets Yisrael be-shilhei ha-tekufa ha-atika*. Jerusalem 1984

– 'The Leadership of the Jewish Community in Eretz Israel in the Fifth and Sixth Centuries'. *PWCJS* 8 (1982) 23-7 (Hebr.)

DANBY, H. *The Mishnah*. Translated from the Hebrew with Introduction and Brief Explanatory Notes. Oxford 1933 and repr.

DAUBE, D. 'The Civil Law of the Mishnah: The Arrangement of the Three Gates'. *TLR* 18 (1944) 351-407

– *'Exousia* in Mark 1:22 and 27'. *JTS* 39 (1938) 45-59

DEBEVOISE, N. *Political History of Parthia*. Chicago 1938

DERENBOURG, J. 'Les sections et les traités de la Mischnah'. *REJ* 3 (1881) 205-10

DIMITROVSKY, H. Z. *S'ridei Bavli. Spanish Incunabula Fragments of the Babylonian Talmud*. New York 1978

DINARY, Y. 'The Impurity Customs of the Menstruate Woman'. *Tarbiz* 49 (1979-80) 306-10 (Hebr.)

DISHON, D. *Tarbut ha-mahloket be-Yisrael*. Tel Aviv 1984

DÜNNER, J. H. *Die Theorien über Wesen und Ursprung der Tosephta kritisch dargestellt*. Amsterdam 1874

EBELING, E. *Aus dem Leben der jüdischen Exulanten in Babylonien. Babylonische Quellen*. Berlin 1914

ELBAUM, J. 'Models of Storytelling and Speech in Stories about the Sages'. *PWCJS* 7,3 (1981) 71-7 (Hebr.)

– 'Shisha inyenei lashon bi-mekorot Hazal'. *Sinai* 86 (1980) 174-80

ELBOGEN, I. *Die jüdische Gottesdienst in seiner geschichtlichen Entwicklung* (3rd ed. Frankfurt/M 1931) repr. Hildesheim 1967

ELBOGEN, I. – HEINEMANN, I *Ha-tefilla be-Yisrael be-hitpathuta ha-historit* (H.T., enlarged, of *Gottesdienst*) Tel Aviv 1972

ELDAR, I. *The Hebrew Language Tradition of Medieval Ashkenaz* 1-2 (HULTP) Jerusalem 1978

ELON, M. *Jewish Law. History, Sources, Principles* 1-3. Jerusalem 1973 (Hebr.)

EPHRATI, E. *The Savoraic Period and Its Literature*. Petah Tikwa 1973 (Hebr.)

EPSTEIN, A. *Mi-kadmoniot ha Yehudim*. 2nd ed. Jerusalem 1957

EPSTEIN, I. (ed.) *The Babylonian Talmud*. Translated into English. 1-18. London 1935-52 and repr.

EPSTEIN, J. N. 'Amru Hakhamim', in *Studies in Memory of A. Gulak and S. Klein*. Jerusalem 1942, 252-61 (Hebr.)

– *A Grammar of Babylonian Aramaic* (ed. by E. Z. Mclammed) Jerusalem 1960 (Hebr.)

– *Introduction to Amoraitic Literature. Babylonian Talmud and Yerushalmi*. Ed. by E. Z. Melamed. Jerusalem 1962 (Hebr.)

– *Introduction to Tannaitic Literature. Mishna, Tosephta and Halakhic Midrashim*. Ed. by E. Z. Mclamed. Jerusalem 1957 (Hebr.)

– 'The Lore of Erets Yisrael. A: Tereifot de-Erets Yisrael. B: Maasim li-benei Erets Yisrael'. *Tarbiz* 2 (1932-3) 308-27 (Hebr.)

– 'Maasim li-bne Erez Israel (Palestinian Halachic Practice)'. *Tarbiz* 1/2 (1930) 33-42 (Hebr.)

– *Mavo le-nosah ha-Mishna* 1-2. Jerusalem 1948. Rev. ed. Jerusalem 1964

FEINTUCH, I. Z. 'The Mishna of the Ms. Leiden in the Palestinian Talmud'. *Tarbiz* 45 (1975-6) 178-212 (Hebr.)

– 'Versions and Traditions in the Talmud'. *Bar Ilan* 23 (1985) 109-27 (Hebr.)

FELDBLUM, M. S. 'Prof. Abr. Weiss – His Approach and Contribution to Talmudic Scholarship', in *Abr. Weiss Jubilee Vol*. New York 1964

FELDMAN, L. 'The Identity of Pollio the Pharisee in Josephus'. *JQR* 49 (1958-9) 53-62

FINKELSTEIN, L. *Akiba, Scholar, Saint and Martyr*. New York 1936

– 'An Ancient Tradition of the Sadducees and the Boethusians', in *Studies and Essays in Honor of A.A. Neuman* (ed. M. Ben-Horin *et al*.) [Philadelphia] 1962, 622-39

– 'The Halakhot Applied to Jerusalem', in *Marx Jubilee Vol.*, Hebr. Section 351-69

– 'The Institution of Baptism for Proselytes'. *JBL* 52 (1933) 203-11

– 'Introductory Study to Pirke Abot'. *JBL* 57 (1938) 13-34

– *Mabo le-Massektot Abot ve-Abot d'Rabbi Natan*. New York 1950

– *The Pharisees. The Sociological Background of Their Faith* 1-2. 3d ed. Philadephia 1962

– 'On the Phraseology of the Tannaim'. *Tarbiz* 20 (1950-1) 96-9 (Hebr.)

FISCHEL, H. A. 'The Uses of Sorites (Climax, Gradation) in the Tannaitic Period'. *HUCA* 44 (1973)
FLUSSER, D. 'Matthew xvii and the Dead Sea Sect'. *Tarbiz* 31 (1961-2) 150-6 (Hebr.)
– 'Pharisäer, Sadduzäer und Essener im Pescher Nachum', in K. E. Grözinger (ed.) *Qumran* (Wege der Forschung 140) Darmstadt 1981, 121-66 (G.T.; Hebr. in *Alon Memorial Vol.*, 133-68)
– *Die rabbinischen Gleichnisse und der Gleichniserzähler Jesus 1. Das Wesen der Gleichnisse.* Bern - Frankfurt/M - Las Vegas 1981
FLUSSER, D. - SAFRAI, S. 'Das Aposteldekret und die Noachitischen Gebote', in *"Wer Tora vermehrt, mehrt Leben". Heinz Kremers zum 60. Geburtstag.* Neukirchen/Vluyn 1986, 173-92
– 'The Essene Doctrine of Hypostasis and Rabbi Meir'. *Immanuel* 14 (1982) 47-57
FRAENKEL, J. 'Hermeneutic Problems in the Study of the Aggadic Narrative'. *Tarbiz* 47 (1977-8) 139-72 (Hebr.)
– 'Remarkable Phenomena in the Text-History of the Aggadic Stories'. *PWCJS* 7,3 (1981) 45-69 (Hebr.)
FRANKEL, Z. *Darkei ha-Mishna. Hodegetica in Mischnam librosque cum ea conjunctos* (Leipzig 1859) repr. Tel Aviv 1959 (Hebr.)
– *Über den Einfluss der palästinensischen Exegese auf die alexandrinische Hermeneutik.* Leipzig 1851
– *Mavo ha-Yerushalmi.* Breslau 1870, repr. Jerusalem 1967
– 'Zum Traktat Abot'. *MGWJ* 7 (1858) 419-30
FRIEDLÄNDER, M. *Die Veränderlichkeit der Namen in den Stammlisten der Bücher der Chronik.* Berlin 1930
FRIEDMAN, M. A. 'Shenei ketaim mi-Sefer ha-Maasim li-benei Erets Yisrael'. *Sinai* 74 (1974) 14-36
FRIEDMAN, S. 'A Critical Study of *Yevamot* X with a Methodological Introduction', in *Texts and Studies. Analecta Judaica 1.* New York 1977, 275-441 (Hebr.)
– 'Two Early "Unknown" Editions of the Mishna'. *JQR* 65 (1974-5) 115-21
FRIEDMANN [ISH-SHALOM], M. *Pseudo-Seder Eliahu Zuta (Derech Ereç und Pirkê R. Eliezer)* (Vienna 1904). Repr. with *id. Seder Eliahu Rabba and Seder Eliahu Zuta.* Jerusalem 1960
FRYE, R. N. *The Heritage of Persia.* New York 1963
– 'Notes on the Early Sasanian State and Church', in *Studi Orientalistici in onore di Giorgio Levi della Vida* (Pubblicazioni dell' Instituto per l'Oriente 52) 1. Roma 1956 314-35
– 'The Political History of Iran under the Sasanians', in *The Cambridge History of Iran* vol. 3/1 (1983) 116-80
FUKS, A. 'Aspects of the Jewish Revolt in A.D. 115-117'. *JRS* 51 (1961) 98-104
FUNK, S. *Die Juden in Babylonien 200-500* 1-2. Berlin 1902-8
GAFNI, I. *Babylonian Jewry and its Institutions in the Period of the Talmud.* Jerusalem 1976 (Hebr.)
– *The Babylonian Yeshiva.* Internal Structure: Spiritual and Social Functions within the Jewish Community in the Amoraic Period (Diss. Hebrew University) Jerusalem 1978 (Hebr.)
– 'The Jews of Babylonia and the Parthian Empire', in M. Stern - Z. Baras (eds.) *The Diaspora in the Hellenistic-Roman World* (Historia shel am Yisrael) [Jerusalem] 1983, 152-157 (Hebr.)
– 'Nestorian Literature as a Source for the History of the Babylonian Yeshivot'. *Tarbiz* 51 (1981-2) 567-76 (Hebr.)
– 'Reinterment in the Land of Israel: Notes on the Origin and Development of the Custom'. *The Jerusalem Cathedra* 1 (1981) 96-104
– 'The Status of Eretz Israel in Reality and in Jewish Consciousness following the Bar Kokhba Uprising', in Oppenheimer - Rappaport, *Bar Kokhva Revolt,* 224-32 (Hebr.)
– 'A Survey of Historical Research on Talmudic Babylonia'. *NWUJS* 21 (1982) 5-17
– 'Yeshiva and Metivta'. *Zion* 43 (1978) 12-37 (Hebr.)
GANDS, S. 'The Dawn of Literature; Prolegomena to a History of Unwritten Literature'. *Osiris* 7 (1939) 261-522
GARTNER, Y. 'The Influence of the Mourners of Zion on Tis'ah Be-Av Customs in the Geonic Period'. *Bar-Ilan* 20-21 (1983) 128-44 (Hebr.)
GEIGER, A. 'Einiges über Plan und Anordnung der Mischnah'. *Wissenschaftliche Zeitschrift für jüdische Theologie* 2 (1836) 489-92

– *Kovets maamarim*. Ed. by S. A. Posnanski. Warsaw 1914 (Hebr.)
– *Lehr- und Lesebuch zur Sprache der Mischnah*. Breslau 1845
– *Urschrift und Uebersetzung der Bibel*. Breslau 1857
GERHARDSSON, B. *Memory and Manuscript. Oral Tradition and Written Transmission in Rabbinic Judaism and Early Christianity*. Uppsala 1961
GIL, M. *Erets Yisrael ba-tekufa ha-Muslimit ha-rishona*. Tel Aviv 1983
GINZBERG, L. *A Commentary on the Palestinian Talmud* 1-4. New York 1941-61 (Hebr.; English introd.)
– 'Derek Erez Rabba/Zuta', in *JE* 4, 526-529
– *Die Haggada bei den Kirchenvätern und in der apokryphischen Literatur*. Berlin 1900
– *On Jewish Law and Lore* (collected papers) Philadephia 1955 , repr. New York 1977
– *Jubilee Volume on the Occasion of His 70th Birthday* 1-2. New York 1945-6
– *Al halakha we-aggada* (collected papers) Jerusalem 1960
– *The Legends of the Jews* 1-6. Philadelphia 1909-28 (various repr.) Vol. 7 (1938) index by B. Cohen
– 'Tamid', in *Journal of Jewish Lore and Philosophy* 1 (1919) (H.T. in *Al halakha we-aggada*, 41-65)
– *An Unknown Jewish Sect*. New York 1976
– *Yerushalmi Fragments from the Genizah* 1. New York 1909
GOITEIN, G. 'Ein Hillel'ischer Spruch'. *MJGL* 1 (1884) 66f.
GOLDBERG, ABR. 'All base themselves upon the Teachings of Rabbi Aqiva'. *Tarbiz* 38 (1968-9) 231-54 (Hebr.)
– *Commentary to the Mishna Shabbat*. Critically Edited and Provided With Introduction, Commentary and Notes. Jerusalem 1976 (Hebr.)
– *The Mishna Treatise Eruvin*. Critically Edited and Provided with Introduction, Commentary and Notes. Jerusalem 1986 (Hebr.)
– *The Mishnah Treatise Ohaloth*. Critically Edited with Commentary. Jerusalem 1955 (Hebr.)
– 'Palestinian Law in Babylonian Tradition, as Revealed in a Study of Perek 'Arvei Pesahim''. *Tarbiz* 33 (1963-4) 337-48 (Hebr.)
– 'Purpose and Method in R. Judah haNasi's Composition of the Mishna'. *Tarbiz* 28 (1958-9) 260-9 (Hebr.)
– 'Rabbi Zeira and Babylonian Custom in Palestine'. *Tarbiz* 36 (1966-7) 319-41 (Hebr.)
– 'The Sources and Development of the *Sugya* in the Babylonian Talmud'. *Tarbiz* 32 (1962-3) 145-9 (Hebr.)
– 'Tannaitic Teachers of Rabbi's Generation Who appear in the Mishna', in *PWCJS* 6 (1977) 83-94 (Hebr.)
– 'Tosefta to the Treatise Tamid', in *B. de Vries Memorial Volume*, 18-42 (Hebr.)
GOLDBERG, M. *Der talmudische Traktat Derech Erez Rabba*. Neu ediert, mit Anmerkungen. 1. Breslau 1888
GOLDIN, J. 'The End of Ecclesiastes: Literal Exegesis and its Transformation', in A. Altmann (ed.) *Biblical Motifs*. Cambridge MA 1966, 135-8
– *The Fathers According to Rabbi Nathan*. New Haven 1955
– 'The First Chapter of *Abot de Rabbi Nathan*', in *M. M. Kaplan Jubilee Vol*. New York 1953
– 'The First Pair (Yose ben Yoezer and Yose ben Yohanan), or, The Home of a Pharisee'. *AJSR* 5 (1980) 41-62
– *The Living Talmud*. Chicago 1957
– 'Mashehu al Beth Midrasho shel Rabban Johanan b. Zakkai', in *H. A. Wolfson Jubilee Vol*. 3. Jerusalem 1965, 69-92 (= 'Session')
– 'A Philosophical Session in a Tannaite Academy'. *Tradition* 21 (1965) 1-21 (= 'Mashehu')
– 'The Three Pillars of Simeon the Righteous'. *PAAJR* 27 (1958) 43-58
– 'Toward a Profile of the Tanna, Aqiba ben Joseph'. *JAOS* 96 (1976) 38-56
– 'Reflections on the Tractate Aboth de R'Nathan'. *PAAJR* 46-7 (1979-80) Hebr. Section, 59-65
– 'The Third Chapter of Abot De Rabbi Nathan'. *HTR* 58 (1965)365-86
– 'Two Versions of Abot De Rabbi Nathan'. *HUCA* 19 (1945-6) 97-120
GOLDSCHMIDT, D. *Mahzor la-yamim ha-noraim* 1-2. Jerusalem 1970

421

GOLDSCHMIDT, L. *Der Babylonische Talmud*. Mit Einschluss der vollständigen Mischnah herausgegeben ...möglichst wortgetreu übersetzt etc. 1-9. Leipzig - Berlin - Vienna - The Hague 1897-1935
GOODBLATT, D. 'The Babylonian Talmud', in *ANRW* II/19.2, 257-336
– 'The Origins of Roman Recognition of the Palestinian Patriarchate', in Rappaport, *Studies 4*, 89-102
– *Rabbinic Instruction in Sasanian Babylonia*. Leiden 1975
– 'Towards the Rehabilitation of Talmudic History', in B.M. Bokser (ed.) *History of Judaism: The Next Ten Years*. 1980
– 'The Story of the Plot against R. Simeon b. Gamaliel I'. *Zion* 49 (1984) 349-74 (Hebr.)
GRAETZ, H. *Geschichte der Juden von den ältesten Zeiten bis zur Gegenwart* (5th ed.) 1-11. Leipzig 1890-1909
GREEN, W. S. 'Palestinian Holy Men: Charismatic Leadership and Rabbinic Tradition', in *ANRW* II/19.2, 619-47
– '"What's in a Name" - The Problematic of Rabbinic Biography', in *id., Approaches to Ancient Judaism*. Missoula 1978, 77-96
GRINTZ, Y. [J.] M. *Sefer Yehudith*. Jerusalem 1957 (Hebr.)
GROSSFELD, B. *A Bibliography of Targum Literature* 1-2. New York 1972-77
GUESNON, A. *Talmud et Machzor*. Paris 1904
GULAK, A. *Le-heker toledot ha-mishpat ha-ivri* 1. *Dinei karkaot*. Jerusalem 1929
– *Toledot ha-mishpat be-Yisrael bi-tekufat ha-Talmud. Ha-hiuv we-shiavudav*. Jerusalem 1939
– *Das Urkundenwesen im Talmud im Lichte der griechisch-ägptischen Papyri und des griechischen und römischen Rechts*. Jerusalem 1935
– *Yesodei ha-mishpat ha-ivri* 1-4 (Berlin 1922) repr. Tel Aviv 1967
GULKOWITSCH, L. 'Der kleine Talmudtraktat über die Samariter, übersetzt und erklärt'. *Anggelos* 1 (1925) 48-56
– 'Der kleine Talmudtraktat über die Sklaven, übersetzt und erklärt'. *Anggelos* 1 (1925) 87-95
GUTTMANN, A. *Das redaktionelle und sachliche Verhältnis zwischen Mischna und Tosefta*. Breslau 1928
GUTTMANN, A. 'The Patriarch Judah I'. *HUCA* 25 (1954) 239-61
GUTTMANN, J. 'The Origin of the Synagogue: The Current State of Research'. *Archäologischer Anzeiger* 87 (1972) 36ff.
– *The Synagogue. Studies in Origins, Archaeology and Architecture*. New York 1975
GUTTMANN, M. *Zur Einleitung in die Halacha*. Budapest 1913
– *Mafteah ha-Talmud* [Clavis Talmudi] 1-4. Csongrad-Budapest 1906-30
HAKOHEN, M. 'Massekhet Avot ba-Halakha'. *Sinai* 50 (1962) 133-51
– 'Perek mi-Massekhet Yirat Het', in *Sinai, sefer yovel le-tsiun hofaat kerah ha-40 shel "Sinai"*. Ed. by Y. L. Maimon. Jerusalem 1958, 418-38
HALEVY, I. *Dorot ha-Rishonim* 1-3 (5 vols.; Frankfurt/M 1897-1918) repr. Jerusalem 1967
HALIVNI, D. W. *Midrash, Mishna and Gemara*. Cambridge MA 1986
HAMPEL, I. *Megillat Taanit* (Diss.) Tel Aviv 1976 (Hebr.)
HATCH, E. - REDPATH, H. A. *A Concordance to the Septuagint and Other Greek Versions of the Old Testament Including the Apocryphal Books* 1-2, suppl. Oxford 1897-1906
HEINEMANN, I. [Y.] 'Die Lehre vom ungeschriebenen Gesetz im jüdischen Schrifttum'. *HUCA* 4 (1927) 149-71
– *Philons griechische und jüdische Bildung* 1-2 (Breslau 1931-2) repr. Darmstadt 1962
HEINEMANN, J. 'Early Halakhah in the Palestinian Targumim'. *JJS* 25 (1974) 114-22
– *Prayer in the Period of the Tannaim and Amoraim* (Hebr. 1966) English revised edition. Berlin 1976
HEINEMANN, J.- PETUCHOWSKI, J. *Literature of the Synagogue*. New York 1975
HENGEL, M. - RÜTER, H. P. - SCHÄFER, P. (eds.) *Übersetzung des Talmud Yerushalmi* 1- . (Vol. 1: *Der Jerusalemer Talmud in deutscher Übersetzung. Berakhoth*) Tübingen 1975-
HERFORD, R. T. *Pirke Aboth. The Ethics of the Talmud: Sayings of the Fathers* (1945) 3rd ed. New York 1962
HERR, M. D. 'Continuum in the Chain of Torah Transmission'. *Zion* 44 (1979) 43-56 (Hebr.)

– 'Persecutions and Martyrdom in Hadrian's Days', in *Scripta* 23 (1972) 85-125
– 'The Problem of War on the Sabbath'. *Tarbiz* 30 (1960-1) 240-56 (Hebr.)
– 'Who were the Boethusians', in *PWCJS* 7 (1981) Vol. 3, 1-20 (Hebr.)
HIGGER, M. *Additions to the Minor Treatises. Hosafot le-Massekhtot Zeirot.* Jerusalem 1935
– 'Massekhet Avot we-Kinyan Tora'. *Horev* 7 (1943) 110-31
– *Massekhet Sofrim.* New York 1937
– *Massekhtot Kalla.* New York 1936
– 'Massekhtot ketanot'. *Otsar ha-Hayim* 11 (1935) 92-6; 165-72
– *Massekhtot Zeirot.* (New York 1929), repr. Jerusalem 1970
– *Otsar ha-Baraitot* 1-10. New York 1930-50
– 'Perek Kinyan Tora'. *Horev* 2 (1935-6) 284-96
– *Seven Minor Treatises.* New York 1930
– *The Treatise Semachot.* New York 1931
– *The Treatises Derek Erez.* New York 1935
– 'Yarhi's Commentary on Kallah Rabbati'. *JQR* 24 (1933-4) 331-48
HOFFMANN, D. *Die erste Mischna und die Controversen der Tannaim.* Berlin 1882. H.T. *Ha-Mishna ha-rishona* (Berlin 1913) repr. Jerusalem 1967. E.T. *The First Mishna*, New York 1977
HOFFMANN, D. SAMMTER, A. (eds.) *Mischnajoth. Die sechs Ordnungen der Mischna* 1-6 (Berlin-Wiesbaden 1887-1933) repr. Basel 1968
HOROWITZ, H. M. *Beth Eked ha-Aggadot* 1. Frankfurt/M 1881
– *Iggeret petuha.* Beth Talmud Suppl 1 (1881)
– *Uralte Tosefta's (Borajta's)* 2-3. Frankfurt/M 1890
HÜTTENMEISTER, F. G. 'Synagogue and Beth Ha-Midrash and Their Relationship'. *Cathedra* 18 (1981) 38-44 (Hebr.)
HYMAN, A. *Toledot Tannaim we-Amoraim* 1-3 (1910) repr. Jerusalem 1964
JACKSON, B. S. 'From Dharma to Law'. *AJCL* 23 (1975) 490-512
JACOBS, L. 'Are there Fictitious Baraitot in the Babylonian Talmud?' *HUCA* 42 (1971) 185-96
– *The Talmudic Argument.* Cambridge 1984
– *Studies in Talmudic Logic and Methodology* 1-2. London 1961
JASTROW, M. *A Dictionary of the Targumim, the Talmud Babli and Yerushalmi and Midrashic Literature* 1-2. Philadelphia 1903 and repr.
JAUBERT, A. 'Le calendrier des Jubilés et de la secte de Qumran'. *VT* 7 (1953) 250-64
JELLICOE, S. *The Septuagint and Modern Study.* Oxford 1968
JEREMIAS, J. *Jerusalem in the Time of Jesus.* Philadephia 1969 (E.T. of *Jerusalem zur Zeit Jesu.* Göttingen 1926)
KAGAN, Z. 'Divergent Tendencies and Their Literary Moulding in the Aggadah'. *Scripta* 22 (1971) 151-70
KAHANA, T. 'Le-havanat ha-baraita al hilkhot Yerushalayim'. *Beth Mikra* 21 (1976) 182-92
KAMINKA, A. *Mehkarim be-Talmud.* Tel Aviv 1951
KAPLAN, J. *The Redaction of the Babylonian Talmud.* New York 1933, repr. Jerusalem 1973
KARA, Y. *Babylonian Aramaic in the Yemenite Manuscripts of the Talmud.* Jerusalem 1983
KASHER, M. M. *Torah Shelemah. Talmudic-Midrashic Encyclopedia of the Pentateuch* 1-34. Jerusalem 1961-81 (Hebr.)
KASHER, M. M. - MANDELBAUM, J. B. *Sarei ha-Elef.* 2nd ed. Jerusalem 1978
KASOWSKI [KOSOVSKY] [KOSOWSKY], B. *Otsar leshon ha-Tannaim* [Concordantiae verborum quae in Mechilta d'Rabbi Ismael reperiuntur] 1-4. Jerusalem 1965-66
– *id.* [Sifra – Torat Kohanim] 1-4. Jerusalem 1967-69
– *id.* [Sifrei Numeri et Deuteronomium] 1-5. Jerusalem 1971-75
– *Otsar ha-shemot la-Talmud ha-Bavli* [Thesaurus nominum quae in Talmude Babylonico reperiuntur] 1-5. Jerusalem 1976-83
KASOWSKI [KASOVSKY], H. Y. *Otsar leshon ha-Mishna* 1-4. Jerusalem 1927
– *Otsar leshon ha-Tosefta* [Thesaurus Thosephtae] 1-6. Jerusalem 1933-61
KASOWSKI, H. Y. - KASOWSKI, B. *Otsar leshon ha-Talmud* [Thesaurus Talmudis. Concordantiae

verborum quae in Talmude Babilonico reperiuntur] 1-41. Jerusalem 1954-82

KATSH, A. I. *Ginze Mishna*. 159 Fragments from the Cairo Geniza in the Saltykov-Shchedrin Library in Leningrad... Jerusalem 1970 (Hebr.)
– 'Unpublished Geniza Fragments of Pirke Aboth in the Antonin Collections in Leningrad'. *JQR* 61 (1970-1) 1-14

KATZ, K. *The Hebrew Language Tradition of the Community of Djerba (Tunisia)* (HULTP) Jerusalem 1977

KAUFMANN, D. *Ginzei Kaufmann. Geniza Publications in Memory of D. Kaufmann*. S. Löwinger - S. Scheiber (eds.) Budapest 1949

KAUFMANN, Y. *Jubilee Vol. Studies in Bible and Jewish Religion...* Ed. M. Haran. Jerusalem 1960
– *Toledot ha-emuna ha-Yisraelit. Mi-yemei kedem ad sof Bait Sheni* 1-8. Tel Aviv 1937-56

KIMELMAN, R. '*Birkat Ha-Minim* and the Lack of Evidence for an Anti-Christian Prayer in Late Antiquity', in Sanders, *Self-Definition* 2, 228-32
– 'The Conflict between the Priestly Oligarchy and the Sages in the Talmudic Period'. *Zion* 48 (1983) 135-48 (Hebr.)
– 'Rabbi Yohanan and Origen on the Song of Songs: A Third Century Jewish-Christian Disputation'. *HTR* 73 (1980) 567-95

KIRCHEIM, R. *Septem libri Talmudici parvi Hierosolymitani* (Frankfurt/M 1851) repr. (*Sheva massekhtot*) Jerusalem 1970

KLAMROTH, E. *Die jüdischen Exulanten in Babylonien*. Leipzig 1912

KLEIN, H. *Collected Talmudic Scientific Writings of Hyman Klein*. Ed. and introd. by Abr. Goldberg. Jerusalem 1979
– 'Gemara and Sebara'. *JQR* 38 (1947-8) 67-91
– 'Gemara Quotations in Sebara'. *JQR* 43 (1952-3) 341-63
– 'The Significance of the Technical Expression *Ella Ey Ittemar Hakhi Ittemar*'. *Tarbiz* 31 (1960-1) 23-42 (Hebr.)
– 'Some Methods of Sebara'. *JQR* 50 (1959-60) 341-63

KLEIN, S. *Toledot ha-yishuv ha-Yehudi be-Erets Yisrael*. Tel Aviv 1946

KLOTZ, M. *Der talmudische Tractat Ebel Rabbati*. Berlin 1890

KOHN, P. J. *Otsar ha-beurim weha-perushim*. London 1952

KOMLOSH, Y. E. *The Bible in the Light of the Aramaic Translations*. Tel Aviv 1973 (Hebr.)

KÖNIG, E. *Einleitung des Alten Testaments*. Bonn 1893

KOSOVSKY, M. *Concordance to the Talmud Yerushalmi (Palestinian Talmud)* 1- . Jerusalem 1979-

KRAUSS, S. *Antoninus und Rabbi*. Vienna 1910
– *Griechische und lateinische Lehnwörter in Talmud, Midrasch und Targum* 1-2 (1898-99) repr. with additions by I. Löw. Hildesheim 1964
– 'Le traité talmudique "Derech Ereç"'. *REJ* 36 (1898) 27-46; 205-21; 37 (1898) 45-64

KROCHMAL, N. *More nevukhei ha-zeman* (Lemberg 1851) ed. S. Rabidowitch. Berlin 1924

KRUPP, M. 'Discussion of Three Text Editions of Mishnaic Geniza Fragments'. *Immanuel* 7 (1977) 68-77
– 'The Relationship between MS Parma De Rossi 138 of the Mishna and MS Vatican 31 of the Sifra, Seder Eliyahu Rabba, and Zutta'. *Tarbiz* 49 (1979-80) 194-6 (Hebr.)

KUTSCHER, E. Y. *A History of the Hebrew Language*. Jerusalem/Leiden 1982
– 'Lashon Hazal', in *id., Hebrew and Aramaic Studies*. Jerusalem 1977 (Hebr.)
– 'Some Methodical Problems of the Lexicography of Mishnaic Hebrew and its Comparison with Biblical Hebrew'. *Archive* 1 (Ramat-Gan 1972) 29-82 (Hebr.)

LAUTERBACH, J. Z. *Midrash and Mishnah*. New York 1916
– *Rabbinic Essays*. Cincinnati 1951

LAZARUS, M. *Die Ethik des Judenthums* 1-2. Frankfurt-M. 1898-1911

LEPPER, F. A. *Trajan's Parthian War*. London 1948

LESZYNSKY, M. *Die Sadduzäer*. Berlin 1912

LEVINE, L. I. [I. L.] 'The Period of Judah Ha-Nasi', in Baras, *Eretz Yisrael*, 94-118 (Hebr.)
– 'Rabbi Abbahu of Caesarea', in Neusner, *Christianity* 4, 56-76

424

– *The Rabbinic Class in Palestine during the Talmudic Period.* Jerusalem 1985 (Hebr.)
LEVINGER, J. *Maimonides' Techniques of Codification.* Jerusalem 1965 (Hebr.)
LEVY, J. *Neuhebräisches und Chaldäisches Wörterbuch über die Talmudim und Midraschim* 1-4. Leipzig 1876-89
LEWIN, B. M. 'Geniza Fragments. I. Chapters of Ben Baboi. II. Maasim li-benei Erets Yisrael'. *Tarbiz* 2 (1932-3) 383-405; 406-10 (Hebr.)
– 'Maasim li-benei Erets Yisrael'. *Tarbiz* 1 (1930) 79-101
– *Otsar hiluf ha-minhagim bein benei Erets Yisrael u-bein benei Bavel* 1. Jerusalem 1942
– *Rabbanan Savoraei we-talmudam.* Repr. from *Azkara. In Mem. of Rabbi A. I. Kook.* Jerusalem 1937
LEWY, I. *Ueber einige Fragmente aus der Mischna des Abba Saul.* Berlin 1876
– *Mavo u-perush le-Talmud Yerushalmi. Bava Kamma perakim 1-6* (Jahresber. des jüd.-theol. Seminars Breslau, 1895-1914) repr. with foreword. Jerusalem 1970
– *Ein Wort über die Mechilta des R. Simon.* Breslau 1889
LICHT, J. *The Rule Scroll.* Text, Introduction and Commentary. Jerusalem 1965 (Hebr.)
LICHTENSTEIN, H. 'Die Fastenrolle. Eine Untersuchung zur jüdisch-hellenistischen Geschichte'. *HUCA* 8-9 (1931-2) 257-317 [Introd.], 318-51 [Text]
LIEBERMAN[N], S. *Greek in Jewish Palestine* (1942) 2nd ed. New York 1965
– *Hellenism in Jewish Palestine* (1950) 2nd rev. red. New York 1962
– *Hilkhot Ha-Yerushalmi (The Laws of the Palestinian Talmud) of Rabbi Moses ben Maimon.* New York 1947 (Hebr.)
– 'How Much Greek in Jewish Palestine?' in A. Altmann, (ed.) *Biblical and Other Studies.* Cambridge 1963
– 'The Old Commentators of the Yerushalmi', in *Marx Jubilee Vol.*, Hebr. Section 287-319
– 'Palestine in the Third and Fourth Centuries'. *JQR* 36 (1945-6) 329-70
– 'On Persecution of the Jewish Religion' ['Redifat dat Yisrael'], in *Baron Jubilee Vol.* Hebrew pt., 213-45
– 'Roman Legal Institutions in Early Rabbinics and in the Acta Martyrum'. *JQR* 35 (1944-5) 20-24
– *Talmuda shel Kisrin. The Talmud of Caesarea* (Tarbiz suppl. 2, 1931) repr. Jerusalem 1968
– 'Tashlum Tosefta' ['Supplement to the Tosephta'], in M.S. Zuckermandel, *Tosephta* (1877-82) repr. Jerusalem (1937) 1970
– *Tosefet Rishonim* 1-4. Jerusalem 1937-9
– *Tosefta ki-Fshutah. A Comprehensive Commentary on the Tosefta* 1-8 (Zeraim-Moed). New York 1955-73 (Hebr.)
– 'A Tragedy or a Comedy?' (Rec. of Neusner, Talmud of the Land of Israel) *JAOS* 104 (1984) 315-9
– 'On the Yerushalmi' [Al ha-Yerushalmi], in *Talmud Yerushalmi. Codex Vatican (Vat Ebr. 133)* Jerusalem 1970
– *Ha-Yerushalmi Kiphshuto* (Sabbath, Erubin, Pesahim) Jerusalem 1934 (Hebr.)
LIFSCHITZ, H. 'Mavo le-Pirkei Avot'. *Sinai* 33 (1943) 178-84
LIFSHITS, B. 'Minhag mevattel le-halakha'. *Sinai* 86 (1980) 8-13
LINDER, A. *Roman Imperial Legislation on the Jews.* Jerusalem 1983 (Hebr.)
LIVER, J. 'Parashat mahtsit ha-shekel', in *Kaufmann Jubilee Vol.*, 54-64 (also in *Studies*, 109-30)
– *Studies in Bible and Judean Desert Scrolls.* Jerusalem 1971 (Hebr.)
– *Toledot Beit David. The House of David from the Fall of the Kingdom of Judah to the Fall of the Second Commonwealth and after.* Jerusalem 1959 (Hebr.)
LOEB, J. 'Notes sur le chapitre Ier des Pirke Avot'. *REJ* 19 (1889) 188-201
LOHSE, E. *Die Ordination im Spätjudentum und im Neuen Testament.* Göttingen 1951
LOWY, S. 'The Confutation of Judaism in the Epistle of Barnabas'. *JJS* 11 (1960) 1-33
MAC-MULLEN, R. *Roman Government Response to Crisis A.D. 235-337.* New Haven 1976
MANDEL, P. *Ha-sippur be-Midrash Eicha* (MA Thesis Hebrew University) Jerusalem 1982
MANN, J. 'Sefer ha-maasim li-benei Erets Yisrael'. *Tarbiz* 1/3 (1930) 1-14
MANTEL, H. *Anshei Knesset ha-Gedola.* [Tel Aviv] 1983
– 'The Development of the Oral Law during the Second Temple Period', in *WHJP* 8, 52-7 (Hebr.)

– 'Ordination and Appointment in the Days of the Second Temple'. *Tarbiz* 32 (1962-3) 120-35 (Hebr.)

– *Studies in the History of the Sanhedrin.* Cambridge MA 1961

MARCUS, R. 'The Pharisees in the Light of Modern Scholarship'. *JR* 32 (1952) 153-64

MARGOLIOUTH, G. 'Gleanings from the Yemenite Liturgy'. *JQR* o.s. 17 (1905) 690-711

MARGULIES [MARGALIOT], M. *Hilkhot Erets Yisrael min ha-Geniza.* Jerusalem 1974

– *Ha-hilukim she-bein anshei ha-mizrah u-benei Erets Yisrael.* Jerusalem 1938

MARX, A. *Jubilee Volume on the Occasion of His 70th Birthday* 1-2. Ed. S. Lieberman. New York 1950

MARX, A. - MARGOLIS, M. L. *A History of the Jewish People.* 3d ed. Philadelphia 1934

MAZAR [MAISLER], B. *Beit Shearim* 1. Jerusalem 1944

– 'Divrei ha-yamim', in *Encyclopaedia Biblica* 2. Jerusalem 1954, 596-606

MELAM[M]ED, E. Z. [E. S.] *An Introduction to Talmudic Literature* Jerusalem 1973 (Hebr.)

– 'Li-leshona shel Massekhet Avot'. *Leshonenu* 20 (1956) 106-11

– 'Nosah, mispar u-mishkal be-Massekhet Avot'. *Sinai* 50 (1962) 152-76

– 'La vie des Tannaim et leurs sentences dans le Traité des Principes', in *Hommage à Abraham …Elmaleh.* Jerusalem 1959. Hebrew section, 49-55

MERCHAVIA, CH. *The Church Versus Talmudic and Midrashic Literature.* Jerusalem 1970 (Hebr.)

MEVAREK, A. 'Seder hakhmei ha-Tora she-beal pe be-Pirkei Avot'. *Shana be-shana* vol. 17 (1978) 267-75

MIELZIENER, M. *Introduction to the Talmud* (1894) 3rd ed. with additional notes and bibliography by J. Bloch and L. Finkelstein (1925) repr. with bibliography 1925-67 by A. Guttmann. New York 1968

MILIK, J. T. 'Textes hebreux et araméens', in P. Benoit *et al.* (eds.) *Discoveries in the Judaean Desert* 2. *Les grottes de Murabbaat.* Oxford 1961, 67-208

MOORE, G. F. *Judaism in the First Centuries of the Christian Era* 1-3. Cambridge MA 1927-30 (repr. in 2 vols. New York 1971)

MOR, M. - RAPPAPORT, U. 'Bibliography to the Bar Kokhba Uprising (1960-1983)', in Oppenheimer - Rappaport, *Bar Kokhva Revolt*, 243-54

MORAG, S. *The Hebrew Tradition of the Baghdadi Community* (HULTP) Jerusalem 1977 (Hebr.)

MÜLLER, J. *Masechet Soferim. Der thalmudische Tractat der Schreiber.* Leipzig 1878

NEUSNER, J. 'Babylonian Jewry and Shapur II's Persecution of Christianity'. *HUCA* 43 (1972) 77-102

– *Eliezer ben Hyrcanus* 1-2. Leiden 1973

– 'Exegesis and the Written Law'. *JSJ* 5 (1974) 176-8

– 'The Formation of Rabbinic Judaism: Yavneh from A.D. 70 to 100', in *ANRW* II/19.2, 21-42

– *A History of the Jews in Babylonia* 1-5. Leiden 1965-70

– *A History of the Mishnaic Law of Purities.* 1-22. Leiden 1974-7

– *A Life of Yohanan ben Zakkai.* 2nd ed. Leiden 1970

– *Method and Meaning in Ancient Judaism.* Missoula 1979

– *From Politics to Piety.* New York 1973

– *The Rabbinic Traditions about the Pharisees before 70* 1-3. Leiden 1971

– (transl.) *The Talmud of the Land of Israel: A Preliminary Translation and Explanation.* 33 (Abodah Zarah) 34 (Horayot, Niddah). Chicago 1982

– 'The Written Tradition in the Pre-Rabbinic Period'. *JSJ* 4 (1973) 56-65

NEUSNER, J. (ed.) *Christianity, Judaism and Other Greco-Roman Cults* (Studies for Morton Smith at Sixty) 1-4. Leiden 1975

– *The Formation of the Babylonian Talmud.* Leiden 1970

– *The Modern Study of the Mishna.* Leiden 1973

– *The Tosefta.* Translated from the Hebrew. 1-6. New York 1977-86

NOACK, B. 'The Day of Pentecost'. *ASTI* 1 (1962) 73-95

OBERMAYER, J. *Die Landschaft Babyloniens im Zeitalter des Talmuds und des Gaonats.* Frankfurt 1929

OPPENHEIMER, A. *The Am-Ha'aretz.* Leiden 1977

– (in coll. with B. Isaac and M. Lecker) *Babylonia Judaica in the Talmudic Period.* Wiesbaden 1983

– 'Benevolent Societies in Jerusalem', in *A. Schalit Memorial Vol.*, 178-90

– 'The Center at Nisibis in the Period of the Mishnah', in M. Stern (ed.) *Nation and History. Studies in the History of the Jewish People* 1. Jerusalem 1983, 141-50 (Hebr.)

OPPENHEIMER, A. - RAPPAPORT, U. (eds.) *The Bar Kokhva Revolt. New Studies.* Jerusalem 1984 (Hebr.)

POLLAK, K. *Rabbi Nathans System der Ethik und Moral.* Frankfurt/M 1905

POLSTER, G. 'Der kleine Talmudtraktat über die Proselyten'. *Anggelos* 2 (1926) 1-38

PORTEN, B. - GREENFIELD, C. *Jews of Elephantine and Arameans of Syene.* Aramaic Texts with Translation. Jerusalem 1974

PRIJS, L. *Jüdische Tradition in der Septuaginta.* Leiden 1948

RABBINOVICZ, R. [N. N.] *Maamar al hadpasat ha-Talmud* (in Vol. 1 of *Dikdukei sofrim*) re-ed. by A. M. Haberman, Jerusalem 1952

– *Sefer dikdukei sofrim. Variae Lectiones in Mischnam et in Talmud Babylonicum* 1-16. Munich - Mainz - Przemysl 1866-97; repr. in 2 vols. New York 1976

RABINOVITZ [RABINOWITZ], Z. M. *Ginzé Midrash. The Oldest Forms of Rabbinic Midrashim According to Geniza Manuscripts.* Tel Aviv 1976

– "'Sepher Ha-Ma-asim Livnei Erez Yisra'el" – New Fragments'. *Tarbiz* 41 (1971-2) 275-305 (Hebr.)

RAD, G. VON, *Das Geschichtsbild des Chronistischen Werkes.* Stuttgart 1930

RAPPAPORT, U. (ed.) *Studies in the History of the Jewish People and the Land of Israel* 4. Haifa 1978 (Hebr.)

RATNER, D. B. *Ahavat Tsion wi-Yerushalayim* 1-12 (Wilna 1901-9) repr. in 9 vols. Jerusalem 1966

REIFFMAN, J. 'Kuntras ruah hadasha'. *Beth Talmud* 4 (1885) 77-84

REINACH, T. 'L'inscription de Theodotos'. *REJ* 71 (1920) 46-56

REINES, H. Z. *Tora u-musar.* Jerusalem 1954

RENGSTORF, K. H. *et al. Rabbinische Texte. Erste Reihe: Die Tosefta.* Stuttgart 1953-

RITTER, B. *Philo und die Halacha.* Leipzig 1879

ROSENBLATT, S. *The Interpretation of the Bible in the Mishnah.* Baltimore 1935

ROTH, C. 'Historical Implications of the Ethics of the Fathers', in *M. Waxman Jubilee Vol.* Ed. by J. Rosenthal. Jerusalem 1966, 102-21

SACKS, N. (ed.) *The Mishna.* With Variant Readings Collected from Manuscripts, Fragments of the 'Geniza' and Early Printed Editions and Collated with Quotations from the Mishna in Early Rabbinic Literature. 1- . Jerusalem 1971-

SAFRAI, S. *R. Akiva ben Yosef. Hayyav u-mishnato.* Jerusalem 1970

– 'And All is According to the Majority of Deeds'. *Tarbiz* 53 (1983-4) 33-40 (Hebr.)

– 'Beth Shearim in Talmudic Literature'. *Eretz-Israel* 5 (1958) 206 12 (Hebr.)

– 'The Decision according to the School of Hillel in Yavneh'. *PWCJS* 7,3 (1981) 21-44 (Hebr.)

– *Erets Yisrael we-hakhameha bi-tekufat ha-Mishna weha-Talmud* (coll. articles) Jerusalem 1983

– 'Halakha le Moshe mi-Sinai – historia o teologia?' *PWCJS* 9 (1986) 23-30

– 'Hasidim we-anshei maase'. *Zion* 50 (1985) 133-54

– 'The Holy Congregation in Jerusalem', in *Scripta* 23 (1972) 62-78

– 'Ha-Ir ha-Yehudit be-Erets Yisrael bi-tekufat ha-Mishna weha-Talmud', in *Holy War and Martyrology. Town and Community* (Historical Society of Israel, Lectures Delivered at 11th and 12th Convention 1966) Jerusalem 1967, 227-36 (Hebr.)

– 'Kiddush Ha-Shem in the Teaching of the Tannaim', in *Baer Memorial Vol.*, 28-42 (Hebr.; E.T. in Th.C. de Kruijf - H. van de Sandt, eds., *Sjaloom. Ter nagedachtenis van A.C. Ramselaar.* Hilversum 1983, 145-65)

– 'Mishnat Hasidim be-sifrut ha-Tannaim', in *We-hinei ein Yosef. Kovets le-zikhro shel Y. Amorai.* Tel Aviv 1973, 136-52

– 'The *Nesiut* in the Second and Third Centuries and its Chronology Problems'. *PWCJS* 6 (1975) 51-7 (Hebr.)

– 'New Research Concerning the Status and Actions of Rabban Yohanan b. Zakkai', in *Alon Memorial Vol.*, 203-22 (Hebr.)

– *Pilgrimage at the Time of the Second Temple.* Tel Aviv 1965 (Hebr.; G.T. *Die Wallfahrt im Zeitalter des zweiten Tempels.* Neukirchen/Vluyn 1981)

– 'The Practical Implementation of the Sabbatical Year after the Destruction of the Second Temple'.

Tarbiz 35 (1965-6) 304-28; 36 (1966-7) 1-12 (Hebr.; *id.* with additions in Admonit, *Kovets*, 117-64)
- 'Restoration of the Jewish Community in the Yavne Generation' in Baras, *Eretz Israel*, 18-39 (Hebr.)
- 'The Synagogue and its Worship', in *WHJP* 8, 65-98
- 'Tales of the Sages in the Palestinian Tradition and the Babylonian Talmud', in *Scripta* 22 (1971) 209-32
- 'Teaching of Pietists in Mishnaic Literature'. *JJS* 16 (1965) 15-33
- 'The Visits to Rome of the Sages of Yavne', in *Scritti in Memoria di Umberto Nahon*. Jerusalem 1978, 151-67 (Hebr.)
- *Wallfahrt* (see *Pilgrimage*)
- 'Was there a Women's Gallery in the Synagogue of Antiquity?' *Tarbiz* 32 (1962-3) 329-38 (Hebr.)
SAFRAI, S. - STERN, M., (eds., in cooperation with D. Flusser and W. C. van Unnik) *The Jewish People in the First Century* (Compendia Section I) 1-2. Assen - Philadelphia 1974-76
SAFRAI, Z. *Pirkei Galil*. 2nd ed. Jerusalem 1985
- 'The Rehov Inscription'. *Immanuel* 8 (1978) 48-57
SALDARINI, A. J. *The Fathers According to Rabbi Nathan (Abot de Rabbi Nathan), Version B. A Translation and Commentary*. Leiden 1975
- *Scholastic Rabbinism*. Chico CA 1982
SANDERS, E. P. *Paul and Palestinian Judaism*. Philadelphia 1977
SANDERS, E. P. *et al.* (eds.) *Jewish and Christian Self-Definition* 1-2. Philadelphia 1980-1
SARFATTI, G. 'On Editing and Vocalising Mishnaic Texts'. *Leshonenu* 31 (1967) 150-54 (Hebr.)
SCHACHTER, M. *The Babylonian and Jerusalem Mishnah textually Compared*. Jerusalem 1959 (Hebr.)
SCHALIT, A. *König Herodes*. Berlin 1969
- *Jerusalem in the Second Temple Period. A. Schalit Memorial Volume*. Ed. by A. Oppenheimer, U. Rappoport en M. Stern. Jerusalem 1981 (Hebr.)
SCHECHTER, S. *Documents of Jewish Sectaries* 1. *Fragments of a Zadokite Work* (Cambridge 1910) repr. with prolegomenon by J.A. Fitzmeyer. New York 1970
- *Ginzei Schechter. Geniza Studies in Memory of Solomon Schechter* (ed. by L. Ginzberg and I. Davidson) 1-3. 1928-9 (Hebr.)
- 'The Quotations from Ecclesiasticus in Rabbinic Literature'. *JQR* o.s. 3 (1891) 682-706
SCHIFFMANN, L. H. *The Halakha at Qumran*. Leiden 1975
SCHOLEM, G. *Jewish Gnosticism, Merkabah Mysticism and Talmudic Tradition*. 2nd ed. New York 1965
SCHÖNBLUM, S. *Shelosha sefarim niftahim*. Lemberg 1872
SCHULZ, F. *A History of Roman Legal Science*. Oxford 1946
SCHÜRER, E. *The History of the Jewish People in the Age of Jesus Christ* 1-3a. Revised ed. by G. Vermes and F. Millar. Edinburgh 1973-86
SCHWAB, M. *Le Talmud de Jérusalem* 1-11 (Paris 1871-89) repr. in 6 vols. Paris 1969
SCHWARTZ, A. *Die Controversen der Schammaiten und Hilleliten*. Vienna 1893
- *Die Tosifta des Traktates Nesikin, Baba Kamma geordnet und kommentiert*. Frankfurt o.M. 1912
SCHWARTZ, J. *Jewish Settlement after the Bar-Kochba War until the Arab Conquest*. Jerusalem 1986 (Hebr.)
SCHWARZ, D. R. 'Josephus and Nicolaus on the Pharisees'. *JSJ* 14 (1983) 157-71
SCHWARZWALD, O. 'Typologie des traductions du traité des Pères en ladino'. *Massorot* 2 (1986) 103-18 (Hebr.)
SEELIGMANN, I. L. 'The Beginning of Midrash in the Books of Chronicles'. *Tarbiz* 49 (1979-80) 14-32
SEGAL, J. B. 'The Jews of North Mesopotamia before the Rise of the Islam', in *Studies in the Bible Presented to M. H. Segal*. Ed. by J. M. Grintz *et al*. Jerusalem 1964, 32-63
SEGAL, M. H. 'Mishnaic Hebrew and its Relation to Biblical Hebrew and to Aramaic'. *JQR* o.s. 20 (1908) 647-737
- *Sefer Ben Sira ha-shalem*. 2nd ed. Jerusalem 1958 and repr.
SEVENSTER, J. N. *Do You Know Greek?* Leiden 1968

SHARVIT, S. 'The Custom of Reading Abot on the Sabbath, and the History of the Baraitot Associated Therewith'. *Bar-Ilan* 13 (1976) 169-87 (Hebr.)

– *Textual Variants and Language of the Treatise Abot and Prolegomena to a Critical Edition* (Diss.) Ramat Gan 1976 (Hebr.)

– 'Traditions of Interpretations and Their Relations to Traditions of Textual Readings in the Mishnah', in *Studies in Talmudic Literature, Bible and the History of Israel. Dedicated to E. Z. Melamed*. Ramat Gan 1983, 115-34 (Hebr.)

SHILOH, S. *Dina de-malkhuta dina*. Jerusalem 1975

SHMIDMAN, M. A. 'An Excerpt from the Abot Commentary of R. Mattathias ha-Yizhari', in *Studies in Medieval Jewish History and Literature*. Cambridge MA 1979, 315-36

SMALLWOOD, E. M. *The Jews under Roman Rule. From Pompei to Diocletian*. 2nd ed. Leiden 1981

SMILÉVITCH, E. - DUPUY, B. *Leçons des pères du monde. Pirqé Avot et Avot de Rabbi Nathan Version A et B*. Texte intégral etc. Verdier 1983

SMITH, M. 'Palestinian Judaism in the First Century', in M. Davis (ed.) *Israel: Its Role in Civilization*. New York 1956, 67-81

SONNE, I. 'The Schools of Shammai and Hillel Seen from within', in *Ginzberg Jubilee Vol.*, 275-91

SPANIER, M. *Zur Frage des literarischen Verhältnisses zwischen Mischnah und Tosefta*. Berlin 1931

– *Die Toseftaperiode in der Tannaitischen Literatur*. Berlin 1922

SPERBER, D. *Great is Peace* (Perek ha-Shalom). Jerusalem 1979

– 'Greek and Latin Words in Rabbinic Literature'. *Bar Ilan* 14-15 (1977) 6-90; 16-17 (1979) 9-30

– *Masechet Derech Ereiz Zutta*. 2nd ed. Jerusalem 1982

– *Roman Palestine 200-400. The Land*. Ramat-Gan 1978

SPIEGEL, Y. S. *Helkam shel Rabbanan Savoraei ba-Talmud ha-Bavli*. Diss. Tel Aviv 1976

SPRENGLING, M. 'Kartir, Founder of Sasanian Zoroastrianism'. *AJSLL* 57 (1940) 197-228

STEIN, S. 'The Concept of the "Fence"', in *Studies. Altmann University*. Alabama 1979, 301-29

STERN, M. *Greek and Latin Authors on Jews and Judaism* 1-3. Jerusalem 1974-84

– 'The Roman Administration in Provincia Judaea from the Destruction of the Second Temple to the Bar Kokhba Uprising', in Baras, *Eretz Israel* 1, 514-20 (Hebr.)

– 'Sicarii and Zealots', in *WHJP* 8, 263-71

– 'Social and Political Realignments in Herodian Judaea'. *The Jerusalem Cathedra* 2 (1982) 40-62

– *Ha-Teudot le-mered ha-Hashmonaim*. 2nd ed. Tel Aviv 1972

STONE, M. E., (ed.) *Jewish Writings of the Second Temple Period* (Compendia II/2) Assen - Philadelphia 1984

STRACK, H. L. *Introduction to the Talmud and Midrash*. 5th ed. (Philadelphia 1931) repr. New York 1970

– *Die Sprüche der Väter*. Leipzig 1915

STRACK, H. L. - STEMBERGER, G. *Einleitung in Talmud und Midrasch*. 7., völlig neu bearb. Aufl. Munich 1982

SUSSMANN, Y. *Babylonian Sugiyot to the Orders Zera'im and Tohorot*. Diss. Jerusalem 1969 (Hebr.)

– 'The Boundaries of Eretz-Israel'. *Tarbiz* 45 (1975-6) 213-57 (Hebr.)

– 'A Halakhic Inscription from the Beth-Shean Valley'. *Tarbiz* 43 (1973-4) 88-158; 44 (1974-5) 193-5 (Hebr.)

– 'The Inscription in the Synagogue at Rehob', in I.L. Levine (ed.) *Ancient Synagogues Revealed*. Jerusalem 1981, 146-53

TALMON, S. 'The Calendar Reckoning of the Judaean Sect', in *Studies in the Dead Sea Scrolls. Lectures ...In Memory of E.L. Sukenik*. Jerusalem 1957, 24-39 (Hebr.)

– 'The Calendar Reckoning of the Sect from the Judaean Desert'. *Scripta* 4 (1958) 162-99

TAUSSIG, S. *Neve Shalom*. Munich 1872

TAWROGI, A. J. *Der thalmudische Tractat Derech Erez Sutta*. Königsberg 1885

TAYLOR, C. *An Appendix to Sayings of the Jewish Fathers. Containing a Catalogue of Manuscripts and Notes on the Text of Aboth* (Cambridge 1900) repr. together with *Sayings*, Amsterdam 1970

– *Sayings of the Jewish Fathers. ...Pirqe Aboth in Hebrew and English with Critical Notes and Excurses*. 2nd ed. (Cambridge 1897) repr. with *Appendix*, Amsterdam 1970

TAYLOR, F. *Tractatus de patribus Rabbi Nathan auctore*. London 1654

TEMPORINI, H. - HAASE, W. (eds.) *Aufstieg und Niedergang der römischen Welt* II: *Principat*. 19/1-2 *Palästinensisches Judentum*. Berlin - New York 1979

TOWNSEND, J. T. 'Rabbinic Sources', in *The Study of Judaism*. New York 1972

TUR-SINAI [TORCZYNER], N. H. 'Gilla panim ba-Tora shelo ke-halakha'. *Leshonenu* 12 (1944) 270ff.

– 'Language and Phraseology in the Tractate of Aboth d'Rabbi Nathan', in *M.M. Kaplan Jubilee Vol*. Ed. by M. Davis. New York 1953, Hebr. Section, 83-93 (also in *Ha-lashon weha-sefer* 3, Jerusalem 1955, 320-34)

URBACH, E. E. 'Class Status and Leadership in the World of the Palestinian Sages', in *PIASH* 2 (1968) 48-74

– 'The Derasha as a Basis of the Halakha and the Problem of the Soferim'. *Tarbiz* 27 (1957-8) 166-82 (Hebr.)

– *Ha-Halakha. Mekoroteha we-hitpathuta*. Givataim 1984

– [Hilkhot avadim] 'Halakhot Regarding Slavery as a Source for the Social History of the Second Temple and the Talmudic Period'. *Zion* 25 (1961) 141-89 (Hebr.)

– Homilies of the Rabbis on the Prophets of the Nations and the Balaam Stories'. *Tarbiz* 25 (1955-6) 272-89 (Hebr.)

– 'The Jews in Their Land in the Age of the Tannaim'. *Behinot* 4 (1953) 61-72 (Hebr.)

– 'Pirkei R. Yoshia'. *Kovets al Yad* n.s. 8 (1976) 79-89

– 'Rabbinic Exegesis and Origenes' Commentaries on the Song of Songs and Jewish-Christian Polemics'. *Tarbiz* 30 (1960-1) 148-70 (Hebr.)

– 'The Repentance of the People of Nineveh and the Discussion between Jews and Christians'. *Tarbiz* 20 (1950-1) 118-22 (Hebr.)

– *The Sages. Their Concepts and Beliefs* 1-2 (E.T. of the Hebrew, which is referred to as *Hazal*) Sec. enl. ed. Jerusalem 1979

VERMES, G. 'The Decalogue and the Minnim', in M. Black - G. Fohrer (eds.) *In memoriam P. Kahle*. Berlin 1968, 232-40

VIVIANO, B. T. *Study as Worship. Aboth and the New Testament*. Leiden 1978

VRIES, B. DE 'The Date of Compilation of the Tractate "Kalla Rabbati"'. *PWCJS* 4,1 (1967) 131-2 (Hebr.)

– *Mehkarim be-sifrut ha-Talmud*. Jerusalem 1968

– *Memorial Volume*. Ed. E.Z. Melamed. Jerusalem 1968

– *Studies in the Development of Talmudic Halakah*. Jerusalem 1962 (Hebr.)

– *Toledot ha-halakha ha-talmudit*. Tel Aviv 1962

WACHOLDER, B. Z. *Messianism and Mishnah*. [n. pl.] 1978

– 'Sippurei Rabban Gamliel ba-Mishna uba-Tosefta'. *PWCJS* 1 (1967) 143ff. (Hebr.)

WEISS, A. *Le-heker ha-Talmud*. The Literary Development of the Babylonian Talmud. New York 1955 (Hebr.)

– *Studies in the Law of the Talmud on Damages*. Jerusalem - New York 1966 (Hebr.)

– *Ha-yetsira shel ha-Savoraim*. The Literary Activities of the Saboraim. Jerusalem 1953 (Hebr.)

– *Al ha-yetsira ha-sifrutit shel ha-Amoraim*. On the Literary Creation of the Amoraim. New York 1962 (Hebr.)

WEISS, I. H. 'Bikoret sefarim'. *Beth Talmud* 3 (1883) 122-5

– *Dor-dor we-dorshav. Zur Geschichte der jüdischen Tradition* 1-5. Vienna 1871-83 (various reprints) (Hebr.)

WELLHAUSEN, J. *Prolegomena zur Geschichte Israels*. 2nd ed. Berlin 1883

WIDENGREN, G. 'The Status of the Jews in the Sassanian Empire'. *Iranica Antiqua* 1 (1961) 117-62

WILLI, TH. *Die Chronik als Auslegung*. Göttingen 1972

WOLFSON, H. A. *Philo* 1-2. 2nd ed. Cambridge MA 1948 (3rd rev. ed. 1962)

YADIN, Y. *The Temple Scroll* 1-3. Jerusalem 1977 (Hebr.; E.T. Jerusalem 1983)

YALON, H. *Introduction to the Vocalization of the Mishna*. Jerusalem 1964 (Hebr.)

ZADOK, R. *The Jews in Babylonia during the Chaldean and Achaemenian Periods according to the Babylonian Sources*. Haifa 1979

ZILBERG, M. *Kakh darko shel Talmud*. Jerusalem 1962

ZIMMER, E. 'Atifat ha-rosh be-evel'. *Sinai* 96 (1985) 148-68

ZLOTNICK, D. *The Tractate 'Mourning'*. New Haven - London 1966

ZUNZ, L. *Die gottesdienstlichen Vorträge der Juden historisch entwickelt.* 2nd ed. (Frankfurt 1892) repr. Hildesheim 1966

ZUNZ, L. - ALBECK, H. *Ha-derashot be-Yisrael we-hishtalshelutan ha-historit* (H.T. of Zunz, Vorträge) Edited with additional notes by Ch. Albeck. Jerusalem 1954

Index of Personal Names

This index contains names up to and including the Gaonic period.

Index of Geographical Names

Index of Sources

Division: a. Hebrew Bible b. Septuagint c. Pseudepigrapha d. Qumran Scrolls e. Philo f. Josephus g. New Testament h. Apostolic and Patristic Writings i. Greek and Latin Authors j. Targum k. Tannaic Midrash l. Amoraic Midrash m. Mishna n. Tosefta o. Palestinian Talmud p. Babylonian Talmud q. External Tractates and Related Works r. Gaonic Works

Of categories m, n, o, and p, only passages quoted or commented on extensively are listed.

a. Hebrew Bible

Genesis

		16:29-30	229
		18:20	64
2:1-3	123, 229	19:1	173
2:15	102	19:3	54n
4:16	111	19:4,	15 54
5:1	112	20:7	231
9:6	107, 112, 268	20:8-10	123
17:5	51	20:8-11	123, 229
18:4	81	20:9	170
25:27	127n	20:13	125
32:33	231	21:2-11	402
45:8	263	21:6	140
		21:18-37	230
Exodus		21:28	203
		21:41	190
4:14	111	22:3-8	230
12:1-2	229	22:6-14	231
12:1-18	229	22:7	140
12:6	141	22:8	140
12:8-10	142	22:16-17	230
12:9	56	22:20	231
12:15	138, 232	22:22	114
12:16	189	22:25	162
12:17	157, 229	22:25-26	231
12:39	229	22:27	139-140
12:43-50	229	22:29	232
13:1-16	158	22:30	231
13:2	232	23:1	83n
13:3-10	229	23:2	49, 231
13:7	159	23:4-5	231
13:11-13	232	23:10-11	228
15:25	134	23:12	229
16:22-26	229	23:13	231

l. Amoraic Midrash

o. Palestinian Talmud (ed. princeps, Venice 1523-24

p. *Babylonian Talmud*

q. *External Tractates and Related Works*